IMPERIALIST JAPAN

The Yen to Dominate

MICHAEL MONTGOMERY

ST. MARTIN'S PRESS
New York

First published in the United States of America in 1988
Printed in Great Britain

Library of Congress Cataloging-in-Publication Data

Montgomery, Michael.
  Imperialist Japan
  Bibliography: p.
  Includes index.
  1. Japan — History — 1868-   .2. Imperialism.
3. Japan — Foreign relations — 1868-   . I. Title.
DS881.9.M58   1988   952   87-23460
ISBN 0-312-01557-7

Contents

List of Illustrations

Introduction

Restoring the Facts

In July 1982 Japan's Ministry of Education published a number of 'corrections' to high school history text books which had been approved by the screening committee set up in 1963 to weed out 'ideological bias'.

They all concerned the presentation of Japanese actions in the three decades leading up to World War Two. For example, the forcible deportation of 700,000 Koreans, following the annexation of their country in 1910, to Japan to work in mines and munition factories was now described as 'the implementation of the national mobilisation order to Koreans'; Japanese incursions into China from 1931 onwards were no longer referred to as invasions, but only as 'advances of the Imperial Army'; an attack by the Japanese fleet on Chinese forces after full-scale war had broken out in 1937 (still to this day labelled in Japan 'The China Incident') was spoken of as 'a battle which broke out between Japan and China'.

Other, even more discreditable, events were to be glossed over altogether, while responsibility for the horrific catalogue of atrocities committed during the infamous Rape of Nanking*, in which over 200,000 Chinese civilians were bestially slaughtered in a calculated campaign of intimidation personally superintended by an uncle of present Emperor Hirohito, was even transferred to the Chinese themselves. 'The cause of the incident was the stubborn resistance of the Chinese troops,' it was now alleged. 'When they inflicted heavy losses on the Japanese army, the Japanese troops were enraged and as a result, they killed many Chinese · soldiers and civilians.'

The revisions provoked a predictable storm of outraged protest not only in China and Korea, but in all the other countries of South East Asia whose civilian populations had suffered similarly in the course of Japanese invasion and occupation. The projected visit of Japan's Minister of Education to Peking was abruptly cancelled, and there was even serious talk of breaking off the diplomatic relations which had finally been resumed in 1972 (when the Japanese Prime Minister of the day had gone so

---

* Since most of the events described in this book occurred before 1942, place names current at the time will be used throughout.

vii

far as to concede that it was 'regretful that for several decades in the past the relations between Japan and China had [contained] unfortunate experiences'). The bitterness was stirred still further by the publication in the Peking Evening News of detailed accounts, complete with grisly photographs, of Japanese blood-letting.

Japan responded in turn by declaring that such criticism represented interference in the country's domestic affairs. An apology was eventually issued to Peking, but this merely repeated the admission of responsibility made in 1972. At the same time it was claimed that it was now too late to halt the offending revisions, but an undertaking was given that 'the necessary amendments' would be made in the 1985 editions.

If any saw this as a gesture of genuine contrition on Japan's part, they were undeceived within a matter of days by the release of the film *The Greater Japanese Empire*, a multi-million-yen spectacular which portrayed Japan's territorial expansion on the mainland as a selfless crusade to rescue Asia from the unscrupulous Westerner. Two weeks later again the Japanese Cabinet cocked a further snook at the outside world by visiting the Yasukuni Shrine commemorating Japan's war dead (including the seven executed in 1948 as major War Criminals). Although they denied that they were doing so in any official capacity, they all wore the morning dress required for State occasions. A Seoul newspaper editor remarked that 'the day will not be far off when the Pearl Harbor attack might be termed an unavoidable act of self-defence'. His prediction was duly fulfilled in an issue of *Japan Echo*, a publication funded jointly by the Japanese Foreign Ministry, Japan Airlines and Toyota Motor Co., which stated that 'Japan, simply to assure its own survival, was given little choice but to wage war with the United States . . . Washington took actions calculated to provoke a fight with Japan.'

In Japan itself, by contrast, this attempt to subvert the facts of history aroused little reaction (except on the island of Okinawa, where up to 75,000 civilians were estimated to have been eliminated in the course of the American invasion in 1945; previously described as having been 'obstacles in the combat', they were deleted altogether). What objections that there were came almost exclusively from the government's political opponents in the Diet (parliament) and in the teaching unions. Among the professional historians, who elsewhere would be expected to raise the most vocal defence of the principle of academic integrity, all but total silence reigned.

Why should this have been so?

A year earlier evidence had come to light in Washington, following the release of previously-classified documents under the Freedom of Information Act, on the existence of a chain of Japanese biological warfare research stations set up in the 1930s to conduct live experiments with lethal bacteria on human beings. Further research in Japan itself had then revealed that Hirohito himself, already well known for his interest in marine biology, had been directly involved in the establishment of the largest of them, code-named Unit 731, where over 3,000 Chinese and Allied prisoners-of-war were recorded as dying in the course of these experiments. As a result, some read into the text-book revisions an attempt to purge the eighty-one-year-old Emperor's record before he finally joined his Imperial, divinely-descended ancestors (although, on the advice of General Douglas MacArthur, the Supreme Commander of the post-war Occupation forces, Hirohito was spared prosecution by the War Crimes Tribunal, its Presiding Judge concluded that his 'outstanding part in starting as well as ending it [the War] was the subject of unimpeachable evidence').

Others, particularly in China, saw them as signalling a revival of Japanese militarism, but while defence spending remained pegged to one per cent of the Gross National Product (in line with the requirements of Japan's post-war constitution) such an interpretation seemed to offer a less than full explanation.

For that one needs to go back further in time — as far back, in fact, as the earliest annals of Japan's recorded history, the eighth-century *Kojiki* ('Records of Ancient Matters') and *Nihongi* ('Chronicles of Japan'). These works represented no more than the first attempts of a primitive society to rationalise the authority of its existing political hierarchy, the ruling house of Yamato, within the context of the prehistoric lore of its native religion, the animistic cult of Shinto. Consequently, they are largely preoccupied with tracing the dynasty's mythological descent from Shinto's central object of worship, the Sun Goddess, Amaterasu.

In imitation of the longevity ascribed to the first Emperors of China the early occupants of the Imperial throne were credited with lifespans of 100 years or more, while the date of the arrival on earth of Amaterasu's grandson (and grandfather of the first Emperor, Jimmu) was set at the equivalent of 1,792,470 BC. This need to outdo the Chinese sprang from an awareness that the cultural heritage of Japan was not the product of an indigenous evolution, but rather a wholesale importation from the vastly older and more highly developed civilisation of her mainland neighbour.

The innate sense of inferiority that it engendered has persisted right down to the present day, and it has to be taken into account before any understanding of the course of Japan's action over the past century is possible. 'There is probably no nation on earth today more conscious of itself than the Japanese,' a contemporary Oriental scholar has written. 'The fact of a strong and isolated ethnocentrism brought suddenly and sharply into conflict with the bewildering culture of the West has accentuated pre-existing tendencies to introspection and has thrown Japan into an introverted psychosis of national proportions as a means of trying to save her own soul.' The assimilation of Chinese script with the Japanese language gave rise similarly to the convention of *inshin denshin* or 'tacit understanding', whereby the spoken word can bear little relation to the meaning intended which is conveyed instead by *haragei*, 'the language of the belly' (in Japanese, the verb is placed at the end of the sentence, which allows the speaker to adapt the sense of his words to what he judges that the listener wishes to hear); in the cultural conflict with the outside world the existence of such a private code would serve both as an extra line of defence against the foreigner and as a confirmation to the Japanese themselves of their own singularity.

This introversion explains how it was that while elsewhere historians gradually developed the techniques of critical evaluation of their sources and the independent expression of objective conclusions, those in Japan by contrast continued to see their function merely as propagators of the unhistorical and intensely chauvinistic Shintoist mythology. The original corpus of the *Kojiki* and *Nihongi* was regularly supplemented by fresh additions in the succeeding centuries, but with no more regard for historical accuracy; their compilers, in the words of another modern scholar, 'selected material according to their own fancy, adjusting the factual with the traditional and never leaving out the overriding need to stress the divinity of the Emperor.'

Japan's geographical isolation was also, of course, a continuing factor, but just when Europe's pioneering navigators bridged the divide and brought her abreast of the achievements of the Renaissance the Tokugawa Shogunate chose to impose a quarantine which effectively removed her from the face of the globe altogether and postponed her own cultural regeneration for a further two and a half centuries. Thus while the Age of Reason was seeing the flowering of independent historical scholarship in the West, Japan's chroniclers remained the blinkered and subservient functionaries of a feudal dictatorship. Worse still, when they were eventually made aware of their country's atrophy, their reaction was to delve even deeper into mythological fantasy in order to substantiate the claims to sovereignty of what was seen to be the only possible alternative to the Shogunate, the Imperial Line.

When Imperial rule finally returned in 1868, shortly after the accession to the Throne of the 15-year-old Meiji, the architects of its Restoration lost no time in inculcating the arguments for those claims into a largely ignorant population. Not only did they decree that Shinto was the only permissible religion in the new order, but they went on to declare that the first function of education was to promulgate 'the Great Way of Obedience to the Gods. Therefore we newly appoint propagandists to proclaim this to the nation...' A Bureau of History was accordingly established within the new Ministry of Education and commissioned with the task of formulating a 'correct' interpretation of the nation's past.

Thanks to the influence of the first European-born Professor of History at Tokyo University, the Bureau was closed twenty years later and for a brief period the spirit of independent inquiry flourished. This rare interlude was brought to an abrupt end in 1911 by another 'History Textbook

Incident' over the question of which side was to be portrayed as representing the legitimate line of succession during a fourteenth-century schism in the Imperial Court. Six years later the author of one such standard work told a visiting American academic that it was 'filled with lies. It bears my name, but it is not the book that I wrote ... Every new edition has more lies and less truth.'

Another distinguished historian published a book which concluded, on the evidence of long and meticulous research, that the *Kojiki* and *Nihongi* should be regarded not as records of historical fact, but as political instruments employed to bolster the legitimacy of the Imperial Line; in particular, he dismissed the first fourteen Emperors as figures of fiction. The reward for his labours was dismissal from his university and, ultimately, conviction on a charge of lèse majesté, along with the country's foremost constitutional lawyer who had dared to argue that the Emperor was 'the highest organ of the State' rather than its transcendental presiding genius.

This reimposition of Shintoist dogma was no coincidence, for it followed, in the wake of Japan's spectacular victories over Russia, Meiji's preparation of a detailed blueprint for territorial expansion on the Asian mainland (entitled, with typical Japanese ambiguity, 'The National Defence Plan'). Meiji had personally directed that campaign in his capacity as Commander-in-Chief, and renewed emphasis was placed on the 'Great Way of Obedience to the Gods' in order to instill in the people an unquestioning acceptance of Imperial authority for the greater undertaking ahead.

'Subjects have no mind apart from the will of the Emperor. Their individual selves are merged with the Emperor', a Professor of Law at Tokyo University pronounced. 'If they act according to the mind of the Emperor, they can realise their true nature and attain the moral ideal.' A College of Shinto was established, where students were taught that loyalty denoted 'the lofty, self-denying, enthusiastic sentiment of the Japanese people towards their august Ruler, believed to be something divine, rendering them capable of offering up anything and everything ... not only their wealth or property, but their own life itself.' The Emperor's previous title of Mikado or 'elevated gate [to heaven]' was simultaneously dropped in favour of Tenno or 'Son of Heaven'.

In such a climate there was clearly no longer room for objective scholarship, and the author of a newly commissioned *National History of Modern Japan* declared that he was motivated instead by the need to record 'the shining example of Emperor Meiji' for posterity and by the ambition to devote his life to 'writing in the service of the nation'. Even scholars in the field of archaeology were pressed into the service of the new orthodoxy: recent Neolithic finds were interpreted to provide evidence for a claim, subsequently dismissed by an American expert as 'entirely unsupportable', that Japan had once shared a common culture with the

whole of Korea and Manchuria and that the three countries were therefore
the home of an 'ancient Eastern race'.

It was then only a matter of time before the pretext for expansion was
broadened into the masquerade of a worldwide anti-colonialist crusade:
'We, the Japanese nation, should be the cyclonic centre of a war of
emancipation of the human race ...' On Hirohito's accession to the
Throne in 1926 the National Defence Plan was updated and enlarged to
incorporate a strategy of 'mass mobilisation,' and the indoctrination of
militant nationalism was correspondingly intensified under the direction
of a Bureau of Thought Control. In 1937 it published a book that was to
become the movement's Bible, *Kokutai No Hongi* or 'The Cardinal Principles of the National Entity of Japan' (the word *kokutai* represents a
concept which has no exact parallel elsewhere, and the traditional
translation 'national entity' cannot convey the religious overtones with
which the word is loaded).

Issued to every school and university in the country and to the by now
numerous colonies of Japanese settled overseas (the first English translation was made from a copy discovered in a secret school buried in the
concrete foundations of an office block in the Brazilian city of Marilia), it
set out to inculcate a theological and historical justification of the 'divine
mission' on which the nation was now embarked. Although its objective
was declared to be the establishment of a 'universal reign of peace' a
widely used commentary accompanying the book (whose archaic language rendered much of it barely intelligible to the average peasant)
explained that fulfilment of the mission 'entails the use of military power,
but history shows that the military might of Japan is always that of a divine
soldiery that is sent to bring life to all things.'

Four years later again, this 'divine soldiery' would be let loose on the
world: the *kamikaze* pilot, the *banzai*-shouting stormtrooper, the 'human
torpedo' submariner, the POW camp guards who looked on their charges
as a sub-species of the human race, the biological warfare scientists who
felt not the smallest scruple in subjecting their thousands of captive
specimens (whom they referred to as 'logs') to experiments which entailed
a lingering and excruciating death.

In all the twelve-hundred-year campaign of imposture and fabrication,
the claim that these were sent 'to bring life to all things' perhaps
stretched credulity furthest in the eyes of the outside world. However,
it must be borne in mind that it was not the outside world, not even the
peoples included in the proposed 'Greater East Asia Co-Prosperity
Sphere', at which this campaign was directed, but only the Japanese
themselves.

That still holds good today, for the alterations to Japanese high school
textbooks described earlier were hardly made for the benefit of audiences
elsewhere — a fact confirmed by Tokyo's massive indifference to the
offence which their publication was certain to give rise to outside Japan.

The explanation for the absence of reaction within Japan itself to such chicanery thus lies in the lack of profession integrity which the Japanese have been inured to expect from their historians — or rather, from their leaders at whose diktat the latter have compliantly subverted the facts — ever since the written word was first introduced into their country.

Clearly the non-Japanese would be equally liable to delusion if he imagined that an attitude formed over the course of so many centuries could be abruptly dispelled within the space of a single generation, even after the traumatic experiences of Hiroshima and Nagasaki. In the light of Japan's subsequent recovery to the point where her trade surpluses are of such a size that they threaten the stability of the entire world economy, he will need to ask whether these most recent mispresentations do not cloak political and conquistadorial designs similar to those of the past (and in particular, whether he should give credence to current Japanese pledges to redress those surpluses).

It is that question which this book, by tracing the correlation between the facade and the reality — between the verbal front presented to the outside world and its inner significance conveyed by 'the language of the belly' — up to the moment when Japan finally revealed her true intentions on December 8th 1941 with the surprise attacks on Malaya and Pearl Harbor, sets out to answer.

Glossary

Bakufu	the executive of the Shogunate
Banzai	lit. 'ten thousand years', and so used to mean 'May the the Emperor live ten thousand years!'
Bushido	'The Way of the Warrior', an ideology developed in the 17th century from a blend of the Zen Buddhist 'bukyo' creed of physical self-discipline with the Confucianist 'shido' tenet of loyalty
CER	Chinese Eastern Railway
daimyo	feudal lord, abolished after the Restoration of 1868
daimyo fudai	allies of the Tokugawa at the battle of Sekigahara in 1600, to whom the top positions in the Bakafu were then confined
daimyo tozama	the defeated opponents at the same battle, who were then excluded from power until the Restoration
DEI	Dutch East Indies
Diet	Parliament, introduced in 1890 and comprising an Upper House of Peers and a Lower House of Representatives
Genyosha	the earliest of the expansionist secret societies and forerunner of The Black Dragon
han	the fiefdoms of the daimyo
hara kiri	ritual suicide by disembowelment (more properly 'seppuku')
Kiheitai	an irregular militia of commoners (i.e., non-samurai) raised in the Choshu *han* to oppose the Bakufu
kokutai	traditionally translated as 'national polity', but perhaps better as 'the nation's essential characteristic', which in the 18th century was developed to include the notion of the Emperor's divine descent
Kojiki/Nihongi	'Records of Ancient Matters'/Chronicles of Japan', the earliest works of Japanese history
Roju	the five-man Inner Council heading the Bakufu
ronin	*samurai* who abandoned their feudal retainerships
samurai	military retainers of the *daimyo*
Seiyukai	New Constitutionalist Party
Shimazu	the honorary title of the *daimyo* of the Satsuma *han*
SMR	South Manchuria Railway
TSR	Trans-Siberian Railway

JAPAN AND
HER NEIGHBOURS

Okhotsk

KAMCHATKA

U. S. S. R.

SEA
OF
OKHOTSK

Nicolaevsk

SAKHALIN

R. Amur

Kurile Islands

Urup

MANCHURIA

HOKKAIDO   Nemuro

Hakodate

Peking

Yalu R.

SEA
OF
JAPAN

HONSHU

Niigata

Gulf
of Chilhi

KOREA

Edo (Tokyo)

Sekigahara   Yokohama

YELLOW
SEA

Kobe Osaka Nagoya
Ise
Nara
SHIKOKU   Shimoda

CHINA

Tsushima St.

INLAND SEA

OCEAN

Nagasaki   KYUSHU

Kagoshima

Shanghai

Loochoo
(Ryuku) Is.

Bonin Is.

Okinawa
Naha

PACIFIC

Iwo Jima

Pescadores
Hong Kong   Is.

FORMOSA
(TAIWAN)

Miles
0   100   200   300   400   500

0   200   400   600   800
Kilometres

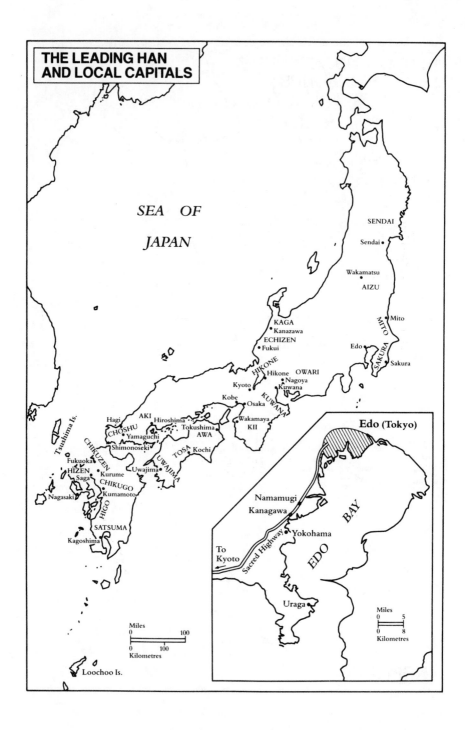

THE LEADING HAN
AND LOCAL CAPITALS

SEA OF

JAPAN

SENDAI

Sendai •

Wakamatsu
•
AIZU

KAGA
• Kanazawa
ECHIZEN
• Fukui

Edo •

Mito

MITO

SAKURA

Sakura

HIKONE
Hikone   OWARI
• Nagoya
Kyoto •   • Kuwana
Kobe   • Osaka
Wakamaya
KII

KUWANA

Edo (Tokyo)

Hagi   AKI   Hiroshima •
CHOSHU   • Yamaguchi   Tokushima •
Shimonoseki   AWA

Tsushima Is.

CHIKUZEN
Fukuoka •
HIZEN   • Kurume   Uwajima •
Saga •
CHIKUGO
Nagasaki •   • Kumamoto

HIGO

TOSA

UWAJIMA

• Kochi

Namamugi
Kanagawa

BAY

SATSUMA

Kagoshima •

To
Kyoto

Sacred Highway

• Yokohama

EDO

Uraga •

Miles
0   5

0   8
Kilometres

Miles
0   100

0   100
Kilometres

Loochoo Is.

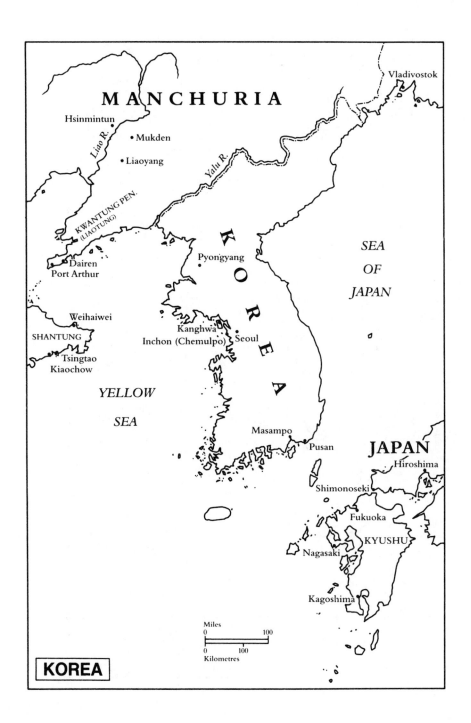

KOREA

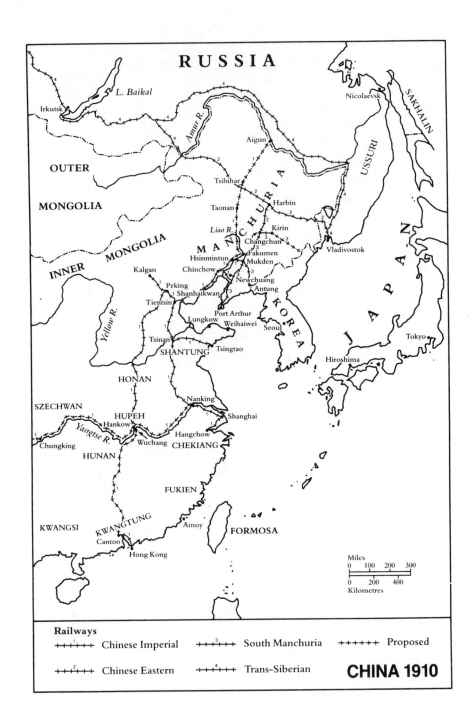

RUSSIA

L. Baikal

Irkutsk

Nicolaevsk

SAKHALIN

Amur R.

OUTER

Aigun

MONGOLIA

USSURI

Tsihihar

Taonan

Harbin

MANCHURIA

MONGOLIA

Liao R.

Kirin

Changchun

INNER

Fakumen

Hsinmintun

Kalgan

Chinchow

Mukden

Vladivostok

Peking

Newchuang

Tientsin

Shanhaikwan

Antung

JAPAN

Port Arthur

Lungkow

Weihaiwei

Seoul

KOREA

Tsinan

Tsingtao

Tokyo

SHANTUNG

Yellow R.

Hiroshima

HONAN

SZECHWAN

Nanking

HUPEH

Hankow

Shanghai

Chungking

Yangtse R.

Wuchang

Hangchow

CHEKIANG

HUNAN

FUKIEN

KWANGSI

KWANGTUNG

Amoy

FORMOSA

Canton

Hong Kong

Miles
0   100   200   300

0   200   400
Kilometres

Railways

+++++ Chinese Imperial   +++++ South Manchuria   ++++++ Proposed

+++++ Chinese Eastern   +++++ Trans-Siberian   **CHINA 1910**

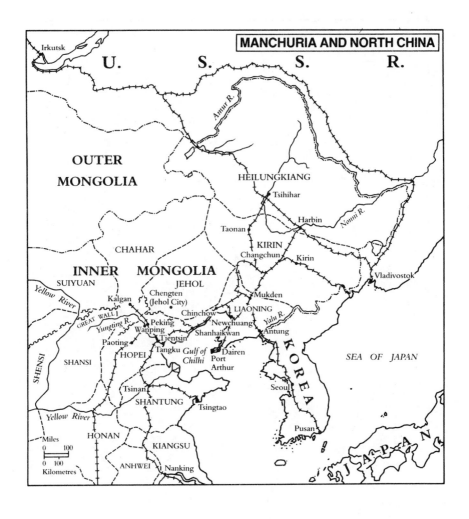

MANCHURIA AND NORTH CHINA

Irkutsk

U.   S.   S.   R.

Amur R.

OUTER
MONGOLIA

HEILUNGKIANG

Tsihihar

Harbin

Nonni R.

Taonan

CHAHAR

KIRIN

Changchun

Kirin

Vladivostok

INNER MONGOLIA

SUIYUAN

JEHOL

Yellow River

Kalgan

Chengten
(Jehol City)

Mukden

GREAT WALL

Chinchow

LIAONING

Yalu R.

Yungting R.

Peking

Newchuang

Antung

Wanping

Shanhaikwan

Tientsin

Paoting

Tangku Gulf of
Chilhi

Dairen
Port
Arthur

SHENSI

SHANSI

HOPEI

SEA OF JAPAN

Tsinan

Seoul

KOREA

SHANTUNG

Tsingtao

Yellow River

Pusan

Miles

0   100

HONAN

KIANGSU

J-A-P-A-N

0   100
Kilometres

ANHWEI

Nanking

CHINA

Controlled by
Japan 12.41

U.S.S.R.

OUTER
MONGOLIA

SINKHIANG

NINGSIA INNER

SUIYUAN

M

KANSU

Tatung
Pa

TSINGHAI

SHANSI

SHANSI

I

SHENSI

Sian

Yellow R.

HONA

H

TIBET

SIKANG

C SZECHWAN

HUPEH

Han

Yangtse R.

Chungking

INDIA

HUNAN

KWEICHOW

Road

Kunning

YUNNAN

KWANGSI

BURMA

Burma

Pearl R.

KWANGTUNG

C

Canto

Hong

Hanoi

Hong

INDO-CHINA

HAINAN

THAILAND

Rangoon

U. S. S. R.

SAKHALIN

H E I L U N G K I A N G

nhan

M A N C H U R I A

K I R I N

Harbin

Vladivostok

L. Khassan

JEHOL

Mukden

LIAONING

Shanhaikwan

ng

ientsin

EI

NTUNG

Tsingtao

Seoul

K O R E A

J A P A N

Tokyo

Hiroshima

ierchwang

chow

KIANGSU

Nanking

Nagasaki

Shanghai

Miles
0   100   200

0   200   400
Kilometres

CHEKIANG

LOOCHOO IS.

IEN

Fuchow

Okinawa

Amoy

FORMOSA

N

Yangtse R.

Airfield

S H A N G H A I

Chapei

International Settlement

French Concession

Bund

Whanpoa R.

Miles
0   1   2

0 1 2 3
Kilometres

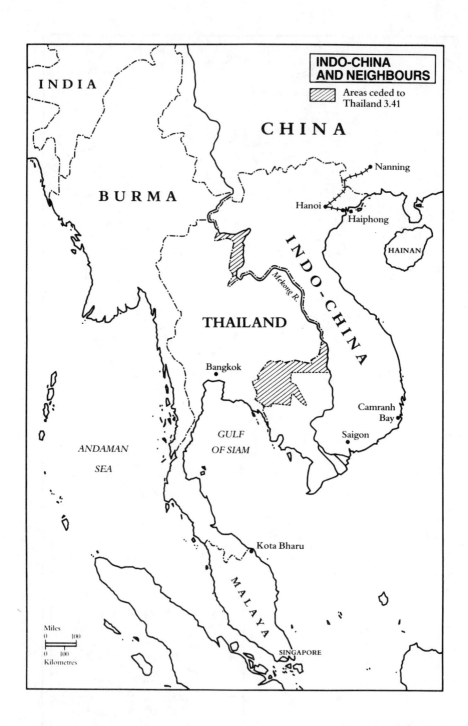

INDO-CHINA
AND NEIGHBOURS

Areas ceded to
Thailand 3.41

INDIA

CHINA

BURMA

Nanning

Hanoi

Haiphong

HAINAN

INDO-CHINA

Mekong R.

THAILAND

Bangkok

Camranh
Bay

GULF
OF SIAM

Saigon

ANDAMAN

SEA

Kota Bharu

MALAYA

Miles
0   100

0   100
Kilometres

SINGAPORE

PART I

Out of the Cocoon

1

The Myth Makers

THE DEBT TO CHINA

'It is six years since we repaired to the East. Through the influence of the heavenly deities the enemies have been subdued. Though the out-of-the-way lands have not yet been pacified and the unsubdued remnants are wild, the central lands are free from turmoil. . . . We hope to establish a capital from which to unite the whole realm, placing the whole world under one roof.'

These words were put by the compilers of the *Nihongi* into the mouth of Jimmu, the mythological founder of the Imperial line. They represented an attempt to give an historical context to the arrival on the main island of Honshu of the original migrants from Korea and the establishment of a capital on the Yamato plain between modern-day Nagoya and Osaka at Nara. The events were assigned to the seventh century BC, but the evidence of recent archaeology and of contemporary Chinese records combines to place them no earlier than the beginning of the Christan era.

Writing had been introduced from China only towards the end of the sixth century AD, and the author of the first translation of the *Nihongi* into English observed of the attribution to Jimmu that his 'whole speech is thoroughly Chinese in every respect, and it is preposterous to put it into the mouth of an Emperor who is supposed to have lived more than a thousand years before the introduction of Chinese learning into Japan.' In a similar sleight of hand, the *Nihongi* credited another pre-historical Emperor with an edict which had in fact issued from a Chinese Emperor several centuries earlier.

The infiltration of Chinese influence had come as an aftermath of the unification of Korea in 562, which had resulted in the expulsion of those who had not followed their kinsmen across the Straits of Tsushima in the original migration. Although legend spoke of an invasion led by an Empress Jingo as re-establishing Japanese influence in the interval, Korea had been under China's dominion for the best part of a millennium, and it did not take long for the superior culture of these latest arrivals to assert itself. Consequently the Regent Shotoku decided to send a mission to Peking in 607 to learn more of it at first hand.

On their arrival they were met by a courtier at the Dragon Throne who questioned them about their own customs. He reported back that 'the King of Wa [Yamato] deems heaven to be his elder brother and the sun his younger. Before dawn breaks he attends the court, and sitting cross-legged listens to appeals. Just as soon as the sun rises he ceases these duties, saying that he hands them over to his brother [the sun]'. Such information was not calculated to impress the occupant of a throne already some three thousand years old; according to the Court historian, 'our just Emperor said that such behaviour was extremely foolish and admonished the King to change his ways.'

As this anecdote illustrates, the indigenous Shinto religion was essentially a cult of sun-worship. Its centre was the shrine of the Sun Goddess Amaterasu at Ise, whose construction was dated by later Japanese historians to 5 BC (thus conveniently predating Christianity). Here were held the Imperial Regalia, including the mirror in which the Sun-Goddess was supposed magically to reveal herself to her descendant on the Throne as a reminder of his divinity. In addition, each of the hundreds of small, isolated communities scattered about the mountainous archipelago maintained their own individual shrines dedicated, as in most primitive religions, to natural objects and the souls of departed ancestors. The name *Shinto* itself was made up of three Chinese characters meaning 'following the will of the Gods without question', and there had been little difficulty in assimilating into it the Confucianist ethic of filial piety which Buddhist missionaries had recently introduced to Japan.

Suitably chastened by the contemptuous reproof from Peking, Shotoku decided to discard Japan's existing way of life in favour of the superior culture of China, beginning with the formal adoption of Buddhism whose deities were easily appropriated by Shinto's animistic objects of worship. His other reforms, spread over a period of forty years, affected every aspect of daily life, ranging from the formal adoption of the Chinese script and calendar, the legal code and tax system, medicine, methods of road and bridge construction to, most importantly of all, the imposition of the Chinese system of administration by a central government working through a network of provincial bureaucracies. The old tribal clans were dissolved, and their members were made citizens instead of the new unified state of Nihon (later Nippon) or 'The Sun-Begotten Land'.

FUJIWARAS AT COURT

Not surprisingly, these reforms met with resistance from the old clan leaders, especially those of the formerly dominant Soga clan who found themselves displaced by a new aristocracy of court officials, provincial administrators and Buddhist priests. The rival Fujiwaras seized on the opportunity of stepping into their shoes, and the remainder of the seventh century was largely dominated by a running battle between the two clans, each side backing different claimants to the Throne but neither daring to go so far as to appropriate the Throne itself. Eventually the Fujiwaras emerged victorious, and they consolidated their dominance of the Court by decreeing that henceforth the succession to the Throne would be decided by primogeniture.

It was the Fujiwaras who were responsible for putting in hand the compilation of the *Kojiki* and *Nihongi*. By emphasizing the divinity of the Emperor and his heaven-ordained mission to unite the population of the archipelago under his rule, they sought not only to legitimise the authority of the Imperial Line, but also to reinforce their own position at the Court. In this they were so successful that their influence there has persisted right down to the present century: of the 76 historical Emperors, no less than 54 have been mothered by Fujiwaras. (The senior member of the line in 1941, Prince Konoye, led Japan as Prime Minister almost to the brink of World War Two, committing suicide in 1945 on the eve of his arrest as a War Criminal, in order to avert the risk of compromising Emperor Hirohito.)

The adoption of Buddhism was also exploited by the Fujiwaras to their own advantage. A network of temples and monasteries was set up alongside the new civil administration, and in 752 the Daibutsu, a 53-foot-high bronze statue of the Buddha, was consecrated at Nara in a lavish ceremony attended by ten thousand priests invited from all over Asia. Thereafter, however, the arrival of new sects from the continent served to diminish acceptance of the Emperor's divinity and, by association, the dominance of the Fujiwaras in government.

In 794 the Fujiwaras attempted to reassert their authority by transferring the capital to Kyoto, but the move only accelerated their decline. The provincial governors grew increasingly independent of the new capital, carving out huge estates of land or *han* for themselves from the public domain, thereby acquiring the title of *daimyo* ('great landlord'). In order to defend their new possessions from rival claimants they recruited their own private armies, thus giving birth to the warrior caste of *samurai*.

THE SHOGUNS TAKE OVER

As the power of the *daimyo* increased, so that of the Court declined even further, until in 1086 the Emperor abdicated in favour of his son and entered holy orders. A century later the leader of the powerful Minamoto family assumed *de facto* sovereignty, and in recognition of his new status the Court accorded him the title of *Sei-i Dai Shogun* or 'Great Barbarian-Suppressing General' (originally conferred centuries earlier on a leader of the Imperial forces who had finally cleared Honshu of its aboriginal inhabitants, the Mongoloid Ainu); on a less formal level, he was referred to as *taikun* (tycoon) or 'supreme ruler'. The administrative capital was moved some three hundred miles east to Kamakura, the forerunner of Edo and modern-day Tokyo, leaving the Emperor in Kyoto with the nominal rôle of overseer of the priesthood and guardian of the Imperial Regalia.

The new regime of the Shogunate and its allied *daimyo* and *samurai* received a further boost to their status from the importation of Ch'en or Zen Buddhism. By 1274 its militaristic philosophy of physical discipline and self-reliance had been sufficiently widely instilled to inspire the country's successful defence against the invading Mongol army of the conqueror of China, Kublai (grandson of Genghis) Khan, a feat repeated seven years later with the help of a *kamikaze* or 'divine wind' which destroyed the greater part of his fleet. Having expected that the mere threat of invasion would have cowed 'the king of your little country' into submitting to his demand for fealty, Kublai withdrew a wiser man, never to return.

These signal victories led to an upsurge of national self-confidence in a Japan which had for so long rested in the shadow of its older and larger neighbour on the mainland. In particular, the *kamikaze* which had saved the day was interpreted as a sign of the divine protection of the Sun Goddess, and led to a revival of interest in Shinto. *The Five Classics of Shinto*, purportedly written in remote antiquity before the introduction of Buddhism (and writing) into Japan, was produced as evidence that Buddhism was originally derived from Shinto. Even more fatuously, its authors had Shotoku, the very man responsible for the adoption of Buddhism as the official religion, declaring that 'Japan was the roots and trunk of civilisation, China its branches and leaves, and India its flowers and fruits. Similarly, Buddhism is the flower and fruit of all laws, Confucianism their branches and leaves and Shinto their roots and trunk. Thus all foreign doctrines are offshoots of Shinto.' These out-and-out forgeries were to be upheld as holy writ by 'scholars' right down to — and indeed, especially during — the present century.

This revival naturally also inspired some further embellishment of Shinto's central dogma, the divine origin of the Imperial Line. In his *Records of the Legitimate Succession of the Divine Sovereigns* Kitabatake Chikafusa* exploited the relative brevity of Japan's recorded history to draw a favourable comparison with the changes of regime chronicled in those of longer-established societies: 'Only in our country has the succession remained inviolate, from the beginning of Heaven and Earth to the present,' he affirmed. 'It has been maintained within a single lineage, and even when, as inevitably has happened, the succession has been transmitted collaterally, it has returned to the true line.'

Kitabatake was writing at the time of the Imperial Schism (the issue at the heart of the 1911 Textbook Incident) and his purpose was to prove the claims of the breakaway Southern Court (of which he was one of the inner circle) by virtue, in particular, of its possession of the Imperial Regalia. In

---

* The Japanese practice of putting the family name before the given name has been followed. In order to make the more frequently recurring names more familiar to non-Japanese readers, sobriquets have been used where appropriate; those in inverted commas are of Japanese origin.

his enthusiasm, however, he went on to make the still larger claim that the integrity of the Imperial Line was 'due to the ever-renewed Divine Oath, and makes Japan unlike all other countries . . . Japan is the Divine Country. The Heavenly Ancestor it was who first laid its foundations, and the Sun Goddess left her descendants to reign over it for ever and ever.' This assertion of Japan's God-given uniqueness among all other nations was to underpin her later claims to a divine mission of world conquest.

At the time, however, this new fundamentalism did little or nothing to advance the claimants' cause, and they were presently obliged to capitulate to an alliance of the rival Northern Court and the powerful Ashikaga clan which had risen to take over the Shogunate. In due course the Ashikagas fell from grace in their turn, and the country became one long battlefield as other *daimyo* rose and threw their *samurai* into the struggle for the Shogunate succession.

Relegated once again to the sidelines, the Court sank to a new nadir of impotence and penury. By the sixteenth century it had fallen so low that one Emperor was obliged to postpone his coronation for twenty-one years before he was in a position to meet the necessary expense. When the Portuguese missionary Francis Xavier visited Kyoto in 1549, he found the Emperor literally scratching a living by hawking examples of his calligraphy in the capital's streets.

FIREPOWER

The traders who brought Xavier to Japan had already introduced something which was to have more immediate and far-reaching impact even than Christianity: gunpowder. Japanese swordsmiths were already as proficient as any in the world, and they were soon turning out copies of, and even improvements on, the original purchase of two matchlocks.

The first to appreciate the tactical scope of the new weapons was the young *daimyo* of a small *han* near Kyoto, Oda Nobunaga, a descendant of both the Imperial and Fujiwara lines. Equipping his *samurai* with 500 matchlocks, he presently took control of the Imperial capital with the Emperor's blessing and set about expanding his sway. By 1575 he was able to put 10,000 matchlocks and several cannon into the field, and at Narashino he mowed down the cavalry of the northern *daimyo* in a battle which opened a new era of military strategy. Oda then turned his attention to the south, but on the eve of a planned invasion of the island of Kyushu he was assassinated by one of his own generals. The command passed to his chief of staff, Hideyoshi, whose humble origins were denoted by the absence of a family name. Although he continued his predecessor's campaign of national unification, he contented himself with securing pledges and tithes of loyalty from the *daimyo* rather than imposing a central administration. With the great wealth that thus accrued to him he built the supposedly-impregnable Osaka Castle (whose massive fortifications stand to this day) and rehabilitated the finances of the impoverished Imperial Court.

In 1591 he felt himself sufficiently established, even though he had failed to secure recognition of his claim to the title of Shogun, to turn his thoughts to conquest overseas on the Asian mainland. 'Though our country is now safe and secure, I nevertheless entertain hopes of ruling the great Ming nation,' he wrote to the Portuguese Viceroy in Goa. 'I can reach the Middle Kingdom aboard my palace-ship within a short time. It will be as easy as pointing to the palm of my hand ...'

His plan of campaign envisaged the occupation not only of China, but eventually of the whole of eastern Asia as far east as the Philippines and as far west as India. Demanding the subjection of these countries, he stated to their rulers that it was 'Japan's destiny to be the sole ruler of the world'; in making this claim, he was motivated not by the Shintoist dogma of Japan's divine mission of world hegemony — he was a devout Buddhist — but by the much more practical concern of easing the acute pressure of her ever-burgeoning population. This had now reached some 25 million, twice that of Spain (then the dominant power in Europe) and five times that of Britain; Japan's land area on the other hand was no larger than Spain's — or that of the modern-day U.S. State of Montana — and because of its predominantly mountainous terrain less than a fifth of it was capable of bearing crops.

A year later Hideyoshi launched an expeditionary force of 200,000 men across the Straits of Tsushima to Korea, but the ensuing campaign proved to be far from the walk-over that he had so confidently predicted. Although his troops took only six months to fight their way up to the northern border at the Yalu River, they there found themselves confronted by a Chinese counter-force of over a million men. Hideyoshi's position was made still more precarious by the havoc wrought to his lines of communication by the cannon of the Korean navy. After two years of unremitting slaughter he dispatched a second expedition, only to see it again outnumbered and driven back by further reinforcements from China. In 1598, just as both sides were settling for an end to the murderous stalemate, he died, taking with him all Japanese thoughts, for the time being, of overseas conquest.

The expense of the expedition in terms of both material and lives had already given rise to mounting disaffection at home, and Hideyoshi's son-in-law Tokugawa Ieyasu quickly pulled back his forces from Korea in order to consolidate his claim to the succession. In 1600 the disaffection degenerated into open warfare, but Ieyasu finally put an end to three centuries of continuous civil war with a decisive victory at Sekigahara over an alliance of his most powerful rivals.

In return for the Emperor's acknowledgement of his right to the title of Shogun and the freedom to appoint his own nominee to the office of Kampaku (Imperial Adviser), Ieyasu completed the restoration of the Imperial fortunes with a handsome grant of land from the territories of his defeated opponents. The Emperor baulked at first at his further suggestion of a marital alliance between their two families, but the union was eventually consummated by the marriage of the new Shogun's daughter to the Imperial heir.

THE TOKUGAWA COCOON

Until his death sixteen years later Ieyasu devoted his energies to the unification of the country under the Tokugawa Shogunate; that this was to last for almost as long as the period of civil war which preceded it is a measure of his success. The most far-reaching of his reforms was the creation at Edo of a central bureaucracy, the Bakufu, headed by a five-man Roju (Inner Council). The top posts were restricted to members of the Tokugawa family and allied 'great lords', the *daimyo fudai*, who were further rewarded by grants of land from the *han* of their defeated rivals, the *daimyo tozama*. The result of this redistribution was to leave 60% of the productive land area in the hands of the *daimyo fudai*, much of it in the prime central plains surrounding Kyoto and Edo. The invidious distinction between the two classes of *daimyo* was to be maintained throughout the Tokugawa Shogunate's history, and it would become a significant factor in its eventual downfall.

Although a convert to the Sung School of Neo-Confucianism which had largely superseded Buddhism on the Asiatic continent, Ieyasu at first continued to tolerate the activities of the Christian missionaries, who in the wake of Xavier's opening crusade had made some half a million converts to their various denominations. In 1614, however, suspicions of Papal involvement in an attempted coup led him to banish the Jesuits and proscribe the Christian faith to all of *samurai* rank and above, although the Protestants from England and Holland were allowed to remain. Twenty years later his grandson Iemitsu was persuaded to intensify this repression; not only were the remaining missionaries expelled, but hundreds of their followers were publicly crucified as a warning to would-be converts, and in 1638 a final orgy of persecution saw 37,000 who still refused to renounce their faith herded on to a remote headland and butchered down to the last woman and child.

Still further measures were taken against the possibility of any future contamination. The expulsion order was extended to all non-Japanese residents, whether Christian or not; all Japanese living abroad were divested of their citizenship and forbidden on pain of death to return to the homeland; all trade with foreigners, except with Chinese in certain very limited categories, was outlawed; no Japanese was permitted to travel outside Japan and to ensure that this prohibition was respected shipbuilders were forbidden to construct any craft capable of sailing beyond home waters.

The Portuguese colony at Macao suffered particularly from the sudden cessation of trade, and a mission was sent to plead with the Shogun to reconsider. It got no further than Nagasaki, however; on orders from Edo, 57 of its members were executed on the spot, 13 alone being spared to report back to the outside world that the Shogun was in earnest. Not surprisingly, the message was taken to heart, and for the next two hundred years Japan would remain sealed as tightly as any silkworm in her cocoon.

This isolationism had much to do with the pervasive influence of one Hayashi Razan. Appointed by Ieyasu in 1608 as Confucianist tutor to the Tokugawa Shoguns (a position which he held for fifty years) and endowed with the hereditary headship of the new State University, a biographer wrote of him that 'there was not a single line in the laws or edicts of the first Tokugawa Shoguns that was not drafted by him.' Neo-Confucianism had developed in China as a strongly nationalistic reaction to the Mongol invasion, and Hayashi saw it as an opportune means both of inculcating popular loyalty to the new regime and of bolstering his own position against the Buddhist establishment. In particular, he sought to present Shinto as the Japanese equivalent, and his *General History of Our State* went so far as to assert that Jimmu's origins were Chinese.

This claim struck the head of the Tokugawa family's important Mito branch (and grandson of Ieyasu) as profoundly unsatisfactory, not to say heretical, and he commissioned a rival *History of Great Japan* in order to re-establish the Imperial Line's divine credentials. 'It was the Sun in person who laid the foundation of this nation over two thousand years ago. Since then divine descendants have occupied the Throne in legitimate succession; never did an imposter or traitor dare to usurp it,' ran its preface. Yet, almost in the same breath, its authors felt themselves able to proclaim that 'arbitrary selection or wilful alteration has no place in authentic history.' The *History* was not completed for another fifty years and not published in full for a century and a half after that, but when it did finally appear, it was to play an important part in the Restoration of direct Imperial rule.

Even this did not go far enough for Yamaga Soko, whose *True Facts Concerning The Central Kingdom* attempted to establish that Japan, not China, was the original source of human civilisation by virtue of Jimmu's divinity, and even that the True Way of Confucius had been received by the sage from Japan's Imperial Ancestors. In order to sustain such a claim Yamaga was obliged to assert that the historical records which would have constituted proof of this had been destroyed in a fire. In another treatise he sought to demonstrate that Neo-Confucianism was an imported version of the original doctrine. Not surprisingly, this was seen as a challenge to the authority of the Tokugawas who had identified themselves so closely with the former, and he was promptly arrested and exiled.

BUSHIDO, 'THE WAY OF THE WARRIOR'

Yamaga pleaded that nothing had been further from his mind, and he was later able to redeem himself by his development of the ideology of Bushido, 'The Way of The Warrior', blending the established Zen Buddhist ethic of physical self-discipline (*bukyo* or 'the warrior's creed') with a new philosophy drawn from Confucianist principles, *shido* or 'the way of the *samurai*'. His central theme was the exposition of the *samurai*'s duties in peace-time: when not serving in a military capacity the *samurai* was still bound to fulfil his obligation to his *daimyo* in return for his stipend, and this he could only do by exercising himself to the best of his ability in the intellectual fields of the arts and philosophy.

This was not, of course, intended to detract from the *samurai*'s primary military function, and Yamaga himself served as military tutor to the future leader of the 'Forty-Seven *Ronin**'. These heroes of succeeding generations of Japanese nationalists forsook their homes in order to avenge their *daimyo* who had been obliged to commit *hara-kiri* after being goaded into an indiscretion in the Shogun's presence; after infiltrating themselves as vagrants into the *han* of his tormentor and lying in wait for over a year for their opportunity, they finally caught him off guard and cut him down.

The Shogunate had little hesitation in giving its blessing to such a redefinition of the *samurai*'s role, the need for which had grown increasingly urgent since Iemitsu, in another move to stamp out dissent, had decreed that the *daimyo* and their *samurai* retinue should reside a third of every year in Edo. As a result, a great many of the latter, unable to meet the cost of maintaining two homes, had abandoned their feudal tenements and taken up the status of *ronin* in the capital, forming a large and potentially subversive element in its population. A diversion of their formidable energies into more peaceable pursuits therefore had seemingly everything to commend it. In the longer term, however, the Shogunate would have cause to regret this: ironically, it was from the *samurai* that the intellectual driving force behind the Restoration would spring.

The nostrums of Hayashi, Yamaga and the Mito School of history on the subject of the Imperial lineage all contributed to a further revival of interest in Shinto, a process also encouraged by Japan's lengthening isolation from the outside world. However, Shinto's emphasis on the Emperor's divinity was not calculated to endear the faith to the Tokugawa hierarchy in Edo. Arai Hakuseki, the leading scholar of his day and cultural adviser to the Shogun, was particularly scornful of the refusal of the authors of the *History of Great Japan* to make use of non-Japanese sources: 'the Mito historians rely on the *Nihongi* and nothing but the *Nihongi*, and so the history of our country is turning into an account of dreams told in a dream.' Another critic of the new mood of chauvinism, who took the precaution of labelling his treatise *The Testament of an Old Man*, was even more outspoken: 'Shinto is what certain medieval Japanese dressed up as ancient traditions of the Divine Ages and called The Way of

---

* *samurai* who left the service of their *daimyo*.

Japan in an attempt to outdo Confucianism and Buddhism . . . it is at once pitiful and ridiculous.'

Such provocative sentiments were too much, however, for the orthodoxy of Tokugawa Yoshimuno who succeeded to the Shogunate in 1715. Arai was summarily dismissed from his post, while the 'Old Man's' pseudonym was unable to save its author from being hounded to an early death at the age of 31. These events encouraged the Shintoist reactionaries to solicit the new Shogun for the creation of a 'School of National Learning' in order to revive the study of early works of Japanese literature. If Shinto was ever to replace the imported Buddhism as a national religion, they argued, it would need the authority of a corpus of basic scriptures with which to rival the Sutras — and purged, of course, of any suspicion of foreign origin.

Their petition granted, the myth-makers went to work with a will, surpassing even Kitabatake and his fellow-fraudsters of four centuries earlier.

'THE AXIS OF THE WORLD'

The new school was immediately faced with the inconvenient fact that not only were the earliest Japanese texts written in Chinese, but they were also very largely Chinese in content. However, this presented little obstacle to the native talent for re-writing history. The high priest of the National Learning movement, Hirata Atsutane, got round it, for instance, by asserting that Japan had all along had its own system of writing before the arrival of the Chinese script, which had therefore developed from the former. Unfortunately, the script which he produced to substantiate this claim turned out on examination to be a 15th-century alphabet from Korea.

Nothing daunted, he went on to adapt passages from Christian theological works in order to demonstrate Shinto's claims to superiority over other religions, merely substituting the word 'Shinto' for 'Christianity'. In addition, he argued that because there was no mention in the *Nihongi* of any Biblical Flood, this could be taken as proof that a divine hand had set Japan on a higher altitudinal plane than the other nations of the world. The theory of Copernicus was likewise held to confirm the correctness of the prominence given to the sun in Shintoist tradition. The art of medicine, he allowed, was first developed in China, but only for the reason that 'the spread of Confucianism and Buddhism, both of them exceedingly troublesome doctrines, worsened and confused men's minds, and as a result of the attendant increase in the number of things to worry about various maladies became prevalent . . .'

Others preferred to postulate, less specifically, that the innate quality of early Japanese works and of the characters which they described was sufficient proof in itself of their freedom from any foreign taint. This was held to be true in particular of the first anthology of poems, the *Manyoshu*, and of the later classic, *The Tales of Genji*; 'They are the natural expression of our ancient heritage,' the argument ran, 'they are the voice of our Divine Land.'

China by contrast, although admitted to be an older civilization, was held to be 'a country of wickedheartedness, so that no amount of profound instruction could keep the innate evil from overwhelming the country . . . Our country in ancient times was not like that. It obeyed the laws of Heaven and Earth. The Emperor was the sun and moon and his subjects the stars . . . However, some knaves appeared, and as a result the Emperor is diminished in power and his subjects too have languished. The ancient texts of the Divine Age, the *Kojiki* and *Nihongi*, are where we may gain knowledge of this.'

The unnamed 'knaves' were probably the Minamoto; the point had not yet been reached where the legitimacy of the Tokugawa Shogunate itself could be called into question. However, the new emphasis on the sanctity of the ancient texts inevitably served to enhance the status of the Throne. A major contribution to this theme came with the publication of a modern version of the *Kojiki* by Motoori Norinaga. Largely ignored until now because of the extreme textual difficulty of its classical Chinese, its rendition into contemporary Japanese was a true labour of love which took him the best part of thirty years.

The *Kojiki* consists almost entirely of accounts of the world's creation by the Sun Goddess and similarly fictitious genealogical reconstructions of the Imperial Line, but Motoori dispensed with any question of their authenticity with the assertion that they were 'miraculously divine acts, the reasons for which are beyond the comprehension of the human intellect.' The scepticism of any non-Japanese could be still more summarily dismissed; 'unable to understand that the truths of the world are contained in the evolution of the Divine Age, they fail to ascertain the true meaning of our ancient tradition,' he maintained. 'That foreign countries revere such non-existent beings [their own gods] and remain unaware of the grace of the Sun Goddess is a matter of profound regret.'

'However,' he went on, jumping from one false premise to another, 'because of the special dispensation of our Imperial Land, the ancient tradition of the Divine Age has been correctly and clearly transmitted in our country in the *Kojiki*, telling us of the genesis of the Great Goddess and the reason for her adoration . . . Our country's Imperial Line, which casts its light over this world, represents the descendants of the Sky-Shining Goddess . . . Thus our country is the source and fountainhead of all other countries, and in all matters it excels all others.'

'It would be impossible to list all the products in which our country excels, but foremost among them is rice, which sustains the life of man for whom there is no product more important. Our country's rice has no peer in foreign countries, from which fact it may be seen why our other products are also superior.' It would perhaps be charitable to suppose that it was the embargo on foreign trade, preventing comparison with rice from other sources, which led him to make such a comical statement.

This theme of Japan's universal superiority had advanced by the first half of the 19th century to the extent that Sato Shinan in his *Confidential Plan of World Unification* could write: 'Our Imperial Land came into existence at the very beginning of Earth and it is the root and basis of all other countries of the world. Thus, if the root is attended to with proper care, the entire world will become its prefectures and provinces. In terms of world geography our Imperial Land would appear to be the axis of the other countries of the world, as indeed it is . . .'

'For Japan to attempt to open other countries, her first step must be the absorption of China. Despite her great strength, China cannot oppose our country. Needless to say, the other countries likewise cannot oppose us, for by the grace of nature Japan is so situated as to be able to unify the countries of the world. I am therefore going to explain in this work how China can be subjugated. After China is brought within our domain, the Central Asian countries, as well as Burma, India and other lands will come to us with bowed heads and on hands and knees to serve us.'

Japan's claim to world hegemony was thus no longer seen simply in terms of spiritual and cultural leadership, but in those of physical conquest by force of arms.

One hundred years later this would find its ultimate expression in *Kokutai No Hongi*. The words, and the phrase 'whole world under one roof' in particular, attributed to Jimmu and quoted at the beginning of the chapter were then made to bear a very different interpretation: instead of being taken to refer to the creation of a single nation by the unification of the scattered communities of the Japanese archipelago in prehistoric times, they were now presented as proof of Hirohito's god-given mandate to bring the entire globe under his dominion.

The myth-makers had cast their spell only too well.

2

'Ugly and Impudent Barbarians'

UNINVITED VISITORS

When Shogun Iemitsu imposed his interdict on commerce with the West, he made a single exception in favour of the Dutch (their Protestant rivals, the English, having earlier withdrawn from the field, unable to compete with the prices of goods shipped from the relative proximity of the Dutch East Indies).

They were permitted to retain a nominal presence on the tiny artificial island of Deshima in Nagasaki Bay, from which they were allowed ashore for the sole purpose of making an annual presentation of gifts to the Shogun. In token of their obeisance they were obliged to enter his presence crawling on their hands and knees; on some occasions they were even further humiliated by being compelled to perform a symbolic trampling of the Crucifix. They were also required to provide him with a summary of the year's developments in the outside world, but they seldom succeeded in arousing his interest; for instance, it was not until 1741 that they were first questioned about a book which had been presented 78 years earlier.

The closure of Japan's ports could not, however, be calculated to forestall the encroachment of a new intruder by land across the continent of Asia.

The Russians had reached the eastern Siberian seaboard to found Okhotsk as early as 1639. By the end of the century they had completed their occupation of the great peninsula of Kamchatka, from where they then began to explore southwards along the Kurile archipelago towards Japan. A shipwrecked fisherman provided their first contact with the Japanese themselves; he was transported all the way back to St. Petersburg in the hope that he could be used to establish a Japanese language and navigation school. The difficulties of staffing it at such an enormous remove eventually proved too great, however, and in 1764 it was transferred eastwards again to the Siberian capital of Irkutsk. Some years earlier, in 1739, the Danish navigator Vitus Bering, who had been commissioned by Peter the Great to explore the west coast of America, had become the first master of a Russian ship to put into a Japanese port.

13

In 1770 an Hungarian adventurer, one Baron Moritz Aladar von Benyowski, organised a mass escape from a penal settlement on Kamchatka, seized one of the warders' ships and set sail for Japan. On his arrival at Oshima he announced himself to be the 'Commander of the Austrian Navy' and wrote to the Shogun warning him that the Russians were planning to invade the northern island of Hokkaido the following year. Taking, in their self-imposed ignorance of European geography, the 'Commander' at his word, the Bakufu were thrown into momentary panic; to his disappointment, however, they recovered their nerve in time to reject his accompanying offer of his services as naval adviser to the Shogun and had him escorted out to sea again.

Though nothing so ambitious as an invasion of the Japanese homeland was in the mind of the Empress Catherine, her ships continued to probe southwards. In 1778 the Russians put into Nemuro with a formal request for permission to trade. Although it met with the customary rebuff, it served to exacerbate the emerging division of opinion between the traditional isolationists and those who had begun to see disaster ahead if Japan continued to cut herself off from the growth in international trade and its attendant benefits.

The argument was further sharpened by a series of disastrous harvests during the following decade and the resultant famine which accounted for over one-and-a-half million deaths. As the taxation imposed locally by individual *daimyo* increased in consequence, so more and more of the poorer farmers were forced to sell up and join the multitudes of *ronin* who had already abandoned their feudal service for the cities. The population of Edo rose as a result to well over one million, making it by far the largest city in the world. Responsibility for its upkeep fell largely on the Bakufu treasury, whose income increasingly fell short of the necessary expenditure. The deficits were met by the time-honoured remedy of debasing the coinage, but the resultant inflation simply gave a further twist to the vicious spiral by driving still more people from the land.

FOREIGN WAYS

In an attempt to find a solution, a group of liberal scholars established the Rangaku or 'Dutch Learning School' and began translating European books obtainable from the Factory at Deshima. In so doing they inevitably brought down on themselves the full wrath of the zealots of the National Learning movement, who accused them of being 'taken in by the vaunted theories of the Western foreigners; they enthusiastically extol these theories, some going so far as to publish books about them in the hope of transforming our civilised way of life into that of the barbarians.'

'What is the meaning of such criticism?' one of the Rangaku scholars retorted. 'Dutch learning is not perfect, but if we choose the good points and follow them, what harm could come of that? What is more ridiculous than to refuse to discuss its merits and to cling to one's past without changing?' Between the two sides the Shogun, or rather, the Bakufu on behalf of the nonentity who currently held that title, wavered irresolutely. Eventually the Rangaku's publication of a book based on Adam Smith's *Wealth of Nations* was considered so iconoclastic that the Bakufu were moved to issue an Act of Prohibition of Heterodox Studies in order to suppress it.

1792 saw the appearance of a second Russian trading mission, this time in a guise which made it impossible for them simply to be turned away, for they had with them the captain of a shipwrecked Japanese junk. After much agonized deliberation, the Bakufu acceded to the castaway's return and informed his deliverers that if they wished to trade they would have to remove themselves to Nagasaki and apply to the authorities there. Being some five hundred uncharted miles distant from that port at the time, the Russians correctly took this for the refusal that it was intended to be and retired to Okhotsk to consider their next move.

Russian sealers had already been active in the north western Pacific for several decades, and in 1795 they obtained the blessing of the Empress to establish a settlement on the Kurile island of Urup, only 200 miles north-east of Hokkaido. This was followed shortly afterwards by the grant of a Royal Charter to the Russian-American Fur Company, an amalgamation of two previous concerns in the area now under the energetic direction of a Captain Vasilii Rezanov. The Bakufu were powerless to prevent such an intrusion, and they could only issue an edict forbidding the inhabitants of Hokkaido to trade with the Company on pain of death.

Not until nine years later did Rezanov present himself at Nagasaki, bearing an official request from the newly-enthroned Tsar Alexander for a full trade treaty. Refused permission to travel to Edo in order to present it to the Shogun, the Captain instead found himself imprisoned in a hastily-erected bamboo shack. Not surprisingly, he fell seriously ill during the six months that it took the Bakufu to arrive at a decision. Once more in the negative, it was accompanied by a note rejecting the many lavish gifts proferred by the Tsar on the grounds that 'Japan already produced all that he [the Shogun] could conceivably want'.

This third rebuff proved too much for the Russian's patience, and in the following year Rezanov launched a campaign of systematic eviction against Japanese settlements on Sakhalin and the Kuriles. In 1807 he went so far as to attack and plunder some junks at anchor in the Hokkaido port of Hakodate. In retaliation, the Japanese seized the captain of a Russian survey ship in the Kuriles and held him in prison until they received an official disclaimer from St. Petersburg of responsibility for the raids. That same year, throwing himself into plans for a still more ambitious drive to extend Russian interests on the western American seaboard as far south as California, Rezanov died.

Others meanwhile had begun to beat a path to the same door, but with no better success, among them a British fur trader and an American ship under charter to the Dutch East Indies Company (Holland itself having fallen to Napoleon). In 1811 Stamford Raffles became Lieutenant-Governor of Java following its capture by Britain and immediately set about persuading the Board of the East India Company to open negotiations with Japan for a commercial treaty. As a first step, he wrote, it would be necessary to 'gain to our interest the present Dutch Resident [Factor] in Japan and the Japanese corps of interpreters at whatever price it may cost'.

A ship was accordingly dispatched to Nagasaki flying Dutch colours and bearing appropriate inducements for the Factor; also on board were an elephant for the Shogun and a Factor-elect who was to take over as soon as it was judged safe to reveal to the Japanese that Java was now in British hands. However, the Factor was no more to be bought than the Shogun, and all, elephant included, shortly found themselves homeward bound again for Batavia. After a similar failure the following year, Raffles was forbidden by the new Governor-General in India to make any further such ventures, and he turned his attention instead to the creation of a British colony at Singapore.

As word had spread of each new visitation over the years, so the spirit of chauvinism fostered by the dogmatists of the National Learning movement had increased until in 1824 Mito *samurai* attacked a British whaler which had been beached by a storm. Managing to beat off their assailants and to put out to sea again, the crew sailed down the coastline to Kagoshima, the southernmost extremity of the Japanese homeland and fiefdom of the Satsuma *han*. To stock up for the next leg of their journey across the open sea, they put ashore and slaughtered some cattle. As they were doing so they were accosted by the owners, and in the ensuing confrontation a number of the Japanese lost their lives.

The Bakufu reacted by issuing a fresh exclusion edict to the effect that any foreign ship found in Japanese waters should now be fired on without warning and its crew killed or at least captured. This proved insufficient, however, to head off the nation-wide storm of indignation aroused by the two incidents. 'Today the ugly and impudent barbarians of the West, the lowly legs and feet of the world, are dashing about across the seas, trampling other countries underfoot and daring with their squinting eyes and limping feet to override the noble nations,' thundered Aizawa Seishisai, the current spokesman of the Mito School.

'Some say the Westerners are merely foreign barbarians, that their ships are trading vessels or fishing boats and they are not people who would cause any serious trouble or harm. Such people are relying on the enemy not coming and invading their land; they rely upon others, not themselves,' he warned of the Rangaku deviationists. 'The weakness of some for novel gadgets and rare medicines, which delight the eye and enthral the heart, have led many to admire foreign ways. If someday the treacherous foreigner should take advantage of this situation and lure ignorant people to his ways, our people will adopt such practices as eating dogs and sheep and wearing woollen clothing ...'

'EXALT THE EMPEROR'

How then was such a horrible prospect to be avoided? For the first time the authority of the Shogun began seriously to be called into question. It was his misfortune that the incidents had taken place within the borders of the two *han* where loyalty to the Tokugawa regime was most susceptible to challenge: in Mito, the repository of the 'evidence' for the divinity of the Imperial Line, and in Satsuma, the most powerful of the *tozama* defeated at Sekigahara by Ieyasu, where secret ceremonies pledging vengeance were still widely held on the anniversary of the battle. As long as the Shogun fulfilled his historic rôle as the 'Great Barbarian-Suppressing General' his writ could be respected as that of the Emperor's surrogate, but once he failed in that, deference to him would be irreconcilable with the subject's overriding duty to his Emperor.

It was at this point that the Mito School joined forces with the National Learning movement to call for the return of the Emperor to his original position of supreme authority as the only figure capable, by virtue of his divine descent, of protecting the nation against the intrusions of the barbarian. Two decades earlier a Mito apostle had been stirred by Rezanov's activities to upbraid the Bakufu for the inadequate condition of the country's defences, but the *han*'s ruling *daimyo* of the time (who was, it must be remembered, still a leading member of the Tokugawa family) had declined to allow any wider expression to such criticism. Now that Mito's own shore had been defiled by the barbarian foot, the latter's successor felt no inhibition in giving his blessing to the publication of Aizawa's *New Proposals*.

In calling for drastic action, even Aizawa still felt obliged to make a token recognition of the Shogun's authority: 'If the Shogun issues orders to the entire nation in unmistakable terms to smash the barbarians whenever they come into sight and to treat them openly as our nation's foes, then within one day after the order is issued, everyone high and low will push forward to enforce it ... This is a great opportunity such as comes once in a thousand years. It must not be lost.' In another section, however, he made it unequivocally clear that it was to the Throne that he was looking: 'The only sure way to protect the Empire is that people should be of one mind, that they should cherish their Sovereign, and that they should be unable to bear being separated from Him. Since Heaven and Earth were divided and mankind first appeared, the Imperial Line has surveyed the four seas generation after generation in the same dynasty ... The duty of subject to sovereign is the supreme duty in Heaven and Earth.'

The slogan *sonno-joi* — 'Exalt the Emperor, Expel the Barbarian' — was to become the clarion call over the next four decades for the restoration of direct Imperial rule. In going on to assert that 'Japan's position at the apex of the earth makes it the standard for the nations of the world' Aizawa was no more than repeating the claim of Japan's divinely-bestowed superiority first made by Kitabatake as far back as the fourteenth century, but in reviving it he provided the inspiration for his near-contemporary Sato Shinan's *Confidential Plan of World Unification* which first stated the case for a strategy of world conquest.

Sato advocated the invasion of China as a means of forestalling further Russian encroachments, but the Tsar would be preoccupied for some time yet with the task of securing his European frontier after the disagreeable experience of seeing Napoleon advance to the very gates of Moscow. In 1827 the British returned to raise the Union Jack over the uninhabited Bonin Islands 500 miles south of Edo and inspire a number of European adventurers to settle there, but as the expiry of the East India Company's charter in 1833 drew nearer, British interest in Japan waned again and the Foreign Office eventually decided against according the settlement colonial status. Seven years later three Japanese castaways on the west coast of Canada were sent on to London by the Hudson's Bay Company's local agent with the suggestion that they might offer the opportunity to negotiate a commercial treaty with Japan; the Foreign Office, however, was still wary of any involvement and ordered them to be returned to Japan.

When the much-travelled trio finally left Canton on the last leg of their journey home, it was on board the American brig *Morrison*. She was carrying a large cargo of U.S.-manufactured textiles; the American commercial community in Canton had expanded rapidly in recent years, servicing over sixty ships with an annual turnover of some sixteen million dollars, and they were only too eager for the chance to force a toe into the Japanese door. Their hopes were in vain, however: no sooner had the three Japanese attempted to set foot again on their native shore than the local defence forces, in accordance with the instructions of the new Exclusion Law, opened up with their cannon. The *Morrison*'s captain, having gone to the trouble of removing the ship's guns below deck as a token of his peaceable intentions, thereupon decided that he had no option but to turn about and make all speed back again to China.

Informing the State Department of their experience, the disappointed Americans pressed for the dispatch of a Navy squadron to Japan with a warning of the very serious consequences that would attend any repetition of such behaviour. Although the suggestion was not in the event taken up, it did induce Washington to formulate for the first time a consistent policy towards Japan. In the course of the next decade this policy was to be given increasingly purposeful expression.

In the meantime Canton continued to be the focus of attention of the Far East, for Japanese no less than Western eyes. In 1839 the Manchu government in Peking appointed a new commissioner there with the specific assignment of putting a stop to the importation of opium which was rapidly undermining all levels of Chinese society; easily transported from the relative proximity of the Indian colony's poppy fields, the drug now accounted for all but a small fraction of British trade with China. Britain saw fit to respond with a series of naval bombardments of the southern coastline, followed by an expedition up the Yangtse to threaten Nanking, the Empire's second capital. The Chinese, their navy non-existent and their shore batteries hopelessly outgunned, quickly capitulated.

The ensuing Treaty of Nanking in 1842 ceded Hong Kong Island by permanent lease to Britain, opened five other Chinese ports to external commerce and abolished the Hong, the local monopoly through which all trade in opium had hitherto been conducted. It also contained a 'Most Favoured Nation' clause which gave Britain an automatic right to any privileges subsequently granted to other nations. Over the next century this was to become a source of ever-growing friction and resentment between the rival Western Powers fighting for a share of China's spoils, similar treaties with France and the United States having followed in 1844.

'FROST ON JAPAN?'

In Japan, the outcome of the Opium War brought a general realisation that the march of events in the world outside was now about to overtake the two-centuries-old Tokugawa strategy of isolation, and the debate on how the Western threat to the Divine Land might be repelled was finally brought out into the open. As a contemporary poet picturesquely put it, 'How can we know whether the mist gathering over China will not fall as frost on Japan?'

The Mito advocates of *sonno-joi* now had a powerful spokesman in their new *daimyo*, Tokugawa Nariaki, who for the next twenty years was to cast himself in the role of national watchdog against the insidious encroachments of the barbarian; the twin corruptions of trade and Christianity, he proclaimed, had been responsible for China's downfall, and hence no price was too high to pay for the protection of Japan's divinely-blessed shores. In reality, however, the price that Japan could afford to pay was severely limited by the parlous state of the Tokugawa economy stemming from another succession of bad harvests and outbreaks of peasant unrest which had flared into open violence, notably in the leading market city of Osaka. In an attempt to resolve the crisis, the Bakufu drafted Mizuno Tadakuni into the Roju (the five-man Inner Council) on the strength of his success in reviving the local economy of his *han*.

Mizuno set about this formidable task by introducing draconian sumptuary laws, debasing the coinage still further, levying forced loans on the merchant class and abolishing the monopolistic powers of their guilds. All this, however, had little perceptible effect, so he then put forward the

radical proposal that all the land in the immediate environment of Edo and
Osaka should be made over to the Tokugawa treasury. Its effect was to provoke such a furious reaction that there was no option but to dismiss him.

The Bakufu had in fact tacitly acknowledged his failure a few months
earlier by relaxing the Exclusion Law to the extent of permitting
assistance to foreign ships in distress, on condition that their crews
undertook not to come ashore nor ever to return to Japan. This modest
concession was, needless to say, strenuously opposed by National Watchdog Nariaki, although even he was prepared to admit that no amount of
expenditure on defence could be effective while Japan's armaments lagged
so far behind those of the West. One of Mizuno's innovations had been the
establishment in 1841 of an artillery school under the direction of Takashima Shuhan of Nagasaki, an early pioneer in the field who had carried
out experiments with cannons and mortars imported from Europe at his
own expense. The school was supported by Sakuma Shozan, one of the
leading lights of the Rangaku, who submitted to the Bakufu a detailed
programme for the adoption of Western technology and the construction
of a modern navy, and whose slogan 'Eastern Ethics, Western Science' was
to inspire Japan's later transformation into an industrial power.

By definition, such a programme demanded participation in international trade, but in advocating the opening of Japanese ports to the ships
of the barbarian Sakuma was envisaging only a temporary abandonment of
the *joi*ist creed; as he saw it, such a step represented a distasteful, but
unavoidable means towards the greater end of safeguarding Japan's sacred
independence. Others, however, began to take his argument a stage
further: although still united on the end, they held that this could only be
achieved by wholesale economic and social reform, which in turn required
freedom to draw on the ideas of the outside world.

BAKUFU AT BAY

As the debate widened, the Bakufu became increasingly divided and
paralyzed. In 1843 a Royal Navy survey ship was reported at work in the
Loochoo (Ryuku) Islands, and the following year King Wilhelm II of the
Netherlands wrote that the British and French were about to establish
trading posts in the islands. In all probability, he warned, they intended to
move on to Japan itself, and the Bakufu would be well advised to lower the
barriers before they were obliged to do so by force of arms — while still,
of course, reserving for his own country the privileged position that it had
enjoyed for the past two centuries.

Mizuno was recalled to the Roju to assist in weighing up the implications of the King's letter. Almost a year passed before they decided on
their response, which was once more to do nothing. By that time Mizuno
had already been dismissed for a second time and his protégé Takashima
arrested on a charge of smuggling foreign weapons and plotting a rebellion

against the Shogun. Ironically, this action only served to increase the likelihood of insurrection, for the Bakufu's refusal to take responsibility for armament development encouraged dissident *daimyo* to do so secretly for themselves; the inventor of Japan's first successful blast furnace was likewise prudent enough to construct it in the privacy of his back garden.

One of the first to respond was Nariaki, who ordered Buddhist monasteries in Mito to melt down their bells to provide copper for the casting of cannon. He did not trouble to obtain the necessary permission from the Bakufu, and when news of this insubordination reached Edo he was directed to stand down as *daimyo* in favour of his son. This did nothing, however, to diminish the National Watchdog's standing either inside or outside his *han*. Indeed, as the attentions of the hated barbarians grew ever more persistent, so Japanese eyes increasingly turned to him as the country's most likely protector. In 1846 he warned Abe Masahiro, the new leader of the Roju, that 'when the safety of Japan is in question, if you do not make your will known clearly and unquestionably, there is no doubt that the *daimyo tozama* and the other nobles will act without waiting for your orders.'

There were two *daimyo* in particular that he had in mind, namely, those of Choshu and Satsuma. After their defeat at Ieyasu's hands in 1600 these *han* had seen the greater part of their territory confiscated, but they had nonetheless retained their full complement of *samurai*. Amounting to some 30,000 in Satsuma and 11,000 in Choshu, their combined total exceeded that of the Shogun's *fudai* allies, and of all the *han* they were the most deeply imbued with the spirit of military tradition (and after the Restoration of 1868 they would dominate the new Imperial Army and Navy respectively).

Furthermore, their economies were in a much healthier condition than that of the central government at this juncture. Satsuma in particular had enjoyed a considerable measure of economic independence since its annexation (with Ieyasu's blessing) of the Loochoos in 1609. The islands continued to pay a nominal fealty to China and had in consequence become the *entrepôt* of a thriving trade between the two countries, to which Ieyasu's successors had been prepared to turn a blind eye. Still more lucratively for the local treasury, the *han* authorities enforced a rigid monopoly in the cultivation of sugar there, which could not be grown elsewhere in Japan; private trade in it was punishable by death, and even a production worker caught licking his fingers was liable to a public whipping.

The Shimazu (*daimyo*) of Satsuma had already begun casting his own cannon using Western techniques, and he now opened a gunnery school which utilised the weapons and drill systems introduced by Takashima. The authorities in Choshu sent several of their *samurai* to study there most notably Yoshida Shoin, a disciple of Sakuma who was to become a prime instigator of the Restoration movement and a hero to future generations of Japanese expansionists.

Nariaki's letter to Abe concluded with the even more ominous threat that 'at such a time the Imperial Court would not remain neutral, and events would soon occur beyond your control.' The Shogun was thus given unequivocal notice that if he failed to fulfil his rôle as 'the great barbarian-suppressor', the nation would look to the Emperor to assume it.

The Throne had recently passed to the sixteen-year-old Komei, an early product of the Gakushain or Peers' School founded by his father to ground the future leaders of Japan in the holy writ of Shintoism. One of his first actions on his accession was to request from the Shogun a full report on the state of the nation's defences, warning him at the same time that the exclusion policy must be maintained at all costs and demanding to be kept informed on every aspect of foreign affairs.

This did not mark any sudden renewal of interest from Kyoto in the outside world. The works of the National Learning ideologues and Mito School had received considerable attention at the Court, which would have thoroughly digested the implications of such statements (of Hirata) as 'the fact is obvious that the Mikado is the true Son of Heaven who is entitled to reign over the four seas and the ten thousand countries', and 'Mediocre leaders see to it that everything appears quiescent, but they let barbarians go unchecked under their very eyes, calling them just "fishing traders". They conspire together to hide the realities, only to aggravate the situation through half-hearted inaction.'

The Bakufu were thus under increasing pressure from three sides: from the warships of the West, vastly superior to anything that could be sent against them and ready to throw Japan open to the world on Western terms; from the more powerful of the *daimyo tozama*, especially the Shimazu of Satsuma, bolstered by well-armed private armies and prepared to make their own external trading arrangements; and from a resurgent Imperial Court threatening — if only as yet by implication — a resumption of direct Imperial rule. Abe, their leader, was by nature a conciliator; like most of his senior officials he recognised that maintenance of the isolation policy by force of arms was totally impracticable, but he felt unable to make public acknowledgement of the fact for fear of arousing the rabid hostility of its fanatical proponents.

His strategy was therefore to run before the wind of events on as even a keel as possible, doing no more than laying an occasional hand on the tiller until the need for a change of tack was beyond argument. He was not to foresee that one of these touches, the confinement under house arrest of Komei's brother-in-law and the latter's father, Prince Kuniye of the Imperial house of Fushimi, would be instrumental in bringing about the Shogunate's fall. Kuniye was himself a figure of very considerable influence, and in the course of the next century his son would become Head of the Army General Staff, his grandson that of the

Naval General Staff and his great-granddaughter the present Empress Nagako.

AMERICA KNOCKS

The previous year (1845), the U.S. Congress, anxious to keep abreast of Britain and France in the East, had passed a resolution 'that immediate measures be taken for effecting commercial arrangements with the Empire of Japan'. Commodore James Biddle was accordingly dispatched to the China Sea with a pair of frigates, the U.S.S. *Columbus* and *Vincennes*.

He arrived in Edo Bay on July 20th, 1846 and presented a formal letter of application from President James Polk. A week later it was returned with a note, undated and unsigned, of brusque refusal; to add to the injury, as Biddle was about to board the Bakufu junk which brought it, one of its crew pushed him over backwards into his own boat. Being under strict orders not to do anything 'to excite a hostile feeling or distrust of the United States', he did not retaliate, thereby giving unwitting support to the contention of the *sonno-joi*ists that Japan had nothing to fear from the barbarians.

Such a rebuff, however, was not enough to dampen the ambitions of New York entrepreneur George Wilkes. The Pacific Mail Steamship Company had been founded in the wake of the recent annexation of the states of Oregon and California, and Wilkes now came forward with a scheme for the construction of a railway to the West Coast in order to promote trade with 'the opulent empire of Japan'. With government blessing, the Company was soon pressing ahead with plans to inaugurate a regular service to China in order to take advantage of the 1844 trade treaty with that country, but much depended on the availability of coaling facilities in Japan.

Consequently Commodore James Glynn, Biddle's successor on the China Sea station, was authorised in 1849 to sail with the U.S.S. *Prebble* to Nagasaki on the pretext of recovering the crew of a shipwrecked American whaler being held prisoner there. He succeeded in securing the crew's release but not the primary objective, and on his return to Washington he persuaded his superiors that a fully-accredited diplomatic mission was called for, to be accompanied by an appropriate naval escort.

The man chosen to lead it was Commodore Matthew Perry, already a national hero by virtue of his capture of Vera Cruz in the recent war with Mexico; the flagship in that action was the *Mississippi*, the U.S. Navy's first steam-driven warship which he himself had helped to design. Known to his naval colleagues everywhere as 'Old Matt', he was a figure of considerable presence both in physique and character who was not above injecting a touch of theatricality when the occasion demanded; he was also a rigorous disciplinarian imbued with a missionary sense of 'carrying the gospel of God to the heathen'. He accepted the commission on one condition, namely, that he was allowed to carry it out as he saw fit without further reference to Washington.

He sailed with his old flagship from Norfolk, Virginia on November 24th 1852, bearing a letter from President Millard Fillmore addressed to 'The Emperor of Japan'. Joined by three more units of the China Sea Squadron en route, he reached Naha, the chief port of the Loochooan island of Okinawa, on May 26th 1853. The British had learnt of his mission, but they were just then preoccupied in quelling the rapidly-spreading Taiping Rebellion on the Chinese mainland. 'Her Majesty's Government would be glad to see the trade with Japan open, but they think it better to leave it to the Government of the United States to make the experiment,' the Foreign Office therefore concluded, 'If that experiment is successful, Her Majesty's Government can take advantage of its success.' By contrast Russia, where interest in Japan had revived over the previous decade following a survey of the Amur estuary opposite the disputed island of Sakhalin, had hurriedly dispatched a squadron under the command of Admiral Evfimii Putiatin.

Well aware that his every move there would be immediately reported back to the homeland by the traders from Satsuma, Perry went to considerable lengths during his stay in Naha to demonstrate that this time America was not prepared to be sent away empty-handed. In an ostentatious show of strength, he paraded his marines up and down the main street, invited himself to the Regent's palace, and carried out a number of practice landings on nearby beaches under the gaze of the suitably-awed inhabitants.

The Bakafu had in fact been given several months' notice of Perry's impending arrival by the new Factor of the Dutch colony at Deshima, one Donker Curtius, who had been instructed by his government to do what he could to facilitate Perry's success so as to be in a position to press for a similar treaty with Holland. Even so, the Bakufu still could not summon the will to take responsibility for the nation's defence. Instead, they merely revoked their order banning the *daimyo* from manufacturing their own armaments and, as a further signal of their abdication, released both Nariaki and Prince Kuniye from their confinement. If this was intended as a gesture of reconciliation to the Court in the face of the common threat, Emperor Komei showed what he thought of it by promptly appointing Kuniye's son Asahiko as his Chief Adviser.

NO 'NO' FOR PERRY

Thus when Perry's 'black ships' (as they were instantly dubbed by Japanese demonologists) finally dropped anchor in Edo Bay on July 8th 1853, the Bakufu were as unsurprised as they were unready. A couple of elderly cannon popped off ineffectually from the opposite shore and a fleet of guard boats rowed out to surround them, but Perry, unlike Biddle before him, made it immediately clear that he would receive nobody on board except authorised representatives of the government, and that he himself would only grant interviews to those of commensurate rank with his own.

When the guards then attempted to make their own way up on deck by the anchor chains and their own grappling lines, they were unceremoniously repulsed with poles and bayonets. Eventually a minor official, the equivalent of a sergeant of police but claiming to be the 'Vice-Governor' of the nearby town of Uraga, was allowed up on board to negotiate with one of Perry's junior officers. On being informed of the contents of President Fillmore's letter, he replied that it would only be considered if it was presented to the proper authorities at Nagasaki, three hundred miles down the coast. He was told in turn that either the letter was accepted on the spot within three days, or the Commodore would go ashore 'with a sufficient force' and deliver it in person.

The three days passed with no sign of any response from the Japanese beyond the feverish work of boatloads of official artists sent out to record every detail of the 'black ships' and their armament. Perry decided to give substance to his threat by moving his ships towards Edo, at the same time taking the opportunity to make a survey of the Bay; an official sent to remonstrate with him was warned that 'if the friendly letter of the President to the Emperor is not received and duly replied to, he will consider his country insulted and will not hold himself accountable for the consequences'. The Bakufu finally acknowledged that they had no option but to acquiesce, and they arranged for a formal exchange of letters to take place in a reception hall hastily erected for the occasion on the shore of the little inlet of Kurigahama.

That of the President contained three requests: for a guarantee of safety for American seamen and property in Japan and her territorial waters, for permission to enter one or more ports and establish a coaling depot, and for the opening of trade between the two countries. The reply, delivered on behalf of the 'Emperor' (i.e., the Shogun; the Americans were not to discover the existence of the real Emperor for another two years) by the Governor of Uraga who was promoted for the occasion to the title of 'Prince of Idzu', was couched in something less than the usual diplomatic niceties.

'The letter of the President of the United States of America, and copy, are hereby received, and will be delivered to the Emperor,' it ran. 'It has been communicated many times that business related to foreign countries cannot be transacted here in Uraga but only in Nagasaki. However, since we have observed that the Admiral [Perry too had received temporary promotion], in his capacity as the President's Ambassador, would be insulted by a refusal to receive the letter at this place — the justice of which has been acknowledged — we hereby receive the aforesaid letter in opposition to Japanese law. As this is not the place to treat with foreigners, we can offer neither to entertain nor to confer with you. The letter being received, you are now able to depart.'

Perry was not a man to be so dismissively fobbed off, however, and on returning aboard he immediately took his ships still further up the Bay to within sight of the Shogun's capital and again put his surveyors to work. Having thus demonstrated that the timing of his departure was to be a matter of his own choosing, he turned about three days later and set sail for Canton. He had also added a letter of his own to that of Fillmore, informing the Japanese that he would return the following spring for a reply to the President's 'very reasonable and pacific overtures' with 'a very much larger force'.

They were left with no room for doubt that he would keep his word.

3

'Exalt the Emperor, Expel the Barbarian'

'THE GREATEST DISGRACE'

The attitude of impervious disdain affected by the Bakufu was not shared by the general populace in Edo, who for several days after the first appearance of the 'black ships' were only with difficulty restrained from taking *en masse* to the surrounding hills. The effect on the Shogun himself was even more debilitating: a week after their departure he passed clean away, as much a nonentity at the end as he had been at the beginning of his sixteen-year term of office.

In an attempt to reassert themselves, the Bakufu ordered a reinforcement of all coastal defences and formally licensed the importation of Western armaments by individual *daimyo*, although their point of entry was still to be restricted to Deshima. They also released the artillery pioneer Takashima from prison and put him in charge of their own programme of armament development. This show of authority was, however, almost immediately neutralised by what amounted to an open and unprecedented confession of impotence: when the *daimyo* made their traditional visit to the Court the following month, they were all, the *daimyo tozama* included, supplied with a translation of President Fillmore's letter and invited to 'express your opinions freely on the matter even though they may be contrary to established policy'.

Although general councils of the *daimyo* had taken place from time to time during the Tokugawa Shogunate, hitherto all discussion on matters of high state had been restricted to the five-man Roju or, when the rare occasion demanded, to a handful of the most influential *daimyo fudai* not already members of the latter. However, the Bakufu's dilemma was now intense: if they bowed to the American demands, it would be seen as a signal to challenge their authority not only by the Western powers but also by potential dissidents at home including, of course, the *sonno-joi* ists; if on the other hand they chose to reject them and offer armed resistance, they faced the humiliation of certain defeat and the imposition of terms similar to those recently inflicted on China by Britain.

If by this novel step the Bakufu had hoped to elicit some kind of

27

consensus with which to reply to Perry, they were to be severely disappointed. The 59 written replies from the *daimyo* that have survived (excluding two which simply pledged allegiance to anything that the Bakufu in its wisdom might decide) fell into three main categories, although even between these there was considerable overlapping. 19 argued for outright rejection of the American demands and the continuation of a rigid exclusion policy, regardless of the consequences; 21 advocated spinning out the negotiations for as long as possible to allow time to build up the country's defences; 19 supported the opening of trade relationships as a means of strengthening the economy, although even they held to the ultimate objective of a military confrontation with the barbarian.

Of the first category, National Watchdog Nariaki was predictably the most uncompromising. The Americans 'were arrogant and discourteous, their actions an outrage,' he stormed. 'Indeed, this was the greatest disgrace we have suffered since the dawn of our history. The saying is that if the enemy dictates terms in one's own capital one's country is disgraced. The foreigners have ignored our prohibition and penetrated our waters even to the vicinity of the capital, threatening us and making demands upon us. If the Bakufu should not only fail to expel them but also conclude an agreement in accordance with their requests, I fear that it would be impossible to maintain our national prestige ... Yet, to my mind, if the people of Japan stand firmly united, if we complete our military preparations and return to the state of society that existed before the middle ages [i.e., before the first Shogunate; Nariaki is here repeating the threat of restoration of Imperial rule], then we will even be able to go out against foreign countries and spread abroad our fame and prestige.'

Going on to argue that foreign trade would amount to no more than the exchange of Japan's reserves of precious metals for 'useless foreign goods like woollens and satin', Nariaki even went so far as to advocate ending the trade with Holland, although in a later passage he contrarily called for the purchase of ships' cannon with the proceeds of the Dutch trade. He also urged that individual *daimyo* be permitted to build warships, and that the two-centuries-old ban on the construction of sea-going ships be abolished.

PLAYING FOR TIME

In the latter he had the support, although with a different strategy in mind, of Ii Naosuke of Hikone, the most powerful of the *daimyo fudai*. 'There is a saying that when one is besieged in a castle, to raise the drawbridge is to imprison oneself and make it impossible to hold out indefinitely,' Ii allegorized. 'We must construct new steamships, especially powerful warships, and these we will load with goods not needed in Japan. For a time we will have to employ Dutchmen as masters and mariners, but we will put on board with them Japanese of ability and integrity who must study the use of large guns, the handling of ships and the rules of navigation. Openly these will be called merchant vessels, but they will in fact have the secret purpose of training a navy ... Forestalling the foreigners in this way, I believe, is the best method of ensuring that the Bakufu will at some future time find opportunity to reimpose its ban on foreigners coming to Japan.'

The Shimazu of Satsuma and Hotta Masayoshi, the *daimyo* of Sakura and a long-standing advocate of some relaxation in the exclusion laws, were others to uphold the advantages of foreign trade, although the former proposed putting a specific time limit on it. 'I think the Bakufu policy should be to seek to obtain some three years' grace, which should be ample,' he declared. 'By that time all the *han* will have completed their preparations; then, I believe, there will be ample means to obtain victory if the Bakufu orders expulsion, for Japan's military spirit has always been heroic.' He went on to suggest that Nariaki be given overall command of defence.

Matsudaira Keiei of Echizen also urged the appointment of a military supremo, but at the same time he rejected out of hand any suggestion of opening the ports on the grounds that if the Bakufu opened them to the Americans, they would then be obliged to open them to all comers. This, he considered, would 'even for a limited number of years be to humble ourselves before all countries. It would be the height of disgrace. And when the time came to withdraw permission, I believe we would find ourselves the object of simultaneous attack by many powerful enemies. This would make it all the more impossible to conduct a successful defence. When it was realised that military weakness forced us to endure such disgrace, I very much fear that it would not only be in foreign countries that men might question the competence of our rulers; it might even be that Bakufu control of Japan would become ineffective ...' The argument had thus come full circle back again to the diehard position of Nariaki.

Faced with the impossible task of squaring this circle, Abe and his colleagues on the Roju, who alone appreciated the full weakness of the national economy and the consequent absurdity of all talk of armed resistance, fell back once more on compromise. They first attempted to appease the more unreasoning *sonno-joïst* element by inviting Nariaki to join them in a war cabinet, officially entitled 'The Commission for Coastal Defence'. Then, having repealed the shipbuilding-limitation statute, they issued a statement to the *daimyo* to the effect that given the state of the country's defences they had no option but to re-enter negotiations with Perry; they would do their utmost to prolong them as far as possible without committing themselves to any definite reply, they promised, but if this tactic failed and Perry attempted to settle the issue by force, then it would be the duty of every Japanese to take up arms in defence of the national honour. A week later a further statement was published, probably at Nariaki's insistence, ordering contingency plans to be drawn up for every possible emergency.

In the meantime a further complication had arisen with the arrival of Admiral Putiatin and his Russian squadron. They too brought a request for the opening of Japanese ports to trade, but it was sweetened by an offer to negotiate on the disputed border in Sakhalin. The fact that Putiatin, unlike Perry, had put into Nagasaki rather than Edo allowed the local authorities to stonewall on the pretext of having to await instructions from the capital, and in their turn the Bakufu eventually replied that no negotiations were possible during the period of mourning for the lately-departed Shogun. This proved too much for the Russian's patience, and he promptly weighed anchor. He returned again in the first week of January 1854, but after five weeks he had still gained no more than an understanding that Russia would be accorded the same concessions as any other country. News of Perry's impending return then convinced him that he had nothing to lose by leaving the running to the Americans, and he headed home again.

PERRY RETURNS

The Bakufu had resorted to the same pretext in an attempt to forestall Perry also, but in the light of their previous experience of him even they could hardly have entertained much hope for its success, and on February 12th their lookouts again sighted the 'black ships' heading for the upper reaches of Edo Bay. Perry had eight vessels with him this time, and when he was joined shortly afterwards by two more he had one quarter of the entire U.S. Navy under his command. The Japanese were not, of course, to know this, and for good measure he put it about that he could call upon a hundred more in the event of hostilities (he had in fact already taken the precaution of establishing a rear base on Okinawa).

Perry was again greeted by the bogus 'Vice-Governor of Uraga' and the familiar request that he should withdraw his ships further down the Bay. He replied by moving them still closer to the capital, and the Bakufu quickly offered Kanagawa, adjoining the then fishing village of Yokohama, as a site for negotiations. The gifts that Perry brought ashore with him were carefully chosen to impress; they included a mile-long telegraph line and a model steam engine capable of doing 25 miles per hour on a track laid out beside the jetty. On seeing these, Nariaki wrote to a fellow *daimyo* that his worst fears were about to be fulfilled: Japan was being brought to the negotiating table in a state of total impotence.

Thus thoroughly intimidated, the Bakufu ordered their team of negotiators, in the words of its leader, 'to undertake discussions and negotiations, giving us secret instructions, however, that we were to handle the matter peaceably'. A wooden conference hall was again run up, although on a somewhat more generous scale than that of the previous year. On March

8th the Shogun's reply to the Presidential letter was finally handed over. Although its preamble warned that 'it is quite impossible to give satisfactory answers at once to all the proposals of your Government, as this is most positively forbidden by the laws of our Imperial ancestors,' the document then went on to concede the requested guarantee of safety for American castaways and the right of American ships to call at Nagasaki, Naha and one other port to be agreed for supplies of coal and other necessities.

Its only significant omission was any concession on the establishment of commercial relations, and Perry immediately countered with a demand for a treaty on similar terms to those which the United States had concluded with China a decade earlier. On this, however, the Japanese were obdurate, and Perry agreed to drop it in return for a Most Favoured Nation clause and a provision for the residence of an American Consul, explaining in his diary that 'commerce brings profit to a country, but it does not concern human life.' He also succeeded — not wishing to see American traders subjected to the same restrictions as those imposed on the Dutch — in substituting Shimoda for Nagasaki, while Hakodate in Hokkaido was agreed as the third port.

The Treaty of Kanagawa was signed on March 31st; its ratification by the two governments was to follow within the next eighteen months. The door was open at last, and others were not slow to take the opportunity to pass through it.

OTHERS THROUGH THE DOOR

Within a month the indefatigable Putiatin was back at Nagasaki, but his country had in the meantime gone to war with Britain and France in the Crimea, and fear of discovery by the British and French squadron which he knew to be looking for him obliged him to depart once more empty-handed. It was with the object of denying Putiatin the use of Japanese harbours (rather than a desire to emulate the American treaty, which the absence of any trade agreement had made rather disappointing in British eyes) that Rear Admiral Sir James Stirling, the British Commander-in-Chief in China, arrived in Nagasaki on September 7th and began parleying with the local authorities. However, when as a result of a mistranslation (the interpreters there being more familiar with Dutch than English) and of Japanese ignorance of the conventions governing international warfare he was offered the use of Nagasaki and Hakodate by British ships — and not merely warships — on terms similar to those granted to Perry, he had little hesitation in accepting.

Hardly was Stirling over the horizon when Putiatin hove yet again into sight, first at Hakodate and then, having received no satisfaction there, in the Inland Sea off Osaka, causing not a little consternation in the Imperial Court at nearby Kyoto. The Bakufu hurriedly drew him off with an invitation to a conference at Shimoda, and on February 7th 1855 he finally extracted a parallel agreement, together with a settlement of the Kurile boundary dispute which gave both parties access to the whole of Sakhalin. The negotiations were interrupted by a catastrophic earthquake, which caught the Russian flagship in a tidal wave and damaged her so severely that she later sank while being towed to another harbour for repairs. The Japanese, rejecting Nariaki's recommendation that they should take the opportunity to seize her crew and put them all to the sword, instead not only supplied a team of shipwrights to help in the construction of a replacement, but also built for themselves an exact replica alongside. In so doing, they laid the keel of a modern navy which barely half a century later would repay Russia by annihilating the Tsar's Baltic Fleet at Tsushima.

The French, under the pretext of returning some castaways, were the next to arrive in the hope of negotiating a treaty, but being without any great strength to show or territorial dispute to settle they received the traditional cold shoulder. The Dutch, however, Japan's sole link with the West for the past two centuries, could hardly be subjected to the same treatment. Donker Curtius had in fact submitted a draft treaty to the Bakufu some months before Perry's first appearance, but they had deemed it analogous to his annual summary of world events and so not requiring a reply. As it transpired, it closely foreshadowed the terms offered to Perry. After the latter's departure the Bakufu, at the prompting of Nariaki, approached Curtius with an order for two modern steam warships. One was presently delivered together with a team of 22 naval instructors, under whose tutelage a Naval College was set up at Nagasaki and 70 young trainee officers selected from the leading *han* enrolled.

Emboldened by this show of goodwill, Curtius renewed his application for a treaty, and this time it was granted. Ratified on January 30th 1856, it gave Dutch ships the right of entry to Shimoda and Hakodate for the purchase of supplies, but all other trade was restricted to Nagasaki as before. As a further mark of favour the residents of the Factory were permitted for the first time to have their families with them and to go ashore into the town; they were also now to be spared the humiliating ritual of trampling on the Crucifix at their annual obeisance to the Shogun, although they were still strictly forbidden to import anything relating to the Christian faith.

The Bakufu had thus succeeded in gaining the three years' grace advocated by the Shimazu of Satsuma. The economy, however, on which all hope of preserving Japan's independence ultimately rested, was still in a precarious condition. Furthermore, this respite had only been obtained at the cost of incurring the implacable, and as it was to prove, fatal hostility of the exclusionists, while it had also wholly failed to assuage the determination of the West to enter into fully-fledged commercial relations with Japan.

THE FIRST CONSUL

In August 1856 Curtius was already writing to warn Edo that the Governor-General of Hong Kong was preparing to visit Japan with a strong Royal Navy force in order to secure a trade treaty, and that same month the U.S.S. *San Jacinto* entered Shimoda harbour to disembark the first American Consul.

The descendant of a long line of New England Puritan stock, the young Townsend Harris fully shared Perry's missionary zeal, adding to it a somewhat dour determination. His arrival was the source of much surprise and dismay to the Bakufu, thanks largely to another mistranslation. Whereas the American version of Article XI of the Treaty of Kanagawa stipulated that a Consul could be sent 'provided that *one or other* (author's italics) of the two governments considers such an arrangement necessary', the Japanese translation stated simply that this could be done 'if conditions made it necessary' without further qualification.

On the Bakufu's instructions, the local governor at first refused Harris permission to land at all; thanks to the recent earthquake, the Consul was informed there was no house available to accommodate him, but if he cared to return again in a year's time there might be one ready. However, when Harris threatened to present himself at the capital, space was quickly found for him in a disused and bat-infested Buddhist temple. Finally taking up his post on September 3rd, Harris wrote in his Journal with foreboding: 'Grim reflections — ominous of change — undoubted beginning of the end. Query: if for the real good of Japan?'

Even then a series of further obstacles lay ahead. The Japanese insisted that three rooms in the temple should be made over to their own officers (in order to spy on him), that no servants should be allowed to remain there after dusk, and that a permanent guard should be stationed in the grounds. Harris, however, overrode them in an unequivocal demonstration that he would allow nothing to stand in the way of the fulfilment of his mission. In the following month he obtained a copy of the recent treaty with Holland from a Dutch frigate which happened to put into Shimoda, and he immediately demanded that similar terms should be granted to the United States by reason of the Most Favoured Nation clause in the Treaty of Kanagawa. The local governor and his deputy, who had been authorised by the Bakufu to negotiate with him on their behalf, at first denied even the existence of the Dutch treaty, causing Harris to write, on January 7th 1857, that 'I am determined to take firm ground with the Japanese. I will cordially meet any real offers of amity, but words will not do. *They are the greatest liars on earth.*' He would not be the last outsider to fail to catch the nuances of the 'language of the belly'.

His persistence was rewarded on June 17th with the signing of an agreement containing the following clauses: American ships were to be allowed into Nagasaki; American nationals were to be permitted to take up residence in Shimoda and Hakodate (where a Vice-Consul was to be installed); they were to come under the exclusive jurisdiction of their own Consuls; the Consul-General in Shimoda was to have unrestricted access into the interior; and an official rate of exchange was to be fixed.

To Harris, however, this agreement was no more than a step in the right direction, as his Journal makes very clear: 'Am I elated by this success? Not a whit. I know my dear countrymen but too well to expect any praise for what I have done, and I shall esteem myself lucky if I am not removed from office, not for what I have done, but because I have not made a commercial treaty that would open Japan as freely as England is open to us.' Two months after he had first arrived at Shimoda he had informed the local governor that he was bearing a letter from the President of the United States to the Shogun 'concerning a matter of the highest consequence to Japan'. At the same time he had left him in little doubt as to the nature of this 'matter' by enclosing a translation into Japanese of a commercial treaty which he himself had concluded with Thailand while en route for Japan.

Harris also insisted that he should deliver the letter personally to the Shogun, a demand that the Bakufu were not inclined to meet; for some months afterwards they had refused even to refer to it. At the time of the agreement in June they were still assuring him that 'it is quite preposterous even to think of an audience with His Majesty, as the laws of Japan forbid it', and it was not until August that they finally gave way. That they did so was due not so much to the threats of force that the exasperated Harris had been intermittently moved to make as to the outbreak of further hostilities between Britain and China; sparked off by the seizure of a British ship on suspicion of smuggling, the so-called 'Arrow War' had led to a retaliatory bombardment on Canton which devastated a large part of the city.

THE BAKUFU COMES TO TERMS

News of this development had been relayed to the Bakufu by Curtius in the hope of persuading them to accept the case for full commercial relations with the West (and with, of course, Holland in particular). The penny now finally dropped. The Roju issued a memorandum to senior Bakufu officials warning that 'if we continue adding to the anger of the foreigners, it is even possible that Japan might suffer the fate of Canton . . . Any attempt on our part to cling to tradition, making difficulties over the merest trifles and so eventually provoking the foreigners to anger, would be impolitic in the extreme. Should we hear the sound of a single cannon, then we will know that everything is up. We have no option, therefore, but to adopt a realistic policy.'

The following month Hotta, the new leader of the Roju in place of the terminally-ill Abe, issued a memorandum which stated baldly that 'it has been decided that we shall open trade'; it remained only, he continued, to discuss the terms to be offered. Two officials were sent to Nagasaki to negotiate an agreement with Curtius, being instructed that if a British squadron should appear there before the terms had been approved by the Bakufu, they were to settle without further reference to Edo and to negotiate with the British on the same basis.

In the event it was not Britain who forced the issue but Russia, in the person once more of Putiatin. Acting on their brief, the two negotiators concluded an agreement with Curtius on October 16th, and with Putiatin eight days later. Under its terms trade was to be opened at Nagasaki and Hakodate unfettered by the restrictions hitherto imposed on the Dutch; also conceded were the right of extra-territorial jurisdiction already granted to the Americans, and the freedom to practise (though not to preach) Christianity.

The Bakufu continued to drag their feet, however, over setting a date for Harris's reception at Edo, until the arrival of the corvette U.S.S. *Portsmouth* at Shimoda opened up the even more unwelcome possibility that he would present himself there at a time of his own choosing. Finally receiving their reluctant blessing, Harris arrived in the capital on November 30th, carried in an official palanquin and escorted by a cavalcade of bearers, guards, porters, servants and local dignitaries for whom the road had been especially cleared. He was surprised to find his allotted quarters furnished with Western-style tables, chairs and beds; they had been minutely copied from drawings secretly made of those in his Consulate.

The audience with the Shogun Iesada took place a week later. Harris, resolutely refusing all requests that he should conform to native practice and enter the august presence beating his head against the floor, presented his credentials, handed over the Presidential letter and made a short speech pledging his commitment to work for friendship between the two countries. The Shogun replied: 'Pleased with the letter sent with the Ambassador from a far distant country, and likewise pleased with his discourse. Intercourse shall be continued for ever.'

On December 12th Harris met Roju-leader Hotta in the first of an altogether more productive series of interviews. He immediately made it clear that he would not be satisfied with the terms recently agreed with Holland and Russia, which he dismissed as 'not worth the paper on which they were written'; in addition to those, he sought the opening of more harbours, freedom of trade from all government interference and the right for himself as Consul-General to reside at Edo. In support of these demands he argued that Britain would certainly not be satisfied with any less, that she was already planning to take possession of Hokkaido for use as a base against Russian encroachment to the south, and that if she was driven to impose her own terms by force of arms she would undoubtedly seek to import opium into Japan with all the disastrous consequences that its introduction had brought upon China.

A memorandum written shortly afterwards shows that Hotta accepted the force of such an argument, although with a quite different objective in mind. 'Even if we were to open hostilities resolutely and without fear of the consequences, we have neither the warships nor the cannon adequate to match the foreigners if large numbers of their warships infest our coasts and begin to burn and plunder,' he conceded. 'I am therefore convinced that our policy should be to stake everything on the present opportunity, to conclude friendly alliances, to send ships to foreign countries everywhere and conduct trade, to copy the foreigners where they are at their best and so repair our own shortcomings, to foster our national strenth and complete our armaments, and so gradually subject the foreigners to our influence until in the end all the countries of the world know the blessings of perfect tranquillity and *our hegemony is acknowledged throughout the globe*' (author's italics).

Hotta also issued a circular canvassing the *daimyo* for their opinions, much as Abe had done on Perry's first appearance in 1853. Their replies were again anything but unanimous. Although there was now a markedly more general recognition of the inevitability of opening the country to trade, violent opposition was voiced against his proposal to allow the 'brutish foreigner' within the walls of the two capitals, Edo and Kyoto.

Nevertheless, Hotta pressed on, and by February 25th 1858 he and Harris had agreed the terms of a draft treaty. Under them Harris gained in addition to the privileges already granted to the Dutch and Russians the right, to be extended to Americans generally in 1862, to reside at Edo; the opening, at intervals between 1859 and 1863, of the ports of Kanagawa, Nagasaki, Niigata and Kobe; permission for Americans to travel inland from them up to a distance of 25 miles; and the removal of all existing restrictions on trade, with the exception only of a total ban on the importation of opium.

THE EMPEROR OBJECTS

When the terms had been submitted to the *daimyo* a fortnight earlier, it was reported to Harris that 'instantly the whole Castle [of the Shogun] had been in an uproar ... the government could not at once sign such a treaty except at the expense of bloodshed.' In an attempt to placate his critics Hotta had acceded to their demand that he should first obtain the approval of the Imperial Court, and he now proposed to Harris that the signature of the treaty should be deferred for another sixty days while he went through the formalities that such a step involved. When Harris, who had only recently been apprised of the Emperor's very existence, inquired what would happen if the Imperial approval was withheld, he was assured that 'the government had determined not to receive any objections from the Mikado ... he has neither money, political power, nor anything that is valued in Japan; he is a mere cypher.'

Later that same week, however, the Consul-General was told elsewhere that on the contrary, 'even those most violently opposed to the treaty will say, if he [the Emperor] decided in its favour, "God has spoken, I submit"', and he observed in his Journal that 'this does not agree very well with the contemptuous manner in which the Japanese speak of this potentate.' Events were to justify Harris's scepticism rather than Hotta's confidence, as the latter was now to discover to his surprise and consternation, for the proposed treaty was to be the occasion for Emperor Komei to make open and common cause with National Watchdog Nariaki and the *sonno-joiists*. After the best part of eight centuries of insignificance, the Mikado was to be a cypher no longer.

Since Hotta's emergence as leader of the Roju Nariaki's influence within the Bakufu had suffered a sharp reverse. In November 1856 Hotta had been given total responsibility for foreign affairs, and he had appointed a commission to consider the implementation of opening the country to foreign trade. When the following August the Roju decided to accede in principle to Harris's demand for an audience with the Shogun, Nariaki once more raised his voice in strident protest: 'Above all to allow a barbarian to come near the person of the Shogun is very dangerous, and as one of the Counsellors [on the Commission for Coastal Defence] duty forbids me to remain silent.' It proved to be his parting shot; within a month he was ousted from the Roju and replaced by a declared opponent.

He was very far from admitting defeat, however, and at once turned to the Imperial Court for support. This he was more than well placed to do, his wife being a daughter of a Prince of the Blood and two of his sisters being married to Kuge (Court nobles) of the highest rank, and he wrote urging that the Emperor should unite the country by issuing a decree ordering 'the brushing away of the Barbarians'. Nor had he any intention of abandoning the plan which he had set in motion in 1847, when he managed to engineer the adoption of his seventh son Yoshinobu into the Tokugawa house of Hitosubashi, to establish a power base for himself within the Shogunate. When it had become clear that the mannikin Iesada was likely to die without issue, Nariaki had sedulously canvassed support for the nomination of Yoshinobu as the Shogun's successor, and he now instructed his agents within the Court to attempt to obtain an Imperial decree to this effect.

Thus the opposition to Hotta's mission was thoroughly marshalled by the time that he arrived at the Court on March 19th; indeed, a week earlier Emperor Komei himself had made clear in a letter to the Kampaku (Lord Chamberlain) that he was thoroughly opposed to the opening of any more ports, especially of nearby Osaka and Kobe, and was prepared if necessary to authorise the expulsion of all foreigners. For some days Hotta found himself unable to obtain an interview even with a minor Court official. Eventually he was informed that he was permitted to submit his arguments in favour of the proposed treaty to the Emperor in writing only.

On April 6th he received the following reply: 'The Imperial mind is deeply concerned. Things having come to the present pass, public sentiment being what it is, and in view of the importance of matters of state,

We desire that the opinions of the Three [Tokugawa] Families and of the *daimyo* be sought.' As he had come to Kyoto with the express purpose of by-passing the latter's opposition, Hotta now saw that his only chance of success lay with the Lord Chamberlain, who was related by marriage to Ii Naosuke, the leader of the *daimyo fudai* and one of the treaty's strongest advocates.

The Chamberlain and his deputy cobbled together the draft of a compromise statement on the Emperor's behalf which, while criticising the Bakufu for having allowed the present situation to develop, at the same time conceded their right to handle it as they saw fit. Komei gave his formal approval to it on April 24th, but he at once made it public knowledge that he had only done so against his better judgement. This immediately brought a storm of protest from the Court nobles, who demanded that it should be redrafted.

The revised document handed to Hotta on May 3rd amounted to a death warrant for the seven-and-a-half-centuries-old rule of the Shoguns, and as such it deserves to be quoted in full: 'The American affair is a great sorrow to our divine land and a matter truly vital to the safety of the State. The Emperor keenly feels his responsibility in this to his Imperial Ancestors. He greatly fears that to revolutionarise the sound laws handed down from the time of Ieyasu would disturb the ideas of our people and make it impossible to preserve lasting tranquillity. The treaty opening the port of Shimoda some years ago was serious enough, but it is the Emperor's belief that the new treaty now proposed would make impossible the preservation of national honour. Furthermore, the Court officials have reported after consultation that the present stipulations would cause immeasurable future difficulties and, more especially, would endanger national prestige. It is the Imperial Command that the Bakufu shall again call the Tokugawa families and other *daimyo* into consultation and report to the Court thereafter.'

THE TREATY GOES AHEAD

Hotta was nonplussed, as he had every right to be: expressions of concern from the Imperial Mind were rare enough, but outright, publicly-recorded opposition to the wishes of the Shogun and his ministers was beyond all precedent. When he had recovered from the shock, he submitted a second memorandum to the Throne requesting in more general terms that the Bakufu be authorised to take whatever steps they considered the situation demanded. This only brought an even more uncompromising reply: if America resorted to violence when she refused the new treaty, war should be formally declared, and in the meantime the Bakufu should press ahead with all speed to strengthen the country's defences.

Recognising that all was lost, Hotta hurried back to Edo. Even as he did so, however, events were already outrunning him. Having seen the agreed deadline for signing the treaty come and go with no indication that the promised Imperial approval was forthcoming, Harris was now threatening to go to Kyoto in person to obtain it. For Hotta himself, however, relief was at hand: even before his return his colleagues on the Roju had taken steps to remove him from office, and on June 4th they announced that *daimyo fudai* leader Ii had been appointed in his place to the emergency post of Tairo or Regent.

Ii's first action was to negotiate with Harris a second deferment of the signature to a new date of September 4th, having first undertaken not to conclude a treaty with any other party until thirty days after that. The pace of events, however, continued to overtake the best intentions. The disparate opinions of the *daimyo* were still being canvassed in compliance with the Imperial Command when on July 3rd the *Mississippi* put into Shimoda with the news that the Chinese had come to terms with the British and French forces, who were now on the point of setting sail to obtain a similarly favourable treaty with Japan.

Harris immediately took ship to Kanagawa to impress on the Bakufu 'the very great importance of having the treaty signed without the loss of a single day'; the new British plenipotentiary Lord Elgin had under him, so Harris informed them, 'several tens' of warships. This invention on Harris's part was another instance of his free play with his trump card of the 'British threat'; in actual fact, Elgin's brief specifically forbade the use of force in order to coerce Japan into a treaty. The Roju went into yet another emergency session, during which Ii summarised the issue at stake thus: 'If we reject the treaty and hostilities break out . . . there could be no greater national disgrace than to suffer defeat and so be forced to concede territory and pay an indemnity. Which would be worse — to reject the treaty now and bring lasting disgrace to our country, or to avoid national disgrace by not waiting for the Emperor's authorisation?' They had no choice, his colleagues agreed, but to forgo the Imperial mandate, and Ii declared himself willing to take personal responsibility for the decision.

The negotiators were accordingly instructed to obtain a further deferment if possible, but if it proved otherwise to go ahead and sign the treaty. Harris was, not surprisingly, in no mood to be fobbed off any further, and on that same day (July 29th) the first commercial treaty between Japan and the United States was finally consummated. After three years of prevarication and procrastination, his perseverance at last had its reward. When the news reached Komei, he, having already declared that such an action would be 'unspeakable, truly deplorable and catastrophic', promptly announced his abdication. He was soon dissuaded however, and instead wrote to the Bakufu abjuring them to unite with the Court in 'preparing the country not to submit to the humiliation of the foreigners'.

As had the first, this new treaty heralded a second round of parallel agreements with the other Powers. Even before it was signed Putiatin had put in yet another appearance, and three weeks later he was granted similar terms, as was Curtius on the same day. Lord Elgin too had now made his much-heralded arrival, although with a much smaller force, of course, than Harris had foretold. It included, however, a magnificently-furnished yacht, the personal gift to the Shogun from Queen Victoria — although, as Elgin's secretary Laurence Oliphant remarked, the former's sickly disposition made this 'a cruel satire upon this unhappy potentate; one might as well request the Pope's acceptance of a wife.' The satire was, as we shall see, crueller than even Oliphant knew. After generous exchanges of saki and champagne a treaty was signed on August 20th, whereupon Elgin took his leave to return to what he considered to be his more pressing responsibilities in China. The round was finally completed on October 9th with the conclusion of similar terms with France.

BATTLE LINES DRAWN

If one crisis had thus been successfully lanced, the other, that of the rival claims to the Shogunate succession, had meanwhile come to a head. On August 14th Iesada had died, as predicted, without issue. In accordance with tradition, no announcement of his death was made for another month (when Elgin had sought an audience with him on the 23rd, he was informed that the Shogun was 'indisposed').

Even before his appointment as Regent, Ii had led the opposition to Nariaki's son Yoshinobu's candidature, having first incurred the National Watchdog's wrath four years earlier when he had publicly ridiculed the suggestion that Perry could be dissuaded from returning by the construction of a row of forts along the Edo seafront; his elevation probably owed something to reports that Nariaki was planning to obtain an Imperial decree in favour of his son, for they had incensed the *daimyo fudai* that the Court should be meddling in so intimate a Tokugawa preserve. When an Imperial Rescript calling for the appointment of a 'full-grown and enlightened' heir (which would have effectively ruled out Ii's own nominee, Iesada's eleven-year-old cousin Iemochi) was prepared for the Emperor's signature, Ii's kinsman the Lord Chamberlain contrived to omit the two adjectives from the final draft, thus leaving the choice still in the Bakufu's hands.

A week after Ii had assumed the Regency he had obtained Iesada's consent to the nomination of his boy cousin and then submitted it to Kyoto for the Emperor's approval. On August 4th, two days before the name of the Shogun's successor was due to be formally announced, Nariaki presented himself at Edo Castle along with the *daimyo* of Echizen and Owari in a last-ditch attempt to plead his own son's case. Ii, whose position had now been strengthened still further by the promotion to the Roju of two staunch supporters, promptly took advantage of this breach of etiquette to put him under house arrest and to remove his two co-sponsors from their positions as *daimyo*. Following the interception of a letter from the Court suggesting that the Emperor might issue a decree ordering Nariaki's release, Ii then launched a full-scale purge of the National Watchdog's adherents in both Edo and Kyoto.

When this had been completed, he sent one of his new placemen on the Roju to Kyoto on a second mission to obtain the Emperor's blessing for the new treaties. Komei's reply, however, demonstrated that even though these were now in force, his opposition remained as strong as ever: 'The treaties providing for friendship and trade with foreigners and other matters are a blemish on our Empire and a stain on our divine land. The present Emperor greatly fears that were such things to start in his reign, he would find it truly impossible to justify himself to his Imperial Ancestors ...' Ii answered in turn with a fresh purge of his opponents, among them Nariaki's chief adviser, who was ordered to commit *hara-kiri*; the National Watchdog himself was banished to his castle in Mito.

'GRASS ROOTS' REBELLION

By now, however, the *sonno-joi* movement was no longer confined to Kyoto and Mito, but was rapidly gaining support throughout the country. This upsurge had been encouraged partly by a second and much more widely-distributed publication of Aizawa's *New Proposals* the previous year, but more especially by the knowledge that the treaties had been signed in disregard of the Emperor's openly-stated opposition and so too of the samurai's instinctive loyalty to the Throne.

Particularly strong was the response in Satsuma among disaffected retainers of the recently-deceased Shimazu, who had been succeeded by his much more conservative, pro-Bakufu brother Hisamitsu (acting as regent for the young heir). Their leader was the spell-binding figure of Saigo Takamori. Six feet tall with a breadth to match, he towered over the mass of his compatriots, his piercing gaze staring down at them from beneath extravagantly-bushed eyebrows; not the least fearsome of his attributes was an already legendary dexterity with the sword. Revered in his own lifetime as 'The Great Saigo', he would be heroized by future generations of Japanese expansionists for his martyrdom in the cause of the *samurai* ideal; even now his memory is still honoured by a daily file of admirers at his graveside.

The movement also now had an articulate ideological mouthpiece in Yoshida Shoin, an apostle of Sakuma's 'Eastern Ethics, Western Science' school. Like Sakuma, Yoshida argued that all contact with the West had to be undertaken with the single-minded objective of improving Japan's defences until she was in a position to maintain her traditional independence. 'In studying the learning of Europe and America, any tendency to idolize the barbarians ... must be rejected absolutely,' he affirmed. 'But the barbarians' artillery and shipbuilding, their knowledge of medicine and of physical sciences can all be of use to us, and these should be properly adopted.' He then went on to add, however, that 'to protect the country well is not merely to prevent it from losing the position it holds, but to add positions which it does not hold.' Among these 'positions' he included not only Japan's immediate neighbours like Korea and Formosa, but also China, Manchuria, the Philippines and even India. 'This,' he declared, 'is an enterprise which must continue so long as the earth shall last.'

With Sakuma's encouragement, Yoshida had attempted to stow away on one of Perry's ships in order to continue his studies abroad, but he was discovered and handed back to be imprisoned by the authorities of his *han*, Choshu. Two years later he was released and allowed to open a school of military studies, to which he soon attracted a considerable following by his zealous, not to say fanatical, brand of scholarship. He would go for days at a stretch without sleep, for example, keeping himself awake at his studies by standing barefooted in the snow.

At this point Yoshida was still prepared to acknowledge the Shogun's authority within the framework of ultimate loyalty to the Emperor: 'If a single subject is insulted by the foreign barbarians, it is axiomatic that the Shogun ... must wipe out this disgrace to the nation and bring tranquillity to the mind of the Emperor.' Even during the treaty negotiations with Harris (to which, of course, he bitterly objected) he had advocated that opposition to it should continue to be expressed through the constitutional channel of the *daimyo* council: 'If when every other effort has been exhausted the Shogun still does not appreciate his guilt, then unavoidably there will be no other course than for my lord, together with those other *daimyo* who realise the crime, to present this matter to the Imperial Court and carry out the Emperor's command.'

It was only after Ii chose to disregard the Emperor's refusal to endorse the treaty that Yoshida's fanaticism took an out-and-out revolutionary turn: 'As things stand now, the *daimyo* are content to look on while the Shogunate carries on in a high-handed manner ... To wear silk brocades, eat dainty food, cuddle beautiful women and fondle over-indulged children is all that the ruling class cares for. They are not in the least concerned to honour the Emperor and expel the barbarian,' he concluded, 'and so our only hope lies in grass-root heroes.' These were the *samurai*, particularly the *ronin* who constituted such a potentially subversive element in Edo's ever-burgeoning population. In appealing to them, Yoshida was calling for a show not of political muscle, of which they had none, but of the power of their swords.

As a first step, he set out to assassinate Ii's emissary to the Imperial Court en route to Kyoto. The plot failed, however, and Yoshida was arrested. Readily admitting to his part in it, he was condemned to death.

His acolytes in the capital then turned their attention to other, easier, targets — the hated 'barbarians' in their midst. In August 1859 three Russian sailors were cut down in Kanagawa, as soon afterwards were an employee of the French Legation and the official interpreter at the British

Legation. In February 1860 the captains of two Dutch merchant ships were hacked to pieces in the main street of Yokohama. In Satsuma 'The Great Saigo' began to draw up plans for a loyalist rising in Kyoto, but before they could come to anything Hisamitsu, already suspicious of his contacts with the *sonno-joi*ists, sent him into exile.

Ii meanwhile had continued to press forward vigorously in his campaign against the Kyoto-Mito axis. Having learnt that the Emperor had addressed a secret appeal over the heads of the Bakufu to Nariaki's eldest son (now *daimyo* of Mito since his father's confinement) to 'expel the barbarian, content the mind of the people and restore tranquillity to His Majesty's mind', he sent his agents to Mito to demand the document's immediate surrender. As father and son temporised, a number of their *samurai* took it into their own possession and went underground, to resurface in Edo in company with some kindred *shishi* or 'men of spirit'. One of them had already tried to shoot the Regent three months earlier, but the bullet had narrowly missed as it passed through his palanquin. Accordingly, they now put in hand a more sophisticated scheme.

The morning of March 24th, when Ii was due at the Shogun's Castle for an audience, was chosen for the attempt. Disguised as ordinary passers-by, one group of conspirators attacked the head of the accompanying procession. As the Regent's bodyguard rushed forward to assist, another group emerged from a side street and quickly surrounded their now unprotected target. Too late the bodyguard realised their mistake as they turned on the snow-covered road, struggling at the same time to draw their swords from beneath their heavy greatcoats. A pistol was fired at point-blank range into the palanquin, followed by a succession of sword thrusts. Ii was dragged out, his head lopped off and borne aloft through the capital's streets.

'If this time it should be my misfortune to die, may my death inspire at least one or two men of steadfast will to rise up and uphold this principle [of *sonno-joi*] after my death,' Yoshida had written after his arrest, and this hope was to be all too amply and bloodily vindicated in the course of the next eighty years. Almost without exception, the leaders who helped to set the country's expansionist course in the succeeding generation were his 'grass roots' disciples, many of them personal pupils; it was through his influence that the Choshu *han* rose to its position of predominance in the new Imperial Army; and it was his insidious slogans that hundreds of thousands of Japanese soldiers repeated to themselves as they poured into Korea in 1894, into Manchuria in 1931, into China proper in 1937 and into the Philippines and Malaya in 1941.

Robert Louis Stevenson hit a prophetic nail when in 1882 he introduced his vignette of Yoshida in *Familiar Studies of Men and Books* thus: 'The name is probably unknown to the English reader, and yet I think it should become a household word like that of Garibaldi or John Brown. Some day soon we may expect to hear more fully the details of Yoshida's history, and the degree of his influence in the transformation of Japan.'

4

Murder on the Highway

'COURT AND BAKUFU UNITE'

The manifesto which was found concealed on the person of one of Ii's assassins spoke not merely of 'the duty of ending a serious evil by killing this atrocious autocrat who has proved himself to be an unpardonable national enemy', but also of his murder being the signal for an outright coup d'état. The Mito *ronin* planned to mount a frontal attack on the foreign settlement at Yokohama, while their Satsuma allies were to surprise the Bakufu garrison in Kyoto and take over the Imperial capital.

Absurdly ambitious the plan may have been, but its implications served wonderfully to concentrate the minds of the wrangling hierarchies in Edo, Kyoto and the leading *han*, giving rise to a new rallying-cry, *kobu-gattai* or 'Unity of the Court and Bakufu'. This new spirit of compromise was further encouraged by the succession of the conciliatory Ando Nobumasa to the leadership of the Roju, together with the death six months later of National Watchdog Nariaki. Although Nariaki's son Yoshinobu had been foiled in his bid for the Shogunate, he had by no means abandoned the hope that his adoption into the Tokugawa family would secure him some high office within the Bakufu, and he immediately distanced himself from the 'men of spirit' calling for its overthrow.

Likewise in Satsuma, when the new Regent-Shimazu Hisamitsu got to hear of the malcontents' planned participation in the coup, he at once issued an order forbidding them to have anything to do with it. In the absence of 'The Great Saigo' in exile, their leadership had passed to his lieutenant Okubo Toshimichi, and the two men presently came to an accommodation: if the latter undertook to restrain his followers, Hisamitsu agreed in his turn to promote the *han*'s involvement in national politics whenever suitable opportunities arose. Okubo was able to keep to his undertaking, but in so doing he was marked down as a 'traitor' by the more fanatical 'men of spirit', a charge which would eventually cost him his life.

The attempt to 'unite Court and Bakufu' was given concrete expression in a proposal that the Shogun should take the hand of the Emperor's sister in marriage. Emperor Komei was at first opposed, but in due course he was won over by the arguments put forward by a young rising star among his advisers, Iwakura Tomomi. 'To date the Bakufu have failed to fulfil their duty to complete our military preparations in order to carry out whole-heartedly the chastisement of the foreigners. Thus the whole country is more and more dissatisfied with them. It is my belief that the Bakufu, growing alarmed at this, have decided to make use of the prestige of the Court to bolster their authority and quell the people's unrest,' Iwakuru asserted.

'Our situation is indeed critical and gives me much concern. To my mind the best way of resolving the crisis would be to order the Bakufu to return in private to the Court the substance of political power. We could thereby unite the people to the Court, and correct and reinforce our national policy.' The proposed match, he went on to suggest, offered a unique opportunity to bring about such a transfer, for by it 'the Court will have succeeded in grasping the reality of power while the Bakufu retains but the appearance of it'.

Komei imposed one condition upon his acceptance: the Bakufu would have to give him a specific commitment to abrogate the treaties with the West. This the Roju felt unable to do, for not only might a unilateral abrogation 'without just cause lose us our good name and make it impossible to preserve our national prestige', but they also 'now had no choice but to seek to gain time; we are gradually completing our military preparations, and our idea is that once this is done we will carry out expulsion in accordance with the Emperor's commands.' After some further negotiations, during which he extracted a pledge from them that 'within seven to ten years action will certainly be taken either to cancel the treaties by negotiation or to expel the foreigners by force', Komei finally gave his blessing to the marriage. As always, only the means was at issue; the end remained constant — 'to expel the barbarians'.

Another objection raised by Komei was that he 'would feel it especially unforgivable to send in marriage a daughter of his own Imperial Father to a place [Edo] where foreigners are resident'; he was also as implacably opposed as ever to the opening of Kobe and Osaka. In order to retain his approval (and the marriage was not celebrated until 1862) the Bakufu felt obliged to make some attempt to negotiate a postponement of the relevant articles of the treaties. The pretext given to the foreign envoys was an alleged upsurge in popular unrest and xenophobic feeling brought about by the accelerating inflation which had followed the opening of the ports (the price of rice had in fact risen by some 50% in the eighteen months after the commencement of foreign trade, but it is an open question whether the two were connected, since foreign trade represented only a tiny propor-tion of the national economy at the time).

The envoys were at first not very accommodating, until in November 1860 they were joined by a treaty delegation from Prussia. Townsend Harris suggested that if any agreement with the newcomers could be confined to the three ports already open (Yokohama, Nagasaki and Hakodate), the other Powers might be more willing to postpone the opening of the others. The suggestion was taken up and a diplomatic mission dispatched to Europe to negotiate with the governments concerned. In making it Harris had doubtless been prompted in part by the murder a week earlier of his secretary in the streets of Edo's diplomatic quarter, which in turn had prompted his fellow envoys to abandon the capital for Yokohama until they received a guarantee of future safety. As a further measure of protection, the British and French obtained permission to station permanent garrisons of their own troops.

Nothing daunted, a gang of Mito *ronin* attacked the British Legation on the night of July 4th 1861, killing two of the British soldiers on guard and almost severing the arm of Laurence Oliphant (recently promoted to Chargé d'Affaires, but the injury would put an end to his career in the diplomatic service). Sir Rutherford Alcock, the Consul-General, at first argued that this assault constituted grounds for rejecting the Roju's proposals since any concession would only offer further encouragement to the *ronin*, and it took the attempted assassination of its leader Ando himself on February 14th 1862 to persuade him to recommend a more conciliatory attitude to the Foreign Office in London. Accordingly the London Protocol was signed in June, granting the desired postponements until January 1st 1868 in return for the payment of appropriate compensation for the attack on the Legation and the removal of all restrictions on trade as already stipulated under the terms of the original treaty. Similar agreements were reached with France, Holland and Russia before the end of the year.

'MEN OF SPIRIT' UNAPPEASED

If the Bakufu hoped that they would thereby disarm their more restive critics, they were soon disappointed. They had earlier attempted to head off the opportunity for violent confrontation on the part of the *sonno-joiists* by establishing trading facilities for Western merchants not at Kanagawa as specified in the treaties, but three miles further south at Yokohama. The latter offered ships a much deeper berth and so was in any case the more appropriate site, but the decision sprang from an altogether different consideration: Kanagawa was a staging post on the Sacred Highway between Edo and Kyoto, and the Bakufu saw only too clearly the likelihood of bloody and compromising clashes if the foreign community should take up residence there.

The ploy was not in the event very successful, nor perhaps did it ever have much chance of being so; the sudden contact between parties who had been kept in ignorance of each other over such a length of time was in itself almost bound to be a source of misunderstanding and conflict. For example, the coins especially minted for the new trade were found, as a result of an overvaluation of their silver content, to be worth only a third of their purported value; silk and other goods paid for in advance were not delivered as contracted; and the Japanese were quick to exploit their age-old talent for imitation (the Worcester Sauce of Messrs. Lea and Perrin was an early victim of this form of piracy).

Nor was the other side by any means innocent of sharp practice. Alcock observed of the first arrivals that they were 'of many nationalities and very few scruples', and he went on to report how 'a ship laden with ruffians from California armed with bowie-knives and revolvers arrived at Yokohama, and these men used to go into the customs house there and would shake the officials as a dog would a rat to make them comply with their demands'. The over-valuation of silver meant that gold was correspondingly under-valued, and this in turn led to a rapid drain of Japan's gold stocks as Western merchants realised that they could make a turn of two hundred per cent without the strains associated with the more conventional lines of business.

Wherever the balance of blame lay, and whatever the cause of the inflation which continued to grow in the wake of the commencement of trade with the West, the distrust and resentment which it sparked soon spread far beyond those immediately involved. This was a considerable source of satisfaction to the *sonno-joï*ists, who, following Yoshinobu's desertion to the cause of Court-Bakufu unity, no longer looked to Mito for their inspiration but to Yoshida Shoin's 'Grass Roots Heroes' in Choshu (where the ruling house of Mori claimed descent from the Imperial Line) and the neigbouring western *han*.

Among the most outspoken and influential of these were Yoshida's brother-in-law Kusaka Genzui, who preached that 'the powers of government must be restored to the Court by establishing an administrative headquarters in Kyoto and referring to the Court all matters of importance'; Maki Izume of Kurume, who advocated the creation of an Imperial Army and the transfer to Imperial control of all the provinces surrounding Kyoto; Takechi Zuizan of Tosa, who urged an alliance of the western *han* and had already formed a loyalist league pledged to 'reactivate the Japanese spirit and bring about the rebirth of our nation'; and Hirano Kuniomi of Chikuzen, who called for the seizure of Kyoto and the extension of Imperial authority over the whole country with the Shogun 'stripped of office, reduced in rank and revenue and given the same standing as the other great *daimyo*'.

The more moderate policy of the official administration in Choshu was outlined by Nagai Uta, supporting the restoration of Imperial authority but dismissing as impracticable abrogation of the treaties and expulsion of the foreigners; instead, he proposed a programme of rearmament, overseas expansion and the creation of buffer zones on the Asian continent against the West. The result, he concluded, would be that 'the misfortunes of the treaties will become a blessing, the Shogun will be fulfilling the "barbarian-subduing" duties of his office, the Imperial glory will shine abroad and the Court will receive tribute from the five continents.' His argument was a reflection of the parting of the ways which had taken place between Yoshida and his mentor, Sakuma Shozan; the latter was now an advocate of Court-Bakufu unity, and he wrote of his hopes for the emergence of a Napoleonic leader acceptable to both parties who 'will devise a practicable plan, enlist co-operation, drive out wickedness and in the end wrap up the world and return it to the Imperial Court, which shall be revered by the world for ages to come'.

In July 1861 Nagai had been authorised to present his suggestions to the Court. He was well received — so well, in fact, that the Emperor sent him on to Edo as an official mediator. In the eyes of the loyalists, however, he was thereby tarred with the brush of Court-Bakufu unity and a plan was laid to assassinate him on his return to Kyoto in March 1862. Its ring leader was the exiled Saigo who, deprived of a power base in Satsuma, had joined his fellow 'men of spirit' in Choshu. The plan failed, but opposition to Nagai within the *han* grew so vociferous that in May the authorities felt obliged to dismiss him, replacing him with Kido Koin, another disciple of Yoshida who was to play a major part in future events. Even now Nagai was not to be spared, and a few months later he was ordered to commit *hara-kiri* to atone for 'his egotism and sins against the Court and Choshu'.

SATSUMA ENTERS THE RING

Saigo was not the only man in Satsuma to resent Nagai's activities, for Hisamitsu was hoping to occupy the rôle of Court-Bakufu mediator himself as a means of honouring his pledge to Okubo to enhance the *han*'s involvement in national politics. He had already drawn up a scheme which included the dismissal of Ando from the Roju and the appointment to high office within the Bakufu of both Yoshinobu and the *daimyo fudai* of the important *han* of Echizen and Aizu, Matsudaira Keiei and Matsudaira Katamori (Matsudaira being a Tokugawa cognomen); to reinforce its merits, he planned to present it in person at both Kyoto and Edo accompanied by a strong force of *samurai*. Before setting out himself, he recalled Saigo and sent him on in advance to explain his purpose to the Satsuma *ronin* in the two capitals lest they misconstrued the presence of his troops.

Predictably, Saigo put his reinstatement to quite opposite ends, revising and expanding his original scheme for a loyalist uprising in Kyoto. In its new version Hisamitsu, in concert with *ronin* of other sympathetic *han* under the leadership of Maki and Hirano, was to 'capture Osaka Castle, advance on Kyoto, put the Shogun's garrison to the sword, drive out all the Bakufu officials, set free the Regent Ii's imprisoned victims and after issuing the Mikado's orders to all the *daimyo* to carry the Imperial palanquin to Edo and punish the crimes of the Bakufu'. When Hisamitsu received word that Saigo had been associating with extremists from other *han* in defiance of his express orders to the contrary, he at once recalled him to Kagoshima (the Satsuma capital) and exiled him again, this time to a remote island.

On May 14th Hisamitsu arrived in Kyoto at the head of about a thousand of his retainers and presented his proposals to the Emperor. Komei had no difficulty in approving them, for they offered a more concrete programme for the advancement of Imperial power than those put forward earlier by Nagai. He also authorised Hisamitsu to suppress any *ronin* conspiracy aimed at jeopardizing the chances of the proposals' acceptance by the Bakufu.

A few days later Hisamitsu got wind of a meeting that was due to take place at the Teradaya Inn in nearby Fushimi between leaders of the Satsuma *ronin* and other conspirators. He promptly dispatched a picked band of swordsmen to dissuade the former from taking part, but they refused to give an undertaking not to do so. Eight of them were then cut down on the spot; the remainder surrendered and were sent back to Kagoshima in disgrace.

The ambitions of the other *ronin*, however, now at a pitch of expectation that the Shogun was about to be forcibly overthrown, were not so easily dispelled. Now that they could no longer look to Satsuma to carry their banner, they began to force the running in their own *han*. In Choshu, as we have seen, they engineered the downfall of Nagai, and in Tosa Takechi successfully organised the assassination of the chief minister, an advocate of Court-Bakufu unity; having survived the bloodbath at the Teradaya Inn, Maki returned to Kurume and began working on a still more ambitious plan to recruit 'righteous followers' from the lower, non-*samurai* classes. In Edo itself *ronin* took it upon themselves to execute former agents of the 'Atrocious Autocrat' Ii, and on June 26th they launched a second attack on the British Legation, fortunately with less lethal effect.

The authorities in Choshu meanwhile, under pressure from *sonno-joi*ists without and Kido within, began a campaign to retrieve their position at Court which had been usurped from them by Hisamitsu. This necessarily involved distancing themselves from the Bakufu, and in July they issued a statement redefining their attitude: 'Our basic policy remains one of "loyalty to the Court, trust to the Bakufu"; but if a situation should arise in which our loyalty to the Court were threatened, then it might be necessary to neglect our trust to the Bakufu.' Having thus reingratiated themselves, they were able to elicit that it was the Emperor's wish that the treaties should be abrogated.

Kusaka, Yoshida's brother-in-law, thereupon submitted a memorial to them demanding that 'the guilt of the Bakufu for having signed the second treaty of Kanagawa against the Emperor's wishes be made clear . . . their lack of respect for over two hundred years must be corrected, the veneration of the Emperor must be established and the duties of rulers and subjects rectified.' The battle-cry of the 'men of spirit' was thus no longer merely that of '*sonno-joi*', which implied a continuing, if diminished rôle for the Shogunate in the nation's affairs; it was now one of *'Tobaku'* or 'destroy the Bakufu'. By August 27th Choshu's rehabilitation was complete, for on that date the *han* was authorised by Komei to mediate with the Bakufu in order to secure their commitment to the abrogation of the treaties.

PLANS AGLAY

In the meantime Hisamitsu had continued to Edo on the second leg of his own mission of mediation. After several weeks of discussion, the Bakufu agreed to a programme of reform which incorporated most of his proposals: Ando was to resign as leader of the Roju; Yoshinobu was to be appointed 'Guardian' of his adoptive cousin, Boy-Shogun Iemochi; Tokugawa kinsmen Keiei and Katamori were to fill a position equivalent to that of Regent and the Military Governorship of Kyoto respectively; foreign affairs were to be entrusted to a commission comprising the *daimyo* of the eight largest *han*; and the Shogun was to make an official visit to Kyoto 'in order to lay the foundations of a complete accord with the Mikado and enable the military prestige of Japan to be developed until she became the most powerful nation in the world'.

In contrast with the rival Choshu stance, there was nothing in Hisamitsu's programme to imply a subordination of the Shogunate to the Throne. Rather, it sought to elevate the *daimyo* to a position in which they would hold the balance of power, and as a mark of this new independence they were now required to spend only one month of the year in Edo — and that without their families — instead of four as previously. The effect of this last reform was that, in the words of a contemporary chronicler, 'in the twinkling of an eye the flourishing city of Edo became like a desert . . . and so the prestige of the Tokugawa family, which had endured so brilliantly for two hundred and seventy years, fell to ruin in the space of one morning.' To discourage any ideas that Kyoto stood correspondingly to gain in status, Hisamitsu then submitted a memorial to the Throne in which he spelt out the catastrophic consequences for both Court and country that would result from abrogation of the treaties.

It was thus a cruel irony that an incident took place shortly afterwards involving his own retainers which not only destroyed almost at a stroke the whole edifice of Court-Bakufu unity which he had gone to such lengths to construct, but which also paved the way for the restoration of Imperial rule in a guise that was to prove so unpalatable to his successors in Satsuma that they would rise in open rebellion against it.

September 14th dawned fine in the foreign settlement at Kanagawa, and a visiting English merchant from Shanghai, Charles Richardson, set out for a ride along the Sacred Way in the direction of the capital with a couple of friends and the sister-in-law of one of them, a Mrs. Borrodaile. As they entered the little village of Namamugi they encountered the considerable entourage of Hisamitsu, who by chance had set out from Edo for Kyoto that same morning. The riders reined their horses into the side of the road, but in the eyes of the Satsuma *samurai* this was very far from showing the proper degree of respect for their *daimyo* and they thereupon drew their swords.

Trapped in the narrow street, the English had little hope of avoiding the murderous blades. Richardson fell, mortally wounded, to the ground, while his two friends were so severely slashed about the body that they could only shout to Mrs. Borrodaile 'Ride on, we can do nothing for you'. She had fortunately suffered no more than the loss of her hat and some of her hair, and so she was able to get back to Kanagawa to raise the alarm. Her two companions also managed to return some time later, but Richardson's dismembered corpse was eventually found by the roadside.

The foreign community were all for calling out the garrison and the crews of the ships in harbour to launch an immediate reprisal, but they were dissuaded in the end by the calmer counsel of Colonel Edward Neale, the Acting British Consul (in Alcock's absence in London for the negotiation of the new Protocol). When news of the incident finally reached the Foreign Office, Lord Russell, the Foreign Secretary, demanded £100,000 in reparation from the Shogun and £25,000 from Satsuma, together with the arrest and execution of those responsible.

When he arrived in Kyoto, Hisamitsu found to his dismay that the incident had already been seized on by the extremists as the opening shot in the campaign to expel the barbarians. Exultant *ronin* had taken over the Imperial capital's streets, and the proponents of Court-Bakufu unity, or rather their unfortunate underlings, ventured outside only at the risk of life and limb. Iwakura, for example, found himself in receipt of an arm severed from one of his retainers, while the head was deposited at the front door of Shogun-Guardian Yoshinobu's residence. Having little means himself of controlling such a volatile situation and fearing that the British fleet might at any moment sail into Kagoshima to exact revenge for Richardson's death, Hisamitsu decided that he had no option but to return there and await developments.

'ABROGATE THE TREATIES'

Emboldened by these events, the Court sent a delegation to Edo demanding the immediate expulsion of the foreigners in order to put an end to 'the unparallelled national disgrace' of their presence in Japan. Its arrival caused a sharp division within the Bakufu; Shogun-Guardian Yoshinobu and the Roju considered that it was more important to uphold the treaties than the Emperor's prestige, whereas Regent Keiei argued that if Komei remained adamant the Shogun ought to resign and join the other *daimyo* in carrying out the Imperial wish — Yoshinobu 'has not realised how ardently the Emperor desires the expulsion of the foreigners,' he asserted.

Eventually, after Yoshinobu had submitted his own resignation and had then been persuaded to withdraw it, they arrived at a compromise. Expulsion was agreed in principle, but no date was to be set for it before the Shogun's visit to the Court scheduled for the spring.

In the meantime the 'men of spirit' in the Shogun's capital set out to match the murderous exploits of their brethren in Kyoto. Yokoi Shonan, who had compromised himself in their eyes by calling for the establishment of a two-tier assembly along the lines of the British Houses of Parliament, was the target of an assassination attempt, which fortunately failed. On February 1st 1863 the new British Legation was burnt down by a gang of Choshu *ronin* acting on the direct orders of Komei himself; included in their number was Ito Hirobumi, the future architect of the constitution which would give Komei's successors a *carte blanche* for their plans to expand the Empire overseas.

As the date of the Shogun's visit approached, 'a body of more than forty *daimyo* came up to the capital . . . Kyoto had not been so crowded since the last visit of a Shogun, that of Iemitsu in 1634,' it was recorded. Among them were the Court-Bakufu unity leaders Yoshinobu, Keiei and Katamori, joined now by Yamamouchi Yodo of Tosa whose release from his detention by Ii had enabled the moderates in that *han* to gain the upper hand. Their presence was intended to bolster the Shogun's position in advance of his own arrival, but instead they found themselves subjected to determined pressure from the Court to nominate a specific date for the foreigners' expulsion. On March 29th they were forced to agree that the expulsion (originally termed 'withdrawal', it was changed at the Court's insistence) should take place twenty days after the Shogun's return to Edo. They received in return a verbal assurance that the Shogun's mandate should run as before, but when it was committed to paper it was found to read 'mandate for the expulsion of foreigners'. Yoshinobu protested, and the offending words were reluctantly deleted.

In their turn eleven *sonno-joi*ist *daimyo* dispatched a memorial to Edo maintaining that the treaties had been granted 'as a great favour and therefore bore no resemblance to a legal contract . . . You say "In fifteen years everything will be ready". Why not say with us that Japan is ready and has ever been ready? What difference is there between today and 250 years ago? Had not the foreigners large ships then as now? . . . The only difference is that they were then propelled by sails, whereas now they use steam. So much the better: they will leave the quicker.' With such a tide running against them, the Court-Bakufu unity party could be forgiven any feelings of despair.

Shogun Iemochi himself arrived on April 21st, and a week later he was ordered by Komei to accompany him on a pilgrimage to the temple of Shimo-Gamo, at which prayers were offered up for success in 'the sweeping away of the barbarians'. On May 1st he was joined by Hisamitsu, who had been detained in Kagoshima by the need to consider the British

Government's demands for reparation and the accompanying threat that if they were not met within twenty days, the considerable force of ships from the Royal Navy's Far Eastern Fleet now assembled in Edo Bay 'will proceed to enter upon such measures as may be necessary to secure the reparation demanded'.

Hisamitsu at once set about attempting to redress the situation, issuing a demand that the *ronin* guilty of atrocities in the Imperial capital should be punished and that the remainder who had no proper business there should be returned to their *han*. Unable, however, in the absence of his own forces (which he had been obliged to leave behind against the threat of the British fleet) to enforce such measures, he very soon saw the hopelessness of the Court-Bakufu unity position and only four days later withdrew again to his *han*.

Choshu's allies in the Court seized on his departure to secure an Imperial Rescript removing Satsuma *samurai* from their post as guardians of one of the nine gates of the Palace. Within a few more days the other stalwarts of the alliance had similarly melted away, leaving only the sixteen-year-old Iemochi and his twenty-six-year-old Guardian Yoshinobu to face the combined forces of the Court, the Choshu 'men of spirit' and their kindred fanatics.

THE GUNBOATS GO IN

Not surprisingly, Yoshinobu gave in, agreeing to a deadline of June 25th for the foreigners' expulsion. In his letter to the Roju explaining his decision he spoke only of '*negotiations* (author's italics) for the withdrawal (*sic*) of the foreigners which are to begin on June 25th'; it was also clearly implied, although never actually stated, that the £100,000 demanded by the British would have to be paid if there was to be any prospect of the Treaty Powers agreeing to negotiate.

Accordingly, on June 24th the first instalment was handed over together with a formal request for a renegotiation of the treaties with a view to closing those ports already open. Even the Bakufu must have been surprised by the vehemence of Colonel Neale's reaction to the latter: he received, he said, this 'extraordinary announcement with extreme amazement ... it is unparallelled in the history of all nations, civilised or uncivilised; it is, in fact, a declaration of war by Japan against the whole of the Treaty Powers, the consequences of which, if not at once arrested, Japan will have to expiate by the severest and most merited chastisement.'

The 'men of spirit', however, were not going to be deterred by mere words, now that a date for action had been fixed. Preparations were centred around the Shimonoseki Straits, the western entrance to the Inland Sea which offered a much safer and shorter passage to ships sailing between Nagasaki and Yokohama than the ocean-going route. A thousand men were put to work erecting batteries along the coastline, while the seat of the Choshu *han* government was moved from Hagi to the more inland

and so less vulnerable Yamaguchi. Similar preparations were put in hand
at Nagasaki by the Hizen authorities, who also lent a military 'Dutch
Learning' expert to Choshu to advise on gunnery technique.

On the appointed day of the 25th the Choshu gunners were ready at
their posts, and as luck would have it they had no more than a few hours to
wait for their first chance of proving their commitment to 'expel the
barbarian'. The American cargo ship *Pembroke* entered the Straits bound
for Yokohama and promptly found herself under heavy fire from the
shore; she was able to escape after suffering some damage both to her crew
and superstructure. When two weeks later the French sloop *Kienchan* and
the Dutch corvette *Medusa* were subjected to similar treatment, the
foreign envoys got together to decide on a joint action in reply. As a result,
three American and French warships on July 16th mounted a retaliatory
bombardment of the batteries, sank two gunboats which had recently been
purchased from Europe and landed troops to spike some of the guns. Most
of the damage was quickly made good, however, and the Straits effectively remained closed to Western shipping.

Meanwhile in Satsuma the 'Traitor' Okubo, who by now had been
appointed to a senior post in the *han* government, was again having
difficulty in retaining control over his more xenophobic followers in the
face of the British demands for reparation. They refused absolutely to turn
over Richardson's murderers, and were raising a considerable outcry
against even the payment of the £25,000. After several abortive attempts to
settle the issue via the offices of the Bakufu in Edo, Colonel Neale finally
presented himself in person off Kagoshima with an escort of eight
warships. After three days of unproductive negotiation, he ordered the
seizure of three Western-built steamers in the hope of speeding matters
up, but the only response was an order to the Satsuma batteries to open
fire.

In the heated engagement that followed, eleven British crewmen were
killed, including the Captain and Commander of the flagship *Euryalus*, and
another fifty were wounded; on the other side, a third of the Satsuma
capital was reduced to ashes in a fire set off by British incendiary rockets.
Honours being adjudged even, the Fleet retired the next day to Yokohama.
A month later envoys arrived there with an undertaking from Hisamitsu
to pay the £25,000 and to 'make a diligent search' for Richardson's
murderers. Relations between the two parties were further restored by the
conclusion of a trade agreement under which Britain was to assist Satsuma
in the purchase of modern warships.

That the British appeared at the time to have withdrawn from Satsuma
with their mission unaccomplished only served to embolden further the
'men of spirit' elsewhere. In Edo the American Legation was burnt down
as the British had been, and in Yokohama a French cavalry officer was cut
to pieces while out riding. In Choshu the *han*'s leading military strategist,
Takasugi Shinsaku, was recalled from China (where he had gone to study

the lessons to be drawn from the 'Arrow War') to raise a militia of farmers and peasants known as the Kiheitai to supplement the regular (*samurai*) forces along the lines of the 'righteous followers' suggested by Maki.

In the face of demands from the Treaty Powers for a guarantee of safe passage through the Shimonoseki Straits, the Bakufu sent a ship to the *han* authorities with an order to desist from firing on foreign vessels. However, it was seized by the Kiheitai, who refused to countenance the order, and when the Bakufu's envoy attempted to return to Edo he was promptly put to the sword. A memorial was dispatched instead to Kyoto requesting the Emperor to put himself at the head of an army of sympathetic *han* and to lead the campaign to expel the barbarian. Should Komei demur, Maki had an even bolder plan in hand: the Emperor was to be persuaded to make a pilgrimage to the Imperial shrine at Ise, then seized en route and conveyed to the heartland of his supporters in the western *han*.

IMPERIAL CLIMBDOWN

In Satsuma meanwhile Hisamitsu had been waiting for a chance to level the score with Choshu for their part in his *han*'s exclusion from the Imperial Palace (his resentment on this count had been a factor in his readiness to settle with the British). On September 28th he learnt of the Choshu plot, and in conjunction with his 'Court-Bakufu unity' ally and Kyoto Military Governor Katamori he applied to the Emperor for permission to forestall it. The demonstration of Western fire-power at Shimonoseki and Kagoshima had given even Komei pause for thought, and he readily assented to their request. Two nights later the combined forces of Satsuma and Aizu seized the Palace gates and obtained an order for the expulsion of Choshu forces and all other *ronin* from the Imperial capital.

Surprised by the speed of this initiative, the latter marched on the Palace and although heavily outnumbered drew up in battle formation opposite the gates. For several hours the two sides confronted each other, each waiting for the other to fire the first shot. The deadlock was finally broken by an order signed by Komei himself to the Choshu men to withdraw, whereupon they reluctantly shouldered arms and retired to their *han*, taking with them seven of the more extremist Court nobles under the leadership of Sanjo Sanetomi. In the meantime their fellow conspirators who were lying in wait at Yamato to intercept the Emperor's person, unaware of the reversal to their plans in Kyoto, raised the flag of revolt and attacked the local Tokugawa garrison, but they were easily suppressed by the 10,000 troops sent against them from the surrounding *fudai han*. In November another band of *ronin* under the Chikuzen activist Hirano met a similar fate; Hirano himself was captured and put to death shortly afterwards.

The turn of the tide against the *sonno-joï*ists confirmed Komei in his new mood of caution, as the following letter indicates: 'The expulsion of

foreigners is certainly the most important thing for our Empire, and we
are doing all in our power in order to bring it about. However, what Sanjo
and his comrades have done wounds us to the depths. They have taken no
account of our advice. That is really Imperial thought coming from below!
Insubordination, nothing less! . . . Now these hateful individuals have been
driven out by my wish; we are profoundly satisfied . . .' In another letter to
Hisamitsu he spoke of his disapproval of the idea of restoring Imperial
rule; he was happy, he asserted, to see the Bakufu continue in government
as long as they 'showed respect' for the opinions of the Court.

The 'Court-Bakufu unity' leaders on the other hand were correspondingly encouraged to reassert themselves. Between November and January they reassembled in Kyoto prior to a second visit by the Shogun
arranged for February 26th, and their united presence persuaded the
Emperor to include them in a newly-created Board of Imperial Advisers.
Hisamitsu and Yamamouchi, the respective leaders of Satsuma and Tosa,
were naturally among them, marking the first entry of *daimyo tozama* into
the highest councils of the Tokugawa Shogunate in its 260-year history.

These two soon took advantage of their new position to reach a
concordat with the Emperor on the approach to be adopted towards
foreigners on the key issue of their expulsion. The retirement of Harris as
U.S. Consul-General and the preoccupation of his successor with the
outbreak of the Civil War at home had increasingly persuaded the
Japanese to look on the British as representing the West. After Colonel
Neale's outraged rejection of the proposal to negotiate the closure of all
three ports already open, the Bakufu had consequently modified it to
relate to Yokohama only, but this too had been dismissed out of hand.
When the French minister then suggested that the Bakufu should take the
matter up directly with the governments concerned in Europe, the idea
was gratefully accepted and a delegation under the leadership of Ikeda
Nagaaki set sail for Paris in February 1864.

The mission was seen as serving a double purpose: not only might it gain
time in the same way that its predecessor had done in 1862, but it would
also convince the Emperor of their support for the principle of *joi*. In the
latter at least it was initially successful; in his first audience with Komei on
February 28th the Shogun was handed a letter stating that 'the subjugation
of the ugly barbarian is our nation's first priority, and we must raise an
army to chastise and overawe them. However, it is not my wish to see
them attacked recklessly . . .'

It was only when Iemochi's reply observed that 'in the matter of the
closing of Yokohama, I have already sent envoys abroad and am most
anxious that success may be achieved, but we cannot tell what attitude the
foreigners will adopt' that divisions began to reappear. In a further
audience on March 21st he was informed that the implication that the
closure was dependent on the success of the Ikeda mission 'was entirely
contrary to the Emperor's wishes. It was not enough that the question be

handled in so irresolute a manner: resolute action must be taken to close the port.' When Shogun-Guardian Yoshinobu then sought to reassure Komei that Iemochi's support for the closure was unconditional, he stirred Hisamitsu in turn to protest that the closure was 'quite impossible. The Bakufu must not accept orders to effect it, and they were quite unable to understand the Shogun's action in submitting his acceptance.'

Yoshinobu answered the Satsuma leader with a drunken tirade of abuse which effectively shattered the fragile solidarity of the 'Court-Bakufu Unity' alliance; within the next three weeks they all departed to their respective *han*, abandoning Yoshinobu, just as they had done the previous year, to carry the battle alone to the Court. This time, however, the Court too was bereft of allies, and in return for a reiteration from Yoshinobu of his determination to see Yokohama closed, Komei was obliged to issue a formal decree confirming the Bakufu's overall authority and granting them permission to take military action against Choshu for having fired on foreign ships.

'MEN OF SPIRIT' UNMANNED

The prospect of a Bakufu-led punitive expedition being mounted against them served to fan the ardour of the Choshu 'men of spirit' into flame once more. Their batteries at Shimonoseki had already opened fire on a Satsuma vessel, and in April Takasugi stole back into Kyoto to assess the possibilities of raising another revolt there and even of assassinating Hisamitsu. He reported back that the time was not yet ripe, but he was overruled by his impetuous followers in the Kiheitai irregulars and even found himself temporarily behind bars. His place at their head was taken by yet another rising star among the former pupils of Yoshida Shoin, Yamagata Aritomo, the man who more than anyone else was to transform the new Imperial Japan into a world military power in the course of the next half century.

Yamagata had already vowed that 'we will defeat the ugly, impudent barbarians; when we unsheath our swords and kill them, they will suffer the force of the divine wind [*kamikaze*] from the Ise shrine and will be thrown into the deep sea like bits of seaweed.' He and twenty-five of his closest accomplices now took a blood oath pledging their lives to the fulfilment of *joi* 'regardless of the dangers involved'. The order was given to the Kiheitai to prepare to march on Kyoto, ostensibly for the purpose of delivering an appeal to the Court; Yamagata also advocated the formation of a military alliance with other sympathetic *han*. An advance guard led by Kido Koin succeeded in infiltrating the capital and assassinating Sakuma Shozan, the chief ideologist of 'Court-Bakufu unity'. Most of them were either killed or captured in a subsequent clash with the Bakufu police, but Kido himself managed to escape.

Relations with the West were simultaneously reaching crisis-point. On May 30th the Treaty Powers sent a note to the Bakufu reiterating their

demands for the reopening of the Shimonoseki Straits to traffic and the
exaction of appropriate penalties from Choshu. When the Bakufu attempted to play for still more time, they threatened to mount an expedition to
Shimonoseki themselves if the Bakufu failed to do so within twenty days.

By chance this ultimatum coincided with the arrival in Edo of the Choshu *samurai* Ito with Inoue Kaoru, his boon companion who would play
Jonathan to the future Constitution-Maker's David in the first generation
of the Restoration leadership. They had been in Britain studying naval technology when they had read of the developing confrontation in the London
papers; having seen for themselves the strength of Western arms, they had
hurried home in an attempt to warn their *han* of the disastrous consequences in store. They offered their services as mediators to Alcock (also now
returned from London) and he, seeing the chance to negotiate directly
with Choshu, promptly accepted. They were provided with a British
warship for the journey, together with a memorandum to the *han* authorities that force would be used if necessary to reopen the Straits and that any
further retaliation carried the threat of reprisal by a foreign army 'just as
similar conduct led the armies of Great Britain and France victoriously to
Peking not five years ago'.

However, they were to find that even this prospect was insufficient to
induce a return to reason among their fellow clansmen, such was the
degree of *joiist* fervour running through the *han*. 'They did not believe that
the matters at issue could be settled without fighting,' Ernest Satow, the
interpreter who had accompanied them from the Legation, recorded.
'They suggested that it would be a good measure for the foreign representatives to throw over the Tycoon [Shogun] and, proceeding to Osaka,
demand an interview with the Mikado's ministers in order to conclude a
direct treaty with them.'

When Satow returned to Edo with this report, Alcock and the other
envoys decided that there was nothing more to be gained by negotiation
and set about preparing a squadron for action, but its departure was
postponed by the return of the Ikeda Mission from Paris. Far from having
been able to win agreement for the closure of Yokohama — indeed, so
strong had been the French opposition to it that they had considered it a
waste of time to go on to the other European capitals — they had been
obliged to sign a convention committing the Bakufu to reopen the Straits
within three months with French assistance if necessary and to secure an
indemnity from Choshu for the attack on the *Kienchan*. 'Our military
preparations are not yet complete by land and sea. It would be disastrous
for us now to incur the enmity of the Treaty Powers,' Ikeda explained in
justification. 'To do so might well jeopardise the safety and very existence
of our whole country.'

Only too well aware of the likely reaction in Kyoto to such a *volte-face*,
the Bakufu were in no mood to accept Ikeda's excuses; he was summarily
dismissed from office and the convention repudiated.

For the foreign envoys this was the last straw, and a few days later a joint force of seventeen warships set sail for the Inland Sea. Unbeknown to Alcock, a dispatch was on its way to him from London in which Lord Russell informed him that 'Her Majesty's Government positively enjoin you not to undertake any military operations whatever in the interior of Japan; they would indeed regret the adoption of any measures of hostility against the Japanese Government or the Princes, even though limited to naval operations, unless absolutely required in self-defence.'

In the meantime three columns of the Kiheitai had advanced on Kyoto and taken up position on the outskirts. Komei issued an Imperial Rescript ordering them to withdraw and Yoshinobu once again attempted to set negotiations in motion, but even the word of the Emperor would not now distract the 'men of spirit' from their self-appointed mission, and on August 20th they launched a concerted attack on the capital.

One column succeeded in penetrating the first precinct of the Palace, and a shell even landed on the Imperial Residence itself (to the terror of the twelve-year-old future Emperor Meiji). In the end, however, the Kiheitai were overwhelmed by the superior numbers of the defending forces from Satsuma and Aizu and were forced to retreat, although not before they had set off a disastrous fire which levelled two-thirds of the capital's buildings. A number of their commanders, including the fanatical Maki and 'Grass-Roots Hero' Yoshida's brother-in-law Kusaka, were killed or committed *hara-kiri*.

Two weeks later the foreign warships reached Shimonoseki and commenced operations. After an initial bombardment from the naval gunners a force of one thousand troops went ashore, destroyed the Choshu guns, dismantled the batteries and threw the shot and shell into the sea. On September 14th Takasugi, who had been released from prison to take command of the Strait's defences, signed an armistice. Pleading that Choshu had all along only been acting under orders from the Court and Bakufu, he undertook to pay an indemnity, to prevent any rebuilding of the batteries and to guarantee safe passage to foreign ships.

The Western envoys demanded an explanation from the Bakufu for this apparent complicity; when the latter answered that the orders in question 'had been transmitted, not by the Tycoon, but by an act of treachery on the part of persons surrounding the Mikado', the envoys retorted that 'either the Tycoon must find the means of bringing the Mikado and hostile party of *daimyo* into accord with him for the maintenance of the Treaties, or the Western Powers might find themselves compelled to go beyond the Tycoon and enter into relations with the Mikado.' This last threat had the desired effect, and on October 22nd a settlement was signed committing the Bakufu to a payment of three million dollars as an indemnity towards the cost of the naval expedition against Choshu or, as an alternative, to the opening of Shimonoseki or another suitable port on the Inland Sea.

A month later the last of the Mito rebels were crushed as they marched across country in a final bid to persuade Yoshinobu to fulfil his filial obligations by abandoning 'Court-Bakufu unity' for the *joiist* stance of his late father, National Watchdog Nariaki. Some four hundred of them were taken into custody by the *daimyo* of Kaga and handed over to the Bakufu, who condemned them to immediate execution; as a final warning to the *han*'s remaining men of spirit, the heads of the leaders were pickled and taken back to Mito to be put on public display outside the *daimyo*'s castle.

5

Imperial Rule Restored

'ENRICH THE COUNTRY, STRENGTHEN THE ARMY'

The Bakufu had reason to look back on the events of the year with some satisfaction. The Choshu threat had, for the moment at least, been dispelled, and if the terms of the settlement with the West had been accepted under some duress, they nevertheless represented a reasonable price to pay for that service (having been so much less equipped to perform it for themselves).

Moreover, the Imperial Rescript ordering the rebels to withdraw seemed to indicate a shift on Komei's part to a more realistic and even co-operative attitude, and when it was followed by another declaring Choshu 'outlawed' and authorising the preparation of a punitive expedition against the *han* under the leadership of Tokugawa Keisho, the ex-*daimyo* of Owari, the Bakufu saw it as offering a unique opportunity to eradicate the menace of the 'men of spirit' once and for all. Demands were accordingly issued to thirty western *han* for a contribution of troops; to ensure the compliance of Satsuma, the post of Chief of Staff was given to 'The Great Saigo' who, on the advice of his ally Okubo, had already been recalled from exile by Hisamitsu to command the Satsuma *samurai* on guard duty in Kyoto.

However, the expedition soon became bogged down by a series of disputes over its leadership. Keisho at first refused it on the grounds of ill health; others then argued that the Shogun should take it upon himself, but in the end Keisho was persuaded to change his mind on the condition that he was given complete freedom of action. There was further argument as to how far the punishment of Choshu should be pressed: some demanded that a portion of the *han*'s territory should be permanently confiscated, while others urged leniency on the grounds that sufficient contrition had already been expressed.

Saigo, as convinced a *joiist* as ever — even before his appointment he had written to Okubo that 'we have no hatred for Choshu because we have set ourselves the objective of increasing Imperial authority' — now used his position to exploit these differences for his own purposes. He was assisted in this by the return to power in Choshu itself of the more moderate element, which enabled him to argue that 'somehow to use Choshu men to

61

punish Choshu men' would be altogether preferable to running down the
country's still slender military resources.

He had no difficulty in gaining support for such a proposition from the
thirty *daimyo* concerned, who were only too pleased to spare themselves
the expense of a contribution, and he was commissioned to negotiate in
person with the new regime. An agreement was reached whereby the
daimyo of Choshu was to make a formal admission of guilt, the Kiheitai
irregulars were to be dissolved, the castle at Yamaguchi destroyed and the
seven Court nobles who had taken refuge there in 1863 expelled. Keisho
pronounced himself satisfied with these terms and on January 24th 1865
gave permission for the expedition to disband.

The Kiheitai, however, predictably refused to comply in their own
dissolution. Within the space of the next six weeks Takasugi, Ito, Inoue
and Yamagata led them to victory over the regular *han* forces of the
moderates and restored their extremist sympathizers to office, whereupon they set about reorganising the Kiheitai and the regular forces into a
unified militia run on Western lines and equipped with Western arms.
When they then heard that the extremists had not in fact been suppressed
at all, a furious Bakufu dispatched a messenger to Keisho with a warrant to
arrest the *daimyo* and his son and bring them to Edo. In a further move to
bolster their authority over the other *daimyo* they again required them to
spend four months of every year in the Shogun's capital.

By now, however, Keisho was already on his way back to Kyoto, and
when the warrant was passed on to the *daimyo* of the three neighbouring
han to Choshu they bluntly refused to accept it. Worse still, in April the
Emperor issued an edict countermanding it, while Shogun-Guardian
Yoshinobu, whom the Bakufu now suspected of having fallen under the
Court's influence, rejected their calls that he should return to Edo. This
was too much for the Bakufu's patience, and on May 13th they issued
orders to the western *han* to join in a second expedition against Choshu, to
be led this time by Shogun Iemochi in person. A month later Iemochi set
out for Osaka with an escort of several thousand troops.

These developments had been observed with close interest by the
Satsuma hierarchy and caused them significantly to alter their previous
stance. Their support for the principle of 'Court-Bakufu unity' had been
based on the expectation that Satsuma would hold the balance of power
between the Court and Bakufu and would so gain a position of decisive
influence in the nation's affairs, but it now seemed increasingly unlikely
that this balance would ever be achieved. As the evidence for the Bakufu's
lack of real authority mounted, so Saigo found it ever easier to bring
Okubo, and through him Hisamitsu, into line with his own objective of
'increasing Imperial authority'. 'Of late the Bakufu has entered the period
of its decline,' he now felt able to assert, 'and it is no longer able to exercise
national leadership. Now, when the barbarians are on all sides of us, if the
great *han* at least do not join together, the Imperial Land will inevitably go

under.' When he spoke of 'the great *han*' he was, naturally, including Choshu.

An equally significant shift had meanwhile taken place there in the attitude of the newly-restored loyalist regime. Their drubbing at the hands of the West at Shimonoseki had at last brought a realisation that 'expel the barbarian' could never be a practical proposition as long as Japan remained so technologically backward. A new slogan now began to be heard in place of the fanaticist cry of *'sonno-joi'* — *'fukoku-kyokei'* or 'Enrich the Country, Strengthen the Army' — although its Choshu proponents still sought to bring this about under the aegis of the Emperor rather than that of the Bakufu.

In April Takasugi actually proposed opening Shimonoseki to foreign trade in order to avoid 'falling into the foreigners' evil toils', but the very idea stirred such outrage among the zealots that he and his fellow Choshu leaders were obliged to go into temporary hiding. In Satsuma the 'Traitor' Okubo was expressing much the same sentiments: 'The eyes of the so-called irresponsible extremists have for the most part been opened and their views changed, so that they recognise the impossibility of expulsion and recommend extensive opening of the country.' Ironically, the Bakufu were simultaneously informing the foreign envoys that Takasugi's return to power meant that Shimonoseki could not be opened, and that they would therefore be paying the indemnity.

SAT-CHO-TO

In the space of a year the two *han* had thus moved from being at opposite political poles to positions very close to each other. In the succeeding months they struck up a dialogue through the intermediation of the leadership in Tosa, creating the foundations of the 'Sat-Cho-To' triumvirate which in turn would be the mainspring for the restoration of Imperial rule.

The catalyst was Choshu's need for Western arms with which to equip its new militia, and which the efficiency of the Bakufu's espionage network was preventing it from obtaining by direct purchase. Satsuma, which had refused point-blank to participate in the second anti-Choshu expedition — Saigo described it as 'a private war' — was already importing considerable amounts of military equipment, including two 750-ton steamers, from Europe via Nagasaki. At the end of August the Tosa intermediaries succeeded in negotiating the delivery to Choshu of 7,300 modern rifles imported by the English firm of Thomas Glover in Satsuma's name; in return, Choshu was to provision Satsuma troops passing through the *han* on any future expedition to the east. It would be some time yet, however, before the long-entrenched feelings of hostility between the two *han* dwindled to a point where a formal alliance could be considered (one Choshu diehard boasted that the soles of his clogs were inscribed with the

words 'Satsuma bandits, Aizu villains' in order that he could enjoy the
sensation of trampling on them with every step).

Meanwhile opposition to the Shogun's expedition had been steadily
mounting elsewhere. Echizen's *daimyo*, Keiei, objected that 'the entire
country felt relieved when the first expedition against Choshu was
concluded without resort to arms. If great numbers of troops are again
mobilised, the various *daimyo* will be impoverished, the people will
disparage the Bakufu, the country will fall into disorder — who knows
what will happen?' On July 14th the Shogun travelled to Kyoto for an
audience with the Emperor, but Komei refused to give his endorsement to
the expedition and Iemochi retired again to Osaka to twiddle his thumbs.
Okubo reported back to Satsuma that both health and morale were both so
poor among the troops who had obeyed the Shogun's call that they offered
little threat to Choshu's forces. 'If the Shogun returns to Edo having
achieved nothing after so bold a beginning,' he went on, 'there is no doubt
that his orders will be more and more ignored, and that the great *han* will
tend to hold themselves aloof from him. We must therefore set ourselves
resolutely to the task of enriching the country and strengthening the
army.'

To compound their difficulties, the Bakufu were now subjected to
further pressure from the foreign envoys under the vigorous leadership of
the new British representative, Sir Harry Parkes. Alcock had been recalled
to London to explain his apparent defiance of his government's embargo
on military operations; although he was able to give a satisfactory account
of himself, he was then transferred to Peking. Parkes had an altogether
more forceful and positive attitude to the promotion of his country's
interests than his predecessor, who had been more narrowly concerned
with the enforcement of the letter of the treaties; years later one of those
who regularly faced him across the negotiating table was to write that 'he
was the only foreigner in Japan whom we could not twist round our little
finger'.

When he received instructions from London empowering him to offer
certain alternatives to the payment of the outstanding two-thirds of the
Shimonoseki indemnity, such as the opening of Osaka and Kobe and the
granting of Imperial ratification to the treaties (which Komei had been
withholding ever since 1858), Parkes persuaded his fellow envoys that
these should be presented to the Shogun not at Edo, but at Osaka: besides
being able to confront him more directly there, he argued that they would
be in a position to cut short any attempt on his part to play for time by
threatening to refer directly to the Palace at nearby Kyoto. This threat,
together with the appearance of a combined escort of nine warships from
the Treaty Powers in the Inland Sea, did indeed have the desired effect,
and the two parties came to a rapid understanding.

When the new terms were then presented to the Emperor, however, they were summarily rejected. Iemochi thereupon submitted his

resignation, an event which was rare enough to cause even such a committed *joi*ist as Komei to have second thoughts. This gave the Bakufu time to rally the Shogun's supporters in Kyoto, and at a council meeting held at the Palace on November 22nd they insisted that any renewal of hostilities with the West 'would in a moment reduce the country to ashes'. The meeting went on for a full 24 hours, and at one point Shogun-Guardian Yoshinobu was reported to have taken hold of the Imperial sleeve and threatened not to let go — and even, according to Satow, to commit *hara-kiri*; finally, however, the Emperor was persuaded to give his assent to all but the opening of Kobe. As a consolation, he was allowed to add a secret rider to the effect that 'there are various unsatisfactory provisions in the treaties previously concluded. They do not conform to the Emperor's wishes. They are therefore to be re-examined...'

This outcome was more than gratifying to Parkes and his colleagues, particularly in view of the fact that the Bakufu also conceded that in the absence of any subsequent agreement to open Kobe the remainder of the indemnity would be paid. On the other hand, the loss of prestige caused to the Japanese by the episode hardly augured well for the stability of relations in the longer term.

When the nature of the proposals had first become known, Saigo and Okubo had spared no effort in bringing the leading *daimyo* to Kyoto in order to stiffen Komei's opposition to them; at the same time Okubo wrote to Prince Asahiko, the Emperor's Chief Adviser, warning him that 'if the Court were to approve these proposals, it would be issuing orders that were contrary to justice. Not one of the *daimyo* who give the Court their backing would obey them ... for an Imperial order that is against justice is not an Imperial order and need not be obeyed.' However, the sheer speed of events had defeated them.

It was at this point that they began to entertain the idea of a formal alliance with Choshu, which had first been officially put forward by the latter a month earlier. Both sides approached the proposal with considerable caution, knowing the opposition that it would provoke among the more reactionary of their respective 'men of spirit'. In the end, it again took the services of the Tosa intermediaries to bring matters to a satisfactory conclusion. One of the latter subsequently wrote, prophetically, that 'I see, as in a mirror, that in the near future the entire country will be following the commands of Satsuma and Choshu'.

Under the agreement signed on March 7th 1866 Satsuma undertook, first, to intercede at Court to obtain an Imperial pardon for Choshu; secondly, should this fail, to send three thousand troops to Kyoto and Osaka to obtain the pardon by force of arms; and thirdly, after the cessation of hostilities to join with Choshu in 'restoring the Imperial prestige'. Seventy-five years later these same two *han* were to lead the Imperial Navy and Army respectively into World War Two.

NOD FROM BRITAIN

One man who played no small part in cementing the relationship between them was Sir Harry Parkes, who had visited Choshu on his way to take up his post at Edo and had quickly made up his mind on the likely outcome of the present power struggle. As his interpreter, Satow, recorded, 'the Tycoon's ministers still persevered in their endeavour to keep the conduct of foreign affairs in their own hands, and had succeeded in persuading Mr. Winchester [the acting Consul-General] that this was an ancient and indefeasible prerogative of the Tokugawa family. Sir Harry Parkes, however, from the first, with clearer insight, held that this was untenable . . .' In arriving at this conclusion, Parkes was no doubt partly influenced by Satow's own opinion, expressed in the light of his experience of the negotiations which followed the Shimonoseki expedition: 'Having beaten the Choshu people, we had come to like and respect them, while a feeling of dislike began to arise in our minds for the Tycoon's people on account of their weakness and double-dealing, and from this time onwards I sympathised more and more with the *daimyo* party, from whom the Tycoon's government had always tried to keep us apart.'

Another factor which weighed with him was the desire to counterbalance the influence which France now held with the Bakufu as a result of their offer of military assistance to the Ikeda mission. A dockyard at Yokosuka and an iron foundry at Yokohama were already in the course of construction under French supervision; a large order for French arms had been placed for use in the campaign against Choshu, and a military mission was now on its way from Paris to organise the equipping and training of the Shogun's army. The supplying of arms to Choshu and Satsuma by Thomas Glover had, of course, had Parkes's blessing; subsequently a trade delegation from Satsuma had departed for London to negotiate the purchase of industrial machinery, to be followed shortly afterwards by a party of young *samurai* sent to study naval and military technology.

The French had already begun to voice suspicions that a secret agreement existed between the British and Satsuma to overthrow the Bakufu when Satow wrote a pamphlet calling for 'a remodelling of the constitution of the Japanese government . . . the Tycoon should descend to his proper position as a great territorial noble, and a confederation of *daimyo* under the headship of the Mikado should take his place as the ruling power,' — thus precisely echoing the new Satsuma line. Satow claimed that the pamphlet had been written for private purposes only and without Parkes's knowledge, but it was soon copied and circulated in the capital, where it was looked on as representing official British policy. In July Parkes paid a formal visit to Kagoshima, where he was received by Hisamitsu with lavish ceremony and hospitality; his tour of inspection included an arms foundry and a glass factory. A percipient naval officer in the party was prompted to remark that 'there is certainly among these people the germ of a future greatness in the manufacturing world'.

NEW SHOGUN, NEW EMPEROR

At the same time matters were reaching a head between the Bakufu and Choshu. The Bakufu were demanding that Choshu should surrender their *daimyo* and his son together with a quarter of their territory, but an ultimatum to this effect brought no response. A whole year had now passed since Iemochi had arrived to set up his headquarters in Osaka, and the cost of maintaining troops in the field over so long a period was having a drastic effect on the national economy; the price of rice had already doubled in 1865 (and was set to treble again in 1866), sparking off a series of riots which spread eventually to Osaka itself. In these circumstances it is hardly surprising that support for the expedition among the *daimyo* dwindled still further. Keiei, for example, considered that to launch it now 'might well endanger the Bakufu's authority and eventually the state itself', while in a letter to the Court Hisamitsu contended that it would recklessly expose the country to the danger of foreign invasion. The young Shogun, however, brushed all such reservations aside and, appointing himself Commander-in-Chief, issued the order to attack on July 23rd.

His numerically superior but ill-equipped and demoralised troops advanced on four different fronts, but on each of them they were repulsed with heavy casualties by the eager and well-disciplined Choshu forces, who had had the benefit of months of intensive training with their new rifles. The campaign was further undermined by the death of August 29th of Iemochi himself at the age of twenty. It was officially reported to have ben the result of a heart attack brought on by chronic beri beri, but given the circumstances, rumours that he had been poisoned by opponents of the expedition were not hard to credit.

As usual, it was not made public knowledge for another month, and on September 22nd the Bakufu even went to the lengths of announcing that 'being extremely ill, the Tycoon has appointed Yoshinobu to take over the direction of affairs'. The latter's succession was duly approved by the Emperor, and on October 4th an armistice was signed putting an end to the hostilities. It was no less timely to the victors than to the vanquished, for the very next day saw the death through a combination of overwork and tuberculosis of the man who more than anybody else had made Choshu's victory possible, Takasugi.

This latest and most humiliating admission of defeat had put it almost beyond doubt that the demise of the Tokugawa Shogunate was at hand, and Yoshinobu was understandably reluctant to take up the appointment. He finally agreed to do so only on the condition that the *daimyo* gave him a free hand to reform the Bakufu and its political institutions, and it was not until January 10th 1867 that he was installed in office. The news of his acceptance served to stiffen the determination of the Satsuma leadership, who, so Parkes reported, 'seem to regard his appointment as the defeat of their policy, which is to place the Tycoon's power under considerable restraint and to secure for some of the leading *daimyo* a share in the administration or in the deliberative portion of it.'

Six days later the Emperor contracted smallpox. Just when it seemed that he was recovering, he took a sudden turn for the worse and died on the night of the 30th. Rumours again circulated that death had not been from natural causes; Satow recorded later that 'several years afterwards I was assured by a Japanese well acquainted with what went on behind the scenes that he had been poisoned. He was by conviction utterly opposed to any concessions to foreigners, and had therefore been removed out of the way by those who foresaw that the coming downfall of the Bakufu would force the Court into direct relations with the Western Powers.' Komei was succeeded by his fifteen-year-old son, Meiji.

The young Emperor's maternal grandfather was Nakayama Takayusu. A man of no particular ability or consequence in himself, he was, however, an intimate associate of a former Lord Chamberlain and kinsman of Hisamitsu who had served as Satsuma's linkman in the Court, and it was through their combined influence that the Satsuma-Choshu alliance was able to secure the return to Kyoto of the two exiles Sanjo and Iwakura. Since his expulsion in 1862 for his 'Court-Bakufu unity' sympathies, Iwakura had undergone a considerable change of heart, as the following quotation from a memorial which he wrote in 1866 indicates. 'Since 1862 the Imperial authority has been in the process of reviving, and Bakufu power has been in decline ... I submit, therefore, that the time has come when we might restore the fortunes of the Imperial House,' he had concluded. 'The purpose of requiring the Bakufu to surrender its administrative powers is to make it possible to reassert our national prestige and overcome the foreigners. To achieve this the country must be united ... the Court must be made the centre of national government.'

By 1867 his 'Destroy the Bakufu' inclinations had hardened still further: 'In the heavens there are not two suns. On earth there are not two monarchs. Surely no country can survive unless authority derives from a single source. If Court and Bakufu continue to co-exist as they do now, we will be able to effect neither genuine expulsion of the foreigners nor genuine friendship with them. Hence it is my desire that we should act vigorously to abolish the Bakufu.' He had thus become one of the prime movers in hastening that process, and until his death in 1883 he would share, with Sanjo and his Sat-Cho-To allies, the highest positions in the Restoration government.

In the wake of his own installation as Shogun Yoshinobu had meanwhile used the free hand promised to him to embark on a wide-ranging programme of reform in a do-or-die attempt to stave off the Shogunate's collapse. He set up departments to direct the various areas of the administration and appointed 'presidents' to be responsible for them; he swept aside the hitherto rigid scales of promotion in the Bakufu hierarchy to advance 'men of talent'; he separated the army and navy and divided the former along Western lines into infantry, cavalry and artillery units; and he inaugurated a series of fiscal and economic reforms to bolster the Treasury, including the procurement of a loan from French banks and the establishment of a joint trading company with them. All this represented only a part of a blueprint drawn up for him by Leon Roches, the French envoy, who also arranged for a Japanese entry in the Paris World Exhibition taking place that summer.

A STRONG ENEMY

The vigour of Yoshinobu's initiative impressed even his most determined opponents. 'The actions of the present Shogun are resolute, courageous and of great aspiration; he is a strong enemy and not to be despised,' Iwakura observed, while in Choshu Kido wrote that 'the courage and resourcefulness of Yoshinobu cannot be under-estimated. If the opportunity to restore Court government is now lost and the lead is taken by the Bakufu, then truly it will be as if we were seeing the rebirth of Ieyasu.' Nor, of course, did it go unremarked in the British Legation, where it caused some anxious heart-searching as to whether their money was after all on the right horse; Satow, who for the past year had kept in regular contact with Satsuma, Choshu and their potential allies, concluded that 'on the whole everything seemed to point to the triumph of the Shogun over his opponents'.

In April, at Parkes's instigation, Yoshinobu invited the foreign envoys to Osaka (where he had put the Shogunate headquarters on a more or less permanent footing) in order to discuss the opening of Kobe, which under the terms of the amended treaties was due to take place the following January. At the same time he wrote to the Emperor requesting the withdrawal of Komei's 1865 veto on the grounds that the opening of ports generally would enable Japan 'to build up the national wealth and strength by adopting foreign methods', and that to renege on the treaties 'would put us in serious difficulties and would in the end plunge all our people into misery and endanger the safety of our country.'

His opponents had until now been looking to the issue of a pardon for Choshu to provide the pretext for a showdown with the new Shogun, but they saw this invitation to the foreigners as too good an opportunity to let pass. Here too it seems that the British Legation lent a prompting hand, for on arriving in Osaka Satow recorded that 'I hinted to Saigo that the chance of a revolution was not to be lost. If Kobe were once opened, then good-bye to the chances of the *daimyo*.' Only in February Satow had been told by a confidant of the 'Traitor' Okubo in the *han* government that Satsuma was privately in favour of Kobe's opening, and that they had even gone so far as to purchase some land there 'of which they would be willing to let us have the greater portion for a foreign settlement'.

For some months past Saigo and Okubo had stationed themselves in Kyoto in order to be able to co-ordinate their plans with Iwakura and the other conspirators; the Satsuma *yashiki* (the *daimyo*'s official residence) gave convenient cover there to those from Choshu, who were still officially outlawed from the capital. They were thus well placed to dictate the manner of the Emperor's reply to Yoshinobu, which was predictably uncompromising: 'It would be impossible to justify to our Imperial predecessor the issue of fresh orders on the subject. Moreover, the views of the *daimyo* are to be sought at once. The Shogun will therefore carefully reconsider his attitude.'

The insistence that nothing should be done until the *daimyo* had been consulted lay at the centre of a carefully-prepared plan, as Okubo's confidant had made clear to Satow: 'If Sir Harry on his arrival would propose to make a treaty with the Mikado, the *daimyo* would at once give it their backing and flock to Kyoto in order to take part in carrying out the great scheme [to restore the Emperor]. All that was necessary was for him to help them to this extent, and they would do the rest.' It has even been suspected that Okubo himself was responsible for drafting the Imperial reply; certainly, he was writing at the same time to the ex-Lord Chamberlain linkman that 'it is in every way necessary that discussion of the desirability of opening this port be set aside for the time being, and that policy be determined only after the views of the leading *daimyo* have been obtained.'

In marked contrast to the urgency which Parkes had originally claimed that the issue demanded, Satow noted that 'the negotiations between the foreign representatives and the delegates of the Japanese Government proceeded satisfactorily though somewhat slowly, and about the middle of May had reached a stage at which it was felt that nothing more could be done for the present.' His account offers no explanation for this change of pace, but it may be assumed that Parkes did nothing to accelerate things; outwardly, he was still assuring the Shogun and his ministers of 'the absence of all disposition on our part to interfere with the choice of the form of government to be adopted', but at one and the same time Satow was writing unequivocally that 'the British Legation are determined that so far as their influence goes, the Mikado should be restored to the headship of the nation.'

Saigo meanwhile had set out for the various leading *han* to execute the next stage of the plan, which was to persuade their *daimyo* to come to the capital with as large a body as possible of their retainers. Hisamitsu was the first to arrive, on May 15th, at the head of no less than 7,000 Satsuma *samurai*. In recent months he had been increasingly happy to leave policy-making in the hands of his subordinates, and so he was not fully apprised of their intentions. Okubo therefore now filled in the picture for him.

'Orders should be issued acknowledging that the lords of Choshu, father and son, acted out of a sincere desire to maintain the interests of the whole country, and that they should be reinstated so that all their retainers may be set at rest and their loyalty assured,' he said. 'To change the Imperial orders with respect to the opening of Kobe is a great and unpardonable crime. Consequently, the Shogun's territories should be diminished and he should be reduced to the rank of an ordinary *daimyo*.' Hisamitsu would have appreciated the need to obtain a pardon for Choshu, for only then would it be possible for their troops to appear openly in the capital again; he may, however, have momentarily raised an eyebrow at being asked to represent the opening of Kobe as a 'great and unpardonable crime' when only a few months earlier he had sanctioned investment in a prime site of real estate there.

Hisamitsu was presently joined in Kyoto in the course of the next three weeks by Keiei of Echizen, Yamamouchi of Tosa and Date Munenari of Uwajima, the three *daimyo* whose support was most essential to the success of the conspiracy. It needed a series of lengthy and sometimes acrimonious conferences before Saigo and Okubo were able to overcome the *daimyo*'s suspicions of Satsuma's motives and to persuade them to present a united demand to the Shogun that any announcement of agreement on Kobe must be preceded by the pardoning of Choshu. In his reply, Yoshinobu countered that the former deserved priority because of its international implications. After further heated debate at the Shogunate headquarters in Osaka Castle a compromise was eventually agreed whereby both decisions were to be announced simultaneously; the signatories would then go on June 25th to the Imperial Palace to obtain the Emperor's approval.

At the last moment, however, Hisamitsu and his lieutenants persuaded the other *daimyo* to abandon the compromise and return to their original demand; possibly they feared that the position of their sympathizers in the Court was not yet so secure as to guarantee its rejection there. In this they were justified, for when Yoshinobu called their bluff and went to the Palace on his own he managed to procure the necessary approval, albeit after some protracted heart-searching on the part of the Court nobles (in the course of which Prince Asahiko recorded in his diary that 'there was a slight earthquake about 2pm'). An Imperial Rescript was duly issued on the 26th sanctioning the opening of Kobe and recommending the adoption of a 'lenient policy' towards Choshu. Outflanked, the four *daimyo* saved what face they could by dispatching a joint letter of protest to the Shogun and retiring to their respective *han*.

TIME FOR ACTION

Watching from the sidelines in Choshu, Ito wrote to Kido of the dangerous implications of the success of this 'clever plot of the Bakufu', and of the need to take action before Yoshinobu completed his programme of

reform. By 'action' he meant military action, and Yamagata was dispatched incognito to Kyoto to sound out the Satsuma reaction to the
disagreeable turn of events. He was soon reassured, being informed by
Hisamitsu in person that 'since the Bakufu is incapable of reconsidering its
position, our two *han* must plan anew for the benefit of the nation'; in a
symbolic gesture, he was also presented with a revolver. Yamagata in his
turn submitted a plan to seize Osaka, assassinate Yoshinobu and join forces
with other sympathetic *han* to launch a direct attack on Kyoto. At the same
time Okubo was writing to his colleagues in Kagoshima that 'the Bakufu
has shown absolutely no intention of adopting the views of the four *han*, or
of repentance, or of upholding the Imperial edicts', and that the time for
applying merely political pressure was past. It was arranged that Saigo
should visit Choshu in the near future to co-ordinate their plans.

Approaches were now also made to Tosa to secure their commitment to
a military alliance. They were well received by the 'Destroy the Bakufu'
element there, led by Itagaki Taisuke, but the dominant figure in the *han*
government, Goto Shojiro, was a supporter of the rival 'Enrich the
Country, Strengthen the Army' camp. Goto had already carried out a
wholesale reform of the *han* economy, setting up a general trading
company in the process which in time was to become the Mitsubishi
conglomerate; he also shared his *daimyo*'s distrust of Satsuma's motives. He
therefore countered with a set of proposals which would give Yoshinobu
the opportunity to abdicate and so avoid the need for bloodshed; powers
would then revert to a two-tier legislature, along the lines first suggested
by Yokoi Shonan in 1861 (the upper house was to be made up of Court
nobles and *daimyo*, the lower of '*samurai* and even commoners who are just
and pure-hearted'), under the ultimate authority of the Emperor. After
some brief and amicable discussion, an agreement was signed on July 23rd
authorising Goto to present these proposals to the Shogun; for its part,
Tosa was to contribute troops to a joint operation should Yoshinobu refuse
to step down.

Nevertheless, the Satsuma leaders continued to push ahead with their
military preparations. In a letter to Yamagata, Saigo explained that the
agreement with Tosa was merely a 'transitional device' in the campaign to
remove the Shogun, while at the same time Okubo proclaimed that 'we
must make ready our troops, rally support in the country and show
ourselves resolute in the Emperor's service'. Saigo also took the precaution
of maintaining contact with his friends in the British Legation, and at a
meeting in Osaka at the beginning of September he informed Satow of a
rumour 'that in two or three years' time money would be collected by the
Bakufu, machinery be provided, French assistance be invoked and war be
begun.' However, he suggested, 'if a report were then spread that England
would also send out troops to protect us, it would be impossible for French
auxiliary troops to be set in motion; therefore it was necessary to come to a
thorough agreement beforehand ...'

Messengers continued to shuttle to and fro between Satsuma and Choshu, and on October 15th Okubo travelled to the Choshu capital to put the finishing touches to their plans. The Bakufu had ordered Choshu to send a minister to Osaka to discuss the issue of the pardon, and this was seen as a convenient pretext for an escort of troops for both *han* to gain admittance to Kyoto. Their first target would be the Imperial Palace, where they were to take possession of the Emperor's person; 'One Sun' Iwakura would give the signal when the moment was ripe. 'If we are robbed of the jewel,' Kido explained, 'we shall be helpless indeed.' October 25th was set as the date for the arrival of the Satsuma contingent in Choshu, both *han* being very conscious of the need to forestall any attempt by the Bakufu to call in foreign help; three months earlier Kido had written of his fear that Japan would 'fall into the toils of the Bakufu and France unless authority is quickly restored to the Court'.

In Tosa meanwhile Goto had taken an unexpectedly long time to gain the approval of his *daimyo* Yamamouchi for his proposals, and he was then still further delayed by complications arising from the murder of two British seamen in Nagasaki for which some Tosa *samurai* were thought to have been responsible. It was October before he finally arrived in Kyoto, by which time the Satsuma and Choshu troops were preparing for the march on the Imperial capital. However, it was agreed that Goto should forward his proposals for reform to the Bakufu as originally planned, allowing the military preparations to be completed in the interval; this he duly did on the 29th.

The disclosure of the proposals did not cause Yoshinobu any particular discomfort, for he had already authorised his officials some months earlier to draw up a scheme incorporating some form of representative assembly. Moreover, there was nothing in Goto's scheme which would reduce the pre-eminent position of the Tokugawa clan among the *daimyo* and so remove the leadership of the executive from the Shogun's hands. Accordingly, on November 8th he announced his intention of surrendering his official powers as Shogun to the Emperor in a statement which was couched only in the most general of terms: 'If the administrative authority is restored to the Imperial Court, if national deliberations are conducted on a broad basis and the Imperial mandate is secured, and if the Empire is sustained by the harmonious efforts of the whole people, then our country will be able to maintain its rank and dignity among the nations of the earth.' Sir Harry Parkes at once divined its implications: 'I doubt very much whether he would abandon the large party and large interests which he doubtless represents, and throw the game of government into the hands of his opponents,' he reported to the Foreign Office, and in another letter he described it as 'a plan to bring him in again to a chief if not sovereign position by the vote of a small packed assembly.'

Two days later an Imperial Rescript announced the Emperor's acceptance of Yoshinobu's submission and a proposal to call the leading *daimyo* to discuss the changes which it entailed; in the meantime 'the territories and cities previously under Bakufu control will continue to be administered as in the past, though subject to orders which will be issued in due course.' None of the *daimyo*, however, answered the summons; the *fudai* were naturally against any dimunition of Tokugawa power, while the *tozama* who were not party to the 'Destroy the Bakufu' conspiracy preferred to await the outcome of events before committing themselves. Thus everything seemed destined to carry on much as before, especially when Yoshinobu's formal submission of his resignation to the Emperor was merely recorded rather than accepted. Goto, finding the rug rapidly disappearing from beneath his feet, retired to Tosa to nurse his disappointment.

SHOWDOWN

The failure of his initiative came as no surprise to the conspirators, and on the very day of the Shogun's resignation Iwakura obtained an order drafted by Okubo and signed by Imperial grandfather Nakayama and two other senior Court nobles (but not by the Emperor) sanctioning Yoshinobu's expulsion by force. Copies were then hurried off to Satsuma and Choshu, representing it as an Imperial Rescript. Satsuma had failed to meet the deadline of October 25th set for the arrival of their troops in Choshu due to the emergence of some die-hard opposition within the *han* to collaboration with their former rivals, which was only disarmed in the end by an assurance from Hisamitsu that the troops were being sent to Kyoto merely for the purpose of 'guard duty'. This delay in turn revived latent anti-Satsuma prejudices among the Choshu forces, and their leaders were on the point of giving the order to march when the Satsuma contingent of 3,000 men under the leadership of 'The Great Saigo' made their belated appearance on December 10th.

The joint force arrived in Kyoto on the 18th, simultaneously with 300 troops from Hiroshima under their *daimyo*. The Choshu contingent of 2,500 men continued eastwards and took up positions in the area of Osaka. An emissary from Satsuma was dispatched to the British Legation with the information that 'all was going on well', and that they 'hoped to be "favoured with a call" as soon as we [the British] reached Osaka' to attend the formal opening of Kobe on January 1st. In fact it was the British who were favoured with a call on their arrival on December 12th, from a lieutenant of Okubo who, as Satow records, 'told us that the coalition, which was determined to push matters to the last extremity in order to gain their points, consisted of Satsuma, Tosa, Uwajima, Choshu and Aki [Hiroshima]'.

The inclusion of Tosa in this claim was a little premature: Goto had returned to Kyoto in the meantime, but when he had been approached by Okubo to fulfil the second part of their agreement, to contribute troops, he had responded non-commitally. When he was approached again on December 27th and given a detailed summary of the conspirators' plans, he replied that while he himself was prepared to go along with them, he was unsure of obtaining the approval of his *daimyo* Yamamouchi, who was not due to arrive in the capital until January 2nd.

Privately, however, Goto was against military action, and he disclosed the plans to Keiei. The latter, a former stalwart of 'Court-Bakufu unity' who still held out some hope of a compromise between the two sides, duly passed them on again to Yoshinobu. The Shogun, however, had 10,000 of his own troops in the Imperial capital and was inclined to dismiss the threat, viewing his opponents, according to Parkes, 'as a coalition who may soon dissolve of its own accord'. At an earlier conference of his *fudai* allies, many of whom had been pressing him to launch a pre-emptive expedition against Satsuma and Choshu, he had warned that any pre-mature military action might well compromise rather than secure his position.

His hope that the opposition would collapse if left to itself might not have seemed unreasonable in the light of Goto's temporising. When Yamamouchi finally arrived in Kyoto, however, and learnt that the other conspirators were about to press on regardless of whether Tosa agreed to participate, he quickly threw in his lot with them for fear that to refuse would entail his *han*'s exclusion from any new government. That same day, January 2nd 1868, the leading *daimyo* and Court nobles were summoned, as Iwakura had prearranged, to an Imperial Council at the Palace, at which they were to approve a decree granting a pardon to Choshu; this would give the *han*'s troops formal access to the capital and so allow the Palace gates to be seized at dawn the following morning.

So confident was Saigo of its outcome that he sent a copy of the decree that evening to the Choshu commander, but in the event the debate became so intense that the Council sat on into the night. As a result, some of the conspirators arrived at their appointed positions before the decree had been issued, and were then obliged to apologize and withdraw. By 10 a.m., however, the gates had been secured and the regular guards from Aizu and Kuwana informed that they had been relieved of duty by an Imperial decree. Another Council was then called to approve a further decree which had been drafted by Iwakura; amongst other things, the document formally accepted Yoshinobu's resignation and abolished the office of Shogun.

There then followed a long and acrimonious discussion on the position of Yoshinobu in the new order. From the Tosa side Goto and Yamamouchi argued that he should be given a place in the government, while from Satsuma and Choshu Okubo and Iwakura demanded that he should surrender all, or at least most, of his territories. Finally — after Iwakura had at one point challenged Yamamouchi to a duel — a compromise was reached whereby Keiei and the *daimyo* of Owari were to visit Yoshinobu, who was himself now in Kyoto, to inform him of the Council's decisions and allow him the opportunity of surrendering his lands voluntarily in return for a share in the new administration.

The Shogun replied that he was quite willing to resign his office, as he had already done two months earlier, and even to consider the question of the surrender of territory in due course, but that for the moment he was prevented from doing so by the opposition of his Tokugawa supporters. The troops of Aizu and Kuwana in particular were in an ugly mood, and in order to prevent the wholesale destruction of the capital which had followed the clash of 1864 Yoshinobu three days later withdrew with them to his headquarters in Osaka.

On his arrival there the Shogun was greeted by Parkes, to whom, in Satow's words, 'he gave but a lame account of the events of the last few days, professing at one moment to have withdrawn his troops from the Palace in accordance with an Imperial order, while refusing to recognise another such order, which he felt was equally dictated by Satsuma . . . he did not appear to claim that he himself possessed any authority, and he did not know whether the other *daimyo* would rally to his support . . . One could not but pity him, so changed as he was from the proud, handsome man of last May. Now he looked thin and worn, and his voice had a sad tone . . .' In a conversation with the commander of the Shogunate troops Satow 'suggested that if the Mikado ordered that there should be no fighting, that order must be obeyed. The significant rejoinder was: "Yes, by the Tycoon, but not by his retainers."'

Back in Kyoto, Goto and Yamamouchi had still not given up the hope that a compromise could be arranged and a clash averted, and they submitted a memorial to the Throne suggesting that if Yoshinobu was to surrender his lands then the other *daimyo* would have to surrender their lands too, and that if this was done it would pave the way for the formation of a *daimyo* council in which the ex-Shogun would be able to take his place as one among equals. This proposal received considerable support among the *daimyo* already in the capital — so much in fact that it persuaded the Satsuma leaders that the time had come again to take matters into their own hands.

In this they received the qualified support of the British Legation; in an interview with a Satsuma emissary Satow advised 'that they should not fight if they could help it, but if they judged it necessary, to do it at once.' In another interview a little later Satow suggested that 'it was only necessary for the Mikado to invite the foreign ministers to Kyoto, and compel the ex-Tycoon to abandon his claim to conduct the foreign affairs of the country.' Okubo then drafted an Imperial decree to this effect, but it was rejected by the majority of the *daimyo*.

END OF THE SHOGUNATE

In the meantime Saigo had sent agents to Edo to recruit a band of 500 *ronin* to stir up trouble in the Shogun's capital with the aim of provoking the latter's forces to take the field. On the 16th the Satsuma *yashiki,* in which the *ronin* had been quartered, was attacked and burnt to the ground. When news of this reached Osaka, Yoshinobu's advisers decided, just as Saigo had planned, that the time for parleying was past.

To the proposal of the *daimyo* of Echizen and Owari that the Shogun should go again to Kyoto under a guarantee of safe passage and confer with the Emperor, they replied that 'no faith can be placed on the declaration of the two *daimyo.* If your Highness determines to go your servants will follow, even at the risk of their own lives. On this expedition we will remove from the Emperor his evil counsellors and try the issue with them by the sword.' The Shogun's 10,000-strong army set out on January 26th from Osaka, reaching the midway point of Fushimi the same day. In Kyoto Okubo drew up a memorial to be submitted by Iwakura to the Emperor forbidding Yoshinobu to enter the Imperial capital, and even before Meiji's response was received orders were given to the Satsuma-Choshu troops to intercept the Shogunate troops.

They met the following day, and although heavily outnumbered (Yamamouchi had forbidden the Tosa contingent to join them, repeating, with some irony, the pretext that it was 'a private war' which Saigo had used to justify Satsuma's refusal to join the second anti-Choshu expedition), the rebels were completely victorious. Yoshinobu fell back again to Osaka with the remnants of his defeated army and four days later took ship for Edo, advising the foreign envoys to do likewise as he could no longer guarantee their safety. On the same day an Imperial decree was issued blaming him for the outbreak of hostilities and releasing his followers from any further obligation to him.

A week later another decree was sent to the foreign envoys , who had retired only as far as their newly-opened customs-houses in Kobe, notifying them that the Emperor was now responsible for the conduct of foreign affairs and implicitly confirming his acceptance of the terms of all existing treaties. In a further secret conference with Satsuma emissaries, Satow advised them 'to get their Note demanding neutrality on the part of all Foreign Powers sent in at once, because they could then request the American Minister to prevent the warship *Stonewall Jackson* being delivered to the Tokugawa people, as well as the two ironclads from France which were expected.'

When the Note was duly submitted, Parkes persuaded his counterparts to accede to it, despite the protests of Roches that 'we must not throw ourselves upon the necks of these people'; he drew not a little satisfaction from the discomfiture of his old rival, whom the turn of events 'had quite thrown on his beam-ends, and he could not bear to stand by and see his policy turn out a complete failure'. Parkes was still more pleased the following month to be the first foreign envoy to be received by the Emperor in Kyoto, notwithstanding an abortive attempt by two *ronin* to assassinate him en route to the Palace.

Yoshinobu's forces retreated along the Sacred Highway towards Edo in the hope of rallying his supporters along the way for a counter-attack. The 'Imperial Army', as it was now called, set out to pursue them under the leadership of Prince Arisugawa, although they were effectively commanded by Saigo. They met with very little resistance until they reached the deposed Shogun's capital, where his supporters were preparing to put up a determined resistance. Yoshinobu, however, had already sent a message to Saigo indicating his willingness to reach a settlement without recourse to further bloodshed, and by late April the terms of a truce had been agreed.

Under them the defeated Shogun was to hand over all his arms and warships, to surrender all but one-tenth of his territories, to renounce the headship of the Tokugawa clan and to retire to Mito. In the course of time he was to receive the title of 'Prince' under a new system of peerages introduced in 1884; he lived on until 1913, presented to the people as an honoured relic of Japan's feudal past. The core of his most loyal supporters withdrew to make a last stand in the northern fastnesses of Aizu, where they were finally forced to capitulate by Saigo in November. This left only some of his warships unaccounted for; they had taken refuge in Hokkaido under the leadership of a former Bakufu official and some French naval advisers, and they were able to hold out there until June the following year.

On September 3rd, at the instigation of Kido and Okubo, it was announced that the Emperor would transfer his throne from Kyoto to Edo, which was to be renamed Tokyo, 'the Capital of the East'. On November 26th Meiji was introduced to his new capital with great ceremony and installed in the ex-Shogun's palace, now to be known as the Imperial Palace, formally bringing to an end seven centuries of Shogunate rule.

The arguments produced in favour of such a move by its authors were not merely those of administrative convenience — that is, that the fount of authority should be at one geographically with the seat of the executive. They had much more to do with the desire of Satsuma and Choshu to consolidate their newly-won position of power behind the facade of Imperial rule, and to remove the Emperor from the closeted and reactionary influence of the Kyoto Court which would be bound to resist the reforms required to make such a consolidation permanent. If the country was to be brought under the centralised control of the two *han* and their allies, the Emperor would have to become their figurehead and not that of the Court; he would have to become like the constitutional monarchs of the West who, in Okubo's words, 'walk about accompanied by only one or two attendants and pay attention to the welfare of their people'.

Meiji was still only a sheltered, hesitant youth of sixteen, and his promoters could be excused for thinking that he would never grow to be anyone of more account. They were to discover differently, however: in the course of time, he would reveal himself to be nobody's figurehead. He was to remain on the Chrysanthenum Throne for forty-four years. At the mid-point of his reign he was raised to the status of an absolute and divinely-ordained monarch, being declared by the Constitution of 1889 to be 'sacred and inviolable'; by its close in 1912 he had masterminded the blueprint for overseas expansion into China and beyond which had first been adumbrated to him by his barbarian-hating father Komei, and which he in turn was to pass on to his grandson Hirohito for its fulfilment.

PART II

Beginnings of Empire

6

The Samurai's Last Stand

NEW BOTTLES, OLD WINE

The dissolution of the Shogunate was a revolution in the sense that it represented the overthrow of an existing order, but, dearly as later ideologues (particularly in Japan itself since 1945) would wish it to have and hard as they have tried to re-interpret the evidence to make it seem as if it did, it bore little or no resemblance to the class revolution of received Marxist terminology in which a lower order rises up against a higher order of oppressors. As we have seen, its main thrust, both intellectual and physical, came from the *samurai*, a military caste which, if it can be meaningfully categorized at all in such terms, represented something akin to the 'upper middle class' in the Japanese society of the day, accounting for only 5-6% of the population.

Furthermore, far from seeking to replace the current system of government by some new and hitherto untried disposition, it sought instead to return to an order which had existed several centuries earlier. All its supporters had looked to end the rule of the Tokugawas established by Ieyasu in 1600, and most of them envisaged a restoration to the Imperial throne of the aegis of authority usurped by Minamoto in 1183. Some even talked of a return to the primitive structure said to have existed before the constitution imported from China by Shotoku in the seventh century, and which was therefore more truly indigenous to the 'Divine Land'; one, for example, proclaimed that 'it is my intention to be guided by the precedents of the age of the Gods, from Jimmu to Tenchi [a later prehistorical Emperor]'.

As for its prime instigators, the leaders of the two *han* Satsuma and Choshu, they saw it only as a means of regaining their former pre-eminence which they had forfeited by their defeat on the field of Sekigahara. The façade had changed, but it seemed — at first, at any rate — that the actual edifice of power was much as before; 'The Tokugawas were exchanged for Saigo, Kido and Okubo. It was only a change in name,' a contemporary observer remarked.

A further reflection of the absence of any preconceived, ideological design among the victorious 'revolutionaries' shows itself in the frequent overhauls to the machinery of government which took place in the early

years of the new order. The decree of January 3rd 1868 abolishing the
Shogunate together with the senior offices in the Court and Bakufu
replaced them with a Senior Executive, Prince Arisugawa, and two
deputies, 'One Sun' Iwakura and fellow Court noble Sanjo; under them
were appointed ten senior Councillors, including Meiji's grandfather
Nakayama and the *daimyo* of Satsuma, Tosa, Aki, Owari and Echizen —
but not Choshu, who had not yet formally received the Imperial pardon —
and twenty Junior Councillors, comprising five Court nobles and three
samurai from each of the above *han*. Only a week later the number of
Councillors was expanded to include representatives from Choshu, and
again thereafter at regular intervals until by June there were 132 in all.

In February the former Bakufu bureaucracy was reorganised into eight
new Departments of State each headed by a Senior Councillor, faithfully
reproducing the Chinese administrative system introduced in 701. June
saw a radical revision of the whole framework under a new constitution,
by which the number of Departments was cut to five and that of the
Councillors to 43 who were then to be re-formed into a legislative upper
house. A lower house of one representative from each *han* was created,
while the executive was divided off into a Council of State under Sanjo
and Iwakura and invested with 'all power and authority in the Empire'.

The introduction of a lower house followed the publication on April 6th
of a Charter Oath legitimising the new order, issued in the name of the
Emperor but largely drafted by Sanjo, Iwakura, Kido and Fukuoka Kotei
of Tosa. Its First Article had promised that 'A widely-convoked assembly
shall be established and all policies shall be decided by open debate', but in
fact it met so infrequently that it was dissolved altogether no more than
five months later. Revived again the following March, its agenda was
largely confined to domestic trivia; one session, for example, voted to
remove the tables and chairs provided on the grounds that 'Japanese
customs should not be abandoned in favour of European customs'. At
another, the motion that the *samurai*'s privilege of wearing two swords
should be discontinued was not only unanimously defeated, but its sponsor,
Mori Arinori, narrowly escaped assassination and was forced to resign. It
was presently replaced in its turn by a similar body under a different name,
which itself duly lapsed into obsolescence and was adjourned for good in
October 1870. (The very promise of a 'widely-convoked assembly' might
be thought to disprove the argument that the Restoration did not represent
a populist movement. However, Fukuoka later confessed that when he
drafted the First Article 'I had in mind the administration of the government by the Court nobles and *daimyo*. It was not that I held the masses
lightly, but I simply did not consider them an important political factor.')

Similarly, the separation of the Council of State from the upper and
lower houses was intended to give the impression of a Western-style
division between the executive and legislature; in practice, however, the
distinction very soon blurred to the point of invisibility. The upper house

had been entrusted with 'the establishment of the constitution, the enactment of laws, the decision of questions of policy, the selection of men to fill the offices of the three higher ranks, the supreme judicial power, the conclusion of treaties and the power of making peace and war', functions which were hardly consistent with the investment of 'all power and authority' in the Council of State. The new constitution laid down that the ministers of the five Departments were to be drawn from the ranks of the Imperial princes, Court nobles and *daimyo*, but as the power of selection for these offices lay with the upper house, the latter effectively held the control of the executive which was nominally vested in the Council of State.

It is therefore not surprising to find Satow complaining that the translation of the new constitution 'had given me a great deal of trouble. I was unable to decide upon the best name in English for the second department [the Council of State]. It might be Imperial Council, Privy Council, or Cabinet . . . there were so many appointments that were held by dummies of high birth, while the real work was done by their underlings. The ancient ranks and precedence had been practically done away with, and I could not help thinking that the Court nobles and *daimyo* would have to be struck out of the list of officials. There was hardly one of them fit to occupy the place of head of a department.'

It did not take long for Satow's prediction, which he may very possibly have passed on as a suggestion to his Satsuma-Choshu intimates, to be borne out: the number of Court nobles in the upper house was reduced to no more than three, and in August 1869 it was merged with the Council of State to form a new and much smaller Executive Committee. Headed again by Sanjo, it consisted otherwise of three Deputies and a number (varying over the next two years from two to six) of *samurai* Councillors; it was given direct control over the Departments, which were increased to six and augmented by a Board of Religion.

EXPLOITING THE IMPERIAL HALO

In a measure to sanctify the restoration of Imperial rule, a Department of Shinto had already been included among the eight originally established in February 1868. It was followed almost immediately by an Imperial Rescript proclaiming that the tenets and practice of the Shintoist faith 'are the great properties of the Empire and the fundamental principles of the national entity [*kokutai*] and education', and proscribing Buddhism and Christianity as 'pernicious sects'. This drew a protest from Sir Harry Parkes, but his opinion for once went unheeded and in the following months some 4,000 Christian converts in the area of Nagasaki were dispossessed and exiled to the remoter regions.

The creation of the Board of Religion — ranked first in importance, above the Departments — marked a further attempt to use the Emperor's 'divinity' to legitimise the new order, and it was accompanied by an Imperial Rescript drawing on the authority of the Sun Goddess herself for the assertion that government and religion 'were one and the same'; at the same time it re-emphasized that education was a primary function of government and that 'the Great Way of Obedience to the Gods must be promulgated. Therefore we newly appoint propagandists to proclaim this to the nation . . .'

The persecution of Buddhism was simultaneously intensified, but it was soon found impossible to dissociate it from Shinto in the popular mind, so intertwined had the two religions become at a parochial level, and in April 1872 Buddhism was rehabilitated and brought under the aegis of the Board. The following month a new joint priesthood was established; in addition to giving religious and moral instruction, it was enjoined to 'lead the people to respect the Emperor and be obedient to His will'. Years later a member of the new government admitted that 'Mikado worship was established to further the political ambitions of the *daimyo* who had been debarred from the exercise of authority by the despotism of the Shogunate. This was the motive activating the Meiji statesmen — not loyalty.'

Just as the Emperor's recognition of the treaties allowed the new government a valuable breathing space in the problem of its relationship with the Western Powers, so this process of its identification with the Imperial godhead helped it to establish its authority on the domestic front; as the new British Chargé d'Affaires remarked, its initial existence was supported 'simply by the halo surrounding his sacred name'. Its leaders, however, were aware that it would need more concrete foundations before long if it was not to collapse in its turn. In April 1869 Sanjo, in his capacity as President of the Executive Committee, warned that people 'on every side were beginning to express a longing for the former government and show contempt for the failures of the new one', and in the following month the future Constitution-maker Ito wrote to Kido Koin that 'if we cannot rule at home, we will be unable to set matters to rights abroad'.

Kido had earlier defined the government's task as a dual one of 'Promoting men of talent on every side and devoting itself fully to the welfare of the people' on the one hand, and putting Japan 'on an equal footing with the other countries of the world' on the other. The crux of the problem facing them, he submitted, was this: they had taken the necessary decisions to these ends, but how could they enforce them when only one quarter of the country — that was, the former Tokugawa territories — lay under their jurisdiction? The solution lay, he proposed, in nothing less than the surrender by the *daimyo* of control of their *han* to the central government.

Even before the fall of the Shogunate Iwakura had arrived at a similar conclusion: 'It will be no easy matter to subordinate them [the *daimyo*] here and now. Yet if we do not subordinate them, we shall be unable to lay the foundations for manifesting to the world Imperial prestige.' There was, however, an historical precedent, dating back to the eighth century, when the country was divided into eight provinces in accordance with the Chinese system. This, he suggested, would make the abolition of the more recent (albeit twelfth century) feudalist structure more acceptable.

DAIMYO DISESTABLISHED

Kido now broached his proposal to his colleagues, and in due course he succeeded in persuading the representatives of Satsuma, Choshu, Tosa and Hizen to put the names of their *daimyo* to a draft memorial to the Emperor. 'Two things are essential to the Emperor's administration. There must be one central body of government, and one universal and integral authority. Since the time when Your Majesty's ancestors founded this country and established a basis of government, all things in the wide expanse of heaven and all things on earth to its furthest limits have belonged to the Emperor from generation to generation. That is what is known as "one central government",' it ran.

'The lands in which we live are the Emperor's lands, and the people whom we govern are the Emperor's people. How then can we treat them as our own? We accordingly surrender our registers to the Throne, asking that the Court dispose of them as it sees fit, bestowing that which should be bestowed, taking away that which should be taken away; and we ask that the Court issues such orders as it may deem necessary ... so that state affairs may be in the hands of a single authority. Thus will name and reality be made one and our country be put on a footing of equality with countries overseas.'

To surrender the registers, on which the administrative systems of the *han* were based, was not quite to surrender all power, nor was the Court debarred, in 'disposing of them as it sees fit', from returning them to their respective *daimyo*, but the repeated reference to 'one central government' left little doubt that this was what was intended. This was certainly how Parkes, who was still in constant touch with the new leaders, interpreted it: 'Several of the leading *daimyo*,' he reported to the Foreign Office, 'have come forward and offered to surrender the government of their own territories — their revenues, forces, jurisdiction, etc. — into the hands of the Mikado's government in order that a strong Central Power may be created.'

Reaction was by no means as enthusiastic in the other *han*, some of whom observed that China's centrally-run provincial system had done nothing to protect her from the West. As a result, a compromise scheme drafted by Iwakura was published by the Court on July 25th 1869. Under this, all the *daimyo* were ordered to surrender their registers and in return were to stay on as 'governors' of their *han*, at the same time being raised jointly with the Court nobles to a new order of nobility. It was in order to force this reform through that the Central Board was formed the follow-ing month, concentrating power in the hands of the Court inner circle and the representatives of the four *han* which had instigated it — Sanjo and Iwakura from the Court, Okubo and Saigo (Satsuma), Kido, Ito, Inoue and Yamagata (Choshu), Goto and Itagaki (Tosa), Soejima Taneomi and Okuma Shigenobu (Hizen). Significantly, many of this tight little band continued to hold major positions of influence well into the twentieth century and in some cases were able to pass them on to their heirs; for example, Okubo's son Makino Nobuaki held the key post of Lord Privy Seal throughout the first decade of Hirohito's reign, and it was sub-sequently inherited for the duration of World War Two by Kido Koichi, Kido's adoptive grandson.

This considerable step towards centralisation paved the way for much needed financial and economic reform. The cost of the mopping-up operations against the Shogunate forces which refused to surrender had accounted for nearly 20% of total expenditure in the first two annual budgets and alone almost exceeded total income, the greater part of which was drawn from land taxes on the former Tokugawa territories. The first head of the Department of Finance observed that 'the expenditure or budget of this Department is a fiction. We have merely resorted to borrowing and our daily expenses are barely met.' Even in the 1870 budget income covered only just over 50% of expenditure. The borrowing mostly took the form of forced loans from the merchant class, and in particular from the three largest corporations headed by Mitsui, formerly bankers to the Shoguns. These loans were redeemed with paper money, which was also issued in loans to various *han* to defray military expenditure which had fallen on the local treasuries. More notes were later printed to cover the central government's outgoings, and being unbacked by any reserves of metal their value decreased inversely with the increase in the central deficit.

It was soon painfully obvious that such a level of borrowing could not continue and that drastic steps would have to be taken to bring the central government's income into line with its expenditure. The task was assigned to Ito and Okuma; the Departments both of Finance and of Civil Affairs were put under their control in order to give them a freer hand in reforming the financial structure of the *han*. After introducing a number of measures to increase central control over the local treasuries, particularly in the disbursement of *samurai* stipends, they made arrangements to replace the multitude of different coinages in circulation by a single unit, the yen; its value was initially fixed at parity on the gold standard with the American dollar.

The task of establishing a new Government mint was given to Inoue, Ito's intimate and his Vice-Minister of Finance. Inoue in turn appointed Mitsui as the mint's agents to supervise the exchange of the old money for the new. His relationship with the company soon grew so close that its rivals began to complain that the Ministry of Finance was located in the company's headquarters. It gave particular offence to the *samurai* asceticism of 'The Great Saigo', who on meeting Inoue at an official function greeted him with a glass of saki and a loud toast of 'This is for you, Mitsui-Man Inoue'. Two years later Inoue brought Mitsui together with another company to form the Dai-Ichi (First National) Bank, which was given an exclusive agency for the Government's exchange business; two years later again he engineered the partner's bankruptcy, leaving Mitsui free to form its own Mitsui Bank.

In spite of these reforms, it became clear that the problem of the central budget deficit would never be satisfactorily resolved until the treasury had complete control over the *han*'s incomes, which in turn entailed the complete abolition of the *han* and the dismantling of the feudal system. Then, as Iwakura remarked to Parkes on May 20th 1871, 'Higo may no longer be Higo, nor Satsuma Satsuma'.

Before the formal announcement to this effect was made, troops from Satsuma, Choshu, Tosa and Hizen were moved into Tokyo as a precautionary measure. When they were all in place, the *daimyo* of the other *han* were summoned to the capital on August 29th. 'In order to preserve the peace of Japanese subjects at home and to stand on an equal footing with countries abroad,' the preamble declared, 'we deem it necessary that the government of the country be centred in a single authority.' The 273 *han* were to be reorganized into 72 prefectures along the lines already introduced in the former Tokugawa territories; all land taxes were to be paid to the central treasury, which in return was to take over the responsibility for *samurai* stipends; and the *daimyo* were also to be relieved of obligation for their outstanding debts while being allowed to retain one-tenth of their former revenue as personal income.

In order to discharge its new obligations as efficiently as possible the leadership of the central government was then concentrated still more tightly in a new Central Board of Sanjo, Iwakura, Saigo, Kido, Itagaki and Okuma. Beneath then a Right Board, comprising the heads of the Departments, was set up, in which Okubo became Minister of Finance, while Ito was moved to the newly-formed Department of Industry to direct the development of railways, telegraph systems and government participation in other industries. A Left Board replaced the defunct lower house, but it was still granted no more than consultative rights and its members were in any case selected by the Central Board.

SAMURAI STIRRINGS

The movement of troops to the capital ahead of the announcement of these reforms was no idle precaution. Although the financial provisions were sufficient to gain the immediate acceptance of all but a handful of the *daimyo* (such as, for example, Hisamitsu, who had been prevented by illness from attending and, it was reported, 'could only grind his teeth with rage'), it did nothing to appease the *samurai*, who had for some time been growing increasingly restive at the direction that the new order was taking.

Their resentment sprang from three sources: first, a loss of stature brought about by the simplification in 1869 of their complex hierarchy to two classes only, those of 'gentry' and 'foot-soldier', and by such measures as the making of sword-wearing optional; secondly, a loss of income resulting from the review of stipends, which had invariably led to their reduction; and thirdly, the abandonment of the principle of *joi*, evinced by the granting of Imperial audiences to the foreign envoys in the early months of the Restoration and by an accompanying policy statement that the new government was no longer prepared to see Japan in the isolationist role of 'the frog looking at the world from the bottom of the well'.

As a result, their swords had soon been unsheathed again in the search for scapegoats. Yokoi Shonan, the original proposer of a two-tier parliamentary system and the target of a previous attempt on his life, was the first to fall, cut down on February 15th 1869 on the grounds that 'he intended to make our splendid Divine Land a vassal state of the ugly barbarians who are like sheep and dogs'. The Vice-Minister for War, whose offence was to suggest throwing the army open to general conscription, was similarly dispatched on October 8th because he had 'arbitrarily introduced barbarian customs, and had remembered foreigners but forgotten his Emperor'. On February 27th 1871 a member of the Right Board was murdered in his bed, the first victim, it was suspected, of a plot to eliminate the entire Board, and in May another plot was discovered aimed at carrying the Emperor back to his former capital in Kyoto.

The unrest centred at first in Choshu, where the Kiheitai irregulars had refused to merge with the regular troops and were eventually put down by loyal *samurai* led by Kido in person. It then resurfaced in Satsuma, where both Hisamitsu and Saigo had begun to voice open criticism of the new policies. 'I feel as if I'm sleeping on a pile of explosives,' the latter warned the 'Traitor' Okubo. A memorial which was popularly supposed to be Saigo's work called for the transfer of all authority from the central government to the Emperor, asserting even that 'we must abandon all steam machinery, railroads, etc.' Their complaints were only silenced when they were persuaded to accept appointments in Tokyo (although Hisamitsu subsequently changed his mind).

Having finally, they considered, set their house in order, the new leadership dispatched a high-powered mission under Iwakura, Kido, Okubo and Ito to America and Europe. Their official brief directed that 'we must restore our country's rights and remedy the faults in our laws and institutions; we must abandon the arbitrary habits of the past ... seeking thereby to achieve equality with the Powers.' Their primary objective, it was saying, was to ascertain what reforms Japan needed to make before the West would be persuaded to treat her as an equal. Of all the inequalities incorporated in the treaties, the one that rankled most was the concession of extra-territoriality, the jurisdiction over foreign residents by their respective Consuls. In Iwakura's words, 'even when foreigners who live in our country violate our laws, we are forced to stand aside while agents of their governments exercise jurisdiction over them. Our country has never before known such a shame and disgrace.' This goal, the revision of the treaties, was to dominate his actions and those of his successor Ito until its eventual fulfilment 23 years later. The mission also had a secondary, but more immediate, objective — that was, to negotiate permission to raise import duties in order to bring in extra income to put towards the heavy new responsibility of *samurai* stipends. In this way it was hoped to disarm the latter's dissatisfaction by defusing their *joïist* objections and by reassuring their fears for their financial security.

As it turned out, the mission had no success on the latter score, but the deep impression made on them by the advances of Western technology and industrialisation confirmed their opinion that direct government intervention was required in Japan's own development; as one of the students accompanying the mission wrote, 'if the country is to be enriched, the army strengthened and education established, production must first be encouraged among the people, products of every kind manufactured and exported overseas, and goods imported that our country lacks.' This participation of government in industry was to play a key rôle not only in raising Japan to the status of a world industrial power within the course of the next generation, but also in maintaining to this day (through the all-powerful medium of the Ministry of International Trade and Industry) the country's ever-growing dominance of the world economy.

At home meanwhile the caretaker government largely ignored an undertaking not to push through any further reforms in the mission's absence. When Iwakura and Ito returned in September 1873, it was to find that their colleagues had introduced compulsory primary education, the adoption of the Gregorian in place of the Chinese calendar, a unified system of calculation of the land tax, the division of the Ministry of Defence into Departments of the Army and Navy and conscription of all men over the age of twenty for three years' service. More presumptuously still, they were preparing to launch a military adventure in Korea under Saigo's leadership amounting to little less than a full-scale invasion.

The pretext for this was ostensibly to punish Korea for her refusal to recognise the new regime, but its real purpose was to offer an outlet for the simmering frustration of the *samurai*; in Saigo's own words, it was 'a far-reaching scheme, which will divert abroad the attention of those who desire civil strife'. Such an enterprise naturally ran quite counter to the increased determination of Iwakura and his fellow delegates that the country's energies should be thrown into industrial development, and after a series of prolonged and heated debates within the Central Board they managed to secure a majority for its abandonment. Saigo, Itagaki and its other proponents thereupon resigned.

DEMOCRACY DENIED

This division, and the announcement made soon afterwards that *samurai* stipends were to be made both liable to tax and commutable into Government Bonds, brought to a head the *samurai's* discontent, compounded as it was by the absence of the 'widely-convoked assembly' in which the First Article of the Charter Oath had promised that 'all policies shall be decided by open debate'. In January 1874 Itagaki and his fellow abdicators (but not Saigo) issued a memorial calling for the immediate creation of a popular assembly, warning that 'if a reform is not effected, the state will be ruined. When we humbly reflect upon the quarter in which the governing power lies, we find that it lies not with the crown on the one hand, nor with the people on the other, but with the officials alone. How is the government to be made strong? It is by the people of the empire becoming of one mind . . . The establishment of a council-chamber chosen by the people will create community of feeling between the government and the people, and they will instinctively unite into one body. Then and only then will the country become strong.' Their conception of the term 'popular' was a limited one, for they did not envisage extending the franchise beyond the *samurai* and the richer class of merchants and farmers.

The need for a written constitution defining the status and function of all sectors of society had also impressed itself on Iwakura and his companions during their tour of the West. On their return Kido formally petitioned the Central Board that this should be put in hand; he had already commissioned a Japanese student in Germany to compile a constitution on the Prussian model (the product, it may be remarked in passing, although obviously authoritarian in character, actually represented a more liberal code than that finally adopted in 1889). Okubo, now elevated to the Board as Minister for Home Affairs, replied that democracy was unsuitable for 'a people who are accustomed to long-standing practices based on old ways and who are unenlightened'; any new constitution, he asserted, 'must maintain the Emperor's position for all ages to come and make the people preserve their natural order.'

As for the Itagaki memorial, it was, according to him, 'a blunder. No one is impressed by it. Even the uninformed are contemptuously amused. I understand that even the foreigners have raised questions. You can generally gauge by the above the seriousness with which the petition is regarded. This is good for us.' Nevertheless, his colleagues did not feel that they were able simply to ignore it and they set up a commission under Ito, also now a member of the Central Board, to explore the subject. In a simulataneous measure to remove it from the public arena, they made it illegal 'to discuss the laws, or to place obstacles in the way of the working of national institutions by the persistent advocacy of foreign ideas'.

By contrast, the Left Board proclaimed the memorial to be 'excellent in principle'. They sought, and obtained, permission to prepare a draft constitution of their own, but nothing more came of it and a year later the Board itself was abolished by Imperial Rescript and replaced by the Genroin or Council of Elders. Under the same Rescript, which promised that 'constitutional government would be established in gradual stages', the Central and Right Boards were divided into the Chief Council, the Lower House of prefectural governors and the Supreme Court. Presented as a separation of government functions into executive, legislative and judicial bodies, the historian W. W. MacLaren remarked of this that 'for effrontery and sheer contempt of the nation's intelligence it would be difficult to find a parallel to this Rescript even in Japanese annals'.

The self-proclaimed 'People's Man' Itagaki had in the meantime returned to Tosa, where in January 1875 he founded the Rissisha, a political party which also served as a kind of mutual-aid society for *samurai* who had fallen on hard times. The title — 'Independence Society' — was borrowed from the Japanese translation of Samuel Smiles's tract *Self-Help* which had sold over one million copies; the party's manifesto, however, was more reminiscent of John Stuart Mill, proclaiming that 'We, the thirty millions of people in Japan, are all equally endowed with certain definite rights.'

If Itagaki can thus take credit for the formation of Japan's first Western-style political party, it has also to be said that he subsequently showed himself to be the first Japanese example of that by-product of Occidental democracy, the political opportunist; a contemporary remarked of him that 'at that time he had no idea of freedom and equality, but later he changed completely and advocated the Social Contract of Rousseau.' The very next month he was back again in Tokyo, lured by a promise from Okubo of participation in the foreshadowed development of an independent legislature, only to resign for the second time the following year when the latter proved to be an illusion.

REBELLION

Elsewhere *samurai* discontent had expressed itself less peaceably. In January 1874 Iwakura narrowly escaped an assassination attempt outside the Imperial Palace by jumping into its moat. The following month a full-scale revolt broke out in Hizen under the banner 'War with Korea, restore the *daimyo*, expel the barbarian', which was quelled with some difficulty by troops of the new Imperial Army under the personal direction of Home Minister Okubo himself. It was rumoured to have been instigated by Saigo, and concern in Tokyo that Satsuma would join it led to an offer of a seat on the Chief Council to Hisamitsu, which he accepted.

Four months later, however, he resigned on the grounds that 'Your Majesty has not shown the slightest sign of adopting my foolish ideas'; amongst his other complaints, he objected to the adoption of Western dress and hair styles, permission to inter-marry with foreigners and 'the non-appointment of a fencing master to the Emperor'. His resignation was followed by a promise from the Government to mount an expedition against Formosa as a reprisal for the murder of some Loochooan fishermen there. It duly set out in May under the command of Saigo's younger brother Tsugumichi, but the temporary truce at home that it bought proved expensive both in terms of the 5.4 million yen outlay and of the resignation of Kido from the Central Board in protest.

Shortly after the abolition of the Boards the Chief Council gave the go-ahead for a second expedition, to Korea, in yet another move to appease the *samurai*, although it did also subsequently succeed in extracting the desired treaty of recognition from Seoul. Even this, however, failed to satisfy the more extreme element, who objected that the fact that Korea still paid tribute to China made Japan 'appear to consent to take lower rank than China, and this is an ineradicable stain on our national character.' 'The Great Saigo' himself had ignored an order to return to Tokyo and busied himself in Satsuma instead setting up a chain of 'private schools', a euphemism for military academies intended to produce an élite force which would enable him to take over the central government and put himself at its head.

1876 saw the introduction of further reforms which raised *samurai* tempers still higher: the wearing of swords was abolished altogether, while the commutation of stipends into Government Bonds was made compulsory. The latter measure in particular led to a wave of protest in the newspapers in defiance of the recently introduced Press Laws which prohibited any criticism of the Government and made it illegal even 'to discuss the laws, or to place obstacles in the way of the working of national institutions by the persistent advocacy of foreign ideas'. One, for example, openly advocated the Government's violent overthrow: 'We must remember that true liberty grows only out of blood and death, not from sterile table discussions.'

It was not long before this advice was given practical effect: in October *samurai* attacked government offices in Higo and killed the prefectural governor. 'Our country differs from all other lands in that it is the country of the Gods, and for this reason it should not even for a moment be held to rank below any foreign land,' they proclaimed. 'However, diabolical spirits now prevailing are bent on abolishing customs which have been cherished and observed from the time of the Gods and on making our people imitate foreigners ...' A month later another revolt flared in Choshu led by a former pupil of 'Grass Roots Hero' Yoshida, but the newly-installed telegraph system enabled the Government to draft in sufficient troops to extinguish it before it could spread further.

Saigo had shown no signs of moving to support either of these insurrections, but in January 1877 the Government thought it wise to transfer elsewhere some arms and ammunition which it held in Kagoshima, the Satsuma capital. However, their authority was still largely unrecognised in the prefecture (as the *han* had now become), and Saigo's private army had no difficulty in pre-empting this precaution and seizing the arsenals for themselves. Saigo then faked an attempt on his own life as a pretext for putting all his 40,000 supporters on the march for Tokyo. The government declared him a rebel and, again using the telegraph to good effect, were able to intercept him in neighbouring Higo with an equal force of Imperial regulars (led by the same Prince Arisugawa who ironically had commanded the Satsuma troops in the final campaign against the Shogun nine years earlier).

A war of attrition followed during the next six months, in which the rebels were stopped and slowly forced back. The opportunist Itagaki came forward with an offer to ally Tosa's troops with the government forces if they would undertake in return to introduce a representative assembly, but this was not taken up. The rebels' resistance was finally broken following the seizure of Kagoshima by a naval force under Ito. Wounded but defiant to the last, Saigo ordered one of his lieutenants to cut off his head and bury it to prevent it from falling into the hands of the enemy — a symbolic gesture which ensured his survival among the pantheon of *samurai* heroes right down to the present day.

A few months later, on May 14th 1878, his defeated supporters had their revenge when their 'traitorous' fellow-clansman Okubo, the man who more than anybody else had worked to break down the *samurai*'s entrenched position of privilege, was hacked to death by six swordsmen while en route for his office. This was the last time that the *samurai* rose to defend their former status as an exclusive military caste, but the tradition of political assassination, and of inventing pretexts with which to justify otherwise unacceptable actions, was to live on far into the twentieth century.

Kido had died a year earlier so that, of the triumverate which had set the break-neck pace of change for the past decade, only Iwakura now survived. Faced with renewed demands for the establishment of representative government, it is not surprising that he and his new colleagues should have sought refuge again in the institution of the Throne. Since his Restoration to nominal sovereignty Meiji's involvement with affairs of state had extended little beyond putting his seal on the reforms carried out in his name. 'If in the past Your Majesty had shown as much care for politics as he had passion for horsemanship, no such criticism from the public as "government by two or three ministers" would have occurred', a senior official told him to his face. They were not to forsee just how deeply the twenty-five-year-old Emperor would take the charge to heart.

7

The Emperor Becomes
'Sacred and Inviolable'

IMPERIAL MENTOR

Since 1871 the young Emperor's education had been taken in hand by the Confucianist scholar Motoda Eifu. Originally appointed as his tutor in classical Chinese literature, Motoda soon extended his influence into other fields and for the next twenty years became his pupil's daily companion. When he himself had been a pupil of Yokoi Shonan he had eagerly imbibed the Mito school's *joïist* dogmas, and he had found it difficult to come to terms with Yokoi's later 'Western Learning' sympathies.

Certainly, the advice that he passed on to Meiji was of a rigidly orthodox Confucianist-Shintoist cast: he spoke continually of the dangers of Westernisation, of the moral shortcomings of the leading reformers in the new government and of the need for the Emperor to exercise his prerogative to override them. Sometimes indeed he would even outbid Confucius himself: 'The ruler looks upon his subjects as his own children; the subjects look up to the ruler as to their parents. Lord and subject, ancestor and descendant are only one body and one spirit, united and inseparable,' he preached. 'This unity of the loyalty between lord and subject with the love between father and son is a perfection . . . something even Confucius was unable to postulate.'

The full extent of his influence is even now impossible to gauge with precision because the Court history of the Meiji reign, compiled by the Imperial Household Ministry, is still not open to public inspection. It can be fairly said, however, that the Emperor's actions can never have strayed very far, if at all, from Motoda's line of advice. In his own cautiously-worded autobiography, Motoda goes so far as to claim that 'regardless of what book I used, I always discussed the essential points of the Emperor's virtue, the importance of duty, reverence for the national entity [*kokutai*], the purity of the Confucian Way, the harm of Christianity, the errors of Buddhism and vulgar studies, the difference between Eastern and Western customs, the reasons why the Imperial and republican constitutions must not be the same and so forth. I explained these repeatedly until I was certain that he believed them firmly.'

In 1873 Motoda informed Iwakura that 'at present the Sovereign's wisdom is not yet extensive and his benevolence is not yet comprehensive', and he urged that the Central Board should hold a daily audience at the Palace because 'the Son of Heaven worries if he does not see his assisting ministers during the day'. Iwakura rejected the proposal, but four years later Okubo agreed to the appointment of eight 'Consultants' (among them Motoda) to the Emperor and to take on himself the post of Minister of the Imperial Household in order to keep Meiji abreast of events.

When Okubo was murdered shortly afterwards, his colleagues on the Chief Council (successor to the Central Board) agreed that the Emperor should be allowed to attend their meetings; they rejected, however, a similar request from the Consultants and later abolished the post altogether, although Motoda, of course, continued in his rôle as Imperial Tutor. In 1876 Prince Arisugawa, the head of the Council of Elders, was instructed by Meiji to commission a study of 'the laws of various nations' with a view to the drafting of a constitution, although it is clear from their correspondence that the inspiration for this came from Iwakura and Okubo rather than the Emperor.

This prompted Motoda to submit his own ideas on the subject. The demands for popular representation had been stirred, he asserted, as a reaction to the oligarchical behaviour of the Restoration leadership: 'If we put them aside today and defer them until later, the mad outpourings of mistaken Western ideas, increasing daily, will finally become uncontrollable and the harm done to the Imperial Household will be incalculable. This is why I consider it essential to establish a constitution today.' The creation of a popular assembly would serve to head these demands off, he thus considered, although it would not, of course, entail any division of sovereignty, which would remain the exclusive preserve of the Emperor as *kokutai* demanded; the assembly's function would merely be to 'have its most reasonable opinions subjected to discussion in the Chief Council and decided upon by the Emperor himself.'

WANTED: A CONSTITUTION

The 'mad outpourings' did indeed continue to grow in volume, fuelled partly by another bout of inflation. In Tosa a section of Itagaki's Independence Society advocated joining the Satsuma rebels, for which they promptly found themselves under arrest. The remainder, convinced by the Rebellion's suppression of the uselessness of violent opposition to the central government, issued a memorial again calling for the establishment of a popular assembly, and in the following year, 1878, they mounted a drive to establish the party as a national organisation under the title of 'The Society of Patriots'.

Their efforts met with a gratifyingly rapid response. In Tokyo alone, for instance, they enrolled 16,000 members, and a year later they felt able to submit another memorial to the central government warning that 'when we seek the reason for the extension of popular rights in the West, we see that the rulers did not grant popular rights, but rather the people themselves took the initiative and seized them.' By the time of its next convention in March 1880 the party's membership had risen to 98,000.

The government, by now thoroughly alarmed, ordered it to disband, whereupon its leaders re-formed under the title of 'League for the Establishment of a National Assembly'. A Metropolitan Police Bureau was set up under Yamagata, who had now resigned as Minister of War to become Chief of the newly-established General Staff. It was decreed that the holder of the new post 'shall be appointed by the Emperor, and will as such be under the direct command of the Emperor'; this prerogative of the military to 'direct access to the Throne', as it came to be called, would fatally undermine subsequent attempts to convert Japan to genuine democracy. One of Yamagata's first acts was to issue an Admonition to all military personnel forbidding them to take part in political activities or even to express 'private opinions on important laws'. Press censorship was made still more severe; the editor of the *Tokyo Azuma* was sentenced to two years' imprisonment for writing that 'the Emperor, the Prime Minister and Ministers are employed, after all, for the protection of the people. That is to say, we regard them as public servants of the state.' In spite of these restrictions, party membership had risen again to 130,000 when the next convention was held in November, and in the following month the League was dissolved and reconstituted as a fully-fledged political party, the Jiyuto or Liberal Party.

This development caused Yamagata to warn Ito, who had succeeded Okubo in the key post of Minister of Home Affairs and was emerging as the new pace-setter in the regime, that the new party 'hoped to overthrow the government at the opportune moment; every day we wait, the evil poison will spread further and further over the provinces, penetrating the minds of the young, and will inevitably produce unfathomable evils'. Even he conceded, however, that 'sooner or later there must be a national assembly', and that only the creation of such a body would confer on Japan sufficient respectability in the eyes of the West to make the goal of treaty revision a reality. Confirming this train of thought, 'Mitsui-Man' Inoue was to write in retrospect that 'constitutional government was not created simply to satisfy the desires of the people. Those in the government also believed that it was imperative to create a constitutional regime to expedite the revision of treaties and the restoration of equal rights.'

After several revisions Prince Arisugawa's draft constitution was completed in 1879. The study of the revolutionary tide in Europe over the past century had left a deep impression on Japan's new masters; in urging the need to conciliate the demands for popular representation, one senior bureaucrat warned, for instance, that otherwise 'mobs will rise and the virulence of the revolution in Paris will make its appearance in Japan. We would then experience not only the needless folly of officials being slaughtered, but, what is more horrible to contemplate, the Imperial House would be endangered.' At the same time, however, they were determined that any constitution to be adopted should be intrinsically Japanese in character, and for this reason Arisugawa's draft found little favour with the Chief Council. Iwakura refused to approve its submission to the' Emperor because there were 'parts which do not conform to *kokutai*', a comment repeated by Ito, who considered that its authors had merely 'rephrased the constitutions of several European nations'.

Ito also drew a firm distinction between conciliation and surrender: 'The method to be adopted by the government today is to fall in with the trends of the time [towards representational government] to take advantage of opportunities when they appear. So, even as we control the trends, there will be no violence, and even when ideas are given free rein they will not lead people astray ... the complete achievement of constitutional government must await the passage of time. In the meantime, everything will be under control.' The draft was accordingly withdrawn, and on Iwakura's advice the Emperor ordered the members of the Chief Council to submit their ideas individually to him.

Ito's faith in the 'passage of time' was reflected in the interval of eighteen months which elapsed while these memorials were prepared. When the last of them was finally delivered in May 1881, they wore, with one exception, a predictably conservative hue. Kuroda Kiyotaka, for instance, the leading representative of Satsuma following the deaths of Okubo and 'The Great Saigo', considered that all talk of popular representation was premature. Yamagata suggested the creation of an assembly of hand-picked members drawn from the local prefectural councils — 'of course, initially such an assembly should not be called a popular assembly and the power of convening and dissolving it should be held by the Government. Furthermore, it should be determined that its decisions may not necessarily be carried out ... As Japan is just beginning a new type of government, you cannot expect a Japanese to have one ten-thousandth of the rights of a European'. Iwakura, whose submission had largely been drafted for him by Inoue Kowashi, the leading scholar of German constitutionalism (but unrelated to Inoue Kaoru), advocated the adoption of the Prussian system, whereby the appointment of ministers would be the sole prerogative of the Emperor and any popularly-elected lower house restricted merely to a consultative function. Ito likewise wished to retain the Council of Elders as an upper house, but, being more concerned to effect a compromise between all the different suggestions, contented himself with general remarks on the need for gradualism, with the one further specific proposal that the Emperor should announce a date for the granting of a constitution and for the opening of a parliament.

ODD MAN OUT

The exception was Okuma, who called for a British-style constitution under which sovereignty would reside with the political party obtaining a majority in a popularly-elected national assembly; furthermore, he argued that elections should be held by the end of 1882 and that the new assembly should be convoked in 1883. In justifying these proposals, he contended that 'the situation has already developed to a point where temporising measures will not suffice to placate the people's sentiments. When a group of people desire something, satisfying their desire piecemeal only serves to whet their appetites and they eventually become uncontrollable. The wiser method is to anticipate their demands and to satisfy them fully . . .' Aware that it would mark a radical departure from those of his colleagues, Okuma at first asked Arisugawa for permission to present his memorial direct to the Emperor. This was refused, although the Prince agreed that it should not be shown to anyone else before the Emperor had seen it.

In spite of this undertaking, however, Arisugawa read the memorial himself and passed it on to Sanjo and Iwakura (as the senior members of the Chief Council); Sanjo in turn 'borrowed' it and showed it to Ito. The latter's reaction was one of indignation. 'In the final analysis your memorial is equivalent to transferring the Imperial prerogative to the people. Such heretical views should not be held by any subject,' he told Okuma. 'I too, in conformity with the Imperial Rescript of 1875, some day hope to see the establishment of a national assembly. However, I desire first to place the Imperial prerogatives on a firm, unshakeable foundation. Since you have your own ideas about this, however, you may assume the burden of carrying out state affairs from this day.' Later he accused Okuma of having 'undercut his friends . . . it was truly an act of betrayal', although he was presently persuaded to withdraw his threat of resignation.

Okuma was thus left in little doubt as to the strength of opposition to his proposals, but by chance a weapon with which to exert pressure in their favour then came conveniently to hand. The Hokkaido Colonisation Commission, with Kuroda at its head, had been granted an annual subsidy of one million yen for a ten-year period with which to develop the untapped resources of Japan's most northerly island. Knowing that the subsidy was shortly to expire, Kuroda now presented Sanjo with a proposal that he and his colleagues on the Commission's Board should be allowed to purchase its assets for a mere 387,000 yen — and payable over a period of thirty years without interest at that. To quote MacLaren again, 'the only conclusion to be arrived at was either that the money [subsidy] had been squandered by members of the Commission or that they were now attempting to get possession of a valuable property on terms so ludicrously inadequate as to amount to theft.'

Okuma was not the only one to voice disapproval when the proposal was discussed in the Chief Council on July 28th, but after Kuroda had threatened to resign and had even assaulted Sanjo with a candlestick, a majority found in its favour and it received Imperial assent two days later. When it was made public, a howl of protest rose even from the pro-government Press and several mass rallies were held in the main cities. Rumours even began to spread that Okuma was about to attempt a coup, but in fact he had already left the capital to accompany the Emperor on a two-month tour of the northern provinces.

If these rumours were not actually put about by his opponents, they were certainly seized on by them as a pretext to plot his downfall in his absence. Although Okuma had been a member of the inner ruling circle since the first months of the Restoration, he had never enjoyed the full support of its Satsuma components; Saigo, for instance, had demanded his resignation in 1870, as had Hisamitsu in 1874. After the resignation of Itagaki in 1876 he had been left as the sole representative of Hizen and Tosa on the Chief Council, and the failure of the rebellions in 1876-7 had only served to increase his isolation within the administration as the ex-*samurai* of Choshu and Satsuma concluded that their best chances of advancement now lay in employment within the central government machine. Another source of friction was his involvement with various subsidiaries of Mitsubishi (he had appointed one of them, the Yokohama Specie Bank, to be the official clearing house for foreign exchange) who were in competition with the Choshu-backed Mitsui interests and stood to lose certain shipping franchises if the Hokkaido purchase went through; rumour also had it that Mitsubishi was putting up the funds behind the 'coup'.

At a meeting on September 18th his opponents concluded that 'we must settle these [constitutional] problems immediately after the return of the Imperial tour. The question will then be whether we adopt Okuma's views or the ideas of the other Councillors ... If we are to take the latter course, we must be resolute, dismiss Okuma from his posts and oust his followers.' At the same time they readily appreciated that they could not simply dismiss Okuma without doing something to appease the anti-government factions which had looked on him as their mouthpiece. Accordingly Kuroda was persuaded to withdraw his proposal for the purchase of the Hokkaido Commission's assets, and it was further agreed that a specific deadline should be set for the publication of a constitution.

The Emperor returned from his tour on October 11th, and that same evening the Councillors (with the exception, of course, of Okuma) presented their memorial to him. Meiji at first expressed puzzlement that the two questions should be seen as interrelated and necessitating Okuma's resignation, but all was quickly explained to him and the Imperial sanction obtained. Soon after midnight Ito called on Okuma to inform him of the decision, and on the following day an Imperial Rescript was issued announcing that a parliament would be opened in 1890 (a date in fact selected by Ito five years earlier).

Okuma wrote of his downfall that the Choshu Ito and Inoue 'allowed themselves to be intimidated by the reactionary Satsuma men. As a result my neck was forfeited.' He was certainly right to see it as marking a decisive shift in the direction of Japan's development. This alignment between Choshu and Satsuma was to remain entrenched on the highest plane of government for the next generation and more, until it was superseded by Satsuma's union with the Imperial Family through the marriage of Hirohito to Nagako.

PRUSSIA PREFERRED

The Rescript concluded with the following words: 'We perceive the tendency of Our people to advance too rapidly, and without that thought and consideration which alone can make progress enduring, and We warn Our subjects, high and low, to be mindful of Our will, and those who may advocate sudden and violent changes, thus disturbing the peace of Our realm, will fall under Our displeasure.' The use of the Imperial 'We' reflected a renewed attempt by the oligarchy (or 'Sat-Cho clan government' as some now disparagingly labelled it) to invest the Emperor and, by association, the constitution which they were about to formulate, with a sanctity calculated to overawe their opponents and critics. Similarly, words previously employed in official documents to denote 'monarch' but which could also be applied to non-Japanese monarchs began to be replaced by *Tenno*, the 'Son of God'.

Public recognition of this godhead in their midst still fell somewhat short of the desired level. A German visitor remarked in his diary of the occasion of Meiji's birthday on November 3rd 1880 that 'it distresses me to see how little interest the population take in their ruler. Only when the police insist on it are the houses decorated with flags. Otherwise house-owners do the minimum.' It had been principally to counter this apathy that the Imperial tour of the North, where loyalty to the Shogun had held out longest, had been undertaken.

Of the allied need to link the Emperor in the public mind with the formulation of the proposed constitution, Ito explained that 'if the Constitution is known to the people as having been drafted by a private individual, not only will this give rise to much public comment and criticism, but also the Constitution will lose the people's respect. It may even come to be said that it would be better not to have a constitution than to have a constitution unrespected by the people.' It was no accident that he spoke of 'the' Constitution, for the essential elements of that eventually promulgated in 1889 *had in fact already been effectively decided.*

The decision to draw on the Prussian rather than the British system can be traced back to the tour of Europe by Iwakura's mission in 1872-3. Iwakura, Kido and Ito had held a number of consultations in Vienna and Berlin with the constitutional scholars Lorenz von Stein and Rudolph von

Gneist, from which they had come away profoundly impressed. In 1878
Stein's protégé Hermann Roesler was brought to Japan to act as the
government's legal adviser, the first of more than twenty Germans to be so
employed, and he remained at Ito's right hand for the next fifteen years.
Roesler's philosophy was centred on the theory that only a strong
constitutional monarchy, or 'social monarchy' as he preferred to call it,
was in a sufficiently independent position to reconcile the different
interests of all sections of society.

Although Prince Arisugawa, when he had received the Emperor's
commission to put in hand the drafting of a constitution, had been given a
copy of Alphaeus Todd's seminal work 'Parliamentary Government in
England' to make available to his fellow drafters, only Okuma had been
persuaded by it to prefer the English system. As the Prussophile Inoue
Kowashi wrote just after the last opinion had been submitted to the
Throne, 'the government plans to reject popular government, which
grants power to the nameless masses, such as is found in England, and to
support a monarchy like that found in Prussia . . .' In the document which
he had drawn up on Iwakura's behalf he stipulated that the Emperor 'shall
have supreme command over the army and navy, declare war, make peace,
conclude treaties, etc.; moreover, the Emperor shall direct the national
administration.' Also included was another feature of the Prussian constitution, a provision that the previous year's budget should be re-enacted if
parliament failed to pass a budget bill. The logic of this von Gneist had
explained as follows: 'If one gives parliament discretionary powers on
financial matters, then the Cabinet becomes subservient to the Assembly,
and the ministers are appointed by the majority in Parliament. This must
be avoided at all costs.'

Meiji passed on all the Councillors' opinions to his tutor for comment.
For Motoda, the Purifier of the Imperial Mind, even the Prussophiles did
not elevate the Emperor's authority high enough, and he foresaw no
function at all for an elected assembly beyond those of supporting the
Imperial prerogatives and acting as a check on his ministers: 'Mass opinion
is not necessarily correct public opinion simply because it is held by many
people . . . even if a national Diet [parliament] is established and the
opinions of the masses are brought together, the only way to decide what
constitutes correct public opinion is for the Emperor to choose.'

He then went on to draw up his own proposals for a constitution
consisting of seven articles. The first laid it down that 'the Japanese nation
is ruled by one divinely descended Imperial line unbroken for ages eternal',
the fourth that 'the Emperor is sacred and inviolable. Whatever disturbances may occur, his person is not affected', and the sixth that 'the
Emperor wields the power of reward and punishment, promotion and
demotion, and life and death over the people of the entire nation.' Taken in
conjunction with the two clauses quoted above from the Iwakura/Inoue
submission, these will be seen to bear a very close resemblance to the main

Articles of the 1889 Constitution; at some points, indeed, they are identical.

'PRESERVING THE PEACE'

In spite of the veiled threat in the Imperial Rescript against 'those who may advocate sudden and violent changes', the pressure for the introduction of representational government continued to mount. When a composite draft of the government's proposals was published in the newspaper *Nichi Nichi*, the recognised organ of the Government, the postulation of the Emperor's divinity was strongly criticised elsewhere in the Press as a pretext for out-and-out despotism. One editor was bold enough to assert that 'even the Emperor, from the point of view of Heaven, is a human being like the rest of us'. He was fined accordingly.

'People's Man' Itagaki had by now been formally elected President of the new Liberal Party, but his antipathy to Okuma was still strong enough to exclude the latter from its ranks. 'I not only disdain combining forces with one segment of the bureaucracy to attack still another segment,' he wrote before Okuma's dismissal from the Chief Council, 'but I am convinced that this is not the path by which we will achieve our aims.' Rebuffed, Okuma formed his own party, the Kaishinto (Progressives), for whom Mitsubishi played banker. The Government retaliated by setting up its own creature, the Teiseito (Imperial Party), under the leadership of *Nichi Nichi*'s editor; Yamagata later defined its function as 'standing between [i.e., dividing] the two large parties and checking their excesses'.

The Government next hobbled the opposition by arranging an offer of 20,000 dollars to Itagaki to enable him to make a trip to Paris 'to study the French Constitution'. He, having just narrowly survived an attempt on his life, understandably accepted. The money was put up by Mitsui Bank, and in return its contract to handle the Army's business was extended for a further two years (it is an open question whether Itagaki was ever made aware of this). A similar offer was made to Okuma, who refused it. In an attempt to undermine his financial support, the Government then set up a company under the Mitsui umbrella to compete with Mitsubishi's transport interests.

This also served to silence unrest in the wake of a drastic and long overdue retrenchment of government expenditure introduced by Okuma's successor as Minister of Finance, Matsukata Masoyoshi (although the military budget was still allowed to take up more than one-third of the total). In a further move to balance the books, Matsukata sold off the Government's interest in the numerous industrial undertakings which it had funded, although it retained a considerable degree of control over their future development through the issue of subsidies, exclusive licences, tax rebates and other privileges. These were made the responsibility of the newly-created Ministry of Agriculture and Commerce, the forerunner of today's economic overlord, the Ministry of International Trade and Industry. One of its first moves was to merge the shipping interests of Mitsui and Mitsubishi into a new company, Nippon Yusen Kaisha (Japan Mail Line). The effect was finally to drive foreign competition, already fighting a losing battle in the face of heavy Government subsidies, out of Japanese waters for good, and it would provide a foretaste of the Ministry's tactics in the years to come.

When, not surprisingly, political opposition began to take more violent forms, Yamagata, now Minister for Home Affairs, seized on the excuse to tighten the restrictions on the Press and public meetings still further. No less than 49 newspapers were suspended, and it became common practice for papers to employ 'jail editors' whose sole function was to serve out the prison sentences imposed on the real editors. Yamagata also reorganised the police service into a para-military force. In the words of one of his biographers, 'it was at this time that he demonstrated a policy of blood and iron'.

His term of office in this Ministry culminated in the introduction of the Peace Preservation Ordinance of December 1887, just when moves were being made to revive the Liberal and Progressive Parties. This draconian statute outlawed all private societies and meetings, gave the police un-limited powers to break up public meetings and provided for the banish-ment from Tokyo of anyone 'judged to be scheming something detri-mental to public tranquillity'. Even his own Chief of Police, himself known as 'Chief of the Devils' for his strong-arm methods of repression, at first baulked at putting it into effect — until Yamagata informed him that 'if you are not strong enough, I can do it myself'. On the same day Yamagata personally ordered the removal from the capital of more than five hundred anti-government politicians and writers, effectively silen-cing all opposition there for the next ten years. This done, he departed shortly afterwards for a tour of military establishments in Europe; the following year he was appointed to the recently-created office of Prime Minister, the first of many such terms.

'HANDS AND FEET' FOR THE EMPEROR

At the time of the Rescript's publication in 1881 Inoue Kowashi had written that 'to put into effect a Prussian-style constitution is an extremely difficult task under existing circumstances; but at the present time it is possible to carry it out and win over the majority and thus succeed. This is because the English-style constitution has not become firmly fixed in the minds of the people ... but if we let this opportunity pass and vacillate, within two or three years the people will become confident that they can succeed, and no matter how much oratory we may use, it will be difficult to win them back.' The following March Ito received an Imperial commission to lead a research party to Europe in order to 'make as thorough a study as possible of the actual workings of different systems of constitutional government,' but it mainly served to conceal the fact that a Prussian-style constitution had already been decided upon. He travelled direct to Berlin, where the Japanese Minister had arranged for him and his colleagues to receive a series of lectures from von Stein, and then to Vienna where he consulted with von Gneist.

In a letter to Iwakura the Constitution-Maker wrote that 'thanks to the famous German scholars von Gneist and von Stein, I have come to understand the essential features of the structure and operation of the State. Apropos the most crucial matter of fixing the foundations of our Imperial system and of retaining the prerogatives belonging to it, I have already found sufficient substantiation for it ... The tendency in our country is toward the erroneous belief that the words of English, American and French liberals and radicals are eternal verities. This misplaced enthusiasm would almost certainly lead to the overthrow of the nation. In acquiring arguments and principles to retrieve the situation I believe I have rendered an important service to my country, and I feel inwardly that I can die a happy man.' Before returning the following year, he paused in London just long enough to hear the conservative constitutionalist Herbert Spencer lecture on representational government.

Ito was still on the high seas when Iwakura died, leaving him the unchallenged leader of the Chief Council. In March 1884 he took under his wing the Ministry of the Imperial Household and with it a newly-created Commission To Investigate The Constitution. The object of placing the latter within that particular Ministry was two-fold: it would enable it to function in conditions of the greatest possible secrecy, and it would help to foster the impression that it was doing so under the direct supervision of the Emperor.

In July Ito announced the creation of a 500-strong peerage in order to lay the foundations of the envisaged upper house. The new peers, styled in five orders borrowed from the ancient Chinese Chou Dynasty, were drawn not only from the former Court nobility but also from sympathetic 'men of talent' among the ex-*samurai*. He had earlier written that 'I believe this is an absolutely indispensable instrument for fortifying the position of the Imperial House ... I hope thereby to take advantage of the fact that as yet the after-glow of the feudalistic pro-Emperor sentiment has not yet completely died down, even though this is contrary to the spirit of the times and goes against the inclinations of the people.' At the same time steps were taken to give the Court a financial independence in keeping with the larger political rôle envisaged for it. In addition to an annual grant of three million yen to cover Court expenses, Government holdings in the Bank of Japan, Yokohama Specie Bank, Nippon Yusen Kaisha and other leading companies were transferred into the Emperor's name, as were some 8.6 million acres of land (to be administered by a newly-established Bureau of Imperial Lands).

In the following year the Chief Council was formally replaced by a Cabinet comprising the ten heads of Ministries, of which Satsuma and Choshu claimed four each; Ito was appointed the first Prime Minister. Although the change was made partly in order to make it appear that Japan was adopting a Western style of government, instead of sharing a collective responsibility each member of the Cabinet was made directly accountable to the Prime Minister, who was in turn accountable to the Emperor (whereas under the old system they had been responsible to the three Ministers of State); leaders of the political parties could be included in it, but as Ministers they would have to be 'above the people and apart from every party,' Ito stated, adding furthermore that their appointment 'is completely in the hands of the monarch, and their dismissal depends entirely on the pleasure of the Emperor.' In his letter of resignation from the old post of Chief Executive, Sanjo explained that the former system 'is not only against the principle of personal government by the Emperor, but also tends to lessen unduly the responsibilities of the various Ministers': the new body, on the other hand, would 'serve as the hands and feet, the ears and eyes of Your Majesty'.

TUTOR TURNS LEGISLATOR

Ito may have believed that he now held the destiny of his country in his own hands, but he had reckoned without Motoda. The Purifier of the Imperial Mind had taken good advantage of Ito's absence abroad to strengthen his position of influence with the Throne. 'Whenever Iwakura and Sanjo intended to present some secret matter to the Emperor,' he wrote of that interval in his autobiography, 'Iwakura spoke to me about it privately so that I could speak to the Emperor when the opportunity arose in order to assist the Imperial decision.' After his return, Ito complained that Meiji was spending so much time with his erstwhile tutor that there was not enough left for Ministers to report to him on affairs of State.

Motoda had also compiled a textbook on Confucian ethics which was published by the Imperial Household Ministry under the title 'Essentials of Learning for the Young' and issued with a personal endorsement from the Emperor to every school in the country; when reports came back of pupils having difficulty in understanding its archaic language, Motoda replied that they should learn it by heart until they were old enough to appreciate its meaning. He was presently able to report with satisfaction that 'the evils produced by American education [the first adviser to the Ministry had been a professor from Rutgers University] have steadily been corrected, and the nation has again turned to the principles of loyalty to the sovereign and love of the country.'

In 1885 it was withdrawn by Ito's nominee for the Ministry of Education, Mori Arinori, on the grounds that it was too old-fashioned and unscientific, but in the following year Motoda was elevated to the new position of Palace Adviser, which gave him formal and direct participation in the drafting of the Constitution. Mori's reward, by contrast, was an assassin's sword; his offence had been compounded in the eyes of the zealots by his declared sympathies with Christianity, and he had anyway been a marked man ever since 1869 when he had initiated the proposal to make sword-wearing for *samurai* optional (on that occasion too he had been cut down, but had survived his wounds).

Having decided in his own mind on the component parts required for his model Constitution, Ito considered that it was now time to assemble them. Just how far his vision of it differed from that of Motoda may be gauged from the first of the guidelines that he issued to the other members of the Commission, Ito Myoji (no relation), Inoue Kowashi and Kaneko Kentaro: 'The constitution should be only a general outline concerning the administration of the Empire; and it should be written in such a way that it may respond flexibly to the development of the national destiny' — in other words, the Cabinet's freedom for manoeuvre should not be made subject to Imperial approval. More ominously, he added that 'the territorial boundaries of the Japanese Empire should not be included in the constitution, but fixed by statute'; they too were to be 'flexible'.

Ito's second guideline laid it down that 'consideration of the national entity [*kokutai*] and the history of Japan should be the fundamental principle which guides the drafting of the Constitution.' It was this that was to be his Achilles heel: *kokutai* incorporated the myth of the Emperor's divine descent and his inheritance of the prerogatives handed down by the Sun Goddess, and so Motoda and others were able to argue that any restrictions on the Imperial prerogatives would be counter to the spirit of *kokutai*.

Roesler submitted his first draft to the Commission in April 1887. In it he embedded the principle that the Cabinet should be responsible not to the Diet, but to the Emperor — the same principle enunciated by Inoue in Iwakura's memorial of 1881, which itself had had the benefit of Roesler's advice. One near-contemporary commentator who had access to some of the participants in the drafting wrote that 'Inoue sounded out Roesler's views on every conceivable matter. It would thus not be an exaggeration to say that our constitution was really drafted with one ear listening to Roesler.' In order to give themselves greater privacy the five of them then retired to the little island of Natsushima in Tokyo Bay, where Ito had had a new house especially built for the purpose. Several more drafts followed, and it was not until the following April that final versions of the Constitution and the Imperial House Law were presented to the Emperor.

The question then arose as to how the finished document should be published. If Ito alone was shown as its author, it would be exposed to the danger already forseen by him of being criticized as the work of a 'private individual'; if on the other hand the responsibility was given to the Council of Elders as some suggested (it was after all their leader, Prince Arisugawa, who had first been commissioned to produce a draft back in 1876, and although they had been made constitutionally defunct by the reforms of 1885 they had continued to exist as an informal body of advisers), it would run the risk of being watered down along the lines of the Arisugawa draft condemned by Iwakura and Ito as 'not conforming to *kokutai*'. In the end the difficulty was resolved by the creation of a new Privy Council especially for the purpose; Ito resigned as Prime Minister to become its President and Motoda, of course, was among its members.

In the following nine months the Privy Council met 44 times, and on all but one occasion Meiji attended in person. To preserve the secrecy of its work, no one was allowed to take any documents away from the conference room, and anyone wishing to put in some extra work on them was compelled to do so in the presence of a secretary. Its discussions were often heated and protracted to a degree that one of its members later predicted would 'perhaps never again be repeated' in the presence of the Emperor. The Emperor's position within the projected constitution remained the central point at issue, and Ito's attempt to relegate it from the Constitution to the Imperial House Law was given short shrift by Motoda and his allies; Ito was later to confess that when he realised just how influential Motoda was, he arrived at an 'understanding' with him.

The first two articles of Roesler's final draft had emerged as follows: '1. The Japanese Empire shall remain an Imperial Monarchy, so that any other form of government, and especially of republican government, can never be made the law of Japan. 2. The Empire of Japan shall be reigned over and governed by the Emperor.' He had deliberately avoided incorporating any commitment to *kokutai* and its mythological implications, justifying the monarchic system instead on the grounds that it alone was suitable to Japan and congenial to the national character; the Emperor's position could be explained more 'naturally', he suggested, by arguing that he derived his powers 'through the medium of his glorious ancestors'.

Such secularised statements of the pre-eminence of the direct descendant of the Sun Goddess were hardly going to satisfy the Motoda school, and indeed Ito himself, as the author of the guideline stating that consideration of *kokutai* should be a 'fundamental principle', was bound to call for their revision. In the Constitution as it was finally promulgated on February 11th 1889 (the day that the first Emperor Jimmu was supposed to have ascended — or rather, descended — to the Throne), they accordingly emerged as 'Article I. The Empire of Japan shall be reigned over and governed by a line of Emperors unbroken for ages eternal', and Article III. 'The Emperor is sacred and inviolable' (Article II covered the rules of the Imperial succession). They thus repeated almost word for word the first and fourth articles of the draft which Motoda first submitted to the Throne in 1881.

QUIS CUSTODIET CUSTODEM?

In his apologia, *Commentaries On The Constitution*, published later that same year, Ito rationalised that the Emperor 'has indeed to pay due respect to the law, but the law has no power to hold Him accountable to it'. This inherent contradiction betrays itself throughout the succeeding Articles which attempted to define the Emperor's status in relation to the Constitution and the proposed Diet. Article IV stated that 'The Emperor is the Head of the Empire, embodying the rights of sovereignty, and exercises them according to the provisions of the present Constitution', but if sovereignty was vested in the Emperor, what was there to compel him to respect the Constitution? Ito could only plead that 'the sovereign power of reigning over and governing the state is inherited by the Emperor from his Ancestors ... and is united in This Most Exalted Personage'.

Similarly, Article V declared that 'The Emperor exercises legislative power with the consent of the Imperial Diet', but Ito was quick to explain that such wording was not to be taken at its face value: 'From the nature of *kokutai* it follows that there ought to be only one source of sovereign power of State, just as there is one dominant will that calls into motion each and every distinct part of the human body. The purpose of the Diet is to enable the Head of State to perform his functions, and to keep the will of the State in a well-disciplined, strong and healthy condition. The legislative power is ultimately under the control of the Emperor, while the duty of the Diet is to give advice and consent.' So the Diet's 'consent' was not a matter of choice, but a 'duty' — a semantic somersault that it would be hard to parallel.

The nub of Ito's dilemma was the impossibility of reconciling the principle of *kokutai* with any accepted concept of constitutional, i.e. representational, government. Elsewhere he claimed that 'the first principle of our Constitution is the respect for the sovereign rights of the Emperor. But at the same time, in order to prevent abuse in the exercise of these sovereign powers, clear checks and limits have been established. The ministers are thus responsible, so that power may not be abused.' Once more the question is begged: the ministers are responsible for checking the Emperor's abuse of his powers, but Article IV laid it down that their responsibility was not to the Diet, but to the Emperor — the very person that they were supposed to check.

Even had the ultimate sanction resided with the Diet, the composition of this bicameral body was such that it was unlikely ever to exert it very strenuously. The upper half, the House of Peers, was to be filled by members of the Imperial family, existing peers and 'persons nominated thereto by the Emperor', while the suffrage qualifications for the 'popularly-elected' House of Representatives were set at a level which limited the electorate to something under two per cent of the adult population. Furthermore, its one chance of exercising direct influence on affairs — by denying supply to the Government — was muzzled by the Prussian-inspired Article LXXI which authorised the re-enactment of the previous year's budget in the event of the failure of a new budget bill to obtain a majority. Other provisions served to strengthen the Emperor's position as absolute monarch still further: Article VII granted him the power to convoke, open, close and prorogue the Diet, Article XI supreme command of the Army and Navy, Article XII the right to decide their strength and composition and Article XIII the sole prerogative for making war, declaring peace and concluding treaties.

The only curb which the Constitution offered against this enormous extension of the Emperor's powers was the provision, in Article LV, that all Imperial decrees, ordinances and rescripts were required to be counter-signed by the appropriate Minister. However, any impression that this might have encouraged that sovereignty resided with a Cabinet appointed by the majority party in the lower house was immediately dispelled by Ito: 'The Emperor stands above the people and apart from every party. Consequently, the government cannot favour one party above the other. It must be fair and impartial. And the Prime Minister ... who assists the Emperor, must not allow the government to be manipulated by the parties.' What Ito envisaged, in the short term at least, was a perpetuation of the Restoration oligarchy by means of the constitutional legitimisation of its figurehead, the Emperor.

FLAWED VISION

Saionji Himmochi, a former Court noble who had accompanied Ito on his research mission to Europe, had written to him of his proposal to introduce the Cabinet system in 1885 that 'your reform plan, which went beyond my expectations and which was so positive, made me literally jump for joy ... Now we may take our place as equals among civilised states; now we need not be worried about the establishment of the national assembly in the near future.' Saionji was to devote the rest of his long life, which extended almost to Japan's entry into World War Two, to the defence of the democratic principle, and his letter demonstrated that Ito also looked forward to the day, albeit at a point somewhat further removed in time than 'the near future', when the appointment of the Cabinet could be safely entrusted to the majority party in the Diet. In a speech delivered only three days after the promulgation of the Constitution, Ito stated that it would only be 'necessary for the parties to develop sufficient discipline before we entrust government to the legislative branch.' One of his fellow drafters, Kaneko, said of him later that 'Ito sought rule by both the monarch and the people, [that is,] the granting by the monarch to the people of the right to participate in government.'

This vision, however, was fatally flawed on two counts. The first was an underestimation of Meiji's determination, inherited from his fanatically-chauvinist father, to reassert Japan's claim to superiority over the 'barbarians', and of the encouragement given to Meiji in this by Motoda's inculcation of a divinely-imposed onus to make effective use of the powers now granted to him. Indeed, far from guarding against the danger of the Crown becoming too powerful, Ito's concern had been to ensure that it was not made too *weak*, as he later confessed: 'In formulating the restrictions on its [the Crown's] prerogatives in the new Constitution, we had to take care to guarantee the future effectiveness of these prerogatives, and not to let the institution degenerate into the ornamental crowning piece of the edifice.' In his defence, it may be argued that he could be forgiven for assuming the permanence of the tradition, going back a thousand years or more, under which the Emperor remained wholly removed from the direction of the nation's temporal affairs.

Ito's other blind spot was his failure to anticipate the implacable opposition of his own Prime Minister, Yamagata, to the concept of parliamentary government. 'The executive power is of the Imperial prerogative, and those delegated to wield it should stand aloof from political parties,' the 'Peace Preserver' unbendingly maintained, and it was on this rock that Ito's whole political career was to founder — and with it the prospect of any real progress towards democracy. Yamagata was to remain either as Prime Minister, Chief of Staff or senior Elder Statesman for the next generation, and by the time of his death in 1922 virtually the whole process of political decision-making hung on the consent of the armed forces.

The powers that Meiji now found himself endowed with would, in the words of one commentator, 'have warmed the heart of a Catherine or Caligula'. Of them all, the supreme command of the Army and Navy probably carried the most far-reaching consequences, complemented, as it was, by the Chief of Staff's prerogative of 'direct access to the Throne', which allowed him to dispense with even the formality of obtaining Cabinet approval for his plans. Just how closely the ambitions of Meiji and Yamagata coincided will emerge in due course.

If Cabinet concurrence in these ambitions was effectively guaranteed by the new Constitution, the co-operation of the population at large still remained to be secured. The first step towards this end was taken the following year through the medium of an Imperial Rescript on Education commissioned by Yamagata. The original draft was prepared by the Prussophile Inoue, but inevitably it was passed on for comment to Motoda, who had already declared his opinion on the subject with characteristic certitude: 'In Japan a system of education which was not mainly directed towards the development of the Japanese spirit would be worse than useless ... we must go back to the fundamentals at once!' He had secretly written one of his own in the meantime, and the final document owed a great deal more to his fundamentalism than it did to Inoue. Its character was epitomized by the injunction to the Emperor's subjects that they should 'always respect the Constitution and observe the laws; should an emergency arise, offer yourselves courageously to the State, and thus guard and maintain the prosperity of Our Imperial Throne coeval with Heaven and Earth.' A copy of the Rescript was hung in every school in the country alongside Meiji's photograph, where they were 'guarded and maintained' so zealously that on numerous occasions teachers sacrificed their lives in attempting to rescue them from the fires which frequently swept through the timber-built classrooms.

His life's work complete, Motoda passed away only three months after the Rescript's promulgation. In the space of 20 years he had seen his charge grow from a 19-year-old figurehead to become the instrument of Japan's envisaged hegemony of the world, 'sacred' by virtue of his divine authority and 'inviolable' in commanding the blind obedience of his subjects. It was Motoda, not Ito, who could 'die a happy man', as Ito himself was very soon to acknowledge. When two years later Ito's proposal for the formation of a government party in order to pave the way for the establishment of party cabinets was overruled by his fellow Ministers, his dismay was such that he refused to succeed Yamagata as Prime Minister.

The Constitution-Maker would spend the rest of his life fighting a rearguard action to defend the principle of representative government. 'The Monarch is not the ruler of the State but is an organ of the State,' he later wrote. 'The fact that the Monarch is the possessor of the nation's Constitution definitely does not mean that his rights and powers are unlimited. The Monarch, in the exercise of his powers under a constitutional system, must first conform to fixed usages and second, must accept the participation of other organs.'

His words would be taken up again in the 1930s in a final attempt to divert the country from the disaster which loomed ahead, but it was already too late. The monster of Imperial power had, like Frankenstein's, grown beyond the means of its creators to control it, and it would ultimately bring destruction to everything it touched.

8

False Dawn
for the Rising Sun

GUNS BEFORE BUTTER

In defining the twin tasks — those of 'devoting itself fully to the welfare of
the people and putting Japan on an equal footing with the other countries
of the world' — which he saw facing the new order in 1868, Kido Koin
made it unequivocally clear which of the two he considered to have the
higher priority: 'If we wish the reforms of a new regime to be realised and
the prestige of the Emperor to be elevated abroad, we must establish the
basis of government by allotting three-fifths of expenditure for military
purposes, one-fifth for the government and one-fifth for the relief of the
people.' The Shogunate might be no more, he was saying, but the
governing philosophy remained exactly as Hotta had expressed it a decade
earlier — 'to foster our national strength and complete our armaments,
and so gradually subject the foreigners to our influence until ... our
hegemony is acknowledged throughout the globe.'

The following year Yamagata and Saigo's younger brother Tsugumichi
were commissioned to make a tour of Europe 'in order for them to become
intimately acquainted with world conditions and to acquire practical
knowledge about warships, artillery, military systems and administration'. They visited Belgium, Britain, France, Holland, Russia and Prussia,
but it was the last of these, 'where the military bearing is the rule' as he
rhapsodized in a poem, that impressed Yamagata most. Elsewhere, by
contrast, he was disconcerted by the advance of the democratic principle.
'Even in England,' he wrote to Kido, 'the King has lost much of his former
power.' On his return to Tokyo he was invited the very next day to the
Imperial Palace to make a first-hand report. This was the first time that a
person without any formal rank, as Yamagata then was, had appeared
before the Throne, and it marked the beginning of a relationship which
was to extend to Meiji's grandson, Hirohito, half a century later.

This invitation was followed by another to become Vice-Minister of the
Army in place of the unfortunate first holder of the office, whose attempt
to create a central army by general conscription had been cut short only
too literally by a band of *samurai* bent on defending their traditional

preserve with their swords. In the light of the reluctance of the individual *han* to merge their separate militia — and of Satsuma in particular, whose forces had already been led back to Kagoshima by Saigo in an expression of protest at the centralist tenor of the new regime's policies — Yamagata at first declined the post. He eventually accepted it, however, on the twin conditions that the *han* were compelled to adopt a unified system of military organisation (up to that point they had variously favoured British, Dutch, French and Prussian systems) and that 'The Great Saigo', as the leader of much the largest, was appointed Minister of Defence. In spite of Yamagata's own preference for the Prussian system, the French was the one selected, and this decision was followed by the creation of an Imperial Bodyguard of 10,000 men drawn from the forces of Satsuma, Choshu, Tosa and Hizen.

It was the presence of this nucleus of a national army whose loyalty was pledged to the central government that finally made it possible to push through the abolition of the *han*. This in turn then paved the way for the introduction of a nationwide recruitment drawing on every class of society; Yamagata's experience with the Kiheitai irregulars of his own *han* had convinced him that good soldiers were just as likely to be found among the non-*samurai* classes as among the 'two-swordsmen'.

Promulgated on January 10th 1873 and blessed by Meiji with an Imperial Rescript, the Conscription Act made three years' service in the new army compulsory for all men over the age of twenty, with a further four years in the reserves. More than any other single measure, this was to provide the springboard for Japan's invasion of the Asian continent; fifty years later one of his severest critics in the democratic movement (but committed nonetheless, it may be noted in passing, to the former's realisation) was to acknowledge that 'if Yamagata were to receive the thanks of the Japanese people a hundred years from now it would be for this one thing alone'.

At much the same time his colleagues on the Iwakura Mission to Europe were being granted an audience with Bismarck in Berlin, at which the architect of *realpolitik* advised them that 'the only way for a country like Japan is to strengthen and protect herself with all her might and to set no reliance on other nations ... When International Law is not to a nation's advantage, it is ignored and resort is made to war.' The next seventy years would demonstrate just how deeply those words were taken to heart.

'PUNISH KOREA'

The opposition of the *samurai* to the dimunition of their status remained as intractable as ever, however, and it was in order to head it off that the expedition to Korea was then mooted. The slogan 'Punish Korea' sprang from Seoul's refusal to recognise the legitimacy of an instruction sent shortly after the Restoration to the effect that since the Shogun had been replaced by the Emperor all official communications should now be addressed to the latter (since Hideyoshi's withdrawal in 1598 diplomatic relations between the two countries had been conducted through the medium of the semi-autonomous *daimyo* of the Tsushima Islands). In reply the Korean Court had retorted that as Korea was a client state of China, only the Chinese Emperor could be accorded such a title. It was, of course, Korea's geographical position which supplied the real motive behind the slogan: divided from Japan only by the 120 miles of the Tsushima Straits, she furnished the obvious starting point for the projected programme of continental expansion. In due course, Korea would be represented to the rest of the world as the aggressor 'pointing a dagger at Japan's heart'.

Japan's new rulers were not the men to take an open rejection of their legitimacy lying down. In March 1869 Kido had told Sanjo and Iwakura that in his opinion it would not be possible to resolve the matter 'without recourse to arms' and that they should anyway aim to open Pusan by force to Japanese trade in order to 'set our country on its course, turning the people's eyes from domestic to foreign affairs and give our army and navy practical experience' but that given the need for the new regime to consolidate 'it is not reasonable to resort to arms at once ... Our national strength is not sufficient.' Yamagata's attitude to the idea of a military expedition was similarly pragmatic: 'Our army is presently in the midst of reorganisation,' he wrote to Saigo early in 1873. 'After one or two years when the foundation of the military system is established, there will probably be no obstacles to sending troops to the continent.'

Saigo, however, was unimpressed by such caution: 'Should Japan's boundaries end at Hokkaido?' he retaliated, at the same time putting forward a plan of conquest which stretched as far north as the Russian port of Nikolaevsk on the mouth of the Amur River and dispatching two of his personal followers to carry out the necessary reconnaissance. In order to conceal its true purpose from the West, he proposed not a direct assault, but a more circuitous tactic: 'Would it not be far better to send an envoy first? It is clear that if we did so the Koreans would resort to violence, and would certainly afford us the excuse for attacking them ... I feel sure that he would be murdered. I therefore beseech you to send me.'

This demonstration of the *samurai* spirit successfully won over the Tosa-Hizen element on the Central Board led by Itagaki and Soejima, who were already resentful of Satsuma and Choshu's appropriation of the highest positions in the new order. In a conversation with Parkes, Soejima boasted that they would be able to subjugate the Korean peninsula 'in a hundred days'. He went on to claim that the maintenance of Japan's independence would also require taking control of the Shantung peninsula and the rest of China, and it was subsequently suggested that Buddhist missionaries should be sent to China and followed up with troops 'for their protection'. Even more significantly, the Korean project received, according to the official history of the secret Black Dragon Society, the 'warm encouragement' of the young Emperor in an early expression of his commitment to the expansionism imbued in him by his father.

At a meeting of the Central Board on August 17th 1873 Saigo's sacrificial appointment as envoy to Korea was approved unanimously, although both Kido and Okubo, who had recently returned from Europe, deliberately stayed away (although the latter, who was not yet a member of the Board, was technically not entitled to attend anyway). On the following day Sanjo, as the Board's President, obtained the Emperor's assent, and Saigo wrote in a note to Itagaki thanking him for his support that 'this is the happiest moment of my life'. However, the undertaking which they had given to the Iwakura Mission required them to await its return before implementing such important decisions, and Iwakura and Ito had already indicated that they would oppose it.

When the former did finally arrive home the following month, his first move was to co-opt Okubo on to the Board; in accepting the invitation, Okubo wrote prophetically that he did so 'at the risk of my life'. As a result, the vote was now tied. Sanjo, who had been working desperately to bring about a compromise between the two sides, then collapsed with a brain haemorrhage. This allowed Iwakura as Vice-President to exercise a casting vote in the opposition's favour; to objections that he was thereby opposing the Imperial will, he replied that 'no matter what His Majesty says, I, Iwakura, will not permit him to do it.' The Emperor was still no more than twenty years old, but never again would he allow his wishes to be so dismissively set aside.

The four defeated protagonists of 'Punish Korea' then resigned in protest, but it must again be emphasized that it was not the cherished goal of expansion which had been called into question, but only its timing. Iwakura and his colleagues on the Mission, having seen for themselves just how much industrial and technological ground Japan had to make up on the 'barbarian' West and so having set their sights more firmly than ever on the revision of the unequal treaties as the first objective, were arguing not for abandonment of expansion, but merely for its postponement. On the other hand they were well aware that time was not on their side; the volatile mixture of *samurai* resentment of reform and conquistadorial zeal was obviously approaching flash point.

FIRST STEPS SOUTH

Saigo's resignation left Yamagata, now Minister of the Army since the separation in 1872 of the Army and Navy Ministeries, as its undisputed commander. He swiftly took over the Imperial Bodyguard and, with the help of a grant of 36,000 yen from the Emperor's private purse, thoroughly reorganised it; he also took the opportunity to replace the 100 officers who had followed Saigo back to Satsuma with his own nominees from Choshu, a move which was the source of Choshu's domination of the first two generations of the Army's senior command.

The ever-growing burden of the military budget (it had quadrupled since 1870) obliged the government to seek private capital in order to finance it. Private companies were invited to subscribe to many of the industrial enterprises which had been taken out of Tokugawa hands after the Restoration, on the understanding that they would later be able to buy out the Government's shareholding — often at an absurdly low price. The leading firms of Mitsui and Mitsubishi benefitted in particular from this largesse: the latter acquired substantial coal-mining interests in this way together with 18 steamships and an annual subsidy of 310,000 yen (to be followed in 1877 by another 9 ships and 700,000 yen as a reward for the help of their troop transports in suppressing the Satsuma Rebellion), while in return for underwriting the Government Bonds offered to the *samurai* in place of their stipends Mitsui was granted a monopoly of the Army's banking business.

The subsequent establishment of Ito's commission to investigate the introduction of a 'popular' assembly did not, as we have seen, succeed in satisfying the *samurai*, and the assassination attempt on Iwakura, coupled with the outbreak of the rebellion in Hizen, persuaded the Central Board that only a military adventure of some kind would serve to divert their energies — particularly those of Saigo and the other malcontents in Satsuma. Korea was for the moment closed, but there was another avenue, it so happened, conveniently to hand.

Two years earlier 69 Loochooan fishermen had been shipwrecked off Formosa, of whom 54 survivors were then murdered by one of the island's aboriginal tribes. Although the Loochoo (Ryuku) Islands had continued to acknowledge Chinese suzerainty and to pay an annual tribute to the Emperor in Peking after their annexation by Satsuma in 1609, Saigo lost no time in taking up their cause and called for a punitive expedition against the offenders; he was supported in this by the former U.S. Consul in Amoy, Charles W. LeGendre, who had been invited by Soejima to serve as an adviser to the Japanese Foreign Office.

LeGendre postulated that as China had never effectively occupied Formosa the island should be the property of whoever was the first to do so; furthermore, he argued, its annexation was essential to Japan's security. Nothing else that he might have said could have been calculated to commend itself so favourably to his new masters. Nor did he stop there: 'His opinion was that Japan should annex Korea, Formosa and Manchuria, thus to make a semicircle around China, threaten Russia in Siberia and take the leadership of Asia,' Okuma was later to recall. 'In those days many *samurai* visited the Foreign Ministry to hear LeGendre talk, forming a long line.'

Saigo's call was followed by an Imperial edict proclaiming the abolition of the Kingdom of the Loochoos and its incorporation as a separate *han* into the Empire of Japan; as a further mark of his loss of independence, the King was provided with an official residence in Tokyo and endowed with a pension on condition that he abrogated the treaties which he had made with the Western Powers in the wake of Perry's visit there in 1854. Soejima then obtained Meiji's permission to go to Peking, ostensibly to ratify the treaty drawn up two years earlier formalising the relationship between the two countries as that of equals, but in reality, as his petition to the Throne reveals, 'to force the Chinese to recognise our [right to launch an] expedition to Formosa.'

The Chinese not unnaturally declined to be so coerced and Soejima thought it wiser not to press the matter, but he was already too late to allay the suspicions of Li Hung-chang, the able and influential Viceroy of Tientsin. Two years earlier Li had expressed the hope that 'China and Japan might help each other in resisting the West', but he harboured no such illusions now: 'Japan's power is daily expanding, and her ambition is not small,' he warned the Court, adding prophetically that 'undoubtedly she will become China's permanent and great anxiety.' Such fears were already only too real, as a memorial which Eto Shimpei, the leader of the Hizen rebellion, had addressed to Iwakura in 1871 demonstrated: 'China is the battleground of Asia. Those who do not take possession of her are endangered; if, however, you do, you control the situation in Asia ...'

On March 1st 1874, the day that the rebels' stronghold fell to government forces, Eto sought out Saigo to enlist his aid. Nothing eventuated, however, although Saigo was reported as being 'very melancholy' about the outcome (which included Eto's execution). Two weeks later Saigo accompanied his *daimyo* Hisamitsu to Tokyo, where the offer of a seat on the Right Board to the latter successfully bought off Satsuma support for the rebellion and ensured its collapse. There is no record of how Saigo was persuaded to accede to it, but it seems hardly a coincidence that plans then emerged for an expedition against Formosa commanded by Saigo's brother Tsugumichi and blessed by the Government's appointment of LeGendre and two other U.S. officers as his advisers.

A mixed fleet of Japanese, American, British and French vessels, including thirteen especially purchased for the occasion (and later transferred to Mitsubishi), had already set sail for Nagasaki to embark the 3,600 Satsuma troops when a protest was received from the U.S. Minister at the employment of the three Americans. The 'Traitor' Okubo was sufficiently disturbed by it to order Tsugumichi not to proceed. In keeping with the attitude of his brother, however, the latter retorted that as the Emperor had approved the expedition so only the Emperor could disband it. He promptly put to sea, although he did agree to dispense with the Americans and to withdraw his troops from Formosa once the expedition's ostensible objective had been achieved.

When news of their departure reached the Chinese Court their reaction was one of simple disbelief. They eventually recovered sufficiently to organise a counter force of several thousand men. Tsugumichi decided, however, albeit reluctantly, to keep to his brief and after subjugating the offending tribe he restrained his men from advancing into the northern half of the island where they would have invited a clash with the Chinese. During subsequent negotiations in Peking China at first refused Japan's demands for recognition of her right of intervention and reimbursement of the cost of the expedition, but after Okubo threatened to take his delegation home the former was conceded and a contribution towards the latter agreed; the issue of Loochooan sovereignty on the other hand was left unresolved. Tsugumichi then sailed home to a triumphal reception, marred only by the death in the interval of several hundred of his men from disease in the Formosan jungle.

Negotiations had also meanwhile been taken up in St. Petersburg to settle the question of Sakhalin, which had been left in joint occupation with Russia under the original treaty of 1855. Influenced perhaps by the prevailing mood of euphoria, Japan was persuaded to exchange her rights in the island for the possession of the remaining Kurile Islands under Russian control. It was later recognised to have been a poor bargain, which it would take another thirty years to retrieve.

'BE ON THE LOOK OUT'

Kido had resigned from the Central Board on the grounds that the expedition represented an unnecessary expense which the economy could ill accommodate. Yamagata also submitted his resignation, arguing that 'unless for the next several years we endeavour constantly to dedicate ourselves to the unfinished task, we cannot build the foundations of our Imperial Army and demonstrate to all nations our dignity. If we should commit more troops and from this situation a clash with China should result, the disadvantages would be beyond description.' It was not accepted, however, and the avoidance of the clash that he feared silenced any further reservations on his part. Likewise, the receipt of a handsome indemnity persuaded Kido to rejoin the Board.

China's concessions, which were viewed as underwriting Japan's claims to sovereignty over the Loochoos, encouraged renewed visions of conquest further afield. In his capacity as Chairman of the Formosa Commission Okuma pronounced that 'if Japan had not taken steps to chastise the savages, a land of cannibals would have been established for ever and Japan would have been disgraced in the eyes of the world. The Emperor should not stop at chastising savages, but should exalt his work to the highest pinnacle of glory.'

In particular, they revived the battle-cry of 'Punish Korea'. Although Iwakura and his colleagues were still as convinced as ever of the inadvisability of a direct invasion, they were equally alive to the need to steal at least some of the *samurai*'s fire, particularly since they were planning to impose further reforms on them. They therefore reopened negotiations with Seoul, but pursued a harder line than previously.

When the anticipated impasse was duly reached in July 1875, they dispatched three warships on the pretext of making a survey of Korean coastal waters. On September 19th a party was sent ashore for water at Kanghwa (guarding the approaches to Seoul) and was predictably fired on by the local defence forces; in the ensuing exchange thirty Koreans were killed. This 'incident' opened the way for the dispatch in January 1876 of a top-level team of negotiators led by 'Mitsui-Man' Inoue, backed by several thousand soldiers and armed with secret instructions that 'if Korea wishes to withhold reply until she has an answer from China, then, while waiting for an answer, Japanese soldiers should be stationed in Seoul, and supplied there and we should occupy Kanghwa Castle.' At the same time Mori Arinori was sent to Peking with the similar object of establishing there Korea's right to negotiate independently of China.

Li Hung-chang, fully appreciating the nature of the Japanese threat and 'poor and weak' Korea's incapacity to oppose it, advised coming to terms, and a treaty establishing full diplomatic and trading relations was duly signed. The Japanese described its purpose as being 'commercial and not territorial, and to secure the perfect independence of the Hermit Nation and to lead it into the light of modern civilisation'; however, their success in having Korea define itself as 'self-governing' would be an important tool in the hands of the expansionists.

The hope that the *samurai* would thereby be satisfied was, of course, less successful, and Saigo was already calling for the subjugation of Manchuria and eastern Siberia in addition to Korea before he took the fatal plunge of leading them into open revolt. Despite its suppression, the Satsuma Rebellion and the subsequent assassination of Okubo (which together with Kido's death removed two of the leading advocates in the government of negotiation rather than force of arms) were to serve as traumatic reminders of the perils of ignoring expansionist sentiments in the future.

The vacuum left by these two outstanding personalities was filled by three elements which combined to propel Japan along the path to ultimate disaster. First, the military headed by Yamagata, who, on receiving approval in 1878 for a ten-year expansion programme to reorganise his all-conscript army into seven divisions (plus 200,000 reservists) along the Prussian lines that he had always favoured, proclaimed that 'at last the military foundation for fighting on the continent has been laid'. Secondly, the Throne in the person of Meiji, the inheritor of his father's conquistadorial dreams, amplified by the ultra-chauvinist dogmas of his tutor, Motoda Eifu. Thirdly, those heirs of Saigo's rebellious *samurai*, the secret societies whose growth as a political force from this point onwards would undermine the democratic movement which alone could have averted that disaster.

The ground won on the Korean front was judged sufficient for the moment, and attention focussed again on the Loochoos. In June 1877, even before Saigo's final overthrow, an order was sent to the King of the Islands forbidding him to send any further tribute to China. The King referred to Peking, where Li again correctly assessed Japanese intentions: 'Although Loochoo in itself is insignificant, the precedent of aggression might be applied to Korea later. Could China always remain silent?' The Chinese ambassador in Tokyo was instructed to open negotiations, but before any conclusion could be reached Japan sent an 'administrator' to the Islands accompanied by 200 gendarmes and then, in April 1879, formally announced their annexation.

China appealed to ex-U.S. President Ulysses S. Grant, who happened to be visiting the country at the time. Grant was reluctant to involve himself and urged the two countries to reach a settlement without recourse to arms; he did, however, offer a mutual-aid treaty to China in order to dissuade Japan from engineering any further such disputes. During discussions in Tokyo on his way back to America, he recorded a conversation with an unnamed Minister in which the latter claimed that 'the Mikado and Ministers were anxious to preserve the peace with China, but there were two million *samurai* very eager for war with a foreign country so that they might find vent for their energies.'

A compromise entailing the division of the Islands between the two countries was then suggested, but the outbreak of war in 1880 between China and Russia encouraged the Japanese to step up their demands. Negotiations dragged on inconclusively for a further two years before they were overtaken by renewed confrontation in Korea. Li summed up the whole affair in a letter to the King of Korea: 'Japan covets Korea and Formosa. Her rapacity, *relying on her skill in fraud*, is well illustrated in the affair of Loochoo. Your country had better be on the look-out ...'

QUISLING 'REFORMERS'

In anticipation of a further Japanese move on Korea Li had instigated a crash programme of warship construction, and he was now further authorised by the Court to put pressure on Korea to enter into treaties with the Western Powers in order to insure herself against the territorial designs of both Japan and Russia (under the 1860 Treaty of Peking the latter had installed itself on Korea's border at Vladivostok). The King of Korea — or rather his Queen, Min, who was much the more dominant partner and had filled the Cabinet with her own family and nominees — privately concurred with such a step, but he feared that the chauvinist majority of his subjects would prevent him from taking it unless it was put in the form of a direct order from the Emperor. Li advised against this on the grounds that it would deprive the Korean negotiators of any bargaining power of their own, and as a compromise he himself was authorised to negotiate with the Powers on Korea's behalf. The Treaty of Chemulpo (Inchon) was duly signed with the United States on May 22nd 1882, to be followed shortly afterwards by similar agreements with Britain, France and Prussia.

Hardly was the ink dry on the last of them, however, when Korean chauvinists under the leadership of the Taewongun, the King's father and former Regent who was bitterly resentful of his daughter-in-law's influence, registered their violent disapproval. On July 23rd a mob attacked the Royal Palace in Seoul, and although the King and Queen both escaped unscathed, a number of their ministers were hacked to pieces. The assault then turned on the Japanese Legation and several of its staff were killed or wounded, but the Minister was able to flee under the cover of darkness to Inchon, where he was lucky enough to find a British ship to give him refuge and return him to Japan.

At an emergency meeting of the Chief Council (as the Central Board had now become) in Tokyo it was decided to send a demand to Korea for an apology and damages 'to the full extent of International Law', and to back it up with a force of 800 troops and 3 warships. When news of this reached Peking the Court, despite the absence of Li on three months' leave, galvanised itself into a rare display of action and commissioned a counter expedition of 4,000 troops under naval escort. Although they were too late to anticipate the arrival of the Japanese, the latter had had no success in pressing their demands and the much larger Chinese force was able to enter Seoul, restore the King and transport the ex-Regent back to exile in China. They then spelt out to the Koreans the terms of compensation to be offered to the Japanese, which included an indemnity of 500,000 yen and the right to station a battalion in Seoul as Legation guards. For want of the prospect of anything better in the immediate future these were accepted, and the second Treaty of Chemulpo was signed on September 3rd.

This settlement came as unwelcome news to the members of the Genyosha, the secret society formed in Fukuoka the previous year by Saigo's surviving followers and the forerunner of the infamous Black Dragon Society, whose shadow was to loom so large over subsequent events. Dedicated to the fruition of their hero's plans for expansion in Asia, it took its name from the sea dividing Korea from Japan (Fukuoka being the nearest port in Japan to the former; having also been Hideyoshi's base for his invasion of Korea, it had remained the natural breeding ground for expanionist zeal). Although Hiraoka Kotaro was nominally its president, the real power behind it was from the beginning exercised by a former *ronin*, Toyama Mitsuru. After his release from imprisonment for his part in the Satsuma Rebellion, this sinister figure had first acquired influence as an underworld middle-man recruiting gang labour for local coal-mine owners. He had already put pressure on 'People's Man' Itagaki to bring his Independence Society out into open revolt against the Government; half a century later his weight was such that Matsuoka Yosuke, who as Foreign Minister was to lead Japan to the brink of World

War Two, admitted that 'I can do nothing before finding out what Toyama's opinion is'.

The sudden turn of events cut short the Genyosha's plans for an operation of their own in Korea. The further news a few weeks later that China had decided to retain her troops there permanently and to appoint a Resident who would dictate the country's foreign policy caused much anguished discussion in the more exalted circle of the Chief Council on the subject of Korea's 'independence', and Iwakura even suggested seeking the opinions of the Western Powers.

Ito, who was in Europe at the time pursuing his constitutional researches, wrote that there was nothing to be gained from that quarter. 'I find that the Europeans would harm and deceive us, and there is precious little sentiment among them for doing anything to profit and benefit us. The European nations, combining together, are trying to outstrip isolated Japan,' he reported. 'If they are going to stress that our level of civilisation is not up to their standards, what about their recognising as civilised and independent states Bulgaria, Serbia, Montenegro and Rumania? These states are peopled by those who do not differ from wild monkeys ...' Therefore, he argued, it was 'very urgent' that Korea's independence should be proclaimed. 'We should give them some help and make them feel some obligation. They have no power and resources, and that is why they have no alternative but to depend on China. Therefore our policy should be to help them declare their independence and remove the declaration by the King that Korea is a dependent state of China.'

However, Ito's colleagues at home felt less emboldened to foster any open challenge among Koreans to China's latest show of authority. Even Inoue, with whom his opinions normally coincided so closely, cautioned that 'though there might be much desire among Koreans for help from Japan to secure their independence, if you go into the matter only Kim Ok-kiun, Pak Young-hyo and Pak Young-kyo [leaders of a nascent pro-Japanese independence party] are really dedicated to this.' While eschewing any direct government involvement, Inoue was on the other hand alive to the opportunity of using other, more devious, channels to the same end, in the shape of the oligarchy's political opponents at home — a ploy which would have the double advantage of diverting the latters' democratizing energies from the domestic front. In particular, Goto, the leader of the main Liberal opposition party in Itagaki's (government-funded) absence abroad, had broken with the oligarchy nine years earlier over the rejection of the plan for direct intervention in Korea and could therefore be counted on to support such a scheme, as could Godfather Toyama and his 'Punish-Korea' acolytes in the Genyosha.

According to one of the many later government-commissioned 'histories', the scheme evolved as follows: 'Some Japanese politicians like Goto now formed the idea of reforming Korea through the aid of Japan, and the Minister of Foreign Affairs, Inoue, was not entirely adverse to the idea. A certain sum of money [170,000 yen] advanced by the [government-sponsored] Yokohama Special Bank was put at their disposal for the purpose of founding political newspapers in Seoul, for training Korean soldiers, and the like; and agents of Goto went out to Korea to produce the papers or corroborate the schemes of reform. The Japanese Government appointed Takezoe Shinichiro, a Chinese scholar of some repute, as Minister in Korea to support the reformers.' In turn, Kim Ok-kiun and the two Paks were brought over to Japan, where they received suitably generous encouragement.

GATE-CRASHERS

The following year Kim applied for another loan of no less than three million yen in order to finance an armed uprising. Inoue declined to lend his government's name to so large and open a commitment, but Goto talked confidently of being able to supply at least one million together with a force of *'samurai* comrades' — referring, of course, to the Genyosha. This was to mark the beginning of an unholy alliance between the Liberals and the secret societies, in which Toyama mercilessly exploited the formers' democractic platform in order to pressurise the government of the day into upholding the commitment to territorial expansion. 'From the very beginning our principle has been *sonno-joi*,' he was later to remind everyone after mounting an assassination attempt on a back-slider.

1884 saw the outbreak of war between China and France in Indo-China and hence the opportunity for Japan to strike in Korea while the former's attention was diverted, an opportunity further enhanced by the subsequent withdrawal of half the Chinese garrison in Seoul. Goto and Kim therefore approached the French Minister in Tokyo, who replied that he did not think that he would be able to help 'officially', but that 'if the opportunity comes, there will be a fund of one million yen and a warship to meet your needs.' Goto was so carried away by the positive nature of this response that he openly boasted about it to Ito (now, since Iwakura's death, the acknowledged leader of the Chief Council). Ito and Inoue decided that if there was to be a successful anti-Chinese coup in Korea, the credit for it must be seen to go to themselves and not to their political opponents. Takezoe was therefore recalled to Tokyo and instructed that he was to cultivate his contacts with Kim and his followers with the idea of wooing them away from the Liberals and the French.

Takezoe, however, seems to have interpreted his new brief rather overzealously, for on his return to Seoul on October 30th he 'began active intercourse with the persons he supposed to belong to the [pro-] Japanese party. He now freely spoke of the approaching destruction of China and of the opportunity for Korea of declaring her absolute independence.' Three days later he announced to the King that Japan would waive the remainder of the indemnity outstanding from the 1882 Agreement provided that the same sum was put towards 'military reforms', and at a dinner at the Japanese Legation the following evening the hosts 'made speeches against China and in favour of the alliance between Japan and Korea. They even ridiculed the Chinese Consul present, who did not understand the Japanese language.'

During his absence in Japan, however, it had become clear that Queen Min and her ruling faction had begun to have second thoughts on the wisdom of too close an involvement with Japan. This persuaded Kim and his associates that the time for violent measures had arrived, and they presented Takezoe with a plan to murder the seven leading members of the Cabinet. According to the official Japanese Foreign Ministry account, he 'strongly warned them against this rash attempt, but observing that their minds were made up he drew up two plans which he submitted to the Japanese government.'

Plan A involved giving the rebels every assistance; Plan B on the other hand was merely concerned to preserve law and order. 'Our Government chose Plan B and so instructed him by telegram on November 28th,' the official account claimed. 'This instruction, however, did not reach him until after the uprising.' The 'uprising' eventually took place on December 4th; we are thus invited to believe that the elusive telegram spent six days in transmission. Even more improbable is the claim of the aforementioned 'history' that Kim revealed the plot in advance to the King and obtained his personal blessing for the massacre of the Queen's family.

The occasion selected was a dinner held to celebrate the opening of the first post office in Seoul. It was attended by all the senior foreign representatives except Takezoe, who excused himself on the grounds of 'sickness'. The American Minister made the following record of what then took place. 'As the dinner drew to a close an alarm of fire was given, and nearly all the guests withdrew from the table and went out of doors to view the fire, which seemed near at hand. A moment later Min Yong-ik [the Deputy Foreign Minister] entered, his face and clothing covered with blood, which was streaming from seven or eight ghastly wounds . . .' Kim's accomplices, several of whom had been dressed up as Japanese guests at the dinner, then doubled round to the nearby Royal Palace and after making out to the King that his life was in danger, they dictated an order for his signature summoning the Japanese garrison. When the troops were in place, 'five of the leading officials of the government were called to the Palace, ostensibly by the direction of the King, and while there they were put to death.'

BOUNCED

The next morning a proclamation was published appointing Kim and the other leaders of the pro-Japan party to the vacant ministries and announcing Korea's independence from China and various other 'reforms'. The conspirators had reckoned, however, without the Koreans' 'three-hundred year hatred' which Isabella Bird, that most remarkable of nineteenth-century British travellers, observed was still nursed against the Japanese in the wake of Hideyoshi's invasion. When word of the coup spread among the general population, they took en masse to the streets crying 'Death to the Japanese!'; they killed several of them and burned their properties to the ground. At this juncture the much larger Chinese garrison arrived from their barracks on the outskirts of the city and requested admittance to the Palace. This was refused by the Japanese commander, and when they eventually decided to force an entry the Japanese opened fire.

As a full-scale battle developed, Takezoe pleaded with the King to take refuge with him and his fellow-conspirators elsewhere, but he declined to do so. The Japanese then had no option but to retire to their own Legation. When their food stocks were in due course exhausted, they were forced to flee in turn to Inchon and thence back to Japan, taking Kim, Pak and four other leading rebels with them. Those that they left behind were subsequently executed on the orders of the King, who at the same time refilled the ministries with his own nominees and wrote to Peking appealing for reinforcements in case the Japanese should attempt to return in force.

Okuma put what gloss he could on the whole episode in his *Fifty Years of New Japan,* an official encomium published in 1909 to forestall reaction in the West to Japan's formal annexation of Korea scheduled the following year. 'After the banquet,' his story reads, 'Prince Min, the leader of the Reactionary Party, was dragged out and murdered, whilst several of the conservative leaders met with the same fate. The city was in a state of turmoil, and the progressives asked for the assistance of the Japanese troops to protect the Palace' (even Okuma forebore to repeat the fiction that the King had done so on his own initiative). 'But the Chinese troops, who numbered more than two thousand, attacked it. The King fled, and the Japanese troops beat a retreat to their Legation, which was attacked and burnt. In Japan the people were furious and clamoured for war, but the self-restraint and caution of the Government fortunately held the upper hand . . .'

This debâcle represented a serious setback to Japanese ambitions in Korea, and the inner cabinet of Ito, Inoue and Yamagata hurriedly met to consider their next move. Ito struck an appropriate note of caution: 'We cannot yet decide whether to risk war with China for Korean independence in the future. But at the moment we must avoid it'. They therefore fell back on their now familiar bluster in order to put as good a face as possible on the whole affair; Inoue was to present the Korean King with 'an accusing letter' and to demand an apology and suitable reparations, together with a promise that the Chinese troops would be evacuated.

In the event, the terms reached with the King amounted to a good deal less than had been extracted in 1882, and an indemnity of no more than 130,000 yen was agreed. Inoue did succeed, however, in excluding the Chinese from the negotiations on the grounds that Korea was an independent state. He was also glib enough to invoke the articles of International Law governing political refugees, following Bismarck's cynical advice a decade earlier, in talking his way out of demands for the repatriation of Kim and his followers. Takezoe was, not surprisingly, replaced as Minister, although no admission of any misdemeanour on his part was made.

Ito then set off for Peking in order to make the necessary peace with China. On his arrival he was informed that the newly-enthroned Emperor was too young to negotiate with him, but that Li was empowered to do so at Tientsin. Before he left, an Imperial Rescript had been issued in Tokyo to all prefectural governors forewarning them that it was hoped that 'a good outcome [of the negotiations] would be achieved in a conciliatory manner' so that, by implication, they should take steps to suppress expectations of a military solution. Ito's entourage included Saigo Tsugumichi, whose presence was designed to convey to the Chinese the contrary impression that he retained the full range of options.

Ito naturally denied to Li that his government had played any part in fomenting the attempted coup in Seoul, and on the question of which of the two garrisons had fired first in the grounds of the Palace he maintained that 'the Japanese were inside and the Chinese outside, so it is clear that the Chinese did the attacking.' He thereby succeeded in putting Li on the defensive, and the latter undertook to enforce appropriate punishment if any such charges could be substantiated.

He then went on to propose that both sides should have the right to return their garrisons in the event of further disturbances on condition only that they informed the other before doing so. He failed in his further attempt to have Korea's independence written into the terms, but the equal right to station troops there could be interpreted as an implicit acknowledgement by China of this. The treaty, or Li-Ito Convention as it became known, was accordingly hailed in Tokyo as a considerable diplomatic coup, and even a leading Chinese historian later conceded that 'it was indeed a victory for Japan'. Certainly, it was to have far-reaching consequences in the next decade.

On his return, Ito acted swiftly to ensure that his success was not put in jeopardy by any disappointed hotheads. Although the Convention was signed on April 18th 1885, no newspaper was permitted to publish its terms until May 27th, and even then they were forbidden to carry any editorial comment. In the same month most of the Korean rebels took ship for America, their fares having been met, it was suspected, from government funds.

Kim, however, refused to go with them, and it was not long before he was laying plans for another coup with a leading member of the Liberal

Party, Oi Kentaro, and an assorted band of desperadoes who volunteered to raise the revolutionary flag in Korea and set the stage for Kim's return. Their chief problem was lack of funds; nothing could now be expected from the French, who had reached a settlement with China, and they were presently reduced to resorting to a series of armed robberies in the Osaka area. The local police were soon on their trail and rounded them up, catching some of them in possession of home-made bombs; the ringleaders were sentenced to six years' imprisonment.

Inoue, however, rejected further Korean demands for Kim's extradition, and instead he had him temporarily confined on Hokkaido — retained, like the bombs, for future use.

9

Democracy Deferred

TREATY REVISION

Yuan Shih-k'ai, the Quartermaster of the Chinese garrison in Seoul, was promoted to the new post of Chinese Resident there in recognition of the part which he had played in thwarting the Japanese coup. Already a man of rare presence among his compatriots, he soon established himself, in the words of one observer, as 'the biggest man in town', with the result that Korea was effectively closed as a political issue in Japan for the time being. The Government's opponents turned instead to that of the unequal treaties with the West as the most effective stick available to them.

Just as Prime Minister (as he had become) Ito was free to turn his attention to the drafting of his promised constitution, so Foreign Minister Inoue was now enabled to concentrate on the revision of the treaties. He had already made a number of tentative overtures over the years to the individual representatives of the Western Powers; the Americans had expressed themselves amenable to revision, but Britain, who at this time held much the largest share of trade with Japan, had refused to consider it until Japan undertook to adopt a European-based legal code.

Inoue now invited all the foreign ministers to settle the issue collectively in a Great Conference to begin on May 1st 1886, and elaborate measures were put in hand to impress them with Japan's progress towards the Western way of life: a large music-hall was built equipped with dance floors and billiard tables, and a grand fancy dress ball was given for foreign residents in Tokyo at which Ito appeared bewigged as an eighteenth-century Venetian nobleman and Inoue got himself up as a strolling minstrel.

Twenty-eight meetings were held in the course of the next twelve months. In exchange for the surrender of the indivious principle of extra-territoriality, Inoue proposed the creation of mixed courts comprising both Japanese and European judges to hear cases involving foreign nationals. However, the idea was roundly condemned as 'prolonging the disgrace we have endured for many years' by the former *samurai* Minister of Agriculture and Commerce, who not only then resigned from the Cabinet but also made public his reasons for doing so.

The Genyosha mobsters seized on the opportunity to organise a series of

130

mass protests, while the former leaders of the now-disbanded Liberal Party voiced their support in the newspapers that were still open to them. 'Our people are no longer Japanese, the country is no longer Japan,' one of them proclaimed. 'If we want Japan always to be Japan, we must preserve Japanese spirit and thought, Japanese customs and traditions.' Another wrote that 'if the coloured races do not now exert themselves, then ultimately the world will become the private possession of the white race.' Nationalistic fervour was lent further force by the shipwreck of an English steamer from which, unlike the crew, none of the Japanese passengers survived; it was put about, and faithfully repeated by ex-Progressives-leader Okuma, that all the latter had been forcibly locked in their cabins before the ship went down.

The storm of protest thereby stirred throughout the country obliged Inoue first to adjourn the Conference, and then, in September 1887, to resign from the Cabinet himself. The Government then stepped in to silence the outcry by introducing Yamagata's Peace Preservation Ordinance, which banished all their leading opponents from Tokyo, and by inviting Okuma to rejoin the Cabinet in Inoue's place and resume negotiations with the Powers. In order to avoid the fate which had overtaken Inoue, Okuma returned to the more discreet tactic of treating with each Power separately. By offering the freedom to travel and reside anywhere in Japan in exchange for a greater autonomy in setting tariffs and an end to extra-territoriality after another five years, he successfully concluded new treaties with Mexico, Germany, Russia and the United States, and he was on the point of doing so with Britain when the terms were leaked in London by *The Times*.

When this report was reproduced in a Tokyo paper, the unholy alliance of the Liberals and Genyosha swung into action again. Two years previously Godfather Toyama had squashed a Genyosha plot on Inoue's life, but whatever considerations had caused him to stay his hand on that occasion were of no account now. A bomb was procured from the recently-released Oi Kentaro's stock manufactured four years earlier in Osaka for use in Korea, and on October 18th 1889 one of his minions hurled it into the Foreign Minister's carriage. Ironically, Okuma was returning from a Cabinet meeting at which Yamagata, just back from his military tour of inspection in Europe, had swung the majority against the proposed revision terms; on the day of Yamagata's disembarkation, Okuma had been on the point of leaving for Yokohama to greet him when his opponents in the Cabinet informed him that the ship had been delayed, thus enabling themselves to beat him to the quayside and gain the homecomer's ear. Okuma was fortunate to lose no more than one of his legs. Kuroda, however, the Prime Minister since Ito's move to the Presidency of the Privy Council and Okuma's chief supporter, took the hint and resigned, to be replaced as planned by Yamagata.

DEMOCRACY'S DIFFICULT BIRTH

The subject of treaty revision was now, like Korea, consigned to limbo, and attention moved on to the first elections for the House of Representatives which were due to take place on July 1st 1890. Yamagata had filled all the leading posts in the new Cabinet with Sat-Cho nominees, but as the election approached he appointed two new Ministers from previously-excluded *han* in an attempt to disarm accusations of perpetrating the ruling oligarchy. In the event, he was far from successful: of the 300 seats contested, 171 were won by the revived Liberal and Progressive Parties, and only 89 by his own allies.

The 'Peace-Preserver', however, was not a man to be deflected by so trifling a reverse from his conviction (enunciated on the day after he took office) that 'the executive power is of the Imperial Prerogative, and those delegated to wield it should stand aloof from political parties.' A month later an Imperial Rescript was issued confirming that Ministers should be accountable to the Emperor rather than to the Prime Minister, and that the Chief of Staff in particular should have direct access to the Throne over the heads of his Cabinet colleagues. For good measure, Yamagata also had it specified that 'in spite of the fact that constitutional government is aimed at open councils and the Diet is designed to be public, Cabinet decisions must be completely secret so that the opinions of no minister will leak out to become the seed of popular debate.'

His contempt for the democratic process could hardly have been made plainer, and less than a month after the result of the elections had been published he issued an amendment to the already draconian Regulations for Public Meetings and Political Associations forbidding any party to ally itself, or even to communicate, with another. Three months later again, on the eve of the opening session of the new Diet, the principle of accountability to the Emperor was further bolstered by the Imperial Rescript on Education decreeing the highest duty of His subjects to be 'to guard and maintain the prosperity of our Imperial Throne coeval with heaven and earth'. Although its author was actually Motoda, in a letter written two days later the Purifier of the Imperial Mind acknowledged the part that Yamagata had played in its preparation. 'I am aware that your achievements are many in both the civil and military fields,' he complimented him. 'Nevertheless, with admiration and respect I express the thought that the support given to this Rescript by you as Prime Minister is the greatest achievement of your life.'

In his first speech before the House on December 6th Yamagata declared that 'if we wish to maintain the nation's independence among the powers of the world, it is not enough to guard only the line of sovereignty; we must also defend the line of advantage . . . and within the nation's resources strive gradually for that position. For this reason, it is necessary to make comparatively large appropriations for our Army and Navy.' By 'the line of sovereignty' he meant Japan's existing territorial limits; by 'the line of advantage' he indicated an unspecified, but obviously extra-territorial area which Japan should seek to dominate in order to create a buffer zone against the encroachment of other powers (three months later, however, he wrote that he had in mind Korea, which he foresaw becoming a centre of conflict in the wake of Russia's proposed construction of the Trans-Siberian Railway). Stripped of its military jargon, his speech represented a faithful restatement of the *sonno-joi* strategy imbibed from his mentor, 'Grass Roots Hero' Yoshido Shoin, thirty years earlier — 'to protect the country well is not merely to prevent it from losing the position it holds, but to add to it the positions which it does not hold'. His expression 'the line of advantage' was to become the catchword for future military expansion.

Three weeks later the parliamentary committee set up to review the government's budget proposals issued a revised draft calling for a cut of more than 10% in the total expenditure put forward, thus immediately setting the scene for the bitter battle in which Yamagata and his henchmen were to engage over the next decade with those who sought to establish the representational principle.

On January 9th 1891 the Finance Minister, Matsukata, who ten years earlier had introduced the sweeping deflationary measures needed to sustain the expansion of military expenditure, rejected the committee's draft on the strength of Article LXVII of the Constitution which decreed that 'already-fixed expenditures based upon the powers appertaining to the Emperor, and such expenditures as may have arisen by the effect of law, or that appertain to the legal obligations of the Government, shall be neither rejected nor reduced by the Imperial Diet without the concurrence of the Government.' Such imprecise terminology was clearly open to differing interpretations, but in the previous year Yamagata had moved to guarantee funds for a new seven-year military expenditure programme by ruling that the latter fell under the Article's provisions. When he now disclosed this during a speech in Matsukata's support, it drew such an outraged reaction from the Opposition that the Diet was suspended for a week.

It also marked a final parting of the ways with Constitution-Maker Ito. During the preparation of the Constitution the two of them had argued long and hard, as we have seen, over the 'transcendental' nature of the Cabinet which it seemed to envisage. Whereas Ito looked forward to some point in time at which the political parties would become sufficiently 'mature' to allow the formation of the Cabinet to be entrusted to the majority party, Yamagata had set his face inexorably against such a possibility. When Ito, who, at his own request, had now temporarily retired to the sidelines as President of the House of Peers, heard of Yamagata's speech, he was 'beyond himself with anger', the more so for having 'recently advised the Prime Minister that to prevent a headlong plunge into danger he should unequivocally state what have been the government's fixed and unchanging national policies for the past twenty years. I did so, believing that this would have a most salutary effect. The Prime Minister did not avail himself of the opportunity. Rather, when he did speak, he gave a short, meaningless, valueless, ineffectual speech ...'

STILLBORN?

A few days later Ito was still further mortified to hear that Yamagata had gone so far as to obtain the Emperor's permission to dissolve the Diet if the Opposition continued to reject the budget. 'When I heard this [from an underling sent by the Prime Minister to explain that he was contemplating such a step for fear that the Opposition would resort to violence], I was positively astounded by the Prime Minister's superficiality and rashness,' he fulminated. 'Even should the situation develop to a point where a dissolution became mandatory, the government must first exhaust all possibilities in an effort to avoid taking that step ... I refuse to be dragged into a purposeless discussion of dissolution merely on a pointless conjecture of future events. In any case the action of the Prime Minister in sending such a person to discuss a matter of such gravity as dissolution leaves one speechless.'

Even as, on February 20th, the *Nichi Nichi* was announcing that the decision to dissolve had been taken, Yamagata drew back from the brink. Goto, who, like the now hobbled Okuma, had accepted the invitation to rejoin the Cabinet in 1887, was authorised to enter into secret negotiations with Itagaki, his co-founder in Tosa of the Liberal Party and now once more the Party's leader. A compromise was reached by which the proposed cut in the budget was reduced to 8%; its passage through the House was then ensured by the support of the 29-strong Tosa element in the Party. It was universally believed that it was bribery which had worked this compromise — Itagaki had already shown himself to be amenable in this way — but just to be on the safe side the 'Peace-Preserver' employed a gang of thugs to prevent a number of known opponents from entering the Diet building on the day of the vote.

No doubt the ferocity of Ito's criticism had played some part in persuading Yamagata to draw back, but a much larger consideration was the likely impact on Western opinion, and therefore on Japan's chances of revising the treaties, of a collapse of constitutional government within three months of its initiation. As Kaneko Kentaro, one of Ito's co-drafters and now a member of the Upper House, was later to write, 'European people ridiculed the idea of Japan's adopting a constitutional government, saying that a constitutional system of government is not suitable for an Asiatic nation and is only adapted to the cool-headed people of northern Europe; even the southern European nations have failed in establishing constitutional government. How can an Asiatic nation accomplish what southern European nations have found impossible? So it was thought that if the Diet was dissolved in its very first session, unpleasant comments would be made by foreign critics. And, in consequence, a compromise was effected between the Government and the Diet.'

If financial inducement did hold some sway with the Opposition side in agreeing to the compromise, they would also have realised that they could not afford to be seen holding out too strongly against it, because the revision of the treaties had, after all, been one of the major rallying cries of the political parties ever since their inception; they could also claim that its terms represented something of a victory for them, for in agreeing a cut of 8% they were retreating not half, but slightly less than a quarter from their original figures. Furthermore, the divisions which it had pointed up within the ruling oligarchy offered the prospect of achieving a much more rapid advance towards genuine parliamentary democracy than even the most progressive might have envisaged.

Such a prospect had not, of course, passed unnoticed in the oligarchy either. Even before the compromise had been arrived at, Yamagata had warned that 'no matter what is decided as a result of the debate, I am apprehensive that this will be a source of grave difficulty in the future.' He was already concluding that, easy enough though it had been to produce the right result, it would be altogether preferable to do without a debate in the first place.

Two months later Yamagata resigned as Prime Minister on the grounds of 'ill health', but in reality the decision sprang from his profound distaste for the machinery of parliament. This did not, of course, mark his retirement from the political battlefield, but only a withdrawal to a strategic viewpoint from where he would be able to oversee more easily the manipulation of the forces at his disposal. Before he took up the Premiership for the second time in 1898 he succeeded in building up a coterie of devoted disciples, both in the bureaucracy and in the military, drawn almost exclusively from his own *han* Choshu. His four leading protégés, Katsura Taro, Kodama Gentaro, Terauchi Masatake and Tanaka Giichi, were all to serve as War Minister and, with the exception of Kodama who died relatively young, as Prime Minister. These men would be the successful agents of his grand design for territorial expansion even long after his death, which was itself still thirty years away.

FURTHER COMPLICATIONS

The choice of his successor was not, of course, made by the Diet, but by the Sat-Cho oligarchy in the guise of the newly-established Genrokaigi or 'Conference of Elder Statesmen' (the old Council of Elders having been replaced by the House of Peers in 1885). This self-appointed body arranged to meet together whenever they considered that the Cabinet 'needed advice and guidance'. In accordance with what was now the tradition of alternation between the two *han*, Satsuma's Matsukata was nominated Prime Minister. Yamagata was, of course, a member of the Conference, and he secured the Home Ministry for Shinagawa Yajiro, his nephew-in-law and fellow-student at the feet of Yoshida Shoin. Shinagawa was at first inclined to turn the post down, but he accepted it quickly enough when Yamagata told him that 'you may consider this an order from your senior'.

Matsukata appears, from the following anecdote, to have been similarly overawed by his elevation. Early on in his Premiership he was summoned to the Imperial presence to answer a request for information on a certain subject. To each of the Emperor's questions the Prime Minister dutifully replied that he would 'have careful investigation made'. Meiji then attempted to strike a more informal note by asking him how many children he had — only to be met once more by the same answer. (The official 'propagandist' who related it did not do so, it may be remarked, in any spirit of jest, but only with the object of depicting how 'His Majesty's stern sense of duty seems to have contributed to his inborn strong personality which reflected itself in the nervousness which the ablest of his Ministers is said to have felt in the presence of their august Master').

Almost at once the military hierarchy started pressing yet again for an increased share of the budget, this time with the added threat that they would otherwise refuse to appoint anyone to the posts of War Minister and Vice-Minister, which under an order of 1888 could only be filled by men of the rank of general (acting or retired). Matsukata threatened in his turn to have this order revoked, a proposal of such profound implications for the independence of the military from the rest of the executive, so carefully nurtured by the 'direct access to the Throne', that even Ito was moved to protest.

'If it is our desire to support the principles of constitutional monarchy and to prevent the transfer of the Imperial Prerogatives to the people, we should not make the military prerogative a plaything of the Diet,' he declared at an Imperial audience. 'If the Sovereign wishes to control the military prerogative directly, rather than entrust ministerial responsibility for controlling it to the political parties and those who are motivated only by the lure of office, we should entrust it to officers of the rank of General . . . It is of the utmost importance that the discords of the political world do not extend to military affairs.' It would not be many more years before Ito was making a bitter meal of his own words; far from becoming a 'plaything of the Diet', the military prerogative would presently be endowed by an extension of this order with a power that mocked the goals of the Constitution itself that he had laboured so hard to establish.

This recurrence of division within the Cabinet led to the creation of a 'Political Affairs Bureau' charged with the task of co-ordinating Cabinet policy and of ensuring, via editorial control of the government-backed

Press, that the Cabinet spoke in public with one voice. Within a month, however, it was disbanded again, such was the antagonism that it roused among the Ministers, who regarded its activities as an improper intrusion. 'I don't like to be told what to do as if commanded,' one of them bluntly informed its head.

The expanded budget, which included proposals for the construction of government-owned steel mills in order to end the Navy's reliance on foreign yards, was duly presented to the Diet when it reconvened for its second session in November. As before, it was promptly rejected by the Opposition majority, but this time the Government made no great effort to achieve a compromise and instead five weeks later ordered a dissolution. Yamagata expressed his predictable satisfaction to Matsukata: 'Since the scheming of the political parties has caused this critical situation, the parties must bear the blame.'

To Ito, however, this represented a further blow to his hopes of a gradual progression towards parliamentary democracy. In a despairing bid to preserve them, he now came forward with a radical initiative. 'The difficulty involved in expelling the present party members from the Diet and replacing them with good people is already known to Your Majesty,' he wrote to Meiji. 'Accordingly, there is but one way to cope with this problem: that is, I must relinquish my titles to become a commoner and organise a pro-Government political party. This party will pledge itself to the great principle of Imperial supremacy and will strive to overwhelm the parties espousing liberal-democratic doctrines and in this manner aid the Cabinet.' The proper way to overcome the Opposition, he was saying, was not to ignore it but to defeat it on its own ground.

In his reply the Emperor also expressed the hope that 'good subjects' would obtain a majority in the forthcoming election, but the methods employed to secure it were rather different to those envisaged by Ito. Having successfully dissuaded him from proceding with his idea the Government, under the direction of Yamagata's protégé, Shinagawa, embarked on a campaign of wholesale bribery, intimidation and suppression. Prefectural governors were ordered to employ armed police and troops for this purpose, and in a secret deal negotiated with Toyama his Genyosha minions agreed to add their own thuggish reinforcements in return for an undertaking of a substantial increase in military expenditures.

This marked an ominous advance in Toyama's influence, for it was the first occasion on which he was able to bind the Government, rather than the Opposition parties, to a commitment to overseas expansion. Opposition rallies were regularly broken up and even fired on; '"Flowers of blood" will bloom in the depths of winter,' Shinagawa predicted, or rather prescribed. The final casualty list amounted to 25 dead and nearly 400 seriously wounded. Against all the odds, however, the Opposition parties still managed to retain 163 seats, giving them a majority of 26.

THE EMPEROR ORDAINS

This result confronted the Government with a fresh crisis. Ito resigned from the Presidency of the Privy Council in protest at the attempts to gerrymander the elections, as did the defeated Shinagawa — although not in any spirit of repentance: 'If similar conditions should prevail in the future, I would do the same again and exterminate the obstructionists,' he bragged. Yamagata tried to persuade his protégé that there was no call for such a step, since 'it would adversely affect the confidence of public sentiment, and as a result both Opposition parties would gain advantage, causing untold damage to the Government'. By way of a compromise Shinagawa was transferred from the Cabinet to the Privy Council, and the post of Home Minister was given to Soejima, the long-time ally of Goto and Itagaki in the early Restoration leadership's Tosa-Hizen minority.

The Opposition was by no means mollified by these moves, however; a motion to impeach the Cabinet was lost by only three votes, and when the budget estimates were presented they were reduced by as much as one third. These were then passed to the Upper House, which promptly made good the cuts, but the question arose as to whether they were empowered to do so. Meiji then took it upon himself to refer it to the Privy Council, who obediently found in the Government's favour.

The possibility of dissolution was once more aired, but both sides recognised that such a step would sound the death knell in Western ears for Japan's attempt at 'respectability'. A compromise on the budget therefore had to be hammered out. No sooner had this been done, however, than the Cabinet was enveloped in yet another crisis, caused initially by the new Home Minister's dismissal of his deputy, another protégé of Yamagata who had played an active part in the manipulation of the election. The Ministers for the Army and Navy thereupon resigned in protest, and when it became clear that no other Generals and Admirals were prepared to come forward to replace them Matsukata saw that he himself had no option but to resign as Prime Minister.

This latest development prompted a hurried Conference of the Elder Statesmen in their rôle of 'advising and guiding' the Cabinet. Ito had deliberately stood aloof from Matsukata's desperate attempts to save himself, believing that only he was now capable of commanding both a united Cabinet and a position of trust with the Opposition, which alone could ensure the resumption of progress towards constitutional democracy. He therefore indicated his willingness to take over the Premiership (which was now due to Choshu anyway via the traditional Buggin's turn with Satsuma) on condition that the other Elder Statesmen agreed to serve under him. After some lengthy negotiations all of them gave their assent with the exception of Yamagata, and even he reluctantly fell into line when Ito threatened to retire altogether from politics unless he did so.

Ito's hopes were to enjoy a short life, however, for when the Diet reconvened again in November his budget proposals, which included an extraordinary item of 3.3 million yen as the first instalment towards the cost of the shipbuilding programme, immediately resulted in the usual impasse. Clearly neither dissolution nor resignation offered any solution; still less did Yamagata's suggestion that the money should be spent regardless of the lack of a majority for it and then be approved retrospectively in the next Diet. When the Opposition then submitted a memorial of censure to the Throne, Ito responded in kind and appealed to the Emperor to use his Imperial authority to enforce the budget.

Meiji summoned the Cabinet, Privy Council and presiding officers of both houses of the Diet and issued them with an Imperial Rescript sternly admonishing that 'in the matter of the nation's defences, a single day's neglect may involve a century's regrets.' To provide the necessary funds for the Navy's shipbuilding programme he decreed that all government officials, both civil (including members of the Diet) and military, were to give up one-tenth of their salaries for the next six years, while he himself would likewise contribute 300,000 yen annually from his private purse. This manifestation of Imperial authority was sufficient to see the budget through the Diet without further demur.

If Ito indulged in any momentary self-congratulation at this seeming master-stroke, he was later to view it in a very different light. Far from advancing the representationalist cause that he cherished, the precedent which it set resulted in the ultimate authority residing not with the people nor even with the tight little circle of the ruling oligarchy, but with the Throne. This overt, as opposed to the previous covert, recourse to the Emperor's person elevated the first Article of the Constitution ('The Empire of Japan shall be reigned over and governed by a line of Emperors unbroken for ages eternal') from being a merely notional, quasi-religious concept into an only too substantial political reality.

CONSOLATION GOAL

Now that the budget had effectively been removed from the jurisdiction of the Diet, the Opposition were obliged to cast about for another stick with which to beat the Government. They found it in the person of Hoshi Toru, the Leader of the Lower House, who was alleged to have benefitted improperly from the establishment of the National Stock Exchange. After a series of stormy debates he was eventually voted out of the House, whereupon a further motion was passed to submit an address to the Throne calling for Ito's dismissal as Prime Minister. In his reply, Meiji left them in no doubt that they were considered to have overstepped their proper function: 'The appointment or removal of Ministers of State is absolutely at the will of the Sovereign, and no interference is allowed in this matter.'

Suitably chastened, the parties' attention reverted to the subject of the revision of the treaties, over which negotiations had now resumed with

Britain. Several motions were tabled which sought to define the terms to be demanded, but Ito judged that public discussion of them in the Diet would hinder rather than help the Japanese cause and he again appealed to the Emperor to order a dissolution. In doing so he appeared to be going back on his previously-stated convictions, but at that juncture his over-riding consideration was to present as good a face as possible to the Western Powers. He was afterwards informed by the British that 'the actions taken against the Diet are evocative of our deepest emotions.' In the subsequent elections Ito positively forbade any recurrence of the manipulation of two years earlier, and once again the Opposition parties won a majority.

They returned at once to the attack and on May 31st, only two weeks after the opening of the new session, forced through a no-confidence motion by the overwhelming margin of 253 to 17. In his consternation Ito turned to Yamagata for advice. The reply was as uncompromising as ever: 'It is useless for the Government to consult this kind of assembly. No matter how conciliatory the approach may be, the Diet has no desire to listen. If this Diet continues, the dignity of the Government will suffer and the confidence of the people will be shaken. Under these circum-stances, I believe there is no other course than to settle unhesitatingly on a policy of dissolution.'

However, it was the Emperor himself who again intervened to secure the desired result by refusing to approve the no-confidence motion; in the face of such an expression of Imperial disapproval, the Diet had no option but to vote through its own dissolution. Six weeks later Ito could point to its justification when on July 16th 1894 a new treaty with Britain was finally signed in London. The extraterritorial courts were to be abolished in five years' time, when Japan would also be allowed to set its own level of tariffs. Similar treaties with other Western nations soon followed.

The goal which Ito had nursed for the 26 years since the Restoration was realised at last.

10
First Rays Over Asia

FIRE RAISING

Yamagata had retired from Ito's Cabinet after only eight months to the calmer waters of the Privy Council, where he was free to join with the Emperor in planning the next stages of territorial expansion. 'On all important military matters I will seek your advice,' Meiji told him, 'so please reply candidly.' The 'Peace Preserver' needed no further invitation.

Taking his cue from Russia's start on the construction of the Trans-Siberian Railway, he submitted a report in which he concluded that 'it is not only for this reason that we must prepare adequate military power within the next eight or nine years; we must also be prepared to grasp any opportunity which may present advantages. This is a truly critical juncture in the fortunes of our nation . . . granted that complications are destined to arise in the Orient at no distant date. Japan's wisest plan is to take some decisive action before other Powers become provided with wings of mischief.'

These sentiments were also given a more public airing in certain newspapers; the *Nichi Nichi*, for instance, expressed the hope that it would not be long before 'the Japanese will be able to enter on a heroic career as a strong and enlightened Power in the East,' while the *Kokkai* criticized Ito for his 'negative policy' and demanded: 'What is to be done to cure this malady?' Its own answer was nothing if not specific: 'Nothing short of a foreign complication can rescue the nation from the plight with which it is now afflicted. The planting of a Japanese flag on some of the South Sea Islands, a fight with China over the Korean question, a conflict with Austria on the Sea of Japan — any of these events would suffice for the purpose.'

The opportunity for such a 'complication' was not long in coming. Due to the increasing stature of her Resident in Korea, 'Biggest Man' Yuan Shih-k'ai, China had steadily re-established her former influence there. On March 28th 1894 a couple of Korean government agents succeeded in luring the exiled leader of the opposition, Kim Ok-kiun, to Shanghai where they promptly shot him as he rested on his hotel bed; a Chinese gunboat then bore off the murderers and victim to Korea. Immediately the news reached Japan his supporters there, Oi and Toyama included, launched a 'Society of the Friends of Mr. Kim' and lobbied the Government to demand the return of Kim's body to Japan. Whether or not their hopes for this were genuine, they were speedily dashed by the further news that the body had been cut up and distributed about Seoul on public display.

One of the Genyosha's bosses thereupon called on Mutsu Minemitsu, the Foreign Minister, and demanded that Japan should go to war to avenge Kim's death. Although Mutsu had also, like Toyama and his cronies, served some time in prison for taking part in the Satsuma Rebellion, he happened at that moment to be embroiled in the final stages of negotiations with Britain over treaty revision; he therefore refused to associate himself with anything that might put their successful conclusion in jeopardy and referred him instead to the Vice-Chief of General Staff, Kawakami Soroku. 'What you say is full of good sense,' the General responded, 'but with a Prime Minister such as Ito we cannot entertain the hope of opening hostilities ... However, if there were only some good men who would cross to Korea and start a conflagration, it would then be my duty, which I would not hesitate for a moment to fulfil, to go and extinguish that fire.'

The gang-leader could hardly have wished to hear anything sweeter, and within a matter of days he had set out for Korea with Uchida Ryohei (who, with Toyama, was to play a key role over the next half century in mobilising pressure for the pursuit of Japan's territorial expansion) and thirteen other hand-picked 'fire-raisers' under the banner of a newly-created 'Society of Heavenly Salvation for the Oppressed'. On their arrival they at once made contact with the leaders of the Tonghak or 'Eastern Learning Society', the Korean counterparts of Japan's *sonno-joi* chauvinists. With the support of the ex-Regent whom Yuan had unwisely been persuaded to repatriate from exile in China, the Tonghak had already raised the flag of revolt against the King (or more particularly, the Queen) and his government the previous year.

The rebels now rose again and on May 31st roundly defeated the government forces sent to suppress them, whereupon the King appealed to Yuan for reinforcements from China. News of this reached the Japanese Cabinet during the meeting of June 2nd at which the decision to dissolve the Diet was taken; Yamagata and the Chiefs of Staff also being present, they were able to persuade their colleagues there and then that Japanese troops should be sent to Korea in accordance with the terms of the Li-Ito Convention and that a General Headquarters should be set up in order to co-ordinate the activities of the Army and Navy. Three days later both these steps received Meiji's personal approval.

Yamagata had already drawn up a broad strategic plan of action, having put in hand the necessary intelligence spade-work as far back as 1879, when he had dispatched a 12-strong intelligence mission to China under Katsura Taro; seven years later he had commissioned an acolyte of Toyama to set up a spy network there under the cover of a chain of drugstores with the diverting tradename of 'Halls of Pleasurable Delights', while the Genyosha's nominal head, Hiraoka, became so familiar a figure to Manchu officials while attempting to suborn them to Japan's interest that he was labelled Tokyo's 'unofficial ambassador'. More recently, Kawakami had dispatched two intelligence officers to Korea and China to make an up-to-date evaluation of the strength of the Chinese forces, and their subsequent findings had convinced him that Japan was now in a position to win a trial of strength.

The Chinese reinforcements amounted to no more than 1200 troops, but in order to ensure Japanese superiority Kawakami deliberately exaggerated their number to 5,000 when he sought Mutsu's approval for the dispatch of a force of 8,000 men. When Mutsu observed that Ito was certain to veto such a large force, Kawakami replied that approval for only one brigade was necessary because 'since the Prime Minister knows that one brigade is about 2,000 men, he will not oppose. However, if we dispatch a "combined brigade", it will really number 7,000 to 8,000 men.' Ito was duly deceived.

Similarly, the Japanese Legation in Seoul was informed that only 300 sailors and 20 police guards were being dispatched; the deputy minister there, however, noted in his diary that 'I could sense from the cable that other forces than the 300 sailors would be sent.' Nor was this the end of Kawakami's duplicity. Before the arrival of the main Japanese force the Koreans and the Chinese between them succeeded in putting the Tonghak rebels to flight, as a result of which Yuan indicated his willingness to the Japanese minister Otori Keisuke to negotiate the withdrawal of troops. Kawakami, however, withheld this information from Ito for fear that the expedition would then be ordered to turn back. When Ito presently discovered this, he threatened to resign; Kawakami apologised that it had been due to 'an oversight'.

As more and more Japanese ships appeared at Inchon Otori cabled to Tokyo that 'the landing of too many troops will cause trouble'. Mutsu appears in consequence to have had second thoughts, but he found himself powerless to countermand the wishes of the General Headquarters, who had assumed overall responsibility for troop movements. Otori was accordingly instructed not to negotiate for a withdrawal of troops, but to propose instead the creation of a joint commission to 'guarantee that the maladministration of the Korean government should be reformed.' When this was rejected by Viceroy Li in Peking as a pretext for 'seizing joint rule in Korea', Otori was instructed to 'take advantage of this opportunity to demand cession of telegraph lines between Pusan and Seoul, abolition of taxes on Japanese in the interior and the like.'

The Japanese minister protested in reply that 'we have no grounds whatever to make such demands against Korea ... It appears that some Powers entertain suspicions of our attitude towards Korea in sending such powerful forces. Hope you will take best possible means to explain our object.' The 'object' was duly defined in a cable from Mutsu on the 23rd:

'In consequence of failure of negotiations with the Chinese government, Japanese soldiers cannot now be withdrawn from Korea on sole condition of withdrawal of Chinese troops, even if Tonghak party disturbance is quelled and even if collision with China should thereby become unavoidable sooner or later. We are bound to do singlehanded what we proposed to Chinese government ...'

On the following day Yamagata submitted his plan to the Cabinet: it incorporated the transfer of Supreme Headquarters to the Imperial Palace, the establishment of a military base at Pusan and the deployment of two full divisions. On the 27th, at a meeting attended also by the Emperor, Elder Statesmen, Privy Council and Chiefs of Staff, the Cabinet drew up a list of 'reforms' to be presented to the Korean government together with a demand that Chinese sovereignty should cease to be recognised and that Chinese troops should therefore be expelled, failing which Otori was instructed to inform them that 'we shall have to take matters into our own hands.'

'THE SUN BREAKS THROUGH'

Two weeks later Otori reported back that the Korean response was negative on every count and the decision to go to war was taken in principle. 'It is now necessary to take decisive steps,' he was told in reply. 'Consequently you will commence active movement on some pretext, taking care to do what is least liable to criticism in the eyes of the world.' This latter proviso was made necessary, of course, by the imminent conclusion of negotiations on treaty revision with Britain (when the Japanese Minister there had tentatively sought out the British attitude in the event of war with China, he had been informed that Japanese control of Korea 'would not be tolerated') and two days later (July 14th) Otori was sternly reprimanded for having demanded the expulsion of a British employee of the Korean Government 'since this may cause the great achievement which is on the verge of being consummated in London to collapse in an instant.' In another two days, however, the new treaty was safely signed and sealed, and the way was finally clear.

On July 23rd Japanese troops forced their way into the Royal Palace in Seoul and compelled the King to sign an order for the expulsion of the Chinese and to instal a new 'reforming' Cabinet appointed by his father, the ex-Regent. Two days later three units of the Japanese Navy under the command of a certain Captain Togo Nakagori engaged two Chinese warships off Inchon, causing one to be beached and the other to return to base for repairs; who fired the first shot was never definitely established. Togo's orders had been to intercept some troop transports which spies had reported setting out from Tientsin. Two hours later one of these hove into sight; she was the British-registered S. S. *Kowshing* under charter to the Chinese. When Togo intercepted her and ordered the captain to follow him, the two Chinese generals on board refused to allow the order to be carried out. Without further ado the Japanese then fired two broadsides and a torpedo at point blank range and sank her with the loss of over a thousand lives.

When news of the incident reached London the British lodged a strong protest with Tokyo, but Japan was eventually adjudged to have acted within the letter of International Law in opening fire. On the other hand, the independent testimonies of survivors established beyond doubt that after the *Kowshing* had gone down Japanese machine-guns had continued to fire on two lifeboats and on individuals swimming in the water, setting a grim precedent for what fifty years later had become almost a rule of conduct for the Imperial Navy.

This outbreak of open hostilities was not accompanied — still less preceded — by any formal declaration of war, nor even was a surprise attack launched by part of the 'combined brigade' four nights later on the Chinese garrison guarding the naval approaches to Seoul. It was only after this operation's successful conclusion (which cleared the way for the landing of further contingents) that one was issued by the Imperial Palace on August 1st, notwithstanding, it stated, 'Our ardent wish to promote the prestige of the Country abroad by strictly peaceful methods.'

Whether or not Ito acquiesced in the decision because he saw the diversion which it offered as the only way out of the impasse which had been reached in the Diet, its immediate effect was to still the political debate and unite the whole country behind the Government. If anyone had a mind to criticize, a leading Opposition magazine wrote, 'they should realise that we are fighting to determine once and for all Japan's position in the world ... If our country achieves a brilliant victory, all previous misconceptions will be dispelled. The true nature of our country and of our national character will emerge in all its strength like the sun breaking through a dense fog.' Another edition asserted that its purpose was 'to build the foundation for national expansion in the Far East ... and to take our place alongside the other great expansionist powers.'

The elections held a month later passed off, in contrast with their predecessors, without incident, and the Diet reconvened at Hiroshima, to where Meiji had transferred the Imperial Headquarters in order to put himself in as close a touch as possible with the front. Another Opposition paper declared that 'we propose that at the very beginning of the seventh Diet session members of both Houses, as representatives of the entire nation, unanimously pass the following resolution: both Houses, in obedience to the Imperial declaration of war, are resolved that they will approve all the measures taken by those in power, so that a glorious triumph may be achieved and the situation in the Far East completely changed.' Accordingly, a special War Budget of 150 million yen was passed in the record time of four days without a single dissentient voice raised against it, whereupon both Houses adjourned. In the next session, in

February, the 1895 budget, including supplementary military expenditure of another 100 million yen, was similarly nodded through.

Yamagata was appointed to the command of the First Army, which comprised the original 'combined brigade' and two divisions which had landed subsequently — 'the happiest moment of my life,' he was later to recall. The Chinese fell back on their stronghold of Pyongyang, but after a week's stout resistance the city fell on September 16th 1894 to an infantry suicide assault on the main gate. On the very next day this victory was complemented at sea when the Imperial Navy caught the Chinese fleet in the mouth of the Yalu River as it was about to head home after escorting a convoy of troopships across the Yellow Sea; in the ensuing engagement the Chinese lost half their twelve warships.

With its flank thus secured against the arrival of any further Chinese reinforcements by sea, the First Army now swept all before it. By the end of October Yamagata had crossed the Yalu into Manchuria and advanced inland, setting up a civil administration as he went. In the following month the Second Army under General Oyama Iwao landed on the Kwantung (or Liaotung) Peninsula to capture Dairen and Port Arthur, and in February 1895 it crossed the Chilhi Strait to the Shantung Peninsula and took the stronghold of Weihaiwei.

'THE LINE OF ADVANTAGE'

Yamagata had by then fallen ill and was ordered by Meiji to return to Hiroshima to serve as his senior adviser. In this capacity he drew up a plan for a pincer movement on Peking to be led by the Emperor in person, but before it could be implemented the Chinese Court took fright and instructed Li to sue for peace. Although there were calls in the Diet (particularly from the Opposition) that the war should be continued until China had been totally destroyed, Yamagata soon recognised that it was a propitious moment to come to terms: 'it is certain that the situation in Asia will grow steadily worse in the future, and we must make preparations for another war within the next ten years,' he reasoned. 'Now is the opportune time to end the war. By ending hostilities in our present condition, before exhausting our resources, we have promises of great progress for the future of our nation — of that I am very pleased.'

On Japan's behalf Ito and Mutsu at first called for the cession of Tientsin and two other cities which guarded the approaches to Peking, but after a *sonno-joi* fanatic had attempted to assassinate Li shortly after he had arrived at the negotiating venue of Shimonoseki, they moderated their demands somewhat in deference to Western alarm (the bandages for the Viceroy were prepared, the world was told, by the hands of the Empress herself). Even so, the terms eventually agreed on April 17th were judged by Yamagata to be 'most satisfactory', including as they did the cession in perpetuity of Formosa, the Pescadores Islands and the Kwantung

Peninsula; the opening of seven Chinese ports to Japanese trade; the payment of 360 million yen and permission to occupy Weihaiwei until this indemnity had been cleared; and recognition of 'the full and complete autonomy and independence of Korea'.

So the first stage of Japan's expansionist programme had been fulfilled; Formosa and the Pescadores provided stepping stones for further advances to the south, while the Kwantung Peninsula and Korea afforded the necessary bridgeheads in the east. Naturally, her propagandists painted a quite different account of the motives for attacking Korea: the Lame Democrat Okuma, for instance, declared that 'they took arms against China only because they believed her supremacy over Korea was a perpetual menace to the security of their Empire and to the peace of the East', while Hishida Seiji maintained that 'Japan fought China mainly for the reform of the corrupt administration of Korea, which was endangering Korean independence and menacing the interests of the world'. Ex-Home Minister Soejima even drew on the continental exploits of the mythical Empress Jingu in order to support his statement that 'all historians know that the claims of Japan [to Korea] were earlier [than China's] in origin and had been exercised for a longer space of time.'

All were at pains to assert that there had been no plans to dispatch any troops there until China had done so, but one Western observer was not so easily deceived. Isabella Bird wrote of the arrival of the first Japanese on June 21st that 'their purpose was well concealed under cover of giving efficacious protection to Japanese subjects in Korea', recording at the same time that 'Japanese agents scoured the country for rice, and every cattie of it which could be spared from consumption was bought in preparation for the war, of which no one in Korea dreamed of at that time.' Describing the march of the main force on Seoul the following month, she commented that 'it was apparent that this skilful and extraordinary move was not made for the protection of her colonies in Chemulpo and Seoul, nor yet against Korea ... there can be no question that Japan had been planning such a movement for years. She had made accurate maps of Korea ... while even as far as the Tibetan frontier Japanese officers in disguise had gauged the strength and weakness of China'. By October *The Times* was agreeing that 'there is evidence to hand showing that the present campaign has been contemplated by Japan for at least fifteen years, and it is therefore not unreasonable to conclude that the Japanese have long since decided what conditions of peace they would make in case of victory'; it went on to predict almost exactly the demands presented at Shimonoseki six months later.

Yamagata, in the privacy of a petition to the Throne outlining the need for a further expansion of the military budget, gave a rather franker account of Japanese ambitions: 'As a result of the present war we have gained new overseas territories which require expanded military forces for their defences. Beyond that, it is necessary, if we are to ride the wave

of victory, to become a leader in the Far East . . . Our military preparedness up to this time has been used chiefly to maintain the line of
sovereignty. However, if we are to make the result of the recent war
something more than a hollow victory and move on to become the leader
of the Far East, it will be absolutely necessary to extend the line of
advantage. Our present military strength is inadequate for maintaining
our new line of sovereignty. It follows that it is inadequate for extending
the line of advantage and becoming dominant in the Far East'.

In the same memorial he also warned that 'of course, Russia, England,
France and other powers with a stake in the Far East will surely alter their
policies . . .' As we shall see in the next chapter, the response of the West
to the implications embodied in the terms of the peace settlement was
indeed a rapid one.

What they were slower — much slower — to appreciate was the extent
of the power granted to Meiji by the new Constitution and the advantage
that he had already begun to take of this *carte blanche* in pursuit of his
father's dreams of overseas conquest. Two years earlier he had prefaced
the Imperial Rescript with which he had bludgeoned the Diet into finding
the funds for the shipbuilding programme with the statement that 'In the
earliest beginnings of the Empire the Sovereign pledged himself to
administer the affairs of state not only within the home borders, but also
beyond the seas'; at the outbreak of the war he had assumed a personal
command of the campaign; and now on its successful conclusion he moved
to perpetuate his direct control over the armed forces by appointing his
cousin Prince Komatsu to the position of Commander-in-Chief.

Thirty-six years later Hirohito was similarly to appoint his uncle
Prince Kanin as Army Chief of Staff to oversee the invasion of Manchuria.

11
Dark Cloud

TRIPLE INTERVENTION

The progress of the war had been closely monitored in the West by the five Powers with interests at stake in China, and even before the fighting began both Britain and Russia had made unsuccessful attempts to mediate between the two sides.

On October 6th 1894 Britain attempted to organise a five-nations intervention, but Germany and the United States refused to take part. German industrialists, however, whose trade with China had grown under the energetic leadership of Friedrich Krupp to a volume second only to that of Britain and who were alarmed at the prospect of losing this hard-won ground to the Japanese invader, persuaded Berlin to offer to send a civil servant, then employed by the customs office at Tientsin, to Japan to negotiate a peace. The Chinese Government accepted his services, and he duly arrived at Kobe in mid-November.

The Foreign Ministry in Tokyo indicated at first that it was prepared to receive the German, but the daily expectation of the news of the fall of Port Arthur was scarcely calculated to put the expansionists in an accommodating mood. After an all-night session of the Cabinet at the Imperial Headquarters in Hiroshima, his credentials were rejected as 'insulting' and he was dismissed without even being informed of Japan's terms for a settlement. China then attempted to meet this criticism by dispatching two Court officials armed with what were considered both by the Court and the Western Ministries in Peking to be the necessary credentials.

The Japanese Cabinet had in the meantime decided on the list of demands to be presented, but the arrival of these two envoys preceded the Second Army's landing on the Shantung peninsula and they were again rejected as insufficiently accredited — indeed, they were even put under arrest. Only Li Hung-chang himself, they were informed, would be considered acceptable, but even his dispatch would be 'wholly useless' unless he was prepared to negotiate on the basis of Japan's demands, which were now finally disclosed.

Their publication gave rise to a further round of hurried consultations in the Western Ministries. The outcome was a pledge of support to Li in resisting them from Russia and France (who had recently concluded an alliance with each other) together with Germany, although Britain and America, suspicious of the others' own territorial designs in the area, continued to adopt a neutral stance. Russian objections centred in particular on the proposed cession of the Kwantung Peninsula, because she was on the point of seeking from China permission to run the Trans-Siberian Railway through Manchuria to Port Arthur (in preference to Vladivostok, which was closed by ice for five months of the year). Armed with the assurance of this support, Li put his signature with an easy mind to the Japanese demands at Shimonoseki on April 17th; their final ratification was set for May 8th.

Six days later the three Powers duly handed in notes to Deputy Foreign Minister Hayashi Tadasu (Mutsu having been taken ill), advising Japan 'in a spirit of sincere friendship' against taking up the Kwantung cession; for good measure, Russia put her Pacific Fleet on 24-hour stand-by. Finance Minister Count Sergei Witte, the moving spirit behind the Trans-Siberian project, had advised the Tsar that 'if Japan should not, contrary to our expectations, listen to our diplomatic insistence, our squadron must be ordered to open hostilities against the Japanese fleet and to bombard Japanese ports without occupying any points'.

Meiji summoned Ito, Yamagata, Saigo Tsugumichi (now Navy Minister) and senior staff officers to an emergency conference the very next day. Although Mutsu wrote from his sickbed that they should 'not yield a step even at the risk of creating a new crisis', the consensus was that they had no option but to back down: 'since our overseas troops are concentrated in Kwantung and our fleet in the Pescadores Islands and our domestic armed forces are nearly zero, we might not be able to defend ourselves,' it was feared. They therefore offered to give up Port Arthur, but when this too was peremptorily rejected, they signalled their surrender of the whole peninsula on May 5th. Four days later the three Powers wrote to express their 'satisfaction' at the decision.

News of the Triple Intervention, as it became known, and the resultant retrocession of what was seen as the choicest prize of the victories on the mainland, had already leaked out to the Japanese public and immediately excited a nationwide storm of protest notwithstanding the Government's closure of all newspapers that gave voice to any criticism. In a further move to quell it Meiji issued an Imperial Rescript declaring that the country had 'accomplished its aim in the war', while Yamagata was given the unenviable task of explaining the order to withdraw to the commanders in the field at Port Arthur, several of whom argued against acceptance of such a humiliation and demanded instead a renewal of hostilities. On his return the 'Peace Preserver' was raised to the rank of Marquis and presented with 50,000 yen as a personal gift from the Emperor. Ito's reward, by contrast, was to receive the attention of Genyosha assassins, although their plot on his life was discovered just in time.

It was not long, however, before these feelings of outraged resentment gave way to a renewed determination that Japan should assert herself on the world stage. A government-inspired slogan, 'Suffer Privations For Revenge', was quickly taken up as the new rallying cry, to which Meiji lent his own encouragement by the creation of a 'Military Virtue Society' under the tutelage of one of the Imperial princes. In the words of one contemporary propagandist, 'it became to Japan as clear as daylight that the new position she had acquired in the Orient by her victory over China could be maintained, and even her independence guarded, only by an armed strength big enough to give her a voice among the first Powers of the world. If she would not retire into herself and finally cease to exist, she must compete with the greatest of nations, not only in the arts of peace, but also in those of war.'

Such sentiments sounded a convenient echo to Yamagata's argument for an extension of 'the line of advantage'. So, even more specifically, did a call from Goto on the Liberal Party benches in the Diet for the annexation not only of Korea, but also of the three provinces of Manchuria. By November the Party had entered into formal alliance with the Government and 'People's Man' Itagaki had joined the Cabinet as Home Minister, assuring an easy passage for the new budget and its proposals for yet another vast increase in military expenditure; the creation of six new divisions increased the Army's share from 10 to 52 million yen at a single stroke, while over the next five years the combined annual budget of the Army and Navy (which was to have 4 new battleships, 16 cruisers and over 600 other craft) was to rise from 20.6 million yen to a staggering 133.1 million — at which level it accounted for over half the entire national budget.

MORE 'REFORMS' FOR KOREA

Given the interest shown by the West in the outcome of the war, the Triple Intervention, profoundly disagreeable as it was, did not take Ito and his Government altogether by surprise, and they had already taken steps to consolidate their hold on Korea long before the inception of peace negotiations. The initial plan of using the ex-Regent to launch the programme of projected 'reforms' had soon foundered when it became clear that that incorrigible reactionary, far from being interested in initiating change, was concerned only to pursue his personal vendetta against his daughter-in-law, Queen Min. The situation, it was decided in Tokyo, demanded the presence of a 'man of great stature and ability'; Otori was accordingly recalled and replaced by 'Misui-Man' Inoue, who as Foreign Minister a decade earlier had given his blessing to Goto's scheme to fund Kim Ok-kiun and his pro-Japanese 'progressive' party.

Inoue immediately ordered the recall from exile in Japan of Kim's former lieutenant Pak Young-hyo and secured his appointment as Home

Minister. A general amnesty was declared for the other accomplices in the abortive coup of 1884, several of whom were also installed in the Cabinet. Inoue then, on January 8th 1895, compelled the King to go through a public ceremony of repeating in person the renunciation of Chinese suzerainty which had been proclaimed in his name the previous July, and of pledging himself to a list of 'reforms', one of which decreed that 'Palace matters and the government of the country must be kept separate', another that 'the Queen and Royal Family are not allowed to interfere'.

This was followed by the third stage of the programme, the drafting in of Japanese 'advisers' to instruct the army, run the railways, administer the post office and telegraph network and revise the taxation system in accordance with Japanese law, leading Isabella Bird to remark that the King was reduced to being 'practically a salaried register of decrees'. Other immigrants were also encouraged to come and set up in private business; over 5000 settled in Seoul during the next two years and in the other main towns Japanese accounted for almost 95% of foreign residents.

An undertaking on such a scale naturally required considerable financial backing, but when Inoue applied to Tokyo for a loan of 3 million yen (to be made available through a pseudonymous bank account), he received to his chagrin a markedly cool response. This did not imply any criticism of his own actions, Ito hastened to reassure him: 'Since you assumed your position, you have carried out a proper policy and set definite principles of reform. This is very good, but one thing I fear is that after the war the financial situation will be difficult to balance ...'

It was not money that was the real sticking point, however, so much as the over-riding need, following the fright of the Triple Intervention, to allay Western, and particularly Russian, suspicions of Japan's designs on the 'full and complete autonomy and independence of Korea' supposedly guaranteed by the Treaty of Shimonoseki. On June 3rd Mutsu wrote in a memorandum to his Cabinet colleagues that 'they [the three Powers] bring up one problem after another. Certainly they will ask about the Korean policy, so before another problem comes up we should decide whether to continue our policy without change or, discontinuing interference, to return to a condition of ordinary treaty relations, conducted actively or passively. At any rate it is urgent that we decide on our objectives, so please obtain an Imperial decision.' Meiji evidently decreed that caution was the order of the day, for 24 hours later Mutsu recorded that 'our future Korean policy will have the objective of discontinuing interference insofar as is possible and causing Korea to stand up by herself. Thus it is decided to take up passive objectives. Consequently, we shall not interfere strongly in Korean railroad and telegraph matters.'

Inoue decided to return to Tokyo to learn at first hand the reasons behind this apparent volte face. He could not have foreseen that his own position would be undermined in his absence.

Secure in the knowledge of Inoue's backing and that of the Japanese troops stationed in Seoul, Pak had grown so much in confidence that he began to entertain the idea of dispensing with such support. 'Inoue will be here only a few years and the army will leave,' he told Sugimura Yotaro, the First Secretary at the Japanese Ministry, 'and then what will I depend on? Therefore I must increase my power, not only to keep my position but also to accomplish the reform of my country.' He systematically ousted his opponents from the Cabinet, eventually obtaining even the resignation of the Prime Minister and his own appointment in his place, causing the American Minister to remark that he had become 'virtual dictator' although he seemed to 'have a sincere regard for his own country and to resent Japan's attempts to take everything to herself'.

Shortly before his departure on June 7th Inoue was heard to complain that 'things had gone too far' and that 'no one listened to him'. However, when Pak tried the following month to coerce the King into replacing the Court Garrison with two Japanese-trained battalions, the latter, prompted as ever by his Queen, seized the opportunity of Inoue's absence to dismiss Pak and order his arrest. Pak duly sought refuge in the Japanese Ministry, where he was taken in despite Sugimura's undertaking to the King 'to do my best to notify the Japanese not to help Pak'. A posse of Japanese plain clothes policemen then escorted him to a ship at Inchon and safety.

On his return Inoue did what he could to mend his fences with the Palace by 'caressing the King' and generally being 'very conciliatory to everybody', but his efforts only succeeded in alienating all parties concerned. On August 29th he again requested Tokyo that '3 million yen should be sent under the [pseudonymous] name suggested', but by then his masters had decided that other, more direct methods were needed to restore the situation, and General Miura Goro, one of Yamagata's most faithful Choshu henchmen, was dispatched to take his place. Inoue at first took it that Miura was being sent as a subordinate rather than as a replacement, and when he was subsequently enlightened he protested his 'embarrassment and dismay'.

In his parting audience at the Palace, he gave the King an assurance that in the event of any attempted treason, 'the Japanese government would not fail to protect the Royal House even by force of arms, and so secure the safety of the kingdom.' Within a month the world would learn just what value to attach to such an assurance.

MURDER MISFIRES

On the night of October 7th the Japanese-trained battalions, accompanied by a number of off-duty Japanese policemen in civilian dress but armed with swords and pistols, rushed the Court Garrison, most of whose weapons Miura had taken the precaution of removing beforehand. The Japanese garrison then arrived to stand guard while their accomplices forced their way into the Queen's quarters, pulling the hair of the Court

Ladies in an attempt to force them to disclose the whereabouts of their mistress and actually killing two of them in mistake for her. When she was finally cornered by a Japanese swordsman, the Minister of the Royal Household tried to shield her and had both his hands lopped off for his pains. The Queen herself was then stabbed repeatedly before being carried outside, thrown still breathing on to a pile of brushwood, soused in kerosene and incinerated.

The helpless King had meanwhile been taken prisoner in his own quarters and the ex-Regent, who by prearrangement with Miura was standing by in readiness, then entered the Palace and issued a proclamation dismissing the 'base fellows' in the Cabinet and replacing them with his own nominees. This was followed three days later by a further Royal edict (although the King absolutely refused to sign it) which attempted to justify the appalling crime and even pretended that the Queen might still be alive.

The Western Ministers in Seoul unanimously refused to recognise the new regime, and in a belated acknowledgement of the universal revulsion which news of the episode had excited, Tokyo recalled Miura, Sugimura and others on the Ministry staff to stand trial at Hiroshima. Sugimura's diary was produced and put the complicity of himself and Miura beyond all doubt; in it, the latter was quoted as having said that 'to cut the evil root of twenty years, the Queen should be disposed of when you enter the Palace.'

Despite this unambiguous admission, they were acquitted on the grounds that 'there was not sufficient evidence to prove that any of the accused actually committed the crime originally meditated by them', while the outside world was assured that the events had come 'as a complete surprise and that the Japanese Government had nothing whatever to do with it'. The imaginations of the official propagandists subsequently had a field day: Soejima, for instance, attributed it to 'a number of Korean rebels joined by a handful of Japanese rowdies', Hishida to 'the result of a plot led by the reform party', and Asakawa Kanichi to 'some bravoes who had escorted the ex-Regent to the King's Palace where he was to present a plan of reform'.

Whoever it was who had sanctioned the atrocity was soon made to see the extent of his miscalculation. Far from securing Korea against Russian encroachment, it effectively delivered control of the country (for the time being, at least) into the hands of the Tsar. Only a month later Miura's replacement, Komura Jutaro, sought Tokyo's permission to 'have Japanese troops enter the Palace to prevent the King from running to the Russian Legation', but this was firmly refused by Saionji, who had replaced the terminally-ill Mutsu as Foreign Minister.

Komura had to be content with redoubling his watch on the Palace, but even in this he was unsuccessful: on February 11th 1896 a loyal maidservant was able to smuggle the King (or 'Emperor', as he now defiantly styled himself) and his son out of the grounds and into the custody of the Russians. Komura was left to look on powerlessly as the Cabinet was dissolved by

Royal decree, the Japanese-trained battalions disbanded and the whole catalogue of Japanese-inspired 'reforms' repealed. In May the monarch formally requested Russia to protect his country.

In the same month Yamagata was dispatched to St. Petersburg (on the pretext of attending the new Tsar Nicholas's coronation) to negotiate an accommodation which would allow Japan to concentrate on her military building programme. The agreement that subsequently emerged committed both sides to guaranteeing Korea's independence and the sovereignty of the King while allowing them to station an equal number of troops in the country. Yamagata proposed setting a specific demarcation line, but the Russians declined the suggestion, and in the end it was agreed merely that there should be an 'unoccupied area' between the two forces.

DOUBLE HUMILIATION

While thus successfully neutralising Japan in Korea, Russia was at the same time pushing ahead with plans for the construction of a railway across the north of Manchuria to cut some 600 miles off the projected route of the TSR (Trans-Siberian Railway). As a first step towards buying Chinese goodwill, Russia combined with France to loan, on strikingly generous terms, the greater part of the money required to pay off the indemnity to Japan imposed by the Treaty of Shimonoseki; in the event of any default, it was agreed that Russia should have a first claim on China's customs revenue. A Russo-Chinese Bank was then set up to handle these arrangements. Viceroy Li was also invited to St. Petersburg for the coronation celebrations. In order to throw Yamagata's spies off the scent, he was transferred to a Russian ship at Port Said and finished his voyage at Odessa.

When the proposal for a railway through Manchuria was put to the Chinese Court, the reply was that they had already determined to build such a line for themselves. Li, however, was to prove more amenable and, wearied perhaps by twenty years of single-handed effort to present China as a credible force to the outside world, succumbed to a bribe, albeit to one of no less than one and a half million dollars. On his return from Russia he was obliged to part with half of this huge sum by Dowager Empress Tz'u-hsi (who represented the real power behind the Throne and was shortly to abandon all formal pretence to the contrary by forcing her son's abdication) before she would put her name to the deal. It was agreed to set up a Chinese Eastern Railway Company under the aegis of the Russo-China Bank; the lease was to run for eighty years, and the Company was to have the exclusive administration of all land deemed necessary for the line's construction and maintenance. In return, China was to enjoy the protection of a mutual defence pact against 'any aggression directed by Japan against the Russian-occupied territory of China or that of Korea'.

As if this news was not galling enough to Japanese ambitions, it was quickly followed by other similar Chinese concessions to the West for railway construction, which encouraged Russia again in her turn to realise her ultimate plan for a branch line from the Chinese Eastern Railway (CER) at Harbin to a port on the Yellow Sea. The Russian envoy entrusted with the negotiations carried a million roubles with him, but he was disappointed to find Li proof against any further such encouragements; the Viceroy was only prepared to offer an undertaking not to grant such a concession to any other Power.

Consolation then came unexpectedly to hand, however, as a result of Germany's seizure of Kiaochow on the pretext of the murder of two Lutheran missionaries in the Shantung peninsula. When she was subsequently granted a 99-year lease on a 30-mile enclave surrounding the city and its port Tsingtao, the Russian fleet was ordered to take up station around Port Arthur in the hope of exacting a similar prize. They did not have to wait very long: on March 25th 1898 Li, swallowing his scruples once more, presented them with a 25-year lease on the whole Kwantung peninsula complete with the right to station troops, build defence works and link it by rail to the projected CER line at Harbin.

Britain, who up to this point had adopted the rôle of the disapproving onlooker in 'splendid isolation' while her rivals picked over the Chinese carcass, now decided to enter the fray, coming away with the rather lesser prize of a 25-year lease on the barely-defensible harbour of Weihaiwei in return for a loan to provide the final instalment of the Shimonoseki indemnity (upon payment of which Japan was committed to evacuating that port). Finally, France also took advantage of another anti-missionary outbreak in the southern province of Kwangtung (not to be confused with Kwantung/Liaotung) to secure a 99-year lease on the port of Kwangchowan and construction rights for a Tongking-Yunnan railway; it was by pleading that this constituted a threat to nearby Hong Kong that Britain was then able to obtain a similar lease on the Kowloon peninsula.

In the space of three years Japan had thus seen all the gains on the mainland which victory had brought her in 1895 first wrested from her by the Western Powers on the pretext of preserving China's independence, and then divided up amongst themselves. On her Pacific flank too she suffered a check which was received as scarcely less of a humiliation. Japanese interest in Hawaii had begun in 1868 with the dispatch of recruits to the labour-intensive sugar cane industry on the islands, which had led ten years later to the first Japanese purchase of land there. While on a visit to Japan in 1882 the Hawaiian king had been so carried away by the scale of his reception as to propose a matrimonial match between the two royal families and even an Asiatic federation under Japanese leadership.

Tempting as such a suggestion must have been (and Meiji declared that such a federation 'cannot only be to the benefit of Japan and Hawaii, but to that of the whole of Asia also'), he felt obliged to decline it for fear of offending America, whom he saw as his best ally in the fight for his first priority of that day, the revision of the unequal treaties. 'However,' he added, 'I ardently hope that such a union may be realised at some future day, and keeping it constantly in my mind I never fail, whenever time allows me, to discuss the means of bringing about that result . . .' By 1896 Japanese immigrants accounted for 60% of Hawaii's labour force. When attempts to stem this flood brought a Japanese warship into Honolulu harbour, America responded by annexing the islands, indignantly as Meiji protested. A few months later the U.S.A. went on to incorporate the Philippines in the wake of her victory over Spain, and the recollection of Bismarck's lecture in *realpolitik* must have rung with a still harsher truth in Japanese ears.

'DESCENT TO DEMOCRACY'

On the domestic front, this mounting series of indignities at the hands of the West not surprisingly proved too much for the spirit of collaboration between the political parties and the ruling oligarchy which had been fostered by the Korean War. The issue between them was one of power rather than policy; the budgets funding the military building programme continued to be voted through almost on the nod, and in calling for the acquisition of Manchuria Goto was publicly enshrining the private plans of the expansionists in the Liberal Party manifesto. When Ito sought to bolster his position in the Diet by offering a Cabinet post to Okuma (who had now enlarged his Progressive Party's representation by merging it with a number of other smaller parties), Itagaki objected so forcibly to the inclusion of his old rival that Ito submitted his resignation.

He was succeeded as Prime Minister by 'I'll Investigate' Matsukata, with the backing of the Progressives, but this alliance in turn fell out over the new party's increasing demands. In January 1898 Meiji once more turned to Ito to step into the breach. In the ensuing general election the Progressives and Liberals won 99 and 98 seats respectively, and when Ito proposed an increase in the land tax to cover a projected budget deficit of 35 million yen, he was defeated by the unprecedented margin of 247 votes to 24. It was now apparent that no administration could hope to govern without a majority in the Diet. Itagaki and Okuma, persuaded at last to swallow their mutual antipathy, decided to capitalise on their joint position of strength by merging their parties into a single anti-oligarchy front, the Constitutional Party.

On completing his tour of duty in the field at Port Arthur, Yamagata had resigned as War Minister before taking off on his diplomatic errand to St. Petersburg. On his return he was advised by his go-between with the Emperor, the Vice-Minister of the Imperial Household, to 'postpone assuming office until a time when the nation is confronted by serious problems' in view of the increasing dependence of any would-be Prime Minister on the collaboration of the political parties. He had therefore

been content for the moment to leave the stage to his own nominees in the
Cabinet (in particular, the War Minister, Katsura) and in the Diet to the
Kokumin Kyokai, a group of ultra-nationalists formed under the leader-
ship of his nephew-in-law Shinagawa and Navy Minister Saigo
Tsugumichi.

However, the formation of the Constitutional Party and its opposition
to the increase in the land tax brought the 'Peace Preserver' hurrying out
of the wings.

At a hastily-convoked Conference of the Elder Statesmen on June 24th
1898 Ito proposed to counter this development by forming his own pro-
Government party. Yamagata at once objected that 'if you organise a
political party, it will probably mark the beginning of party cabinets. Isn't
the system of party cabinets opposed to our national entity [*kokutai*] and the
spirit of the Imperially-bestowed Constitution, and a descent to democratic politics?' For Yamagata the concept of Cabinet dependence on
political parties was as noxious as ever, but when Ito replied with the
suggestion that Yamagata himself should appoint a cabinet, he was caught
off guard and obliged to decline. The only other alternative, Ito then
declared, was to leave it to the leaders of the Constitutionalists, as the
majority party, to form a government — a proposal so radical that his
colleagues were reportedly 'struck dumb with astonishment'. In a black
mood Yamagata wrote to a friend of 'the downfall of the Meiji Government . . . I believe retirement is the only course open to me.'

MARRIAGE OF CONVENIENCE

He soon recovered from his despair, however, when on reconsidering the
position he saw that there was still one way of ensuring the survival of the
military building programme and its ultimate objective, territorial expansion. Three days later he instructed his Court go-between (now promoted
to full Minister of the Imperial Household) that 'when the Emperor orders
Itagaki and Okuma to form the next Cabinet the order must ask them to
select [all the] Cabinet Ministers except the Army and Navy Ministers'.
The current holders of those offices, Katsura and Saigo, were being urged
to resign by Chief-of-Staff Kawakami and by withholding recommendations for their successors to make it impossible to complete the new
Cabinet, but they now received an Imperial order to remain at their
posts. Duly reappointed, they lost no time in extracting as a condition of
their service a pledge from Itagaki and Okuma that they would 'agree to
supplement the shortage of funds for the post-war projects and to provide
the essential things'. The new government was thus effectively hobbled
even before it had taken office.

Katsura then bent his considerable energies to ensuring its downfall by
exacerbating the differences which soon arose between its component
parts and driving a wedge between them. A senior member of the

Constitutionalists wrote of him that 'I long ago perceived that he was not merely a soldier, but was without doubt scheming for the oligarchy ... When the balance of power argument occurred within the party and the struggle between the two factions became intense, he would adopt a fair, impartial attitude in public, but in private he would act in concert with the Elder Statesmen outside the Cabinet and continually attempt behind-the-scenes manoeuvres. His plan was to organise the next Cabinet during the disturbance over the split in the Constitutional Party, and in this he was conspicuously successful.'

One incident in particular which he was able to turn to advantage was a speech by the Education Minister, Ozaki Yukio, during which, in warning against an over-emphasis on economic success, he depicted the ultimate degeneration of the country into a republic governed by Mitsui. Although it was, of course, presented as pure hypothesis, the mere suggestion that Japan might ever become a republic was seized on as constituting blasphemy, an accusation which Katsura then reinforced by spreading false reports that it had given rise to talk of mutiny in the Army. On October 23rd he was able to report to his patron Yamagata that the Emperor had ordered the unfortunate Ozaki to be dismissed, and that a fierce argument between the Progressive and Liberal factions could be expected to ensue over the choice of a successor. His highest hopes were fulfilled, for the subsequent dissension became so bitter that within a week Itagaki had submitted the Government's resignation.

Katsura's next step was to call a Conference of the Elder Statesmen who, with the exception of Ito, who had taken himself off to China, decided together that Yamagata's moment had come. Knowing that Ito would very probably oppose such a choice, they had to move quickly. Yamagata was summoned from his Kyoto villa that same day and received the appointment as Prime Minister at an Imperial audience on November 5th. In anticipation of such a move Okuma had telegraphed to Ito to return immediately the Government had fallen, but Ito's ship did not reach Nagasaki until the 7th.

The need for funds to cover the budget deficit was now critical and, distasteful as it was to him, even Yamagata acknowledged that the means of raising them required the approval of a majority in the Diet. Outwardly he remained as uncompromisingly hostile as ever to the idea of collaboration with the political parties. He filled his Cabinet almost entirely with admirals, generals and peers, announcing that 'I do not consider Cabinets organised on a party basis as consistent with the spirit of the Constitution enacted by the Emperor ... People talk of an alliance with the Constitutionalists. If their policies and ours agree, we may march in step. But there is no alliance.' Behind the scenes, however, he soon involved himself in some prolonged horse-trading with Itagaki and his party. Being the more rurally-based of the two parties (after the fall of the coalition Okuma had at once revived the Progressives under the new title of Real Constitutionalists), their support for an increase in the land tax was seen as the more important, although Itagaki's previous record of venality was no doubt another factor taken into account.

After fêting the 'People's Man' as the spectator of honour at the annual Army-Navy manoeuvres, Yamagata retired with his guest to the home of a friendly tycoon to negotiate a formal agreement. Two weeks later its terms were published: in return for the Constitutionalists' support for an increase in the land tax, Yamagata undertook to arrange the passage through the Diet of several major items of Constitutionalist policy and to extend the franchise, at present restricted to little more than 400,000 (males) out of a total population of 42 million, to just under one million. Only on Itagaki's request for places in the Cabinet for himself and his colleagues did Yamagata refuse to budge.

'A LIFE-AND-DEATH HOLD'

Even with the votes of the Constitutionalists in his pocket Yamagata was still some way short of commanding an absolute majority in the Diet, especially as Okuma had now joined forces with the other Opposition groups to form an Anti-Land Tax Increase League and was busily mobilising a nationwide campaign in its support. The 'Peace-Preserver' countered along familiar lines: he ordered the League to be disbanded, banned all its supporters outside Tokyo from coming to the capital and forbade all public discussion on the subject.

When even these measures appeared unlikely to secure a majority, he fell back on another well-tried ploy: he procured almost a million yen from the Imperial Household purse via his go-between, its Minister, to buy the necessary votes. A large part of this sum found its way into the pocket of former Stock Exchange Insider Hoshi Toru, who on the formation of the Constitutionalists had arbitrarily abandoned his post as Ambassador in Washington and returned to Japan to press his nose into this new trough. Failing to win a place for himself in the Cabinet, he had built a power base instead on Tokyo City Council, and in return for the gift of a monopoly of the city's railways he contracted to deliver the votes of the councillors' allies in the Diet. The budget could now be safely laid before the House, and it was duly passed by a majority of 37.

Neither side in this marriage of convenience harboured any illusions as to its durability, and indeed both began almost from the day of its consummation to make provision for the inevitable divorce. Even before that Hoshi had confided to a friend that 'there is no choice but to have Ito become Prime Minister', and Saionji had written to his patron (Ito) that both [parties] ardently wish to combine forces with you. However, it is extremely doubtful that they desire to rely on your statemanship because they have undergone sudden enlightenment. Their range of vision does not extend outside their diverse party interests.' Realist that he was, perhaps even Saionji would have been surprised at the frankness of Hoshi's next sentence: 'However, we must not let old men lead us for long; once the foundations have been laid let us expel all the old men, beginning with Ito, and do as we please.' Even to Yamagata's face he was scarcely less frank (anticipating Stalin's oft-quoted remark): 'At the very least I control forty men in the Diet. Pray tell me, how many soldiers can you mobilise there?'

On his side Yamagata had taken steps to consolidate his position in advance by creating the Board of Admirals and Marshals to serve as the highest advisory body on military affairs; besides himself, it comprised Prince of the Blood Komatsu, Oyama and Saigo, all of whom were then raised to the appropriate rank. As Prime Minister, he now pushed steadily ahead with a series of measures designed to ensure that the fulfilment of his plans would not be subject to interference from the political parties.

Before embarking on this programme, he naturally took the trouble to arm himself with the Emperor's authority. 'The affairs of state would be handled competently by a politician like Ito, but without Ito's ability I rely on your aid in the conduct of political affairs,' he informed Meiji in a secret message. 'My only aim is that Imperial authority should be extended and Imperial prestige should not decline. I hope you approve of these things.' His first step was to stiffen the entry exams to all grades of the Civil Service to a degree that members of the political parties would be effectively excluded from it. This action in itself almost drove the Constitutionalists to withdraw their support there and then, and, anticipating the worst, Yamagata re-formed his supporters in the Kokumin Kyokai into a political party of his own, the Imperialists. However, the promised extension of the franchise was not yet on the statute book, and Itagaki was accordingly persuaded to knuckle down for the moment.

Thus emboldened, Yamagata next greatly increased the powers of the oligarchic Privy Council so that it became no longer a merely advisory body on constitutional questions, but an arm of the executive over whole areas of government and a further barrier to the participation of the political parties. His final move, embodied in Imperial Ordinances 193 and 194 and promulgated on May 15th 1900, had the most far-reaching consequences of all: under them only generals and admirals on the *active* list were now allowed to serve as War and Navy Ministers. Although the 1888 order had limited those offices to men of that rank, they were still, in theory at least, open to those who had retired and were no longer under the thumb of the military establishment. Now, by withholding nominees to fill these posts, the establishment would be able to block the formation of any government which refused to promote its territorial ambitions.

In the words of one commentator, 'this Ordinance, more than any other single piece of legislation, gave the militarists a life-and-death hold over all subsequent Cabinets.' It was modified slightly after Meiji's death in 1913, but restored in full by Hirohito in 1936; the invasion of China followed a year later, the attack on Pearl Harbor four years after that.

12

Black Dragon

'OPEN DOOR' IN CHINA

Thanks to the successful passage of each new and larger budget, the military building programme was now well on its way to completion.

The implications had not gone unnoticed abroad in the meantime, particularly in St. Petersburg. 'It cannot be doubted that the immense armaments of the Japanese are directed against us and that Japan is eagerly preparing for an armed conflict with us,' the Tsar's new minister in Tokyo had reported in 1897. 'It is equally unquestionable that this conflict will break out over the Korean question.' He must have been further sobered the following year to read a letter in the *Hochi Shimbun* which declared that 'whatever reasons existed to fight China in 1894 exist with incomparably greater force to fight Russia today ... To look back upon events since the Retrocession of Liaotung [Kwantung] must make every Japanese thrill with indignation. If ever there was a time when the country should assert itself, this is it.'

Having finally obtained the right to run a line through Manchuria, Russia's entire Far Eastern policy now hung on the completion of the Trans-Siberian Railway, making it imperative that Japan's rapidly expanding army should not be given the slightest pretext for interference. The more conciliatory attitude that sprang from this realisation was readily reciprocated by a Japan which had been made acutely aware of her isolation in the international field by the Triple Intervention and subsequent events in China. Only a month after her acquisition of the Kwantung lease Russia came to an agreement with Japan whereby both sides undertook not to assist Korea either militarily or financially without the other's consent, but no bar was put on Japan's economic development of the country in view of the scale of her established commercial activities there.

The expansionists needed no second invitation to reassert a dominating Japanese presence. By the end of the year Japanese outnumbered all other foreign residents in Korea by a ratio of six to one, the Japanese share of total imports rose to 65% and the Dai Ichi Bank, by issuing a silver yen coin valid only in Korea which rapidly became the accepted currency, virtually assumed the role of the country's central bank.

The biggest push of all was made in the field of railway construction.

Plans for lines from the capital to Inchon and Pusan had been drawn up immediately after the invasion in 1894, but they had been cut short by the King's escape into Russian custody and the concession for the Seoul-Inchon line was subsequently granted to an American entrepreneur. Although he was able to complete it in 1898, the Japanese labour force that he was obliged to employ became so unco-operative that he was then compelled to sell out to a Japanese syndicate led by Mitsui. The latter approached Yamagata with a request for government funds, and a sum of 1.7 million yen was duly made available to the company. Negotiations were also then successfully concluded for the construction of the Seoul-Pusan line. Shortly afterwards the American adviser to the King received an ultimatum from the new Japanese Minister that the American owners of the Seoul Tramways Company should forthwith remove their tracks where they crossed those of the railway; unless they did so, he was warned, Japanese soldiers would be sent to do the job and he himself might become the victim of an 'accident'.

Not unnaturally, Russia viewed these developments with some unease, and she attempted to counter them with plans for establishing naval facilities at the southern port of Masampo, which the Tsar's Navy had long coveted as offering the best guarantee against Japanese interference with their line of communication between Vladivostok and Port Arthur. However, no sooner had the most appropriate site been selected than the land was found to have already been bought by Japanese nominees. When all attempts at persuading the Korean government to rescind the purchase failed, the Pacific Fleet was sent in to secure the lease of an alternative site, but this proved so inferior to the original choice that it was never in fact developed.

Since their acquisition of interests in China, France and Germany had grown somewhat cooler in their support for their Russian ally's ambitions there, while Britain positively welcomed what she saw as a check to them. The same sentiment was echoed by U.S. Secretary of State John Hay in his famous declaration that the principle of 'Open Door', as opposed to the establishment of exclusive spheres of interest, should be applied in China by outside Powers.

The result of this apparent indulgence by the West towards her fresh activities in Korea was to encourage Japan to probe further afield. In spite of the American annexation, Japanese immigration to Hawaii more than doubled in the succeeding four years, as it did indeed to the West Coast of America itself, leading to riots in Vancouver and the inauguration of the 'Stop The Yellow Peril' movement being held in California, where one seventh of the population was now of Japanese origin. Her efforts to penetrate southwards, on the other hand, had run up against the 'White Australia' policy of the new Dominion government there, provoking protests in the Diet. However, it was to China that the closest attention soon returned once more.

STIRRING THE POT

After the failure of a rebellion in Canton against the Manchu administration in 1895, its leader Sun Yat-sen had taken refuge in Japan, where in the course of the next three years he was taken up by a variety of backers. They ranged on the one hand from the misty-eyed idealist Miyazaki Torazo, for whom the regeneration of China was an essential means of 'reviving human rights and establishing a new reign of justice throughout the universe', to, on the other, the bosses of the Genyosha, who saw in him a promising tool in the service of their rather less altruistic ends. Miyazaki had already obtained secret government funds from the Matsukata-Okuma coalition via Inukai Ki, one of the Lame Democrat Okuma's co-founders of the Progressive Party, to permit him to travel to China in order to make contact with revolutionary groups there, and the still-thriving unholy alliance of Liberals and mobsters now combined to set Sun up in a house in Tokyo.

Okuma himself saw more promise in backing the reform movement of K'ang Yu-wei, who in May 1898 at last succeeded in gaining the Chinese Emperor's ear and persuading him to embark on 'A Hundred Days of Reform', a programme of root-and-branch modernisation which would leave no field of the old mandarin system untouched. However, it was met with the predictable opposition of the Dowager Empress, who on September 21st overthrew her son in a coup, leaving China to her fate and K'ang to join Sun as a refugee in Japan.

His arrival there was marked by the foundation of the 'East Asia Common Culture Society' under the patronage of Prince Konoye Atsumaro (the President of the House of Peers), Ito, Okuma and, of course, the Genyosha. In subsequent years it set up a network of offices in China, ostensibly for the purpose of 'study and research', but in practice they were to provide a vital intelligence service alongside the already-established 'Halls of Pleasurable Delight'. The two exiles, however, soon made it clear that they were far from natural allies; whereas K'ang still envisaged the maintenance of (an albeit reformed) constitutional monarchy, Sun had dedicated himself to nothing less than its total overthrow and the establishment of a republic. This division was reflected among their Japanese backers; while Okuma's Progressives, or Real Constitutionalists as they now were, continued to give their support to K'ang, the Genyosha held on to Sun as the best bet, a view which was strengthened by the fall of the Okuma government.

The first opportunity to put this judgement to the test came not in China, but in the Philippines, where the rebel leader Emilio Aguinaldo was continuing to resist the new American administration. Miyazaki had already made contact with him during his travels, and he was soon able to persuade Sun that 'any victory against Western imperialism would be a victory for all Orientals, and a friendly Philippine republic would provide an ideal proving ground and staging area for work in China.' Inukai also gave his blessing, although the Foreign Minister in the incoming Yamagata Cabinet, Aoki Shuzo, declared himself unable to give any official assistance for fear of offending America.

This was taken as a hint to refer the matter to Chief of Staff Kawakami, who was duly found to be much more accommodating — just as he had been in 1894 over the dispatch of the 'fire-raisers' to Korea. Ten thousand rifles, six million rounds of ammunition and ten field guns were made available from the Imperial armoury. Having passed through a chain of ever more anonymous hands, including those of Genyosha-boss Uchida Ryohei, they were loaded on board an elderly Mitsui freighter for dispatch to the field; Uchida was also instrumental in procuring the necessary coal for her bunkers. The ship, however, proved unequal to such a weighty assignment and on July 26th 1899 she foundered in a storm off the Chinese coast, taking all Aguinaldo's hopes to the bottom with her.

BOXER REBELLION

Undaunted, the conspirators began to press ahead with plans for a second attempt at raising a rebellion in China. Three years earlier Katsura, in his capacity as Governor-General of the new colony of Formosa, had drawn up a plan for a landing at Amoy, the leading commercial centre in the adjacent mainland province of Fukien. In the wake of the concessions wrung from China by the West in 1898 Japan had secured a promise from Peking not to alienate Fukien to any of the Powers. Katsura's plan was now enthusiastically revived by his Choshu successor and fellow protégé of Yamagata, Kodama Gentaro, under Katsura's watching brief at the War Ministry.

In Japan Uchida set about recruiting Genyosha toughs to serve as the landing's storm-troopers, while Sun and Miyazaki took ship for China with the aim of co-ordinating the support of the various reform groups there under the banner of Hsing Han-hui or the Rise Han Society. In this they were not altogether successful, for K'ang refused to see them in the belief that they had been sent to assassinate him, while the leaders of the Society in Hankow were prematurely uncovered by the Manchu authorities and executed. Those in Kwangtung fared better, however, and having established a base in the mountains east of Canton they defeated the Manchu forces sent against them and headed towards Amoy to link up with the expected landing there.

The enterprise had in the meantime drawn encouragement from developments in the north. One of the first acts of the Dowager Empress on her reoccupation of the Throne was a reorganisation of local militia companies in the provinces which had been most exposed to the depredations of the Powers. Known as 'Righteous and Harmonious Fists' and so labelled more simply as 'Boxers' by the foreigners, they soon became an instrument of her intense chauvinism under the banner, so reminiscent of its *sonno-joi* counterpart in Japan, of 'Preserve China, Destroy The Foreigners'.

Beginning with attacks on the Christian missionaries and their converts, their targets soon widened to include all 'foreign devils' and their works, railway and telegraph lines coming in for particular attention. When in November 1899 the European ministers in Peking protested at this 'illegal rebellion', the Empress countered with a secret order to all provincial viceroys to 'fight for the preservation of their homes and native soil from the encroaching footsteps of the foreign aggressor'; thus, far from constituting a rebellion, these activities were in fact directly authorised by the Throne. A delegation was dispatched from the Chinese Court to Tokyo to seek support and was duly accompanied on its return by forty Japanese officers; The East Asia Common Culture Society seemed to its patrons to be about to pay some early dividends.

Early in May 1900 Tientsin was attacked, the railway station was burnt, telegraph lines were cut and a number of the railway workers killed. It was now apparent that the Europeans in the capital were in danger of being cut off, and the British Admiral Sir Edward Seymour set out with a relief force of 2,000 men from the Far Eastern Fleet anchored at Tangku. He soon ran into heavy opposition, however, and was obliged to turn back. The Boxers then began to lay siege to Peking itself. The Imperial troops were openly thrown in alongside them, creating a de facto state of war between China and the Powers. On June 10th the German Minister and a Japanese Secretary were killed in the streets, whereupon most of the foreign diplomatic community took refuge in the more easily defended British Legation.

When the news reached Europe, considerable panic ensued as the Powers cast about for means to redress the situation, while in Japan there were loud calls for revenge. Yamagata, however, very mindful of the need not to reawaken European suspicions of Japanese territorial ambitions, decided that 'in this instance our best policy is to adopt a cautious attitude and refrain from sending troops ourselves unless the Powers request our assistance'. He therefore contented himself with polite notes indicating willingness to make Japanese troops available if it was considered that they were needed. With varying degrees of reluctance the Powers realised that they had little option but to accept such an offer, whereupon a force of 8,000 men was rapidly mobilised under General Terauchi Masatake (another of Yamagata's inner circle of protégés) and dispatched to Tientsin with stern instructions to put their best feet forward in front of Western observers.

They were joined in due course by 4,800 Russian, 3,000 British, 2,100 American and 800 French troops. On August 4th they set out for the capital under the overall command of the Russian General Nikolai Linevich, having decided not to wait for the German contingent which had only put to sea a week earlier. In his parting speech on the quayside to them Kaiser Wilhelm had somewhat betrayed himself by urging them to give no quarter 'just as the Huns a thousand years ago, under the leadership of Attila, gained a reputation by virtue of which they still live in historical tradition'; his chagrin may be imagined when he was informed that the German-less force had reached Peking and successfully raised the siege in the space of the next ten days.

AMOY ADVENTURE

The Russian contingent in fact represented only a minor proportion of the total number of troops which St. Petersburg had sent into the area, the rest being deployed in Manchuria on the pretext of protecting the Chinese Eastern Railway from Boxer attacks. Formosa-Gauleiter Kodama happened to be in Tokyo at the time, and he capitalised on fears that Russia was about to entrench herself permanently there to argue that now was the time for Japan to stake her claim in the south of China. If any objections were raised in the West, then surely it could be answered, he postulated, that Japan had as much right to protect her nationals in Amoy as those in Peking. The Cabinet was successfully persuaded, and he hurried back to Formosa to finalise the arrangements.

On August 15th, the day after Peking was relieved, he received a telegram from Katsura authorising him to proceed with his preparations; their purpose, Yamagata wrote in a Cabinet memorandum, was 'to build up opposite Formosa a formidable presence which will serve in time of peace as the focus for trade and industry within China. Thus we can hold in our grasp the "throat of the Far East" [the Straits of Formosa] and keep in check any intrusion by an enemy.' A naval officer was to proceed to Amoy in advance, the telegram went on, with instructions that 'in certain eventualities' he might call for reinforcements 'in order to protect Japanese interests'.

A week later the abbot of a Japanese temple in Amoy fled to the Japanese Consulate and reported that the building had been burnt to the ground by a Chinese mob. Kodama, having in the meantime received the Emperor's authority to commit the equivalent of a full battalion and two artillery batteries, immediately dispatched a small force of Uchida's storm troopers, who succeeded in provoking further anti-foreign demonstrations. On the 27th Katsura telegraphed again with orders to proceed with the main landing. Kodama commandeered all the mail transports in Formosa and embarked the remainder of his men and supplies. Everything was now set. (The U.S. Consul was later able to establish the facts of the original incident, which threw a rather different light on it. The 'abbot' was a former *samurai* and the 'temple' no more than an old house which he and two companions had taken on a short lease; on the day before the fire they had been seen moving out all their belongings.)

The next day, however, yet another telegram arrived from Katsura ordering a postponement: the warships could anchor in Amoy harbour, but the troopships were to be kept at sea. It transpired that a report had reached Tokyo to the effect that Russia was on the point of withdrawing her troops from Manchuria, and that Ito in his capacity as President of the Privy Council had been able to use this to persuade both the Emperor and Cabinet that the West would take grave exception to any unilateral Japanese adventure elsewhere in China. (There had in fact been a considerable division of opinion among the Tsar's advisers over what policy to adopt: the new War Minister Alexeii Kuropatkin was all for taking the chance to seize Manchuria and turn it into a Russian province, while Witte argued that a guarantee of protection for the Railway should be negotiated with Li.)

A furious Kodama telegraphed back that it was now or never, but the Cabinet insisted on staying his hand while they established the truth or otherwise of the Russian report. The wires from the U.S. Consulate in Amoy were also humming in the meantime, reporting to Washington 'Situation critical. Japanese landing troops, guns. Chinese had kept faith. "Mob" disproved. Thousands fleeing.' Shortly afterwards the undersea cable was cut in the vicinity of the Japanese warships, but the outside world had been successfully alerted and within a week British warships arrived to land a force of marines, putting an end to Kodama's plans for an operation whose first requirement had been that it should be brought off out of sight of Western eyes.

Kodama's immediate reaction was to cable a request for a transfer to another post and then, when it was turned down, his resignation on the grounds of 'illness'. This too was refused, and Meiji dispatched a Court Chamberlain to Formosa to 'express solicitude for the Governor-General's health'; Kodama was thus obliged to withdraw his resignation and to enter into the charade by travelling to Tokyo to 'express his appreciation of such a demonstration of Imperial favour'. News of the 'attack' on the Amoy 'temple' had now been leaked in the Japanese Press, and the Government were even more seriously embarrassed when it became clear that Russia, far from withdrawing from Manchuria, was energetically consolidating her position there. On September 11th Yamagata informed Kodama that he and his Cabinet accepted the blame for the failure of the operation and were resigning in consequence.

The resignations were not made public until the 26th, and then quite other reasons were advanced for them. Yamagata was represented as having wished to resign earlier in the year, again because of 'ill health', but as having stayed on in order to see the Boxer crisis through, and then as having been moved by Ito's announcement on the 15th of his formation of the new Seiyukai Party* from the rump of the old Constitutionalist majority to consider that Ito was now the country's 'natural leader'—a remarkable conversion, this, to the democratic principle. In fact, as Ito was the first to acknowledge in a letter to Yamagata begging him to stay on, the real reasons represented a shrewd calculation: not only was Yamagata shuffling off any further responsibility for the Amoy debâcle on to Ito, but he was doing so before the new party would be able to organise itself sufficiently to handle it. The expurgated account of events has once again been perpetuated by the official historians and biographers, and the researcher will seek in vain for any mention in them of the planned operation.

The measure of Ito's predicament may be gauged from the fact that he was obliged to take the self-same Kodama on board his new Cabinet as War Minister, while the outgoing Foreign Minister Aoki (who had contributed to Yamagata's decision to resign by seeking over his head Meiji's permission for a move to pre-empt Russian encroachment in Manchuria) was elevated to the Privy Council. The rebel force in Kwangtung had in the meantime swollen into an army of 20,000 men, but robbed now of the prospect of receiving reinforcements and, more particularly, arms via Amoy, Sun was soon forced to the conclusion that its cause was hopeless and ordered it to disband.

Shortly afterwards an order arrived from Tokyo to remove himself from Formosa, and he returned to Japan to console himself that the seeds of a successful revolution in China were there if only they could be allowed to take root; a promise from Kodama of Japanese support 'if there was a serious outbreak in the future' also helped to keep his hopes alive. The disillusioned Miyazaki, by contrast, took up the life of a travelling minstrel to support himself while he composed his autobiography, *My Thirty-Three Years' Dream*, which was to become a cult book among future generations of Japanese youth.

RUSSIA STEALS A MARCH

Manchuria, where the Russian presence was estimated to have grown to no less than 50,000 troops, was now the focus of Tokyo's attention. Not content with merely putting down the last shows of Boxer resistance there, they had occupied the International Treaty port of Newchuang before crossing south into China proper at Shanhaikwan and taking control of the whole length of the railway to Peking, previously managed by British interests. At this point Witte managed to gain the upper hand in the Tsar's council chamber and persuaded him that such open rapacity would surely invite the other Powers to follow suit and so undermine the

---

* New Constitutionalist, but the Japanese title will be retained to avoid confusion with the opposition Real Constitutionalist Party.

long-established policy of gradual encroachment and consolidation. The
Russian contingent in the international relief force was therefore ordered
to withdraw to Tientsin. Their partners were invited to do likewise and to
open negotiations there with Li for a settlement.

Britain and Germany, however, mindful of Li's weakness for roubles,
were now so deeply suspicious of Russian intentions that they were
persuaded to lay aside the antagonism created by the Kaiser's open support
for the Boers in South Africa, issuing a joint statement committing
themselves to the protection of the 'Open Door' principle 'for all Chinese
territory'. At the insistence of Germany, who wished to avoid any direct
offence to her Russian ally, any specific reference to Manchuria was
excluded, and although the other partners presently added their signatures
this vagueness was very soon seen to render the whole exercise
meaningless.

Russia did eventually hand back the Peking-Shanhaikwan railway to
British control, but in Manchuria itself she continued to press on with her
own dispositions regardless. While she joined the other Powers in the
negotiations which were presently opened with the Chinese Court, she at
the same time authorised the local commander, Admiral Evgenii Alexeieff,
to treat with the Viceroy of Mukden, Tseng-chi, and on November 9th
these two signed a secret agreement which, while nominally restoring the
civilian administration of Manchuria to China, by stipulating the withdrawal of all Chinese troops and their replacement with Russian 'guards'
along the railway effectively endorsed Russia's occupation of the entire
region. When a garbled version of the terms appeared in *The Times* on
January 3rd 1901, it was greeted with an outcry of protest from the other
capitals involved. St. Petersburg thereupon issued a denial that any such
agreement existed.

A month later a formal draft treaty couched in very similar terms was
presented to Li, but this time even another million roubles was not
sufficient to persuade him to connive in so blatant a surrender of his
country's interests. Instead, he advised the Court to lodge an appeal for
protection with the other Powers. Britain, Germany and Japan duly
responded with a warning to the Chinese government not to conclude a
separate agreement 'affecting territorial rights in the Chinese Empire'
with any individual Power outside the joint negotiations still in progress,
although Germany still insisted on excepting Manchuria.

Nevertheless, this was sufficient to induce Russia, who was relying on
raising a loan in the London market to relieve her growing financial
difficulties, to announce on April 8th the withdrawal of the terms put to
China, although any withdrawal of troops from Manchuria would be
dependent on the outcome of the joint negotiations in Peking. These
continued to be prolonged by inter-Power bickering, but an agreement
was finally reached in September under which Russia secured the lion's
share of the indemnity exacted to cover the cost of the relief expedition;

she also insisted on all parties withdrawing their contingents before she would put her signature to it.

This course of events had been watched in Japan with growing alarm and resentment. As soon as the Amoy landing had been aborted Uchida had hurried off to Manchuria to investigate the situation at first hand. His subsequent reports of a deal in the offing which would set a seal on Russia's control of the region led to the inauguration on September 24th 1900 of The People's League under the patronage of the ubiquitous Prince Konoye, leaders of the Real Constitutionalist and Imperialist parties and, of course, Godfather Toyama. Purportedly dedicated to unifying public opinion behind a policy of 'maintaining the integrity of China and upholding Korea', its immediate objective was in fact to persuade Ito's newly-installed Cabinet to send troops to Korea. At the same time six Law Professors, under the leadership of Tomizu Kanjin and with the active encouragement of Konoye, drew up a memorial to present to the Prime Minister urging that 'we should not miss this opportunity. Today our Imperial nation must make the first move in a great leap forward' and advance into Manchuria in order to forestall Russian imperialism. To solve the Manchurian question was to solve the Korean problem, not vice versa, they argued.

Ito, however, was still optimistic that an acceptable agreement could be negotiated with Russia, and he refused to bow to such pressure. Indeed, he even went so far as to designate, with a nice touch of irony, The People's League a political association and therefore subject to the restrictions of Yamagata's Peace Preservation Ordinance.

THE DRAGON CUTS ITS TEETH

Undeterred, the Professors turned their attention instead on the new Foreign Minister, Kato Takaaki. They found him altogether more sympathetic; two years earlier he had resigned as Ambassador in London in protest at the rejection of his suggestion of an anti-Russian alliance with Britain. 'A peaceful agreement with Russia will mean a defeat for Japan,' he now declared. 'A firm attitude on our part, even a resort to arms if necessary, is the only policy left to us.' Thus even in his own Cabinet Ito rapidly found himself in a minority of one, while in the Upper House Yamagata's lieutenants began to block his proposed budget as a means of forcing the resignation of Hoshi, the Stock Exchange and Tokyo City Council fixer and new Minister of Communications.

In January 1901, while Kato was attempting without success to elicit from St. Petersburg an admission of the existence of the Alexeieff-Tseng agreement, Uchida completed his reconnaissance in Manchuria and ventured into Siberia as far west as Irkutsk before returning to Tokyo to report his findings to his chief, Toyama. The outcome of their reunion was the foundation under Uchida's nominal presidency of the secret society to end all secret societies, the Kokuryukai or 'River Amur Society', dedicated to the extension of Japan's boundaries to that river, which bounded Manchuria and ran almost to Lake Baikal. By a coincidence, the Chinese characters for it also represented the phrase 'Black Dragon', and it was the latter translation which was adopted in the West.

Its inaugural manifesto pronounced that 'in view of the situation in East Asia and the mission of Imperial Japan, and in order to check the expansion of the Western Powers in the East, and to promote the development and prosperity of East Asia, it is the urgent duty of Japan to fight Russia and expel her from the East, and then to lay the foundation for a grand continental enterprise taking Manchuria, Mongolia and Siberia as one region.' Its activities soon spread into so many different fields — for example, the establishment of Russian language schools, the publication of pamphlets, the organisation of public meetings, the financing of agents in Russia — that in fact it rapidly lost all pretensions to secrecy, and under Toyama's guiding hand it became the juggernaut which over the next generation succeeded in pulling public opinion towards the achievement of his chosen goal. In 1945 General MacArthur made a point of proscribing it even though it had effectively disbanded after Japan's entry into World War Two, its objective fulfilled.

As reports of the terms that Russia was attempting to force on China continued to dribble out, the pressure on Ito to abandon his conciliatory stance was stepped up from all sides. When he appealed to Yamagata to draw off the opposition in the Upper House to the budget, the 'Peace Preserver' responded with a missive as two-edged as any *samurai*. 'Because at the present time we cannot foresee what changes will occur in the Far Eastern situation in the near future, it is, of course, improper to oppose the tax increase,' he told the Peers. 'However, it is your responsibility to take a firm stand in the enforcement of official discipline when the administration and the foundation of the Nation are being corrupted.' The deadlock was only finally resolved by an Imperial Rescript ordering the budget's passage; it was not countersigned by Ito and indeed he disclaimed all prior knowledge of it, thus disproving the claims of later Japanese historians that Imperial Rescripts were issued on the initiative of Ministers rather than of the Emperor.

In the Cabinet Foreign Minister Kato brow-beat his colleagues into permitting him to send a formal note of protest to St. Petersburg, while further afield the Black Dragon circulated a pamphlet entitled *On the Relative Merits of War and Peace Based on the Estimated War Potential of Japan and Russia*. At the beginning of April the Board of Field-Marshals and Admirals met in secret with the Emperor to consider an intelligence report on Russia's combat strength in Manchuria. The atmosphere in Tokyo was now so charged that the Russian Ambassador prepared to pack his bags and advised his government to double its troops along the Manchurian border. When Kato's protest was rejected, further anguished Cabinet sessions ensued in which he demanded the right to reply in still firmer language, but eventually he was persuaded to state merely that 'Japan reserved its opinion under the present circumstances'.

Russia's announcement of the withdrawal of her terms to China followed two days later, but it brought only the most fleeting relief to Ito; within a month he finally admitted defeat and resigned. The Elder Statesmen conferred at length over the question of his successor; given the Seiyukai's resentful majority in the Diet, none of them felt inclined to pitch their reputations into the fray by taking on the task themselves. Instead, their choice fell eventually on Yamagata's favourite, Katsura.

On the face of it, this first appointment of a Prime Minister from outside the inner circle of the Restoration oligarchy seemed to constitute an important break with the past, but the reality was rather less impressive. Not only was the new Cabinet packed with Yamagata's nominees, including the three Peers who had led the opposition to Ito's budget, but it failed to contain a single representative from the Seiyukai majority. Furthermore, the Elder Statesmen laid down that all issues of foreign policy were to be referred to themselves, and that the most important questions were to be decided by an Imperial Conference attended by the Emperor, Elder Statesmen and the relevant Ministers. With good reason did it become known as 'the Curtain Cabinet'.

Yamagata was well pleased with his handiwork; it was as if the political parties had never been.

PART III

Into the Big League

13

Alliance With Britain, Victory Over Russia

ITO'S FOG

In the minds of the expansionists, the decision for war with Russia had already been as good as taken. Only a week before Ito resigned Yamagata had written to him that 'sooner or later there will undoubtedly be a collision of major proportions. If Russia, overconfident of her strength, should penetrate our line of sovereignty, we must be resolute and prepared for such an eventuality.' Given the fact of Russia's alliance with France, however, he readily perceived that Japan was not in a position to enter such a trial of strength single-handed, and he went on to propound that 'it would be advisable immediately to sound out the British and discuss with the Germans a plan to establish an alliance ... Then, when an opportunity arises, it would not be difficult to establish spheres of influence in Fukien and Chekiang ...'

The concept of an alliance with Britain was by no means a novel one; as far back as June 1895 the *Jiji Shimpo* had published an article by Hayashi Tadasu in which he declared that 'In order to oppose Russia, England has not hesitated to join hands even with decadent countries like Turkey and China. How much more then ought she be willing to co-operate with Japan,' adding with characteristic bluster that 'we do not hesitate to assert that England would derive more benefit than Japan from the proposed alliance.'

By that date Britain's initiative in renegotiating the unequal treaties and her refusal to join the Triple Intervention had already done much to restore the goodwill lost by her earlier opposition to treaty revision, and subsequent events had only served to confirm her as a natural ally in Japanese eyes. Since British assets in China lay to the south (in Hong Kong and the Yangtse basin) they were not going to conflict with Japanese ambitions in the north, while Japan's rapidly-growing strength as the foremost naval power in the area was seen by Britain as offering the best protection of those assets against Russia's seemingly insatiable imperialism.

This recognition of the two countries' identity of interest had been reflected in 1898 in their co-operation over the surrender of the Weihaiwei lease to Britain and again, even more conspicuously, in the mobilisation of the relief force to Peking two years later. On that occasion Britain had been much the most enthusiastic of the Western Powers in requesting Japan's assistance, and she had even gone so far as to make a covering offer of a million pounds when Japan used the pretext of poverty to give an appearance of hanging back while she tried to assess the reaction of the other Powers to such an invitation. Both Ito and Yamagata had inclined towards acceptance, but Aoki as Foreign Minister had taken it upon himself to refuse it 'in order to avoid national disgrace for a hundred years'. However, Aoki had been replaced by Kato, like Hayashi a proponent of an alliance with Britain, while Hayashi himself was now the Ambassador in London. With the pro-Russian Ito out of the way, Kato lost no time in authorising Hayashi to take up the idea with the British government, although he instructed him to make it appear as if he was doing so on his own initiative.

Hayashi began to test the water in Whitehall with due circumspection. Finding it at an agreeable temperature, he helped to warm it a few degrees further with a hint that if no alliance with Britain was forthcoming Japan might then have to consider entering one with Russia. When he was then asked to outline what terms his government had in mind, a Conference of the Elder Statesmen on August 5th took advantage of Ito's absence to draw up a list of proposals; Yamagata in particular was insistent that no further time should be lost. When Ito was eventually brought abreast of these developments he did not go so far as to declare his outright opposition to them, but he still expressed himself as very much more strongly in favour of an arrangement with Russia. He was due to sail for America the following month to receive an Honorary Doctorate at the Yale Bi-centenary and he obtained his colleagues' permission to go on to Europe and make an approach to the Russian government. Yamagata insisted, however, that he should refer back to Tokyo before coming to any final agreement, to which Ito is reported to have replied tartly that 'I am not going abroad for my own pleasure.'

Once Ito was safely out of the country, Hayashi was given the full-steam-ahead signal, together with plenipotentiary powers to open formal negotiations. These proceeded so amicably that by early November the British government presented Hayashi with a first draft of the proposed terms. On referring them to Tokyo, he was instructed to take them to show to Ito in Paris where the latter had paused in order to sound out French opinion on the possibility of his reaching an agreement with their Russian ally.

Ito was predictably astonished, as he confessed to Hayashi: 'I am now informed by you of the Anglo-Japanese Alliance negotiations, which have made such progress that withdrawal from them is no longer possible. It is contrary to my expectations.' Hayashi in turn was hardly less surprised by

Ito's claim that he had been authorised to negotiate an agreement with Russia, but he was soon reassured by Tokyo that this was not the case. 'When I received this telegram and showed it to Marquis Ito, he was still more puzzled,' he related in his *Secret Memoirs*. Before parting he gave Ito an undertaking that he would not pursue the negotiations in London until he had learnt the outcome of the latter's conversations in St. Petersburg.

A fortnight had now elapsed since the presentation of the British draft, and on Hayashi's return the Foreign Office made no bones of its displeasure that Ito had chosen to go on to St. Petersburg rather than to London. When he offered the excuse in reply that 'in November the London climate was at its worst, and fogs were general, and would prejudice Marquis Ito's health which was not good, Lord Lansdowne [the Foreign Secretary] evidently did not think very much of my explanation ... "Why, if he was travelling for his health, did he go to St. Petersburg in the winter?"' British suspicions were only allayed by a second telegram from Tokyo disclaiming 'any intention of playing a double game', and in a further effort to demonstrate their sincerity the Cabinet quickly buckled down to the preparation of their response to the British draft.

MATTER FOR CONGRATULATION

On November 30th Hayashi received a list of amendments to present to the Foreign Office, which he was also instructed to forward to Ito for his comments. On receiving it Ito found a number of grounds for criticism and replied that 'I think that all negotiations for an Anglo-Japanese Alliance ought to be suspended until we are quite sure that it is hopeless to attempt to conclude a satisfactory convention with Russia ... for which [in my opinion] the prospects are very favourable.' By the time that his cable was received in Tokyo, however, the Elder Statesmen had already met to endorse the Cabinet's amendments. Ito's one ally, Inoue, was brought into line by the disclosure that it had been Japan who had initiated the negotiations; to withdraw now, he conceded, would be to incur an unacceptable loss of face. The matter was then referred to the Throne. Meiji, seeing the danger that if word of the negotiations reached Russia Japan would be left between two stools, ordered the amendments to be submitted to Britain without further delay.

Ito, outmanoeuvred once again by the expansionists, was left to wring his hands all the way back to Tokyo. 'I certainly wish to congratulate you,' Prime Minister and First Protégé Katsura wrote to Yamagata in recognition of his patron's rôle as formulator of this successful strategy, 'on the unanimity which was achieved among the Elder Statesmen in regard to this important matter.' The Emperor also acknowledged his gratitude by bestowing on the Field-Marshal the Grand Order of the Chrysanthemum.

After some further minor discussion, including the possibility of German participation which was quickly dropped following another sharp deterioration in Anglo-German relations over events in South Africa, the Anglo-Japanese Alliance was formally concluded on January 30th 1902. Under its terms, which were to remain in force for five years, both parties were empowered to take any necessary measures to protect their respective interests in China and Korea, while the other was to remain neutral if such measures involved one of them in war; if on the other hand another Power entered such hostilities they were pledged to go to each other's assistance. The accompanying preamble spoke of 'a desire to maintain the status quo and general peace in the Far East, especially the independence and territorial integrity of China and Korea, and in securing equal opportunities in those countries for the commerce and industry of all nations'; in answer to subsequent questions in Parliament, British Ministers made it clear that, as before, Manchuria was considered to be an integral part of China.

On the day that the Alliance was made public three weeks later Katsura spoke of it in the Diet as an 'internationally important matter' which would secure Japan's objectives in Eastern Asia. If in his satisfaction he allowed himself the luxury of under-statement, the Japanese Press was less reserved in expressing its welcome; the *Jiji Shimpo* hailed it as 'a great honour' and the *Nippon* urged its readers to look on it also as providing a unique opportunity for Japanese business to invest and expand on the Asian continent, although the *Kokumin Shimbun* at the same time warned against the temptation to rely too much on Britain which might lead Japan to lose sight of her primary objective — the build-up of the nation's military capacity. All over the country, the British Ambassador in Tokyo reported home, its publication was greeted with 'immense enthusiasm'.

Eight years earlier the expectations of Japan's acceptance as an equal by the West aroused by the revision of the treaties and the victory over China had been peremptorily dashed by the Triple Intervention. Now she had been accorded the status, in a form which guaranteed it from outside interference, of partner by the most powerful nation in the world.

The official writ was quick to term it 'obviously a defensive alliance', but this was hardly as its instigators conceived it or as detached observers saw it. A British correspondent of the *Contemporary Review* wrote a month later that 'there is in Japan much talk of an attack some day on Port Arthur, followed by an invasion of Manchuria'. A leading Chinese historian was later to describe it as 'without doubt the most important single factor in international relations in the Far East in the first two decades of the twentieth century ... An instrument which ordered a third Power, Russia, to get out of Manchuria while giving Japan a free hand in Korea could hardly be said to be purely defensive.' With Russia successfully isolated, all that remained now was to complete the military build-up.

RUSSIAN COUNTER

Ito's would-be allies in St. Petersburg put the best face on the news that they could muster. The *Official Gazette* published a statement that the Russian Government had received the announcement 'with the most perfect calm', which was followed by a joint declaration with the French reaffirming their commitment to maintenance of the status quo and the 'Open Door' policy. Negotiations had in the meantime been resumed with China on a settlement of the Manchurian question. The Russians began by offering to withdraw their troops over a period of three years and to return the railways to Chinese control, but when an agreement on this basis was almost ready for signature they suddenly made the evacuation conditional upon a Chinese undertaking not to award railway or any other commercial concessions in Manchuria to any foreign concern except the Russo-Chinese Bank. When Li showed signs of resisting these strong-arm tactics a further 300,000 roubles were pressed into his ever-open palm, but even as his fingers closed around them the sensation of illicit gold finally proved too much for his elderly heart and on November 4th 1901 he expired.

The loss of their one reliable partisan in the Chinese Court virtually removed the prospect of concluding an agreement with China on anything like the Russians' own terms, and the true scale of their disappointment at the subsequent dashing of their hopes for an accommodation with Japan needs little divining; the completion of the Trans-Siberian Railway was still some way off, and the terms which were eventually reached with China on April 8th 1902 did no more than recognise the realities of the position created by the new Alliance. Russia was to withdraw her troops in three stages over a period of eighteen months 'provided that no disturbances arise', at the end of which total administrative control of Manchuria including the railways (apart from the Chinese Eastern Railway and the International Treaty Port of Newchuang) would revert to China.

This retraction on Russia's part was inevitably taken as a signal by the expansionists in Japan to press on with their preparations. The stage had been reached where deference to the niceties of parliamentary procedures for the benefit of foreign observers could be dispensed with, so Yamagata informed Katsura: 'At this time it would be most desirable for our nation if a strongly united Cabinet would face the opposition squarely and openly engage it in hostilities ... We should gradually advance by encouraging the fighting spirit of the Cabinet ministers and strive to realise the nation's plans with unbending spirit.' The next budget, calling for a further expansion of the naval building programme and an increase in the land tax to finance it, was bitterly opposed in the Diet by both Ito and Okuma at the head of the two major parties. Katsura tried first to reason with them and then to buy them off, but when both these ploys failed he obtained Meiji's permission to dissolve the Diet and re-apply the previous year's budget.

In the resultant election the Seiyukai and Real Constitutionalist parties won no less than 384 out of a (now enlarged) total of 476 seats. Yamagata and Katsura recognised that they had no option but to give some ground to the Opposition, for if the same budget was re-applied a second time the building programme would be left seriously short of funds. Ito was therefore informed that his previous demand, that any increase in the military budget should be met by a corresponding reduction in government spending elsewhere and not by an increase in the land tax, would now be met. This proved sufficient, despite Okuma's indignant accusations of treachery, to swing the Seiyukai into line and secure, on June 5th 1903, a majority for the new budget.

Ito was not to enjoy for very long any satisfaction that he had derived from this apparent reassertion of his influence, for his opponents moved swiftly to ensure that he would never again command the same capacity to obstruct their plans. On June 24th Katsura demanded that he should either retire from the Conference of Elder Statesmen or give up his leadership of a political party, on the grounds that the two rôles were incompatible. When Ito refused to do either unless he received a direct order to do so from the Emperor himself, Katsura submitted his own resignation. Yamagata then suggested to Meiji that the problem could be resolved by appointing Ito to the Presidency of the Privy Council, a position which would automatically debar him from the Lower House. The Emperor agreed.

On receiving the Imperial appointment, Ito made a proviso that he would accept it as long as Katsura withdrew his resignation. This, of course, the Prime Minister immediately did, for it was expressly to secure Ito's removal from the Lower House that he had resigned in the first place. Ito also imposed a second condition, namely that the rest of the Elder Statesmen should join him in the Privy Council, but this too was only playing into their hands for, while it served to maintain the status of that body, it also ensured that there too he would be outvoted. A party colleague correctly noted in his diary that 'Ito's entry into the Privy Council is a trick of the Yamagata clique aimed at saving the Cabinet and leaving it free to carry out its policies by separating Ito from the Seiyukai and destroying the party.' To all intents and purposes, this marked the end of his struggle over a quarter of a century to establish, however tentatively, the principle of parliamentary government.

Another factor which had influenced Ito in withdrawing his opposition to the new budget had been Russia's failure to carry out the second stage of her evacuation of Manchuria, which had been due to take place on April 8th under the terms of the agreement with China. Indeed, far from withdrawing her troops from the region, she had merely transferred them either to the leased enclave of Port Arthur or to the land allotted to the Chinese Eastern Railway under the articles of the Company's incorporation. The British Consul in Mukden reported that the number of troops re-classified as 'railway guards' had risen to 30,000 and that 'depôts' containing barracks for as many as 6,000 men were being constructed at regular intervals along the Company's tracks.

At the same time the Chinese Court informed the other Powers that it had been presented with a new list of demands by Russia which would, if granted, effectively concede to her a total monopoly over Manchuria's economic development. When they in turn lodged formal protests in St. Petersburg at this contravention of the 'most favoured nation' clauses in their respective treaties with China, Foreign Minister Vladimir Lamsdorff denied the existence of such a list, but following its rejection by the Court Peking soon reported that it had been re-presented as before except for the concession that each demand might be considered separately.

This new assertiveness on Russia's part had its origins in the displacement of Witte and Lamsdorff from the Tsar's favour by a triumvirate of Kuropatkin, Alexieff and Captain Alexander Bezobrasov, a freewheeling entrepreneur who, since his success in persuading the Tsar's private treasury to take over the Yalu timber concession on the Manchuria-Korea border (first granted to Russia interests by the King of Korea in 1896), had drawn up a blueprint for the economic development of Manchuria backed by military occupation; in April the Tsar had appointed Bezobrasov Secretary of State and had advanced him a further two million roubles for the development of his project. Japanese observers now reported that a sizeable force of Russian troops had crossed the river into Korea for the ostensible purpose of lumber-cutting, but that they had then gone on to Yongampo on the river's mouth and were engaged in constructing what appeared to be a barracks.

These events stirred a predictably swift reaction in Japan. On the very day that the news reached Tokyo of the presentation of the Russian demands in Peking, the People's League was reconstituted as the 'Comrades Society For A Strong Foreign Policy' under the familiar tutelage of Prince Konoye and Godfather Toyama. Soon afterwards Tomizu and his fellow-professors, after conferring with Konoye, called on Katsura and pressed for an immediate declaration of war. Although they undertook to the Prime Minister to keep this request secret, it soon leaked out and the demand was widely taken up by the Press.

Katsura was not best pleased at this attempt to pre-empt his own plans and he told Tomizu in so many words to stick to his lecture room. At a Conference of the Elder Statesmen on April 21st it had been agreed that negotiations should be reopened with Russia on the basis of recognising the preponderance of their respective interests in Korea and Manchuria, although Katsura, unlike Ito, had expressed no confidence that Russia could be brought to accept such an arrangement. The Army General Staff, meeting a few days later, also concluded that war was inevitable and pressed for immediate action, but Chief of Staff Oyama would not commit himself to do more for the moment than put the armed forces on the alert.

The following day he submitted a memorial to the Throne 'On the Replenishment of Military Preparedness'.

'THE LIMIT OF ENDURANCE'

Impatient with such caution, a number of his subordinates got together with like-minded colleagues in the Naval General Staff and Foreign Ministry to form a secret pressure group, named the Kogetsukai after the restaurant in which they first met. Their attitude was summed up by a participant Major General thus: 'There is no longer room for discussion. We must fight Russia even if it means defeat. Our struggle for arms expansion has had only one purpose: to fight Russia . . . If we do not fight now, it is evident that Russia, which has been invading the Far East in full force, will soon replenish its strength in Manchuria and advance into Korea. In that case, an agreement between Japan and Russia will come to be only a piece of paper, and Japan will inevitably be shut out of the Continent . . . Japan will become another India or Burma. When we think of this, there is no choice but to fight. Even if we should lose, we can avenge ourselves against Russia within a hundred years, if we work at it with tightened belts. This is no time for compromise.'

The group arranged among themselves to lobby the Elder Statesmen and members of the Cabinet individually, and to commit *hara-kiri* if their efforts should fail and war not eventuate. In most cases they were met with expressions of polite indifference, but they elicited a more positive response from War Minister Terauchi, Home Minister Kodama (the instigator of the Amoy adventure) and Foreign Minister Komura; one of the latter's closest aides was heard to remark during a drinking bout that 'we must kill the pro-Russian Ito'.

Whether or not it was due to any of their influence, the next meeting of the Army General Staff on June 8th evinced a harder line which ruled out any idea of a mutual recognition of interests in Korea and Manchuria. Oyama still refused to commit himself publicly to any more positive stance, and a fortnight later he submitted another memorial to the Throne entitled 'My Opinion Regarding the Solution of the Korean Problem' in which he again advocated a negotiated settlement.

The following day, June 23rd, Meiji summoned an Imperial Conference of the Elder Statesmen and leading Cabinet Ministers to consider a memorandum prepared by Komura. In it the Foreign Minister restated the case for opening negotiations with Russia but their objective, he asserted, would have to be the Russian concession of Japan's right to suzerainty over Korea. 'It will be extremely difficult to obtain Russia's concurrence in such an agreement,' he concluded. 'Consequently, I believe it to be essential that, in commencing negotiations, Japan be firmly resolved to achieve its objectives whatever the costs.' Only Ito expressed any reluctance to go along with such a conclusion and for his pains, as we have seen, he was promptly kicked upstairs to the confines of the Privy Council. When this manoeuvre had been completed, Katsura reshuffled his Cabinet to reinforce the hard-liners.

After a preliminary note conveying Japan's desire to 'consult the Russian Government in a spirit of conciliation and frankness' had drawn a response which indicated a similar willingness to negotiate, the Japanese proposals based on Komura's memorandum were presented at St. Petersburg on August 12th. The first four Articles proposed no more than a mutual recognition of interests and a commitment to the 'Open Door' policy, but the fifth demanded 'recognition on the part of Russia of the exclusive right of Japan to give advice and assistance in the interest of reform and good government in Korea, including necessary military assistance'.

Even the official propagandist Asakawa conceded a year later that this Article provided 'grounds for possible misinterpretation' — before going on to assert that 'the task of reform could not safely be left either with the indolent Korea or with another Power, be it China or Russia, whose ultimate object would best be served if Korea was to remain feeble. The reform of Korea may truly be called the penalty of Japan's geographical position . . . and nothing seems to kindle the Japanese nation with a higher ambition than their profound determination to perform what they deem their historic mission in the fairest spirit of human progress.' In a similar attempt at deception the American adviser to the Japanese Foreign Office, Henry W. Denison, eliminated all provocative-sounding phraseology from the English translation of the proposals in order to present to the rest of the world a picture of Japanese reasonableness and sincerity.

Whoever may have been deceived subsequently by these honeyed glosses, the Russians had at the time no hesitation at all in 'misinterpreting' (i.e., correctly divining) the intentions that lay behind the proposals. Within twenty-four hours of their receipt Alexeieff was appointed Viceroy of the Far East and endowed with supreme civil and military authority, answerable only to a special committee nominated by the Tsar and presided over by himself. Witte, by contrast, was shunted from the Ministry of Finance into the non-executive Council of Ministers. The Russian counter-proposals, when they were eventually transmitted on October 3rd, were uncompromising to the point of bluntness: Japan was 'not to use any part of the territory of Korea for strategical purposes', the whole country north of the 39th parallel was to be a neutral zone prohibited to the troops of both sides and Manchuria was to be recognised 'as in all respects outside Japan's sphere of interest'.

The expansionists had made good use of this interval to bring Japanese public opinion to the boil. The 'Comrades Society For A Strong Foreign Policy' was renamed, even more unequivocally, 'The Anti-Russia Comrades Society' and enrolled the support of the whole political spectrum, from Prince Konoye and Professor Tomizu to Opposition leaders Itagaki and Okuma. Indeed, it was the Opposition who now took up the running, just as they had done ten years earlier in the drive for war with China. The Opposition paper *Yorozo Choho*, for instance, which until now had taken an anti-war stance, on September 15th did a smart editorial about-turn, demanding: 'What positive action has our government taken in this critical situation? We have endured the Russians too long. Just because we have borne the unbearable, their licence, rapacity, insults and contempt have fallen upon us endlessly. We have now reached the limit of our endurance. Does the present situation still leave any room for discussion? Certainly not . . .'

Two days after the Russian counter-proposals had been received, The Anti-Russia Comrades Society held a mass meeting, at which the following resolution was unanimously approved: 'In view of the present situation, we deem that the time has now come for us to take measures of the last resort. We shall no longer permit hesitation and indecision on the part of the government.'

It must have been satisfying indeed to Katsura and his patron Yamagata to see the pace set so effectively for them. Yamagata now took steps to place another of his protégés, Amoy-Adventurer Kodama, in a key position when the post of Assistant Chief of Staff fell vacant. Even though it represented a demotion for him, Kodama obediently stepped down from the Home Ministry; 'Present conditions require a war-time policy,' Yamagata explained in a letter to War Minister Terauchi recommending the appointment.

One of Kodama's first actions in his new post was to study the findings of Uchida's reconnaissance in Siberia with a view to disrupting Russia's lines of communication, and he enthusiastically took up the Black Dragon boss on his offer to mobilise the numerous tribal bandits active in the area of Lake Baikal with the object of cutting the already-completed section of the Trans-Siberian Railway. Since his return Uchida had been busying himself with the establishment of a 'Japan-Russia Society' aimed at cultivating the 'co-operation' of the Russian people in the anticipated event of a Japanese victory. In this enterprise he had been able to enlist the support of Ito who, somewhat naively it might be thought in the light of Uchida's past activities, saw it as a vehicle for fostering a negotiated settlement.

DECISION FOR WAR

By now Ito and his dwindling band of supporters could have harboured few illusions as to the hopelessness of such a cause, but as President of the Privy Council he was in a position to withhold ratification of all treaties and alliances and so still represented a considerable obstacle to the expansionists. Toyama decided that it was time to stretch a hand from behind his curtain.

Accompanied by three burly underlings, he paid an uninvited call on Ito's house. On being answered at the front door, he announced in a loud voice: 'I don't know whether there is going to be a beating up or not...' According to the official Black Dragon history, the conversation which then ensued between the two men 'virtually determined the decision for war with Russia'. Whether this was so or not, the visit was followed up by a letter from the 'warning committee' of The Anti-Russia Comrades Society accusing Ito of interfering as an Elder Statesman with Cabinet decisions and threatening 'public indignation' if he did not desist. When the letter was published in the Press, it created such a furore that Katsura called in three of the Society's leaders (including, of course, Toyama) and publicly declared to them that the Cabinet and Elder Statesmen were 'of one mind'.

Katsura too was favoured by a letter from the Society reminding him that the responsibility for the 'ultimate decision' was his and that he was not to be absolved of it by any opposition from the Elder Statesmen. This followed Japan's reply on October 30th to the Russian counter-proposals, which had marked something of a retreat from the original demands: Japan would recognise Manchuria as being outside her sphere of interest in return for a reciprocal declaration by Russia regarding Korea; she was prepared to accept the concept of a neutral zone if it was shifted north to span the Korea-Manchuria border; and, while reserving the right to use the rest of Korea for strategic purposes, she would undertake not to construct any military installations on the coast which would threaten naval lines of communication through the Tsushima Straits.

Publication of these terms stirred the Press to a fresh wave of denunciations of government weakness. Two weeks earlier the *Kokumin Shimbun*, in an editorial entitled 'A Warning to Government Leaders', had declared that 'should our government show signs of making further concessions to Russia, the righteous indignation of our people could not be held back even by ten thousand oxen. If this should occur, our nation would fall into confusion like a broken-up nest of a thousand bees.' Even the economic journal *Toyo Keizai Shimpo*, which less than two months earlier had written that 'knowledgeable people would never join those fellows who excitedly advocate war with Russia', now concluded that 'the possible effects of war upon the national economy are indeed grave, but the prestige and independence of our nation are of even more concern. If fighting is inevitable, we must of course bear the burden.' On November 22nd a conference at Osaka sponsored by the Press (following Army manoeuvres held nearby under the personal supervision of the Emperor) passed a resolution stating that 'a peaceful solution of the Manchurian question through indecisive diplomatic measures and humiliating conditions is meaningless. This is not what our nation wants.'

On December 10th the Emperor opened the new session of the Diet with the customary Speech from the Throne. The President of the Lower

House, one Kono Hironaka, an Anti-Russia Society sympathizer, then rose to make the formal reply, which had become so much of a convention over the years that its composition had been left to the Chief Secretary of the House. On this occasion, however, Kono stuffed the Secretary's script into his pocket and read out a prepared speech of his own which amounted to a motion of censure on the Cabinet and which called on Meiji to 'bring your enlightened judgement to bear on the situation'. The half-listening members, inured by tradition, then passed it unanimously, unaware that it had marked any departure from the usual ceremonial. When the true nature of its contents was eventually realised, the Government attempted to submit it to a second vote; failing in this, they then obtained an Imperial Rescript to dissolve the Diet. Kono's action received widespread popular acclaim; ten years later he would be finally rewarded with a place in the Cabinet.

The Diet's dissolution freed the Cabinet from parliamentary pressure and allowed them to prepare for war in their own good time, following the receipt the next day of a second Russian reply which contained nothing more than a restatement of their previous proposals. This insouciance is reflected in a story told of the Russian Ambassador in Seoul, who asked of the King rhetorically: 'Where in the world is Japan?' Affecting to examine a map through a pocket magnifying glass, he then declared: 'Oh, I find a tiny country called Japan in a corner of the Pacific Ocean. My Russian Empire is the greatest country on the globe, spreading over two continents. If Korea relies upon our Empire, she will be as safe as in navigating a sea in a colossal vessel. Should Japan object to it, our Russia will only have to do this.' He then placed some matches on the palm of his hand and blew them off. Such misguided overconfidence was repeated a generation later by the British, whose organisation of the defence of Singapore was undermined by the belief that Japanese pilots suffered from a congenital defect of the eyesight which debarred them from flying by night.

The leading ministers conferred with the Elder Statesmen on December 16th, and it was agreed that Japan should offer no further concessions but should merely invite Russia to 'reconsider her position'. Five days later Katsura wrote to Yamagata to tell him that unless Russia accepted the current Japanese proposals 'the last resort' should be taken. Yamagata expressed a little doubt in his reply as to whether the time for that had quite arrived, but on the 21st he gave Katsura the go-ahead to put all the necessary preparations for war in hand.

Katsura also called on Ito the same day and at last received an undertaking of unequivocal support for the decision; having seen the Seiyukai vote for Kono's 'motion of censure' a fortnight earlier, Ito had finally brought himself to acknowledge that he would isolate himself even from his own party if he persisted in holding out for a negotiated settlement. A week later the Cabinet called a special meeting, attended for the first time by the Vice-Chiefs of Staff, to establish a Supreme War Council. Yamagata proposed the immediate dispatch of troops to Seoul in a pre-emptive move to secure Korea, but this was turned down after the Navy Ministry, Yamamoto Gombei, pleaded that he was not yet in a position to furnish the necessary transports.

A further exchange of notes took place between Tokyo and St. Petersburg without producing any shift in the stance of either side, and on January 12th 1904 an Imperial Conference decided on the dispatch of one further note to allow time for the assembling of the transports. This was completed by the 30th, and in the absence of any further Russian reply Yamagata, Katsura, Komura, Yamamoto and Ito met to draft a memorial to the Throne submitting that the time had come for a 'resolute decision'. Before they parted, the 'Peace Preserver' was reported to have thrown his arms around his old adversary Ito, exclaiming 'if Japan loses, I'll be dead, but you'll be left to pick up the pieces'; this rare display of emotion may be explained by the fact that it was all of thirty-three years earlier that he had first drafted plans for war against Russia. Two days later Chief of Staff Oyama advised the Emperor that it was essential that Japan should strike first.

SURPRISE ATTACK

On February 6th Japan formally broke off diplomatic relations with St. Petersburg and reserved the right to 'take such independent action as they may deem best to consolidate and defend their menaced position'. Within hours the Japanese Fleet put out to sea under the command of Admiral Togo. During the night of the 8th it launched a surprise torpedo attack on the Russian Pacific Fleet of seven battleships and six cruisers anchored in Port Arthur, succeeding in grounding three of them for the loss of a destroyer. On the same day the Twelfth Division under General Kuroki Tametomo landed in Korea at Inchon; the escorting squadron of warships also engaged a Russian cruiser and gunboat stationed there and damaged them sufficiently to cause their crews to scuttle them.

It was the moment that all Japan had been whipped up to anticipate by the expansionists ever since the humiliation of the Russian-led Triple Intervention nine years earlier. 'I don't know why, but my blood boils and my eyes burn,' a young poet wrote ecstatically. 'What joy! What joy!'

An official Declaration of War was not issued to Russia until three days later, and then it was claimed that 'it is entirely against our wishes that we have unhappily come to open hostilities'. Most of the official apologists of the time chose to gloss over this embarrassing discrepancy altogether, while in his *Fifty Years of New Japan* Okuma preferred to relate the declaration's timing to 'the day to be long remembered as that on which our first Emperor, Jimmu, ascended the throne of Japan 2564 years before'. In their reply to Russia's formal note of protest the Japan Government claimed that Japan had already reserved her right to take independent action which 'implies all, including, as a matter of course, the opening of hostile acts. Even if Russia were unable to understand it, Japan had no reason to hold herself responsible for the misunderstandings of Russia. The students of International Law all agree that a declaration of war is not a necessary condition for beginning hostilities, and it has been customary in modern warfare for the declaration to follow the opening of the war. The action of Japan had, therefore, no ground for censure in international law ...' Thirty-seven years later very similar arguments would be trotted out to defend the duplicity of Pearl Harbor.

Just as he had done ten years earlier, Meiji moved his headquarters to Hiroshima in order to take personal charge of the campaign, taking with him Yamagata (in place of Oyama, who had been given command of the Army in the field) as Chief of General Staff. Further night attacks by sea on Port Arthur were followed by attempts to block the harbour entrance by sinking old hulks in the narrows, but these were only partially successful. On April 13th the Russian fleet broke out, but while returning from an inconclusive engagement with the enemy the flagship struck a Japanese mine and went down, taking the admiral in command with it. Thereafter they were content to remain in harbour and await reinforcement by the Baltic Fleet, which after a seemingly interminable series of delays eventually set sail in October under Admiral Zinovii Rozhestvenski.

On land the failure to complete the Trans-Siberian Railway had left the Russians heavily outnumbered, and in early May Kuroki drove them back over the Yalu River and crossed into Manchuria. Within a week two more Armies were landed at the base of the Kwantung Peninsula, the Second to drive north on the Russians' other Manchurian flank and the Third under General Nogi Maresuke to advance south on Port Arthur. Before the railway could be cut Viceroy Alexieff took train for the Russian headquarters at Liaoyang to join War Minister Kuropatkin, who had arrived from Europe to take personal command of his forces. Under the overall command of Oyama the two Japanese Armies linked up to advance on Liaoyang, and after three weeks of stiff resistance Kuropatkin was obliged to fall back on Mukden.

Everything now hinged on Port Arthur, whose speedy capture, Yamagata wrote to Nogi, 'is the most important element in the victory or defeat of our whole army'. Since Alexieff's departure the military command of the enclave's defences had fallen under the erratic direction of General Anatolii Stoessel, who then persistently ignored orders to hand over to the general specifically appointed to the post. Nogi's heavy artillery had already penetrated to within range of the harbour, but his subsequent attempts to advance closer were beaten back by the well-entrenched defenders.

When the Baltic Fleet (denied the use of the Suez Canal by Japan's British allies) rounded the Cape to enter the Indian Ocean, Nogi received a personal order from Meiji to take the citadel at whatever cost. Obediently resorting to the human wave tactic, he saw two of his own sons fall in another unsuccessful assault which cost 15,000 lives in all. One of the many Japanese agents behind the lines then approached three of Stoessel's aides and after offering them a promissory note bearing Yamagata's signature undertaking to pay the staggering sum of 65 million dollars in eleven years' time, he obtained a map of the Russian minefields. (The undertaking was never met, each of the three traitors being eliminated before they could redeem it).

At last, on December 5th, the vital 203-Metre Hill commanding the harbour was taken at the cost of yet another 11,000 lives, and after seeing all his remaining ships picked off one by one Stoessel capitulated. The terms of the unconditional surrender had actually been drafted two years earlier in anticipation of the event.

Nogi's Army, or what was left of it, was immediately transferred north again to reinforce the assault in Manchuria, and on March 16th, after weeks of bitter fighting which saw no less than three quarters of a million casualties, Mukden fell. All this time the Baltic Fleet had been continuing on its slow but steady progress, and to make up time Rozhestvenski decided to take the most direct route to Vladivostok through the Tsushima Straits. Togo was lying in wait for him, however, and by executing the classical manoeuvre of 'crossing the enemy's T' he was able to score a devastating victory. Out of six Russian battleships and six cruisers, only a single cruiser evaded destruction or capture.

Despite the successive Russian reverses on land Yamagata had recognised that the enemy was still very far from defeated, such was the magnitude of their resources. The Trans-Siberian Railway had at last been completed, and a further half million troops were even now on their way eastward. Japan on the other hand had lost a quarter of her already-outnumbered army and an even higher proportion of her officers. The production capacity of her munitions factories was falling further and further behind the demand at the front, and her economy as a whole was now totally dependent on foreign loans (the final cost of the war exceeded government revenue six times over).

After the fall of Mukden, Kodama, now Chief of Staff of the Manchurian Army, had been secretly summoned home by Meiji to give a first-hand assessment of the situation. He admitted, 'Mitsui-Man' Inoue recorded, that 'any further advance by the Army is impossible' and that it was time to put out peace feelers. Coming from the Adventurer of Amoy, this was sufficient to extinguish any lingering optimism among the high command. Katsura and his Foreign Minister, Komura, had already drawn up in private lists of terms to be put to Russia, but they felt bound to acknowledge the dizzy heights to which public expectations had been raised by the news of seemingly unending Japanese victories. Rather than make a direct approach to the enemy the Cabinet therefore decided, with Meiji's approval, to enlist the services of U.S. President Theodore Roosevelt, who had already declared his willingness to mediate between the two sides.

JAPAN'S HALF LOAF

While the Baltic Fleet was still afloat to carry his hopes of a dramatic reversal of Russian misfortune Tsar Nicholas had refused to entertain any talk of peace, but when it was dispatched to the bottom at Tsushima even he was brought to face reality, which included the ever-growing threat of revolution at home. When Roosevelt issued his formal invitations on June 9th, they were therefore promptly accepted by both sides and the venue of Portsmouth, New Hampshire agreed.

Their public announcement, however, came as a profound shock to the Japanese population at large, buoyed up as they were by hopes of a final, conclusive victory. Professor Tomizu was predictably to the fore in stirring opposition with an article entitled 'Has The Occasion For Peace Really Arrived?', for which he was suspended from his post at Tokyo University. The strength of criticism that it engendered played a part in the selection of the leader of the Japanese delegation to the Peace Conference. As the man who had negotiated the treaty after the war with China, Ito was the natural choice, but when Meiji asked Katsura if he would be able to cope with the critics in Ito's absence, the Prime Minister replied none too confidently. The Emperor thereupon ordered Ito not to go, and the choice fell instead on Komura.

When the fact of the coming Conference finally sank into the Japanese consciousness, projection of the terms to be demanded from Russia became more extravagant than ever. At the head of everyone's list was an indemnity running as high as 5,000,000,000 yen coupled with an acknowledgement of Japanese control over Korea and Manchuria. On top of these the Anti-Russia Comrades Society, which now merged with seven other nationalist societies under the Black Dragon umbrella to form 'The Joint Council of Fellow Activists on the Peace Question', demanded the cession to Japan of the whole of Sakhalin (which the Japanese had overrun in the last month of the war), the territory of the Chinese Eastern Railway in Manchuria and the Russian maritime province of Ussuri, while Professor Tomizu and his six colleagues called for the surrender of all Russian territory as far west as Lake Baikal. Even they, however, were outdone by a journalist who contended that the Imperial Army should march into St Petersburg itself and dictate its terms to the Tsar in person.

The instructions given to Komura were very moderate by contrast: only Japanese control of Korea, withdrawal of Russian troops from Manchuria and cession of the Kwantung Peninsula with the connecting railway to Harbin were categorized as 'absolutely indispensable', the payment of an indemnity and the cession of Sakhalin being deemed only 'relatively important'. Even these limited aims were recognised to be 'extremely difficult to secure', and it was with good reason that Katsura instructed the Foreign Secretary and his team that they 'should never let their deliberations be known to the populace'. Because of his previous links with the expansionists some of the Elder Statesmen were suspicious that Komura would exceed his mandate, and they accordingly extracted an undertaking from him that in no circumstances was he to break off negotiations without reference to Tokyo.

When the Conference got under way on August 9th, Witte, as leader of the Russian delegation, expressed a readiness to meet most of the Japanese demands, but on the Tsar's instructions he flatly refused to concede either an indemnity or any part of Sakhalin. In spite of the fact that these two items were not among the 'absolutely indispensable' conditions of his brief, Komura reported to Tokyo that negotiations had reached 'a complete deadlock' and declared his intention of terminating them the following day.

In the meantime, however, Yamagata had visited the front in Manchuria to see the position for himself, and what he found confirmed his worst fears: reinforced by three army corps of élite troops, the Russians now enjoyed a numerical superiority of three to one and a corresponding revival of confidence. Worse still, the Japanese Ambassador in Washington was informed by American bankers that the financial markets of the West would not support any further Japanese bond issues; in order to fund the war the national debt had soared to a figure of 1,370,000,000 yen (the equivalent then of £137 million, or £2,000 million in today's terms). The reluctance of foreign underwriters to increase it further stemmed partly from doubts surrounding the claim made a year earlier of a massive gold discovery at a mine which had been sunk by the government-backed Industrial Bank on the personal orders of Katsura. The value of the strike had been put at £400 million by a Home Affairs Ministry 'expert'. It ultimately proved totally worthless.

An Imperial Conference held on August 28th in Tokyo accordingly decided to withdraw the demand for an indemnity and to accept, purportedly 'out of respect for humanity and civilisation', a last-minute Russian offer to cede the southern half of Sakhalin. On receiving these new terms Komura, who had from the outset been the most determined of all to hold out for the original brief and was not party to the larger considerations behind its abandonment, could only remark despondently that 'I thought it might come to this.'

The Treaty of Portsmouth was concluded the following afternoon. Under it both sides also agreed to evacuate their troops from all areas of Manchuria except the railway territories under lease to them (the Port Arthur line was ceded to Japan as far as Changchun rather than Harbin as at first demanded). They also undertook not to obstruct any Chinese industrial or commercial development, and not to use the railways (except within the Kwantung Peninsula) for strategic purposes; and in Korea, Russia was pledged not to interfere with 'any measures of guidance, protection and control which Japan found it necessary to take.'

The reasoning behind this 'sacrifice for the sake of peace' (as the propagandist Hishida labelled it) owed more to cold calculation than any high-mindedness. 'Japan regarded peace as indispensable to her rapid recovery,' a later historian explained. 'Furthermore, in order to carry out her plans in China — the real object of her policy — Japan keenly realised that Russian co-operation was a prerequisite.'

A month later it was revealed that Japan had simultaneously been involved in negotiations with two other Powers. Following discussions in London, the Anglo-Japanese Alliance was renewed for a further period of ten years and greatly extended in scope: both sides were now obliged to go to the other's assistance in the event of an attack by a third party on either's interests, which were mutually recognised to be paramount in India and Korea respectively. Although not made public until September 27th, the final draft had been signed on August 12th. In early September advantage was taken of the visit of the U.S. Secretary of War, William Taft, to Tokyo while en route for the Philippines to conclude a pact whereby, in return for American recognition of Japanese suzerainty over Korea, Japan renounced all territorial designs on the Philippines. The Taft-Katsura Agreement, as it became known, was formally endorsed by Roosevelt on September 21st.

Secure in the protection of this new and formidable triple alignment, the Imperial Army high command immediately set about drafting under Yamagata's guidance the strategy for a second, much wider offensive against Russia in the event of the envisaged 'co-operation' failing to materialise. Their deliberations were to result in the presentation a year later to the Emperor of a blueprint for further expansion on the Asian continent, and a fifteen-year programme to bring the Army's standing strength up to 25 regular divisions.

14

Korea and Beyond

'RUNNING DOGS'

When the news reached Japan that the demands for an indemnity and for the northern half of Sakhalin had been dropped, the country, fed a censorship-controlled diet of endless victories and limitless expectations of reward, was struck dumb. Even the Press was at first rendered incapable of doing more than publishing the bare announcement in banner headlines without comment.

When it did recover its powers of speech twenty-four hours later, it was seized with a collective apoplexy that made its reception of the Triple Intervention ten years earlier seem positively stoic by comparison. Many of the leading papers appeared edged in black, with headlines to match: 'The Unpardonable Crime', 'Ah, Great Humiliation! Great Humiliation!' 'We Are More And More Enraged', 'Head Of A Dragon, Tail Of A Worm', 'Ito And Katsura, Running Dogs', 'Reject The Peace, Manchurian Army, Keep On Fighting', 'We Shall Shake The World With Our Public Opinion', The People Should Rise As One Body And Urge The Government To Cancel The Peace'. A number even went so far as openly to advocate the assassination of the Cabinet.

Godfather Toyama and his cronies on the Joint Council of Fellow Activists needed no further invitation. On the very next day, August 31st, 1905, they set up an Anti-Peace Society and dashed off a memorial to the Imperial Palace, the gist of which appeared thus in the *Osaka Asahi Shimbun*: 'We, His loyal subjects, are at the extremity of tears, blood and indignation. We are willing to fight to the last man, even if Japan must become a scorched land ... Whether the agreed peace is to be ratified or rejected is the prerogative of His Majesty. We, His subjects, humbly request His Majesty to order cancellation of the peace agreement, which is contrary to His Will, before it is signed, to order wise men to form a new Cabinet and to command the military men to fight on.' A resolution was simultaneously passed calling on the Cabinet to 'apologize for their crimes to the Emperor above and to the people below.'

Three days later, having received no response from the Government, they drew up plans for a mass protest rally in the capital's Hibiya Park on September 5th, the day set for the formal signature of the Treaty. A nearby theatre was hired for a 'get-acquainted meeting' of prospective speakers; application was made for permission to use the Park 'to shoot off two fire-crackers in the bushes'; banners were ordered bearing such slogans as 'The Whole Nation, One Heart' and 'We Have Swords To Cut Down Traitors'; and 30,000 'invitations' were distributed to 'anyone who is patriotic'. The Press also took up this call: 'Come, those who have blood. Come, those who have backbones. Come those who have strong wills . . . and all together raise a voice of opposition to this humiliating and shameful peace.'

The Government replied by issuing free copies of its mouthpiece, the *Kokumin Shimbun,* approving the Treaty terms, but the paper was uni-versally boycotted. An order to the Directors of the Tokyo tram com-panies to decorate their vehicles with celebratory flags was similarly foiled when the Streetcar Workers Association threatened to destroy the whole fleet if a single flag was raised. As a last resort an order was issued banning the rally and instructing the police to barricade the Park entrances.

By 10 am on the appointed day, however, a crowd of some 30,000 had already gathered and had little difficulty in rushing the wooden barriers to cries of 'Port Arthur 203-metre Hill fell, Banzai!' Speeches were due to begin in the theatre at 2 pm, but the crowd both inside and outside grew so dense that the police ordered it to disperse before the first speaker could take the stage. Fighting then broke out as the crowd turned its attention elsewhere. The *Kokumin Shimbun* offices were stormed and its presses smashed; the house of the Home Affairs Minister was then attacked and burnt to the ground, at which point three companies of soldiers of the Imperial Guards Division were sent in. As the demonstrators scattered into the suburbs, they took their revenge on police stations and boxes, destroying over 70% of the total in the metropolitan area in the course of the next twenty-four hours. For the first time since the Restoration, martial law was declared and all newspapers critical of the Treaty were closed down.

Total casualties amounted to over a thousand, including 17 dead (all demonstrators). The report of the official investigation into them was suppressed; finally published in 1938, it was found to exonerate the police of all blame. A number of the rally organisers were arrested and charged under the Peace Preservation Act, but they were all released again without standing trial after they explained that the development into a riot had been 'indeed a surprising consequence . . . something that is extremely regrettable.'

Elaborate security measures were taken on the return of Komura who, notwithstanding his own disappointment at the outcome of the negotia-tions, had become the prime target for vilification: 'It is our plenipoten-tiary who has smeared the face of the ever-victorious nation,' the *Yorozu Choho* accused. 'On the day of his return he should be met with flags of mourning. Every person in the city should shut the door of his house and turn away from him. Any who welcome this soft fellow, who has invited unprecedented humiliation upon our nation, are wretched people with no blood ...' A large crowd of officials having been assembled on the Yokohama customs quay as if to greet him, he was smuggled ashore elsewhere, driven in a closed carriage to the station and put on a special train to Tokyo.

HANDS UNDER THE POLITICAL COUNTER

On September 7th more than a hundred Opposition members in the Lower House called on Katsura with a demand for an extraordinary session of the Diet. Amid all the sound and fury, however, the leaders of the majority Seiyukai Party had been conspicuous by their silence — for the very good reason that they were already bound by a secret deal with the Government. This had its origins in approaches made by Katsura the previous November to the Opposition in an attempt to gain all-party support for his war budget. Lame Democrat Okuma's personal vanity persuaded his Real Constitutionalists to reject him, but the Seiyukai, led by Saionji (who had succeeded his patron Ito as party president) and their astute secretary-general Hara Kei, recognised the opportunity to strengthen their claim to a voice in the Cabinet.

Having first satisfied himself on Katsura's motives, Hara (who was related to both Ito and Inoue among the Elder Statesmen) then struck a deal with him: in return for the party's support for the duration of the war, Katsura would resign as Prime Minister when it ended and recommend Saionji to succeed him on condition that the new Cabinet contained a majority of non-party members. Even at this stage Katsura foresaw that 'when peace comes, the people will certainly be dissatisfied with the terms', and he stipulated that after the resultant unpopularity of the outgoing administration had died down, Saionji should stand aside and return the premiership to him. This pact was to hold good almost up to the time of Katsura's death eight years later.

Unaware of these secret commitments, the leaders of the Real Constitutionalists suggested to their counterparts in the Seiyukai that the two parties should join in a motion of censure on the Treaty terms in an attempt to topple the Government. Their consternation may be imagined when Saionji replied that 'I cannot help congratulating the Government, which for the sake of civilisation and humanity has restored peace ...' Scarcely less surprised must have been the rank-and-file members of his own party, who earlier that same day had passed a resolution condemning the terms and calling on the Government to resign. Hara left Tokyo in the evening announcing that he was 'going to inspect mines in the north-eastern region'. Next day Katsura invited the leaders of both parties to his official residence and gave them an account of the reasoning behind the conclusion of the Treaty; the meeting also served to make it plain to Okuma and his colleagues that their opposition to it had been effectively isolated.

Waves of indignation continued to radiate outwards from the capital in the wake of the Hibiya Park riot and the imposition of martial law, causing the Government to take further steps to bring the country to order. The rally-organiser, Kono, undertook to distribute leaflets appealing for calm and to disband The Joint Council of Fellow Activists, while Yamagata requested Chief of Staff Oyama to 'take appropriate measures to ensure that this wave of excitement will not affect the Army in Manchuria'. The 'Peace Preserver' followed this for good measure with a rare public statement of policy published in the Government mouthpiece *Nichi Nichi* justifying the decision to come to terms. 'To continue the war would have involved heavy sacrifice, and would not have attained results greater than those attainable by making peace now,' he explained to the nation. 'We shrank therefore from wasting the resources which the country would need for its future enterprises in Korea and in the leased regions of Manchuria ...'

The Taft-Katsura Agreement was announced on September 21st, to be followed a week later by the news of the renewal of the Anglo-Japanese Alliance. On October 16th an Imperial Rescript was issued to mark the formal ratification of the Portsmouth Treaty expressing Meiji's pleasure with it and concluding: 'We strongly caution Our subjects against manifestations of vainglorious pride and command them to attend to their lawful vocations and to do all that is in their power to strengthen the Empire.' The seal of Imperial approval was sufficient to still the most outraged hothead, and on November 29th martial law was finally lifted and the freedom of the Press restored. A motion in the Diet went so far as to attribute Japan's victories in the field to 'Your Majesty's almost superhuman wisdom ... We, whose happiness it is to witness these great things, dance with joy and cannot contain our delight.'

Katsura still felt unable to hand over the premiership until he had secured the acknowledgement of the other parties concerned in the Treaty, namely, China and Korea. If he were to resign before this was done, he feared that they might interpret it as a sign of internal opposition within Japan to the Treaty and thereby be encouraged not to recognise it. Komura was accordingly dispatched to Peking where he obtained the required imprimatur, together with a secret clause which bound China not to build any railway 'in the neighbourhood of or parallel to' the Port Arthur-Changchun line until the Japanese lease on the latter expired, while Japan was given an additional 15-year lease on the Mukden-Antung line which she had constructed during the war as a link to Korea.

Ito's parallel mission to Seoul was rather more of a formality, for in the early days of the war Japan had forced the Korean King to put his signature to a protocol conceding the right to establish a military protectorate there, and this had been followed a few months later by another which gave Japan control of the country's economy. The benighted monarch was now confronted with a document incorporating not only these, but a further clause which put all direction of Korea's foreign affairs in the hands of a Japanese Resident-General. He appealed in desperation to Britain and America for help, but in vain; the former was bound by the new terms of the Alliance to recognise Japan's paramountcy, while Roosevelt felt so powerless to intervene that he ordered the U.S. Legation in Seoul to close down. Two of the Korean Cabinet committed suicide rather than be party to it, and the signature of the King himself was only finally obtained at two o'clock in the morning (some even asserted later that it had been forged by the Japanese). Its announcement later that day provoked riots in various parts of the country, but these were quickly squashed by the Japanese forces already in occupation. On December 21st an Imperial Rescript was issued in Tokyo promulgating the appointment of the first Resident-General — none other than the Constitution-Maker Ito himself.

His mission fulfilled, Katsura made way for Saionji, as agreed, on January 6th 1906. The secret had been kept so successfully that it came as a surprise to most members of his own Cabinet. Even Yamagata had not been included in it, and this assertion of independence from his patron on Katsura's part was to lead to a growing coolness between the two men. However, Yamagata was still able to register his baleful influence in the new Cabinet via two other protégés, War Minister Terauchi and his own adopted son, Communications Minister Yamagata Isaburo. Saionji kept to his side of the deal by appointing only three ministers out of a total of ten from the ranks of the Seiyukai.

CHANGE OF TACK

Yamagata, who had already resigned as Chief of General Staff in order to take over from Ito as President of the Privy Council, made his support for the new administration conditional upon its continuation of the expansionist programme; at any time, it must be remembered, he could engineer its downfall by getting Terauchi to resign and refusing to nominate a successor. The conclusions of the High Command's study for a second offensive against Russia were first drafted by another protégé (and member of the Kogetsukai pressure group) Tanaka Giichi, and then presented to the Emperor by Yamagata himself on October 16th 1906. Entitled *The Plan of National Defence for the Empire*, it envisaged a campaign to drive the Russians out of northern Manchuria together with a naval assault on Vladivostok, to be followed by the conquest of southern China and the closure of the Straits of Formosa (in his original draft Tanaka had also called for attacks on French Indo-China and the Philippines). Obtaining the Imperial blessing, it was then submitted for comment to Saionji, who demurred only to the extent of asking that the timetable for the required expansion of military and naval capacity should not be fixed in advance but decided as and when funds became available.

In making this qualification he could hardly be accused of overstepping his responsibilities as Prime Minister, given the parlous state of the national economy at the end of the war. The initial tranche of funds was only found by resorting to the device of nationalising the country's railways; the sudden flood of Government scrip issued to meet it set off a runaway surge in economic activity, from which the projected increase in tax revenue was then earmarked for the military building programme. Such dubious practice led Anglo-Ally Kato, who had returned to the Foreign Ministry in place of the outcast Komura, to resign in protest, and its discussion in the Diet became the occasion for a free fight in which furniture was smashed and a number of members injured before the Seiyukai majority saw it through.

Inevitably, the boom collapsed in due course as spectacularly as it had begun, bringing in its wake a depression which was only relieved by the outbreak of World War One seven years later. The Government was accordingly obliged to turn to the alternative strategy of seeking Russia's co-operation, first envisaged during the Portsmouth negotiations.

The leading proponent of this policy was Hayashi, who had been recalled from the London Embassy to take over the vacant Foreign Ministry. In the words of Reuter's correspondent in Tokyo at the time, 'the whole foundation of Japanese policy as he enunciated it lay in simultaneous political and commercial penetration ... He saw in a commercial and economic campaign in China an invaluable aid to, and in certain spheres a substitute for, diplomatic [or military] activity. His policy was to combine the two, and to reinforce their advance by agreements with the various Powers, which should give Japan control over every other nation's affairs in China.' Another veteran Tokyo hand, Ernest Satow, described it even more bluntly: 'Japan proposes to secure as large a share of the trade of China as she can, by all contrivances she can think of.'

This change of tack brought Hayashi almost immediately into collision with the military over the question of the evacuation of Manchuria. In spite of the undertaking enshrined in the Portsmouth Treaty and of a decision taken at an Elder Statesmen Cabinet conference on May 22nd 1906 to complete it before the agreed date of April 15th 1907, the High Command opposed any attempt to enforce it. Hayashi thereupon submitted his resignation, only to be ordered to retract it by the Emperor. The Kwantung Army, as it was now called, reluctantly bowed to the Imperial Will and agreed to withdraw from the non-leased areas, reducing itself to the 13,000 men permitted as railway guards on the South Manchuria Railway by the Treaty.

His strategy thus confirmed, Hayashi began to move towards the desired rapprochement with Russia. Tentative feelers had in fact already been put out by St. Petersburg, but Hayashi, not wishing to give an impression of over-enthusiasm, preferred to make an indirect response via

Russia's ally France — a tactic, so he recorded in his Memoirs, that met with the approval not only of the Russophile Ito but even of Yamagata.

As it happened, the French had their own reasons for reciprocating this show of goodwill, having somehow got wind of Japanese designs in Indo-China. In an agreement signed in Paris on June 10th 1907 ritual obeisance was made to the principle of maintaining China's independence and the policy of 'Open Door', but both sides went on to pledge themselves 'to support each other in preserving peace and security' *inside* those parts of China adjacent to areas where they held rights of 'sovereignty, protection or occupation' — Indo-China and southern Manchuria respectively. Just how lightly the notion of China's independence was held is indicated by the fact that neither side saw fit to seek Peking's approval for the agreement.

Seeing this recognition by Japan of France's right to a sphere of influence in China's southern provinces, Russia was not slow to seize the bait which was now offered concerning her own interests in northern Manchuria. Barely three days later agreement was reached between the two countries on the linking of their respective railway systems at Harbin, to be followed in another six weeks by the Russo-Japanese Convention of St. Petersburg. Outwardly, this did no more than bind the parties to uphold the 'Open Door' and maintain the status quo as defined in the Treaty of Portsmouth 'by all pacific means in their power'. However, a number of secret clauses were appended to it which not only recognised their respective spheres of influence in Outer Mongolia and Korea, but also divided up Manchuria between them by a specific line of demarcation; each party, 'desiring to avert the complications likely to arise from competition', undertook not to interfere with the other's development of railway and telegraph lines on either side of it.

RAILWAY DIPLOMACY

Having thus received, as he saw it, *carte blanche* from the Powers that mattered (the United States held no direct interests in China and those of Germany were considered to be so small as to be insignificant), Hayashi lost no time in pushing forward with his objective of economic and political penetration. The South Manchuria Railway Company had already been incorporated the previous year to take over the Port Arthur-Changchun and Mukden-Antung lines; five-sixths of its capital was held by the Japanese government, and out of the 7,354 holders of the remainder (which was nominally available to the Government and citizens of China) all but 25 were Japanese. Japan was also vested with the right to appoint its principal officers, the first president being Goto Shimpei, the former Governor of Formosa; as was the case with that colony, however, real control was exercised by a military Governor-General, the commander of the Kwantung Army.

The SMR's field of operations was extended beyond the rights granted to Russia under the terms of the original lease in 1896 to work mines and run telegraph lines alongside the railway and now encompassed the construction of warehouses, freight depots, electric power stations and even of hotels and restaurants. Similarly, the civilian administration under the Governor-General was vastly expanded to include not only the supervision of customs and police, but also civil jurisdiction (a 'mild form' of torture could be applied during the trial of Chinese defendants, who made up 95% of the population of the leased territories), tax collection, public health, local government and schools management.

The deadline of April 15th 1907 for the evacuation of non-leased territory had not been met, the troops there being merely reassigned to 'gendarmerie duties' at the Japanese consulates set up in the ten towns which China had agreed to open to international trade. Their presence was made necessary, according to the propagandist Asakawa, by 'a most strenuous and persistent policy of obstruction' on the part of the Chinese authorities, with whom 'no argument to the effect that Japan has, by an enormous sacrifice, saved Manchuria for China has much weight'. Likewise, Japanese immigrants continued to pour into areas outside the lease in flat violation of the Peking Agreement; these were explained away as 'unscrupulous adventurers' and so beyond the power of the Japanese government. Under the Agreement the guards on the SMR were also to be withdrawn 'when tranquillity shall have been re-established in Manchuria and China shall have become herself capable of affording full protection to the lives and property of foreigners'; that they had not been so already was due, in Asakawa's words, 'to the inadequacy of the Chinese police and military forces in the face of the still great dangers from the "mounted bandits"'.

The SMR was to be Hayashi's spearhead, and he made it his first priority that nothing should be allowed to blunt its edge. Its coastal terminus was at first closed to all but Japanese ships, and prohibitive rates of tariff were imposed on all but Japanese goods. In further contravention of the Portsmouth Treaty, it was used to transport troops, who were represented as protecting passengers against the 'mounted bandits'.

In November 1907 China responded to these flagrant infringements of her rights by inviting the British firm of Pauling & Co. to construct an extension of the Imperial Railways network (which served Port Arthur's rival port of Newchuang) from Fakumen to Hsinmintun, which would have the effect of by-passing the junction of the SMR lines at Mukden. In protesting at this threatened competition, Japan was obliged to reveal to the world the existence of the secret clause in the Peking Agreement forbidding the construction of any line 'in the neighbourhood of or parallel to' the SMR. China remained unmoved, however, pointing out that as the distance between the two was 35 miles they could hardly be construed as being 'in the neighbourhood' of each other, and that furthermore they were separated by the natural barrier of the Liao River.

Japan then appealed to her British ally. The Foreign Secretary in the new Liberal administration, Sir Edward Grey, found himself torn between supporting his own country's commercial interests and maintaining the wider advantages of the Alliance. Coming down eventually on the side of the latter, he instructed his Ambassador in Peking not to support the project, which was accordingly dropped. In the wake of this important diplomatic victory a question was put to the Foreign Minister in the Diet as to whether the leased territories were now considered to be part of the Japanese Empire? The implications of this were held to be so sensitive that Hayashi would only give his answer behind closed doors. Asakawa hastened to reassure the world that 'it is impossible to infer any ulterior design on Japan's part to create a situation favourable for an indefinite retention of the territory or its ultimate annexation'.

STOCKING THE CABINET

On the domestic front, however, there was less cause for satisfaction. As the depression deepened, so industrial unrest began to manifest itself, culminating in a riot of 15,000 copper miners which troops had to be brought in to quell. This was followed by a decree ordering the fledgling Socialist Party to dissolve and banning all literature which smacked of subversion, particularly by Russian authors. The Party's activists continued to meet in secret, however, and on June 22nd they staged a public parade through the streets of Tokyo. 'The Red Flag Incident', as it became known, was broken up by the police with their customary ferocity and most of its organisers imprisoned, but even worse was to follow — namely, an attempt on the life of the Emperor himself. The object, as its ringleader Kotoku Shusui explained at his trial (held in camera), was to prove Him mortal and so destroy the myth of His divinity. Striking as he was at the first article of faith in the official dogma, his retribution was as swift as it was merciless; he and eleven of his fellow-conspirators were all executed within three days of the verdict being found against them.

Yamagata especially was disturbed by these developments. He had never approved the deal which had brought Saionji to the Premiership, and he now felt even less confident in the ability of one who, albeit a quarter of a century earlier, had himself edited a radical newspaper (until receiving a direct order from Meiji in person to desist). It was time, the 'Peace Preserver' advised in an audience at the Imperial Palace, to invoke the other side of the deal and recall Katsura. The fact that in the general election of only a month earlier Saionji and his Seiyukai had won an overall majority for the first time was not, needless to say, seen as presenting any obstacle.

The pretext chosen was once again the budget, which called for further expenditure cuts in the face of the continuing depression. Ostensibly in protest at the economies imposed on his department, Yamagata's adopted son obediently resigned as Minister of Communications. 'Yamagata's trickery is no longer a cause for surprise,' the Home Minister and Seiyukai secretary-general Hara observed. 'After all, he is annoyed that he has not succeeded in running the present Cabinet as he wished, so it is not strange that he resorts to such scheming methods.' When this failed to trigger the fall of the Cabinet as he had anticipated, Yamagata played his trump card, the resignation of War Minister Terauchi and refusal to nominate a successor. Saionji accepted the inevitable and announced his retirement on the well-worn grounds of 'ill health'.

Katsura was duly reinstalled, together with Komura, his old running mate in his first Cabinet, who replaced Hayashi as Foreign Minister; the rest of the Cabinet was almost entirely filled by other non-party nominees of Yamagata. Japan's stance in foreign affairs immediately took on a more positive and apparently open attitude; as Asakawa would have it believed, her previous policy had been 'widely misunderstood by the outside world ... Since the change of Cabinet the situation has begun to improve on all sides.'

PUSHING THE OPEN DOOR

Nowhere had the 'misunderstanding' run deeper than in the United States, particularly over Japan's attempt to obtain a stranglehold on Manchuria by means of the SMR. Not only did this conflict with Hay's cherished principle of 'Open Door' and with the Roosevelt-inspired Portsmouth Treaty, but it also threatened American dreams of a 'trans-world' railway conjured up by railroad magnate E. H. Harriman. The resulting animosity was reciprocated no less passionately by Japan over the discrimination imposed on Japanese immigrants in California. This had culminated in an order issued on October 11th 1906 by the San Francisco Board of Education segregating the children of Orientals into separate schools. The order was condemned by Roosevelt with all the Presidential authority that he could muster, but even so he was obliged to introduce an amendment to the Immigration Act barring entry to all but existing passport-holders before the Board would agree to withdraw it.

The *Tokyo Mainichi* thereupon called for the dispatch of the Japanese Fleet, while for his part Roosevelt took the talk of war seriously enough to order a review of the Philippines' defences and to warn Tokyo that 'the United States will no more submit to bullying than it will bully'. In case the Japanese were tempted to dismiss this as mere bluff, the U.S. Battle Fleet of sixteen battleships was then sent out on a tour of the Pacific. Consequently even the expansionists in the High Command conceded that the time had now come to eradicate the 'misunderstandings', for the state of the economy clearly ruled out any further large-scale military undertakings in the foreseeable future.

There was a second, equally pressing incentive for doing so. Following the abandonment of the Fakumen-Hsinmintun project in the face of Japanese objections, the Chinese Court realised that the establishment of a nation-wide railway system under their own auspices offered the best prospect of holding the Empire together against the threat of further encroachments. A development plan was accordingly drawn up under the supervision of the newly-appointed Director of the Imperial Railways, Chang Chi-tung, while the former 'Biggest Man' in Korea, Yuan Shi-k'ai, was switched from the command of the new National Army raised by the Dowager Empress after the Boxer Rebellion to head the Foreign Ministry.

Yuan at once set in motion negotiations for the necessary loans (China had still to pay off a considerable portion of the Boxer indemnity). America, the proponent of 'Open Door' policy, and to a lesser extent Germany, were the obvious sources to tap first; recent agreements with Japan made Britain, France and Russia less promising prospects, and in any case an Anglo-French consortium had already been granted in principle a concession to build a line from Hankow to Canton. In August 1908 the U.S. Consul-General in Manchuria (and agent for Harriman), Willard Straight, and the Chinese provincial governor reached an agreement for the construction of a line from Chinchow to Taontan, to be backed by a loan of $20 million; the contract for the survey work was given to Pauling.

As this proposed line ran parallel with the SMR and only slightly further west than the abortive Fakumen-Hsinmintun project, it was not calculated to find favour with the Japanese. An instruction was hurriedly cabled to Tokyo's Ambassador in Washington to negotiate a settlement of the two countries' current differences so as to forestall the ratification of Straight's agreement. They were assisted in the race by the apparently fortuitous deaths in mid-November of both the impotent Chinese Emperor and, within the space of 48 hours, the Dowager Empress herself. A fortnight later, on the very day that the Chinese arrived in the American capital to finalise the Chinchow-Taontan contract, Japan and the United States exchanged notes recommitting themselves to the principle of Open Door in China and to 'the maintenance of the status quo'.

This Root-Takahira Agreement, Straight predicted gloomily, would be used by Japan as a tool 'to convince the Chinese of the existence of confidential relationships between the United States and Japan and of the hopelessness of securing American assistance against Japanese penetration'. The failure to put any definition on the 'status quo' would, he thought, be seen in Japanese eyes as conferring tacit approval on their designs on Manchuria, while obeisance to the 'Open Door' now held no more than 'a ceremonial meaning'. Certainly, ensuing events in China did nothing to contradict such a conclusion. The Dragon Throne passed to the three-year-old Pu-Yi, nephew of the late Emperor, who was appointed Regent, and the greatest obstacle in Japan's path, 'Biggest Man' Yuan, found himself dismissed from office and in fear of his life. 'Within three years there will be a revolution in China' was Ito's confident prediction.

In the meantime the Constitution-Maker was happy enough to settle into his new post as Resident-General in Seoul and, secure in the Treaty of Portsmouth's guarantee of Russia's non-interference, to implement those 'measures of guidance, protection and control which Japan found it necessary to take'.

KOREA'S FATE SIGNED

The decision formally to annexe Korea had been taken in principle as early as 1904 by the first Katsura government, but it was to be implemented over a period of years in order to minimise offence to the West; the same consideration had dictated the choice of Ito as the first Resident-General. The conditions that he imposed for his acceptance of the post, particularly that he should have direct command over the occupying forces, indicate that he foresaw his rule as a relatively benevolent one. They also caused considerable misgivings among the military hierarchy, as the Chief of Staff recorded: 'When Ito demanded the position of field-marshal it started a big argument. Yamagata was opposed, but because he wanted Ito to be the first Resident-General, there was no way out ... Kodama was also reluctant. He approved on the surface, but told me by telephone to oppose it publicly, which I did. Afterwards I also reluctantly gave in.' As a check on his independence, it was arranged that the Black Dragon boss Uchida should be included on Ito's staff.

Uchida immediately set about organising a 'Unite Japan and Korea Society' among the remnants of the Tonghak rebels (who had been used to provide the spark for the Japanese 'fire-raisers' in 1894), but he was obliged to dissociate himself from it in public when Ito learnt of his connection. In spite of this he was able to obtain a grant of 100,000 yen from the Army to fund the Society's activities and even to persuade the Korean Prime Minister to include its president in his Cabinet.

This moved the King to send a secret mission to the International Conference held at The Hague in July 1907 to complain of Japan's interference in his country's affairs and to invite assistance from the Western Powers. The Japanese managed to stop the mission being ad-mitted to the Conference chamber, but they were unable to prevent them from gaining the informal ear of the delegates. When news of this reached Tokyo Prime Minister Saionji was bombarded with memoranda calling for 'decisive measures', including one from Toyama 'asserting and con-firming' that the sovereignty of the Korean King 'should be delegated to our nation'.

In Seoul, Ito awaited the outcome of a series of conferences between the Elder Statesmen and Cabinet (also attended by Katsura, although he was at that time a member of neither). Growing restive at the inaction, Uchida and his Korean stooges decided that 'now is the time. We must force the abdication of the King.' Concluding that neither Ito nor the Korean Prime

Minister would approve such a step, they cabled Tokyo on July 17th 1907 with a fictitious claim that 'last night Ministers pressed for abdication, but were rejected.' In fact, Ito had become severely disillusioned with the King after the Hague mission, and he was prepared to fall in with this account. He himself thus reported two days later that 'nine of the Cabinet went into consultation with the King at 1 am today. They got his agreement to abdicate and promulgated it at 3 am.' Even if it is accepted as fact (and it bears an ominous resemblance to the account of the King's early-morning signature of the 1905 'agreement'), this behaviour of the Ministers is rather more likely to have been inspired by the arrival from Tokyo the previous afternoon of Foreign Minister Hayashi than to have been a spontaneous initiative of their own.

Later that same day Ito reported that some Korean soldiers had attacked Japanese gendarmes in the streets of the capital. On the 22nd in a cable to Saionji, he expanded the incident into an attempt by the King to regain his throne 'by various underhand measures', including an order to the palace guards to assassinate the Cabinet; the attempt had failed, he alleged, 'due to the arrival of Japanese soldiers thirty minutes before it was due to take place'. Unfortunately he seems to have got his lines crossed with Hayashi, whose account read somewhat differently: 'There was an attempt to go into the Palace and kill all the Ministers. They fled and were barely able to arrive at the Resident-General's residence at 11.30 pm asking for protection ... our soldiers took up position at 11.58 pm.'

Whichever of the two, if either, is to be believed, the intention behind them was plain enough, for on the following day the Elder Statesmen and Cabinet met to discuss sending more troops to Korea, a step which Ito had suggested in his cable. On receiving their approval, Ito summoned the Korean Cabinet and presented them with the draft of a seven-article agreement conferring vast new powers on the Resident-General, including the right to appoint Japanese to posts in the Government. He doubtless also passed on to them Saionji's assurance that the requested troops were on their way, giving them even less option but to sign. This done, Yamagata and Saionji presented their copy of the agreement to Meiji, who bestowed his Imperial sanction on it.

The formal announcement of the King's abdication (in favour of his feeble-minded son), followed closely by that of the disbandment of the Korean Army, led to further widespread unrest, and an English visitor described how Japanese troops toured the countryside burning scores of villages in search of 'rebels'. One particularly well-informed crowd gathered outside the Japanese Legation shouting 'Kill Uchida!' Even when not branded as 'rebels', many leaseholders on the Royal estates, some with tenancies several centuries old, shortly found themselves summarily evicted to make way for Japanese settlers.

SEALED

A measure of the extent of Ito's *volte-face* is provided by his treatment of Pak Young-hyo, the veteran survivor of the failed coup of 1884 and puppet government of 1895. The previous year Ito had obtained the King's blessing for Pak's return from his long exile in Japan and had even gone so far as to confide that he planned to 'make him Prime Minister'. By June 1907 Pak was back in Seoul awaiting the call to office. When the news of the King's abdication reached Tokyo, a 'Japan-Korea Friendship Society' was hastily organised to press for Pak's appointment as Prime Minister. Pak's reaction, however, was to decline to play the subservient rôle intended for him, just as he had begun to show signs of doing in 1895. Instead, he accepted an invitation from the King to join a government-in-abdication. This was too much for Ito, who promptly had him arrested and banished to a remote island. Back in Tokyo, the embarrassed members of the Japan-Korea Friendship Society were obliged hurriedly to roll up their banners and disband.

Uchida, however, was still very far from satisfied. The new 'agreement' was, he complained, 'still a long way from the final objective', while he was 'disappointed' that Ito had declined the offer of help from the United Japan and Korea Society in suppressing the unrest. Despite the savage measures taken against them, the number of 'rebels' continued to mount, reaching a total of 70,000 in 1908 (of whom almost 12,000 were killed). Many of the survivors crossed into Manchuria to regroup.

In August, while Ito was in Tokyo, his deputy, Sone Arasuke, cabled for permission to arrange with the Chinese for the dispatch of troops over the border in pursuit of them, but Ito refused. Sone then contacted the War and Foreign Ministers, Terauchi and Komura respectively, direct and asked them to consider the matter. Uchida too was busy at work behind Ito's back, accusing him in a letter to Katsura (now again Prime Minister) of forgetting his 'great mission'. In September he returned to Tokyo to co-ordinate a behind-the-curtain campaign for Ito's removal.

In due course Ito became aware of his subordinate's activities, and returning again to Japan in April 1909 he made a speech defending his Korean policy and accusing Uchida of disloyalty. Such an open attack on the Black Dragon-Army-Emperor nexus was not to be tolerated and, according to the Black Dragon's official history, 'shortly afterwards an unofficial decision that he should resign was made'. In a letter dated April 17th Katsura wrote to Yamagata that 'the sooner the day of his replacement, the better for the next step in our policy ... Now is the best time. Terauchi and Komura agree with me.' Ito was experienced enough to know a *fait accompli* when he saw one, and in June he duly submitted his resignation in exchange for a return to the office of President of the Privy Council (conveniently vacated for him by Yamagata).

'The next step in our policy' could mean only one thing, and in fact

Komura had already prepared a draft giving the go-ahead for Korea's annexation. 'The policy of Japan towards Korea is to establish our power in the peninsula and firmly hold this power,' it read. 'Since the Russo-Japanese war our power has been increasing . . . but it is still not enough and our relationship with Korean officials is not satisfactory. Therefore from now on it is necessary to try to increase our actual power and make a deeper foundation . . . The surest means to establish our power in Korea is to annex the peninsula and make it a part of our territory.' Komura and Katsura kept this draft secret between themselves until they had had an opportunity to sound out Ito on his return in April.

Until now Ito, with his lifelong preference for civilian rather than military rule, had resolutely opposed the attempts of the expansionists to strengthen their position in Korea, and they were understandably apprehensive of his reaction. They were therefore 'rather taken aback', in the words of his private secretary, when 'Ito said that he completely agreed with them'. The meeting did, however, take place after he had learnt of the decision to replace him; furthermore, he also extracted a pledge from Katsura in return that the annexation would not take place 'for another seven or eight years'. The draft was then shown to Yamagata, and it eventually received the Emperor's sanction in July after it had been endorsed by the Cabinet. Contingency plans were drawn up in case of a Korean refusal to put a signature to it.

The choice of Ito's successor as Resident-General had also been decided upon in advance. 'An influential person is not necessary,' Katsura told Yamagata in the same letter just quoted. 'I recommend Sone, because it will be easy to direct him as we wish.' Sone, of course, was a bureaucrat rather than a soldier, but Uchida was assured by the high command that if he proved 'not sufficiently committed to the final plot, we will just dismiss him.'

The Black Dragon Boss returned to Seoul to ensure for himself that all went according to plan, and he quickly found reason to question whether the new Resident-General was indeed 'sufficiently committed' after the latter refused to approve further Government funds for the Unite Japan and Korea Society. As a result, a letter was soon on its way back to Tokyo suggesting that Sone should be required to resign. At the same time a henchman of Yamagata began broadcasting doubts on the degree of co-operation to be expected from Ito, but, according to the Black Dragon history, 'fortunately he was invited to Ito's residence for dinner and there he obtained Ito's approval' for annexation. What words were used at the front door to gain admittance was not this time recorded.

Shortly afterwards Ito set out for Manchuria to meet the Russian Ambassador to China with a view to initiating a further rapprochement between the former enemies. As the two men greeted each other at Harbin railway station, a young Korean pushed through the crowd of onlookers and shot the Constitution-Maker dead. Rumour had it afterwards that his bodyguard had deliberately allowed the assassin through; the latter's motives were never publicly established because he himself died while being held in police custody for interrogation.

AND DELIVERED

Whether or not there was any Japanese involvement in the affair, it was immediately seized on as a pretext for proceeding with Korea's annexation without further ado. At the funeral a 'Korean Problem Friends Society' was formed, which immediately drew up a memorandum calling for annexation. Uchida sent a draft of it to Tokyo, where it was passed on to Katsura, Yamagata and Terauchi in turn. Sone wrote to Yamagata complaining of Uchida's activities but to no visible effect, for the Black Dragon Boss then organised a pro-annexation petition to be presented to the Korean Prime Minister by the president of the Unite Japan and Korea Society. This was rejected on Sone's advice, whereupon Uchida returned on December 26th to Tokyo to press once more for the Resident-General's dismissal.

Yamagata and Katsura were at first reluctant to take this suggestion further because 'they had not yet reported Sone's failures to the Emperor'. On February 2nd 1910, however, Katsura assured Yamagata's henchman that 'annexation would be accepted in due course and all contrary views rejected'; further funds were then forwarded to the Unite Japan and Korea Society in order to 'harmonize the opinion of the newspapers' in Seoul.

In due course Sone was recalled to Tokyo and made aware of his 'failures' so forcibly that he suffered a nervous breakdown. Katsura thereupon took the opportunity to call on him and suggest that he should resign because of ill health, but the Resident-General 'pretended not to understand and merely stayed in his sickbed'. His obstinacy was to no avail; the Cabinet and Elder Statesmen met and simply appointed War Minister Terauchi to take his place. Thus armed, Terauchi confronted the unfortunate invalid on May 25th and obtained his formal acquiescence.

The following week the Cabinet met to discuss the system of administration to be imposed after annexation. Steps were also taken to stifle the anticipated outcry in Korea, and a further 600 gendarmes were dispatched to Seoul for good measure. A fortnight later a Bureau of Colonial Affairs was set up under the direct supervision of Katsura himself; the Minister of Communications and former President of the South Manchuria Railway, Goto, was appointed Vice-Director. By July 8th the last details of the proposed 'treaty' were finalised, and a week later Terauchi set out for Korea under a heavy guard of still more gendarmes.

The Western Powers drew the obvious conclusion from his appointment. The previous December Komura had assured the British Ambassador that 'the Japanese Government had not the slightest intention of departing from the line of policy they had decided upon, and you may rest assured that the status quo would be maintained in Korea, at any rate for some time to come.' By now, however, the West had learnt to recognise the public word of the Japanese for the double-speak that it was and to cock an ear for the private 'language of the belly', so that when even as late as May 19th Komura described annexation as 'the only possible sequel' but still insisted that no date had been decided upon, the Foreign Office in London concluded that this 'was a good deal more definite than anything they have said before, and they evidently do not mean to wait very long.'

By July it was recognised to be 'imminent', and Britain indicated that her acquiescence would be conditional upon an undertaking from Japan that the existing tariffs agreed with Korea would remain unchanged for the next ten years. This was eventually conceded with reluctance, although in the subsequent session of the Diet Komura denied that it had been as a result of any pressure from Britain. (Only two years later the duty on Korean rice imported to Japan was abolished, giving it a substantial advantage over rice imported from elsewhere; when Britain and France protested, it was explained that 'unchanged' was assumed to mean 'not raised'.) In Russia the kopek had dropped even more quickly, and by July 4th, nearly two months before the formal announcement of the annexation, a second agreement with Japan had been signed. It made no mention of Korea, but in binding both sides to 'maintain the status quo' it implicitly reaffirmed Japan's claim to the country.

'It was as though a chill had passed over the city,' the British observer quoted earlier recalled of Terauchi's arrival in Seoul. 'He said little in public, but things began to happen. Four newspapers were suspended in a night ... every day brought its tale of arrests.' On August 13th Terauchi informed Tokyo that everything was in place, and he was authorised to open 'negotiations' with the Korean Cabinet. A week later he had a draft of the 'treaty' agreed by the Prime Minister. This was considered at length by Yamagata, Katsura and Komura the following day, and after it had been submitted to a conference of the Privy Council attended by the Emperor Terauchi was instructed to sign it jointly with the Prime Minister in Seoul. It was then endorsed by the Cabinet in Tokyo within 24 hurs, sanctioned by Meiji and finally promulgated on August 29th.

The excuses advanced to justify it to the outside world were as varied as they were fraudulent. Vice-Foreign Minister Ishii Kikujiro, a former member of the 'War with Russia' Kogetsukai pressure group, claimed that 'the peace of the Far East could not be made secure' without it; Katsura asserted that the Koreans 'were absolutely unfitted to govern themselves', while Terauchi, taking his cue from Uchida's Unite Japan and Korea Society stooges, went one better with the statement that 'the Korean people, seeing that without Japanese assistance they would be unable to keep abreast of the times, asked the Japanese government to annex the country.' Okuma, however, was for once less concerned with masking his satisfaction: 'For many years we have tried to control Korea, even at the cost of blood, and now we have accomplished peaceful annexation. It is like a dream,' he exulted.

In the course of the next 35 years at least 700,000 Koreans were to find themselves shipped to Japan as forced participants in the drive towards the realisation of the 'divine mission'. A Shinto shrine would be set up in every Korean school, the pupils given Japanese names and forbidden to speak in other than Japanese; their parents would be obliged to recite an oath of loyalty to the Japanese Emperor before they were allowed to purchase the everyday necessities of life.

In 1984, on the first-ever visit of the President of South Korea to Japan, Emperor Hirohito went so far as to acknowledge that 'there was an unfortunate past between us for a period in this century'. It was small wonder that the '300-year-old hatred' had taken on an even more enduring bitterness, so that this occasion was marked by, according to some, 'the biggest security operation that the world has ever seen'. It included a round-the-clock surveyance of the streets of Tokyo by a fleet of six helicopters and an airship flown all the way from Britain for the purpose. To this day all Japanese films and songs are banned in South Korea, while conversely all box office records there were broken by a film heroizing the assassin of Ito — ironically, the one Japanese who had momentarily stood in the way of the fate being prepared for the country.

15

Speeding Revolution in China

GODFATHER AND SUN

To Toyama and his Black Dragon minions the pace of the Hayashi strategy of political and commercial penetration in China — or 'shrinking diplomacy', as they disparagingly labelled it — felt irksomely slow.

Despite previous setbacks, actively helping to bring a revolution about still seemed to offer a much quicker route to the common objective than merely making provision for its eventuality. Once revolution succeeded, they reasoned, their own participation in it would entail that 'the Manchu race would be eliminated, and their former home in Manchuria would be left to an uncertain fate . . . Japan, allied with a China whose revolution she had made possible, would put Manchuria and eastern Siberia under Japanese control, and Japanese power would expand into the continent.' Furthermore, time was of the essence: 'Biggest Man' Yuan's new National Army already had 100,000 regular soldiers under arms, and it was eventually scheduled to reach a full strength of half a million. As a preliminary move to counter this potentially formidable obstacle, a secret military academy was established for Toyama's chosen revolutionary standard bearer, Sun Yat-sen, and his fellow exiles in Japan; these now included Huang Hsing, the leader of another abortive rebellion in the southern provinces.

Another of the Dowager Empress's belated reforms was, ironically, to make no small contribution towards the eventual downfall of the Manchu dynasty. The progressive abolition of the centuries-old Civil Service entry examination and a switch of emphasis to foreign learning led to an exodus of Chinese students seeking to complete their education abroad. Japan made an obvious first port of call, particularly after her spectacular victories over Russia, and by the time that Sun returned from a fund-raising mission to Indo-China, Hawaii (where he managed to obtain a U.S. passport) and America in July 1905 their numbers had swollen to over 10,000. Shortly afterwards he was introduced to Huang Hsing by 'Dreamer' Miyazaki, whose idealistic visions of a new China had been revived by recent events, and the two revolutionary leaders agreed to form a joint organisation.

The inaugural meeting of the Tung Meng Hui or 'Sworn Brotherhood' was held the following month under the auspices of the Black Dragon. Sun and Hsing were appointed President and Vice-President respectively, and in addition to Miyazaki several hundred students were sworn in as charter members. Within a year membership had risen to 10,000 and branches had been established in America, Hong Kong and Malaya as well as in every province of China itself. The movement also boasted a newspaper, The People's Paper, under the editorship of the young radical Wang Ching-wei.

Everything now seemed well set to the conspirators and their Japanese backers; Sun expressed 'confidence that my revolutionary work might be completed in my lifetime', while Genyosha-Boss Hiraoka so far forgot himself as to warn a high-ranking Chinese government official, 'with a force of eloquence that caused greasy sweat to flow down his face', that it was 'superficial to consider affairs in Japan as being decided in accordance with the wishes of men like Ito and Yamagata' rather than those of 'the pillars of the State' — i.e., the Emperor and his acolytes in the secret societies.

Early in 1906 the local branch in the central province of Hunan instigated a rebellion, but it was put down by the authorities before the Tokyo headquarters were able to mobilise support for it. As a result, a special committee was set up to organise future rebellions; it was decided that operations should be concentrated in the south-west because the French authorities in Indo-China were prepared to connive in the use of their territory for cross-border bases. Miyazaki was commissioned to negotiate the purchase of arms following another fund-raising campaign by Sun, in which he succeeded in winning the backing of Mitsui.

ECLIPSE

In its manifesto the Brotherhood had called not only for the overthrow of the Manchu dynasty and the co-operation of China and Japan, but also for 'the solution of the agrarian question on the basis of the equitable redistribution of the land'. Such a radical stance had succeeded in attracting the support of Japanese socialist leaders such as Kotoku and Kita Ikki and even a number of Russian anarchists who had fled to Japan after the abortive 1905 Revolution. On January 16th 1907 Sun gave an address to an audience of 5,000 people on the theme of 'Three Principles of the People', which he had adapted from Abraham Lincoln to suit his own purposes; he also suggested that Japan might expect to be rewarded with the whole of Manchuria for her help in a successful revolution.

The publicity which this speech aroused brought it to the ears of the authorities in Peking, prompting them to ask the Japanese government to expel him. The latter's attitude had changed, in the light of Sun's growing radicalism, from passive benevolence to one of active alarm, and they were ready to issue an order of permanent banishment against him.

However, Toyama's lieutenant, Black Dragon Boss Uchida, interceded and was able to commute it to one of four years — and even to win for him a grant of 60,000 yen from government funds towards his cause.

Sun and Huang departed together for Hanoi to take charge of operations on the ground. By a stroke of luck, their arrival coincided with a spontaneous anti-tax insurrection in the border province of Kwangsi. The Brotherhood's forces were quickly on the scene to foment it, and at one stage even appeared to be on the point of persuading the Manchu soldiers sent against them to change sides and join the revolution. Sun's optimism soared: 'with the combined forces we should have a very powerful army, and with additional training we could easily occupy Kwangtung and Kwangsi. From there we could proceed to the Yangtse valley and join the modern [National] armies in Nanking and Wuchang. It would not be difficult at all to occupy the entire country.'

Once again, however, he was to be disappointed. Of the arms expected from Japan some were lost at sea and many were not sent at all due to a rift at headquarters with members who considered that Shanghai would make a more promising base of operations. The Manchu soldiers then put discretion before valour and drove the insurgents back into Indo-China, whereupon the French authorities finally bowed to a demand from the Chinese government that they should be banished.

Even more embarrassing to the Japanese was the interception in February 1908 by a Chinese warship off Amoy of a consignment of arms intended for Huang, who was gathering the remnants of his followers for one last sally over the border into the province of Yunnan. The incident was eventually smoothed over when the Chinese government proposed that they would buy the arms for its own use provided that Japan halted all further shipments to the rebels, but the ill feeling that it aroused among the general population against Japan led to a boycott of Japanese goods throughout southern China. Its effect was sufficiently serious for the Head of the Commerce Department in the Tokyo Foreign Ministry (and soon to be Vice-Foreign Minister), Ishii Kukijiro, to ask Uchida to use his influence with the revolutionaries to put an end to it.

PLAYING AT TRAINS

The perception of the Chinese Court that the establishment of a national railway network offered the best prospect of preserving the Empire as an independent entity was inevitably flawed by the need to seek the necessary finance from external sources. After the November 1908 U.S.-Japan agreement scotching the Court's own project for a Chinchow-Taontan line in Manchuria, this gave way to the much more pessimistic realisation that their only hope lay in the tactic of playing off one Power against another.

Thus on March 7th 1909 Chang Chi-tung, the Director of the Imperial

Railways, signed a preliminary agreement with Germany for the construction of the Hankow-Canton line. He had originally promised this to Britain and France, and it was understood that if these two Powers protested, Germany could have instead the concession for a line running along the upper Yangtse valley from Hankow to Szechwan; this in fact was what Chang was really after, for he was anxious to break up the existing British monopoly in the Yangtse valley, but he was afraid of the international storm which might arise if he offered the upper Yangtse (or Hukuang as it became known, 'Hukuang' being a composite of the adjoining provinces of Hupeh and Hunan) line to Germany over the heads of the other two. Britain and France did indeed protest, but then accepted the concession of the Hukuang line to Germany, as Chang had hoped, on the promise that any extension of it would go to them.

The news of this new agreement sparked off a protest from the United States in turn, on the grounds that Chang had made a promise of participation to them as far back as 1904. On his elevation to the White House earlier in the year, President William Taft had declared his intention of making a more active defence of the all-but-moribund principle of 'Open Door' in China. With the aid of railroad magnate Harriman the State Department organised a banking syndicate to pursue this policy. Willard Straight was allowed to resign from the Department and was dispatched again to China to act as the syndicate's agent.

On June 6th Chang initialled a draft agreement with the Anglo-French-German consortium, but Taft then appealed directly to the Prince Regent and succeeded in getting the negotiations re-opened. This caused considerable resentment among the other three Powers, and the American insistence on an equal share not only in the loan to be raised for its construction but also in the running of the line resulted in the negotiations being even more protracted — so much so, indeed, that they were finally overtaken in November by Chang's death.

In the meantime Taft, who shared none of Roosevelt's sympathy for Japan, had initiated a still more forceful intervention against what he saw as the Japanese threat to the 'Open Door' in Manchuria, which had been further increased by permission obtained from China on September 4th to construct a line from Kirin to the Korean border. His proposal was for a line running the length of the region from Chinchow in the south to Aigun on the Russian border, and on October 2nd Straight succeeded in obtaining a provisional contract for it from the Viceroy of Manchuria. In order to forestall Japanese objections that this would represent unacceptable competition to the South Manchuria Railway, the Americans also proposed that Japan should be invited to participate; the Chinese Court, however, saw this as offering too great a hostage to fortune and turned it down. Taft, through his Secretary of State Philander C. Knox, then came forward with an even more ambitious proposal; namely, that the six Powers concerned in China should together raise a loan which would enable China to buy back both the South Manchuria Railway and the Chinese Eastern Railway from Japan and Russia respectively; the entire railway system in Manchuria would then be run by an international board of management until such time as China was able to repay the loan.

AMERICA SIDETRACKED

However well-intentioned this might have been, the effect was precisely the opposite to that intended, in that it made Japan and Russia, whose 1907 agreement had parcelled up Manchuria between them, only more determined to ward off outside interference. The threat that Knox's proposal posed was sufficient to overcome any qualms that Russia might have entertained at the growing certainty of Japan's annexation of Korea and led directly to the conclusion of their second agreement, on July 4th 1910.

The result of this was to make the prospect of China's reasserting control over Manchuria more remote than ever, as a writer in the *Japanese Diplomatic Review* made abundantly clear: 'We cannot now say what will happen when the Japanese lease [on the Kwantung Peninsula and SMR] expires, but this much I can say for certain — Japan will apply to continue it and will be backed by Russia. In return Japan will back Russia when the latter refuses China permission to repurchase the CER at the end of the 30 years provided for under the Russo-Chinese Contract. China certainly is not bound to grant the demands of Japan and Russia, but in that case she will have to resist Russia and Japan united.' 'My Government does not understand Japanese sentiment, and I do not think they would take any notice of it if they did,' the U.S. Ambassador in Tokyo remarked sorrowfully on the same occasion. 'To them a railway is just a railway'; another commentator observed, apropos the American argument that the scheme offered Japan's island empire security against Russian aggression, that it apparently escaped Washington's notice that Japan 'did not wish to remain merely an island empire'.

The 'Knox Neutralisation Plan', as it became known, was also responsible for a sharp deterioration in Anglo-U.S. relations. The American Press, in a campaign largely orchestrated by the disappointed Straight, roundly condemned Britain for her lack of support, to which the Foreign Office replied that it could hardly have been expected to encourage Japan, as an ally, to give up the greatest prize of her victory over Russia five years earlier. Taft attempted to heal the rift with the suggestion of an arbitration treaty to resolve the differences between the two countries. Since any such treaty threatened to conflict with the existing terms of the Anglo-Japanese Alliance, Grey suggested in reply that the invitation should be extended to include Japan. When this was put to him, however, Foreign Minister Komura rejected it out of hand on the grounds that Japan 'could not possibly accept an arbitration award on matters which might possibly affect the very existence of the nation and [which might] place Japan in an unfavourable position, since most of the arbitrators would be Europeans and Americans who had different cultural, racial and religious backgrounds.'

In a note to his predecessor Kato, who had returned to London as Ambassador for the second time after his resignation, Komura reminded him that it was 'the kernel of our foreign policy ... to strengthen the foundations of the Alliance more and more, and to work towards the preservation of peace in the Far East and support for our Imperial interests.' The Foreign Minister was concerned that if the vital shield which the Alliance provided Japan was seen by Britain to be an obstacle to the proposed arbitration treaty, she might decline to renew it when it expired in 1915. His fears were compounded by vociferous protests by socialist sympathisers in Britain at Kotoku's execution and by widespread criticism of Grey for his apparent failure to protect British commercial interests in Manchuria from unfair Japanese competition. He therefore proposed to Grey that it should be revised to provide an escape clause relieving Britain of an obligation to assist in the event of hostilities arising with America and that it should be extended to run for a further ten years in this new form.

To Grey the proposal could hardly have been more opportunely timed, since it offered Britain freedom to concentrate her naval forces in Europe against the threat of the rapidly expanding German fleet. There was also the further thought that 'if our Alliance is terminated in 1915, Japan will have her hands free to act in the Far East without restraint or control by us. It is possible that we might in that case find the Japanese fleet arrayed against us in the Pacific or allied with that of some other power. These are changes that are unpleasant to contemplate ...' This argument was particularly useful in answering Australasian fears of Japanese designs, expressed at the Imperial Defence Conference in June 1911, which had been prompted by large-scale emigration into the area; indeed, so anxious was Grey to placate them that he indicated his willingness to Kato to encourage its diversion into Korea and Manchuria instead. Negotiations proceeded smoothly along the lines proposed, being completed with a formal signing on July 13th. Three weeks later the Anglo-American Arbitration Agreement was concluded — only then, ironically, to be refused ratification by the Senate.

END OF THE MANCHUS

The rumoured imminence of a new Russo-Japanese agreement, together with reports of growing hostility to the Hukuang concession among the local population, who had begun to call for permission to build the line themselves, had finally concentrated the minds of the four Western participants sufficiently to work out a compromise to put to Peking in May 1910. In reply, however, the Prince Regent required that the loan should cover rather more than just the line's construction; it should be extended, he argued, to finance both industrial development in Manchuria as a counter to the anticipated consolidation of Russian and Japanese interests there and the general programme of reform belatedly initiated by the Dowager Empress, including the establishment of a two-tier central parliament and reform of the currency and army. This immediately incited Russia and Japan to exert pressure on their allies, France and Britain respectively, to oppose the loan. Russia even threatened to send her army into northern Manchuria on the pretext of stamping out an epidemic there, but Japan, anxious not to compromise the prospects of renewing the Alliance with Britain, countered with the less bellicose proposal of a rival loan.

Threatened from every direction without and with bankruptcy within, the Prince Regent had little option but to accede to the terms put before him. In particular, the Four-Power Consortium insisted that the advance of the other two loans which he sought was conditional upon the conclusion of the Hukuang contract. On May 20th 1911 the Regent finally put his signature to the contract. No sooner had he done so than Russia and Japan demanded to be included in the Consortium. Before agreement on this could be reached, however, the Prince Regent and the three-centuries-old Dynasty of the Manchus were no longer.

As the negotiations ran on, Sun Yat-Sen's Sworn Brotherhood had again raised the revolutionary flag in Canton with an attack on the Manchu garrison led by Huang (Sun himself being abroad at the time on another fund-raising mission). Although they succeeded in taking over the garrison, the anticipated support failed to materialise and they were soon driven out again with the loss of seventy-two dead. Huang himself managed to escape with the other survivors into Szechwan, where resentment against the concession of the Hukuang contract to foreigners was rapidly coming to a head. On August 4th a Provincial Railway League was set up there to demand cancellation of the loan. When this was refused, they announced the withholding of taxes to the central Government, in turn sparking off widespread and sometimes violent disorder.

When Peking issued orders to suppress the insurrection, they were informed that the local militia and even the Provincial Governor himself had gone over to the other side. Troops were then sent in from neighbouring provinces to disarm the rebels. The Brotherhood's Hankow cell saw its chance, although their planned outbreak was almost forestalled on October 9th by an explosion in one of their secret arsenals. When the viceroy of nearby Wuchang ordered the arrest of the ringleaders, however, the garrison mutinied and within 48 hours the whole city was in rebel hands.

Within another two days Hankow and the neighbouring city of Hangyang had also fallen, and a 'Military Government of the Republic' was proclaimed. By the end of the month they had been joined by ten other provincial capitals along the Yangtse valley and southern coast, including

Canton. In desperation the Prince Regent appealed for help from his old enemy Yuan and appointed him Prime Minister with authority to negotiate with the rebels. The 'Biggest Man', however, was in no hurry to oblige, gradually raising his terms in order to give himself time to gauge the likely extent of the revolution's success, and it was not until December 6th that the frantic Regent at last conceded the final condition, his own resignation as the representative of the infant Emperor.

The speed of these developments caught the Japanese government uncomfortably off guard. The growing unpopularity of the Katsura Cabinet's severely deflationary economic policy, which included a quite arbitrary reduction of interest on existing government bonds, had made for a correspondingly increasing reliance on bribery in order to retain the necessary support of the Seiyukai majority in the Diet. When earlier in the year the prospectus of a new corporation entrusted with the Tokyo electric light franchise had revealed that the Board was packed with party members, the public outcry was such that the appointments were hastily cancelled and a new list of directors published. With a general election due the following year, it was recognised by both sides that it was time to put an end to the association if the Seiyukai were not to spoil their chances.

Katsura therefore waited only until after the successful renewal of the Anglo-Japanese Alliance in July before resigning once more in favour of Saionji. The last of the former Court nobles among the Restoration leadership and a life-long supporter of the democratic principle, Saionji was by instinct unlikely to heed calls for a bold military initiative in China to take advantage of the turn of events there, and his scope for action was further constricted by the fact that his new Foreign Minister was still on his way back from his previous post as Ambassador in Washington. When Black Dragon Boss Uchida called at the Foreign Ministry on October 18th to elicit the Government's response, he was told that it was weighing up all the relevant factors but had not yet arrived at a decision.

A QUESTION OF HORSES

Even the expansionist camp was deeply divided over how best to respond. Toyama organised a mass rally in Hibiya Park in support of the rebels and dispatched several agents to China to report on their progress and lend what help they could. These included the socialist Kita Ikki and an ex-head of a Japanese police school in Peking. The latter travelled via Korea where he won Resident-General Terauchi's blessing for a scheme to help the rebels take all of China south of the Yellow River and to establish a puppet Manchu regime north of it under Prince Su, the dynasty's last Minister of the Interior. As a first step he arranged for the Prince's safe passage to Port Arthur, in return for which he was allowed to adopt one of Su's daughters, the eight-year-old Yoshiko who twenty years later was to play a spectacular role in Japan's establishment of the puppet state of 'Manchukuo'.

The military establishment, personified by Yamagata, on the other hand adopted a quite different response, maintaining their deep distrust of Sun and his radical associates (when Sun had returned on a visit to Japan the previous year they had kept him under minute surveillance and eventually required him to leave the country). Yamagata's thinking was governed by two principle considerations. One was his perception of the need to rebuild the country's resources before embarking on its next programme of 'future enterprises'. The other was a growing conviction, inspired by the anti-immigrant legislation in California and the British Dominions together with the Kaiser's ever more frequent utterances on the subject of the 'Yellow Peril', that the white race was setting out to dominate the world at the expense of all others.

'Thus, if the coloured peoples of the Orient hope to compete with the so-called culturally advanced white peoples, to preserve their heritage and to retain their independence ... China and Japan, culturally and racially alike, must be friendly and promote each other's interests,' he reasoned. If the Western Powers moved to take advantage of the Manchu Dynasty's collapse, then 'Japan could not remain quietly and look on with folded arms ... the Japanese people must harmoniously, earnestly and sincerely join in the peaceful warfare (*sic*) ...' If on the other hand the outcome fell short of actual war, 'we must gradually draw closer to China, by careful cultivation, and quietly realise our future plans.'

Whereas Toyama and his acolytes advocated the immediate subjection of their defenceless neighbour, Yamagata saw the need to hold it together as a shield against the West while gradually subverting it to Japan's own purposes. While the former held to Sun and his revolutionary republic as their tool, Yamagata envisaged 'a politically reconstructed China which, in step with world progress, means a constitutional monarchy'. In his eyes, there was only one man qualified to occupy such a throne, and that was 'Biggest Man' Yuan, a military leader like himself; he was therefore prepared to bury old animosities in favour of support for his long-standing adversary. Anything, after all, was to be preferred to a republic based on the democratic principle.

Caught in this crossfire, Saionji and his Cabinet continued to waver between one side and the other. As early as October 13th — that is, before Yuan's recall — the Manchu Government had transmitted a request to Tokyo for arms and ammunition in the fight against the rebels. The Cabinet decided to compromise: they would supply arms to the value of 2.7 million yen to the Government unofficially via private dealers on condition that Peking formally acknowledged its 'respect' for Japan's position in Manchuria, and 3 million yen worth to the rebels via similar channels. Home Minister Hara explained of the thinking behind this that 'there was no sympathy whatsoever for the cause of the rebel army. The feeling was that we could honestly give our sympathy only to the legitimate government in Peking, but the tendency has also been to recognise that honesty alone would not help in achieving our objectives.'

The desire to ride both horses at once was a reflection of opinions held within the Japanese Embassy in Peking: its head, Ijuin Hikokichi, had struck up a close relationship with Yuan and naturally saw him as the most promising carrier of Japan's hopes, while the Military Attaché argued for the dispatch of arms and even of troops to the rebel side. To compound the confusion still further the Foreign Ministry's Adviser in International Law urged that 'the government should intervene and take up a definite attitude, helping one party or the other, obtaining in return an advantageous foothold for Japan.'

UNSEATED

When Yuan finally accepted the Premiership, Ijuin suggested to him that he should appeal to Japan for aid in putting down the rebels; Yuan, however, replied that he hoped to arrive at a settlement with them by negotiation rather than by force of arms. Tokyo then put out feelers to London with a proposal for a joint Anglo-Japanese intervention, at the same time putting three divisions on 24-hours standby. Before they were able to elicit a response, and greatly to their chagrin, it was announced that an armistice between the two sides had been arranged.

This setback was then compounded for Tokyo by two grotesque errors of judgement on the part of the Foreign Ministry. First, a note seeking support for the argument in favour of a Chinese monarchy was dispatched to Washington, which was perhaps the least likely of any capital in the world to lend it a sympathetic ear. Then almost simultaneously support for a republic was pledged to the rebels in Shanghai in return for exclusive mining and railway concessions, an offer which was contemptuously rejected. When its terms presently became public knowledge Tokyo indignantly denied their authenticity, but the damage to the last vestige of Japan's reputation for sincerity was already done.

Toyama decided that it was time to apply the whip to the revolutionary horse, which had begun to show unmistakable signs of antipathy to Japanese ridership. Sun had finally arrived at the scene of the action on December 24th, bringing with him to serve as his Chief of Staff a young American hunchback named Homer Lea. Having been turned down by West Point because of his deformity, Lea had organised a militia of revolutionary Chinese in his home state of California, in the course of which his sympathies had taken a passionately anti-Japanese turn. In 1909 he had created a considerable sensation with the publication of his book *The Valor of Ignorance,* which warned of Japanese schemes to invade California and even described in detail their likely plans of attack on the state's major cities.

Clearly, the influence of such a man so close to Sun could not be allowed to go unchecked, and although 'Dreamer' Miyazaki had joined the entourage when it paused at Hong Kong he was thought unlikely to provide a sufficient counterweight. As they approached Shanghai Toyama himself therefore set out to join them, accompanied by Inukai who, as leader of the Genyosha's old allies the Real Constitutionalists, had formed a new Nationalist Party with a number of Seiyukai members disgruntled by their leadership's horse-trading with Katsura. Inukai had intended to travel incognito, but during an argument with the station-master at Nagasaki he let slip his true identity.

Hardly had they set foot in China than the Republic was proclaimed at Nanking, and on New Year's Day 1912 Sun was inaugurated as its first President. Negotiations were still proceeding for a settlement with Yuan, an outcome that Toyama was determined at all costs to prevent, and he attempted to do so by a two-pronged approach to the rebels via their minds and their pockets. Uchida, his ever-ready lieutenant, was to act as his dual spearhead.

Having rapidly put together a mass-circulation booklet in Chinese which called for a partition of the country between the Manchus and the new Republic, the Black Dragon Boss then set about hustling his big business contacts into offering the Republic loans. Mitsui had been quickly on to the scene with the offer of a facility for the purchase of arms, and with a few well-directed nudges Uchida was able to raise a total of 3 million yen. An even more ambitious scheme was hatched around the Hanyehping Iron Company which had been set up with the help of loans from Mitsui in 1899 to supply iron ore to the government-built Yawata Steelworks conveniently situated near Fukuoka to receive it: the Company was to be reorganised under joint Sino-Japanese management and its assets mortgaged to Japan in return for further loans to the Republic.

By now Sun could have had few illusions as to the motives behind Japanese offers of assistance, and he was finally undeceived for good by a telegram from the Brotherhood's Tokyo headquarters warning him that the Elder Statesmen were planning a military intervention in China in support of the Manchu throne. 'Peace-Preserver' Yamagata, having seen his chosen mount (Yuan) reject the Japanese bit and run instead in tandem with the revolutionaries, was still determined that Japan should ensure for herself at least a share of the prize at stake. On January 14th he accordingly submitted a memorandum calling for the dispatch of an expeditionary force to Manchuria and for negotiations with Russia for a mutually-agreed division between them of Inner Mongolia. Two days later the Cabinet and Emperor approved the proposal, and shortly afterwards reports began to filter through of a sudden surge in Japanese purchases of rice in Manchuria.

When the telegram was first seen in Shanghai by one of Sun's lieutenants, his face was reported to have turned ashen grey. Certainly, its effect was to bring Sun and Yuan rapidly to terms with each other: Sun was to step down from the Presidency of the Republic on condition that Yuan agreed to the final abolition of the Throne even in its present merely ceremonial role. When news of the agreement broke, Toyama hurried to Nanking in a last-ditch attempt to dissuade Sun; whether by coincidence or not, Yuan found himself the target of an assassination attempt, while Homer Lea was suddenly taken ill with a mysterious fever to which he succumbed a few months later. On February 12th Sun duly resigned, and Yuan was elected President of the Republic of China by the new National Council in Nanking; simultaneously in Peking the boy Emperor Pu-Yi announced his own abdication from the Dragon Throne. He least of all was in a position to foretell that two decades later he would be restored to it as Emperor of the Japanese puppet state of 'Manchukuo'.

EXIT MEIJI

The sight of Toyama and Yamagata being unseated by their respective mounts was mortifying enough, but that of Saionji and his Cabinet being left at the start without a ride at all (except for Japan's eventual inclusion with Russia in the International Consortium) was even more damaging to Japanese self-esteem. Plans at once therefore began to be laid for the Last Noble's replacement (the fact that his Seiyukai Party won an even larger majority in the May election was not, of course, considered to be of any account), but their consummation was delayed by a still greater blow — the death on July 30th 1912 of Emperor Meiji himself at the age of sixty. Whatever the cause, Court practice did nothing to prolong his life: no doctor was permitted to touch the Imperial flesh even in the hour of death, nor did anyone dare to suggest raising him from the floor on to a Western-style bed.

After the traditional 45 days of mourning the body was taken to join those of the Imperial Ancestors in the old capital of Kyoto. As the cortège set out from Tokyo, it was discovered that General Nogi, the captor of Port Arthur, had committed *hara-kiri* together with his wife. It was put about that they had done so partly to honour a secret pact of requital to their two sons and the countless thousands of other young Japanese who had been sent to their deaths in that campaign, and partly as an example to the nation as a whole to uphold the principles of self-sacrifice enshrined in the Bushido ethic. Nogi had indeed left a note beside him deploring the decadence and self-indulgence of the present younger generation and exhorting them to abide by the ancient warrior code of the *samurai*, but the explanation for his act ran a little deeper than that.

After his retirement from the Army Nogi had been appointed head-master of the Peers School and as such had become the personal tutor to young Prince Hirohito, the eldest son of the new Emperor Taisho. It was to this young charge that his act was especially directed, to serve as a perpetual reminder of the obligations of Japan's Imperial mission of world hegemony — a fact confirmed by Nogi's official biographer: 'The thought of these very duties [as tutor] was an added incentive to his deed.' Just how deeply that message was taken to heart was evinced as recently as 1984 when Hirohito was asked who had exerted the biggest influence on him; he replied without hesitation 'My grandfather Meiji' — the very man who did most of all to set Japan on the road to that mission's fulfilment.

The suddenness of Meiji's death had left Yamagata temporarily stranded. His First Protégé Katsura was 6000 miles away in St. Petersburg at the time, ostensibly on a pleasure trip, but in reality to put the seal on a third agreement with Russia which not only reconfirmed the secret demarcation line in Manchuria but also decided the partition of Mongolia between the two countries. Yamagata himself, caught as he was in the middle of preparing the downfall of the Saionji Cabinet, was more than reluctant to court publicity by taking on the task of guiding the new Emperor's first steps. Katsura was hastily recalled and, somewhat to his surprise, found himself on his return appointed to the twin posts of Lord Chamberlain and Keeper of the Privy Seal. These gave him the power both to arrange the Emperor's audiences and to be present at them himself. To allay any suspicions that the appointments might have aroused, Katsura announced to the public that his acceptance of them stemmed from a decision to retire from politics for good.

The compliance of the Palace thus secured, Yamagata was ready again to proceed. At his bidding the War Minister, another leading protégé, on November 22nd submitted a demand for the two new divisions still to be raised under the National Defence Plan approved by Meiji in 1907. In the same week the 'Peace Preserver' abandoned his villa in Kyoto to take up residence again in the capital. Saionji had pledged himself at the election to a further reduction in government expenditure, and when his Cabinet rejected the demand as expected, the War Minister submitted his resignation. No serving officer could, of course, be found to take his place, and Saionji's direct appeal to Yamagata to nominate a successor met only with the bland reply that 'this is no time for me to interfere ... While it was a different matter when the Meiji Emperor was alive, we must avoid worrying the present Emperor about such things because he is still young.' Without a War Minister, Saionji had no option but to resign.

The other Elder Statesmen, in whose gift the appointment of a new Prime Minister lay, were uneasy at these tactics. None of them, however, felt bold enough to take up the office, and it fell to Katsura as Yamagata had intended. The announcement of his appointment on December 17th 1912 provoked a storm of criticism accusing him of 'hiding behind the sleeve of the Dragon' — in other words, of abusing his position at the Court to procure office. Even the Satsuma-dominated Navy, seeing the issue as 'a struggle between Choshu and the Nation', at first refused to nominate a Navy Minister, and it was only when he received a direct order from the Throne that Saito Makoto finally agreed to serve. For all his denials to the contrary, few were prepared to believe that Yamagata's hand did not lie behind all this. He received several death threats through the post, and early one morning a would-be assassin was discovered attempting to break into his Tokyo residence (although the official explanation of the latter's action was that it represented a protest against the unemployment situation).

By the time that the Diet reconvened the following week the Seiyukai had united with the Opposition Nationalists to form a 'Society for the Preservation of the Constitution'. The Emperor promptly adjourned the session until January 20th 1913. In the interval Katsura, who had over the years grown increasingly resentful of his role as Yamagata's cat's-paw, attempted to answer the criticism first by announcing that he was 'now on a footing of absolute independence', and secondly by forming a political party of his own. In order to give himself more time for this he procured a further adjournment of the Diet until February 5th on the pretext that the draft of the Budget had not yet returned from the printers, but when the day of reckoning finally arrived he had still gathered no more than ninety recruits to his flag. Not the least of his obstacles was the 150,000 yen made available by the Satsuma admirals from Navy funds to the Seiyukai to counter any attempts to buy off their members.

A huge crowd filled the streets surrounding the Diet, and the Seiyukai lost no time in moving a no-confidence motion when the session opened. For the Nationalists the 'Blasphemer' Ozaki again accused the Prime Minister of hiding behind the Throne and imputing to it responsibility for his own mistakes (the official stenographer was subsequently dismissed for refusing to alter the record in such a way that Ozaki would be laid open to another charge of blasphemy). Before the motion could be put to the vote yet another Imperial order arrived for a five-day adjournment.

Katsura turned to Yamagata to intervene, but his formation of a political party had not endeared him to his patron and the 'Peace-Preserver' replied stiffly that 'the function of the President of the Privy Council is to respond to the summons of the Emperor and not to mix in political turmoil'. Katsura then appealed to Saionji (who was still President of the Seiyukai) to withdraw the motion. When the Last Noble declined, he found himself summoned to the Imperial Palace and confronted with the same demand. Loyal though he was to the advance of constitutional government, he could not contemplate defiance of his Emperor and duly resigned his Presidency.

FILLING THE VACUUM

On the morning of the 10th Yamamoto, the senior member of the Satsuma Naval hierarchy, called on Katsura and after accusing him of bringing about a 'national calamity' urged him to resign also. The Prime Minister replied that he was not averse to doing so. When this was reported to the Diet, they became even more determined to force the issue. Massive crowds again surrounded the building, and when word came out that Katsura was again threatening adjournment if the no-confidence motion was not withdrawn they quickly broke into open riot, storming and burning police boxes, pro-government newspaper offices and the homes of Cabinet ministers. The following day similar disorders flared in other major cities. Faced with a real prospect of civil war, Katsura finally threw in his hand.

His fall came as a crushing blow not only to himself (and within six months he would be dead) but also, even more importantly, to the ambitions of the young Emperor Taisho to maintain the omnipotence of the Throne established by his father. Never the most robust of men, his health now went into a steady decline culminating six years later in a cerebral haemorrhage which would leave him semi-incapacitated.

The next twenty years would be taken up by a struggle to fill the resulting power vacuum between the military and the politicians — or more accurately, between those who looked only to force of arms to advance Japan's position in the world and those who believed that the same end could be best attained under cover of a token show of representational government — much as the first two decades of Meiji's reign had been, before he was enshrined as absolute ruler by the 1889 Constitution. Yamagata, already 76 years of age, would not live to see the outcome; had he done so, he would have died well satisfied. For the moment, however, he could only retire again to his villa until the odium stirred against him by Katsura's maladroit behaviour had spent itself. He went so far as to submit his resignation as Privy Council President, but Taisho refused to accept it.

As a leading instigator of Katsura's downfall, Yamamoto was the obvious choice as his successor, but the nation was soon to discover that the change was merely that of the Navy for the Army, of Satsuma for Choshu. 'Now we shall see some big naval contracts,' one newspaper editor remarked on the appointment, but even he must have been surprised by the speed at which his cynicism was vindicated.

Two years earlier the Navy had submitted a building programme of eight battleships and a similar number of cruisers, but had been allotted only a quarter of the necessary funds. It now seized the chance to make up the shortfall, although another year would pass before the full implications of the decision were revealed, when it emerged during a court case in Berlin that two senior Naval officers had accepted bribes in placing the construction contracts with German firms. They were subsequently court-martialled and the senior of the two was ordered to repay the staggering sum of 410,000 yen. The Army-dominated House of Peers immediately slashed the Naval budget almost in half, but the Lower House refused to endorse such a drastic cut and instead passed a motion of no confidence in the government. Serious rioting ensued, and on March 23rd 1914 Yamamoto submitted his resignation.

Yamagata canvassed far and wide for a suitable replacement, but none
of his own henchmen proved capable of forming a Cabinet and in the end he
was obliged to settle for the compromise choice of the Lame Democrat
Okuma. For all his protestations of commitment to the principle of representational government over the years, he had shown, whenever the occasion demanded, that he was as devoted to the expansionist cause as any of the
other Grand Old Men of the Restoration. Inspired by a desire to better
his old rivals in the Seiyukai, he made himself no less accommodating
this time; not only did he pledge his support for the Navy's '8–8'
building programme, but he also agreed to put through the Army's
demand for the two new divisions. In addition, he accepted Yamagata's
nominee for the post of Home Minister, while the key Foreign Ministry
was to go to Anglo-Ally Kato, who had already served in that office twice
(in Okuma's first Cabinet of 1900 and Katsura's last of 1913). As leader of
the new party set up by Katsura, Kato would enable the coalition with the
Nationalists almost to match the Seiyukai's numbers in the Diet.

Kato's other recommendation was that he had long taken an aggressive
stance on Japan's interest in China. As early as 1905 he had called for the
extension of the Manchurian leases to a term of 99 years, and in January
1913 as Ambassador in London he had informed Sir Edward Grey that
'Japan is determined on having permanent, exclusive possession . . . it is the
immutable policy of any Japanese government, based, in the final analysis,
upon the will of the Japanese people. The Japanese people feel an affinity
towards Kwantung the way one feels an affinity towards a tree one has
planted . . .' Japan would, he added, bring the subject up for discussion with
China 'at the psychological moment'. On his way home to Japan he had
called at Peking to instruct Ambassador Ijuin to establish 'convenient
grounds for a settlement of the problem'. Katsura, during the short life of
his government, had approved wholeheartedly: 'the rapid settlement of
problems with China in order to preserve peace in the Pacific is just the
thing to become the most important policy of the Cabinet.'

SECOND REVOLUTION

Since the debâcle over the Manchu abdication, events in China had,
from the Japanese point of view, taken a more promising turn. The early
days of the new Republic appeared to be blessed with sweetness and light
between its two leading figures, Yuan and Sun: the President had
appointed a member of the Sworn Brotherhood to be Prime Minister, and
by mutual agreement the National Council had been moved to Peking.

In August 1912 the two men met there for the first time in an aura of
ostentatious cordiality. Sun submitted a programme for the construction
of 75,000 miles of new railway track, and in return for his magnanimity in
having surrendered the Presidency he was appointed Director-General of
Railway Development on a salary of $30,000 per month. It remained,

however, to find the funds to finance such a grandiose scheme. Yuan's negotiations with the International Consortium on the terms of the proposed Reorganisation Loan were proceeding painfully slowly, and Sun decided that a visit to his old contacts in Japan would bring quicker results. It was a step that would soon bring the two men's suspicions of each other to the surface.

Unseated though they may have been by Yuan, Yamagata and his allies were still very far from switching saddles to Sun and his radical colleagues. They refused to make any formal recognition of his arrival in Japan, although he was granted a series of private interviews with Katsura in which it was agreed that Japan and China should work together to eliminate Western interests in the Far East. Sun's backers in big business and the secret societies felt no such inhibitions, however, and the scale of the reception organised for him led Sun to rhapsodize that 'the patriots of your country have led and taught me, and I deem Japan my second fatherland and your statesmen my mentors. China awaits your saving help.' Negotiations were quickly completed for the formation of a Sino-Japanese Industrial Corporation under his presidency, its capital to be provided by Mitsui, Mitsubishi and two other leading conglomerates. At the end of his five-week-long triumphal tour he was so carried away as to declare that 'the protestations of friendly sentiments by the Japanese are not superficial, but come from the bottom of their hearts . . . What Japan wants is not territory in China but increased trade, and the Japanese are following a policy of peace.'

Even before his return to China Sun's relations with Yuan had reached breaking point. The National Council had been superseded by the National Assembly, and in the first elections held for it the largest share of seats had been won by the Kuomintang or People's National Party, which had been formed by an alliance between the Sworn Brotherhood and a number of smaller factions. On March 20th one of the Brotherhood's co-founders was about to board the Shanghai–Peking express to take up the Premiership when he was assassinated. Yuan was immediately suspected of having hired the gunman, and when the Assembly met two weeks later it refused to approve the terms which had finally been agreed with the International Consortium for the Reorganisation Loan (the newly-elected Democratic U.S. President, Woodrow Wilson, in a rush to demonstrate his anti-colonialism to the world, had revoked America's participation). Yuan retorted that as they had already been approved by its predecessor, the National Council, they had to stand, and he went ahead with the agreement regardless.

Unrest soon broke out again in the Yangtse valley, which moved Yuan to dismiss three Kuomintang Provincial Governors there. Sun responded with an ultimatum to the President to resign. When it expired on July 14th without response Nanking declared its independence, to be followed shortly afterwards by four southern provinces. Sun's Japanese allies were also quick to swing into action; a chemist was set to work in Peking to concoct a poison for Yuan (even before the hostilities had broken out the socialist and Black Dragon agent Kita had publicly vowed to kill him, and had been deported by the Japanese consul in Shanghai for his indiscretion), while an offer of twenty million yen was wired to Sun in return for the cession of Manchuria. Sun rashly accepted, and plans were put in hand to send a warship to bring him to Tokyo to put his signature to the deal.

Before they could be realised, however, Yuan succeeded, with the considerable help of the Consortium who issued funds to buy off other potential rebels, in crushing this 'Second Revolution', and Sun was obliged to set course for Japan aboard a rather less imposing conveyance, a Mitsubishi collier. He found refuge once again under Toyama's ever-accommodating roof; Huang joined him in due course along with a number of other Kuomintang stalwarts, among them the young Chiang Kai-shek.

Sun's defeat, however, at least provided a pretext for his backers in Japan to urge the Government to adopt a much more uncompromising attitude towards Yuan. They had already succeeded in forcing the replacement of Ijuin in the Peking Embassy by a Genyosha acolyte, Hioki Eki, and Toyama teamed up with Nationalist leaders Inukai and Ozaki in a revival of the unholy alliance of old to form a 'League of Those Agreed on the China Problem'.

An incident during the recapture of Nanking, in which three Japanese hawkers had broken the curfew to rescue their belongings and had been murdered by some of Yuan's soldiers on the rampage, supplied the looked-for *casus belli*. A huge protest rally assembled in Hibiya Park before moving on to the Foreign Ministry. When an official emerged from the building to issue a placatory statement he was promptly cut down by a young 'man of spirit', who then seated himself on a large map of China and committed *hara-kiri*, cutting his stomach in such a way that his blood spilled out over Manchuria and Mongolia.

As a result of their efforts Sun's backers, in the words of an official propagandist, 'finally awakened the Japanese Government to the need to adopt positive measures to settle the question of Manchurian and Mongolian railways'. These 'positive measures' resulted in turn in a secret agreement under which China conceded to Japan the right to finance the construction of five further lines in Manchuria extending into the Inner Mongolian province of Jehol.

This concession apart, however, they could only look on helplessly as Yuan remorselessly consolidated his position. On October 10th he was elected President for the next five years by the National Assembly; three weeks later he had eight Kuomintang Assembly members arrested, its three hundred other members unseated and the party proscribed as a seditious organisation. In January 1914 he suspended the Assembly indefinitely and replaced it with his own Political Council.

The sight of such a long-standing enemy of Japan so firmly entrenched in control of China had also contributed to the dissatisfaction which led to the fall of the Yamamoto Cabinet. Plans were revived for the restoration of the Manchu dynasty in the north and of Sun's republic in the south. It was reported to Peking that Kuomintang cadres were planning to dress up as Yuan's troops and burn Japanese buildings in order to provide a pretext for Japanese military intervention, and a letter was intercepted with the information that 'the members of our [Kuomintang] party at Shanghai have decided that half of them should go to a conference at Nagasaki and should unite with the Japanese in finding funds and purchasing weapons; Formosa is to be used as a base, and operations are to begin from Chekiang and Fukien.'

In February Sun entered into a contract for the loan of 1.5 million yen to finance the purchase of 100,000 rifles, the security for which was to be provided by bonds issued in 'the occupied territory'; Japan would furnish military advisers and a 'volunteer force', whose assistance would be repaid in the event of a successful outcome by an undertaking that all industrial development in China would be jointly financed with Japanese capital. When Okuma succeeded to the Premiership shortly afterwards, Sun followed up with another letter offering nothing less than a full military alliance and customs union.

Yuan presently got wind of the deal, and he issued an order to the provincial authorities 'to execute on the spot everyone who takes in payment notes circulated by Sun Yat-sen and alleged to be secured by an internal loan.' Many of Sun's own supporters with a better grasp of Japan's real intentions dissociated themselves from so far-reaching a commitment and returned to China. Even some of his more idealistic Japanese admirers were quick to condemn it; Kita, for instance, accused him of combining with Japanese capitalists to betray the socialistic principles which he had formerly espoused.

What chance of success such an ill-considered scheme might have had was never put to the test, being overtaken by an event which offered the expansionists an altogether more promising vehicle for their ambitions — the outbreak of World War One.

AN 'IMMENSE AND UNIQUE OPPORTUNITY'

'Japan is going to take advantage of this war to get control of China,' Yuan predicted to the U.S. Ambassador in Peking. The Black Dragon indeed had already drawn up just such a plan of action. 'We should induce the Chinese revolutionists, the Imperialists and other malcontents to create trouble all over China. The whole country will be thrown into disorder and Yuan's government consequently overthrown. We shall then select a man from among the most influential and most noted of the 400 million Chinese and help him to organise a new form of government and to consolidate the whole country', it ran. 'We consider the present to be the most opportune moment. The reason why these men cannot now carry on an active campaign is because they are insufficiently provided with funds. If the Imperial Government can take advantage of this fact to make them a loan and instruct them to rise simultaneously, great commotion and disorder will surely prevail all over China. We can then intervene and easily adjust matters . . .'

Yamagata, however, continued to differ on the choice of horse. 'Some people,' he wrote in a pointed rejoinder, 'place too much faith in the armed might of our Empire and believe that against China the use of force alone will gain our ends . . . Our present plan should aim primarily at improving Sino-Japanese relations and inspiring in China a feeling of abiding trust in us' by accepting the fact of Yuan's suzerainty. He had no difficulty on the other hand in agreeing that 'now is the opportune time for the Empire to settle on a policy towards China, correct the mistakes and omissions of the past and plan a complete revision.'

It was not only to China that the planners looked. 'Our best plan of action is to make skilful use of the War to erect a lasting national policy [of expansion] for the Empire,' Army Chief of Staff Oyama asserted. Thus while the eyes of the West were focused on the European bonfire, Japan would tip-toe silently about in the background with her own box of matches, to the discomfiture of the British in India, the Russians in Finland, the Americans in Mexico.

Even where no flames took hold as a result, she would have her salesmen placed ready to show off a full range of Japanese manufactures which the war-orientated factories of Europe were no longer able to supply. At the outbreak of the War Japan's national debt stood at over 1,500 million yen; by the time of the Armistice four years later, that had been converted into a surplus of 2,000 million, and when the West's salesmen returned to re-establish their former markets they would find that they had been supplanted, sometimes for ever.

In the words of Sir Edward Grey, 'the opportunity for Japan was immense and unique', and it was seized with both hands.

16

World War One: Perfect Camouflage

'JAPAN UNABLE TO REFRAIN'

Archduke Ferdinand of Austria had been dispatched by a student's bomb in Sarajevo on June 28th 1914. Precisely a month later Austria declared war on Serbia, and by August 4th Germany had joined Austria against an alliance of Britain, France and Russia.

Three days earlier Sir Edward Grey had informed his opposite number Kato in Tokyo that although it was probable that Britain would intervene, he 'did not see we were likely to apply to Japan [for assistance] under our alliance'. Immediately after the British Declaration of War, wishing to cover himself against all possible contingencies, he added that if 'hostilities spread to the Far East and an attack on Hong Kong or Weihaiwei were to take place, we should rely on your support.' The Elder Statesmen met with the Cabinet that same day to consider this statement, and in reply they assured Grey that in such a case 'the Imperial Government will be ready at once to support His Majesty's Government if called upon.' He in turn replied that Britain 'should, if we could, avoid drawing Japan into any trouble, but should a case arise in which we needed her help, we would gladly ask for it and be grateful for it.'

In his memoirs Grey was later to write that 'in the early days [of the war] the Japanese Alliance was a matter of some embarrassment and even anxiety. Japan was ready to take her part in the war as our Ally; the Far East and the whole of the Pacific Ocean lay open to her and were her natural sphere of operations. But the prospect of unlimited action was repugnant to Australia and New Zealand ... Equally important, the effect of Japanese action on public opinion in the United States might be disastrous.' In the light of the recent revelation of her expansionist ambitions in Korea and elsewhere it was vital that Japan should enter the war, if at all, only by express invitation, and then that her field of operations should be rigorously restricted. By her reply she appeared to indicate that she was willing to accept these conditions. The appearance, however, was not to last for very long.

Even more optimistically, China had approached America with a view to having herself, the areas leased to the Powers included, declared a neutral zone, but this had already been ruled out by the vigorous steps that Germany had begun to take in defence of her garrison at Tsingtao. As early as August 1st German reservists from all over China had begun to pour in to join the 3,500 regular troops stationed there, while several units of Admiral von Spee's Far Eastern Squadron were being fitted out for action. In a lightning sortie a few days later, the cruiser *Emden* put out from the harbour and captured a Russian auxiliary with a number of merchant ships. She then turned south and before the British squadron based on Hong Kong could intercept her she linked up with the heavy cruisers *Gneisenau* and *Scharnhorst* in the Caroline Islands.

Together they represented a formidable threat to British shipping in the area, and only three days later Grey, after consultations with the First Lord of the Admiralty, Winston Churchill, felt obliged to send another note to Tokyo requesting the assistance of the Japanese Navy 'in hunting out and destroying' them; it was realised, he added, 'that such an action on the part of Japan will constitute declaration of war with Germany, but it is difficult to see how such a step is to be avoided.' On its receipt Kato immediately persuaded Prime Minister Okuma that if Japan was to enter the war, her part in it could not be limited to the pursuit of German warships, and this proposition was then put to the Cabinet, Elder Statesmen and Emperor in rapid succession for approval.

The only person to question it at all seriously was Yamagata — not, of course, through any misgivings on its legality, but because of a nagging suspicion that the German war machine that he so much admired might put Japan on the losing side. Kato then put through an additional proposal of his own: an ultimatum should be sent to Germany to surrender the whole Tsingtao concession to Japan, and that if it was not met Britain should then join with Japan to seize it and so 'base their [Japan's] participation in the war on the broad grounds stated in the Agreement of the Alliance'.

Grey's worst fears were thus confirmed. With a typical Foreign Office euphemism the U.S. Ambassador in London was informed that 'Japan finds herself unable to refrain from war with Germany'. Grey repeated his request that Japanese action should be limited to the protection of Allied shipping on the high seas and that Japan should 'postpone for the time being hostile activities under the Anglo-Japanese Alliance'. Kato brusquely rejected this, however, arguing that 'public opinion' would not allow him to back down; still less would he entertain Grey's next suggestion that a boundary should be set on Japan's field of operations.

The ultimatum, calling for the surrender of Tsingtao by September 15th with a view to its 'eventual' restoration to China, was approved by an Imperial Council on August 15th and dispatched to Berlin, to be followed by a public statement by Okuma that 'Japan's object is to eliminate from the continent of China the root of German influence, which forms a constant menace to the peace of the Far East, and thus to secure the aim of the Alliance with Great Britain. She harbours no design for territorial aggrandisement or entertains no desire to promote any other selfish end . . .'

The words must have left the ears of the British Foreign Secretary red hot. To have invited Japan to join the hostilities, on however limited a scale, betrayed an unforgivable misapprehension of her avowed goals. As one of his own officials lamely admitted, 'we did not at first realise how keen they were to come in'. (After the war was over, his successor Lord Curzon was to order the suppression of a report from the Ambassador in Peking to the effect that 'we do not appear to be in urgent need of Japanese assistance'.) Grey was left to salvage what he could with a unilateral statement, for the benefit of his anxious audience in Australia and New Zealand, that 'it is understood that the action of Japan will not extend beyond the China Seas . . . nor to any foreign territory except territory in German occupation on the continent of Eastern Asia.' Not unnaturally, Kato promptly disavowed any such 'understanding'.

In the meantime there had been moves afoot in Peking for Germany to forestall Japan by retroceding Tsingtao to China, but when Tokyo got wind of them the Chinese Government was warned in no uncertain terms to drop the idea. The ultimatum thus expired on August 23rd without response from Berlin; in line with his outspoken racial prejudices, the Kaiser vowed that 'it would shame me more to surrender Tsingtao to the Japanese than Berlin to the Russians'. An Imperial Rescript was issued that same day formally declaring war.

'SECOND RESTORATION'

Japan thus entered the Great War — still referred to there as 'The German-Japanese War' — in a theatre largely removed from the inconvenient gaze of the other participants and on terms which amounted almost to a *carte blanche* to pursue her expansionist ambitions. The propagandists were put busily to work again to convince a now thoroughly sceptical world of the high-minded nature of Japanese motives. Perhaps the most remarkable of their efforts was that of one (the same that had described Terauchi, the Gauleiter of Korea, as 'honest, gentle, artless, fair and conscientious') who proclaimed that 'Japan declared war on Germany solely and purely in order to remain true to the spirit of her obligations. The course which led to Japan's taking such a momentous step shows no trace of the influence of the so-called militarists . . .' Not even he, it should be noticed, felt able to point to any written evidence of such an 'obligation', and when Kato was questioned on the subject in the Diet he refused to reply on grounds of 'diplomatic secrecy'.

It was left to Kato's successor Ishii eventually to admit that the

Declaration of War had been made 'in obedience to the general spirit of the Alliance, and not under any particular article'. Ishii's own *Diplomatic Commentaries* may be thought to give a more accurate record of Japanese motives: 'the measures adopted were not only suited to the emergency but calculated as well to advance the interests of the Empire for years to come.'

During the past month both France and Russia had approached Japan with the suggestion that they too should formally ally themselves with her, but they had been firmly rejected by Kato on the grounds that such a move would diminish the value of the Anglo-Japanese Alliance. The two suitors had to be content instead with signing a joint declaration with Britain in London that they would not make a separate peace with Germany while the others were still engaged in war; Japan was not invited to add her signature because such a provision was already contained in the terms of the Alliance (although she was to do so a year later).

In contrast with Kato the Elder Statesmen, particularly Inoue and Yamagata, had been in favour of the proposed quadrilateral alliance. 'I approve wholeheartedly', the latter had enthused. 'In particular, the formation of a united group with England, France, Russia and ourselves, and the importation of capital from France, are most urgently needed.' Having harboured reservations as to the wisdom of declaring war on Germany at all, he was all the more critical of Kato's ultimatum to Berlin. 'It is useless,' he complained. 'Our foreign relations have been wrecked.' The final straw came when, after his refusal to answer questions in the Diet on the justification for declaring war, Kato issued instructions forbidding the circulation of diplomatic correspondence even to the Elder Statesmen on the grounds of wartime security. To have to share the process of decision-making on matters of high state with a party politician was irksome enough, but then to be excluded altogether was intolerable. The Elder Statesmen demanded a meeting with Prime Minister Okuma.

It was held on September 24th at Inoue's private residence. Afterwards a summary of their conclusions was circulated. 'Since the death of the late Emperor and the advent of the present Emperor the prestige of Japan among the Powers has declined,' it stated. 'The Okuma Cabinet has not yet been able to realise its desire for a second Restoration. Yet the present offers an immense and unique opportunity for improving Japan through domestic and foreign policies. With the aim of developing long-range goals for the nation ... the Prime Minister and each Elder Statesman should be completely open and candid, conferring closely and exchanging ideas.' Even more specifically, it laid down that 'the Foreign Minister, Baron Kato, will faithfully carry out the foreign policy agreed upon unanimously between the Prime Minister and the Elder Statesmen.' It served notice, in other words, that it was the Elder Statesmen and not the political parties who would fill the vacuum left by Emperor Taisho's increasing disengagement from public affairs. If Kato imagined — and he continued to behave as if he did — that the role of the Elder Statesmen was played out, he was soon to discover otherwise.

BRIDGEHEAD

On the day that Kato's ultimatum was transmitted to Berlin the Chiefs of Staff, who as far back as July 2nd had met with Taisho in a newly-established Council of National Defence to co-ordinate their preparations, reported on their respective states of readiness to the Palace. When the Declaration of War followed a week later, an infantry division and cavalry brigade were immediately mobilised for an attack on Tsingtao and the Navy ordered to sea to blockade the harbour. Kato had already hedged the undertaking to restore the concession to China 'eventually' with a statement that 'even if we were to return it to China, it would be necessary to attach many conditions,' and he dropped a heavy hint that British participation in the operation would not be welcome. The further suggestion that France and Russia should also be invited to join it received even shorter shrift. Grey, however, was determined not to compound his original mistake and insisted on sending a British contingent. Comprising a battalion of the South Wales Borderers and a company of Sikhs, it was dwarfed by the Japanese force, but it was thought that its very presence, even when placed, as agreed, under Japanese command, would serve as some sort of check on them.

The first Japanese troops landed on September 2nd at Lungkow, some 60 miles north of the concession's perimeter. With no troops of her own on hand to meet them, China's response was necessarily limited to vehement protests at this violation of her neutrality and the declaration of a war zone to cover the anticipated field of Japanese operations, roughly corresponding to the Shantung peninsula. The British contingent landed within the concession's perimeter on the 24th, and by then Kato had already assured the Diet that he had made no commitments whatever to any other Power on the return of Tsingtao to China. From the outset the British were relegated to a subordinate role and kept in ignorance of the general plan of campaign; on frequent occasions they found themselves coming under fire from Japanese patrols.

On November 7th they were surprised to learn of the German garrison's surrender, having been given no advance information of, let alone been permitted to participate in, the final assault. This fact was seized on by pro-German elements in Tokyo as a pretext for accusing the British of having been 'cowardice itself'. In reply the Foreign Office contented itself with the observation that the campaign had shown 'our Japanese allies in a very unfortunate light as co-operators in the field'.

The Japanese fleet had also been busily engaged in the meantime, not so much in pursuit of von Spee's cruisers as in the occupation of the German-held Caroline, Marshall and Mariana archipelagoes, all of which lay hundreds of miles to the east of the limit publicly set on Japan's operations at the outset of the war by Okuma's restriction to 'the elimination from the continent of China of the root of German influence'. This was another serious embarrassment for Britain who had allotted precisely the same task to the Australian Navy, and even more of one when Kato then announced that Japan intended to retain all the islands north of the Equator *in perpetuum*. In spite of the very real alarm which this aroused in Australia, Grey felt unable to do more than acquiesce 'on the understanding that all occupation of German territory will be without prejudice to the final arrangements [at the end of the war]'. It was a card that Japan would play for all that it was worth.

After Tsingtao's fall it was announced that the concession would remain under the control of the Japanese Expeditionary Commander-in-Chief for the duration of the war. His field of operations by no means stopped there, for he had earlier detached a force to seize the entire 240-mile length of the German-run railway from Tsingtao to its junction with the Imperial Railways network at Tsinan, on the pretext that the Germans had used it to ferry in supplies and reservists. To Chinese protests that since Tsingtao was now surrounded 'the concurrence of your government in the railway's protection is quite unnecessary', Japan replied flatly that she considered the line 'indivisible'. President Yuan thereupon appealed to Britain and America to use their good offices to intervene.

In his meeting with the Elder Statesmen on September 24th Okuma had agreed with them that 'the major objective of our China policy should be to dispel the distrust and doubts harboured towards Japan by the Chinese, beginning with Yuan Shih-k'ai, and to demonstrate our sincerity.' Kato's intentions remained quite otherwise, however, and he was still determined that that body should not interfere with their execution. The 'psychological moment' that he had spoken of two years earlier to Grey for establishing Japan's 'permanent, exclusive possession' of the Manchurian leases had now, he considered, arrived.

THE TWENTY-ONE DEMANDS

Ambassador Hioki, who like his predecessor Ijuin had been detailed to establish 'convenient grounds for the settlement of the problem', was accordingly recalled from Peking on November 12th to receive instructions. He brought with him a list of suggested requirements drawn up by the military attaché there. Shortly afterwards Okuma was favoured by a similar list presented to him by Black Dragon Boss Uchida, who pressed in addition for the overthrow of Yuan and the establishment of a puppet monarchy under Prince Su. These two documents were then welded together to produce the composite draft of the infamous 'Twenty-One Demands' to be presented to Yuan.

These were arranged under five separate headings. Group One demanded that Japan should be permitted to 'dispose of' the German leases in Shantung as she saw fit, that China should not cede any part of the province to any other Power and that she should grant Japan certain other commercial concessions there. Group Two would extend all existing Japanese leases in Manchuria to a period of 99 years, and would grant land ownership and extra-territorial jurisdiction in Manchuria and Inner Mongolia to Japanese nationals, together with mining concessions and the right of veto on railway development by other Powers. Group Three would grant Japan joint ownership of the Hanyehping Iron Company and all adjacent iron ore deposits, which China was to undertake neither to nationalise (as Yuan was already proposing to do) nor to develop with any but Japanese capital. Group Four would require China not to cede any territory along her entire coastline to any other Power. Group Five would give Japan the right to appoint Japanese political, financial and military advisers to the Chinese Government, to establish a joint administration of the police, to supply at least half of China's war material requirement together with the appropriate experts, to build a new network of railways serving the Yangtse valley, to veto all commercial developments in Fukien province with non-Japanese capital, to buy land for Japanese missions and to propagate the Shinto faith.

They were designed, in short, to give Japan a stranglehold over her neighbour. Their effect would be, according to the U.S. Ambassador in Peking, Paul Reinsch, 'to place the Chinese State in a position of vassalage through exercising a control over important parts of its administration and over its industrial and natural resources, actual and prospective'; it was no accident, he also remarked, that the paper on which they were presented bore the water-mark of a machine-gun. Nor were the Chinese themselves any less alive to their implications: 'Never a Chinese, rich or poor, high or low, stupid or intelligent, but knew that Manchuria was going as Formosa and Korea had gone, and that Mongolia and Shantung and Fukien were going too, and that henceforth no Chinese would be master of his own soul,' the *North China Herald* warned.

Certainly the Demands represented everything that the Black Dragon expansionists could wish for, and if they perhaps exceeded the bounds of what Okuma (although not by very much, to judge by his description of the Chinese as 'outwardly and inwardly filthy') or even Kato had in mind, there were pressing political reasons for their putting their names to them. Since Kato's refusal to answer questions in the Diet on the grounds for declaring war, the Opposition Seiyukai majority had grown increasingly unco-operative, finally refusing to pass the budget with its provision for the creation of the promised two new divisions and so forcing Okuma to dissolve the Diet and call an election. The Seiyukai had then joined with Uchida to form a National Foreign Policy Association backing his 'solution to the China problem', making it obvious to Okuma and his colleagues that their only hope of retaining office lay in stealing the Opposition's thunder. Kato had the additional incentive of being the son-in-law of the head of Mitsubishi, which was already heavily involved in the Hanyehping Iron Company.

Hioki was handed the draft of the Demands on December 3rd with instructions to return to Peking and present them to Yuan in person 'whenever a suitable opportunity arose'. Groups One to Four were to be settled 'in principle'; Group Five, the most obnoxious of all, was to be kept rigidly secret, but its acceptance was 'not absolutely necessary'.

The 'suitable opportunity' was not long in coming. On January 7th 1915 the Chinese government announced the cancellation of the Shantung war zone in view of the cessation of hostilities there and requested Japan to withdraw her troops from the area, including, naturally, the Tsinan-Tsingtao railway. Protesting that this represented 'a want of confidence in international good faith and friendly relations', Hioki a week later presented the Demands to Yuan together with a warning that if he failed to keep them to himself Japan would take immediately steps to carry them out.

'Why does Japan treat China like a pig dog of a slave?' the Chinese President is reported to have protested, but he quickly realised that his defence against such a brazen threat lay not in any physical opposition that he himself might be able to muster, but in the force of international opinion among the other Powers with interests in the area. Within a matter of days, therefore, he saw to it that a copy of the Demands reached Reinsch's hands, from where they were quickly revealed to the outside world.

Hioki at first denied all knowledge of them and even, according to one source, tried to recover the original draft from Yuan, but the damage was done. Tokyo attempted to retrieve the situation by publishing their own version omitting Group Five altogether. When this was duly laughed out of court, it was explained that the latter were not meant as demands at all but merely as 'wishes', and that 'while Japan would continue to press them, she did not expect to compel obedience by force' — adding, with a picturesqueness sufficient to open the eyes of any still blind to Japan's designs, 'when there is a fire in a jeweller's shop, the neighbours cannot be expected to refrain from helping themsleves'.

'UNPRECEDENTED MAGNANIMITY'

Negotiations opened in Peking on February 2nd. China refused to take them further until Group Five was withdrawn, and was then accused by Japan's propagandists of 'adopting her usual intransigent policy'. After seven weeks of minimal progress, 7,000 additional Japanese troops were dispatched to Manchuria and Shantung in order to concentrate the Chinese mind; these, Hioki explained, were only 'reliefs' for those already there, although he was quick to add that they would not be withdrawn 'until the negotiations could be brought to a satisfactory conclusion'. The Minister of War, another Yamagata placeman, decided that matters should be pushed still harder and used his prerogative of direct access to the Throne to obtain Taisho's blessing for an even larger force, but when Kato got to hear of this he interceded to persuade the Emperor to countermand it. The Foreign Minister was still determined to keep control of affairs in his own hands, and his position and that of the Okuma Cabinet as a whole was considerably strengthened by their victory in the General Election of March 25th.

The negotiations continued to drag on. In April Kato submitted an Amended Project to Peking which made a number of concessions, but still did not withdraw Group Five. On May 1st the Chinese replied with a Final Amended Project of their own. This in turn was found to be unacceptable, and on May 7th Kato issued an ultimatum giving China 48 hours to accept the new terms or face their imposition by force of arms; Japanese residents in China were simultaneously warned to prepare to leave the country. Group Five, however, was not included in the ultimatum, being merely 'reserved for future discussion', while the new draft of the first four Groups now represented a significant retreat from the original Demands. Feeling that they were unlikely to gain any further concessions, the Chinese signalled their acquiescence.

In the agreement signed on May 25th Japan undertook to return Tsingtao on condition only that it was declared an open port within which a Japanese settlement was to be set up. Rights of land ownership and extra-territorial jurisdiction in Manchuria and Inner Mongolia were not conceded, while Japanese participation in the latter's economic development was to be strictly limited. China was to retain ownership of other iron ore deposits in the area of Hanyehping, and she made no commitment on the use of her coastline other than that no foreign Power would be allowed to construct a naval dockyard in Fukien.

The mere fact that she had provoked Japan into issuing an ultimatum at all was something of a coup, because it enabled her to plead at the end of the war that she had only come to terms under the threat of *force majeure*, and that these were therefore invalid. Their effect at the time was to confirm the world's worst suspicions of Japan. Sir Edward Grey spoke of a violation of the spirit of the Anglo-Japanese Alliance, while the United States warned that 'it cannot recognise any agreement or undertaking which has been entered into . . . impairing the treaty rights of the United States and its citizens in China, the political or territorial integrity of the Republic of China, or the . . . Open Door policy.' Ishii, shortly to be the next Foreign Minister, put what gloss he could on it: the Demands were 'just and reasonable' and had been the subject of 'world-wide misunderstanding', while the climb-down on Shantung and Mongolia was an act of 'magnanimity unprecedented in history'.

On the domestic front too the agreement set off furious criticism of Okuma's government from all sides. The withdrawal of Group Five and the failure to establish a puppet regime in northern China made Kato the object of such enduring odium to the Black Dragon hierarchy that when all of ten years later he became Prime Minister, Uchida was arrested on a charge of complicity in an attempt to assassinate him. The Elder Statesmen were scarcely less determined to have his blood, for despite Okuma's undertaking of the previous September Kato had still found no necessity to keep them abreast of events. 'Since negotiations with China began, I have come across references here and there in the newspapers,' Yamagata observed with massive sarcasm to the Prime Minister, and to his colleague 'I'll Investigate' Matsukata he wrote that 'I still have no authoritative information on the negotiations with China ... That even you have received no reports is truly shocking.'

Hearing on May 4th through the Home Minister that an ultimatum was in the offing, Yamagata had called a meeting of the Elder Statesmen with the Cabinet, at which he spoke once more of the need to maintain as friendly relations as possible with China and to avoid giving offence to world opinion. His sharpest words were reserved for the Group Five Demands, which in his opinion 'would disgrace the honour of Japan which stands for justice (*sic*) in the world', and it was following Yamagata's intervention that Group Five had finally been withdrawn.

Not content with this reassertion of their influence, the Elder Statesmen pressed ahead with demands for Kato's dismissal. 'Choose between changing the Foreign Minister and severing all connections with me,' 'Mitsui-Man' Inoue bluntly demanded of Okuma; the threat was particularly pointed because it was Inoue who had first put forward Okuma's name for the Premiership a year earlier. Okuma duly bowed, but in order to conceal the Elder Statesmen's part in it Kato's resignation was bracketed with that of the Home Minister, who was discovered in July to have bribed officials in his Ministry on a massive scale to rig the March election in the Government's favour.

A SECOND BITE

In China itself, however, Tokyo was powerless to undo the damage to Sino-Japanese relations wrought by the Demands. May 25th, the date of the agreement's signing, was to be proclaimed National Humiliation Day, and it was followed by another nationwide boycott of Japanese goods and commercial institutions. As domestic support for Yuan had been greatly strengthened by his resistance to the Demands, so Sun became increasingly discredited by his Japanese links. The numbers of the Sworn Brotherhood in Tokyo dwindled rapidly as they, including even Sun's lieutenant Huang Hsing, slipped back to China to take advantage of Yuan's offer of money and an amnesty. In a desperate attempt to halt the decline Sun accused

Yuan of having actually invited Japan to present the Demands in order to bolster his own position, and when that misfired he wrote to the Japanese Foreign Ministry warning them of the bad faith of Yuan's 'evil government' and offering them terms whose effect would have been to bind China even more tightly to Japan than the Twenty-One Demands.

Just when it seemed that Japan had forfeited her opportunity to interfere in China for the foreseeable future, an act of over-confidence on Yuan's part presented her with another one. A month after Kato had been forced out of office, Yuan's eldest son set up an organisation in China to press for the restoration of the Dragon Throne with his own father as Emperor. Outside the Elder Statesmen, who still favoured the cultivation of friendly relations with him as China's established leader, the reaction in Japan was predictably unenthusiastic. Although Okuma issued a non-committal statement that it was a question for China to settle for herself, he added ominously that 'if it proved prejudicial to Japan's interests, we would not shrink from immediate measures.'

The first such 'measure' was an attempt to persuade the Allies to join in a refusal to recognise the proposed monarchy. The response was distinctly lukewarm; the British Ambassador in Peking, for instance, complained that 'the Japanese have been making themselves and us ridiculous by all these representations which have produced no effect except antagonizing the Chinese . . . we all feel that we are so many puppets pulled by Japanese strings'. This lack of interest did on the other hand allow the new Foreign Minister, Ishii, to claim that 'the Allies were too occupied on the European fronts to give attention to this distant complication, and consequently the duty of nipping the Chinese upheaval in the bud fell entirely on the shoulders of Japan.' Another justification found for this 'duty' was an improbable rumour put about that Germany was negotiating with Yuan for permission to build a submarine base at Canton; at that stage of their development the U-boats were having difficulty in penetrating as far as the Mediterranean, let alone the Indian and Pacific Oceans.

When in the face of 'all these representations' Yuan refused to do more than postpone his inauguration as Emperor until the Chinese New Year in February, Vice-Chief of Staff Tanaka (the architect of the 1907 National Defence Plan of future expansion) detached the Commander of the Kwantung Army and ordered him to Shanghai, ostensibly to 'investigate German plots' but in reality, as Tanaka's official biographer was to relate, 'to support anti-Yuan movements throughout the southern part of China'.

At the end of December a revolt duly materialised in Yunnan, led by the province's Governor, Liang Chi'i-ch'ao. Liang had arrived in Japan in 1898 with K'ang Yu-wei after their short-lived reform movement had been cut short by the Dowager Empress's coup against her son, and throughout his long exile he had held aloof from Sun's Brotherhood, which he regarded as subversive; he had returned to China to support Yuan when the new Republic was first declared, and he had only now broken with him over his monarchical ambitions. K'ang, it will be remembered, had been taken under the wing of the Real Constitutionalist Party, forerunner of the present Nationalists (whereas Sun and his supporters had been adopted by the secret societies), and since the Nationalists' leader, Okuma, was now by good fortune Japan's Prime Minister, he could look with confidence to that quarter for assistance. The British Embassy in Peking reported that the revolt was 'engineered with the connivance of the Japanese who are naïve enough to think we don't know it.' The neighbouring province of Kwangtung also declared itself independent the following month, but when the rebel army moved on into Szechwan it found itself faced by far superior forces.

Sun's Black Dragon allies had also meanwhile taken steps to claim a share of the action. After an attempt, led by several Japanese officers, to seize Chinese warships at Shanghai and take over the city in preparation for Sun's return had been easily scotched, their attention turned to reviving the plan to place the captive Prince Su on a restored Manchu throne in the north; a new splinter group, 'The Mountain of Sweat Society', was set up to co-ordinate it. When they approached Okuma with a suggestion that German arms captured at Tsingtao should be made available for a rebellion, he publicly dismissed it as 'completely out of the question'; privately, however, he sent an order to the Japanese commandant there to do all that he could to assist. Mitsui provided the necessary ships to smuggle the arms across to Manchuria, where an advance guard of junior officers and 'men of spirit' had gone on ahead to prepare the ground. Their first objective was the removal of Yuan's ally, the Manchu 'Old Warlord' Chang Tso-lin, but in spite of raising a force of 3,000 men all their attempts on his life were frustrated.

In expectation of their success Tanaka had submitted a memorandum to the Cabinet calling for non-recognition of Yuan as Emperor regardless of the attitude of the other Powers. It was duly endorsed. When informed of this by Ambassador Hioki, Yuan, concerned perhaps that the West might react similarly, consented to postpone his inauguration for a further two months. Prodded again by the military, the Cabinet then adopted a seven-point programme for the 'Establishment of Awesome Power in China' aimed at the elimination of Yuan on the grounds that 'whoever comes after him will serve Japan's interests better.' Although direct intervention was eschewed, all possible aid was to be given to the anti-Yuan forces and plans were drawn up for a co-ordinated, three-pronged attack on Peking from Manchuria, Shantung and the Yangtse valley.

Three more provinces had by now gone over to the rebels, and the prospect of further defections finally, on March 22nd, persuaded Yuan to abrogate the proposed monarchy. This concession, however, only served to encourage the rebels, who interpreted it as a sign of weakness, as did their Japanese collaborators who felt correspondingly less constrained to conceal their activities. A thousand-strong force was openly drilled by

Japanese instructors in Tsingtao before being put on the railway, machine-guns and all, to Tsinan. At the same time permission was refused to Government troops to travel on the line in the opposite direction on the pretext of 'preserving neutrality'. When this contradiction was pointed out, it was explained that the rebels must have travelled 'as civilians'. Elsewhere countless 'incidents' were staged, of which only the Japanese version ever appeared in the largely Japanese-dominated Chinese Press.

By the end of May five further provinces had deserted. When the Chinese Ambassador in Tokyo pleaded that the country would disintegrate if Yuan was forced to step down, Foreign Minister Ishii replied that Yuan would be welcome to bring his family to Japan and live out the rest of his life there. Even this dubious consolation was to be denied to him, however; already a broken man, he died on June 6th at the early age of 56. His death was greeted with open jubilation in Japan; Prime Minister Okuma even boasted in public of his own contrasting longevity.

DOUBLE DEALINGS

If Yamagata had done nothing since procuring Kato's dismissal to avert the destruction of the 'Biggest Man', it was because his attention had been taken up by events further afield. German successes in Europe had rekindled his doubts on the capacity of the Allies to win the war, 'so the policy of relying solely on the Anglo-Japanese Alliance to maintain continued peace in the Far East may be inadequate. The most urgent task for Japan, therefore, is to have in addition an alliance with Russia which would provide us with adequate means to gain our objectives.' He was particularly concerned with the poor performance of the Russians on the Eastern Front and the evident unpopularity of the war among them; if Russia was to make a separate peace with Germany, Japan's position in China would, he considered, be put under great threat. Kato had represented the greatest obstacle to such an alliance; Russia's critical shortage of war material, which only Japan was in a position to make good, augured well for a favourable response.

Yamagata seized on the visit of the Tsar's uncle to Japan in January 1916 to put forward this suggestion. He was greatly put out by Ishii's cool response to it, but after complaining to Okuma of the Foreign Minister's 'impudence' he saw to it that negotiations were put in hand. Thanks mainly to his persistence, they were eventually concluded on July 3rd.

As published, this fourth Russo-Japanese Agreement did no more than renew the protection of the two parties' mutually-recognised interests against the interference of any third party. However, the secret clauses attached to it went a great deal further than that: not only were these interests now designated 'vital' rather than merely 'special' as before, but they were extended to cover the whole of China and not just Manchuria and Mongolia, including, of course, the concessions wrested by Japan from

China the previous year. In return, Japan engaged to supply Russia with arms, including 700,000 rifles, and other equipment to the total value of 300 million yen. These provisions only came to light when they were revealed by the Bolsheviks in the wake of the Russian Revolution.

Yamagata professed himself 'overjoyed', and he now moved on to re-establish the authority of the Elder Statesmen once and for all. Okuma's position had continued to come under fire both from the House of Peers for his financial policies and from the expansionists for his failure to take a more active part in Yuan's downfall. Earlier in the year he had been the target of another Genyosha bomb, and in an understandable desire to see out his remaining days with at least one leg still intact the Lame Democrat was happy enough to come to an accommodation: in return for Yamagata's undertaking to draw off the opposition of the Peers, he agreed to resign the Premiership at the end of the present parliamentary session in July. The Gauleiter of Korea, Terauchi, was lined up to succeed him.

When the time came, however, Okuma was not prepared to surrender the interests of the political parties quite so easily. He proposed instead that the office should go to Kato, who had now taken over the leadership of the largest party in the Diet. This was rejected by Yamagata on the familiar grounds that a political appointee would impair 'the strength of national unity', whereupon Okuma moved to take the matter out of the Elder Statesmen's hands by suggesting to the Emperor that he should invite both Kato and Terauchi to form a coalition. Terauchi, acting on his patron's instructions, declined the invitation; Okuma's response was to nominate Kato as his sole successor and resign, on October 4th. Yamagata, however, had been forewarned of this move, and summoning the Elder Statesmen to a hasty conference with the Emperor he obtained the Imperial blessing for his own choice.

Terauchi was, if anything, even more convinced than his patron of the prospects of a German victory. Exploratory talks for an agreement between the two countries had been initiated through their respective Ambassadors in Stockholm as far back as January 1915, but these had been abruptly terminated when it was discovered that Japan was passing their conversations on to her Allies in an attempt to restore her credibility with them after the debâcle of the Twenty-One Demands; 'There is no point in negotiating with the Japanese, one can get more by thrashing them!' Kaiser Wilhelm had exploded — a sentiment that Hitler would echo a quarter of a century later. With the advent of Terauchi this chicanery was soon forgotten and both sides began to put out tentative feelers again — only to be brought up short in February 1917 by the interception of the 'Zimmermann Telegram', which revealed that moves were afoot to bring about a German-Japanese-Mexican alliance, whereby Mexico would be helped to recover her 'lost' territories in Texas, Nevada and New Mexico in the event of an American entry into the war.

Japan in her usual tones of injured innocence protested that it was a plot got up by the Germans to create dissension between her and her allies, but at the same time she felt no inhibition in accepting a large order for arms from Mexico — and this in spite of a previous undertaking that she would only sell to the Allies. German prospects were now rather less promising, while Japan's position had grown so strong that she felt able to make a positive virtue of her duplicity and pressurise the Allies into paying a larger price for her allegiance.

In the space of four years her exports had doubled as factories worked 24 hours a day to meet the demands of markets starved of their usual supplies from Europe. No orders were ever turned away, and in the rush to meet them quality was often sacrificed for quantity, earning Japan a reputation for shoddiness which in some areas has persisted to this day. Thanks to the success of the U-boats in the Atlantic, the greatest demand of all was for ships in which to carry these goods, and Japanese yards had only to name their price.

In the very first month of the war Britain, aware that her naval resources were already overstretched, had asked Japan for the loan of a number of her warships for use in the Mediterranean and, two months later, for her assistance in setting up a blockade of the Baltic, but Japan had declined to do more than offer escorts for convoys in the Indian Ocean. In February 1916 Britain had made a fresh request for a larger force to be sent there, and Japan agreed on condition that Australia and Canada relaxed their restrictions on Japanese immigrants. In the event, Australian Prime Minister William Hughes could not be persuaded to do so.

Britain now, in January 1917, came forward with yet another request, for the dispatch of a destroyer flotilla to the Mediterranean. This time Japan felt able to raise her price: in any post-war settlement, Britain was required to support the continuation of the Japanese occupation of Tsingtao and the former German Pacific islands north of the Equator. In return, Britain extracted a Japanese pledge of support for her claims to the German islands south of the Equator. The Foreign Office in London tried hard to justify this deal to themselves: 'If we have made an unpleasant virtue of necessity, Japan has, as far as her southward Pacific penetration is concerned, come up against an almost equally unpleasant condition of finality.'

A quarter of a century later this 'condition of finality' was to prove about as 'unpleasant' to the aggressor as the Maginot Line had done further west.

17

Versailles: Easy Pickings

CHINA DIVIDED

If the Foreign Office also deluded themselves into believing that Japanese aid and comfort to revolutionary movements in the British Empire would now cease, they were to be swiftly undeceived — just as the Russians were by the continuing flow of funds to Lenin's associates in Finland and Islamic groups in Turkestan in spite of their newly-signed Agreement with Japan. The most significant of the former was that led by Rash Behari Bose in India, which had come out in open rebellion in 1915. This had been suppressed following an unsuccessful attempt on the life of the Governor-General, Lord Hardinge, and Bose had fled to Japan, where he found refuge under Godfather Toyama's capacious roof.

On British insistence an extradition order was reluctantly granted against him, but before it could be served Goto, formerly Director of Colonial Affairs and now Home Minister, saw to it that he had moved on to a less obvious hideaway. Bose would stay on in Japan plotting further rebellions in his homeland, even becoming a paid-up member of the Black Dragon; in World War Two he assumed the leadership of an Indian government-in-exile until handing over to his namesake, Chandra Bose, whose Nationalist Independence Army would serve as the path-clearer for a Japanese invasion. An accomplice was smuggled into Afghanistan to co-ordinate revolutionary movements there, while the activities of the network of Japanese agents in Tibet (then a British protectorate) remained the source of frequent British protests. Not for nothing was the Anglo-Japanese Alliance now generally referred to in Tokyo as 'the wastepaper basket alliance'.

After her success with Britain, Japan went on to persuade both France and Russia to lend their support to her post-war claims to Tsingtao and the former German Pacific islands. Both countries agreed to do so on condition that she put pressure on China to declare war on Germany. However, this was a development that Japan was determined to oppose at all costs because it would automatically give China a say in any post-war settlement and so allow her to put Japan's claims at the mercy of international opinion. The new Foreign Minister, Motono Ichiro, who as Ambassador in St. Petersburg had successfully negotiated the Agreement with Russia and its secret clauses, made appropriate noises of assent and even went so far as to claim that Japan had already made 'every effort from the beginning' to do so — while proceeding, of course, to do nothing of the sort.

On Yuan's death the Presidency of the Chinese Republic had passed to his faithful lieutenant and fellow northern warlord Li Yuan-hung, while General Tuan Chi-jui continued as Prime Minister. Another key figure in the government was the Japanese-educated Minister of Communications, a post which also encompassed that of finance minister (the Bank of Communications being the country's central bank). One of Li's first acts was to reconvene the Assembly which had been suspended in 1913; this encouraged Sun Yat-sen to return to Shanghai from Japan and take his place once more at the head of the Kuomintang, the majority party. The prospect of a democratic, republican China led the Japanese military attaché in Peking to recommend to Tokyo military intervention, but Terauchi already had a scheme in mind which reverted to the earlier formula of economic and commercial penetration favoured by Hayashi.

The Prime Minister selected as his chief agents in this two men who had been instrumental in consolidating Japan's penetration of Korea during his Governorship there — Shoda Kazue, the President of the Bank of Korea, and Nishihara Kamezo, the head of a textile importing company. Nishihara was dispatched to Peking with offers of loans to the hard-pressed Chinese Treasury, while Shoda was appointed Vice-Minister of Finance with orders to organise a consortium of banks to provide them. The first, for 3 million yen, contained a secret provision which gave the Japanese the right to match the lowest price of any other bidder for contracts with the telegraph service; copper coinage was demanded as collateral, which was then shipped to Japan, melted down and sold on the world market for twice its face value.

This deal had already stirred opposition in both the Chinese and Japanese parliaments when it was overtaken by a larger event on the world stage, America's entry into the war on April 17th 1917 (following the disclosure of the 'Zimmermann Telegram' and Germany's announcement of unrestricted submarine warfare against neutral shipping, which had resulted in the sinking of the liner *Laconia* with the loss of several hundred American lives). Washington's invitation to China to declare war herself, backed by a loan of $10 million to help meet the necessary war expenses and a promise of remission of the outstanding Boxer indemnity, immediately reopened the newly-healed divisions in Peking. Prime Minister Tuan and the northern warlords were eager to accept this opportunity to increase the military budget; the Kuomintang on the other hand wished to remain neutral in order to retain the benefits of the growing trade with Germany conducted through the International Settlement at Shanghai.

For his part, President Li, anxious to preserve the fledgling Constitution, insisted that any decision on the matter should rest with the
Assembly. Tuan summoned the warlords to Peking for a show of strength,
and on the day that the debate was due to take place they surrounded the
parliament building with a hired mob to intimidate the members into
voting for war. The latter, however, refused to meet under such conditions. Most of the Cabinet then resigned; when Tuan refused to do
likewise, Li dismissed him. The warlords then threatened to declare their
provinces independent, obliging Li to dissolve the Assembly.

A month of confusion followed, in which the nine-year-old Pu-Yi even
found himself placed back again on the Dragon Throne for a few days. It
ended on July 14th with the entry into Peking of Tuan at the head of a
northern army and the flight of the Kuomintang to Canton, where Sun
announced the establishment of an independent Southern Republic. Tuan
formally declared China's entry into the war a month later.

AND BETRAYED

These events had been watched with close interest and growing alarm in
Tokyo. 'If China listens to advice from America,' the Japanese military
attaché in Peking warned at one stage, 'she will have Japan to deal with.'
Faced nonetheless with the unpalatable fact of America's and China's
entry into the war and the prospect of their participation in any post-war
settlement, Japan saw it as vital to obtain prior recognition from America,
as she had already from the other Allies, of her claims to Tsingtao and the
Pacific islands.

Ex-Foreign Minister Ishii was accordingly dispatched with all speed to
Washington, ostensibly on a mission to co-ordinate details of war strategy
and supply. When, during his interview with President Wilson, that
unwordly idealist mounted his favourite hobby-horse, the immorality of
the creation of spheres of interest in China by outsiders, Ishii seized the
opportunity to suggest a joint declaration by both countries reaffirming
their commitment to the principle of the 'Open Door'. However, if it was
not to be merely an empty repetition of the Root-Takahira Note of 1908, it
would have to define, he suggested, Japan's preferential position as a near
neighbour.

Wilson readily assented and deputed his Secretary of State, Robert
Lansing, to prepare an appropriate draft. Ishii proposed to Lansing that
Japan's position should be described as 'paramount', just as America's
position in relation to Mexico and the other American nations was in the
Monroe Doctrine. When Lansing objected to this as being too strong, it
was agreed to substitute the word 'special'. According to the Note which
then emerged on November 4th, both governments 'recognised that
territorial propinquity creates special relations between countries, and
consequently the U.S. Government recognises that Japan has special

interests in China, particularly in the part to which her possessions are contiguous.'

However unimpeachably high-minded this choice of words might have appeared to Wilson (and, when questioned in the Senate, Lansing denied that it had any 'political significance'), that was certainly now how it struck the rest of the world. As Ishii himself insisted, 'whether it be civil war, or epidemics, or political heresies which afflict China, the contagion will spread to Japan and the Japanese will suffer as well. These considerations are what lie at the bottom of Japan's special interests in China ... As the primary meeting of the term "special interests of Japan in China" is political, so is the chief *raison d'etre* of the Ishii-Lansing agreement political.' His government colleagues spoke of his 'great diplomatic victory', and the Lame Democrat Okuma boasted that America 'will not now repeat such follies [as advising China to enter the war] in disregard of Japan's special position in China.'

In Peking U.S. Ambassador Reinsch, who was best placed to advise on its likely interpretation but who was not even consulted on its preparation, reported that 'relays of Chinese have thronged to see the American consul, all sounding one note — that they have been betrayed by America ... it is quite generally interpreted as indicating a withdrawal of the American Government, in favour of Japan, from any desire to exercise any influence in Chinese affairs.' Tuan's government felt obliged to issue a disclaimer to the effect that it refused to accept that the Note represented any extension of the rights granted under existing treaties. This was not enough to satisfy some of his warlord supporters, who declared their independence, thus forcing the Prime Minister to resign.

LOAN SHARK

Nishihara had gone to ground in the meantime to wait for the smoke to clear before coming forward with offers of further loans. When he now emerged again, he saw that he had the field to himself. America was unable to fulfil the promise to remit the Boxer indemnity because the other parties concerned would not agree to waive their (larger) shares, while investment by private American companies was held to be in contravention of the Lansing-Ishii Note. No other Allied Power was forthcoming with loan offers, which would, it was seen, be inevitably used only to fund the campaign of the northern warlords against the Kuomintang.

Nishihara's accomplice, the Minister of Communications, was still in charge of the Peking Treasury, and the two of them went to work again with a will. An initial advance of 20 million yen was used to purchase 40,000 rifles; this was followed in the next twelve months by others amounting to a further 125 million yen in all, ostensibly to be used in railway, mining, forestry, telegraph and other industrial developments. They were backed up by secret Military and Naval Agreements signed in

May 1918 giving Japan freedom of movement to deploy her forces in northern Chinese territory against the 'enemy influence' of the Bolshevik victors of the October (1917) Revolution; no more money, it was made plain to Tuan, would be forthcoming until he put his signature to these.

In all this Nishihara acted on the direct authority of Terauchi and the War Ministry, and without the knowledge even of the Foreign Ministry. When the subject had first been broached in the Diet, Foreign Minister Motono had dismissed it as a figment of the imagination, and all mention of it in the Press was thereafter rigorously suppressed. Details were only finally released in October 1918 following Terauchi's resignation in favour of his recent Seiyukai allies under the leadership of Hara Kei, who as the first untitled Prime Minister earned himself the sobriquet 'The Great Commoner'. (His appointment marked no loosening in the military's hold on the Cabinet, however, for Yamagata engineered the installation of another protégé, Tanaka, in the key post of War Minister.)

Terauchi had dissolved the Diet the previous year when it failed to approve his budget and had secured a majority for the Seiyukai in the resultant election by the usual strong-arm methods, but a wave of strikes and riots mounted in protest at the effects of his financial policies won such widespread support that even the Gauleiter of Korea was persuaded that it would be unwise to stand in its path. The loans, it was now disclosed, had been issued to the Peking regime on no more security than promissory notes supposedly backed by gold; the latter never materialised, and of the 145 million yen lent, only 5 million was ever recovered. In order to redeem them, the Government raided the funds of small savers deposited with the Post Office. Japan would never again invest money overseas for so little return.

RED ALERT

A month later peace at last descended on the battlefields of Europe, and the combatants, with the exception of Soviet Russia, which had already made separate terms with Germany in March, adjourned to Versailles to settle their respective claims. For Japan, however, who, since mopping up Tsingtao in the early days of the war, had been happy to sit back and count her profits as her rivals fought each other to destruction, the real fighting was just about to begin.

Even before the October Revolution had presaged Russia's exit from the war, the Allies had made appeals to Japan to send some men to prop up the crumbling Eastern Front, but the Army General Staff had rejected them because they held the first priority to be the establishment of 'Japan's political and economic supremacy in China'. The spread of Bolshevism into Siberia and the Russian leaseholds in northern Manchuria put a very different complexion on the matter, however. On December 12th Lenin ordered the local soviet to take control at Harbin from General

Horvath, the Governor of the Chinese Eastern Railway Zone, and it was only prompt action by the local Chinese forces that restored the situation.

Plans were immediately drawn up in Tokyo for the dispatch of two mixed brigades to northern Manchuria and the Russian maritime province of Ussuri, ostensibly 'to protect foreign residents', while Nishihara in Peking had no difficulty in persuading Terauchi to provide support for an anti-Bolshevik White Russian force being organised in the Trans-Baikal Province by the young Cossack officer Gregorii Semenov. At the same time a network of agents were infiltrated into the two areas to assess the prospects of success for a Japanese expeditionary force.

Another focus of considerable concern to Tokyo was the need to prevent the Bolsheviks from laying their hands on the enormous, ¾ million-ton arsenal which the Allies had stockpiled at Vladivostok to await transfer along the Trans-Siberian Railway to the Eastern Front. Britain suggested to Japan and America that they should send a joint naval force for the purpose, but the idea of sharing command was unacceptable to Tokyo. However, when it was learnt that a Royal Navy cruiser had then been ordered there independently, Terauchi declared that 'somehow our ships have got to enter Vladivostok first!' Two ships and a force of marines under Rear Admiral Kato Kanji were ordered to sea post haste, and by steaming at full speed all the way he made port on January 12th 1918, beating *HMS Suffolk* by two days. A month later they were joined by *USS Brooklyn*. Kato's instructions were to liaise with the Japanese consul and 'to coerce with silent pressure' the local population of 'ignorant masses, especially the greedy and depraved Jews' into resisting the Bolsheviks.

On February 28th a Siberian Planning Committee was set up in secret under Tanaka (still then Vice-Chief of Staff) to co-ordinate plans for a military expedition. The first need, it was recognised, was for a military agreement with China in order to give Japanese troops freedom of movement in Manchuria, which was in danger of being pre-empted by the prompt deployment of Chinese forces there. Loan-Fixer Nishihara was instructed to deploy his moneybags to secure first the appointment of the co-operative Tuan to the head of the War Participation Board in Peking and then his return to the Premiership. This was achieved by the end of March at the cost of a further 'loan' of 20 million yen and the resignation of Foreign Minister Motono in protest at the Army's assumption of responsibility for foreign affairs. He was replaced by Goto, whose loyalty to the expansionist cause had never wavered since his notoriously tyrannical Governorship of Formosa a quarter of a century earlier.

A few days later three Japanese clerks were killed in the course of a robbery at a Japanese-owned store in Vladivostok. Signalling to Tokyo that 'order was completely destroyed, so that there did not exist ashore the means for protecting the lives and property of Japanese,' Kato promptly landed his marines; on the following day the commander of the *Suffolk* followed suit. Kato's action, however, was not well received by the Advisory Council on Foreign Affairs, a body which had been set up after the previous year's General Election to co-ordinate policy between the Cabinet and its Seiyukai backers in the Diet, and which only a fortnight earlier had decreed that in the absence of American support for a military expedition action should be limited to the supply of arms to the anti-Bolshevik forces of Horvath and Semenov.

As they had anticipated, the landing only succeeded in destroying their original objective (of salvaging the arsenal) and, worse still, in confirming Russia's new rulers in their worst suspicions of Japanese intentions. Following the receipt of a telegram from Lenin warning that 'the Japanese will certainly advance. That is inevitable. All the Allies will assist them without exception. Therefore you must begin to prepare yourselves . . . most of all you must give your attention to the best way out, the carrying off of stores and railroad material,' the local soviet moved in to take control of the port. The marines were hurriedly withdrawn; every city in eastern Siberia was now in Bolshevik hands.

Events in Manchuria were hardly more encouraging to the expansionists. Despite the receipt of 20,000 Japanese rifles and financial support from Britain and France, Horvath had made little progress in raising an anti-Bolshevik force — so little, in fact, that Semenov, who had been chased out of Trans-Baikal and briefly interned by the Chinese, refused to recognise his authority any longer and set off with a second expeditionary force (which included 49 Japanese 'instructors') on his own initiative. Furthermore, Horvath absolutely refused to meet Tokyo's demand that any Japanese expeditionary force should be granted unrestricted use of the Chinese Eastern Railway.

This demand had been made the more urgent by the presence of the Russian Railway Corps, a 300-strong squad of American engineers who had been invited by the short-lived Kerensky regime to help reorganise the TSR and its CER branch, both seriously disrupted by the Revolution. In spite of American denials, the Japanese Army General Staff persuaded themselves that this represented the spearhead of an American move for 'the eventual control of all continental transportation' and as such posed a grave threat to their ambitions in the area.

SIBERIAN SORTIE

It was clearly time, the Generals decided, to take the matter out of the hands of the politicians. Yamagata had until now insisted on international approval as a pre-condition for any military expedition, but he now informed Hara that 'in order to create a military spirit in the nation, it will be necessary to send some troops.' The Advisory Council on the other hand remained resolutely opposed to such an operation. Caught between the two, Foreign Minister Motono was given little option but to resign; the

'Peace-Preserver' then brushed aside the nominations of the Cabinet for the post to secure the appointment of Goto.

Goto immediately drew up a programme for a 'policy of aggressive defence' centred around a plan to take over control of the TSR at least as far west as Irkutsk and to secure China's acquiescence in freedom of movement for Japanese troops in Manchuria. Drafts of the proposed Military and Naval Agreements had been presented to Peking shortly after Nishihara had successfully engineered the return of Tuan to the Premiership, but the powers which they would grant Japan in Manchuria were so sweeping that even the normally-compliant Tuan had rebelled against putting his name to them. However, when the Loan-Fixer made it plain that no more sorely-needed yen would be forthcoming he soon kowtowed, and the signature of both Agreements was completed on May 19th. Not only was Japan given a *carte blanche* to take whatever action in Manchuria she deemed necessary to combat the 'common enemy' (the Bolsheviks were represented to be agents of Germany on the grounds that they were about to co-opt all German prisoners-of-war held in Siberia into the Red Army), but she was even given command of Chinese troops in the area.

Ex-Foreign Minister Ishii was again dispatched to Washington, this time as Ambassador, to disarm American suspicions of Japanese motives in advance of such an expedition. At the same time a force of 500 'volunteers' was rushed into Trans-Baikal to assist Semenov's second sortie, but he was already on the retreat again and was soon forced back into Manchuria. This was by no means seen in Tokyo as an unmitigated disaster, however, because it provided a pretext for bringing the newly-signed Military Agreement into play. The news that a large part of the Kwantung Army was preparing to move into northern Manchuria caused the U.S. Government to inform Tokyo that it 'trusts that the Imperial Japanese Government shares its opinion that a military occupation of Manchuria would arouse deep resentment in Russia ...'

At the same time another development was taking place which caused America not merely to swallow her distrust, but even to invite Japan to join her in launching an expedition to Siberia. The well-disciplined Czech Army of some 50,000 men had been left stranded on the Eastern Front by Russia's withdrawal from the war. Denied access to their homeland to the west, they had been given permission by the new regime in Moscow to make their way east on the TSR to Vladivostok, from where a fleet of Allied ships would return them to Europe. A third of them reached the port by the end of May without incident, but when the Bolsheviks, fearing that they might go to the assistance of Semenov and other resistance movements in Siberia, attempted to disarm them, they quickly seized control of large sections of the railway. To Britain and France this turn of events was seen as creating an ideal opportunity to consummate the earlier proposal for an Allied expedition through Siberia to prop up the Eastern

Front, while in America the Czechs' struggle to establish an independent state struck a deeply sympathetic chord.

The invitation proffered to Japan on July 5th envisaged an international force of a division of 7,000 men from each Allied Power. The objective would be limited to safeguarding the Czechs' evacuation from Vladivostok. This was clearly rather different from the operation that Tanaka's Siberian Planning Committee in Tokyo had in mind, and they argued that the situation called for the dispatch of a second Japanese force to Trans-Baikal 'in self-defence', and that since 'America looks on the Czech forces as its own army' Japan was entitled to put equivalent numbers to both of them in the field. At a meeting of the Advisory Council on July 16th the War Minister therefore proposed sending no less than twelve divisions in all, a suggestion which provoked strenuous opposition from the political party leaders; 'I can see that the true intent of the Government is not to respond to the American proposal, but rather to contrive to intervene in Siberia,' one of them correctly divined. In order to appease them Terauchi felt obliged to reply that the Minister had been speaking of 'a distant emergency', and it was agreed that the American terms should be accepted, with the provision that a second force would be sent 'if called for by further exigencies of the situation' — and with the usual disclaimer to any 'political or territorial designs therein'.

This climbdown drew an equally outraged response from the Army General Staff, who accused the Cabinet of throwing away the chance of 'a great war in Siberia to decide the fate of the nation'. The Chief of Staff even threatened to resign. Terauchi reassured him that the dispatch of the Trans-Baikal force was not subject to American approval since it had not formed part of the invitation; it was therefore a matter between Japan and China alone, which was fully provided for by the Military Agreement — and which, given Horvath's recent removal from Chinese soil to set up an all-Russian government at Irkutsk, was not likely to encounter any objections from Peking. Washington had indeed refused to agree to any provision for a second force, and a compromise formula was eventually worked out whereby it was agreed that 'in order to support the Czech forces, it will be necessary to advance beyond Vladivostok and to increase this assistance in response to circumstances as they develop.'

Such well-meaning but imprecise terminology was an open invitation to the Japanese to put their own pre-planned interpretation upon it, the nature of which was rapidly communicated to Ishii in Washington: 'The Empire anticipates in its above-mentioned reply to America that in time of emergency it may be necessary to move its forces beyond Vladivostok or to increase their strength *without waiting every time to confer with the United States* (author's italics), but, of course, in every case we shall endeavour to inform the Unites States Government of the circumstances as soon as possible ...'

Thus it was that by mid-October Japan had already landed three divisions in Siberia without the least hint of consultation with her Allies, or even with her own Advisory Council. Even as President Wilson in Washington and Opposition members in the Diet protested, the troop wagons continued to roll along the TSR and CER into the interior, until by the spring of 1919 the whole length of the two railways east of Irkutsk was in Japanese hands. A few months later again yet another division landed to occupy the northern half of Sakhalin, making a total of some 100,000 Japanese troops in the field, although Tanaka would admit to the dispatch of only a third as many (not until 1927 would their true number be revealed).

IDEALISM UNDONE

As the delegates of the victorious Allies gatherd at Versailles in January 1919 to divide the spoils and to give substance to the Wilsonian dream of a League of Nations, they were thus uncomfortably aware that Japan already held a lien upon the proceedings. In recognition of this she was invited to join the 'Big Four' (Britain, France, Italy and the United States) in seating two representatives on the Council of Ten, the governing body of the Conference. The claims that she put on the table centred around three items: the Shantung peninsula, the former German Pacific islands and the inclusion of the right to equal treatment with other races in the League of Nations charter.

Of these the first represented much the most important objective. Ever since her seizure of the railway to Tsinan outside the Tsingtao concession at the outset of the war Japan had steadily consolidated her hold on the peninsula with the establishment of her own civilian administration. This, in the words of U.S. Ambassador Reinsch, had been set up 'without a scintilla of right. It was later withdrawn for new concessions and privileges wrung from the Peking Government. The Japanese are old masters of this trick. Seize something which you do not really want, and restore it to its owner if he will give you something you do want.' What Japan wanted was permanent possession of the Tsingtao concession, and for this she had already indicated to China that she was prepared to give up what she had claimed for herself in the rest of the peninsula.

She now played a similar trick at Versailles. The first of the three items to come up for serious discussion was the demand for racial equality. When this failed to obtain the necessary unanimous vote in its favour thanks to the obdurate refusal of Prime Minister Hughes to depart from his 'White Australia' policy, the Japanese put on a great show of indignation (even though she herself had no intention at all of relaxing her own stringent restrictions on immigration into Japan). In the Diet Anglo-Ally Kato spoke of Hughes as a 'peasant', while several of the more unenlightened dailies warned Saionji as leader of the Japanese delegation to take out a life insurance policy if he failed to secure the demand. The Last

Noble was anything but intimidated, for he foresaw only too well that a refusal to press this issue further would predispose the other Powers much more favourably to his side on the one that really mattered.

The Japanese case on Shantung was already a strong one. Although the Chinese could argue, as they did, that the concessions there which had been granted as part of the 'Twenty-One Demands' in 1915 had been extracted by *force majeure*, they could not do so of a further agreement which they had foolishly signed in September 1918 in return for yet another Nishihara loan. This, while providing for the eventual return of the leasehold to China, confirmed the transfer to Japan of Germany's economic rights there, including the joint control of the Tsinan-Tsingtao railway. Furthermore, Japan could rely on the support of Britain and France which had been pledged to her in the secret treaties of 1917. Finally, as if her hand was not already strong enough, she threw in the threat of staying out of the League if her demand was not met, just as Italy had done only three days earlier, on April 24th, over the Conference's decision to award the province of Fiume to Yugoslavia.

Wilson was caught in a cleft stick: to give in to Japan would represent a betrayal of the 'Open Door' and all the other principles of independent republicanism that he stood for, but if on the other hand Japan were to follow Italy his cherished hopes of a meaningful world forum would be stillborn. In the end it was the latter consideration that weighed most heavily with him, and Japan had her way; she was required to give no more than 'her word of honour' for the return of the leasehold, nor was any deadline set on her retention of the economic rights. Almost as an afterthought, the Pacific islands north of the Equator were ceded to her under a Class C mandate. This forbade the construction of (above-ground) fortifications, but as the islands were ear-marked for a network of submarine bases this was scarcely received as a hardship.

Of all the War's combatants, Japan thus emerged the least scathed and the best rewarded. She had greatly consolidated her position in Manchuria; she had secured her first foothold in China proper; she now had a vast stretch of the Pacific Ocean to herself; she virtually controlled the whole of eastern Siberia, where she would continue to retain her troops as a bargaining counter until she had won more valuable concessions at the Washington Disarmament Conference of 1922; and having entered the War as one of the most heavily indebted nations, she had come out of it as the world's banker.

For China, by contrast, the outcome was the exact reverse, as her citizens were quick to signal in a nation-wide orgy of riots and anti-Japanese demonstrations. In one incident near Changchun 18 Japanese soldiers were killed, but this time Japan could offer to stay her hand; it was clearly only a matter of months before the opposing forces of the northern warlords and Sun's Kuomintang would be doing battle again and prostrating the country still further.

On a personal level, no one perhaps suffered more bitterly for the defeat of his high-minded idealism than President Wilson. He had been looked on as China's surest protector not only by 400 million Chinese, but also by his fellow countrymen, and for him the cruellest blow was still to come: in March 1920 the U.S. Senate refused to endorse the Versailles Treaty, and America was left outside the League which he had staked everything to create.

In a few more months he was dead, but almost simultaneously a new figure entered to take the centre of the Pacific stage: the man who would led Japan into World War Two and who still sits today, 67 years later, on the Chrysanthemum Throne.

PART IV

Strike North v Strike South

18

Enter Hirohito

LOCAL DIFFICULTIES

If Japan's continuing aggrandisement on the Asian continent thwarted the best intentions of the peacemakers at Versailles, it also brought no peace on her own domestic front.

The advantages to the nation's economy which had been garnered from the 'German-Japanese War' were rapidly dissipated by the extravagance of the Siberian adventure, which amounted in all to the enormous sum of 700 million yen. It was then further undermined by the general recession which followed in the wake of a brief post-war boom, and in particular by the slump in demand for Japanese products as the West began to recover a share of its former markets. The rate of inflation, which had increased steadily during the war, now accelerated sharply. The price of rice, for instance, the rise in which had brought about the fall of the Terauchi Cabinet even before the hostilities had ceased, doubled in the course of the next year in spite of the best efforts of 'The Great Commoner' Hara to control it; in unhappy contrast that of the country's largest single export, silk, collapsed by no less than 75% in the first six months of 1920.

Under such circumstances it was hardly surprising that the spirit of self-sacrifice in the expansionist cause should have begun to wane, particularly when it was seen that the industrial magnates and commodity profiteers were not sharing the privations of the rest of the population. 'The attitude of the majority of our people is completely different from their attitude when they have met with so-called hardships in the past,' the *Asahi* observed. 'The people are not asking "What will become of the country?", but they have risen to cry out "What will become of us?"'

This disillusionment manifested itself most noticeably in a mounting wave of industrial unrest and in the propagation of socialist ideology inspired by the Russian Revolution. 1919 saw the formation of sixteen illegal trade unions, which led to strikes in shipyards, railways and mines in pursuit of higher pay and better conditions. The unrest continued to escalate over the next two years, affecting such key units as the government-owned Yawata Steelworks and the Tokyo Municipal Railway and culminating in a 45-day strike in the Kawasaki and Mitsubishi shipyards which was finally suppressed by the Army.

263

It also spread to the countryside, where the Japan Farmers Union was set up to improve the lot of the peasant; even the 'untouchable' Eta class, who were condemned from birth to a lifetime's drudgery in the most menial functions that society had to offer, were sufficiently encouraged to form their own Equality Society. The workers' demands, including that of universal male suffrage, were co-ordinated by the Labourers Friendly Society; established some years earlier as a mutual aid organisation, it increasingly began to fill the rôle of a general workers' representative body, and in 1921 its title was changed to that of the General Federation of Labour.

The government's initial response to these pressures was to set up a conciliatory body, 'The Capital-Labour Harmonisation Society', headed by a textile magnate and endowed with an initial capital of ten million yen. When, hardly surprisingly, all its attempts at mediation were forestalled by its identification as a 'bosses league', appeal was then made to more traditional sources of support.

In establishing 'The National Essence Society', the Home Minister enlisted the ever-reliable services of Toyama. It was soon able to boast a nationwide network of branches enlisted, in most cases, from the work-forces of local labour contractors and the membership of the Ex-*Ronin* Society which Toyama had created as an offshoot of the Black Dragon some years previously. Ostensibly cast in the same conciliatory rôle, it quickly abrogated to itself the function of 'maintaining law and order and no damned nonsense'. Having successfully 'settled' a number of strikes with familiar strong-arm methods it then took to the wider political arena, helping the police to break up the May Day rallies of 1920 and 1921 and to disrupt gatherings of the newly-formed Socialists Union by distributing handbills which invited bystanders to 'Kill The Socialist Traitors!'

These 'men of chivalrous spirit', as their allies in the police described them, made a particular target of the supporters of the Universal (Male) Suffrage Bill introduced in the Diet by veteran opponent of the oligarchy 'Blasphemer' Ozaki. His age, advanced though it was, could not save him from their violent attentions, while the editor of the *Asahi* was dragged bodily from his office and bound to a telegraph pole in the main street of Osaka. Even the Annual General Meeting of the Nippon Yusen Kaisha shipping line was made an occasion for a free-for-all — until it was realised that the Company's largest single shareholder was none other than the Emperor.

Hara, who had been one of the most fervent advocates of earlier moves to extend the franchise, was induced to have second thoughts, not least by Yamagata, who advised him that 'universal suffrage would destroy the country', and he quickly dissolved the Diet before a vote on the Bill could be taken. In revenge a disappointed railway worker stole up behind the Prime Minister as he was about to board a train at Tokyo Station and stabbed 'The Great Commoner' through the heart.

1. Commodore Matthew Perry as he was ...

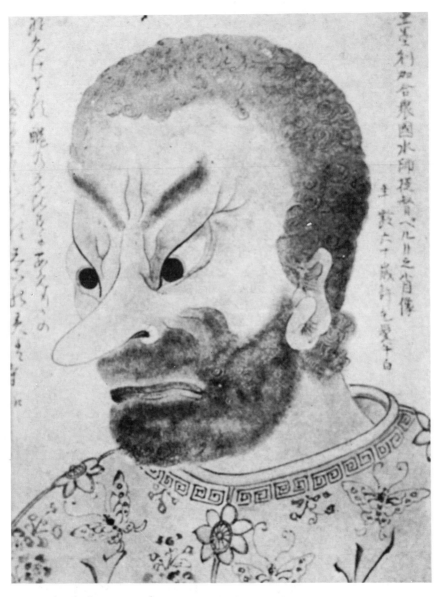

2. ...and as the Japanese saw him

THE OUTRAGE ON THE BRITISH EMBASSY AT JEDDO, JAPAN : ATTACK ON MESSRS. OLIPHANT AND MORRISON.

3. The attack on the British Legation 4th July 1861

4. Western navies spiking the Choshu guns at Shimonoseki 16th July 1863

5. A western envoy presenting his credentials to the invisible Shogun

6. Emperor Meiji opening the first Diet 29th November 1890

7. The sinking of the British-owned S.S. *Kowshing* 25th July 1894

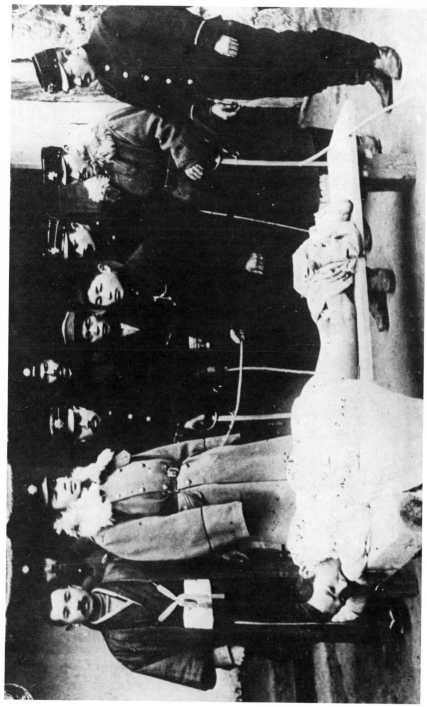

8. Japanese troops torturing a Korean prisoner

9. Japanese shells for use in the siege of Port Arthur 1904

10. The battered Russian battleship *Tsarevich*, sole survivor from the Battle of Tsushima 27th May 1905

11. Toyama Mitsuru, godfather of the Black Dragon Society, with Chinese President-to-be Chiang Kai-shek

12. Korean schoolboys being marched off to a Japanese labour camp

13. Emperor Taisho with Yamagata (2nd left) and Katsura (2nd right)

14. Emperor Hirohito leading the Army on manoeuvres

The assassination was followed a few months later by the death of Yamagata himself. He was hailed by one official obituarist as 'a most misunderstood man and a pioneer advocate of popular government', a description which might have brought a smile to the stony lips of the 'Peace Preserver' himself. Hara was succeeded by his Finance Minister, Takahashi Korekiyo, but whatever talents had qualified him for that post were soon found to fall short of those demanded by the more exacting office of Premier (and even his qualifications for the former might be thought questionable in the light of his call to 'get rid of foreign products, money, traders and ships!'). As a result, the political argument continued increasingly to be fought out on the streets rather than in the Diet. The Army, robbed now of the guiding hand of its creator, began to drift into internal dissension, while the economic burden of its Siberian campaign brought about a sharp decline in its stock with the population at large.

Even the institute of the Throne itself, the fulcrum of the social order at home and the standard bearer of the programme of expansion overseas, began to be called into question when it became no longer possible to conceal the fact that 'The Son of Heaven's disability was a more than physical one. During a parade at the annual Army manoeuvres Taisho embarrassed his entourage of generals by descending from the review dais and insisting on making a minute inspection of the contents of a private soldier's pack; even more disconcertingly, at an opening session of the Diet he suddenly rolled up his inaugural speech into a telescope and peered through it at the dumbfounded members. It seemed, in short, that anarchy stared Japan in the face.

It was into this chasm that Taisho's son, Hirohito, now stepped.

A NAVAL SPLICE

After the suicide of General Nogi, the post of personal tutor to the young Prince had been entrusted to Admiral Togo, the victor of Tsushima. The change brought no relief to the Spartan routine of his charge's upbringing, a feature of which was being made to stand naked under a waterfall for a quarter of an hour in mid-winter. It at least had the effect of turning him, in the words of a close neighbour to the Imperial seaside retreat who was able to observe him on the beach, into 'a good physical specimen' who became in due course a strong swimmer, a skilled horseman and an enthusiastic golfer — in sharp contrast to the frail-seeming, baggy-trousered image which has been presented to the world since 1945. Another member of the tutorial staff, ethics instructor Sugiura Jugo, exercised an influence similar to that which Purifier-of-the-Imperial-Mind Motoda had exerted on the Emperor Meiji two generations earlier. No less of a Shinto dogmatist, Sugiura sought to stamp on the impressionable mind of his young pupil the proposition that 'China is degenerate and therefore cannot be our partner and stand with us against the West. Our Empire must decide to match arms with the Aryan clan alone.'

In 1915 Hirohito went to sea for the first time with the Imperial Navy on a gunnery exercise, and a year later an official photograph of him dressed in Captain's uniform was issued to the nation to mark his formal installation as Crown Prince. On February 4th 1918 his betrothal was announced to Nagako, the fifteen-year-old sister of one of the select band of his fellow-pupils at the Peers School. Her father, Prince Kuni, was the son of Prince Asahiko, Emperor Komei's confidant who had urged him to dissociate himself from the attempted Choshu coup of 1863, while her mother was the daughter of the last Shimazu of Satsuma.

The match had been engineered by the Lord Privy Seal, Makino, himself a member of the Satsuma hierarchy, in a bid to loosen the rival hold of Choshu on the Emperor's counsels. It was naturally unwelcome news to Yamagata, who had already lined up two eligible Choshu candidates of his own, but he could hardly come out publicly in opposition. He therefore bided his time, until some two years later he began to put it about that the Shimazu family suffered from congenital colour blindness. He then wrote to Prince Kuni with a proposal that such a defect should not be allowed to contaminate the Imperial blood; 'The cancellation of the engagement would certainly bring public applause,' he concluded. 'Your reconsideration is sincerely urged.' Kuni, however, retorted that in that event the honour of his family name would compel him to commit *hara-kiri*, an action which was rather more likely to attract adverse publicity to the matter (which until now had been the subject of a rigorous Press embargo). For good measure, he enlisted the aid of Toyama, between whom and Yamagata little love had been lost since their difference over the choice of leader in the Chinese revolution.

In February 1921 Hirohito was due to set out on a tour of Europe which had been arranged with Yamagata's blessing (partly too with the object of laying the ground for a renewal of the Anglo-Japanese Alliance), and in a further bid to defer the threatened wedding Yamagata made moves to bring forward the date of the Crown Prince's departure; 'I can work much more effectively when he is out of the way,' the 'Peace Preserver' is reported to have said. When Toyama heard of this, he immediately countered by having his minions in the Press mount a furious campaign against the whole concept of the tour. Hirohito would be defiling his Divine Ancestry by soiling his feet on barbarian shores, it was argued, and he would be demeaning himself in the eyes of his subjects by associating with lesser breeds who were incapable of appreciating the inherent superiority of the Japanese race.

Some suggested in addition that he would be exposing himself to the risk of assassination at the hands of Korean extremists; this was not in fact so far-fetched, because a year earlier 4,000 of their compatriots had been mown down in cold blood on the streets of Seoul by Japanese occupying troops on the occasion of the King's funeral. Others even hinted darkly that 'certain opponents of the engagement' might take the opportunity of his absence to do away with his fiancée. Toyama reserved his greatest effort for the National Foundation Day celebrations, when he marshalled hundreds of Black Dragon henchmen and student hirelings to march through the capital's streets with banners proclaiming 'The Emperor Is Insulted! Death to Yamagata!'

Alarmed at the prospect of violent public opposition, the Government had already mounted a police guard on Yamagata's villa (much to the old *samurai*'s indignation), and on the day before the demonstration was due to take place it announced the resignation of his linkman at the Court, the Imperial Household Minister, together with an official confirmation of the engagement; this followed an Imperial audience at which it was made plain that there was to be no change of the Imperial mind. Along with his fellow Elder Statesmen, 'I'll Investigate' Matsukata, Yamagata then submitted his own resignation from all public offices and titles, but this was rejected by the Throne. His main objective achieved, Toyama withdrew his opposition to the royal tour, and on March 3rd Hirohito set sail for Europe.

The episode marked a decisive turning point in the direction of Japan's thrust overseas, for in 1941 it would be the 'Strike South' strategy of the Satsuma-led Navy rather than the Choshu-based Army's 'Strike North' that received the Imperial sanction. The future Empress's father, Prince Kuni, would oversee the development of the Japanese Air Force, while her other princely relatives who were now added to the Imperial family included Fushimi and Kanin, who became the Chiefs of Staff of the Navy and Army respectively throughout the decade leading up to World War Two; Asaka, who was to enter history's Chamber of Horrors as the Rapist of Nanking; and Higashikuni, who would acknowledge the Court's responsibility for all that had transpired by stepping in as Prime Minister to sign the Surrender in 1945. The new Chief Aide-de-Camp appointed to accompany the Crown Prince was, like four out of the next five holders of the post, an old China hand from a non-Choshu background.

Stopping at Hong Kong, Hirohito made a point of inspecting the colony's main reservoir, which twenty years later would prove to be its Achilles' heel against the besieging Japanese; likewise at Singapore he borrowed a yacht to circumnavigate the island, which one of his staff noted was 'separated from Johore by a narrow strait'. The European itinerary included visits to a number of World War One battlefields and at least two reunions with uncle-to-be Prince Higashikuni, who was studying incognito at the St. Cyr Military Academy in Paris.

When the royal party finally re-embarked for the return voyage at the end of July, Higashikuni stayed behind to co-ordinate an anti-Choshu Army cell among the military attachés stationed in Europe. It included Tojo Hikedi, who as Prime Minister would usher Japan into World War

Two, and whose propensity for fighting was early recognised by a childhood nickname of 'Scrapper'; Yamashita Tomoyuki, the future captor of Singapore; Nagata Tetsuzan, a key figure in the preparations for global conflict; Komoto Daisaku, the eventual assassinator of Manchurian 'Old Warlord' Chang Tso-lin; and Itagaki Seishiro and Doihara Kenji, two leading conspirators in the 'Mukden Incident' which would pave the way for the absorption of Manchuria.

Shortly after Hirohito's return to the homeland, three weeks after the assassination of Prime Minister Hara, formal recognition of the new Satsuma-based leadership was served by the announcement of his appointment as Prince Regent; the death two months later of Yamagata served to complete the change. His father's incapacity had never, of course, been publicly admitted, for such an acknowledgement would have at once demolished the whole premise of Japan's claim to world hegemony; instead, the expansionists had sought to conceal it, and at the same time to counter the spread of socialism, by making ever greater play of the Throne's 'Divine Mission' and the subject's duty of unquestioning obedience to it.

THE IMPERIAL ROAD

The two central exponents of this new ultra nationalist movement were the socialist and Black Dragon agent Kita Ikki and the future 'Doctor Goebbels of Japan' Okawa Shumei, who early in 1919 had come together to found 'The Society To Preserve The National Essence'. In the previous year Okawa had joined with a number of leading members of the Seiyukai to set up The Imperial Road Society, and his new creation was in turn to spawn a whole new breed of patriotic societies which over the next decade combined to harmonise the energies of the political and military leadership in a single-minded pursuit of the objective of world hegemony under the banner of the new Prince Regent, or Emperor as he would presently become.

On succeeding to the Throne in 1926 Hirohito would choose the honorific title of Showa or 'Enlightened Peace' for his reign, and the new movement would adopt the slogan of 'Showa Restoration'. Just as the Restoration of Imperial authority under his grandfather Meiji (whose title meant 'Enlightened Rule') marked the sweeping away of the antiquated Shogunate, so Hirohito's accession was looked on as the signal to put an end to the sterile and debilitating experiment in democracy in favour of the 'restoration' of the goal of the Divine Mission. No contradiction was seen between the choice of the word 'Peace' and the events thus foreshadowed: although it was promised that the achievement of the Mission heralded for the world an era of unprecedented tranquillity, Kita observed that 'peace without war is not the Way of Heaven'.

After recounting his experiences in China in *A Private History of the Chinese Revolution*, Kita had applied their lessons in *A Plan for the Re-*

organisation of Japan, and it was after reading the latter that Okawa had proposed that they should join forces. 'At present the Japanese Empire is faced with a national crisis unparallelled in its history,' its opening sentence ran. 'The entire Japanese people should, in planning how the great Japanese Empire should be reorganised, petition for a manifestation of the Imperial prerogative establishing "a national opinion in which no dissenting voice is heard, by the organisation of a great union of the Japanese people". Thus, by homage to the Emperor, a basis for national reorganisation can be set up.'

The central features of the *Plan* that he went on to propound included the suspension of the Constitution for three years while the 'Reorganisation' was carried out, the abolition of the House of Peers and its replacement by an Imperially-appointed Council of Deliberation of 'distinguished men' with the power to overrule the House of Representatives, universal suffrage for all men (but not women) over 25, the nationalisation of all companies with assets of more than ten million yen (including all banks, mines and shipping lines) and of all individual estates of land worth more than 30,000 yen (including that of the Imperial Household), the enforcement of an 8-hour working day in all industries and the introduction of profit-sharing and worker-participation schemes.

Abroad, the Divine Mission demanded that Japan became 'the leader of Asia' in the struggle of liberation against the West, for 'our 700 million brothers in China and India have no path to independence other than that offered by our guidance and protection. And for our Japan, whose population has doubled within the past 50 years, great areas adequate to support a population of at least 240-250 millions will be absolutely necessary 100 years from now, . . . Japan claims possession of Australia and eastern Siberia.' A similar work published in the same year looked even further afield, urging that 'attention should be devoted to the question of colonisation on the Amazon and in South America.'

In spite of attempts by the authorities to suppress it, Kita's *Plan* quickly became the bible of the ultranationalist movement; it remained so until its eventual replacement by *Kokutai No Hongi* in 1937 — the year which would also see Kita executed on a charge of sedition.

It will be observed how strikingly closely the programme prescribed in it foreshadowed the manifestoes being simultaneously hatched by two fellow socialists in Europe, Benito Mussolini and Adolf Schicklgruber. Indeed, the only fundamental difference between them was the central position that Kita reserved for the institution of the Emperor. In time, of course, both Mussolini and Hitler would themselves occupy the central position in their respective regimes, but neither of them could claim for themselves the status of an aristocrat — still less that of a hereditary monarch. Were it not for that, Kita would equally qualify for the label of 'fascist'. The confusion engendered by this similarity has led one present-day commentator to make the remarkable statement that 'of all Japan's *rightists* (author's italics), Kita came closest to the national socialism that was emerging in Italy and Germany. Like his European counterparts, Kita had been influenced by *Marxism* . . .'; he has clearly fallen victim to the remorseless campaign waged by the Left to live down the 1939 Nazi-Soviet Pact by transferring the slur of fascism from their own revolutionary/proletarian movements to the oligarchic/monarchic orders of the Right.

It was Kita's philosophical justification for Japanese expansionism that most attracted Okawa; he was less enthusiastic about some other aspects of the *Plan*, notably the nationalisation of leading companies, which was unsurprising in view of the fact that as Director of the South Manchuria Railway's Oriental Research Institute he himself was an employee of just such a company. The manifesto of their newly-formed Society proclaimed that 'we do not consider it sufficient to pursue reorganisation and revolution for Japan alone, but because we really believe in the Japanese nation's destiny to be the great apostle of mankind's war of liberation we want to begin with the liberation of Japan itself.' Soon after Hirohito's assumption of the Regency the Institute was transferred to the grounds of the Imperial Palace. Here, still under Okawa's directorship but under the new title of University Lodging House, it would become the forcing house behind the strategy of world conquest, and its 'students' would include every one of the seven men eventually convicted in 1947 as Class A War Criminals.

AMERICA THE OBSTACLE

The Seiyukai government, demoralised by the assassination of its leader, harassed by the mounting disorder in the streets and embarrassed by scandals surrounding the administration of the opium monopoly which it had established in Manchuria as a further means of debilitating the native population, resorted to desperate methods in its attempts to silence the Opposition in the Diet, where Ozaki had proposed a motion calling for a cut in the military budget in line with the United Nations Covenant. In one debate it planned to rout them with the help of a live snake thrown from the public gallery; however, the hoodlum hired for the purpose lost his nerve at the critical moment and dropped the writhing reptile among the Government's own supporters. Undaunted, the 'Blasphemer' carried his campaign to the electorate outside, where he received overwhelming support, despite the counter arguments of naval and military reservist associations proclaiming 'the inevitability of a Japanese-American war'. In June 1922 the Government finally felt obliged to resign, to be replaced by a non-party Cabinet headed by the Navy Minister, who had recently returned from leading the Japanese delegation at the Washington Disarmament Conference.

The Conference had opened in November 1921, but in an attempt to keep the potentially embarrassing subject of the continuing Japanese military presence in Siberia off the agenda — without removing its threatening implications — Japan had already set in motion negotiations at Dairen with the Soviet-backed Far Eastern Republic. As the last of the Allied troops in the international expeditionary force were withdrawn in the early months of 1920 Japan had installed puppet White Russian regimes in the main towns. That in Nicolaevsk, at the mouth of the Amur River, was attacked shortly afterwards by Soviet partizans and the 600-strong Japanese colony and garrison were put to death before their compatriots were able to relieve the ice-bound port.

In retribution the Japanese seized Vladivostok and the northern half of Sakhalin. Since one of the preconditions set for their withdrawal was the outlawing of Communism in the whole of eastern Siberia the Dairen negotiations were clearly doomed to fail from the start. When they duly broke down on April 21st 1922 they had already served Japan's purpose — those at Washington having concluded two months earlier without binding Japan to anything more definite than an undertaking to withdraw her troops 'before long'.

The first item settled at Washington was the replacement of the Anglo-Japanese Alliance by a Four-Power Pact including the United States and France. When the subject had been raised at the (British) Imperial Conference in June Foreign Secretary Lord Curzon had warned that if the Alliance was discontinued Japan might 'seek future friends in another quarter; and this, in another ten or twenty year's time, might alter the whole face of the Eastern world.' Canada, however, had adamantly refused to countenance its renewal on the grounds that it would, in theory at least, commit her to taking sides against the United States, and it was agreed that a more general arrangement to cover the Pacific should be sought.

Japan was at first opposed to such a suggestion, but her delegation eventually accepted it in return for an embargo on all fortifications in the Pacific within a radius of some 2,000 miles of Japan, effectively removing the threat of any attack on her by the West. The same consideration allowed them to add their signature to a Naval Treaty imposing a ten-year moratorium on the warship construction race which had been sparked off by the launching of Japan's 'eight-eight' programme; nearly two million tons of shipping either already in commission or on the stocks were to be scrapped by the five major navies, and Japan was to limit her tonnage of capital ships to 60% of that of America and Great Britain.

It remained now only to settle the matter of China, on which the new U.S. President Warren Harding was determined to see the vague undertakings extracted at Versailles made a good deal more specific. While Japan was happy enough to go along with the other eight Powers involved and to sign yet another pledge to uphold the principle of 'Open Door' and the maintenance of the status quo, she once again refused to admit the

Chinese argument that the 1915 and 1918 agreements between the two countries had been signed under duress. In return for the recognition of the rights that these agreements had conferred on her in Manchuria and Inner Mongolia — which, she maintained, was implicitly confirmed by the commitment to the status quo — Japan was, however, prepared to restore in principle the sovereignty of Shantung to China and to withdraw her troops while still retaining her economic privileges in the province. Advised by Harding that they could not hope to obtain any further concessions, the Chinese reluctantly settled on these terms.

The overall outcome of the Conference was viewed with little satisfaction in Japan; indeed, the British Ambassador in Tokyo reported that it was regarded as 'a secret coalition between Great Britain and the United States at the expense of Japan'. The 60% warship ratio was a particular source of resentment (Japan having originally put in for one of 70%); Kato Kanji, future Chief of Naval Staff and a member of the delegation, is reported to have remarked that as far as he was concerned, World War Two began on the day that the 60% ratio was adopted. Certainly, it was now recognised that America had become the greatest obstacle to Japanese expansion in the Pacific.

With the elevation of the Navy Minister to the Premiership, the way was now clear for Satsuma to cut down the military influence of their Choshu rival. Even before he actually took office he had submitted a new defence programme severely reducing the Army's budget, but preserving that of the Navy, by switching the funds released by the Washington embargo on warship construction into fields not restricted by the Treaty such as submarines, naval aircraft and torpedoes. Prince Regent Hirohito duly gave this his approval; charge of the naval air development programme was entrusted to a rising star in the Naval General Staff (and a protégé of his future father-in-law), Yamamoto Isoroku, the future mastermind behind the attack on Pearl Harbor.

The evacuation of Siberia (although not of northern Sakhalin), the prerequisite for a reduction in the Army's standing strength, was finally completed in October, after a vain attempt to pass the arms stockpile at Vladivostok into the hands of the anti-Soviet White Russians. Ten months later the Premiership was taken over by Yamamoto Gombei, who had briefly held it in 1913, on the death of his fellow Satsuma Admiral in office.

TURMOIL IN TOKYO

The new Prime Minister was still selecting his Cabinet when at noon on September 1st 1923 Tokyo began to sway to the tremors of an earthquake. At first they were no more significant than any of the others which register almost daily on the capital's seismographs, but after a few minutes they suddenly intensified until whole districts lay devastated. Beneath the piles of matchwood to which the typical Japanese home had been reduced lay buried the still-burning cooking stoves lit for the midday meal. In next to no time the entire city was ablaze. A strong wind fanned the flames and carried the sparks further and further afield, so that even the largest open spaces offered no refuge to the panic-stricken inhabitants. In Yokohama thousands plunged into the waters of Tokyo Bay to escape, only to meet with an even grislier death as 100,000 tons of fuel oil gushed into the sea from the fractured tanks of the nearby Yokosuka naval base, ignited and roasted them alive. Some 140,000 died in the inferno, which should have served as an awful warning of what was to come; the number exceeded the total of atom bomb victims at Nagasaki and Hiroshima put together.

Hardly was the last fire extinguished than the search for scapegoats began. A rumour was put around that Korean immigrants had been responsible for spreading the flames, with the result that over four thousand of them were hunted down and done to death with clubs, spears and even bare hands, guilty of nothing more than speaking Japanese with an accent. Another rumour had it that socialist malcontents had been the instigators, and 1300 of them were promptly rounded up and thrown into jail. One of them had led a march at the height of the fire to seek the safety of the moated grounds of the Imperial Palace, and while he was held in custody he was strangled to death by a captain of the secret police, Amakasu Masahiko, who for good measure proceeded to do the same to his wife and seven-year-old nephew who were being held in adjacent cells. Their screams were overheard, and the authorities consequently felt obliged to bring him to trial on a charge of infanticide; he was sentenced to ten years' imprisonment, but the term was later commuted to one of only three years on Hirohito's orders, and he was lauded in the Press as a national hero.

Grandiose schemes of reconstruction were discussed in the Cabinet, including the sinking of a deep-draught harbour in Tokyo to rival that of Yokohama. However, the necessary funds were not so easily to be found, especially as the Government was obliged to bail out insurance companies who had rashly promised to meet all claims in full in the naïve expectation that their reinsurers in London would foot the bill (earthquake risks being specifically excluded in all Lloyds policies).

A new session of the Diet was called on December 27th to debate the question of raising a loan abroad. While the Prince Regent was on his way to perform the opening ceremony, he narrowly escaped death when one of the spectators lining the route darted forward and fired a number of pistol shots into the State Carriage. The would-be assassin was duly tried and executed, and it was put about by the secret police that he had been a socialist out to avenge the murder of his strangled comrade. He was no socialist, however, but the son of a well-known Diet member from Choshu — the *han* that Hirohito was set on ousting from its position of influence in favour of the Satsuma kinsfolk of his future wife.

The Yamamoto Cabinet resigned en bloc in token acknowledgement of their responsibility, to be replaced by one made up entirely from members of the House of Peers, with the single exception of War Minister Ugaki Kazushige, the first non-Choshu occupant of that office since 1912. In a further move to obliterate the memory of the unfortunate incident, the royal wedding was brought forward to January 26th 1924. The seven hundred invitations to the ceremony were limited to the families of the royal couple and members of the government, but it was no surprise that a place was also found for Godfather Toyama among this honoured company.

The attempt on Hirohito's life had led to a fresh surge of popular veneration of the Throne, which the ultra nationalists were quick to exploit with a new clutch of patriotic societies in place of the now defunct Society To Preserve The National Essence (Kita and Okawa having finally parted company over the nationalisation issue). The most influential of these was The National Foundations Association, founded under the auspices of the Minister of Justice, Baron Hiranuma Kiichiro. In due course its membership was to rise to a total of almost 200,000 and include such notables as Admirals Togo and Kato, Generals Ugaki and Nagata and the future President of the Seiyukai, Suzuki Kisaburo.

ONE CHEER FOR DEMOCRACY

The pressure for colonisation of the Pacific received a further impetus a few months later from the introduction in Washington of a General Immigration Bill which debarred U.S. citizenship to all aliens who were not already naturalised. The Japanese Ambassador in Washington hardly helped his country's case against it by threatening 'grave consequences' if it was passed by Congress. Japan presently retaliated with a new Nationality Law permitting her emigrants to both North and South America to renounce their Japanese citizenship, thus throwing them on the mercy of the governments concerned.

These early pioneers not only provided the nucleus for the colonies of the future — by the end of the next decade almost every country in South America had a Japanese population of at least 20,000 — but they also established intelligence networks in their respective domiciles behind facades similar to the 'Halls of Pleasurable Delights' that Toyama's first agents in China had used. Elsewhere, in a report to the Australian Naval Board the First Naval Member posed some prescient questions: 'If Japan is only concerned with legitimate defence precautions, why does she place a Rear Admiral as Governor of her newly-acquired islands in the Pacific? Why does she discourage shipping from other countries trading there? Why does she try to obtain land in strategic positions in the Malay Straits? Why does she carry on a system of espionage in Australia?'

The 'Cabinet of Peers' not unexpectedly failed to survive the general election held in June 1924, and the Premiership passed to Kato Takaaki, the former Anglo-Ally and author of 'The Twenty-One Demands', whose Real Constitutionalists emerged as the largest single party and allied with Inukai's Nationalists to secure a majority. Unlike the Seiyukai Opposition, both parties were in favour of the long-promised and oft-postponed introduction of universal male suffrage, which now at last took its place on the statute book. This triumph for democracy was, however, rather more apparent than real, for the new government felt obliged to counterbalance it simultaneously with an amendment to the Peace Preservation Laws which gave the secret police such sweeping and draconian powers that it rapidly became known as the 'Dangerous Thoughts Bill'. One of its first victims was the peasant-based Farmers Labour Party, which was ordered to disband only 30 minutes after its inaugural meeting. Mere mention of socialism was outlawed in schools and universities, as was any criticism of the armed forces; several distinguished liberal professors were black-listed and forced to resign, and scores of students found themselves arrested and held without trial. Those who remained free were even forbidden to take part in theatrical performances.

Another feature of the new, so-called 'Mitsubishi Government' (both Kato and Foreign Minister Shidehara Kijuro were married into the conglomerate's controlling family) was the severely deflationary stance of its economic policy. No less than 15% was slashed from the previous year's spending despite the considerable sum earmarked for the reconstruction of Tokyo and Yokohama, while the sudden surge in the country's trade deficit, brought about by the loss of export production in the wake of the earthquake, was cut back by the introduction of a 'national thrift week' and of a prohibitive tariff on imported 'luxuries'. In a move to revive exports, the Ministry of Commerce and Agriculture was divided by its new head, former Premier and Finance Minister Takahashi, into a Ministry of Commerce and Industry (MCI) and a Ministry of Agriculture and Forestry; the former was then given powers, closely foreshadowing those enjoyed by MITI today, to form export unions among the smaller companies and to organise cartels among the conglomerates which, by improving their margins in the domestic market, would enable them to increase the competitiveness of their export prices.

The decision was also taken to put an end to the occupation of northern Sakhalin, the expense of which had greatly increased as a result of the Soviets' *de facto* control over the rest of Siberia. In a treaty signed at Peking on January 20th 1925 Japan agreed to withdraw her forces from the island and to enter diplomatic relations with the Soviet Government in return for certain oil and mineral concessions there and Soviet recognition of the 1905 Treaty of Portsmouth. Added to the recent anti-Western outpourings of the patriotic societies, the suddenness of this reconciliation (three earlier attempts had ended in failure) led Stalin to rhapsodize on the prospect of a Soviet-Japanese alliance which would, he declared, 'mean the beginning of the end for world capitalism'; his words would have rung somewhat hollow in the ears of the hundreds of communists then languishing in Japanese jails as a consequence of the 'Dangerous Thoughts Bill'.

FRESH BLOOD FOR THE ARMY

The War Ministry was still in the hands of Ugaki, and the return of the occupying forces in Sakhalin now allowed him to press forward with the long-planned Choshu faction purge in the Army under the cover of demobilisation; this had now become a matter of urgency since the *han*'s Army hierarchy, conservatively-inclined at the best of times, were venting their resentment at the alliance of their Satsuma rivals with the Imperial Family by blocking moves to modernise the Service along the lines of the revision which Hirohito had made of the 1907 Meiji-Yamagata National Defence Plan on assuming the Regency (a proposal, for example, to introduce a panoramic sighting telescope allowing operations to be directed from concealed command posts was opposed on the grounds that all orders in the field should be given by officers leading from the front). Four complete divisions were disbanded, but the majority of their non-Choshu elements were then redrafted into newly-commissioned tank, air and intelligence corps. Of the remainder, many were posted as instructors to schools and universities where military training was now made compulsory.

Many others were transferred to specialist assignments in a chemical and bacteriological warfare section set up, in the aftermath of Japan's refusal to sign the 1925 Geneva Protocol banning the offensive use of such weapons, under Hirohito's personal sanction. Some 3,350 were to graduate from the Narashino School of Chemical Warfare, whose main production plant was established on the small island of Okuno-Jima. This plant was capable of manufacturing two tons per day of mustard and other toxic gases, which accounted for some 37,000 casualties (2,068 of them fatal) in the subsequent war in China. From 1932 onwards the island was deleted from all Japanese ordnance survey maps.

On the bacteriological side, the central research station was later moved to Pingfan, near Harbin, after the takeover of Manchuria, where it was run by the infamous, brigade-sized Unit 731 known as 'The Devil's Gluttony'. Here human guinea pigs, usually prisoners of war, were exposed to anthrax, cholera, smallpox, typhus, gas gangrene, bubonic plague and other lethal diseases. Over 3,000 of them, including not only Chinese but also Americans, Britons and Australians, died in the course of these experiments, either from the diseases themselves or during vivi-section to check their progress.

To this day Hirohito's interest in the natural sciences is still assiduously presented to the world as having been exclusively confined to the innocent field of marine biology; before 1945, however, it ranged very much wider to include the study of disease-carrying fungi, bacilli and culture tissues, and recently-declassified documents put it beyond doubt that he personally monitored the progress of the section's researches. In 1984 a former member of Unit 731 testified that the Emperor's youngest brother, Mikasa, paid an official visit there, and that the order establishing it bore Hirohito's personal seal.

The 1927 budget set the share of military expenditure at only 27% compared with the figure of 42% five years earlier. The brunt of this reduction fell on the Army, and it was not to be expected that the Choshu hierarchy would take such a diminution of their influence lying down. In casting about for political leverage with which to redress matters, they soon found willing allies in the Seiyukai. Having long regarded themselves as the natural party of government, the Seiyukai had grown increasingly restive since their exclusion from office in 1922 and they were now none too squeamish in the choice of partners who might be of assistance in securing their return to power. Thus it was that the party Presidency was put into the hands of Tanaka, the prime mover of the Siberian expedition and the Choshu standard-bearer since the death of Yamagata. It was also subsequently revealed that Tanaka for his part had helped to bring about this unlikely match by diverting 3 million yen of secret Army funds into the party's coffers.

NEW ENEMY IN CHINA

Their chosen line of attack on the Government was Foreign Minister Shidehara's allegedly 'rubber-kneed' policy towards China. The division there between the northern warlords and southern republicans had shown little sign of resolving itself in the intervening years — indeed, that prospect had grown if anything even more remote as both sides became themselves victim to internal divisions of their own. On winning control in Peking in 1922 Wu Pei-fu had restored Li Yuan-hung as President of the Republic and had invited Sun Yat-sen to join with him in another attempt to reunify the country.

Sun, however, had declined. Not only was he still suspicious of Li's part in the failure of the first attempt, but he had responded with typically uncritical enthusiasm to the first tentative approaches of the new regime in Moscow and had buoyed himself up to believe that with their assistance he would again be able to place himself alone at the nation's head. At his invitation, a team of high-level Soviet advisers arrived in Canton the following year led by Mikhail Borodin, who proceeded to reorganise the Kuomintang along soviet lines into a network of activist cells drawn from the Chinese Communist Party, which had been established two years earlier. Returning the compliment, Sun dispatched his young Chief of Staff, Chiang Kai-shek, to Moscow to study Soviet military organisation.

Within a year Communist control of the Kuomintang was complete, and its forces set out northwards to join with 'Old Warlord' Chang Tso-lin in a pincer movement on Peking. Hardly were they on the march, however, than their enemy Wu was removed by an internal coup. Sun again received an invitation to discuss reunification, which he this time accepted.

He travelled north via Japan, where he made an impassioned call for an Asiatic alliance with his new-found friends in Moscow against Western imperialism. 'Russia symbolizes and practises a "live and let live" policy,' he asserted. 'We Asiatics must emancipate Asia from European and American oppression. Japan and China must join hands ...' The speech stands as a monument to a lifetime of muddle-headed, well-meaning innocence, and three months later Sun died of cancer. Had he lived a few months longer, perhaps even he would have been finally undeceived, for when the new regime in Peking moved to follow up a Soviet-inspired revolt against Chang in Manchuria, the Japanese Kwantung Army stepped in and refused to allow its forces access to the South Manchuria Railway. Russia had earlier signed an agreement to withdraw her troops from the Chinese Eastern Railway in the north; under the Peking Treaty of 1905 Japan was then bound to withdraw hers likewise from the SMR, but she had failed to do so.

The leadership of the Kuomintang passed to Sun's former fellow-exile in Japan and heir apparent, Wang Ching-wei, who shared his complacent appraisal of Moscow's motives. Chiang Kai-shek, however, having seen the workings of the Kremlin at first hand, was a good deal more accurately informed. 'The Russian Communist Party cannot be trusted,' he had warned Sun on his return, and he now set about weeding out its representatives from his command, the First Army based in Canton. Having completed this to his satisfaction within the year and mobilised his forces for another northern expedition on the pretext of capitalising on a new wave of anti-foreigner demonstrations and riots, he then took advantage of Borodin's temporary absence to arrest all the remaining Soviet advisers and assume full military control of the party.

He soon succeeded in securing control of the great industrial centres in the Yangtse valley, but as he advanced further north the Communist element in the party attempted to reassert themselves by establishing local administrations of their own; in particular, the Central Executive Committee moved its base up from Canton to Hankow and began reversing many of the steps that he had taken to eliminate the influence of the Communists within the party. They also whipped up further Communist support by inciting attacks on the International Settlements. The most violent of these took place in Nanking, where six Westerners were killed and a number of foreign Consulates burnt to the ground; the Japanese Consul was forced out of his bed, but he was spared any further indignity.

In Shanghai the Communists under Chou En-lai seized control of the Municipal Council, whereupon Chiang marched on the city and seized it back. Although Chou managed to escape to join Mao Tse-tung in the hinterland, 5000 of his comrades were captured and publicly executed on April 12th 1927; the day is still remembered in China as Black Tuesday, and it marked the beginning of an irreversible split between the Kuomintang and the Communist Party. A few weeks later such severity was lent justification by the interception of a telegram from Stalin calling for an agrarian revolt to recapture the military leadership of the Kuomintang from Chiang, and even the party's political leadership under Wang were now persuaded to rid themselves of Moscow's fellow-travellers.

A 'POSITIVE' RESPONSE

In Japan the expansionists had seen in these events ample pretext for further intervention in China — and in Manchuria in particular, where they felt that some price should be extracted from 'Old Warlord' Chang for the protection which the Kwantung Army had given him. Foreign Minister Shidehara, however, remained determined that this action should not be allowed to set a precedent. 'By taking such a course, we should forfeit our national honour and pride,' he insisted. 'Once and for all, in no case and by no means can we be party to so ill-advised a step.' Unfortunately, he could no longer rely on the support of Prime Minister Kato, who had died in office in January 1926 and whose successor, Wakatsuki Reijiro, presently became embroiled in a financial crisis stemming from the insolvency of the Suzuki conglomerate. When this sparked off a run on Suzuki's chief creditor, the Bank of Formosa, the Government agreed to make the Bank an emergency loan of 200 million yen. Under the rules of the Constitution, however, such an issue had to have the prior approval of the Privy Council, where the expansionists and their Seiyukai allies held a clear majority. The Government felt obliged to resign when the Council duly refused its sanction. Its fall, however, did nothing to stem the mounting panic, and the Seiyukai Cabinet which entered office on April 20th 1927 under Tanaka had to print a special issue of well over 1,000 million yen to stave off a total collapse of the economy.

In order to avoid a repetition of such a dangerous sequence of events a Commerce and Industry Deliberation Council was set up within MCI to formulate future economic policy. Although loans of some 30 million yen were authorised as a result to smaller companies, it was the surviving conglomerates who benefitted more, both from the elimination of rivals caught in Suzuki's wake and from the concept of government-directed rationalisation introduced by the Council. Another development which was to have even more far-reaching consequences was the creation alongside the Council of a Resources Bureau, to which companies were required to report their productive capacity and which would provide the military with a ready-made entrée into the field of economic planning.

Having disposed of the crisis, Tanaka set about preparing the ground for what he saw as his first priority, the adoption of a much more 'positive' policy in China. In addition to the Premiership he also took on the office of Foreign Minister, although he delegated much of the responsibility for foreign affairs to Mori Kaku, a Seiyukai party insider who had been sent to China the previous year to join Suzuki Teiichi in assessing Chiang's potential as a leader of a unified China. Mori had reported back that the odds were indeed running strongly in favour of Chiang being able to unify the country, a prospect which did not bode well either for Japan's territorial interests in Manchuria or for her commercial interests in China proper. Consequently Tanaka decided to do what he could to encourage 'Old Warlord' Chang, in the shape of the offer of a loan to finance further railway development in Manchuria; Chang had now taken over the northern administration in Peking and was on the point of marching south to fight a final eliminator with Chiang.

The two armies met in the plains of Honan. After a bloody but indecisive encounter, Chang fell back on Peking to regroup. Worried by the prospect of the Warlord's total defeat, Tanaka dispatched another emissary advising him to take advantage of the Kwantung Army's protection and pull back further into his Manchurian base. Chang, however, replied indignantly that 'my war is Japan's war. What am I to make of Japan's good faith when in spite of this fact Japan is assisting Chiang Kai-shek, who has turned Red, and is advising me to return to Manchuria?'

Mori, whose capacity for intrigue in the expansionist cause had already won him the sobriquet of 'The Arch Schemer', then came forward with the suggestion that Japan should land troops in Shantung on the pretext of protecting Japanese nationals there in order to prevent Chiang from marching on Peking. Tanaka was at first lukewarm and suggested instead merely transferring two battalions already stationed at Tientsin, but Mori persisted and finally had his way. On May 30th some 2,200 troops were detached from the Kwantung Army and landed at Tsingtao, provoking protests at this violation of Chinese sovereignty from both 'Old Warlord' Chang in Peking and Chiang in Nanking.

'If Tanaka will not send the expeditionary force, I'll make him resign from the Presidency of the Seiyukai,' Mori had boasted, and the fact that he prevailed was an ominous precedent. From then on, the greatest pressure in the Army for expansion overseas would no longer come from the Choshu hierarchy schooled in the more gradualist strategy of Yamagata, but from the junior, non-Choshu commanders working in tandem with their allies in the ultra nationalist societies and the Imperially-connected Navy.

Now Hirohito was Emperor in name as well as in fact, his crippled father having suffered a final, fatal stroke on Christmas Day 1926. The era of 'Enlightened Peace' had begun.

19
Exit Democracy

ALL EYES ON MANCHURIA

On June 27th 1927 Prime Minister Tanaka, acting once again on the promptings of 'The Arch Schemer' Mori, called the top echelons of the War and Foreign Ministries together for an 'Eastern Regions Conference'.

Throughout the ten days that it met its discussions centred on the policy to be adopted towards Manchuria. It was chaired by Mori's close ally and former fellow-spy in China, Suzuki Teiichi, who had recently returned to Tokyo to report his findings on Chiang Kai-shek's prospects. Since his arrival he had drawn up his own plan of action in consultation with a group of junior staff officers who had graduated from 'Doctor' Okawa's University Lodging House, and who included such leading participants in Manchuria's eventual absorption as Komoto Daisaku, Ishihara Kanji and Itagaki Seishiro. 'The consensus was to cut Manchuria off from China proper and bring it under Japan's political control,' Suzuki related. 'This meant that Japan's whole policy — domestic, foreign and military — must be directed toward the attainment of this single objective. We knew that the execution of the plan called for circumspection and finesse, since it was obvious that no minister in Tanaka's Cabinet would support such a plan . . . Unless Japan waged war, she would find it difficult to solve her continental problems.'

Tanaka by contrast entered the Conference proposing nothing more ambitious than the projects for railway development which he had already put before 'Old Warlord' Chang, and the measure of the influence which Mori and Suzuki succeeded in exerting on him may be gauged by the following exchange between the Prime Minister and General Muto Nobuyoshi, the Commander of the Kwantung Army:

Muto : 'Although this is not a pleasant prospect, Japan must be prepared to face a world war if such a drastic programme [as that of Mori and Suzuki] is to be carried out. To begin with, America will not tolerate it. If America will not acquiesce, neither will England nor the rest of the Powers. Are you

281

prepared to cope with America and the eventuality of a world war?'

Tanaka: 'I am prepared to face the consequences.'

Muto : 'You are sure you will not waver later on, are you?'

Tanaka: 'I am all set to face the worst.'

Muto : 'If this Government is so determined, I have nothing else to add. We shall wait for the order to come and simply carry it out.'

The Kwantung Army Commander's subsequent willingness to acquiesce in orders from Tokyo without questioning their wisdom would earn him the title of Muto 'The Silent'.

On the final day of the Conference Tanaka announced an eight-point programme which included affirmation of the right to intervene in China generally for the protection of Japanese nationals, to uphold the peace in Manchuria and Inner Mongolia and to support any regime which she deemed capable of defending her interests in those two areas. This he submitted to Hirohito on July 27th. Four years later a document which purported to be a copy of it was published in China and subsequently caused a considerable stir in the West, although independent Oriental scholars have since almost unanimously condemned this so-called 'Tanaka Memorial' as a forgery. Certainly, it is most unlikely that such statements as 'In order to conquer the world, we must first conquer China' and 'If we want to control China we must first crush the United States' would have been formally committed to paper at this stage, but the detailed proposals which it goes on to list for the economic penetration and development of Manchuria do bear a striking resemblance to the programme carried out after the eventual seizure of the region, and it has been suggested that they were drawn not from Tanaka's submission to the Emperor, but from the minutes of a series of meetings which Mori held in August with commanders in the field in Manchuria.

Before these meetings had taken place a second contingent of troops had been landed in Shantung, bringing fresh protests from both 'Old Warlord' Chang in Peking and Generalissimo Chiang in Nanking and an intensification of the boycott of Japanese goods which had been initiated by both halves of the country in response to the first landing. In return Mori and his associates demanded yet more 'positive' measures, including the isolation of Chang's arsenal at Mukden by cutting the railway from Peking where it crossed the tracks of the South Manchuria Railway. Tanaka this time refused to be brow-beaten, however, and even made a statement to the Press that 'our government is taking the position that we negotiate with Chang Tso-lin so long as he prevails in the north and likewise with Chiang Kai-shek so long as he is in control of the south'. The troops were accordingly withdrawn the following month.

As Chang prepared to launch himself south again against the Kuomintang, both Chiang and Wang Ching-wei decided to resign from the leadership of their respective wings of the party in order to facilitate a rapprochement which would allow it to confront the enemy with a united front. Chiang travelled to Japan to negotiate with Tanaka for support; both Mori and Toyama also attended the discussions. A bargain was struck whereby Japan undertook to recognise the Kuomintang or Nationalist regime as the legitimate government of China south of the Great Wall on the proviso that they gave a similar undertaking on Japan's interests in Manchuria and continued to eradicate their Communist former comrades. Armed with this assurance, Chiang returned to Nanking where he was at once restored to the leadership of the now united party. By March 1928 he was ready to set out again for Peking at the head of an army of ¼ million men to confront the 'Old Warlord'.

KWANTUNG ARMY 'PIQUED'

Mori now once again demanded the dispatch of troops to Shantung; if the agreement with Chiang meant that they had nothing to fear from the Nationalist army, there was still the danger, he argued, that the Japanese community there might be molested by the retreating Manchurians under Chang. Rumours that another expedition was about to be sent had already led to demonstrations on the streets of Tokyo and caused Tanaka to dissolve the Diet before the matter could be put to the vote.

In the ensuing election, despite the disbursement of 10 million yen in bribes and the usual intimidatory tactics, the ruling Seiyukai won an overall majority of only two. The rival Nationalists and Real Constitutionalists had now merged into a single party, the Democratic Nationalists, while eight seats went to the newly-formed, communist-inspired Proletarian Party. The latter was seen as an even more unwelcome development, and the Government reacted with a further savage crackdown on trade unions and other radical associations. Under an Imperial Ordinance issued by Hirohito, some 1500 people were arrested on a charge of harbouring 'dangerous thoughts', a crime which was now made liable to the death penalty by yet another amendment to the Peace Preservation Laws. This would lead in due course to the establishment of the infamous Bureau of Thought Control and the arrest of a further 60,000 on similar charges over the next decade.

Once more too Tanaka bowed to his subordinate, Mori, whose demands were now backed up by the War and Navy Ministers (but not by the Foreign Minister). As the Nationalist army advanced into Shantung in mid-April, the 17,000 strong 6th Division was dispatched from Japan 'to protect [2000] Japanese nationals residing in Tsingtao and other places along the Tsingtao-Tsinan Railway'. The commanders in the field played their part in sustaining this fiction: for instance, the execution of 13

Japanese opium-smugglers was reported back to Tokyo as the 'murder of 300 Japanese civilians'.

When on May 2nd Chiang entered Tsinan and found the Japanese already in the possession of the city, he demanded their withdrawal. The Japanese made as if to comply, but the following day fighting broke out between the two sides. As a result of the mediation of the American and British Consuls, the Chinese agreed to withdraw some six miles from the city. On the 7th, however, the Japanese, on the signal of a rooftop pistol shot from a Special (i.e. secret) Service agent, opened fire on the 4,000 Chinese troops still remaining and then proceeded to run amok among the civilian population; in the space of the next five days some 7,000 Chinese were massacred and a large part of the city destroyed.

Chiang appealed to the League of Nations to intervene, but that body declined to take action since his regime had not yet been universally recognised as the rightful government of China. Terms for a settlement of the affair were eventually reached a year later, although no thanks for that were due to Mori, who, as the chief Japanese negotiator recorded, 'said to me in an overbearing tone of voice "It's all wrong to try to reach a settlement over an incident like the one at Tsinan ..." Mori's idea was diametrically opposite to the briefing I had received from Prime Minister Tanaka ... It seemed as if Mori was already in league with the extremists of the Army and was trying to create disorder in China in order that they might capitalise on the confusion to extend Japan's influence there.'

With a quarter of a million men still at his back, Chiang decided to swing further to the west and resume his march on Peking. The 'Old Warlord' Chang was ill-prepared to meet an opposing army of such strength, and the Japanese feared that if he insisted on trying to defend Peking he might be so thoroughly routed that there would be nothing to stop the Nationalists taking control of Manchuria and reuniting it with China — a prospect to be averted at all costs. They therefore advised him to withdraw into his home base while he had the chance, threatening that if he failed to do so in time they would disarm his retreating troops at the Manchurian border; at the same time the Kwantung Army moved its headquarters from Port Arthur to Mukden in readiness for action. Chang had little option but to accede, and the opportunity was also taken to extract his agreement to the plans for railway development which had been presented to him the previous year.

At this point the U.S. Government began to take alarm and issued a request to be informed in advance of any further action which Tokyo contemplated taking in Manchuria. An equally alarmed Tanaka reconvened the Eastern Regions Conference on May 20th. Day after day Mori urged that the time to seize control of Manchuria had now arrived. In Manchuria itself the Kwantung Army, which had been led to expect an Imperial Order to mobilise at any moment was, in the words of its Chief of Staff 'bursting with spirit and piqued at the government's indecision', while the recently established Manchurian Youth Congress called for the creation of a new state of 'Manchuria and Mongolia* bought by the blood of the whole nation'.

On the 25th the decision to go ahead was taken — only then to be vetoed by Tanaka, who had finally concluded that he could not risk the prospect of war with the United States. An eye witness has described the scene when the order 'to suspend completely the previously decided plan' arrived at the Kwantung Army Headquarters the following morning: 'Colonel Komoto clutched the telegram in his hand and bit his lip ... the Commander-in-Chief and Chief of Staff hardly spoke the rest of the day. Even the normally voluble Ishihara and easy-going Itagaki were silent.'

MURDER ON THE MUKDEN EXPRESS

In Tokyo a furious Mori called for the abrogation of the Washington Treaty and that same day he got an ally in the War Ministry to submit an alternative plan, under which an expeditionary force was to be landed at Shanhaikwan to cut off Chang's line of retreat: the Kwantung Army would then have a free hand to occupy the rest of Manchuria. When this was blocked in Cabinet on the 27th by the Navy Minister, Okada Keisuke (on the recommendation of the Chief of Naval Operations, Suzuki Kantaro), Komoto told Ishihara and Itagaki of an even more audacious plan which had been drawn up by Tatekawa Yoshiji, Chief of European and American Intelligence on the General Staff — nothing less than the assassination of the 'Old Warlord' himself.

A military attaché in Harbin was assigned to the task, but when he reached the Army's Headquarters at Mukden he was persuaded by Komoto that it would be a great deal more easily carried out there rather than in the much more public environment of Peking as originally planned. 'The malignant cancer today in Japan's Manchuria and Mongolia policy is Chang Tso-lin,' Komoto had told a select audience at the Yamato Hotel, Dairen. 'If we get rid of him somehow, after that there will be no difficulty in manipulating his young son.' Chang himself then became an unwitting accomplice: his general offensive had failed all along the line against the superior numbers of the Nationalists, and June 2nd he gave the order to withdraw to Manchuria.

The site chosen for the deed was the bridge which carried the SMR over the Peking-Mukden line just outside the city, and which was patrolled only by Japanese guards. The 'Old Warlord's staff at Mukden requested permission from the Japanese to mount their own guard beneath the bridge. This was of course refused, and three Manchurians were picked up off the streets, dressed in uniforms planted with ostensibly incriminating

* Referring to the Inner Mongolian province of Jehol; from now on the 'Conquer-Manchuria' propagandists would automatically lump it together with the three Manchurian provinces.

orders from one of Chang's rival warlords and added to the Japanese guard. Captain of Intelligence Tanaka Ryukichi was posted at Peking railway station to signal the departure of Chang's personal train. There is evidence that Chang had already received warning of the plot from his agents in Tokyo, but when his senior Japanese adviser undertook to accompany him he concluded it to be groundless.

The anticipated signal came through on the morning of June 4th. As the train approached Mukden in the early hours of the next day Chang and his adviser were engaged in a game of mah-jong, but a few miles short of the city the game broke up and the Japanese retired quickly to the rear coach. Minutes later a massive explosion brought the bridge down on the compartment where Chang still sat; he was carried unconscious from the wreckage and died in hospital within a few hours. During the day more bombs were set off in Japanese meeting halls in the city, to be followed by insistent telephone calls from Komoto to the Consul-General, Hayashi Kiyùjiro, urging that he should mobilise the Army 'to protect Japanese residents'. This he politely declined to do; it was the last time that it would be considered necessary to seek out his permission for such a move.

The conspirators had lined up the 'Old Warlord's Chief of Staff in his place to head a puppet Manchurian republic, but the plot now began to backfire. Two of the Manchurian 'sentries' were bayonetted and laid out beside the track as planned, but in the confusion following the explosion the third managed to escape into the night, eventually making his way to the dead Warlord's son, Chang Hsuen-liang, to reveal the truth. The 'Young Warlord' wisely decided to conceal his knowledge for the moment while he established his own succession above the claims of his Chief of Staff. He arranged for statements to be issued from the hospital indicating that, far from being dead, his father was well on the way to a full recovery. If he was to succeed, he saw that it would be essential to match the support of the Japanese Government against that of the Kwantung Army for his rival, and to this end he began to address appropriate overtures to Tokyo.

YOUNG WARLORD FOR OLD

The concealment of his father's death also served to defer proposals by Manchuria's provincial leaders to abandon their former allies in China, the northern warlords, and to throw in their lot with Chiang's Nationalists — a move which clearly might invite a full-scale Japanese intervention. On being elected Commander-in-Chief in his father's place Chang's first action was therefore to persuade them that an accommodation with Japan was essential, at least for the time being, if they were 'to obtain their own independence'. When, however, the victorious Chiang Kai-shek swept on to establish himself in Peking and almost immediately announced that he would not be renewing the trade treaty with Japan which was about to expire, Chang reported to Consul-General Hayashi on July 16th that the public pressure for a union with the Nationalists was such that if he ignored it he 'would be in a very embarrassing position, and might perhaps be forced to resign.' At the same time he opened negotiations with Chiang, who showed every sign of wanting to speed them to a successful conclusion.

For Japan the prospect of a reunited China and Manchuria was objectionable enough, but the possibility of the Chinese boycott being extended to her commercial interests in Manchuria struck at the roots of the strategy of economic penetration which represented the very minimum of her people's expectations. Hayashi was therefore instructed to advise the 'Young Warlord' in the strongest possible terms not to enter into any such agreement; in return Japan would then be willing to 'consider sympathetically measures to strengthen his position.'

In the face of so unambiguous a threat, Chang felt obliged to inform Peking that 'regrettably, because of Japanese intervention, negotiation towards reaching an agreement has had to be postponed. However, there has been no change in my own attitude towards seeking the eventual peaceful reunification of China.' If Tanaka hoped that this would be sufficient to avert the danger, he was soon to find that he had underestimated both Chang's determination to free himself from the tainted embrace of his father's murderers and his commitment to the vision of himself as a partner in a united, independent China. 'The provinces here are as much a part of China as those south of the Great Wall,' the 'Young Warlord' told a Western interviewer. 'I shall release all but local powers to the central authority.'

In Tokyo meanwhile the Prime Minister's attention had been diverted by an unexpected development on the domestic front. On July 20th he had agreed to join fourteen other leading nations in signing a declaration, which became known as the Kellogg-Briand Pact, renouncing war as an instrument of national policy. This initiative had come from the American Government who were anxious to make heard the voice in international affairs which had been denied to them since the refusal of Congress to join the League of Nations. The signatories were described in it as acting 'in the names of their respective peoples', but as soon as the text was released in Japan it provoked the outcry that it violated the Constitution, under Article XIII of which the sole prerogative for signing treaties lay with the Emperor.

In vain did Tanaka explain to the next session of the Diet that the phrase should be understood as meaning 'on behalf of' and not 'by agency of' and the Pact was condemned even by the veteran liberal 'Blasphemer' Ozaki as infringing the Imperial Prerogative and the national entity (*kokutai*): 'In the case of monarchies like Great Britain and Belgium, where the monarchs simply preside and do not rule, it is proper that the peoples should be the subject of treaties to be concluded,' he told the House. 'But in the case of this country, where the Emperor controls and exercises the supreme sovereignty and monopolizes the right of concluding treaties, it is impossible . . . the present Cabinet ought to go into sack cloth and ashes and await the Emperor's pronouncement on its offence.'

Hirohito in due course referred the issue to the Privy Council. Under the lead of two of the original drafters of the Constitution, Ito Myoji and Kaneko Kentaro, the Council voted overwhelmingly to ratify the Pact only on condition that a qualification was inserted stipulating that the offending phrase was 'inapplicable in so far as Japan is concerned'. The incident marked one more nail in the democratic coffin, when even so 'positive' an expansionist Prime Minister could be overruled by the Emperor's agent, the Privy Council; and the resurrection of *kokutai*, after lying largely dormant for a quarter of a century, was an all-too-ominous portent of what the era of 'Enlightened Peace' would entail.

When the first report of the facts behind the 'Old Warlord' Chang's assassination eventually reached Tanaka in October he found himself placed in an even more invidious position. 'What fools!' he was heard to exclaim. 'They [the Kwantung Army] behave like children. They have no idea what the parent has to go through.' Recovering himself, he made a more considered assessment of the implications to Navy Minister Okada: 'If the Army takes such measures as that *we will never be able to develop our plans* (author's italics)'. He was referring to the National Defence Plan's blueprint for territorial expansion on the Asian continent which he himself had drafted in 1907 and which, in the wake of Hirohito's 1923 revision, had recently been updated again to incorporate a 'general mobilisation plan' prepared by Nagata Tetsuzan, then Chief of the General Staff's Military Affairs Section, to give effect to the conclusions reached by the Eastern Regions Conference the previous year. Based on the thinking of the German General Staff, this new draft called for a programme of economic and technological development to replace the mass-attack strategy of a fanatical *kokutai*-inspired soldiery, such as had won the day at Port Arthur in 1905.

Tanaka first turned for advice to Saionji, whom the death of his fellow Elder Statesman Matsukata in 1924 had left as the lone survivor of the Grand Old Men of the Restoration. The Last Noble had no hesitation in urging him to inform the Emperor and to punish those responsible 'even if, for a time, feeling against China becomes worse. This is necessary if we are to win confidence internationally.' When he was informed Hirohito too was concerned about the likely international reaction and, more particularly, the threat that it posed to 'our plans' for territorial expansion. 'Military discipline must be rigorously maintained,' he told the Prime Minister.

When Tanaka attempted to put the necessary wheels into motion, however, he found himself opposed by the General Staff who, while agreeing to carry out an investigation, claimed that any decision on military discipline belonged to them. He even found that a majority of his own Cabinet was against him; any admission of the Kwantung Army's complicity, they argued, would be seen as dishonouring the Emperor in his capacity as Commander-in-Chief of the armed forces. When on October 23rd Komoto was first named as the leading instigator at a meeting of the government-appointed 'Committee to Investigate the Death of Chang Tso-lin', such uproar ensued that his good ally 'The Arch-Schemer' Mori was able to suspend it. When Tanaka again reported to Hirohito, what passed between them was so secret that the Grand Chamberlain was for once excluded from the audience.

In the meantime Tokyo's warning against a China-Manchuria reunion had, far from diminishing local pressure in its favour, only served to encourage it further. By mid-August the 'Young Warlord' had resumed negotiations with Nanking. In return for his recognition of the Nationalist regime, he was offered full local autonomy in Manchuria and a share in the administration of the Inner Mongolian province of Jehol. These terms were judged more than acceptable both in themselves and in the light of the current Japanese preoccupation with domestic problems and on December 29th the Nationalist flag was raised throughout the three Manchurian provinces for all the world to see.

Even now the Kwantung Army conspirators refused to accept that their hands had been bloodied in vain, and handbills began to appear in the leading cities accusing Chang and his late father of misrule (for which 'heavenly punishment was inflicted upon him and he fell under a bomb') and calling for his replacement by the Chief of Staff. Chang moved swiftly to scotch such a scheme, taking a leaf out of the assassins' own book: on January 10th 1929 he invited his rival to an evening of mah-jong and had him shot at the table.

IMPERIAL GALL

Tanaka's embarrassment may be imagined as he faced the reconvened Diet on the 31st. He attempted to win himself a respite with a request to the Opposition not to raise the issue of Chang Tso-lin's death, but the Democratic Nationalists rejected it and throughout the session he was obliged to fend off questioners with the statement that 'a certain grave incident' (the euphemism adopted by the censored Press) was still under investigation. On May 22nd, following a demand from a bipartisan Diet committee for a date to be set for the publication of the War Ministry's report, it was finally handed to the Prime Minister, but there was still no end to his predicament in sight as the Supreme War Council simultaneously required that it should not be published. On June 11th he promised a committee from the House of Peers that he would publish it; on the next day the Army's 'Big Three' (the Chief of Staff, War Minister and Inspector-General of Military Education) refused his request to reconsider their stand.

It was Hirohito who finally resolved the impasse; exactly how he did so must remain a matter of conjecture for the fifteen relevant pages were removed from the original draft of the Memoirs of Saionji's secretary, Harada Kumao, which represents the best Court source over this period. At any rate, Tanaka was summoned to the Palace on June 27th.

Unable to bring himself to admit to the truth, he informed the Emperor that, happily as it had transpired, no Japanese had been involved in the assassination, but that certain officers were to be disciplined for their negligence in allowing it to occur. The Emperor expressed surprise at this unexpected conclusion and sought confirmation of it the next day from the War Minister. The latter repeated the gist of the Prime Minister's story but apparently slipped up over some important details, and that same afternoon Tanaka found himself onçe more on the Imperial mat.

'So what you first told me was incorrect, was it?' Hirohito demanded. Tanaka was struck so dumb by the accusation that Hirohito turned to the new Grand Chamberlain, Suzuki Kantaro (who had just been transferred from his former post of Chief of Naval Operations), and remarked: 'Prime Minister Tanaka seems to have lost his tongue for the moment.'

'Allow me to explain matters further to your Majesty,' Tanaka was eventualy able to stutter.

'There is no need for any further explanation,' the Emperor replied curtly and thereupon withdrew into his inner chambers.

Now in tears, Tanaka begged Suzuki to submit a request for a further audience.

'I shall convey your wishes to His Majesty,' the Chamberlain replied, 'but I am afraid that it will be useless.'

It was, and three days later Tanaka submitted his resignation along with that of his Cabinet. Within three months he was dead, the victim, it was widely rumoured, of his own hand.

Some years later Hirohito was heard to express a fear that he had been too harsh with Tanaka. He had every reason to do so, for the all-but-total absolution of the conspirators at the Prime Minister's expense gave the green light to the Kwantung Army to press ahead with its own impetuous plans of conquest in defiance of the military (not to mention political) authorities in Tokyo; this in turn divided the Imperial Army into bitterly-opposed factions for the best part of a decade and threatened to compromise the programme of carefully-controlled expansion overseas laid down in the Meiji-Yamagata blueprint.

Warlord Assassin Komoto was nominally suspended from duty, but he was allowed to stay in Manchuria where he was already urging his comrades that 'war with China and moreover with the United States must be expected.' He would remain there for the rest of his career as a leading string-puller above the Manchukuan puppet show, and by the time of the 1945 Surrender he was actually about to be appointed to the highest post in the administration. His son was to become a prominent industrialist in postwar Japan, a member of the Diet and one of the inner caucus of the ruling Liberal Democratic Party.

NAVAL MANOEUVRES

By what had become a standing convention, the resignation of the Government was followed by an invitation to the leader of the main Opposition party to form the next administration. The Democratic Nationalists were now led by Hamaguchi Osachi; although a man of diminutive stature, his passionate commitment to the democratic principle had earned him the popular sobriquet of 'The Lion'. 'Rubber Knees' Shidehara returned to the Foreign Ministry as did Demobiliser Ugaki to the War Ministry, while the party's close links with Mitsubishi were maintained through the appointment as Finance Minister of Inoue Jannosuki, the son-in-law of the conglomerate's proprietor.

The party at once returned to the policies of monetarist rectitude which had characterized its last administration in 1924-7. Japan was returned to the gold standard (which it had abandoned in 1917), and an overall cut of 10% was ordered in government expenditure, defence not excluded. It was a cruel stroke of misfortune that these measures were followed almost at once by the great crash on Wall Street which would plunge the world, and particularly nations like Japan that depended heavily on foreign trade, into the Depression of the thirties. Before this had taken its full effect the party was able to win an absolute majority in the next general election, but by an even crueller irony this feat also carried within it the seeds of ultimate destruction. Much of the credit for this victory went to a certain Adachi Kenzo, whose career as a political gangster stretched all the way back to his recruitment of Korean Queen Min's murderers in 1895. As a reward for his efforts Hamaguchi felt obliged to offer him the Home Ministry, a position which Adachi would soon exploit with fatal consequences to his own party.

In foreign affairs Shidehara resumed the conciliatory approach to China which had earned him the vilification of the expansionists during his last term of office. One of the last acts of the Tanaka Cabinet had been finally to recognise the Nationalist regime as the legitimate government of all China, and Shidehara followed this by agreeing to the Chinese demand for a revision of the 1915 and 1918 treaties. After some weeks of amicable negotiation, the Japanese Ambassador returned to Tokyo with a set of proposals to lay before the Cabinet.

Suddenly, on November 29th, it was announced that he had committed suicide. However, the pistol which shot him was not his own, which was discovered packed in his suitcase; furthermore, the weapon was found in his right hand, whereas the bullet had entered his head from the left side. Chinese suspicions that he had paid the penalty of offending the advocates of a more 'positive' policy were amplified by the announcement that he was to be replaced by one of the officials who had been responsible for serving the 'Twenty-One Demands' in 1915. Indeed, Chiang went so far as to reject this man's credentials, and relations between the two countries returned once more to a state of mutual hostility.

The 'China Question', however, was soon submerged under still larger problems created by the opening on January 21st 1930 in London of a new Five Power Naval Conference with the object of setting limitations on the construction of warships not covered by the 1922 Washington Treaty — cruisers, auxiliary ships and submarines. A similar attempt in 1927 had foundered on the failure of America and Britain to agree on weight limits for cruisers.

The Japanese Naval General Staff submitted a demand that the ratio of 60% of American and British strength set for Japan in 1922 should be increased to 70% for the surface ships, and that no cut should be imposed on her current submarine tonnage. Its Chief was now that bitter critic of the Washington Treaty, Kato Kanji, who was so opposed to the whole principle of limitations that he refused to go to London as part of the Japanese delegation. His job, he said, 'was to wage war, not to prevent it'. It was led instead by ex-Premier Wakatsuki and Navy Minister Takarabe Takeshi, the son-in-law of the Satsuma patriarch and twice-times Premier Yamamoto Gombei. Another member was the future Pearl Harbor Mastermind Yamamoto Isoroku, who made it his business to see that the subject of naval aircraft was kept off the agenda.

After two months of hard bargaining, a compromise was reached which gave Japan a 60% ratio in heavy cruisers, one of 69.75% in all other surface ships and one of 100% in submarines (which, since Japan's tonnage already exceeded that of America and Britain, entailed a six year moratorium on further construction in this category). When it was referred to Toyko for approval, it was opposed not only by Kato, but also by his fellow Admirals Togo and Prince Fushimi. Saionji, however, was able to impress on the other members of the Emperor's inner circle of advisers the advantages of acceptance both to Japan's international standing and to her domestic economy.

'A nation's military preparedness depends in the first instance upon its financial policies. The strength that derives from reckless plans and emergency ad hoc preparations is virtually no strength at all,' he argued, and he went on to quote the example of Bismarck 'who firmly believed that it was Germany's future to expand. Yet he was well aware that such expansion was not immediately possible because his state lacked the essential power. Hence, while he seemed to pay unnecessary deference to Disraeli in London and Napoleon III in Paris, he was actually an astute statesman . . . Right now we have both the United States and Great Britain grabbing for the leader's baton. Precisely because of that situation we can step in between the two and gain appropriate advantages for ourselves.'

Even that doyen of the liberals, the Last Noble, let it be noted, was committed to expansion, and his emphasis on economic strength as a necessary precondition was reflected in the introduction of the Important Industries Control Law which greatly enlarged on the scope given to MCI four years earlier by authorising it to set up cartels in no less than 26 designated industries. Its effect was to increase still further both the power of the conglomerates and the opportunity of the military to direct the economy.

When Hamaguchi was summoned to the Palace on March 27th he was told that the Imperial wish was for the treaty to be concluded as soon as possible 'for the sake of world peace'. This was, of course, the 'peace' that was envisaged to follow the ultimate 'unification' of the world under Japan's hegemony, and Hirohito was fully alive to the threat which would be posed to its realisation by any precipitate aggression.

After much anguished breast-beating in the face of the Prime Minister's 'unshakeable' determination to accept the terms, even the Navy hardliners conceded the Government's right to make the ultimate decision. 'The American plan cannot be accepted,' a memorandum issued by the Navy Ministry and General Staff stated, but it then went on to acknowledge that 'the Naval agencies have, of course, no right to go beyond the proper boundaries of state and military matters. They will, of course, follow official regulations and do the best they can within the limits set by government policy.' 'After all,' Kato consoled himself, 'if we concentrate on aeroplanes, we can maintain our national defence.' As a condition of their compliance, they submitted a list of measures to be undertaken to offset the 'deficiences' imposed by the terms; these included improved training, maintenance and research facilities and 'full provision for air power'. Hamaguchi and Finance Minister Inoue promised to make the necessary funds available.

Secure in the knowledge of the Court's support and the Navy's acquiescence the Prime Minister called his Cabinet together on April 1st to approve the Treaty. Two hours before they met, the draft of the instructions to be sent to Wakatsuki and Takarabe in London was shown to the Naval members of the Supreme War Council. When the latter then withdrew to the Naval Ministry to discuss it with the General Staff, Kato absented himself and went instead to the Imperial Palace to request an audience.

However, he was informed by Grand Chamberlain Suzuki that the Emperor's timetable for the day was already full, and by the time that he was able to obtain an audience the following morning the draft had already received Imperial sanction and been transmitted to London. The 'deficiencies' entailed by the Treaty's acceptance, he declared to Hirohito, would lead to important changes in the operational plans based on the revised defence programme which had been approved by the Emperor in 1923, and the matter would require 'very careful consideration'.

ADMIRALS COLLIDE

Whether or not Kato's original object had been to persuade Hirohito to withhold Imperial approval, he soon made it clear that his acquiescence was a very temporary one, and that the rift between the hardliners, the so-called 'Fleet Faction', who held that the 1923 programme was sacrosanct, and the gradualists, the 'Shore Faction', who maintained that Japan should stand by her treaty obligations, was as wide as ever. 'It's as if we had been roped up and cast into prison by Britain and America,' he complained a week later to Saionji's secretary Harada. 'There should be discussion of the obstacles to Japan's expansion in the Far East ... It is essential that we build sufficient strength to constitute a threat to any opponents.'

The Chief of Naval Staff next drew up a memorial to the Throne protesting that the Emperor had been denied his constitutional right as Supreme Commander to receive advice of his General Staff before sanctioning any decision that affected the Navy's standing strength; at the same time he also put it about that his request for an Imperial audience had been deliberately blocked until after the Treaty's approval and threatened to resign in consequence along with his Vice-Chief Suetsugu Nobumasa — a move which would force the resignation of Navy Minister Takarabe and, by the old trick of refusing to nominate a successor, of the rest of the Cabinet too. He made no attempt to conceal that this was now his ultimate objective. 'No cabinet of political parties can resolve this situation,' he told Harada. 'The Cabinet should be limited to officials. Absolute monarchism is the only solution.' Ex-Navy Minister Okada, however, was able to persuade him to stay his hand at least until Takarabe had returned from London.

Behind this sudden reversal of Kato's attitude it is not difficult to detect the opportunistic hand of 'The Arch-Schemer'. Even before the Cabinet had met to consider the terms Mori had announced to the Press that the Seiyukai 'must adamantly reject them', and only a day after their acceptance was signalled to London, he had raised the issue of constitutional impropriety; there is in addition clear evidence that he had foreknowledge of the contents of Kato's memorial. Certainly, it was no coincidence that as soon as the Diet reconvened on April 21st the emotive cry of 'violation of the Imperial Prerogative' rose from the Seiyukai benches, coupled with a demand that in the light of his continuing absence in hospital Ugaki should resign as War Minister (in the expectation that his replacement would be of a more vigorously expansionist stamp). Outside the Diet Mori busily propagated the fiction that the Government had been responsible for blocking Kato's request for an Imperial audience.

Takarabe had in fact already indicated an intention to resign before he set off back again for Japan on the Trans-Siberian Railway, but he was intercepted at Harbin by an envoy from Hamaguchi who persuaded him that this was no time to yield to the Government's opponents. It was also suggested that he should delay his re-appearance until after the Diet had adjourned on May 16th. He accordingly 'fell ill'.

When he finally stepped ashore at Shimonoseki on the 18th, he was presented by a 'patriot' with a dagger and the suggestion that he should commit *hara-kiri* for having 'endangered the national defence'. Arriving in Tokyo the following morning, however, he was almost mobbed by wildly cheering crowds, and when he reported to the Palace Hirohito personally requested him to remain in office and to 'do all you can to have the Treaty approved by the Privy Council'. He was then bearded by Kato, who handed him his memorial to the Throne with the request that the Navy Minister should pass it on to the Emperor.

Takarabe held on to it, however, and Kato was eventually induced to apply again for an Imperial audience in order to be able to submit it in person together with his resignation. In the knowledge that Takarabe would now accept Kato's resignation without following it with his own, Hirohito referred it back to the Navy Minister; it was arranged that the Chief of Staff should join the Supreme War Council in exchange for relinquishing his office. Less confidence was placed (with good reason, as it soon transpired) on Kato's accompanying promise 'henceforth not to be of embarrassment to you [Takarabe] as Minister', and when Ugaki announced that he considered that he was now also free to resign as War Minister he was rapidly persuaded by his Cabinet colleagues to change his mind.

The Privy Council, still savouring the part which it had played in the fall of the last Democratic Nationalist government and in forcing through the qualification to the Kellogg-Briand Pact, remained a major hurdle. In particular, its Vice-President, Baron Hiranuma, was a close ally of Kato, and his other rôle as President of the National Foundations Association gave him a behind-the-curtain influence which almost now rivalled that of the octogenarian Godfather Toyama (in 1947 he would receive a life sentence as a Class A War Criminal). Before Hirohito passed the Treaty to the Council for ratification, it was therefore imperative to show that it had the support of the Navy's highest body of command, the six Admirals on the Supreme War Council. Not only was Kato himself now a member, but it also seemed that he could count on the support of both Togo, who had already pronounced that 'this Treaty should never have been signed', and of Fushimi, who had attempted to intercede on his behalf when Kato's resignation was submitted to the Throne. When informed of Togo's new attitude, Hirohito remarked that 'the Fleet Admiral should take a long-term view on all matters. Besides, we will have freedom of action at the 1935 [Naval] Conference.'

SAMURAI SECOND FLOWERS

For weeks the issue hung in the balance while a 'replenishment' plan was drawn up diverting the funds which would be saved in meeting the Treaty's restrictions into the development of aircraft and other areas. On July 22nd Takarabe was finally able to win the day with a pledge from the Prime Minister that 'the greatest effort will be made to realise these objectives by utilising finances and such other means as may be necessary'. This allowed the Privy Councillors to agree on a report to the Throne which, while acknowledging that the Treaty would create deficiencies in the maintenance of the 1923 defence programme, was able to demonstrate to Hirohito that these would be made good by 'the full development of non-limited categories and aircraft, research facilities, amphibious equipment, arrangements for dispatching expeditionary forces . . .' 'I will not neglect to provide fully for the Empire's armaments,' Hamaguchi reaffirmed on the 25th to the Emperor. 'I pledge to do everything in my power to assist your Majesty in carrying out the broad plans for the advancement of the nation.' The Treaty was duly referred to the Privy Council for ratification that same day.

The battle was still very far from over, however, for Hiranuma saw to it that the sub-committee appointed to examine the issue was packed with opponents of the Government, including the Constitution-drafters Ito and Kaneko. 'In the Privy Council the Government has at last struck a hidden rock,' Mori confidently asserted. 'The Cabinet will surely founder within the next four or five days.'

The sub-committee first demanded to see the Admirals' report to the Throne, and when the constitutional expert and Dean of Law at Tokyo University, Minobe Tatsukichi, ruled this to be *ultra vires* they requested that Kato should be allowed to present his opinion in person to them. The Council's secretary saw to it that the committee's deliberations were kept very far from confidential, and Kato had in fact been standing by in Tokyo for some days, having absented himself from the Naval manoeuvres then in progress on the grounds of the illness of his niece (although it was noted that no other member of the family showed such concern for the girl's health). When permission was refused by Prime Minister Hamaguchi, Ito threatened to suspend the committee's hearings until the Government's budget could be demonstrated to honour the pledge to fulfil the replenishment programme. 'The Lion' again stood firm, however, and total deadlock seemed imminent.

Ito was faced with the prospect, if the committee refused to ratify the Treaty, that their decision might be overturned by the full Council (on which two of Hirohito's brothers sat) or, worse still, that if its refusal was confirmed by the Council, the Emperor might grant a request for ratification from the Prime Minister over their heads (as he was constitutionally entitled to). In either event, he was suddenly brought to realise, only massive humiliation could ensue for himself and his allies. The rest of the committee were reluctantly persuaded to see likewise, and on September 17th they signalled their acceptance of the Treaty. So unexpected was their *volte-face* that only the previous day the Seiyukai had organised a major rally calling for its rejection. His task fulfilled, Takarabe was at last able to submit his resignation. Greeted for a second time with Kato's fulsome apologies, he demanded that 'you must absolutely stop all contact with politicians of low class and scheming minds.' 'I shall never again see such persons,' his ex-Chief of Staff assured him, but he would break this pledge even more rapidly than his last one.

The forces of democracy were not to enjoy their triumph for very long. Confronted with the need to reduce the overall budget by 150 million yen, Finance Minister Inoue proposed to cut that of the Navy and Army by 54 and 31 million yen respectively. 'With an allocation like this the Navy can move neither hand nor foot,' its new Vice-Minister protested, and Kato jumped in to demand that the full replenishment plan should remain intact. After prolonged and ill-tempered haggling, the cuts were finally reduced to 45 and 25 million yen. Hardly had these been agreed when on November 14th a young affiliate of the National Foundations Association stepped forward from the crowds at Tokyo station and, almost on the same spot on which the 'Great Commoner' Hara had been cut down nine years earlier, fired a pistol into Hamaguchi's stomach as he was about to board a train.

The Prime Minister did not this time die immediately, lingering on for another year. However, even before the bullet was fired an event had taken place which struck another, larger nail into democracy's coffin. Shortly after the London Naval Treaty's ratification had been announced, a group of some eighty younger Army officers of field rank met to form the Sakurakai or Cherry Society, so named because the colourful but brief life of the cherry blossom was held to be emblematic of the *samurai*'s readiness to die a glorious death.

Their leader was Hashimoto Kingoro, another of 'Doctor' Okawa's ex-pupils at the University Lodging House, who seven years later would earn himself worldwide infamy by his unprovoked attack on the American gunboat *Panay* as it stood by in the Yangtse to evacuate neutrals caught up in the Japanese assault on Nanking. 'That the politicians in their ultimate degeneracy have been able to strike a foul blow at the military establishment can clearly be seen in the London Treaty,' he proclaimed. 'Yet the military establishment is paralyzed, lacks courage to come forward against the decadent politics, and can do no better than depend on the Privy Council, doddering old men of a past generation . . . it is clear that the foul blows which the party politicians have recently struck at the Navy will be turned next on the Army.'

Their naval counterparts in the 'Fleet Faction' added their support for the overthrow of the parliamentary system, but their effectiveness was limited by a number of factors. Foremost among these was the continuing dominance of the Satsuma *han* whose link to the Throne through the Empress served to reinforce their commitment to the gradualist strategy of the Meiji-Yamagata blueprint. In the Army, by contrast, the pressure for more radical action had been increased not only by the loosening of the traditional Choshu influence, but also by the fact that the new generation of officers were much more closely linked to the agricultural classes who were now bearing the brunt of the economic recession — agricultural income in 1930 fell by an average of no less than 30%.

'SOMETHING REALLY BIG'

'Things will go on from this point till something really big breaks next February or March,' a leader of one of the patriotic societies informed Prince Konoye Fumimaro, who had inherited his father's mantle as the principal patron of such bodies; the same man had warned of an impending attack on Hara only a few days before it took place in 1921, so that he was clearly a well connected source. It was at this juncture that Konoye stepped into the rôle of go-between for Hirohito and the militarists. It would in due course cast him twice as Prime Minister in the run-up to World War Two; charged in its aftermath as a major War Criminal, he would commit suicide rather than run the risk of revealing the extent of the Emperor's involvement. To facilitate the link, he secured the appointment of Kido Kiochi to the office of Secretary of the Lord Privy Seal.

The adopted son of Restoration leader Kido Koin and a member of the influential aristocratic Eleven Club, Kido was also a fanatical golfer and one of Hirohito's favourite partners on the nine holes laid out in the Imperial grounds, where they could be sure of not being overheard as they discussed the highest affairs of state. A few months later he was told by Saionji that in his opinion Hirohito sometimes had a better grasp of these affairs than his Ministers or even his grandfather Meiji had. Elevated to the office of Lord Privy Seal itself in 1940, he would join Konoye in the dock six years later, to be condemned to life imprisonment by the evidence of his diaries — but, unlike the Imperial Go-Between, he had no need to take cyanide, knowing that they contained not a single word that could be taken to implicate the Emperor.

When it became clear that Hamaguchi would not recover in time to attend the next session of the Diet, the problem arose of choosing a stand-in for the Prime Minister. Saionji, whose responsibility it was as the only surviving Elder Statesman, at first toyed with the idea of proposing Ugaki (who had now recovered from his own illness) in order to appease the unrest of the military and to foil the claims of the Queen-Murderer Adachi, but in the end he decided that such a choice would give fortune too many hostages and he plumped for Foreign Minister Shidehara. Far from reducing the possibility of 'something really big' occurring, however, this decision served only to make it more certain.

Even before the session opened, Shidehara had made himself a fresh target for the zealots by his refusal to sanction the dispatch of troops to Manchuria to settle a clash which had taken place in October between Chinese and Japanese police units in the area of Chientao where several thousand Koreans had been transplanted. The clash was no accidental collision, being the handiwork of Doihara Kenji, who had already earned the sobriquet of 'The Lawrence of Manchuria' for his subversive activities behind the lines.

In the Diet itself, a speech by Matsuoka Yosuke, who had exchanged his post as Vice-President of the South Manchuria Railway for a seat on the Opposition benches, provided an even more ominous pointer to the direction of future events. 'We feel suffocated as we observe the internal and external situations,' the future Foreign Minister and enthusiastic accomplice of the dictators Hitler, Stalin and Mussolini declared. 'We are seeking room that will let us breathe.'

On February 3rd 1931 the flak aimed at Shidehara redoubled when in answer to criticism of the London Naval Treaty he defended it on the grounds that the Emperor had sanctioned it and therefore it could not possibly be held to endanger the nation's security. Immediately 'The Arch-Schemer' Mori leapt to his feet with a charge of *lèse majesté* for implying that the 'sacred and inviolable' Emperor was responsible for such a contentious decision, and the debate ended in such violent fisticuffs that the House was suspended. By law the Budget had to be passed by February 11th, and it was clearly Mori's intention to force its postponement and so bring the government down. Before that point could be reached, however, Seiyukai leader Inukai thrashed out a settlement with Adachi which forced his Secretary-General to toe the line and allowed his Foreign Minister to withdraw 'his slip of the tongue'.

However, Mori already had a much higher card up his sleeve — a plan for an outright *coup d'état* which was at that moment being put together by activists in the Army and Okawa's patriotic societies. On the appointed day (fixed eventually at March 20th) the headquarters of the two main parties and the Prime Minister's Residence were to be bombed, the Diet seized by troops under the command of the Cherries and then surrounded by a crowd of 10,000 Seiyukai party members under Mori and 'patriots' under Okawa, a motion of no confidence in the government passed, parliament dissolved, military law declared and a new Cabinet appointed under the leadership of Ugaki.

The extent of Ugaki's complicity is still to this day a matter of some conjecture, such was the veil of secrecy subsequently drawn over the episode. No disciplinary measures were ever taken against its participants; even Saionji heard nothing of it until August, and it was not until the War Crimes Tribunal in 1947 that it was first discussed in public. What can be said with certainty is that the conspirators were not confined to the Cherry Society, but included some of the highest ranking officers in the War

Ministry — in particular, Vice-Minister of War (and World War Two Chief of Staff) Sugiyama Hajime, Vice Chief of Staff Ninomiya Harashige, Director of the key Military Affairs Bureau and wartime Prime Minister Koiso Kuniuki and Intelligence Chief Tatekawa Yoshiji.

On January 15th Ugaki had held a meeting with these four to discuss the subject of 'national reconstruction'; whether any mention of a coup was made has never been established, although the additional presence of Chief Cherry Hashimoto might be taken to suggest that it was. At any rate, on February 11th Koiso arranged for a further meeting between Ugaki and Okawa, at which the latter revealed the detailed plans and asked the War Minister to arrange for the requisite supply of bombs. In the version of what transpired between them which Ugaki told Saionji's secretary Harada nine months later, he dismissed Okawa's request for his support as 'an outrage', but the entry in his diary written immediately afterwards is a good deal more ambivalent: 'I am keenly aware of the fact that party politics has degenerated, and for the sake of the nation I feel that something ought to be done about it.' Moreover, Okawa reported back to Hashimoto that Ugaki 'did not seem disinclined about the venture'.

Whatever the War Minister's attitude was, the bombs were presently obtained from Staff Headquarters and in the first week of March Okawa marshalled his patriots for a dress rehearsal. Far from the planned 10,000, however, he was able to muster no more than 4,000. As a result, he appealed to Koiso to make up the numbers with troops, but when the request was passed to Ugaki for approval he replied 'Don't be a fool! Do you think you can use His Majesty's troops for such a purpose?' The plot was thereupon abandoned.

Ugaki's change of heart may possibly be explained by more than just the poor turnout of the supporting cast, since he was at that time considering a suggestion that he should take over the presidency of the Seiyukai. He may also have been influenced by the opinions of Nagata, Suzuki and Tojo who had been commissioned by Koiso with the detailed planning of the conspiracy and who, it appears, eventually concluded that it was unlikely to succeed. Doubt also surrounds the extent of Imperial Go-Between Konoye's involvement; although he was earmarked as Home Minister in the proposed military Cabinet, it has yet to be established that he actively assisted in its preparation.

Others in the military hierarchy, notably Lieutenant Generals Araki Sadao, Mazaki Jinzaburo and Minami Jiro, had refused to participate not so much from doubt of the prospects of success as from a personal animosity to Ugaki originating from his cutbacks in the Army's manpower during the previous decade. This resentment and the failure of the attempt at 'national reconstruction' combined to bring very much nearer the long-threatened split in the Army's ranks between zealots and gradualists, which would culminate in the 1936 Mutiny (and even beyond; when in the following year Ugaki was appointed to form a Cabinet, nobody would come forward to fill the War Ministry and he was obliged to resign).

Thus thwarted on the home front, it was only to be expected that the zealots would turn now to Manchuria and their natural allies in the Kwantung Army.

20

Kwantung Army Steals a March

A QUESTION OF PRIORITIES

In December 1930 the Kwantung Army's General Staff had already conspired to approve an outline programme for the occupation of Manchuria. It was based on the studies of 'Doctor' Okawa, the product of his work as Director of the South Manchuria Railway Research Institute, and of two of its own staff officers, inseparable companions and fellow expansionists, Ishihara Kanji and Itagaki Taisuki.

The occupation was seen as an essential bulwark against the spread of communism from Soviet Russia — only in May the Chinese Communist Party had given directives for the establishment of regional Soviets throughout Manchuria; once that was completed, it was reasoned, Japan would be free to expand southwards. Only the United States was then likely to present a serious obstacle, and it was imperative that everything should be in place before the London Naval Treaty expired in 1936 when America would be able to embark on a massive extension to her fleet. War with America, according to Ishihara, was 'inevitable': it would begin as a 'war of endurance' over China and then develop into a 'war of decision, [in which] we can devote ourselves to the great task of unifying the world': Japan should first 'try to make America fight alone' and to reach an 'understanding' with Britain and the Soviet Union, but if that should fail 'we shall not fail to engage [them] in all-out war.' In addition, Okawa considered that the exploitation of the natural resources of Manchuria would not give Japan the self-sufficiency needed for such a conflict, and that only the seizure and development of northern China as well would make good the deficiency.

Where they differed was on the question of whether military action in Manchuria should have priority over political 'reorganisation' on the home front. 'Internal reform is extremely difficult to undertake without national unity ... History has proved that military success at the initial stage of war arouses and unites the public,' Ishihara argued. 'Conditions in our country make it more appropriate to drive the nation to foreign expansion, in the course of which internal reform can be accomplished.'

With Itagaki he then drew up a detailed plan of action: a night-time explosion on the SMR outside Mukden was to provide the pretext for the storming of 'the nearby North Barracks housing the 'Young Warlord' Chang's main garrison, followed by the occupation of Mukden itself, Changchun and other key cities. 'When the military preparations are complete, we need not go to great lengths to find a motive or occasion,' they asserted. 'All we need to do is to pick our time and then proclaim to the world our absorption of Manchuria and Mongolia as we did the annexation of Korea.'

For his part, Okawa continued to work on plans for a second attempt at a political takeover while at the same time, with the assistance of 'The Arch-Schemer' Mori, raising financial backing for the Conspirators in Mukden. Warlord Assassin Komoto busied himself in Tokyo winning over supporters in the War Ministry and General Staff, notably Vice-Minister of War Sugiyama, Chief of Operations Tatekawa, Director of the Military Affairs Bureau Koiso and his Section Chief, mass mobilisation strategist Nagata. Tatekawa subsequently recalled Child-Strangler Amakasu from his exile in Paris and dispatched him to Mukden to liaise with the Conspirators.

In April 1931 the General Staff in Tokyo adopted a 'Situations Estimate' in Manchuria. First drawn up by Nagata and Chief Cherry Hashimoto the previous November, it had received a final polish from Tatekawa, who as Operations Chief would mastermind its execution. It posited three alternative strategies: 1) the removal of the 'Young Warlord' and the installation of a pro-Japanese regime, which would then negotiate a settlement of Japan's current demands; 2) the establishment of an administration which would be completely independent of China (and, nominally at least, of Japan); 3) a military occupation.

In its original version, it too had called for a 'reorganisation' in Japan as an essential precondition, but after the failure of the March Plot this was omitted and the following sentence added in its place: 'In the event of the Government not taking action on the basis of this document, the Army should devise its own means of dealing resolutely with the situation.' It was then submitted to the Throne, where it seems to have been favourably received, for immediately afterwards Hashimoto felt able to declare that it had been decided to 'deal resolutely with the situation'.

This rather vague promise of action was not enough to satisfy the bolder spirits in Mukden, who grew still more impatient when Nanking's Foreign Minister announced a programme to recover all territorial rights currently leased to foreign Powers in China including, it was made clear to Japan, the SMR and the Kwantung Peninsula. The Conspirators were also acutely conscious of the need to forestall the World Disarmament Conference, which was due to take place in Geneva in February 1932. In response to their representations, the new Minister of War, Minami (in the wake of the March Plot, Ugaki had been transferred to the less conspicuous post of Governor-General of Korea) called a conference at the Ministry on June 11th to prepare a more specific programme of action. The resulting document, entitled *A General Outline of a Solution of the Manchurian Problem* and based on the assumption that 'military action will probably be necessary', detailed the preparatory steps to be taken 'with a view to achieving results in approximately one year's time, that is, by the spring of 1932.'

A PRETEXT TO HAND

Even this, however, constituted too long a wait for the restless Conspirators, and a staff officer was dispatched to Tokyo to argue for a September deadline. Since he was travelling in an unofficial capacity, he was careful to contact only known sympathizers within the high command. They agreed to set a date of September 28th, which was to be kept as a top secret between them for the time being. Blessing was also given to Nagata's suggestion for the transfer of two huge 9·5″ howitzers from Port Arthur, where they had been deployed in the siege of the Russians in 1905, to the Kwantung Army garrison in Mukden. A large shed was run up to conceal them from any watching Chinese who were told that it was to contain a swimming pool. When the guns were safely installed, one was trained on the North Barracks and the other on the airfield where the 'Young Warlord' had stationed several squadrons of the latest fighter planes just delivered from France.

In a further bid to capture the support of the local population, a team of speakers were sent into the other leading cities of Manchuria in order to 'awaken the eighty million brothers at home where party politics "ran riot", to appeal to the entire nation on the existing state of affairs in Manchuria, and to prepare for the liquidation of the international root of the calamity by striking a blow at the Chinese Government.' Okawa added his voice at the same time, urging also that the time was ripe for a 'reorganisation' in Japan itself. Despite his years, Godfather Toyama too was as busy as ever behind the curtain, forming a 'Society for the Ultimate Solution of the Manchurian Question'; it was presently to merge with Okawa's organisations to form the Japan Production Society under the presidency of his henchman, Black Dragon Boss Uchida.

Meanwhile a certain Captain Nakamura Shintaro had been dispatched on a reconnaissance mission to north-western Manchuria by the Tokyo General Staff. Equipped with a false passport describing him as a 'school-teacher', he was joined at Harbin by an assistant and two interpreters. Towards the end of June they were arrested at a restaurant by a suspicious detachment of Chang's Chinese regulars. They were duly searched and discovered to be carrying surveying materials, 100,000 yen in cash and a liberal quantity of opium. Some days later they were accordingly executed as spies, although it was not until July 20th that word of their death reached the Japanese.

Chang, well aware of the possible implications that this carried for the currently delicate Sino-Japanese relations, promised Tokyo assistance in investigating it. Foreign Minister Shidehara, no less awake, imposed a Press embargo, and the War Ministry cabled the Kwantung Army Headquarters that it was on no account to be used as a pretext for military action. The Conspirators, however, were determined to extract every inch of mileage from it, and Ishihara sent an indignant letter of protest to Nagata. A few days later the news was leaked to the Press, who duly seized on it as an 'outrageous provocation'. As if this was not bad enough, another clash had meanwhile occurred in Manchuria over the rights of Korean immigrants, provoking anti-Chinese riots in Korea and, in retaliation, a stiffening of the anti-Japanese boycott in China.'The Arch-Schemer' Mori set out for the scene of the incident — not, he explained, in order to investigate it, but 'with something else in mind'.

It was in this highly-charged atmosphere that the Kwantung Army's new Commander-in-Chief, Honjo Shigeru, arrived with his Staff in Japan for a Commanders' Conference in early August. At a secret meeting with the Conspiracy's collaborators inside the high command, Sugiyama, Ninomiya, Koiso, Tatekawa and Commander of the Korean Army Hayashi Senjuro, he obtained their support for military action; to avoid the risk of compromising the Emperor, Chief of Staff Kanaya Henzo and War Minister Minami were for the moment excluded.

Two days later, however, whether by coincidence or otherwise, Minami gave an address to the Conference which put him firmly on the Conspirators' side. Having rejected the arguments of Finance Minister Inoue for a further cutback in the Army's budget as 'proposals for a sell-out', he went on to speak of a 'serious turn' of events in Manchuria and a 'decline in external prestige of the nation resulting from a relapse in national vigour,' urging that 'at such a time those who engage in military affairs should strengthen their spirit of service to the nation and should resolve to be prepared to fulfil their duties ...' He was followed by Sugiyama, who demanded 'a forceful solution' of the incidents in Manchuria. Hayashi readily agreed to supply reinforcements from his Korean Army, whose transfer across the border had the added advantage, in Minami's view, of 'not exciting the feelings of the Powers so greatly as would the dispatch of troop ships from Japan itself'.

ON THE BRINK

Minami's address (which, contrary to precedent, was open to the Press) immediately gave rise to popular talk of war, and the Conspirators now set the agreed date of September 28th as a definite deadline. For all his efforts, the Consul-General in Mukden, Hayashi Kyujiro, had failed to turn up any concrete evidence on Nakamura's murder, and on August 24th the War Ministry issued a statement threatening to carry out a 'security occu-pation' of the area if the Chinese did not admit responsibility. On September 3rd the Chinese investigators also reported that they had drawn a blank. The Kwantung Army alleged that they had deliberately concealed the evidence, and in order to appease them Shidehara felt obliged to present demands for a public apology and compensation.

Realising the urgency of the situation Chang, who was at that time recovering from a bout of typhoid in Peking (where he had returned after helping Generalissimo Chiang quash a revolt by his old enemies among the northern warlords the previous year), dispatched one of his personal staff to lead a second investigation. Furious though he was at Minami's behaviour, Wakatsuki, who had taken over the Premiership from Shidehara following an abortive return to office by the bullet-ridden Hamaguchi, had decided to let is pass rather than risk inflaming actions and emotions further, and instead he contented himself with an appeal to 'work together and devote ourselves to our country'.

The traffic between Mukden and Tokyo meanwhile intensified. A delegation of the Manchurian Youth Congress arrived to present their case for action, and were duly reassured by Tatekawa that 'the military have already prepared for a final decision'. Inseparable Itagaki took leave of the Conspirators' headquarters to satisfy himself of the level of domestic support. When Hashimoto asked him, 'Is the Kwantung Army going ahead with it?' he answered with a categorical 'Yes'. The Chief Cherry took this response as a green light to continue with his plans for a coup on the home front.

The Collaborators in the high command, however, were more concerned to see the 'solution of the Manchurian question' achieved first, and they were understandably anxious that its success should not be jeopardised by a repetition of the March fiasco. 'I hope you know what you're getting into,' Nagata warned Hashimoto. Shortly after his return to Mukden Itagaki dispatched an intermediary to ask that the War Ministry should 'not interfere too closely when the Japanese and Chinese armies clash'. 'We don't know how far we can check the Government, but we'll do our best to back you up,' was the encouraging reply. 'We're all set and ready to go ahead as planned', the intermediary then informed Hashimoto, at the same time revealing the site of the planned bomb explosion.

After a Cabinet meeting on September 4th Minami told the Press that he couldn't say whether the situation demanded a resort to armed force, but the Army would act 'in accordance with the wishes of the people'. Thanks to the propagandist work of Mori and Okawa, there was now little doubt what interpretation would be put on those 'wishes'. Their efforts had been further boosted by a grant of 50,000 yen from secret Army funds authorised by Kanaya, and military aeroplanes dropped 100,000 leaflets over several cities entitled 'Wake Up To National Defence!' and including maps of Manchuria. 'However much Japan may try by compromise and concessions to establish Sino-Japanese relations on a basis of reasonableness, it is a fact that the situation is already beyond settlement by such means', Mori told a meeting of the Seiyukai board. 'Beyond doubt it has reached the brink of war.' The party's leader, Inukai, slanted his next policy speech accordingly, sailing as close to the prevailing political wind as he dared: 'For us Japanese, who are suffering from over-population, to seek an outlet in neighbouring regions as peaceful merchants, industrialists and farmers will be asserting merely our minimum right to national existence . . .'

The first concrete news that 'a plot is afoot among young officers in the Kwantung Army to thrash the Chinese Army' reached the government in Tokyo that same day, causing Shidehara to cable Consul-General Hayashi in Mukden with orders to 'make further arrangements to control these adventurers'. As soon as Last Noble Saionji got wind of it, he passed it on to the Imperial Palace. This was not the first inkling that the Court had received that something was in the air, for two months earlier some young officers' manifestoes calling for action had come to the attention of Prince Kanin, Hirohito's uncle and the Imperial Family's senior serving member in the Army. Hirohito had requested him 'to take extra precautions regarding the actions of the [Kwantung] Army in Manchuria and Mongolia'.

The Emperor now summoned Minami to question him on the state of military discipline. The War Minister, who was still not directly party to the Conspiracy, assured him that 'we are controlling them very carefully,' and to Saionji the following day he was similarly bland: 'I will exercise my responsibilities and be extremely careful.'

Rumours got as far as the League of Nations, where the Chinese delegate called for sanctions against Japan. Dismissing them as 'entirely groundless and absurd', the Japanese Minister in Nanking claimed that his country's policy towards her neighbour was rooted on the principles of 'self-defence', an argument that was endorsed by Privy Seal Secretary Kido.

MUKDEN PREPARES TO JUMP

On September 10th 'The Lawrence of Manchuria' Doihara, who had now been appointed by Honjo, his former instructor at the Military Academy, head of the Kwantung Army's Special Service Agency, arrived in Tokyo for a meeting with the high command. It was agreed that they should await the outcome of the current negotiations with China over the Nakamura Incident and that a resort to force should be made in the absence of a satisfactory outcome. At the same time Doihara implied to the Press that the Kwantung Army had intended to enforce their own 'solution', but were refraining from doing so because of Government opposition. At a subsequent and somewhat less formal meeting, he brought the Collaborators up to date with the latest plans. Hashimoto again entered a plea that the plot should be deferred until October, by which time he was hoping to have carried out the overthrow of the Government in Tokyo. After addressing a committee of the House of Peers on the theme that 'communist power is spreading throughout China', Doihara set out again

for Mukden bearing 20,000 yen raised by Okawa to go towards the
expenses of the plot; Warlord Assassin Komoto had departed the previous
week with a further 30,000 yen from the same source.

On September 13th the 'Young Warlord's' personal investigator set out
for the scene of Nakumura's disappearance with a force of 20 military
policemen, and Consul-General Hayashi expressed his confidence to
Shidehara that the incident could be settled by negotiation. Such an
outcome threatened, of course, to leave the Conspirators high and dry, and
the next day they signalled to the General Staff in Tokyo to complain that
'Chang's offences and insults have become extremely difficult to bear'.
Almost simultaneously, the Foreign Ministry received this warning telegram from Consul-General Hayashi: 'Kwantung Army assembling troops,
bringing out munitions, seem likely to start action near future.' When
Shidehara then confronted Minami with this, the War Minister replied
casually that 'we can't put any confidence in this without checking it out.'

Nevertheless, Minami was sufficiently perturbed to call an emergency
meeting of the General Staff and inquire whether they thought that 'there
is any chance that the Kwantung Army would take action without
consulting Army Headquarters'. Tatekawa airily dismissed such a possibility, but he was more than a little flustered when the War Minister
retorted that 'it seems as if you have some inside information on the
Kwantung Army'. The alarm of the Collaborators increased still further
when he then went on to say that 'we had better advise Honjo of the
Emperor's caveat by telegram'. Koiso hurriedly objected that a telegram
might be 'misinterpreted' and instead suggested a letter to be delivered by
Tatekawa, 'the only one who can control these young fellows'. After some
hesitation, Minami put pen to paper and handed the completed letter to the
Conspiracy's mastermind to pass on to his fellow Conspirators.

The meeting over, Tatekawa hurried back to his office and ordered
Hashimoto to send a telegram to Itagaki in their private code forewarning
him of his impending journey and its purpose. To this the Chief Cherry
added one of his own: 'Plot discovered, Tatekawa coming, strike first to
avoid implicating him. If Tatekawa arrives [prematurely], take action
before receiving his message.' Tatekawa also arranged with Okawa to
dispatch an underling to Port Arthur to sound out Honjo's attitude.

The telegrams caused consternation in Mukden, and it was debated
whether it would be wiser to await Tatekawa's advice before starting
anything. Eventually, however, the Conspirators concluded that to do so
might risk having to abandon the whole enterprise for good, and they
immediately launched a series of practice manoeuvres in preparation for
an attack on the 18th, the day of his expected arrival. At the same time
Child-Strangler Amakasu was sent to Harbin with the 30,000 yen brought
from Tokyo by Komoto with the object of setting up 'incidents' which
would provide pretexts for an extension of the fighting into northern
Manchuria.

Two days later Chang's investigator returned to Mukden with the local commander of the troops responsible for Nakamura's death and placed him under arrest pending court martial, and on the same day the Nationalist's Foreign Minister in Nanking called for 'stern punishment in accordance with military law in the event of his being found guilty'. Thus encouraged, Consul-General Hayashi urged the local Governor to come to a speedy settlement in order to 'deprive the Kwantung Army of an excuse for going into action'.

It was not to be speedy enough. Hayashi had also taken the precaution of sending a warning to Honjo in Port Arthur of the developments in Mukden, but a Conspirator on the Commander's staff kept it in his pocket until it was too late.

Having left Tokyo on the 15th, Tatekawa had made leisurely progress through Korea in order to give the Conspirators ample time to complete their arrangements. He finally arrived at the Manchurian border on the morning of the 18th. In spite of travelling in mufti, he was recognised there as he boarded a train for Mukden, but when challenged he denied his identity. At 11.30 am he disembarked again at a town some forty miles short of Mukden, where he was met by Itagaki and briefed with the latest preparations (the other Inseparable, Ishihara, had remained in Headquarters at Port Arthur to mind Honjo).

Six hours later they boarded another train and reached Mukden shortly after 7 pm.

For the benefit of the junior officer sent to meet them they went through a little exchange of 'belly language'.

'Aren't the young officers very worked up over the Nakamura Incident?' Tatekawa pretended to inquire.

'Oh no, Sir, not at all.'

'That's good then, I can catch up on some sleep. We'll go into it all tomorrow.'

They drove to an inn where a liberal supply of *saki* and *geisha* had been laid on for the ostensibly weary General. Having seen him satisfactorily installed, Itagaki took his leave and doubled back to the office of the Special Service Agency, which was to serve as the nerve centre for the night's operations.

BUMPS IN THE NIGHT

Shortly afterwards a patrol from the 3rd Company of the 2nd Railway Battalion armed with 42 packs of explosives set out under cover of darkness for a point on the track of the South Manchurian Railway equidistant from the city walls and Chang's garrison in the North Barracks, and only a mile from the bridge where three years earlier Komoto had blown the senior Chang to his death; it was perhaps less than a coincidence that the patrol was led by a younger cousin of Komoto. It was planned to detonate the charge beneath the carriages of the next south-bound express, which was due in to Mukden at 10.30; the rest of the Company was stationed one mile further north to launch the first attack in the wake of the explosion.

The train was punctual, and at approximately 10.25 the charge was set off beneath it. It blew out a section of one rail, but the train's momentum was enough to take the rear carriages over the gap and it carried on to Mukden unscathed. The noise of the explosion had, however, been sufficient to catch the attention of the Chinese guards in the North Barracks, and a detachment was sent out to investigate. Minutes later they came under fire from the main body of the 3rd Company as it too hurried to the scene of the explosion after being informed of it by a runner from the patrol. (It may be thought more likely that the explosives had not been set in a position to damage the track at all; certainly no foreigner was allowed to inspect the scene until after repairs had been allegedly completed four days later. The Japanese were also, of course, to allege that the explosion was the work of the Chinese, who were purported to have positioned a force of some 400 men at the junction of the Barracks wall and the track to open fire on their patrol immediately afterwards; how the runner could then have made his way unchallenged through these 400 men to reach the main body of the 3rd Company further up the track was never explained.)

As soon as the opening of fire was reported to Itagaki by field telephone he ordered the 29th Regiment and the remaining companies of the 2nd Battalion to attack the North Barracks and the city fortifications respectively in accordance with the standing plans laid down to cover any such 'incidents'; for the sake of security only the 3rd Company had been allowed to know that this was to be the night. Mobilisation orders were also issued to all the other units stationed along the line, and the first shells from the two 9.5″ howitzers were soon raining down on their pre-aligned targets, the Barracks and the airfield.

Shortly afterwards an agitated Deputy Consul — General Hayashi was away attending a funeral wake — arrived at the Agency demanding to know what was happening. Itagaki replied that a Japanese patrol had been fired on by Chinese forces from the Barracks and that 'as it's an emergency situation and the Commanding Officer's in Port Arthur, I issued an order [to engage] on his behalf.' When questioned as to his authority to do so, Itagaki retorted 'Does the Consulate-General wish to interfere with the prerogative of the Imperial Command?' To emphasise the point, a junior officer drew his sword and threatened to kill any 'meddler'.

The Deputy retired suitably abashed to seek out his superior, but when Hayashi himself presently telephoned to demand a stop to the fighting, Itagaki replied that 'the Army will deal with this in the way that it has planned.' Having fended off the Consul-General, he then took steps to maintain Tatekawa's cover, so that when the Mastermind appeared in the inn's vestibule to inquire into the source of the gunfire which had, he claimed, disturbed his slumbers, he was escorted back to his room by a posse of soldiers; 'It's dangerous outside,' their leader explained to him, 'so we've been ordered to keep you indoors.'

Thanks to the destruction of the main gate by howitzer shells, it did not take the 3rd Company long to gain entry to the North Barracks. Confident that events had gone beyond the point of no return, Itagaki now, one hour after the opening of fire, considered it safe to inform Headquarters at Port Arthur. His telephone call caught the Army Commander in his bath, which allowed the insiders on the Staff time to win over those not already in the know with the argument that 'we must not let Itagaki and Ishihara down the way we did Komoto' (after his assassination of the 'Old Warlord' in 1928). When Honjo eventually completed his toilet he was thus greeted with the unanimous opinion that 'we must resolutely make ourselves the masters of the enemy garrisons'.

'All right,' he replied after a few moments' contemplation, 'let it be done on my responsibility.' He did, however, stipulate that the action should be confined to Mukden, rejecting Ishihara's request for a full-scale occupation of the whole of Manchuria. As with other senior officers who had not been directly involved in the planning of the operation, it may never be possible to establish accurately the degree of his complicity; any claim, however, that he was totally ignorant of what was in train must be set against an address which he had made that very afternoon to an inspection parade in which he declared that 'with the present uneasiness in Manchuria and Mongolia growing daily more pronounced, we cannot be complacent. If violence should break out, I trust that each unit will take resolute action and adhere to its goals with unwavering determination.'

On the confirmation from Headquarters of Itagaki's original orders, the 29th Regiment launched its attack on Mukden's city walls, and shortly after midnight the rest of the 2nd Battalion joined the 3rd Company's assault on the North Barracks. Five hours later they were reinforced by the arrival of the 16th Regiment from their garrison 50 miles to the south, and by 7.30 am the entire city, Barracks and airfield were in Japanese hands. When the local Chinese Commander tried to telephone for reinforcements, he found, of course, that the line had been cut.

MUFFLED RESPONSE FROM TOKYO

The first news of the 'Incident' reached Tokyo shortly after 1 am on September 19th, and six hours later the Collaborators there gathered to discuss it. 'The Kwantung Army's action is entirely just,' Koiso pronounced to unanimous approval. Reinforcements should be sent immediately, it was agreed; troops from the Korean Army, being nearest to the action, could be diverted as a first step.

The Korean Army Commander Hayashi Senjuro, however, had not

waited even this long for such an invitation, having at first light dispatched
two companies of an air regiment and given orders for a mixed brigade to
mobilise. Having informed Tokyo of this, Hayashi two hours later sent a
second telegram, stating that 'I am about to send my troops across the
border. Request is made to secure promptly His Majesty's sanction'; like
his counterpart in the Kwantung Army, the Commander-in-Chief of the
Korean Army came under the direct control of the Emperor, rather than
of the War Minister or Chief of Staff, in operational matters. For this
initiative, he would subsequently be lionised as 'The Border-Crosser'.

From the wording of the telegram it seemed that Hayashi was seeking
Imperial approval after, and not before, he crossed the border, and even
the Collaborators on the General Staff considered that this might lay him
open to a charge of violating the Imperial Prerogative. Accordingly Chief
of Staff Kanaya (who, although not a Collaborator, was by now of course
abreast of events) ordered him to wait for an Imperial order, but it took
two more telegrams and another fifteen hours to persuade Hayashi finally
to stay his hand.

A similar clash of wills was meanwhile taking place at Mukden, whither
Honjo had hastily decamped with his Staff to join Itagaki at the centre of
operations. Before he arrived there he eventually yielded to Ishihara's
arguments for a full-scale occupation and gave his sanction to the
mobilisation orders which Itagaki had already issued to all other units in
the SMR zone, at the same time appealing to Tokyo for an extra three
divisions in order that he could 'positively assume the responsibility of
maintaining public order over the whole of Manchuria'. When, however,
he learnt of the interception of Consul-General Hayashi Kyujiro's warning
telegram to him and saw the contents of War Minister Minami's letter
which Tatekawa now belatedly delivered into his hands, he promptly
reversed his decision. He was fully supported in this by Tatekawa; 'The
establishment of a new administrative regime in South Manchuria comes
first,' he declared. 'If we delay on that, some third power will intervene.
Northern Manchuria can wait for the moment.'

In arguing thus, Tatekawa was adhering to the Number One Plan in his
Situations Estimate (the installation of a pro-Japanese regime) as against
Number Three (military occupation), and in a telegram to Tokyo he
suggested Pu Yi, the last Manchu emperor of China, as a possible candidate
to head such a regime. It seems that the other Collaborators back in Tokyo
had arranged with him to take the same attitude, for when Sugiyama and
Ninomiya met at much the same time to confer with the Inspector-
General of Military Education, Araki Sadao, they agreed that while the
'Incident' should be used to bring about a solution of the Manchurian
problem, that solution was to consist of 'completely upholding the existing
treaty rights and was not to imply military occupation of the whole of
Manchuria'.

Honjo must also have been influenced by orders of an even more constraining nature which were now arriving from the War Ministry. At an emergency meeting of the Cabinet called at 10 am that morning, Minami had assured his colleagues that the Kwantung Army's actions had been of a purely defensive nature taken in response to Chinese 'violence and provocation'. This claim was then rapidly demolished, however, when Foreign Minister Shidehara read out Consul-General Hayashi's latest reports which put it beyond doubt that on the contrary they were the prelude to a carefully rehearsed conspiracy. It was then unanimously decided that Honjo should be ordered on no account to expand the area of hostilities.

The War Minister, according to one observer, was left 'dispirited', and 'he lost the courage to propose reinforcements'. At a meeting of the General Staff held shortly afterwards Chief Kanaya declared that 'while circumstances beyond control have brought about this incident, we should quickly settle it and return to the status quo.' In other words, he was saying, even the Number One Plan was now out of court. This in turn allowed the Japanese delegate at the League of Nations, where China had lost no time in raising the subject, to claim that 'the Japanese Government has taken all the measures possible to prevent this local incident from leading to undesirable complications'.

Nine hours later, however, the boot seems to have been firmly on the other foot, apparently as the result of an audience which Hirohito held with Kanaya in the afternoon (it will be remembered that Hirohito had approved the 'Situation Estimate' when it had been submitted to him in April). In this the Chief of Staff, while expressing 'extreme regret' for 'Border Crosser' Hayashi's precipitate action, sought the Emperor's sanction for the dispatch of the Korean Army. In reply Hirohito voiced satisfaction with the Cabinet's decision to limit the hostilities, but he evidently did not set any veto on the deployment of troops from Korea, for by seven o'clock that evening Prime Minister Wakatsuki was telling Saionji's Secretary Harada how Kanaya had returned with Minami after his Imperial audience to urge the dispatch of reinforcements, emphasising the precarious situation of the 10,000-strong Kwantung Army (its strength was actually nearer 20,000) in relation to the quarter of a million on the Chinese side and hinting that 'troops might have already been sent from Korea'. When Wakatsuki had described the latter as 'an outrage', the War Minister had justified it by the precedent of the dispatch of troops to Shantung in 1928 without the sanction of the Tanaka Cabinet. 'So you can see, I am unable to restore order under the present circumstances,' the Prime Minister bewailed. 'It's not that I'm asking you to consult Prince Saionji, but I really am in a nice mess.'

When Harada reported the conversation back to the Court, they were none too pleased at this apparent attempt to implicate the Emperor. Kido complained in his diary that 'the unity of the Cabinet seemed weak, but the only way to control the Army is through constant Cabinet supervision,' while Saionji urged that if the Cabinet should throw in its hand and submit its resignation 'the Emperor should absolutely not allow it until the Incident is completely settled.' In tendering this line of advice, however, the two men were motivated by very different considerations: whereas Saionji, the last survivor among the pioneer standard-bearers of the representationalist principle, was concerned to uphold the sovereignty of parliament, Kido saw that his first duty as one of the inner circle of Court advisers was to shield the Emperor from open involvement in so momentous an issue. 'In view of such circumstances', he went on, 'It was decided amongst us that the Emperor had better not say anything further unless necessary ...' Thus when Kanaya sought a further audience with Hirohito the next day, he was informed that the Emperor was 'indisposed'.

'NOTHING CAN BE DONE'

This refusal to intervene was naturally taken by the Army as a signal to proceed. That same day Minami drew up the following policy statement: 1) 'Cabinet approval must be obtained before Japanese troops stationed in Korea cross the Korean frontier. *In the case of necessity, however, if approval from Tokyo cannot be obtained in time, the Commanders in Chief of the Kwantung and Korean Armies are given the authority to take appropriate measures* (author's italics). 2) The solution of problems pertaining to Manchuria should be sought *at the local level and not between Nanking and Tokyo*. 3) The Army agrees with the Government in its policy of non-aggravation, but desires to point out that the non-aggravation of the situation *does not necessarily mean the non-enlargement of the theatre of operations ...*'

The qualifications to the pious pronouncements of respect for the sovereignty of the Government effectively converted it into a *carte blanche* for the Kwantung Army to pursue its ambitions, an interpretation which a telegram from Korean Army Headquarters duly confirmed at 8.35 that same evening: 'In order to treat the issue as a local problem, it would be more expedient to take the form of unilateral troop mobilisation. We hope you will give us enough leeway to dispatch part of our forces unilaterally if occasion should arise.'

The Conspirators in Mukden lost no time at all in manufacturing just such an 'occasion'. In a late night conference in Itagaki's bedroom, they agreed to extend hostilities to Kirin, which lay outside the SMR zone (although *agents provocateurs* had already been hard at work there). Honjo was then roused from his bed and confronted with the decision. The Commander-in-Chief at first refused to give it his sanction. 'An atmosphere of great strain prevailed,' one of those present recorded. 'The Commander told all except the Chief of Staff and Itagaki to leave, and they conferred for two hours. He finally decided upon a Kirin expedition. The time was 3 am ...' Had he not done so, the same source reveals, the Conspirators would have resigned en masse.

The chief consideration behind his change of mind was the need 'to involve the Korean Army and thereby increase the manpower available' (which was already uncomfortably stretched); by sending the main body of his own troops to Kirin, he could then plead that reinforcements from Korea were an absolute necessity. The 2nd Division was immediately ordered north, but Tokyo was not informed for another three hours because 'interference was feared'. No such hesitation in informing 'The Border-Crosser' Hayashi was judged to be necessary, and by 1 pm that afternoon (on the 21st) the mixed brigade which had been poised at the frontier crossed the Yalu River into Manchuria.

Hayashi had informed the high command of his intentions some hours beforehand, explaining that he had been 'impelled by a sense of justice', in order to give them time to cancel the order if they wished. No such counter order arrived; on the contrary, four junior officers on the General Staff were put to preparing the draft of a statement demonstrating that he was not violating the Imperial Prerogative. It was also suggested that Kanaya should seek the Emperor's approval because 'the Emperor has long [since April, when he had approved the 'Situations Estimate'] given the Commander of the Korean Army the duty to dispatch part of his troops to Manchuria in case strategic and tactical needs required it'; but Nagata vetoed this proposal on the grounds that Hirohito would be seriously compromised if the Cabinet decided to withhold its approval. Should they do so, it was agreed that both Minami and Kanaya should resign as War Minister and Chief of Staff respectively and so bring down the Cabinet.

Last of all to be allowed into the picture was Prime Minister Wakatsuki, Minami waiting until after the Cabinet had adjourned for the day before passing the news on to him. Thus when they met again the following morning their chief preoccupation was to decide their response to the League of Nations, whom China had now called upon to take immediate action to redress the situation. It was agreed that they should reject any attempt by outside parties to effect a settlement, and their delegate was instructed to 'keep the dispute outside the domain of the League' when the Council met later in the day.

The Chinese assertion that the Japanese action had been without provocation was duly denied, the Nakamura incident and a catalogue of other alleged sources of conflict being quoted instead and coupled with a warning that 'premature intervention would in the circumstances only have the deplorable result of needlessly exciting Japanese public opinion, which is already over-excited, and thus impede the peaceful settlement of the situation.' The Council therefore contented itself with a declaration that it would 'endeavour, in consultation with the Chinese and Japanese representatives, to find adequate means of enabling the two countries to withdraw troops immediately.'

The arrival meanwhile of the mixed brigade from the Korean Army in Mukden had encouraged the Conspirators to extend the front even further north to Harbin. The *agent provocateur* activities of Amakasu, including bomb attacks on the Japanese Consulate and Bank of Korea office there, had provided the pretext, but when the Conspirators sought Tokyo's sanction they received the uncompromising reply that such a move was 'strictly forbidden'. Minami and Kanaya were alarmed not only that it might provoke intervention from Russia, but also that it might jeopardise their chances of obtaining Cabinet approval for the involvement of the Korean Army.

They need not have worried on the latter score, however, for even before the Cabinet convened to consider it on the 23rd Wakatsuki told Koiso that 'there is nothing that can be done now'. Although both Shidehara and Finance Minister Inoue registered strong protests at Hayashi's unauthorised action, it was accepted that they had little choice but to give it their retrospective approval and vote the necessary funds, since 'soldiers could not live for a day without the government providing for their expenses'. They did, however, succeed in extracting a pledge from Minami that the Kwantung Army would not advance beyond Kirin. When Wakatsuki reported to the Palace, Hirohito told the Prime Minister that 'the government's policy not to aggravate the situation is indeed an appropriate one. You will see to it that this is carried out.' To Kanaya, however, he expressed a rather less wholehearted commitment to such a policy of moderation, merely cautioning the Chief of Staff 'to behave discreetly in future'.

As for 'The Border-Crosser' himself, he donned his ceremonial *kimono* in readiness to commit *hara-kiri* on the least word of Imperial displeasure. None came, however, even though Hirohito was advised by the Grand Chamberlain Suzuki that he was beyond doubt guilty of violating the Imperial Prerogative. He would go on to end his career as Prime Minister, while his partner-in-crime Honjo would receive an even more personal mark of Imperial approval, becoming the Emperor's Aide-de-Camp; not for them the 'I don't wish to hear any further explanations' with which the unfortunate Tanaka had been dismissed two years earlier.

Hirohito's connivance (to put it at its mildest) not only sealed the fate of Manchuria, but destroyed the democratic government's last chance of wresting the wheel from the military and diverting his nation from the road to disaster.

21

'Manchukuo'

'PARADISE' IN MANCHURIA

In Geneva, Japan's delegate seized on the high command's veto on the extension of hostilities to Harbin to inform the League of Nations that his Government had 'firmly pursued the object of preventing an extension of the situation', and that it 'intends to withdraw its troops to the Railway Zone in proportion as the situation improves'.

The sole purpose of sending troops outside the zone to Kirin had been, he went on to explain, 'to prevent a possible flanking movement on the South Manchuria Railway', while he also claimed that even after the dispatch of the mixed brigade from Korea the total number of Japanese troops in Manchuria still did not exceed that permitted as railway guards under the Treaty of Peking. Denying once again that Japan harboured any territorial ambitions there, he repeated his warning that any intervention by the League could only 'run the risk of adversely affecting the situation which already shows signs of improvement'.

China countered with a plea for the dispatch of neutral observers to attest to the promised withdrawal, but this found little favour with the other member states who were largely preoccupied with their internal economic problems in the onset of the Great Depression. The Council did agree to refer the issue to the United States as a signatory of the Kellogg-Briand Pact, but there too it aroused little sympathy, Secretary of State Henry L. Stimson going so far as to rationalise that 'the army in Manchuria was proceeding without authorisation from Tokyo, and therefore the Japanese Government could hardly be accused of violating the Kellogg Pact'.

The veto had, by contrast, been the cause of considerable heart-searching among the Conspirators in Mukden, oblivious as they were to the need both to obtain Government approval for the involvement of the Korean Army and to pull the wool over the eyes of the outside world. In another emotionally-charged conference on September 22nd Tatekawa had attempted to persuade them to lay aside their ambitions to occupy all Manchuria (Plan Three) for the time being in favour of establishing a pro-Japanese administration. The outcome was a compromise agreement, approximating to Plan Two, to create a nominally-autonomous state

317

under Pu-Yi divided into five provinces (four in Manchuria plus Jehol in Mongolia) which 'would be made a paradise for all races existing in Manchuria and Mongolia'.

Within days each of the four Manchurian provinces were visited and potential leaders of the independence movement contracted to the scheme — in the case of Kirin, with the help of a revolver held to his head. To ensure the continuing commitment of the puppet selected in Mukden, 'The Lawrence of Manchuria' Doihara was temporarily appointed Mayor of the city. Orders were also sent to the commander of the Japanese Boxer Protocol Garrison in Tientsin to put Pu-Yi under guard, and his removal to Manchuria was presently to be another of Doihara's special assignments; Chinchow would then 'be bombed by aeroplane to exert a threat' — it was reported that the 'Young Warlord' Chang, isolated now from Mukden, was intending to set up a new seat of government there.

The scheme quickly received the approval of the Collaborators in Tokyo, qualified only by the caveat that 'it has to be carried out secretly'. War Minister Minami, by contrast, simultaneously issued an order forbidding 'participation in the movement to establish a new regime in Manchuria,' and he followed this up on September 29th 1931 with a signal that 'the Kwantung Army should have absolutely nothing to do with a movement, rumoured by Cabinet Ministers to involve the Commander-in-Chief, to restore the Emperor Pu-Yi'; for his part, Chief-of-Staff Kanaya assured the Prime Minister that 'participation of Army officers in such a movement is a total lie.'

These disavowals were made with an eye to the closing session of the League of Nations Assembly, which was due to take place that same day, and they successfuly deceived the Council President into talking of 'the real progress achieved in the last few days'. The Assembly then unanimously adopted a resolution that 'recognises the importance of the Japanese Government's statement that it has no territorial designs on Manchuria, and notes that it will continue as rapidly as possible the withdrawal of its troops, which had already been begun . . .' Deciding to consider the situation again on October 14th, the delegates broke up for the recess with easy minds.

Minami evidently felt that the need for pretence was now over, for when Foreign Minister Shidehara suggested in Cabinet the following day that the Army should withdraw again to the Railway Zone by that date, the War Minister retorted: 'Why on earth don't we withdraw from the League instead? If we are set on engaging the rest of the world in a war — that is, if we have the guts to do so — what's there to be afraid of?'

The Conspirators felt even less cause for restraint than hitherto, declaring on October 2nd that the rapid creation of the new state was to be realised 'by making every effort to promote the various nascent independence movements, especially by providing considerable assistance to those that resort to military action'. The following day they received an order from Minami and Kanaya to leave major policy decisions to Tokyo, coupled with a warning that the 'weak policy' of Shidehara 'was dominating the Cabinet, and that the atmosphere of the Court was suddenly becoming unfavourable to the Army.' Consul-General Hayashi Kyujiro, who was now persona non grata with the Kwantung Army and even under threat of death for having reported his suspicions of their intentions, had told Tokyo that it was now 'impossible to bind them to Government policy', and Hirohito had evidently woken up to the threat that loss of control over this juggernaut posed to his longer term plans for territorial expansion by drawing the attention of the world to Japan's plans for further aggrandisement.

If the warning was designed to give them pause for thought, however, it had precisely the opposite effect. Within 24 hours Inseparable Ishihara issued a public policy statement that he and his fellow Conspirators intended 'to make the Army especially resolute and, if necessary, to lead it into a clash with the [Chang] Government' which 'the people, though they all praise the dignity of the Japanese Army, do not make the least attempt to support.' The Kwantung Army, he declared, although 'it stands aloof from politics and diplomacy ... sincerely wishes to realise rapidly the paradise of co-existence and co-prosperity for the thirty million residents of Manchuria and Mongolia.'

BOMBS AWAY

Four days later Kanaya received a signal from Mukden stating that 'Chinchow is the headquarters of Chang. It is the centre of disturbances in Manchuria. The Kwantung Army contemplates taking some sort of action against it. Please be so advised.' If this had come as a surprise to him, how much more so must have a second signal a few hours later informing him that 'Chinchow has been bombed. We beg your thoughtful disposal of the matter.'

Ishihara himself had taken part as an observer in the raid; 75 bombs had been dropped resulting in considerable civilian casualties, together with leaflets describing Chang as a 'most rapacious and stinking, wanton youth' and threatening ruthlessly to destroy the town if its people did not 'submit to the kindness and power of the Army of the Great Japanese Empire'. In a later report to Tokyo, Mukden claimed that its purpose had been 'to observe Chinese troop movements and military plans in the area. As the planes were attacked by ground fire, they bombed the Chinese army' — forbearing, of course, to mention that the bombing had been planned over two weeks earlier.

News of the attack sent a predictable thrill of horror around the world. 'For all their promises, the Japanese army was expanding rather than contracting its operations,' U.S. Secretary of State Stimson remarked, and he swiftly revised his previous decision to stand aloof. 'I am afraid we have got to take a firm ground and aggressive stand toward Japan', he told his colleagues, and in a protest note to Tokyo he declared that 'bombing of an unfortified and unwarned town is one of the most extreme of military actions, deprecated even in time of war.' This opening of Stimson's eyes to the true nature of Japan's ambitions was to have far-reaching consequences, for he would become the sternest opponent in the White House of those who argued in favour of appeasing her in the negotiations preceding her entry into World War Two.

The League of Nations Council was sufficiently galvanised to bring forward its next meeting (scheduled for the 14th) by a day, and in order to forestall isolationist opposition on the domestic front Stimson arranged that American participation should 'appear to come [as the result of an] unprompted' invitation. The Japanese delegate, of course, strenuously opposed the invitation, but it was upheld by the other thirteen members. Pleading that 'the Japanese railway guards (*sic*), in taking military measures in Manchuria since the night of September 18th, have been actuated solely by the necessity of defending themselves, as well as protecting the SMR and the lives and property of Japanese subjects, against wanton attacks by Chinese troops and armed bands', he declared once more that the issue was one which Japan and China should be left to settle for themselves.

His Chinese counterpart replied that by her very actions Japan had ruled out such negotiations, as a result of which 'China has put herself in the hands of the League and abides the issue with confidence in her destiny and in the moral forces of civilisation'. Invoking the Kellogg-Briand Pact, which bound its signatories to settle all disputes 'by pacific means', the Council passed a resolution again calling on Japan to withdraw her troops and this time setting a deadline of November 17th, the date of their next scheduled meeting. The Japanese delegate, finding himself again in a minority of one, retorted that as the vote had not been unanimous, he considered it to have no force.

TOKYO TAKES COVER

Meanwhile in Tokyo the matter's 'thoughtful disposal' was a source of no less anxiety to the Government. Just as they had done over the original Mukden action and the Korean Army's crossing of the Yalu River, the high command lent their retrospective approval rather than side with the critics of militarist opportunism, declaring that 'bombing those who obstruct reconnaissance activities into sources of public disturbance is a local problem and a proper military action', and it contented itself with cautioning Mukden that 'bombing of cities creates a strong impression on Europeans and Americans, who are sensitive to air raids as a consequence of the World War and do not understand the situation in Manchuria'.

Prime Minister Wakatsuki saw the attack as final proof that there was now no stopping the juggernaut. 'We are in real trouble,' he bemoaned to Saionji's secretary Harada. 'I would summon the Minister of War to explain to him at great length the necessity of maintaining discipline among our troops overseas. He would agree, "Quite right, I'll send out an order to that effect at once." Then what would happen? The troops would then do something completely to the contrary. This is followed by immediate repercussions at Geneva. Both I and Japan's reputation are as good as betrayed. I am at a loss to know what to do . . .' This further attempt to appeal to the Court for advice and so to implicate the Emperor was again criticised by Privy Seal Secretary Kido as most reprehensible.

A few days later, on October 17th, he was confronted with evidence that those behind the juggernaut were preparing to push it down paths that even he had not suspected, when Chief Cherry Hashimoto and several other officers on the General Staff were arrested on charges of plotting another coup to be coupled with a simultaneous declaration of independence from Tokyo by the Kwantung Army. As we have seen, Hashimoto had been planning such an operation ever since the failure of the first attempt in March, and the Kwantung Army's unconcealed resentment at the latest restrictions imposed by Tokyo persuaded him that the moment was ripe. The scope of the plot, which had allegedly been scheduled for October 21st, was a good deal more extensive than had been the case in March: not only was it planned to wipe out the entire Cabinet with an aerial bombing attack on the Prime Minister's Residence, but the whole of the inner circle of Court advisers were also to be eliminated on the grounds that they had conspired to divide the Emperor from his subjects.

Its declared object was to 'seize the reins of government by military means and thereupon bring about a dictatorship through which to execute political reform', entailing, of course, the abolition of the political parties. The new Cabinet would be led by Inspector-General of Military Education Araki as both Premier and War Minister (it may be doubted whether he was in fact ever a party to the plot — indeed he had positively disowned it only the previous evening after Hashimoto had appealed to Vice-Chief of Staff Sugiyama for the high command's support. Sugiyama appears to have acted more equivocally, because he was afterwards stigmatized as 'The Toilet Door' on the analogy of being open to pressure from either side), while Hashimoto himself, Tatekawa and Okawa would take the Home, Foreign and Finance Ministries respectively. It was to be an entirely military operation; Okawa's civilian 'patriots' were this time to be excluded lest, as Hashimoto explained at his War Crimes trial in 1947, 'they became a source of leakage'. Rather than have this latest example of Army indiscipline advertised by a court-martial, the instigators were released shortly afterwards and merely transferred to other postings.

'You might make arrests in Tokyo, but in Manchuria the Kwantung Army will attain independence just the same,' one of them had boasted.

'While they are fighting a sacred war in order to expand national power and prestige, the Emperor does not approve and the Government obstructs our every move.' They had therefore 'resolved that if the first signal for internal reform is fired in Japan, they would make the Commander-in-Chief declare the independence of the Kwantung Army, abandon Japanese citizenship and entrench themselves in Manchuria.'

That it was no idle boast was confirmed by a Foreign Ministry official who had been sent to investigate the situation in Manchuria; he reported back a conversation of the two Inseparables in which they declared that 'since we have succeeded in this project [the Mukden action] we shall next undertake a *coup d'état* when we return to Japan, destroy parliamentary government and establish a state based on so-called national socialism centred around the Emperor. We shall overthrow such capitalists as Mitsui and Mitsubishi and carry out equal distribution of wealth.' Further confirmation came with the discovery that Warlord Assassin Komoto had been dispatched to Japan with 200,000 yen filched from Chinese Salt Tax revenues to foster subversive activities.

Accordingly the high command took action that same day to quell such a movement. 'Any act of conspiracy, such as one aimed at the attainment of independence of the Kwantung Army or such like, will not be tolerated,' Mukden was informed. 'We are determined to achieve fundamental settlement of the Manchuria-Mongolia problems by contemplating, if necessary, the formation of a government compatible with our wishes. Trust to our zeal and be patient ...' In reply Commander-in-Chief Honjo indignantly denied any such intention, protesting that the high command's attitude 'signifies lack of confidence in myself and my Staff and is greatly deplored', while the latter expressed themselves as even more deeply outraged: 'We absolutely could not yield to allowing the glorious Kwantung Army to be regarded with ineradicable suspicion ...' In an attempt to soothe their wounded feelings, Hirohito dispatched his Aide-de-Camp to Mukden to express His appreciation of their services.

The improbably grandiose scale of the plot suggests that its instigators had little serious intention of carrying it through, and that by prematurely disclosing it to the high command its real objective was to intimidate the opponents, both in the Army and in the Government, of the Kwantung Army's ambitions. If this was in fact the case, it was certainly successful. Not only did it produce a noticeably more accommodating attitude in the high command, but it led to the rapid rise to power of Araki as the one man there who was seen capable of keeping their zeal within bounds. It was he who would now take over the leadership of the younger, more radical element in the Army whose call for immediate action, encapsulated in the battle-cry 'Strike North', was already putting them in open conflict with the more gradualist proponents of the Imperial-Satsuma 'Strike South' strategy. Its effect in the political arena was even more profound, for the Government would now abandon all attempts to pretend that it was still in control of events and that it was therefore capable of satisfying the requirements of world opinion at Geneva.

ACROSS THE RUBICON

The Conspirators in Mukden had even so already taken steps to expand the field of their operations still further in open defiance of Tokyo. On October 10th Doihara had been given the go-ahead to proceed to Tientsin to arrange the abduction of Pu-Yi, on the pretext of assisting the Garrison there to organise their defences against a possible attack by Chang. Two weeks later, on October 24th, they adopted a memorandum outlining the proposed constitution of his new empire.

It was to be 'an independent new state separated from China proper, which will outwardly be under unified Chinese administration but actually under our control' through the appointment of Japanese advisers who were 'to seize the key positions of the various organs'. Its institutions would be 'democratic', but since its citizens' 'political consciousness' left something to be desired there would naturally be no place for any form of representative government. The employment of such an anachronistic, not to say comic, figurehead was adamantly opposed by Shidehara for the adverse impression that it was bound to give to the rest of the world, and for once he enjoyed the full support of his War Minister colleague, but this was still a considerable climb down from the total prohibition that Minami had imposed on Mukden only a month earlier.

The last of the Manchus was captivated by the offer to restore him to his throne; he would style himself 'Henry' in admiration of the English kings of that name, he announced (although his own failure to produce any issue might be thought to have made this a somewhat bizarre choice). His wife, however, resolutely refused to go along with the scheme, and in the end 'Henry' had to be persuaded to make the journey alone by a series of threatening telephone calls and two hand-grenades not-too-thoroughly concealed in a basket of fruit and purportedly delivered by the hand of the treacherous Chang.

'The Lawrence of Manchuria' hired some coolies to stage a nocturnal 'attack' on the Japanese Concession in Tientsin, and under cover of the resulting confusion Pu-Yi was spirited away to a Japanese freighter waiting off Tangku. Disembarking in Manchuria, he acted out his allotted part by appealing to the Japanese for protection, and he was duly escorted under guard to Port Arthur; by a grim stroke of humour, the man assigned to this 'humanitarian' task was none other than Child-Strangler Amakasu. With an eye to the possibility of further developments in China itself the commander of the Tientsin Garrison also took the opportunity to ask Tokyo for reinforcements.

It was to the Northern front, however, that all eyes now turned. On October 15th the man earmarked by the Conspirators as the puppet

Governor of the northern province of Heilungchiang was persuaded to launch an expedition into that province. Retreating before it across the Nonni River, the Chinese provincial army under Ma Chan-shan burnt the two bridges which carried the Taonan-Tsihihar railway. Since this line had been built with Japanese capital and was linked to the SMR, their destruction was seized on as the sought-after 'excuse for dispatching troops to North Manchuria' (in the words of a staff officer at Mukden).

Omitting to mention that Ma had subsequently offered to repair them himself, Mukden informed Tokyo on October 24th that 'we have urged the SMR to start repair work immediately. They are in general agreement with such a policy but seem worried about the League of Nations' response ... We hope you will exert pressure where needed to carry out this plan. If repair work is to be carried out, the Kwantung Army will assist ...' At the same time an ultimatum was presented to Ma threatening that if he did not repair the bridges within a week the work would be carried out by Japanese forces, who were already being moved up into the area on the familiar excuse that the line was being threatened by bandits.

The high command was only too well aware of what lay behind this request and the danger which it carried of Russian reaction, not to mention that of the League of Nations. Consequently Kanaya informed Mukden that 'the dispatch of troops away from the Nonni River and far into North Manchuria will not be permitted without my authorisation regardless of the circumstances', for such a move 'would stimulate the anxiety of those at home and abroad and might lead to interference with the further course of development' — expansion overseas. A second signal instructed that the repairs should be carried out as rapidly as possible 'so that they are finished by the 14th [the League's Council being due to reconvene on the 17th] and the covering forces completely withdrawn'. More 'indirect' methods of winning over Ma were suggested, for which 3 million yen would be provided.

Ishihara, who had arrived to take personal charge of the operation, had no intention of brooking any interference from Tokyo in his plans, which were that 'while we are repairing the bridges, we shall quietly assemble the Kwantung Army's main strength around Taonan and crush Ma's forces with a single blow. Russia has no intention of intervening at this stage [so he had learnt from the Russian Consul at Harbin]. Therefore, if we can't advance on Harbin directly, we might as well clinch the control of northern Manchuria from the north-west'. As he had anticipated, Ma ignored the ultimatum and on November 2nd he was ordered to withdraw six miles while the Japanese carried out the repairs. This too he declined to do, and when the Japanese advanced across the river two days later the inevitable clash occurred.

Meeting unexpectedly stiff resistance, Ishihara called headquarters for reinforcements, but this time Honjo refused to be railroaded by his Staff and in turn encouraged the high command to take an even firmer stand. In an explanatory telegram of his own to Mukden, Tatekawa, who had now rejoined the Collaborators in Tokyo, stated that it was 'essential to give due consideration to intricate political conditions at home and abroad . . . His Majesty is especially concerned about this matter. Therefore it will be only proper for the Chief of Staff to report for Imperial consideration every instance of action on your part that exceeds your original functions . . .'

At an Imperial audience the following day, Hirohito granted Kanaya's request that he should temporarily delegate the right of command to the Chief of Staff on the grounds that 'to obtain an Imperial sanction for each command decision not only would be troublesome for His Majesty but where an urgent decision is needed, might even fail to procure that decision in time'. In agreeing to it, Hirohito may be assumed to have been influenced not only by the need to prevent the Kwantung Army from jeopardising his own plans for expansion, but also by the wish to prevent his own person being compromised in so sensitive a situation.

Notwithstanding Tatekawa's attempt to reason with them, the Conspirators immediately protested at this 'extreme violation of the right of supreme command'. Honjo too was indignant, feeling that his competence was being impugned; pointing out the impossibility of running a campaign from a position one thousand miles behind the lines, he told Kanaya that 'I sincerely hope that you will trust me and other officers of the Kwantung Army and leave operational details against the Heilungchiang Army to our discretion.'

Slightly taken aback by his sudden reversal of attitude, Tokyo amended the veto on any advance across the Nonni River and gave him their permission to pursue the enemy as far as the Chinese Eastern Railway. The Conspirators naturally interpreted this as meaning that no serious restriction on their activities was intended after all, and when Ma refused a demand that he should withdraw his forces from the provincial capital of Tsihihar they signalled Tokyo for yet more reinforcements on the curious argument that 'if the request is not granted quickly, we may be forced to resort to unilateral action in self-defence'.

Tsihihar lay to the north of the CER, and to the Government in Tokyo this marked their Rubicon. 'So far I have made every effort to maintain our country's face by offering to the League explanations regarding the Kwantung Army's actions which, though at times rather flimsy, still had some semblance of truth,' Prime Minister Wakatsuki told Harada when Minami presented the demand from Mukden to the Cabinet. 'But if the Army should ever advance beyond the Chinese Eastern Railway and attack Tsihihar I can no longer assume responsibility for its actions.' The demand was duly rejected by the Cabinet, but in the War Ministry Tatekawa took advantage of the absence of most of the high command at the Army's annual manoeuvres to authorise a further demand to Ma that he should evacuate Tsihihar and give up his command.

When Ma again refused, the high command accepted that an attack on Tsihihar was now inevitable and mobilised the required reinforcements, three air regiments and a mixed brigade; they added the qualification, however, that the city was not to be permanently occupied once the Chinese had been driven out, after the Cabinet threatened to resign if this was not done. In order not to compromise Hirohito, the request as presented for his signature mentioned only the air regiments and not the mixed brigade. He had, however, learnt of the proposed attack on Tsihihar, but even so he raised no objection to it. Fearing that Ma might back down if he knew that reinforcements were on their way, Ishihara launched the assault on November 17th without waiting for their arrival, and two days later the city was in Japanese hands.

GENEVA STIRS

The Conspirators had no intention of heeding the Cabinet's requirement that they should now withdraw, for their plans called for the total suppression of Russian influence in northern Manchuria, particularly in Harbin, where they still maintained a considerable presence. To this end they were even prepared to provoke the Soviet Army into crossing the border for a once-and-for-all encounter. Vice-Chief of Staff Ninomiya was dispatched to see that the withdrawal was carried out as ordered but on his arrival in Mukden he was persuaded to ask Tokyo for two weeks' grace. This was refused, but the Conspirators again demurred, pleading that a withdrawal could not be undertaken while there was a danger of Ma being allowed to regroup.

Faced once more with open defiance, Kanaya signalled back an order in Hirohito's name demanding immediate obedience 'in order to preserve the honour of the Nation and the Army and in consideration of the overall international situation'. This show of resolution on Tokyo's part caused consternation in Mukden, where Honjo agreed with his Staff that they should submit their resignations en masse; he differed from them, however, in insisting that the evacuation should be carried out before they did so.

While they were agonizing over the issue the timely machinations of Doihara in Tientsin contrived to extricate them from the impasse. Following Tokyo's refusal of the Garrison Commander's request for reinforcement, he had joined with the Conspirators in a scheme to engineer another clash in the area of Chinchow with Chang's forces. This duly took place on November 23rd, provoking a strongly worded note of warning from Secretary of State Stimson against any further moves on Chinchow. When Foreign Minister Shidehara referred to Kanaya for reassurance, the Chief of Staff disclaimed the possibility, asserting that any Japanese action in the area was directed against 'bandits'.

The very next day Doihara staged the second Tientsin 'incident', and hardly had the news been relayed to Mukden than the major part of the 2nd

Division was ordered south from Tsihihar 'to assist the Tientsin Garrison in its danger'. In response to a request from the Conspirators, 'Border-Crosser' Hayashi also stood by to move part of his Korean Army into the area. On the same day the air regiments raided Chinchow for the second time; not content with merely dropping bombs, they descended and machine-gunned trains heading out of the city packed with refugees.

Minami at first denied all knowledge of their action, but when confronted by Wakatsuki and Shidehara with the facts he replied that the Army had to defend itself. The news prompted Stimson to lodge a second protest and to make public his earlier note. As a result, the Foreign Minister requested Kanaya to signal Mukden immediately to withdraw its forces back across the Liao River 'regardless of existing circumstances'. The order had to be repeated in the Emperor's name before it was finally heeded, and it would prove to be Shidehara's last throw.

Stimson's protests had been preceded by regular appeals to Japan (and even to China) from the President of the League of Nations' Council 'not to aggravate the situation further' after each new expansion of Japanese operations, and when the Council reconvened on November 16th talk began to be heard at an unofficial level of imposing economic sanctions on Japan. In order to head off this uninviting prospect, Tokyo decided to reverse its previous stand against outside intervention and invited the dispatch of a Commission of Inquiry. It was at this juncture that China produced the 'Tanaka Memorial' as evidence of Japan's duplicity, and this change of attitude was designed to substantiate the reply that the document was 'a forgery from beginning to end'.

This show of sincerity was almost immediately nullified by the news of the advance on Chinchow, especially as the Japanese delegate had only a day earlier labelled it as 'entirely unfounded and, in fact, absurd'. When China then proposed the establishment of a neutral zone around Chinchow to be manned by an international peace-keeping force, Japan replied that if China withdrew her forces south of the Great Wall she too would undertake not to enter the zone 'except in the event of a serious and urgent threat endangering the safety of the lives and property of Japanese nationals'. Having seen such a proviso used by Japan so many times in the past as a pretext for violating her sovereignty, nothing would induce China to put her name to one again, and the proposal lapsed.

With deadlock threatening, pressure was applied on China to accept the earlier Japanese proposal for a Commission of Inquiry. Reluctantly, and much against her better judgement, China agreed, and on December 10th the Council appointed five Commissioners under the Chairmanship of Lord Lytton; China and Japan were each invited to add an 'assessor' of their choice.

Once again Japan had succeeded in warding off the threat of external interference in her designs. Not only had the time limit for her withdrawal from the newly-occupied areas now been dropped, but in affirming the resolution establishing the Commission her delegate had even been able to reserve the right to take military measures 'against the activities of bandits and other lawless elements in Manchuria', giving her *carte blanche* to complete her absorption of the country at her leisure in the certain knowledge that nothing would be done in the international arena while the League waited for the Commission's conclusions. The last slender hope that the diplomatic approach of a representative government might prevail over the conquistadorial ambitions of the militarists had been swept away; as the Last Noble Saionji bitterly observed, diplomacy was now dismissed 'by the entire nation as mistaken and wrong'.

TOO LATE

Even as the Commission was being voted through in Geneva, the Wakatsuki Cabinet in Tokyo was being finally undermined. For some weeks the Home Minister, Queen-Murderer Adachi, had been advocating a coalition with the Seiyukai, but the suggestion was strongly opposed by Wakatsuki and Shidehara who saw that it would entail the surrender of their policy of diplomacy. Finance Minister Inoue was no more enthusiastic because on November 11th the Seiyukai caucus had passed a resolution to abandon the gold standard. These fears were well grounded, for Adachi had established a close relationship with Araki, the rapidly emerging spokesman of the hardline expansionists. On December 10th Adachi refused to attend a Cabinet meeting and Wakatsuki called on him to resign, but the Home Minister refused to do so unless the rest of the Cabinet did likewise.

The flight into dollars quickly reached panic proportions, and in the month after the announcement of the Seiyukai resolution the Bank of Japan saw its gold reserves nearly halved. In order to stave off a total collapse of the currency, Wakatsuki and his colleagues saw no option but to submit to Adachi's arm-twisting. Shop assistants in Tokyo spent all weekend marking up prices in anticipation, and when the export of gold was duly embargoed on the Monday morning the conglomerates were able to thank the incoming Seiyukai Cabinet headed by Inukai for a paper profit of some 60 million yen. Neither were to enjoy its fruits for very long, however; for the population at large, and for the military in particular, it provided the final proof of the corrupt collusion between party politics and big business, whose days were now correspondingly numbered.

Inukai, with an eye only on maintaining himself in office, once again bound himself to the militarists' coat-tails, appointing Araki Minister of War, his *alter ego* Mazaki Jinzaburo Vice-Chief of Staff and 'The Arch-Schemer' Mori to the key position of Cabinet Secretary. The Prime Minister was persuaded by his past contacts with Sun Yat-sen and Chiang Kai-shek that he was uniquely qualified to negotiate a settlement with China which met Japan's economic demands; by the same token he also believed that these appointments would leave him better placed to fulfil Hirohito's injunction to correct 'the lack of discipline and despotism of the military' and to subordinate their territorial ambitions. Their effect was, however, quite the opposite: it would be he who was made the Army's prisoner rather than vice versa, as he would discover within the week.

On December 17th the Conspirators ordered an attack on 'soldier-bandits' across the River Liao north of Chinchow, and the high command issued another order in the Emperor's name not restraining them as before, but actually sending in reinforcements. In the absence of any response from the Cabinet, a general advance on Chinchow commenced four days later. Britain, France and America lodged forceful protests, but Japan dismissed them by pointing to the right to take military measures which she reserved for herself in putting her name to the League of Nations resolution, adding that 'we trust that this sincerity and forbearance are in accord with the spirit and faithfulness to obligations based on the aforesaid resolution'. Hearing that a division from the Korean Army was also about to be thrown into the attack, Chang decided to evacuate the temporary capital and fall back behind the Great Wall. By January 3rd 1932 Chinchow had fallen.

The news roused Stimson to issue an even more strongly-worded censure, and in warning Japan that the United States would refuse to recognise any outcome in Manchuria which contravened established international treaty rights he put himself well in advance of the League, whose support for his new stand was decidedly lukewarm. Noting this, the Japanese delegate replied, with an effrontery that must have strained even his adamantine facial muscles, that his Government was 'glad to receive this additional assurance that the Government of the United States can always be relied on to do everything in their power to support Japan's efforts to secure the full and complete fulfilment in every detail of the Washington and Kellogg treaties for the outlawry of war'. In the longer term, however, Stimson's initiative was to be an important influence on the rest of the world's adoption of a policy of non-recognition towards the puppet regime that Japan was shortly to establish.

Two weeks later the action moved into China proper with the staging of another 'incident' in Shanghai (which will be described in the next chapter). Its purpose was two-fold: to satisfy the increasingly strident demands from the more radical elements in the Navy for a share in the glory, and to divert the world's attention from the Kwantung Army's final thrust into northern Manchuria. This was the attack on Harbin, where the local Chinese leader had refused every Japanese blandishment to change sides. The high command ordered that the attack should be handled with 'extreme caution', for they still harboured a real fear of Russian intervention. Hence it was preceded by the usual activities of *agents provocateurs* and an assault by Chinese troops in the pay of a local collaborator, but when the international headlines were safely preoccupied with Shanghai the 2nd Division moved up and occupied the city on February 5th 1932.

NEW ROBES FOR HENRY

All Manchuria was now under the control of the Kwantung Army. Even before Harbin fell a Supreme Administrative Council had been set up together with a 'Self-Government Guiding Board' which was to foster 'independence movements' in the four proposed provinces. By February 17th each of the puppet 'Provincial Governors' had declared their independence, and the following day the creation of a new independent State was announced. The Inukai Cabinet had eventually accepted the Conspirators' constitutional blueprint of October 24th 1931 in its entirety, declaring that 'Manchuria and Mongolia will be made an essential part of the existence of the Empire; the area will be closely related to the political, economic, defence, transport and communications affairs of the Empire, and it will be under Japanese protection,' and in order to conform with Japan's international treaty obligations the establishment of the new state 'was to take the form of voluntary action by the Chinese'.

Inukai had at first attempted to set negotiations in motion for a settlement with China which would recognise Chinese sovereignty over Manchuria, but these had been abruptly terminated when they became known to Mori, who promptly leaked them to the Army. This had followed a visit from Itagaki to press for the need to cut all Manchuria's existing ties with China; such a step was, he conceded, in contravention of the Washington Treaty and the League of Nations' Covenant but he argued that 'it is not against the spirit of the respective international agreements for the Chinese themselves to break up internally (*sic*)'. In early February the new Foreign Minister had asked Ishihara to postpone independence because of the likely international repercussions, but he had replied that everything had now been arranged and was past the point of no return.

The Cabinet also finally accepted the Conspirators' proposal of Pu-Yi as the nominal head of the new State, and some discussion now ensued on what political form his position should take. Some argued for one of outright monarchy, but in the end it was decided, in deference to world opinion, that a republic should be declared and that 'Henry' should hold the title of 'Chief Executive'. He was threatened with 'drastic action' by Itagaki should he decline to fall in with the scheme.

His wife was still stoutly refusing to join him, and Doihara had been obliged to call in the services of Princess Yoshiko, the daughter of the earlier Japanese cat's-paw in Manchuria, Prince Su. Now the mistress of Japan's master spy in China, Tanaka Ryukichi, and already herself a practised promoter of the Japanese cause, the beguiling 'Eastern Jewel', as she was known, was soon able to cajole her childhood companion out of her fears. The unfortunate couple were not to be reunited for long, however, for 'Henry' had to be rehearsed in his new walk-on part on the world stage, and his opium-addicted wife was not considered likely to make a favourable impression as a royal consort.

The new State of 'Manchukuo' was proclaimed on March 1st 1932. Under the ever-watchful eye of Child-Strangler Amakasu, Pu-Yi was taken by special train to his new capital of Changchun, now relabelled Hsinking. Nine days later he was formally inaugurated as Head of State. Flanked on either side by Commander-in-Chief Honjo and the President of the SMR, he remained silent throughout the ceremony, which, although declared to be representing 'the will of 30 million people', was witnessed by no more than 200 carefully-selected and heavily-guarded guests. The next day saw an exchange of letters (actually signed four days earlier) between 'Henry' and Honjo, in which the 'Chief Executive' formally requested the services of Japanese advisers. In accordance with the blue-print, these advisers 'were to supervise and direct operations' in every department of government with the approval of an overseer 'who was constantly to maintain contact with the Kwantung Army Staff office'; they were to take care, however, to see that 'Japanese supervision and direction should as much as possible be below the surface and be limited to behind-the-scenes manipulation'.

'Henry' was later to describe the sum total of his duties as 'Chief Executive' thus: 'When the Kwantung Army made a decision, they would write it down and tell me to sign it. Edicts, laws, treaties, everything was managed in the same way. When I was first appointed, I used to go into my office about nine o'clock in the morning and wait for an hour or so. Then, as there was nothing to do, I would return to my quarters. Later, I just stayed away from the office altogether.' To compensate him for such exertions, he was paid an annual sum of £90,000, over 100 times more than the salary of the Japanese Prime Minister of the day. Two years later he would be further exalted by the title of 'Emperor'. His autobiography recalls his child-like joy at the news: 'My first thought was that I would have to get a set of Imperial robes . . . the robes that I had been dreaming of for 22 years.'

IN THE DOCK

Despite the distraction of events in Shanghai, the absorption of Manchuria had not, of course, gone unnoticed in Geneva, and on March 11th the League Assembly passed a resolution incorporating the American prin-ciple of non-recognition of the new State. In the face of this fresh hostility (and the as yet unstated but obvious threat of economic sanctions), a committee was set up under the Chairmanship of 'The Arch-Schemer' Mori to review the question of Japan's own (public) relationship to 'Manchukuo'. Its conclusion, approved by Hirohito, was that Japan 'for the time being should not grant recognition within the meaning of International Law'.

The recent arrival of the Lytton Commission was also looming large in Tokyo's considerations, and great lengths were taken to see that it received the right impression. Wherever the Commissioners travelled in Manchuria they were attended by a heavy police guard, ostensibly for their own security but in reality to prevent them making contact with anyone not previously vetted. The attention given to China's assessor Wellington Koo was particularly heavy-handed; his escort comprised Japanese soldiers with fixed bayonets, and even inside his hotel he was followed from room to room by a posse of plain-clothes agents.

In spite of this rigid quarantine, some 1500 letters were smuggled through to the Commissioners, and of these all but two were bitterly hostile to the new 'paradise for all races'. Even more embarrassingly, Ma took to the northern hills again with the $2m that had been used to buy his acceptance of the post of War Minister in the 'Cabinet' and launched another vigorous campaign to demonstrate that the new State represented the will of rather less than the whole population. Araki evidently decided that all the precautions had gone for nothing. 'Let the League of Nations say whatever it pleases,' he proclaimed in a speech to the National Foundations Association, 'let America offer whatever interference, let Russia attempt to disturb the peace in Manchuria as hard as she will, and let China decry Japan's action at the top of her voice, but Japan must adhere to her course unswervingly.'

After yet another Prime-Ministerial assassin's bullet removed Inukai on May 15th, the demand for 'Manchukuo's recognition grew ever more insistent. Deeply compromised as he was by his currying to the expansionists in his drive to gain office, Inukai was still the last holder of the office by virtue of the leadership of a political party to offer any prospect of a restraining influence on their ambitions. On the instigation of his successor, Admiral Saito Makoto, a former Aide-de-Camp to the Emperor Meiji, the Lower House in the Diet unanimously passed a motion calling for immediate recognition.

When the Lytton Commission returned to Japan on July 4th to assess the attitude of the new Cabinet, they were greeted by a well-orchestrated series of mass demonstrations parading the same demand, while the new Foreign Minister, who as President of the SMR had given his blessing to the use of the railway for troop movements in flagrant violation of the Treaty of Peking, left them in no doubt that recognition was only a matter of time and that it was 'regarded as not in conflict with the Nine Power Treaty'. 'There is no longer any room left for direct negotiations with China', he went on, and therefore China should be told that she 'should not rely on the League for settlement of the present case.'

The following month Honjo gave up the Command of the Kwantung Army and returned to Tokyo to become Hirohito's Aide-de-Camp. He was succeeded in the field by the man he himself had replaced two years earlier, Muto 'The Silent'. As Commander-in-Chief and unaccredited 'ambassador' to 'Manchukuo', Muto was commissioned to negotiate a 'treaty' between Japan and the new State. On the 25th the Foreign Minister informed the Diet that the final preparations for recognition were on the point of completion, declaring that the Japanese people need not be worried by an adverse reaction overseas because they were 'solidly determined not to concede a foot even if the country is turned into scorched earth'. This attitude was expressed even more uncompromisingly by Mori, who asserted that it would serve notice to the world that Japan 'now defiantly rose from her traditional diplomacy characterized by servility and sixty years of blind imitation of Western materialistic civilisation'. More ominously still, the Cabinet announced that it was 'to take early measures with regard to the replenishment of armaments, and to give full consideration to emergency economic and national mobilisation'; it also spoke of the need for 'various internal as well as external preparations to be rapidly made against the United States'.

When the newly-promoted Major-General Itagaki cabled two weeks later that everything was ready at his end, Hirohito had the draft of the proposed 'treaty' referred to a Privy Council committee under the National Foundations Association's President, Baron Hiranuma, for examination. Within the space of three more days it was redrafted, Imperially sanctioned, signed and published to the world, thus pre-empting the publication of the Lytton Report.

When they appeared on October 2nd the Commission's findings hardly took the world by surprise. They disclosed that 'the military operations of the Japanese troops cannot be regarded as measures of legitimate self-defence' . . . the Japanese 'had a carefully prepared plan to meet the case of hostilities between themselves and the Chinese. On the night of September 18-19th, this plan was put into operation with swiftness and precision. The Chinese had no plan of attacking the Japanese troops or of endangering the lives and properties of Japanese nationals . . .'

As for the 'Independence Movement' that Tokyo had made so much play of, they decided that it 'had never been heard of in Manchuria before September 1931 . . . The evidence received from all sources has satisfied the Commission that, while there were a number of other factors which contributed to the creation of Manchukuo, the two which, in combination, were most effective and without which, in our judgement, the new state could not have been formed, were the presence of Japanese troops and the activities of Japanese officials, both civil and military. For this reason, the present regime cannot be considered to have been called into existence by a genuine and spontaneous independence movement.'

Their verdict was unequivocal: 'It is a fact that without declaration of war, a large area of what was indisputably Chinese territory has been forcibly seized and occupied by the armed forces of Japan and has in consequence of this operation been separated from and declared independent of the rest of China.' In conclusion, the Report recommended that a largely autonomous administration should be set up which would still formally acknowledge Chinese sovereignty, that all armed forces should be withdrawn and replaced by a local gendarmerie, and that Japan should be guaranteed the right to develop her economic interests 'without carrying with it a right to control the country either economically or politically'.

The reaction in Tokyo was equally predictable. When it was first released at a Press Conference, those journalists present almost without exception expressed their surprise at its completeness and objectivity, but their editorials the following morning of course contained nothing but indignation and ridicule. In the Diet only the frail voice of the 'Blasphemer' Yukio, the doyen of the liberal parliamentarians, could be heard in the Commission's defence, declaring that it was 'a high act of nonsense to suggest that Manchukuo had been formed by the free will of its people'. In the Cabinet War Minister Araki dismissed it as 'a travelogue'.

SELF-DISCHARGE

A committee was set up under Araki and his Foreign Minister colleague to draft Japan's response, and after receiving Hirohito's approval it was forwarded to Geneva. The task of presenting it to the League's Assembly was allotted to the ever-voluble Matsuoka, whose facility for verbal gloss had already caused his fellow members of the Diet to dub him 'The Talking Machine'. He had also stepped into the shoes of the recently-deceased 'Arch-Schemer' Mori as the leading Fifth Columnist within the parliamentary system. The following year he would resign his seat and, in an article entitled 'Dissolve the Political Parties', would openly proclaim that 'the day is fast approaching when the nation, spewing out the evil results of contact with Western civilisation, will become what its true nature would have it be ... We must throw aside any institution, organisation or notion that interferes with co-operation [under the guidance of the Emperor]. If the political parties fall into this category, why not get rid of them? ... The national spirit is politically rooted in the concept of the whole nation as a single family which has always had the Emperor as its patriarch ... government by parties, being based on Western individualism, liberalism and democracy, does not suit Japanese conditions or the nature of the Japanese people.'

The Lytton Report was, Araki's committee concluded, 'marked by omissions, inconsistencies and misapprehensions', and to the familiar claims to the spontaneity of the 'independence movement' and its exemption from the provisions of the Paris and Washington Treaties they added the novel one that because of China's continuing internal disharmony she no longer held to the description of an 'organised state' as defined therein.

In Geneva, Matsuoka followed up with his own pungent observations, asserting that Japan had never entertained a policy of continental expansion, but that, on the contrary, she had 'an innate love of peace'; that peace, however, was 'not peace on paper, but peace based on realities' — and those 'realities' were embodied in the recognition of 'Manchukuo'. He concluded by declaring that 'Japan has been and is a loyal supporter of the League, and hopes to remain so if she does not find it absolutely incompatible with the existence of Japan, as well as with her great policy of maintaining and preserving peace and order in the Far East.'

This not-so-veiled hint that Japan would opt out of the League if it refused to recognise 'Manchukuo' was followed by an even more overt threat when a motion of censure was proposed after the issue was passed to the Assembly; its passage would, Matsuoka warned, result in consequences 'which were perhaps unintended or unanticipated by its sponsors'. In making these, he was reflecting not the collective attitude of his Government at home, but only that of the War Minister, Araki. Indeed, the rest of the Cabinet were anxiously searching for a formula that would head off a collision. Once again, however, the rug was to be pulled from beneath them by the Kwantung Army.

Taking their cue from a speech on Christmas Day 1932 by Araki in which he declared that 'any part of Jehol which the Kwantung Army feels forced to occupy in defence of its flank, it will undoubtedly keep,' its forces breached the Great Wall on New Year's Day 1933 and seized the Chinese half of the border town of Shanhaikwan. The pretext for this action was that 'someone hurled two bombs and fired two rifle rounds' into the yard of the Japanese garrison on the north side of the Wall, but it quickly transpired that the 'someone' had been a member of the garrison acting under the direct order of its commander.

Nothing daunted by this revelation, the 6th and 8th Divisions (which had been dispatched to Manchuria as early as April with secret orders to occupy Jehol) prepared to move inland along the Great Wall, and on February 9th 1933 the Kwantung Army Commander, Muto, drafted his 'Jehol Subjugation Plan', explaining that 'the affairs of Jehol are unquestionably an internal problem of Manchukuo . . . Because subjugation of the province is designed to strike a fatal blow to anti-Manchukuo, anti-Japan elements, these elements purposely confuse the distinction between Jehol and North China. They move troops in to the province and, glossing over these matters, raise a loud outcry that Japan harbours designs of territorial aggression.' Air raids had already been softening up the province for some months (not least with leaflets inviting its inhabitants to join the 'paradise' of Manchukuo), and Chang's demoralised and ill co-ordinated defenders offered little resistance. On March 4th Jehol City (Chengteh) fell and the campaign was over. Plan Three of Ishihira's and Itagaki's blueprint for Manchuria and Inner Mongolia had been completed.

With the lie so effectively given to all Matsuoka's protestations of injured innocence, the League of Nations Assembly was moved, in a rare display of unanimity, to pass a resolution refusing recognition to 'Manchukuo' and incorporating the recommendations of the Lytton Report by 42 votes to nil, with the single abstention of Thailand. Even Saionji now accepted that 'withdrawal is inevitable', and a draft ordinance to that effect was submitted to the Imperial Palace.

Conscious of the danger that as a non-member of the League Japan might be required to surrender her mandate over the former German Pacific islands, Hirohito hesitated, until the country's leading jurists assured him that in their opinion Japan had obtained her title to them not from the Treaty of Versailles but from the secret treaties made earlier with Britain and France. Accordingly he summoned the Privy Council on March 27th to the Palace, where they voted unanimously in favour of withdrawal.

The decision was then announced in an Imperial Rescript. According to this, it had been necessitated by 'a wide divergence of views in regard to the need to respect the independence of the new state and to encourage its healthy development in order that sources of evil in the Far East may be eradicated and enduring peace thereby established...' After the ritual lip-service to the wish to maintain 'mutual confidence' with the rest of the world, Hirohito went on to warn His subjects to prepare themselves for a quite different scenario: 'Our Empire is confronted by a situation fraught with momentous possibilities. It is indeed an hour that calls for intensification of effort on the part of our entire nation. We command that all public servants, whether civil or military, shall faithfully perform each his appointed duty ...'

A few hours later in Geneva 'The Talking Machine' Matsuoka rose from his seat to concede that all his flights of oratory had been in vain. Having given two years' notice of his country's withdrawal (as required by the League's Articles) he beckoned to the rest of the Japanese delegation and led them briskly out of the Assembly Chamber.

Japan was not to remain the lone outcast for long, however, for that same month Adolf Hitler's National Socialists became the largest party in the German Reichstag.

22

Dissension in the Ranks

ULTIMATUM IN SHANGHAI

As the Kwantung Army prepared early in January 1932 for the assault on Harbin, Inseparable Itagaki had returned to Tokyo to win approval for his 'Manchukuo' blueprint. The consequences of flouting international opinion had at last given even the Conspirators in Mukden some food for thought, impressing them with the need to divert the eyes of the world from this final and least easily disguised stage of the occupation of Manchuria.

On January 10th, a day before his scheduled audience with Hirohito, he accordingly signalled to Master-Spy Tanaka in Shanghai to set the wheels of the planned diversion in motion. 'The Manchurian Incident has developed as expected, but the opposition of the major Powers is still giving certain persons at the centre doubts,' his telegram ran. 'So please use the current tension between China and Japan to bring off your incident and turn the eyes of the Powers towards Shanghai.'

That tension was certainly at an all time high. The fall of the Wakatsuki/Shidehara Cabinet had virtually removed any prospect of a settlement of the 'Manchurian question' being reached by diplomatic negotiation, while the Chinese boycott of Japanese goods instigated in the wake of the 'Mukden Incident' had resulted in a drop in sales of nearly 40% — in Shanghai its effect had been even more marked, forcing the closure of 90% of Japanese-owned factories there. Relations had been still further strained only the previous day, when a Korean nationalist had made a second attempt on Hirohito's life; a Chinese news agency had written of it that 'unfortunately he threw it at the wrong carriage,' giving the local Japanese residents the pretext for a field day of indignation. The fact that Itagaki happened to be in Tokyo that same day has been seen as more than a coincidence; on the other hand, little play was made of it in Shanghai when events presently began to unfold there (in Tsingtao, by contrast, a Japanese mob set fire to the local Press office and then refused the fire brigade access).

It was eight days later that Tanaka engineered a pretext for action in Shanghai. As five Japanese priests of the aggressively nationalistic Nichiren sect passed in noisy procession alongside a towel factory in the central commercial district of Chapei, they were set upon by a number of the factory's labour force hired by Tanaka for the purpose. One of them subsequently died from wounds received in the fracas. That same night a gang recruited from the Japanese Young Men's One Purpose Society attacked the factory and burnt it to the ground; when a force of Chinese police arrived on the scene, a thorough-going battle developed in which two Chinese and one Japanese were killed.

Almost before dawn had broken the Japanese Consul-General issued a protest and demanded an apology, full reparations, the arrest of those responsible for the deaths of his compatriots and an end to the boycott and all 'anti-Japanese feeling'. The Mayor of Shanghai promised to comply as far as he was able to, pointing out, however, that he was not in a position to control the private sentiments of individuals. This was not judged to be sufficient, and he was warned that 'in the event of such compliance being refused, we are determined to take such steps as may be necessary'. That same afternoon a meeting of Japanese residents called for the dispatch of reinforcements from Japan for their protection.

The Imperial Navy was only too ready to oblige; if they continued to allow the Army to hog the glory, the Naval Staff feared that their own share of the military budget would be correspondingly reduced. As early as October 1931 the local commander of Japanese marine forces in Shanghai, Rear Admiral Shiozawa Koichi, had threatened 'decisive action' to protect Japanese interests there, but at that stage Shidehara had felt himself in a strong enough position to ignore his calls for reinforcements. With Shidehara Foreign Minister no longer, the new Vice-Minister of the Navy felt able to assert that 'it is now the Navy's turn to get to work'. Within a week an aircraft carrier, a cruiser, four destroyers and a torpedo squadron had dropped anchor in the Yangtse roads, together with a full regiment of marines.

With this impressive armada at his back, Shiozawa now issued an ultimatum giving notice that unless his demands were met in full by 6pm the following day (the 28th) he would take military action. He would 'blast the Chinese out of Chapei in 48 hours', he confidently informed Western journalists. An alarmed Municipal Council of the International Settlement promptly declared a state of emergency and mobilised their individual garrisons. This was exactly the reaction that Shiozawa had counted on, for by involving the other Powers he hoped to avoid giving the impression to the outside world that Japan was acting unilaterally. That he was set on action regardless of the Chinese response could already have been inferred from the fact that all Japanese residents had been evacuated from Chapei two days earlier, and with an hour still to run he himself confirmed to the correspondent of the *New York Times* that the total acceptance of his demands was 'beside the point'.

Early the next afternoon the Mayor notified the Japanese Consul-General that he was prepared to concede even the demand to force an end to the boycott and to dissolve all the organisations behind it. The Consul-General announced this to be 'fully satisfactory', but when he was asked whether the threat of military action was now removed he would only reply 'for the present'. At dusk Shiozawa brought the last of his marines ashore and at 8.30 pm issued the following declaration: 'The Imperial Navy, feeling extreme anxiety about the situation in Chapei where Japanese nationals reside in great numbers [but had already, of course, been evacuated], has decided to send out troops to this district for the enforcement of law and order in the area. In these circumstances I earnestly hope that the Chinese authorities will speedily withdraw the Chinese troops now stationed in Chapei.' The marines would move in at midnight, he added. The official copy of the declaration was not delivered to the Mayor until 11.25; he was thus given 35 minutes to evacuate 30,000 men. Indeed, he had even less, according to one Western eye witness who saw the Japanese advance out of their sector of the Settlement only twenty minutes later.

BLITZKRIEG

Shiozawa was doubtless hoping to complete the operation within the hours of darkness, but he had reckoned without the fighting qualities of the defending 19th Route Army which had recently been transferred to Shanghai after successfully driving Mao's Communists back into the mountains of Kwangsi (from where it would shortly set out on its Long March into the hinterland of the North West). In anticipation of a Japanese attack it had concentrated its defences around the North Station, and as the Japanese advanced across the main line they were quickly cut off and routed.

The sight of his marines discarding their arms and fleeing back into their own sector must have come as a disagreeable surprise to their commander, and at first light he brought in his 70 carrier planes. All that day they flew non-stop bombing sorties, concentrating first on the Chinese defences around the North Station but then spreading outwards over the whole of densely-populated Chapei; having released their bombs, they then dropped down to machine-gun fleeing civilians. Thousands of women and children died in the carnage and Shiozawa would be labelled 'Baby-Killer' by the rest of the world. The raid on Chinchow had given a premonition of such tactics, but this was the first time that the world had witnessed the systematic and indiscriminate bombing of a civilian population from the air; unhappily, it set an all too familiar precedent. Another notable casualty was the Commercial Press building housing the Oriental Library and its priceless collection of ancient scrolls and manuscripts; it was completely gutted by incendiaries.

Not content with devastating Chapei, Shiozawa called up the 4,000 reservists in the Japanese colony and gave them the task of putting the

International Settlement under Japanese control. Having disarmed the Settlement's international police force, these set about terrorising the Chinese residents, concentrating particularly on traders who had refused to stock Japanese goods; their shops were burnt, their houses looted and their families pulled out and driven away, in many cases never to be seen again.

The news of these atrocities naturally heightened fears of Japanese intentions in the rest of the world, particularly in the United States. At Geneva Japan's representative announced that it had been the Chinese who had opened fire first and that 'our forces were thus compelled to reply and conflicts occurred ... We have not in any sense made use of the International Settlement as a base for attack on the Chinese.' While admitting that 'excesses have been committed when feeling was running high and chaotic conditions prevailed', he went on to reassure fellow delegates that his Government 'are prompted by no other motive than that of discharging their international duty and of safeguarding the large number of Japanese nationals and Japanese property ... They have already declared that they cherish no political ambitions in the region of Shanghai nor any thought of encroaching there upon the rights and interests of any other Powers.' Similarly, the Navy declared that they were only motivated by 'a policy of seeking the sincere co-operation and friendship of our dear neighbours, the Chinese'. Not every Japanese who had witnessed the events was prepared to go along with these lies, however: one member of the Legation in Shanghai asked to be recalled in disgust at his compatriots' behaviour.

A truce was arranged the following day through the offices of the American and British Consuls, but Shiozawa used it merely as an opportunity to regroup and to appeal to Tokyo for further reinforcements. A squadron headed by two more aircraft carriers under the command of Nomura Kichisaburo (the man who eight years later would be dispatched to Washington with the thankless task of convincing America of Japan's commitment to peace even as Yamamoto's carrier force steamed towards Pearl Harbor), duly set sail within 24 hours. For the succeeding three days the marines attempted to advance out of different sectors of the Settlement under the cover of further blanket bombing, but each sally only stiffened the resistance of the 19th Route Army. Outnumbered by a factor of some eight to one, Shiozawa was forced to swallow the bitter truth that only the Army could now rescue him from failure.

The Navy asked for the dispatch of a mixed brigade, but the War Ministry decided that a full division was needed. A protracted argument followed as to which service had the right to determine the size of the force, but the seriousness of the situation eventually forced the Navy to back down. Hirohito gave his approval, but at the same time, in a move to ensure that this development would not threaten his own plans for future expansion, he elevated his wife's cousin, Prince Fushimi, to the post of Navy Chief of Staff — just as two months earlier, he had secured the promotion of her uncle, Prince Kanin, to that of Army Chief of Staff. It was the Chief of Staff, rather than the Minister for the Army or Navy, who had the decisive say because it lay in his gift to appoint the third member of the 'Big Three' of each service.

The 9th Division landed at Shanghai on February 16th with orders to persuade the Chinese to withdraw peacefully if possible and to permit the creation of a neutral zone. The city's determined defenders refused, however, even when presented with an ultimatum. The Japanese then attacked again, but even with their greatly increased numbers they could still make little impression on the 19th Route Army. The situation was now critical, for the Lytton Commission was due to call at Shanghai on its way to Manchuria in less than three weeks' time. Nomura, who had taken over from the disgraced Shiozawa, appealed desperately for yet more reinforcements. Despite the opposition of Takahashi, the incumbent once more at the Finance Ministry, the military had their way — when Hirohito himself was reported to be expressing some unease, the Navy Minister told Fushimi 'not to worry the Emperor with politics' — and two further divisions were mobilised.

The advance guard landed on February 28th and immediately joined the 9th Division in a sweep south to cut off the gallant Chinese, who were now preparing to withdraw in the face of this new and vastly superior force. On the same day 'The Talking Machine' Matsuoka arrived to initiate a new round of truce negotiations in advance of the next session of the League of Nations Assembly on March 3rd. Tokyo was on the point of declaring the independence of 'Manchukuo', and that fiction was seen as more likely to be swallowed by the outside world if hostilities in Shanghai were brought to a close before that date. It was hoped that a decisive vistory could be scored in the few days remaining, but in fact most of the retreating Chinese were able to slip through the net. Both sides accepted the truce which the League duly called, although the Japanese continued to land the remainder of the two newly-arrived divisions.

An International Committee was appointed to draw up terms for a settlement, and China succeeded in having the negotiations transferred to Geneva. When the Committee set a deadline of May 31st for the withdrawal of all troops Japan bitterly protested that this constituted an infringement of the Imperial Prerogative, but her hand was eventually forced by the need to rush the divisions in Shanghai to northern Manchuria in order to deal with the outbreak of a serious guerrilla campaign there. As they pulled out, construction work began on an enormous new barracks in the Japanese sector of the Settlement and, perhaps even more ominously, on the erection of a grandiose Shinto shrine.

PATRIOTS' PUTSCH

This palpable climbdown in the face of external opinion brought to a new head the simmering battle of wills between the established hierarchy wedded to the gradualist programme of expansion and the more radical, impatient element typified by the younger officers and their acknowledged leader, the new Minister of War, Araki. The outcome was a rash of new nationalistic societies dedicated to the realisation of the 'Showa Restoration', that uniquely Japanese compound of left-wing fascist anti-capitalism and right-wing monarchist authoritarianism simultaneously committed to sweeping away both the monopolistic conglomerates and the political parties, and exemplified by the claim that 'the Monarchy in Japan is unlimited and all-embracing'.

In the services, the most important of these organisations was the Kodoha or Imperial Road Association, and its formation brought the division in the ranks firmly into the open. This division was made still wider by Araki's action in purging the high command of its remaining Choshu components, and it led to the counter-formation of a Purification Group under Mukden-Collaborators Koiso and Tatekawa ostensibly dedicated to the removal of all *han* cliques. This claim was viewed somewhat sceptically, however, by the non-Choshu element, and the main opposition to the Imperial Roadsters rallied round the more astute figure of Mass-Mobiliser Nagata; known as the 'Control Group', this faction represented the brains behind the plan approved by the Emperor for harnessing the old-style zeal of the *samurai* to a force as modern in its strategy as in its equipment.

Among the civilian activists, by contrast, dissatisfaction with the Government's performance led to a harmonisation of the disparate factions, notably between those represented by 'Doctor' Okawa Shumei and the quasi-socialist Kita Ikki. Kita had long since retired into monastic seclusion, but he had left behind him the 'Society of the White Wolf', a terrorist organisation committed to 'resolving all social problems by actual force on the basis of justice and the *samurai* spirit'. It had subsequently been taken over by an agrarian activist, Tachibana Kozaburo, and transformed into a 'School of Love for the Native Soil' in Mito, the repository of terrorist tradition dating back to the assassination of the 'Atrocious Autocrat' Ii in 1860. Another of its leading lights was an ex-Black Dragon agent and Buddhist priest, whose brother had established a similarly-committed cell among the naval pilots at the nearby 'Misty Lagoon' School of Experimental Flying (whose research with torpedo bombers would prove itself so spectacularly a decade later at Pearl Harbor). The two had then combined to recruit 'The Blood Brotherhood', an élite band of dedicated terrorists.

The issue over which Okawa and Kita had fallen out was, it will be remembered, that of nationalisation, but criticism voiced by the conglomerates at the cost of the Shanghai expedition had finally persuaded Okawa that they could no longer be allowed the rôle of free agents. On February 11th he launched the Jimmu Society, whose manifesto pledged it to 'destroy the abuses of the political parties and work for an Imperial political and economic organisation' and, on a wider scale, to 'secure the emancipation of the non-white races and moral unification of the world'. In its short life, it would take over the running among the patriotic societies from Uchida's Japan Production Society and even from the Black Dragon itself, whose original aims had now been fulfilled with the absorption of Manchuria and the extension of Japan's border to the River Amur of its title.

In calling for the end of political parties the Jimmu Society matched the proclaimed objectives of the Imperial Road Association, and although the latter in due course recruited members from the civilian population, as it did also from the 3 million strong Reservist Association, the Jimmu Society acted for the moment as its civilian arm. Even inside the parties themselves a strong movement developed for their own subjugation at the hands of the military when, thanks to the Army's interception of his signals, it was revealed that Inukai was engaging in secret negotiations with the Chinese for the withdrawal of Japanese troops from Shanghai. 'The Arch-Schemer' Mori warned the Prime Minister that 'the Army is highly indignant', hinting even that his life was in danger. Araki in his new rôle as War Minister made little effort to conceal his own sympathies: while guaranteeing to see that military discipline was maintained, he told the Imperial Go-Between Konoye that he 'could not leave the Young Officers to their fate, when they were truly of pure intentions and were sincerely concerned for the nation'.

Mori began to conspire with Araki for Inukai's removal and his replacement by Baron Hiranuma at the head of an Army-dominated Cabinet. Konoye suggested that Inukai should be replaced as Prime Minister by Navy Chief of Staff and Imperial Cousin Prince Fushimi, but both Mori and Araki, perhaps wishing to counter the Imperial Family's commitment to the gradualist blueprint, saw the Big Baron as the most effective prosecutor of the Imperial Road programme. 'The Arch-Schemer' proposed that a committee should be set up under Hiranuma with the ostensible purpose of examining the problem of Army discipline, but it was to be invested with such wide powers that it would in fact represent a rival Cabinet. When Inukai rejected the suggestion, Mori retaliated by leaking a proposal by Inukai that Hirohito should dismiss thirty of the leading recalcitrants among the Young Officers, leading to furious accusations that the Prime Minister was 'attempting to control the Army by resorting to Imperial authority'.

On May 1st Inukai declared in a radio broadcast that, while he was well aware of 'the demoralised and corrupt social conditions that enraged the high-spirited people', the solution to them lay in the reform rather than the rejection of parliamentary government and that his majority in the recent election left him well placed to carry out this reform. The Prime Minister was effectively signing his own death warrant. The dedicated assassins of Tachibana's Blood Brotherhood had already found two successful targets in the Mitsui head, Dan Takuma, and former Finance Minister Inoue Jannosuki, and they now had Inukai firmly in their sights; indeed one of them had already been assigned to the task two months earlier, but had apparently lost his nerve.

The string-pullers of the patriotic movement moved in to ensure that there was no second failure. Toyama's association with Inukai stretched back to the turn of the century when they had jointly taken the refugee Sun Yat-sen under their wing, and on the fall of the Wakatsuki Cabinet he had cautioned his old friend against taking up the Premiership. Inukai had chosen to ignore the warning, and he could therefore, Toyama doubtless rationalised, only blame himself for the consequences. If the Godfather himself was not directly involved in the conspiracy (and he was now 79), both his son and his secretary certainly were, for it was they who provided Tachibana with the necessary funds; furthermore, both Toyama and his son were on record as wishing to see Mori Prime Minister, and Saionji's secretary Harada later alleged that Mori too was an active collaborator. Further funds were also provided by Okawa's Jimmu Society, as were the necessary murder weapons and bombs after they had first been obtained by Chief Cherry Hashimoto from sympathizers in the Kwantung Army.

The plot was set for May 15th. It had originally been planned for the previous day when the Prime Minister was due to hold a reception for the visiting Charlie Chaplin; if a bullet could find this 'darling of the capitalist class' as well (the Little Tramp would have been mortified to hear himself so described), so much the better — it would guarantee the greatest possible publicity for the cause. In the end, however, it was decided that security for the occasion would be prohibitively tight, whereas the following day was a Sunday and most policemen would be off duty. The assassination was entrusted to a group of Misty Lagoon officers and Military Academy cadets, while the Blood Brotherhood were to bomb power stations and some principal public buildings.

The Prime Minister was duly hunted down and dispatched in the supposed privacy of his official Residence. The Blood Brotherhood had less success, most of their bombs failing to explode and those that did caused little damage. Their mission over, they all dutifully surrendered to the police. Another group of officers confronted Vice-Chief of Staff Mazaki and demanded a military coup under Araki's leadership, but he was eventually able to give them the slip and have them arrested. In due course Okawa was also taken into custody, along with Toyama's son and secretary; Tachibana at first took flight to Manchuria 'to write a book', but presently returned and gave himself up.

HIGHEST TREASON

Those of The Blood Brotherhood still at liberty attempted to organise a direct appeal to the Emperor on behalf of their arrested 'kinsmen', only to be arrested in turn on a charge of *lèse-majesté*. This rejection inspired a still more audacious plot — nothing less than the removal of Hirohito himself from the Throne and his replacement by his more charismatic brother Chichibu.

The planners of the attempted October 1931 coup had not only accused the Imperial Household Ministry of dividing Hirohito from his subjects, but they had actually gone so far as to criticise the Emperor himself, calling him 'a mediocre person' and 'a pacifist'. Another source of dissatisfaction was his failure to date to produce a male heir (a fourth daughter had been born that March). When six months later it emerged that the Palace was pressing for a withdrawal from Shanghai, this disrespect for the Imperial personage had grown to such proportions that Saionji considered it a real danger that 'even if the Emperor were to caution them now, the Army probably would not obey him.'

Chichibu by contrast had already demonstrated himself to be un-ambiguously sympathetic to the young Army radicals over a number of years. While still a cadet at the Military Academy in 1923 he had obtained a clandestine copy of Kita's *Plan for the Reconstruction of Japan*, and after he had graduated, he told a leading Young Officer serving in the same regiment that 'I agree with your idea about the necessity to reform Japan. Please regard me as your comrade.' Imperial Aide-de-Camp Honjo's diary records that Chichibu had a 'fierce argument' with Hirohito after Inukai's murder, during which he told his brother that he should suspend the Constitution and impose direct Imperial rule. In September 1932 Konoye recommended Chichibu for the post of Lord Keeper of the Privy Seal where he would have been able to bring his influence to bear on Hirohito even more directly; the proposal was vetoed by Saionji, however, and he was assigned instead to the General Staff. The radicals' disenchantment became complete when in May 1933 Hirohito issued a direct order to Chief of Staff Uncle Kanin not to allow the Kwantung Army to advance beyond Jehol.

The plot, to take place on July 11th, also had as its object the liberation of the Blood Brothers, whose trial opened on June 28th, and it was organised in conjunction with a branch of Uchida's Japan Production Party who labelled themselves 'The Soldiers of God'. They were to storm the courthouse while police attention was diverted by a demonstration elsewhere in Tokyo by several hundred supporters; at the same time the cell-leader in the Misty Lagoon Flying School was to wipe out the Cabinet with an aerial attack on the Prime Minister's Residence, and on the ground bomb parties would account for leaders of the political parties and members of the Imperial Household. According to some accounts, not even Araki was to be spared, his offence having been to have allowed the arrest of the Blood Brothers in the first place. Hirohito would then be removed to the old Imperial capital of Kyoto and Chichibu placed on the Throne; the new Cabinet was to be headed by another Imperial Prince,

Hirohito's uncle, Higashikuni, who had established firm connections with the radicals and actually sheltered one of the plot's ringleaders under his own roof, an action which he later conceded to have been 'a great mistake'. Some months earlier Higashikuni had met with Tachibana's 'Land Lovers', even though Tachibana himself was then in police custody awaiting trial.

The plotters had also counted on the police being taken up with a visit that Hirohito was due to make the same day to the Military Academy, but this calculation proved in fact to be their undoing. The police had already been put on alert for the occasion, and it was as a result of this extra vigilance that the unusual number of Japan Production Party members were seen congregating the previous evening at a hostel which was well known to be a favourite activists' meeting place. A week after their arrest Higashikuni was invited to dinner with Konoye, Harada and Privy Seal Secretary Kido, who gently suggested to him that 'members of the Imperial Family should not act thoughtlessly' (he did not, as we shall see, interpret this as a warning to cut off his radical associations). The birth at last of a male heir to the Throne on December 23rd finally put an end to talk of a change of Emperor. No word of the affair was released in the Press until over four years later, when the trial of the accused opened; granted bail, they were finally sentenced in 1941, only to be immediately released again.

When the trial of the Blood Brothers eventually got under way, no time limit was placed on the defence and the whole process became a pro-paganda exercise for the virtues of the Imperial Road — Tachibana, for instance, was allowed to harangue the court for over a month. Their guilt was not contested, and their justification was the familiar one of having acted in the national interest — 'which is more important, the nation or the law?' The Osaka Bar Association pushed this curious logic to its ultimate extremity, advising a plea of 'self-defence'; if it takes a lawyer to subvert the law, perhaps only a Japanese lawyer would actually turn it on its head. Appeals for clemency flooded in from every quarter, some of them accompanied by severed little fingers as tokens of fellow-feeling; Araki declared himself in favour of obtaining an Imperial edict decreeing that they 'should be acquitted of all charges and allowed to resume their political activities afresh'.

For all his eloquence, Tachibana was sentenced to life imprisonment, and Okawa and the two Misty Lagoon ring-leaders to fifteen years apiece. The military cadets got only four years on the grounds that they had been misled by the doctrine of the Imperial Road — a plea which it would not have occurred to Araki to enter. The assassins of Inoue and Dan were similarly indulged; the former took advantage of the platform allowed to him to proclaim that 'Japan is the greatest country in the world and will eventually conquer the world'.

DOWN THE IMPERIAL ROAD

Two days after Inukai's death the General Staff had announced that it would refuse to nominate the War Minister in any Cabinet headed by a party politician. This represented the formal obituary of the parliamentary system, although the Seiyukai's willingness to pander to the demands of the military in pursuit of office had effectively sealed its death years earlier. Even Nagata, who characterised himself as 'possessing the weakest opinion in the Army', declared that 'a government by the existing political parties is absolutely rejected'. Mori immediately engineered the succession to the Seiyukai Party Presidency of Suzuki Kisaburo and at the same time pushed forward his proposal once again for a joint Seiyukai-military Cabinet under Hiranuma. Saionji, whose task it was to recommend a Prime Minister to the Emperor, refused absolutely to consider the Big Baron and settled for Suzuki as the lesser evil.

Hirohito himself set no conditions other than that the new man should have a clean personal record without fascist sympathies; the only *sine qua non* was that the Constitution should be maintained at all costs, 'otherwise I should not be able to justify myself to the Emperor Meiji'. In indicating that it was immaterial whether the new Cabinet was drawn from a single party or a coalition he seemed to be stating a preference for a politician, but the Army still refused to back down. In the end the deadlock was broken by the compromise choice of Admiral Saito; his record as a uniquely lenient governor of Korea recommended him to the Diet, while his fellow Admiral Togo pronounced him 'tolerable' to the Supreme Command by virtue of his membership of the advisory board of Hiranuma's National Foundations Association. Saito wanted the 'Border-Crosser' Hayashi as his War Minister, but he was quickly made to bow to the General Staff's insistence that Araki should continue in the office; unlike his Naval counterpart, Araki had felt himself under no obligation to resign in recognition of responsibility for the part of the military cadets in Inukai's murder.

Prime Minister now in all but name, Araki lost no time in attempting to frogmarch the country down the Imperial Road. His first priority was to secure an enormous increase in the military budget, which he justified by contending that the country should be mobilised for war with Russia in four years' time, on the strength of a convoluted argument that America would embark on a new programme of naval construction on the expiry of the London Treaty in 1936 and that Russia could then be expected to enter into an anti-Japanese alliance with her. 'Thus, should any dispute arise in the Far East it might easily assume calamitous proportions. The only way to forestall disaster is to increase our armaments,' he advised. In the eyes of his radical followers this carried the further advantage that it would provide a convenient excuse to mulct the hated conglomerates.

'At every Cabinet meeting he presents a new list of demands which leaves the [other] Ministers pale and speechless,' it was reported. 'It sometimes happens that Araki is the only one to take the floor.' 'The Crisis of 1936' became his catch-phrase; a 1936 Club was formed in the Reservists Association, which published a news-sheet every ten days expatiating on the inevitability of war with Russia. Despite the protests of veteran Finance Minister Takahashi, the military budget more than doubled in the years 1932-3 to a level where it accounted for 70% of the government's income and created an annual deficit of almost 1 billion yen, which another raid on Post Office savings accounts was only partially able to cover. The resultant fall in the value of the yen from 2 to 5 against the U.S. dollar led to an enormous upsurge in Japan's exports, arousing accusations of dumping from her competitors and, ironically, earning Takahashi the sobriquet of 'The Keynes of Japan'. He consoled himself that 'it is much harder to nullify the results of an economic conquest than those of a military conquest' — a remark which he was not to know would exactly describe the central theme of post-1945 Japanese policy after the attempt at military conquest failed.

Side by side with this demand for more arms came its natural corollary, the call that 'we must have national unity, exalting the spirit of nationalism'. The concept of *kokutai*, which had lost some of its momentum over the period of the 'democratic' experiment, was now to receive its second wind. 'I think that for Japan to get out of the present difficult situation, there is no other means than that the entire Japanese people decidedly and fully realise that they are Japanese. Only then will the development of Japan get into full swing,' Araki pronounced. 'The fundamental essence of the Japanese system of government is the unity of high and low, of the Ruler and His people. This points clearly to the aim of the Japanese which amounts to the glorification of the Emperor, for which purpose public welfare must take precedence over private, personal welfare ...'

'The Imperial Road is the embodiment of the union between the true soul of the Japanese state and the great ideal of the Japanese people, which must be preached and spread over the whole world. All obstacles interfering with this must be resolutely destroyed, not stopping at the application of real force.' This 'application of real force' did not stop at the coercion of Japan's own unfortunate citizens, Araki went on to make abundantly clear: 'Different countries in Eastern Asia are the objects of oppression on the part of the white race. Awakened Imperial Japan can no longer tolerate the arbitrariness of the white race ... The thought must here be expressed clearly and frankly that whatever enemy opposes the spread of the Imperial idea must be destroyed.'

Such a naked appeal to the nation's endemic chauvinism inevitably inspired the appearance of a fresh rash of patriotic societies, united under the umbrella organisation 'The Patriotic Movement United Consultative Society'. Their common slogan proclaimed that *kokutai* demanded 'the rendering of assistance to the Emperor', a theme which led seven years later to the creation of Konoye's Imperial Rule Assistance Association and heralded the arrival of the one-party state. One of them was the ominously-named 'Society of Enlightened Ethics' dedicated to curbing the influence of 'dangerous thinkers', 2,200 .of whom were arrested on October 10th 1932 alone. A particular target was a lecturer at Kyoto University who suggested that the Constitution was more important than the Emperor; when his fellows in the faculty threatened to resign in protest at his dismissal, Minister of Education Hatoyama Ichiro coolly replied: 'Let all the professors resign if that is how they feel. We don't mind closing the universities altogether.' The same Hatoyama would go on to serve two terms as Prime Minister in post-war Japan.

Of all these new bodies, it was the 'Great Asia Association' which lent the frankest expression to Araki's uncompromising expansionism. Patronised once again by the ubiquitous Konoye, it would serve as the forerunner to that ultimate embodiment of Japan's conquistadorial designs, the Greater East Asia Co-Prosperity Sphere.

23

Hirohito Takes Command

NAVAL COUNTER SALVO

Araki moved swiftly to consolidate the position of the Imperial Roadsters by removing the likely 'obstacles' within the Army high command itself. Every senior Choshu general on the General Staff, including Ninomiya, Sugiyama and Koiso was reassigned to the field, as were Control-Groupers Nagata and his faithful lieutenant, 'Scrapper' Tojo. Their replacements were chosen not on any merit, but by reason only of their membership of the Tosa or Hizen *han*.

His 'Crisis of 1936' strategy cut right across that of the Control group, whose blueprint for total war, endorsed by Hirohito, called for a long period of military mechanisation and industrial modernisation in which any major war, and especially with the massed infantry of the Soviet Union, was to be avoided at all costs. His Choshu purge had the effect of infuriating even the non-Choshu Purification Group, who had pledged themselves to the removal of all *han* influence within the service; as one critic charged, 'while chanting effortlessly that he must invest the Emperor's Army with integrity and abolish all cliques within it, he has in fact built up his own large faction.'

He was scarcely more popular with the ruling Shore Faction in the Naval Ministry. Although as part of his 'Crisis of 1936' strategy he had asked the Navy 'to take care of America', the memory of having to be rescued by the Army in Shanghai still rankled and they were disinclined to involve themselves too closely with Araki and his Imperial Road faction. 'We are annoyed by the young officers who are trying to entice the Navy,' Navy Minister Osumi Mineo told Harada. 'We are taking the utmost precautions against the Army.' Chief of Staff Fushimi had fallen in enthusiastically with the call for a naval war against America, causing Saionji to remark that 'I'd like to remove him somehow or other', but the Shore Faction were concerned that their own plans for advancing towards the south would be jeopardised by the implausibility of striking in both directions at once.

Finally, the enormous budget deficits run up to accommodate Araki's demands and the consequent inflation stirred a growing resentment in the civilian population, particularly among the peasants and farmers, whose living standards were still declining drastically; 'the welfare of the farmers

350

is being sacrificed for the sake of the military budget,' was another accusation increasingly to be heard.

It was therefore not surprising that pressure for Araki's removal increased from all sides, and it was finally capped by the birth of the Crown Prince (on December 23rd 1933) which dashed his plans to replace Hirohito with Brother Chichibu on the Throne. A month later he resigned after an unsuccessful battle to have his henchman Mazaki appointed in his place.

He was succeeded by the 'Border-Crosser' Hayashi, although he did manage to secure a place for Mazaki among the 'Big Three' as Inspector-General of Military Education. Hayashi immediately made a clean sweep of Araki's nominees from the General Staff and brought back Nagata to head the key Bureau of Military Affairs. He also put a veto on the 'Crisis of 1936' slogan in military publications and on all plans for a war with Russia; instead, he gave his approval to the resumption of diplomatic relations with Moscow and, in particular, of the negotiations for the purchase of the Russian interest in the Chinese Eastern Railway.

Moscow had made an offer to sell it the previous year for 250 million yen, to which Tokyo had replied with an offer of 50 million. Almost at once the railway began to suffer from a series of concerted attacks from 'bandits', which caused it a severe drop in income, but when Moscow complained that Japan was deliberately engineering these in order to reduce its value, Tokyo naturally absolved itself from responsibility for anything which took place inside the 'independent' state of Manchukuo. After some further prolonged exchanges of accusations and counter-accusations, a sum of 140 million was finally agreed.

This new conciliatory attitude towards Russia did not, of course, signify any abandonment of Japan's expansionary plans, but only a shift in their direction from north to south. Expanding on a practice initiated by Araki with the object of 'promoting a better understanding among the people regarding national defence', Hayashi issued a series of pamphlets soliciting public support for a continuing growth in the military budget. 'War is the Father of Creation and the Mother of Culture,' one of them proclaimed. For Japan war was not a matter of 'might makes right', but a 'heaven-sent mission to participate in the great work of helping the life of the universe to unfold and infinitely develop.'

The strengthening of national defence was not merely a matter of increased armaments, it was agreed, but it also 'includes the promotion of social security. It is imperative that we set our house in order by effecting social and economic stabilisation.' When this was interpreted as threatening an outright military dictatorship, causing a slump on the Stock Exchange, Hayashi hastened to reassure the nation that 'the fundamental direction indicated in the pamphlet must be carried out gradually, according to legal procedures. Moreover, I personally shall do my best to realise the plan within legal means.'

Araki's downfall came as an even more welcome relief to the Navy's Imperial-Satsuma hierarchy, for they now saw the way clear for the implementation of the 'Strike South' strategy. Fushimi described its basic objectives as follows: 'The policy of operations against America is first . . . to clear out the enemy's seaborne military power in the Orient and at the same time, in co-operation with the Army, attack their bases, thereby controlling the western Pacific; then while protecting the Empire's trade, to harass the enemy's home fleet and defeat it through surprise attack.'

This new confidence in the ability to 'take care of America' sprang from the successful development of new weapons such as the prototype of the Zero carrier-plane, oxygen-driven torpedoes with a range of 24 miles and 2,000-ton submarines equipped with seaplanes and a cruising range of 20,000 miles. With these they calculated that they would be able to eliminate the American fleet's numerical superiority before it reached the western Pacific for a decisive battle, in which the survivors would be accounted for by a new 18″ gun created to sink a 16″ battleship with a single shell. As for the fleets of the European colonial Powers, it was foreseen that they would be preoccupied with the containment of the menace of Germany signalled by Hitler's withdrawal from the World Disarmament Conference in October 1933.

Navy Minister Osumi, at Fushimi's bidding, had throughout 1933 been pressing for a larger naval budget. In August, however, Hirohito decided that the time had come to restrain the influence of his cousin by introducing a regulation obliging the Chief of Staff to consult with the Navy Minister and, by extension, the other Ministers involved (principally the Finance and Foreign Ministers) before presenting plans affecting Naval strength for the Emperor's sanction; by this means it was hoped that he would be able 'to do nothing without their approval'.

It was quickly to prove a forlorn hope. Two months later Finance Minister Takahashi attempted to slash the Navy's proposed budget in half; the outraged Osumi threatened to resign, and in the certain knowledge that Fushimi would refuse to nominate a successor, Prime Minister (and Shore Faction sympathizer) Saito capitulated.

TREATY ABROGATION

The second London Naval Conference was due to take place in two years' time, and in September Osumi proposed to the Cabinet that Japan should enter a demand for a 10 to 7 ratio in capital ships, 10 to 8 in heavy cruisers and complete parity in all other categories. However, because Japan, unlike America and Britain, had implemented the maximum building programme allowed to her under the existing treaties — since 1922 she had launched 164 new warships as opposed to America's 40 — she in practice already enjoyed such ratios, and the Fleet Faction (led, just as it had been at the time of the 1930 Conference, by Kato, Togo and Suetsugu) proclaimed that they would be satisfied with nothing less than full parity in all categories. Since it was inconceivable that the other Powers would agree to this, they were effectively demanding an end to all armament limitations and the abrogation of the existing treaties.

At a Military Council on June 8th 1934 Suetsugu put their position unequivocally: international disarmament, he asserted, represented 'nothing more than the dreams of fools', and those who argued in its favour were simply playing into the hands of Britain and America. Now was the time to 'abrogate the existing treaties and have no treaties and no restrictions', not only because Japan's geographical position 'gives us an extremely favourable position for national defence,' but also because 'we have been piling up a considerable amount of research concerning what types of independent armaments we ought to produce if a treaty is not signed.' Here he was referring in particular to the blueprints drawn up for a colossal 62,000-ton class of battleships to house the all-conquering 18" guns. In order to lay them down legally before 1937, notice of abrogation would have to be served to the other Powers by December 31st 1934.

Another of his demands was that the Government 'should control public opinion and manage it completely'; a Naval Affairs Reporting Division had already been recently created to control the release of all information to the Press, who were now to be forbidden any discussion of shipbuilding programmes and comparative naval strength. Finally, he added the threat that if the Government still insisted on attempting to reach an accommodation with the West at the Conference, 'we cannot guarantee that, with the military and the people angered, a misfortune even greater than that of May 15th [1932] would not occur.' As Commander of the Combined Fleets, he was better placed than any to gauge the feelings of the Navy's younger officers.

The demand for abrogation met with the support of the Army General Staff, although War Minister Hayashi and Mass-Mobiliser Nagata were less enthusiastic at the prospect of seeing a large proportion of the available funds diverted from their carefully-laid programme of Army mechanisation into the construction of this new breed of naval leviathans. This joint pressure proved too much for the Saito Cabinet, which was already tottering as a result of a financial scandal involving the Minister of Commerce, and on July 3rd the Prime Minister submitted his resignation.

He was succeeded by his fellow-Admiral Okada, a choice which had been agreed by the Court several weeks earlier. Okada was, of course, a member of the Shore Faction, and Hirohito was just as concerned as he had been in 1930 to cloak the expansionary blueprint behind the façade of commitment to international armament limitation. In forcing through the appointment, Saionji had faced a stiff battle with the Imperial Road supporters of his *bête noir*, Hiranuma, whom only two months earlier he had managed to prevent succeeding to the key post of President of the Privy Council. The Big Baron's nomination had had the support of War Minister

Hayashi, Fleet Faction leader Kato and even Lord Privy Seal Makino. 'I don't know whether it is because they are both from the Satsuma *han*, but Makino seems to feel an attachment for Hiranuma,' Saionji observed, and it had taken all the 84-year-old Last Noble's powers of persuasion to wean Makino away to his own nominee.

It was not to be expected that the Imperial Road/Fleet Faction camp would take this reverse lying down, and it soon became clear that the Shore Faction had won for themselves the most temporary of respites. Okada's vulnerability was exposed when his attempt to replace Osumi as Navy Minister with his own nominee was roundly rebuffed by the Fleet Faction majority on the General Staff; 'Their unity is extremely solid and we'd better be careful,' the chastened Prime Minister reported to Harada. His position was further weakened when Takahashi, that staunch upholder of budgetary prudence, decided that his years were now beyond continuing the fight and nobody more impressive than a Treasury bureaucrat could be found to fill his position as Finance Minister.

The new Cabinet had barely had time to take office before Osumi presented a demand for immediate abrogation of the existing Naval Treaties and full parity in any new treaty, accompanied not only by a threat to resign if it was refused but also with a claim that Fushimi had already secured its approval from Hirohito, which was therefore 'the end of the matter'. On investigation, however, it was found that when the Chief of Staff had presented the proposals at the Palace, Hirohito had in fact refused to consider them and returned them to his cousin unopened. Osumi then worked on Hayashi and eventually succeeded in winning an admission from the War Minister that, although he considered the proposals extremely dangerous, they had the support of the Army as a whole.

Confronted with this, and the implied threat of another attempted coup by the Young Officers, Hirohito conceded that 'because the military is demanding it, we have no choice', but he insisted that the abrogation should be carried out in a way which would transfer the onus of responsibility for it to the other Powers. This could be done, it was suggested, by coupling the demand for parity with a proposal for the abolition of capital ships and aircraft carriers; there was no danger that the West, given their existing numerical superiority in battleships, would agree to such a scheme, and as for aircraft carriers, did not Japan already have any amount of those, albeit stationary, in the Mandated Pacific islands?

To bolster the impression of being ready to compromise, the Japanese delegation to the Conference was put under the leadership of the Harvard-educated Yamamoto. This strategy was amply justified by events: after three months of proposals and counter proposals which brought the added bonus of driving a wedge between Britain and America, the future Pearl Harbor Mastermind announced on December 30th that he saw no way out of the deadlock and that Japan therefore had no option but to serve notice of her abrogation of the Washington and London Treaties. This, Kato exulted, would see 'the dawn of the regeneration of the Imperial Navy'.

'ORGAN' CONTROVERSY

While their allies in the Fleet Faction were thus calling the tune in the Navy, the Imperial Road 'Strike North' radicals began to reassert themselves in the Army after the demotion of their spokesman Araki. Plots were laid to assassinate both Makino and Saionji, but these were then superseded by the much more ambitious plan of a group of Staff College officers at the Military Academy to attack the Diet and eliminate the leading politicians. Another officer at the Academy, however, tipped off the Military Police and on November 20th the ringleaders were arrested.

No word of the 'Military Academy Incident', as it became known, was revealed to the public until 1946 — the fact that Hirohito's youngest brother, Prince Mikasa, was then a cadet at the Academy, was no doubt a contributory factor to the silence — when Araki's Number Two, Mazaki, alleged that it had been fabricated by the Control Group in order to discredit him and force his resignation as Inspector General of Military Education. It is true that on taking over the Premiership in July Okada is on record as having told War Minister Hayashi that 'I want you to move swiftly and use your powers . . . to get rid of Mazaki, who is the root of all evil in the Army', but the credibility of Mazaki's allegation is rather undermined by his similar accusation that the much more serious mutiny of 1936 was engineered by the Control Group with the same purpose in mind.

Another compelling motive for keeping the affair from the public eye was the involvement of one of the ringleaders in the attempted coups of March and October 1931, who if brought before a court martial was only too likely to retaliate by revealing the complicity of Nagata, Koiso and other leading Control Group members in those conspiracies. The conspirators were therefore released after a couple of months and merely transferred to the Reserves. Not unnaturally, the Imperial Roadsters saw this leniency as an invitation to hit back.

On February 18th 1935 an acolyte of Baron Hiranuma made a statement in the House of Peers which suggested that Professor Minobe, the leading scholar in Constitutional Law at Tokyo University since 1902 and one-time tutor to Hirohito himself, was guilty of blasphemy. His works had been accepted as the standard authority on the subject by a whole generation of university students, but by defining the Emperor merely as 'the highest organ of the State', it was now claimed that he was contradicting the Shintoist teaching of the Emperor's divinity, which automatically rendered Him transcendental to, not part of, the State. Minobe was therefore, his accusers argued, 'theoretically a materialist individualist and morally an anarchist', who sought to deny Japan's unique position in the world and to reduce the Emperor to the status of any European constitutional monarch or even republican president.

In vain Minobe, who was also a member of the Upper House, protested that his definition was merely an amplification of Article IV of the Constitution which declared the Emperor to be 'the head of the Empire'. The accusations were quickly taken up in the Lower House by the Seiyukai Opposition and then orchestrated throughout the country by Imperial Road members in the 3-million-strong Reservists Association. A party of Reservists ceremonially burnt a complete set of his works at the Meiji Shrine, proclaiming that they represented 'a non-Japanese, blasphemous, Europe-worshipping ideology which ignores our 3,000-year-old tradition and ideals'. Minobe found himself in court on a charge of *lèse-majesté*, in which other leading figures, including Okada, were named as accomplices, while the Diet passed a motion calling for the 'clarification of *kokutai*'. Minobe was, of course, merely a scapegoat; the real targets were the ruling 'Strike South' faction, and in particular the man who had been drafted in to prevent Hiranuma from occupying the Presidency of the Privy Council.

The strategy succeeded in placing the establishment in a most embarrassing position, for although Hirohito could describe the issue in private to his Aide-de-Camp Honjo as 'a very silly business', he could hardly associate himself in public with any disavowal of his divinity without simultaneously undermining his own authority and with it the argument for the 'Strike South'. They were rescued, however, by none other than Number Two Roadster Mazaki, who was so confident that they would be forced into a humiliating climb-down that on April 4th he issued a directive to all Army commanders decreeing that 'the organ theory [of the Emperor as part of the State] is incompatible with *kokutai*'. In thus preempting the Government's decision, he gave them a pretext for removing him as Inspector-General.

Under Army regulations, the appointments of Generals had to be agreed by the 'Big Three'. The vote of Chief of Staff and Imperial Uncle Prince Kanin was not in doubt, but Nagata was worried that when the moment came Minister of War Hayashi 'is so influenced by others that he may hesitate in his decision'. However, his resolution was successfully stiffened by Okada, who urged him 'to go ahead boldly ... and do it now'. This left only the agreement of Mazaki himself to be obtained, and in return for it he was offered a say in the forthcoming annual promotions; when he refused, Hirohito himself issued an order on July 15th transferring him to the relative backwater of the Supreme War Council.

SWORDS UNSHEATHED

In a last-ditch attempt to save their idol, the ringleaders of the Military Academy Incident had published a pamphlet revealing the complicity of the leaders of the Control Group in the 1931 plots. Although they failed in their objective, they did succeed in identifying some, and particularly Nagata, as targets for the revenge of Imperial Road fanatics. One of these, a certain Aizawa Saburo, travelled to Tokyo immediately on hearing of Mazaki's dismissal and remonstrated with Nagata; for his pains, he found himself posted to Formosa.

On August 12th Aizawa returned again to the War Ministry. On the first occasion he had toyed with the idea of murder and had thought better of it, but this time, after some encouraging words from Mazaki, his mind was made up. Having established that his target was in, he marched into Nagata's office unannounced and cut him down with several strokes of his *samurai* sword (he spoke later of his shame that, as a fencing instructor, he had failed to dispatch him with a single stroke). He himself had cut a finger in the scuffle and after it had been bound up by a medical orderly he asked permission to return to Nagata's office for his cap, explaining that he was about to embark with his regiment for Formosa; he gave every appearance of genuine surprise when it was refused and he instead found himself under arrest.

In order to increase the impression of the enormity of the crime, the public announcement of Nagata's death was delayed for several hours while the Emperor approved his promotion to the rank of Lieutenant-General. The scene was now set for a final showdown between the rival camps of 'Strike North' and 'Strike South'. Being now so closely identified with the latter, Hirohito saw only too clearly that his own position was again at stake and he accordingly began to assume a much more explicitly direct authority than hitherto. When Hayashi resigned in customary acknowledgement of his responsibility for the outrage, warning at the same time that 'if decisive steps are not taken immediately, the situation will drift into chaos', Hirohito lost no time in ordering the new War Minister 'to deal with the Young Officers more firmly' and Chief of Staff Uncle Kanin 'to help the War Minister in this matter'.

Prime Minister Okada reported to his Cabinet that the Emperor now 'wished to supervise personally all diplomatic and military affairs'. The birth of a male heir to the Throne had not wholly removed Hirohito's suspicions of his brother Chichibu, and, contrary to the precedent that gave serving Imperial Princes postings within easy reach of Tokyo, he had him transferred to the far north of the main island of Honshu. To judge by the following remark that Chichibu was reported to have made on leaving the capital to a fellow officer, these suspicions were amply justified: 'In case you stage an uprising, come to welcome me at the head of your men.'

For all their precautions, however, the loss of their leading spokesman was to serve as a crippling blow to the 'Strike South' faction and a corresponding stimulus to their opponents.

Even before Nagata's death Okada had been pressurised by the Reservists Association into issuing a statement agreeing that the 'organ theory' was inconsistent with *kokutai*, but far from being mollified, they roundly condemned him for failing to mention the unfortunate Minobe by name. The Professor himself increased their excitement still further when on September 17th he finally resigned his university chair and his seat in the House of Peers. The Procurator-General, who had had little success in demonstrating that Minobe had actually violated any law, took this move to be an admission of guilt on his part and promptly dropped all charges against him. Far from recanting, however, Minobe announced that his only reason for resigning was that the current atmosphere made it impossible for him to carry out his duties.

The enraged Imperial Roadsters in the Reservists Association bombarded Tokyo with demands for Minobe's imprisonment and the resignation of the 'insincere' Government. On October 13th their leaders joined with the kindred spirits of Araki's 1936 Club in calling on Okada in person and abusing him as 'a wicked and worthless person'. While refusing to bow to their demands for his resignation, the Prime Minister did feel obliged to accommodate them to the extent of making a further statement conceding that any 'foreign' ideology which ran counter to the God-given concept of *kokutai* and the Emperor's absolute sovereignty had to be exterminated.

One fanatic went so far as to apply this ruling to Minobe in person, but his indignation was not matched by his aim and the professor escaped with no more than a bullet wound in the leg. Rumours of plots being laid against the lives of the original target, the Privy Council President, and of Lord Privy Seal Makino grew so insistent that both men submitted their resignations to the Throne; the former was again persuaded to stay on for the moment, but the latter's was reluctantly accepted and he was replaced by the recently retired Premier Saito.

Even worse for the Control Group was the revelation of new War Minister Kawashima Yoshiyuki's sympathies for their rivals. Not only did Kawashima appoint Imperial Roadsters to the key posts of Chief of the Military Affairs Bureau and Commander of the Tokyo Garrison, but he also allowed Nagata's murderer, Aizawa, the full glare of a public court martial at the First Division's Tokyo headquarters. When it opened on January 28th 1936, it immediately became a public relations outlet for the whole Imperial Road catechism, accompanied by the familiar flood of letters demanding clemency and jars containing pickled little fingers.

Making no attempt to deny his guilt, the defendant positively gloried in it. 'I marked out Nagata because he, together with senior statesmen and financiers and members of the old Army clique like Generals Minami and Ugaki, was responsible for the corruption of the Army', Aizawa boasted. 'He was the headquarters of all the evil. If he would not resign, there was only one thing to do. I determined to make myself a demon and finish his life with one stroke of my sword'. His defence was therefore not one of fact but of motive, namely, that he acted 'to save the nation from a crisis.'

Whenever he was asked to elaborate, he would simply repeat the dogma that 'the Emperor is the incarnation of the Great God that made the Universe. The Emperor is Absolute.' When it was put to him that it was from the Emperor that the law derived and that in breaking it he was therefore acting against the Emperor's wishes, he was reduced to a rare moment of silence.

MUTINY

Particular emphasis was put throughout on 'the evil men surrounding the Throne' who were alleged to be subverting the Emperor's Supreme Command of the Armed Forces for their own ends, and the leaders of the 'Military Academy Incident' were already hatching a plan to assassinate the new Lord Privy Seal, Saito. When Quasi-Socialist Kita was brought out of his decade-long retirement and invited to participate (his fellow ideologist 'Doctor' Okawa was still serving his sentence for his part in the 1931 plots), the plan expanded into something altogether more ambitious — a full-scale revolution 'which will soon destroy the ruling military clique'.

The very success of Aizawa's trial as a public relations exercise, however, persuaded them that its realisation should be postponed until after that had ended, and Aizawa himself asked that they should not do anything 'silly' which might jeopardise his acquittal. The fact that a general election was scheduled for February 20th was seen to be of no account; as one of them explained, 'revolutionary officers should not depend on elections, but rather rise with swords in our hands'.

What finally forced their hand was the news that the ruling Control Group majority on the Army General Staff were about to transfer the First Division, in which most of the conspirators were concentrated, from Tokyo to Manchuria in order to bolster the Kwantung Army (now commanded by Minami in place of Muto 'The Silent') for a new push south into northern China. Some argued that they should wait until the Division returned to Japan, but the majority were for action in advance of its departure, and although he judged it to be premature Kita gave his assent when he saw that nothing would deflect them.

Number Two Roadster Mazaki was kept in close touch with the preparations although he was careful to distance himself from any actual involvement. One of the ringleaders hinted to War Minister Kawashima himself that something on the scale of 1932 was about to take place, and was given the impression that 'when we go into action, he [Kawashima] will not be our opponent'. Another to indicate his approval — even adding that Prime Minister Okada should be killed — was the future 'Tiger of Malaya' Yamashita Tomoyuki, although it had been suspected in view of his subsequent career that he was playing the part of *agent provocateur* on the Control Group's behalf.

It is certainly true that the Court and Government had good notice of the conspiracy. As early as late December Privy Seal Secretary Kido recorded in his diary precise details of the objectives assigned to the various rebel regiments; at the beginning of February the Chief of the Tokyo Military Police was informed that the Young Officers would attempt another coup at the end of the month, and the Mitsui and Mitsubishi conglomerates both reported that they were being dragooned into paying protection money to finance the Mutiny. On February 17th one of the regiments carried out a dress rehearsal attack on the Police Headquarters with fixed bayonets and penetrated as far as the second floor; when a complaint was lodged with the Tokyo Garrison, it was explained that this was merely a 'night drill' in preparation for the transfer to Manchuria.

In spite of all this evidence, no pre-emptive measures were taken by the authorities beyond moving a few extra policemen into the capital. If it is safe to dismiss Mazaki's later contention that the whole affair was actually engineered by the Control Group, it is quite easy to believe on the other hand that they decided to allow the Imperial Road/'Strike North' faction its head in order that they would then be able to catch it in the open and suppress it for good.

The deadline was set for 5 am on the morning of the 26th February 1936, which was scheduled to be the final day of Aizawa's court martial; hopes of his acquittal had been severely diminished by his inability to cope with the more penetrating questions of the prosecution. Another important factor in the choice was that on that day all three of the ringleaders happened to be the Duty Officers of the rebel units concerned.

The plan of action closely followed that of the abortive Military Academy Incident. The 1st and 3rd Regiments of the First Division were to take over the administrative heart of the capital; they would then join with the 3rd Regiment of the Imperial Guards to seize the gates of the Imperial Palace and, just as the conspirators had done in the Revolution of 1868, seal off the Emperor from contact with any but the 'right people'. Parties from the same units would simultaneously dispatch the six leading 'evil men surrounding the Throne'; Saionji was originally included on the death list, but it was then decided that he should be spared in order that he should give legitimacy, in his rôle as Premier-maker, to the appointment of Mazaki as the new Prime Minister.

The 1400 soldiers to take part were woken at 2 am and told for the first time of the conspiracy and its purpose (their NCOs had been informed of it the previous day). Outside it was snowing heavily, just as it had been 86 years earlier when the Mito *ronin* had cut down the 'Atrocious Autocrat', Ii. This was taken as a good omen, and most of the primary objectives were already in rebel hands when the deadline arrived.

The death squads, however, were rather less successful, for only three of the six targets — Lord Privy Seal Saito, Mazaki's replacement as Inspector-

General of Military Education and Finance Minister Takahashi (who had been brought out of retirement again by Okada) were dispatched according to plan. The former Lord Privy Seal Makino was alerted in time by his bodyguard and hustled to safety out of a back door. Lord Chamberlain Suzuki was shot and left for dead, but eventually recovered, to become the last Prime Minister in World War Two. Okada enjoyed an even more remarkable escape thanks to the courage of his brother-in-law, who drew on himself a hail of machine-gun fire while the Prime Minister was being hidden in a garden shed; after comparing the bullet-shattered face with a photograph of Okada, the assassins departed in the conviction that they had killed the right man.

Back in the centre too things began to go wrong for the rebels. The men from the Imperial Guards regiment successfully talked their way into the Palace grounds on the pretext of reinforcing the Palace Guards against attack, but their leader's connection with the rebels was then discovered and they were ordered out again at gun-point; thus the all-important tactic of seizing the Emperor's person, which had been such a decisive factor in the 1868 Revolution, was frustrated.

DIVINE INTERVENTION

Hirohito moreover, now that he was bereft of the two key members of the inner circle who had served to cloak his position of absolute authority in the past, was compelled to exercise it openly and unambiguously. When Kawashima arrived at the Palace at 9.30 with the rebels' manifesto and a list of their demands (which included the arrest of Ugaki, Minami, Koiso, Tatekawa and other leaders of the Control Group, and the appointment of Araki to the command of the Kwantung Army in order to pursue 'a tough policy towards Russia') the Emperor's reply was uncompromising to the point of brutality: 'This is mutiny,' he told the War Minister. 'I will give you one hour in which to suppress the rebels. Any soldier who moves Imperial troops without my orders is not my soldier, no matter what excuse he may have.'

It had been at the bidding of Mazaki that Kawashima had gone to the Palace ('At last you have done it!' he had congratulated the War Minister), and the rebels' idol now set about mobilising the support of senior officers for their cause. Having sent a message to Hiranuma to secure his assent to be nominated as the new Prime Minister, he then met with Fushimi to suggest that the Naval Chief of Staff should recommend to his cousin Hirohito a new Hiranuma Cabinet with himself (Mazaki) as War Minister. Finally, he convened a meeting of the Supreme War Council.

Dominated as it was by Araki and other forcibly-retired 'Strike North' advocates (Chief of Staff Kanin was absent ill), he had no difficulty in brow-beating the 'Strike South' minority into adding their names to the following proclamation to the rebels: 'The purpose of your decisive action has been reported to the Emperor. Your motives, based on your desire to clarify *kokutai*, are approved. The Supreme War Councillors, realising the present disgraceful state of our national prestige, have resolved to strive together to achieve that same purpose. We are now waiting to hear the Imperial will.'

Araki would afterwards claim that this represented no more than a confirmation that Kawashima had informed the Emperor of the rebels' goals, but anyone familiar with this kind of Japanese double-speak would instantly recognise it as a statement of approval. Furthermore, the word 'actions' was afterwards substituted for 'motives' in the second sentence by the 'Strike North' majority in the certain knowledge that the 'Strike South'-ers would have refused to put their name to such a change. Similarly, it was later argued that an order from the First Division Headquarters authorising 'the units which have gone into action' to maintain law and order in the city centre was a device to get the rebels under control, but at the time the rebels greeted it as an unambiguous official endorsement of the mutiny.

When Fushimi went to the Palace with Mazaki's suggestion for a new Cabinet, he too received short shrift from Hirohito. Both the Chief of Staff and the Navy Minister, Osumi, as members of the Fleet Faction, were regarded as sympathetic to the rebels, but they were heavily outnumbered by the Shore Faction on the General Staff. As soon as he received word of the mutiny, Yonai Mitsumasa, the commander of the Yokosuka Naval Base dispatched a contingent of marines to guard the Navy Ministry building; after the War he also disclosed that he had drawn up a contingency plan for them to rescue Hirohito from the Palace if the need arose and to bring him on board a battleship.

After Fushimi returned from his Imperial audience, the Naval General Staff ordered the First Fleet to stand by in Tokyo Bay and train their guns on the rebels' positions. They also entered a strong protest with the War Ministry at the published form of the War Council proclamation, for the new word 'actions' implied approval of the assassination of three senior Admirals (Saito, Suzuki and, as was then presumed, Okada). Thus when Kita claimed in a 'Showa Restoration Bulletin' which the rebels put out that evening that the Navy was siding with them, he was being hopelessly optimistic.

The War Council's proclamation was similarly unrepresentative of the attitude of the Army's General Staff. The majority, led by Vice-Chief of Staff 'Toilet Door' Sugiyama not only opposed the mutiny but favoured the use of force to suppress it. A junior officer on the Staff cabled military units outside Tokyo for support 'for the glorious uprising in the capital', but he met with no response except from the Eighth Division in which Chichibu was serving; a delegation of Young Officers asked that the Prince should be allowed to return to Tokyo, a request that it was thought wiser not to oppose if the mutiny was to be kept from spreading outside the capital. In Manchuria the Kwantung Army Commander Minami ordered his Secret Police Chief, 'Scrapper' Tojo, to squash the first signs of any insubordination.

During the afternoon Sugiyama obtained Hirohito's permission to move reinforcements into the capital. At the same time the Cabinet, still unaware of Okada's survival, met to appoint the Home Minister as provisional Premier before submitting their resignations to the Emperor in acknowledgement of their collective responsibility for the mutiny. Hirohito, however, refused to accept them for the reason that, as Privy Seal Secretary Kido recorded, 'the rebels and those who support them might then try to set up a new Cabinet [as indeed they already were] which would achieve their goals. To prevent this one should advise the Emperor to reject any suggestion of a new Cabinet and insist that the present authorities suppress the mutiny.'

Hirohito needed no persuading, summoning each War Councillor to the Palace and demanding of them 'Why haven't the rebels been suppressed yet?' The 'Strike North' majority on the Council, however, were naturally reluctant to take such a step and they then conferred with the rebel leaders in the hope of persuading them to withdraw their troops in return for a promise that they themselves would do everything they could to bring about a Cabinet of the rebels' choice. The proposal, however, met with a cool reception from the mutineers, who were still toying with the idea of a second attempt at occupying the Palace. In any case, the idea of such a deal was then rejected out of hand by Hirohito. By now it was past midnight, and the Cabinet and Emperor agreed to declare Martial Law in the capital as a temporary stop-gap; the 'Strike North'-supporting Commandant of the Tokyo Garrison was made directly responsible to the Throne for its imposition.

The Commandant's first order, issued at 8.15 the next morning, charged 'the units which had gone into action' with maintaining law and order in the central area which they controlled against possible disruption by 'communist elements'. As all known communists had long since been put away under lock and key, this was interpreted by the rebels as conferring legitimacy on them as part of the forces charged with imposing Martial Law. The 'Strike North' majority on the Supreme War Council again conferred with the rebel leaders, who now agreed to withdraw their troops on condition that the Council put forward Mazaki's name as the new Prime Minister; since they were now recognised as part of the official martial law forces, it was explained, they could obey an order from the Commandant to return to their barracks without any loss of face.

In the meantime Hirohito, after conferring with the General Staff, had issued an order to the Tokyo Garrison Commandant that he should 'immediately evict the officers and men who have occupied the central area and make them return to their respective units'; the use of the word 'occupied' put it beyond all doubt that the latter were regarded by the Palace as having acted illegally. Sugiyama, aware of the negotiations carrying on between the War Council and the rebels, was at first reluctant to pass the order on to the Commandant, but Hirohito threatened that if no move was made against the rebels, he would assume personal command of the Imperial Guards Division and go to crush them himself. Accordingly, the loyal units of the First and Imperial Guards Divisions were moved up opposite the rebel positions.

UNCONDITIONAL SURRENDER

At 5 pm Chichibu finally reached Tokyo and was driven under heavy escort to the Palace for an audience with the Emperor. His arrival caused the rebels to proclaim that 'Prince Chichibu, who supports our cause, has arrived in the capital. Now the Restoration is near'. Once again, however, their hopes were outrunning events. What passed between the two brothers that evening has never been disclosed, but Hirohito was later to remark that Chichibu's behaviour during the mutiny was 'better than it had been during the May 15th [1932] Incident'. At any rate, Chichibu was told to remain in the Palace until the situation had been dealt with because of the unsafe position of his own palace, and he was thus kept from communicating with the rebels.

Another source of consternation to the rebels was the reappearance of Okada alive and well as a result of an ingenious ruse. The mutineers guarding his official Residence allowed in a number of his friends for the purpose of conducting a memorial service; during the rituals it was announced that one of the mourners had fainted, and the Prime Minister, having meanwhile been led out of his hiding place in the garden shed and dressed up in a hat and glasses, was carried out past the unsuspecting guards to a waiting car.

The War Council's deal with the rebels was not surprisingly turned down by Sugiyama on the grounds that the Emperor was opposed to the appointment of any new Cabinet before the mutiny had been suppressed. For good measure, Hirohito then summoned Mazaki to an Imperial audience and upbraided him for the Army's continuing failure to take decisive action. Mazaki returned to the rebel leaders and told them that there was now nothing for it but to submit, warning them that if they failed to do so he would be obliged to lead the loyal units in person against them.

The mutineers still found it almost impossible to accept that the embodiment of the Showa Restoration, the Showa Emperor himself, opposed their actions; 'This stupid thing cannot be true,' one of them remarked. In desperation, some of them proposed mounting an attack on the Martial Law Headquarters, but they were overruled on the grounds that such a move would undermine the claim to be recognised as part of the martial law forces. Kita, however, persuaded them that they should not surrender until their demands had been met, claiming that 'thousands of letters of support' were being received from all over the country and that his clairvoyant wife had received a message from the spirits describing them as 'The Righteous Revolutionary Army'.

The following morning (the 28th), when it was apparent that there was going to be no surrender, the General Staff met with the commanders of the martial law forces to discuss their plan of attack. The Supreme War Council still advanced pleas against the use of force, but Sugiyama again dismissed them and ordered the rebel leaders to present themselves at the Prime Minister's Residence to hear the Imperial Command.

Some of them still refused to acknowledge it, claiming that it must have been forged by 'the traitors around the Throne', and that even if it was genuine they should disobey it for the sake of Japan just as 'The Great Saigo' had done in 1877. The majority, however, finally voted to give in and commit *hara-kiri* as long as the Emperor sent a chamberlain formally to witness their self-sacrifice. Imperial Aide-de-Camp Honjo recommended acceptance of these terms 'with tears in his eyes' — his own son-in-law was implicated in the mutiny — but Hirohito remained adamant: if they wished to kill themselves that was their own affair, but as rebels against the Throne they could not expect any token of legitimacy for their actions. Honjo noted in his diary that 'I have never seen such severity and anger in the Emperor before'.

Still Kita urged defiance, asserting that 'all the Gods and Buddhas' were praising them and predicting their victory. His words were again decisive, and the rebels set about preparing a last ditch defence, in spite of receiving a plea from Chichibu that the officers should 'act gallantly' by releasing their troops and then committing suicide. Greatly to Hirohito's annoyance, the General Staff then decided that it was already too late to mount an attack that day. Sugiyama was informed by the Cabinet that any further delay would provoke a run on the banks and an economic collapse, and he promised them and the Emperor that it would be carried out 'immediately' the following morning; further reinforcements were then summoned into the capital.

At dawn on the 29th central Tokyo was sealed off and the rebels' positions surrounded by tanks and artillery. Local residents were ordered to evacuate their homes, and Hirohito, taking Chichibu along with him, moved up to supervise operations in person. Overhead, three bombers circled dropping thousands of leaflets addressed to the NCOs and soldiers. 'It is still not too late, so return at once to your units,' they were told. 'All those who fail to do so will be considered traitors and will be shot. Your parents, brothers and sisters all implore you not to become traitors.' Similar messages were put out at regular intervals on the radio, while a huge advertising balloon bearing the inscription THE IMPERIAL COM-

MAND HAS BEEN ISSUED, DO NOT RESIST THE ARMY COL-
OURS! was suspended from the roof of a nearby building.

This stark confrontation with the fact of their treason against the man of
whose cause they had believed themselves to be the only true upholders
was too much for the great majority of the rebels. By noon they had all,
sometimes with the blessing of their officers and with the exception only
of a unit of the 3rd Regiment, laid down their arms and returned to their
barracks; an hour later even that unit's commander had given in and, after
ordering them back, shot himself in the head. The remainder were told to
report to the War Minister's residence, where Yamashita asked them if
they intended to do likewise. They replied that they did, but soon
afterwards they decided to change their minds on the grounds that if, like
Aizawa, they were granted a public court-martial, they too would be
able to use it as a platform for the Showa Restoration.

In his determination to crush the opposition to the Strike South strategy
once and for all, however, Hirohito was in no mood to grant them any such
licence. On March 4th he issued an order setting up a Special Court
Martial. This was to be held under strict censorship, the defendants were
not to be allowed the help of counsel, they would have only two hours each
in which to put their case and they would have no right of appeal against
the verdict.

Of the 124 prosecuted, the great majority were released with a
reprimand on the grounds that they had acted only under orders. The full
weight of Imperial retribution fell on the officers: 13 of the 19 on trial
were condemned to death and of the remainder only one received less than
life imprisonment. Four civilians, Kita included, were also executed as
collaborators. Mazaki too, the patron saint of the rebellion, was charged,
but quietly released again fifteen months later on the succession to the
Premiership of his ally, Imperial Go-Between Konoye. A new court
martial was also set up for the unfortunate Aizawa, who was still awaiting
the verdict of his first one; this one was both swift and secret, and he went
in front of the firing squad nine days before the other condemned men.

If the 'Strike North' movement was not, as we shall see, wholly
exterminated, there was no longer any doubt as to the direction
that Japan's territorial ambitions would now take. Even Imperial
Roadster Araki, the movement's acknowledged leader, was obliged
to concede that to expect Japan to halt her expansion south into
China would be 'like telling a man not to get involved with a certain
woman when she is already pregnant by him.'

Still more significant was the open demonstration of personal authority
which Hirohito had made in suppressing this most important challenge to
it, after he had been deprived of the services of the Court circle which at
all other times had served to preserve the myth of the Emperor's
remoteness from the apparatus of power. When five years later he
launched Japan into the final phase of his grandfather Meiji's blueprint for

expansion, that circle was again, of course, on hand to present him to the world as the helpless witness of an unstoppable juggernaut — just as, when four years later again he took the decision to surrender, they would stand aside to allow him to project himself to the world as a lifelong champion of peace.

PART V

'The Great, Decisive War'

24

Across the Great Wall

FIRST FOOTHOLD

With the conquest of Jehol on March 4th 1933 and the capture of 250 miles of the Great Wall along the province's southern border, the whole of northern China had lain within Japan's grasp. That very same day Kwantung Army Commander Muto 'The Silent' issued orders to 'make preparations for operations in North China,' and, as if the thrust of her ambitions was not already obvious enough to the outside world, Imperial Roadster Araki two weeks later commandeered the front page of the *Tokyo Asahi* to announce that 'it is inevitable that an advance across the Great Wall must be made in order to ensure control of the district, and to wipe out the [enemy] forces in the neighbourhood.'

Inseparable Itagaki, his work in Manchuria now complete, was in place in Tientsin ready to pave the way at the head of the Special Service Agency there, armed with a budget of no less than two million yen with which to buy the loyalties of the local warlords and stir up popular disaffection with Chiang Kai-shek's Nationalist Government in Nanking. Belatedly, the Generalissimo rushed 50,000 reinforcements north into the border area under Ho Ying-ch'in, while the 'Young Warlord' Chang, his once 200,000-strong army now dispersed to the winds, retired to console himself in the fleshpots of Europe.

On April 1st, five days after Japan had formally announced her resignation from the League of Nations, the 6th Division crossed the Great Wall some sixty miles inland, to be followed a few days later by the 8th in a sweep thirty miles further west aimed at cutting off Ho's supplies. By the 18th, when the Kwantung Army Chief of Staff, Mukden-Collaborator Koiso, ordered an all-out offensive to coincide with an anti-Chiang coup planned by Itagaki in Peking, the Chinese were already in full retreat. Squadrons of Japanese bombers had become a daily sight over the capital; the treasures of the Forbidden City were hastily crated up and moved south to Nanking for safekeeping while its long-suffering citizens braced themselves for the worst.

Suddenly, at midnight, an order was received to pull all forces back again to the Great Wall. It originated from the Vice-Chief of the General Staff, Number Two Roadster Mazaki, in Tokyo following an Imperial audience in which Hirohito had threatened to issue a direct Imperial command if the General Staff refused to do so. In Geneva China was already demanding that the League should adopt economic sanctions against Japan, and the Emperor was determined to forestall any repetition of the Korean Army's unauthorised move into Manchuria in 1931 which could provoke the West into jeopardising the longer-term expansion plans enshrined in the National Defence Plan blueprint. Faced with such an unequivocal declaration of the Imperial Will, the Army had no choice but to obey, and Hirohito was able to reassure the Naval Chief of Staff that 'I have issued the necessary orders to the Army Chief of Staff, so set your mind at rest.'

The order to withdraw was issued as a demonstration of the Emperor's authority and of his intention to take personal control of Japan's continental expansion. It did not, of course, signify any disapproval in principle of advancing into northern China, which was wholly consistent with the approved 'Strike South' strategy; indeed, it went on to instruct that the Kwantung Army should continue 'to maintain a menacing attitude towards hostile forces in North China'.

Accordingly, as soon as they were seen to have come to heel, Hirohito on May 3rd approved a further order to resume the advance. Three days later the Army General Staff drew up a 'Draft Plan of Emergency Measures for North China', under which the Chinese forces were 'to be compelled to make a substantial surrender or to dissolve, thereby resulting in the withdrawal of the Chinese army along the China-Manchukuo border and in the establishment of peace in this area.'

That same day the Kwantung Army launched itself across the Great Wall in response, Commander-in-Chief Muto explained, to the 'contemptuous attitude' of the Chinese. Within a week Ho's forces had again been routed, this time with the help of false radio signals put out by Itagaki's Special Service Agency in Tientsin ordering the Chinese to withdraw at critical junctures in the battle. As the Japanese consolidated their new positions Muto issued a declaration that 'if the Chinese Army immediately abandons its hitherto provocative attitude and withdraws some distance from the border, our Army will quickly return to the line of the Great Wall.' This was shrewdly timed, for it drew most of the sting from a speech by the recently-elected U.S. President, Franklin Roosevelt, the following day reviving the threat of galvanising the West into economic sanctions.

That danger past, the advance once again resumed until by the 25th the Japanese front line directly threatened both Peking and Tientsin, and the Chinese finally sued for peace. On the political front Itagaki had been rather less successful: not only was the collaborator chosen to take over Peking in the wake of the planned coup assassinated before it could take place, but a fragment of a grenade thrown by an *agent provocateur* at the office of the Japanese Naval Attaché was recovered by the Chinese and found to bear the stamp of the Tokyo Artillery Arsenal. He was promptly ordered to desist from any further subversive activities for the time being.

The General Staff had already drafted its terms for a cease-fire: whereas it was stipulated that the Chinese were to withdraw to a line only forty miles north of Peking and Tientsin, the return of the Kwantung Army to Manchuria was to be 'voluntary'. In addition, the venue of the proposed truce negotiations was not to be 'convenient to the gathering of foreign diplomatic officials and press correspondents and to meddling intervention by third powers'. In order to verify their compliance with the first condition, the Chinese were required to provide facilities for aerial observation. As for the second, the port of Tangku was selected where, as a warning to would-be 'meddlers', Japanese warships were able to anchor offshore with their main guns trained on the building in which the negotiations were to take place.

In such an atmosphere the Chinese delegation were not surprisingly unwilling to hold out for very long against the demands put before them. The Foreign Ministry was under the already conciliatory direction of Wang Ching-wei, who after his ouster from the leadership of the Kuomintang had put himself at the head of a breakaway regime in his native Canton until the Japanese invasion of Jehol persuaded him to bury the hatchet. His declared policy towards Japan of 'resistance on the one hand and negotiation on the other' was well-suited at that juncture to Chiang's preoccupation with the Red menace over and above the threat from the Japanese, encapsulated in his slogan 'first internal pacification, then resist external aggression'.

Indeed, after the delegations had formally exchanged their credentials on the afternoon of May 30th, the following day's negotiations were opened and concluded almost within the hour. The Japanese, dominated by the representatives of the Kwantung Army, simply presented their demands and rejected all Chinese attempts to amend them. The north-eastern corner of the province of Hopei, roughly described by the Peking-Tientsin-Shanhaikwan triangle, was to become a Demilitarised Zone policed by a Chinese 'Peace Preservation Corps' of gendarmes armed only with pistols, rifles and bayonets, who were not to be 'constituted of armed units hostile to Japanese feelings', and who were to 'exercise strict control over anti-Japanese activities [especially the boycott of Japanese goods], which are the basic cause of Sino-Japanese conflict'. The Japanese forces were 'voluntarily to withdraw, in general, to the line of the Great Wall', but some units would remain 'in case of disturbances which the police force would be unable to cope with'.

Japan thus gained her first military foothold in China proper as well as *de jure* recognition of her control of Jehol. Wang attempted to justify his submission on the grounds that China was too weak to defend the northern provinces, and by continuing to attempt to do so she would only put provinces to the south in jeopardy. 'Therefore we decided to find a means of stopping the war temporarily' in order, he explained, to gain time in which to 'reconstruct our material resources and enlarge our capacity for a war of resistance'. By no means all his fellow-countrymen were convinced by the wisdom of such appeasement, but it did allow Chiang to turn his energies again to the 'extermination' of the Communists in Kiangsi and to force them to embark on the Long March into the hinterland.

AN 'AGREEMENT'

Other negotiations followed in the succeeding months, as a result of which political control of the Demilitarised Zone was transferred from the provincial authorities to a Political Affairs Council which Chiang had earlier established in Peking, but which the Japanese considered easier to manipulate. In a further move to consolidate their hold on the area and demoralise the resistance of its inhabitants, they required the Chinese to remove all restrictions on trade across the Great Wall. In the subsequent surge of imports into the Zone, much the most significant item was the traffic in opium. The capture of the 'poppy province' of Jehol had given a huge boost to the production of the drug under Japanese control, which was now directed to Tientsin to be processed under the protection of Itagaki's agents; from there the refined heroin and morphia were distributed all over northern China through a hastily-established network of drug-dealers.

With the downfall of Araki and the rise of Mass-Mobiliser Nagata's Control Group, the emphasis in Tokyo on a policy of economic, as opposed to military, penetration in China received a further boost. This once again brought Japan into conflict with the League of Nations, which had set up a Committee of Technical Assistance to promote China's economic development. On April 17th 1934 the Japanese Foreign Ministry declared that since 'Japan must necessarily share with China the responsibility for maintaining peace in the Far East', Japan was bound to oppose any 'joint operations undertaken by foreign Powers in China, even in the name of technical and financial assistance', which she construed to be a threat to that peace. This attitude was amplified five days later by a further statement from the Japanese Ambassador in Washington, which pronounced that any country would have to consult Japan first before seeking to conclude commercial transactions with China, and that failure to do so would be regarded as an 'unfriendly act . . . Japan alone must act and decide what is good for China.'

This was received by the outside world as tantamount to a declaration of suzerainty over China. In America in particular, it was branded by the Press as 'an Asian Monroe Doctrine' and 'a second Twenty-One Demands'. The Foreign Minister and former Black Dragon activist, Hirota Koki, accordingly hurried to the U.S. Embassy with a revised translation of what 'was said or should have been said', which deleted all reference to foreign

economic aid to China. His efforts at reassurance were somewhat undermined, however, when shortly afterwards a Japanese graduate at Harvard
revealed to, of all people, President Roosevelt himself, that Japan planned
to take over the whole of the Far East and the Pacific, including Australia,
New Zealand and a few outposts in South America. In Britain, where the
appeasers were now calling the tune in the coalition National Government
(following the defeat of its candidate in a by-election at East Fulham, an
area not previously noted for its grasp of international affairs), the Foreign
Secretary declined to make any comment on the grounds that the original
declaration had not been formally communicated to him through the
official channels. When Hirota then issued a further statement denying
any intention of interfering with foreign interest in China and reaffirming
Japan's allegiance to the principle of 'Open Door', the Western Powers
returned again to their own post-Depression economic problems.

When the dust had safely settled the Inner Cabinet of the five leading
(Prime, Home, Finance, Army and Navy) Ministers drew up a 'General
Outline' of their Chinese policy. Not only should Japan, they agreed,
'exploit internal strife in China to bring about a change in China's anti-
Japan policy' and 'not refrain from disturbing the political situation in
order to protect her rights and interests in China', but she also 'must
uncompromisingly oppose actions by China based on its traditional policy
of befriending distant nations and antagonizing its neighbours, and resist
any support by other powers for this policy.' They went on to declare that
'the guiding principles of the Nationalist Government are in fundamental
conflict with our China policy ... we should induce that Government to
become more friendly towards Japan and to appoint persons friendly
towards Japan to various offices within the Government. We desire a state
of affairs in which local governments, such as that in North China, will not
obey orders from the Nationalist Government ...'

In January 1935 Hirota initiated a new round of negotiations with
Nanking with the aim of 'inducing' a more conciliatory Chinese attitude,
at the same time making a point of declaring in the Diet that he was
offering 'no threat, no invasion'. The following month, 'The Lawrence of
Manchuria' Doihara, still the head of the Special Services Agency in
Mukden, made a tour of northern China, at the end of which he
recommended that Japan should 'insist on safeguarding our interests
established in the Tangku Truce agreements and, by this means, lead the
local regimes in North China into absolute obedience.' As a first step in
this process, the Kwantung Army in April unilaterally inaugurated a
regular air service to Peking from Jehol and Manchuria. When the Chinese
protested, they were referred by way of justification to the 'aerial
observation' clause in the Truce — even though the last Chinese troops
had, of course, been withdrawn from the Demilitarised Zone two years
earlier.

The Japanese Tientsin Garrison under its commander, Umezu Yoshijiro, also took the opportunity to adopt a more assertive presence, when on May 2nd the collaborating editors of two pro-Japanese news-sheets were murdered in their beds. Umezu was elsewhere at the time, but his Chief of Staff immediately issued a series of demands to Ho Ying-ch'in, who had stayed on after the Tangku Truce as Chiang's Commander-in-Chief in North China, including the incorporation of both Tientsin and Peking into the Demilitarised Zone, the dismissal of the head of the Hopei civilian administration and the total withdrawal of all Kuomintang offices and Nationalist Army units from the province. Conspicuous by its absence was any demand for the arrest and punishment of the murderers, adding to the evidence that they had in fact been hirelings of Itagaki.

Ho indicated that he was prepared to yield on most points, but the withdrawal of the military 'would be most painful and is completely impossible'. The high command in Tokyo, not wanting to see matters develop into a confrontation at this stage, stepped in with a modified demand that the Nationalist Army should only be required to withdraw as far as Paoting (about 70 miles south of Peking), and that the civilian administration should enforce a strict control of all anti-Japanese movements. The Imperial–Satsuma guardians of the 'Strike South' strategy took additional measures to safeguard their plans: Chief of Staff Uncle Kanin instructed that any use of force should be limited to clear-cut acts of self-defence, and the Navy dispatched a number of warships to Tientsin to reinforce Imperial authority.

Far from backing down, however, the Tientsin Garrison on June 9th issued Ho with an ultimatum that he should complete the withdrawal of all Nationalist forces within the month. For good measure, it was reinforced by another show of righteous indignation over a light-hearted magazine article entitled 'Idle Conversations About Emperors', in which Hirohito was described as 'a puppet of the real rulers of Japan' and 'a lover of biological study, whose being Emperor is a great loss to science'.

Since this was precisely the image of him that Tokyo was so sedulously projecting to the outside world, no offence had been taken when it had first appeared in Shanghai the previous month, but when it was reprinted in Tientsin the Garrison, taking its cue from the 'organ controversy' then raging in the homeland, eagerly seized on it as yet another stick to lay across the back of the unfortunate Ho. Receiving only the most muted support from Chiang, who was still preoccupied with the pursuit of the Communists on their Long March and had mistakenly seen the arrival of Japanese warships at Tientsin as a gesture of support for the Garrison's demands, Ho finally capitulated on all fronts. With the conclusion of this 'Ho-Umezu Agreement', military control of all Hopei passed into Japanese hands.

'AUTONOMY'

This show of strength by the Tientsin Garrison had already encouraged a further flexing of muscles from the Kwantung Army in the neighbouring Inner Mongolian province of Chahar. On the instructions of Doihara, Master-Spy Tanaka had moved into the area with the aim of placing the tribal leader Te, who could claim to be a direct descendant of Genghis Khan, at the head of a pro-Japanese Mongolian 'independence movement'. On June 11th, following a number of 'incidents' on the Jehol border, Doihara demanded the immediate withdrawal of all the pro-Chiang local warlord's forces from the province.

The high command in Tokyo, aware of possible Western reactions if the demands for a Chinese withdrawal from Chahar and Hopei were presented simultaneously, urged discretion; 'If we shun excessive publicity at this time, we should, in view of the present situation, be able to achieve practical results without publicity,' they advised. In spite of two further border clashes immediately afterwards, Minami, who had now taken over the command of the Kwantung Army from Muto, took a cautious line and urged that nothing more should be sought other than a guarantee against any further encroachments in Jehol.

Nanking, however, was expecting something much tougher and in a move to pre-empt it Chiang's warlord was replaced and his forces ordered southwards. Seizing on this attitude of appeasement as a sign that further concessions could be wrung from them Doihara then presented the warlord's successor, Ch'in Te-ch'un, with a new set of demands that entailed that 'measures for maintaining peace and order in the region evacuated should be modelled on those taken in the Demilitarised Zone'. Nanking once again signalled its acquiescence to the 'Ch'in-Doihara Agreement'; the Chinese forces were withdrawn to Peking, and their place taken by Japanese-controlled Peace Preservation units.

'The Lawrence of Manchuria' next set about inciting anti-Chiang unrest with the purpose of creating a pro-Japanese autonomy movement which would give Japan the same political control over the whole of the two provinces which she already held in East Hopei. This goal was given an extra urgency by the monetary reforms introduced by Nanking in early November in response to a growing currency crisis which had culminated in a panic run on silver triggered by an assassination attempt on Wang and his enforced retirement from the Foreign Ministry. On the advice of a British Government economist, all remaining holdings of silver were to be handed in to a Currency Reserve Board in exchange for a new paper currency; as a further measure of support, all British banks in China were ordered to back the reforms. Not only was this seen in Tokyo as an attempt to restore Britain's economic influence there at Japan's expense, but it was feared too that it would also serve to give a strong boost to China's political unity which Japan was seeking to destroy.

In spite of Doihara's pressure on the northern warlords not to co-operate, the reforms were soon acknowledged even by the Japanese to be 'proving considerably successful'. Doihara's next move was to summon the warlords to a 'State Founding Conference' for an autonomous North China (to include not merely Hopei and Chahar, but Shansi, Shantung and Suiyuan as well). However, on the appointed day he found himself sitting on his own at the conference table. A dismayed Minami thereupon cabled a request to Tokyo for 'stronger measures'.

'In order to cause the Nanking Government to abandon this policy, which will place China under the economic control of Britain and which, at the same time, tramples on the welfare of the people and menaces Manchukuo, we have no alternative but to demand that the provinces of North China be separated economically from the Nanking Government, as was previously recommended by the Chief of Staff,' Minami explained. 'Accordingly, this Army believes the outrageous action of the Nanking Government affords a splendid opportunity to execute the North China operation planned by Japan. We must put it into effect with the utmost determination and with absolute unity between central headquarters and the field army ... Of course we recognise that any move beyond the Great Wall should be carried out with the utmost caution and appropriate justification, and in particular, that any advance beyond the Demilitarised Zone should be done only on the Emperor's orders.'

The high command, however, was still worried that any premature move into China would jeopardise their long-term strategy, and the Vice-Chief of Staff, 'Toilet Door' Sugiyama, replied that Minami's arguments were 'not easy to recognise as sufficient reason for the movement of troops by the Kwantung Army. As you know, our national policy has not yet developed to the point of carrying out our aims in North China by the use of military force ...'

Minami tried another tack, representing that there was a danger of the Nationalist Army intervening in Shantung and that Japan 'must be firmly prepared to send troops' there on the usual pretext of protecting local Japanese residents. He even requested the dispatch of warships, but the Naval high command was even more chary of compromising the 'Strike South' and refused to co-operate.

A few days later, however, Press reports, doubtless originating in Mukden, began to appear, claiming that the 'North China Autonomy Movement' was due to be launched on November 20th. As a result Tokyo was persuaded to shift its stance and agreed to 'advise' Chiang to grant some form of autonomy to North China; at the same time Minami was warned that 'in view of its major domestic and international impact, the Autonomy Movement must be implemented as part of a controlled national policy and must not be carried out independently by the Army.'

In a move to save face, the Army General Staff put out a statement claiming that the initiative had come from themselves and purporting to discredit 'the clever propaganda of the Nanking Government and various foreign press reports, based on their own ulterior motives, to the effect that "the Autonomy Movement is only a creation of our Army" ... The Chinese people, hitherto as mild as sheep in the face of the authority of [Nationalist] Government officials, will no longer put up with this suppression and have launched a fierce movement against it ... Although Japan has declared its friendly feelings and sympathy towards this Autonomy Movement, Japan has never provided any substantive aid. It has in fact endeavoured to observe and control the activities of certain unruly Japanese.'

These 'unruly Japanese' were not, of course, identified, and the northern warlords hastily assured Chiang that the 'Autonomy Movement' was entirely the creation of the Japanese, and of Doihara in particular. At the same time they informed the Japanese that they would have nothing to do with it, while Wang's successor at the Foreign Ministry announced bluntly that 'the plain fact is that if Japan would recall General Doihara ... the Autonomy Movement would probably come to a sudden end.'

Determined to have something to show for all their efforts, the Japanese fell back on claiming 'autonomy' for the Demilitarised Zone which they already controlled, and on November 28th they announced the creation of an East Hopei Anti-Communist Autonomous Council. The puppet placed at its head was immediately branded by the Nationalist Government as a traitor, and orders were issued for his arrest.

Doihara, however, was still not satisfied that nothing more could be achieved, and two days later he forced the warlords to inform Nanking that 'present conditions in North China necessitate autonomy' and that they should discuss the establishment of an appropriate governing body. When the Nationalist negotiators arrived in Peking a week later, they were greeted by a storm of student demonstrations; 'we must fearlessly stand up and resist Japanese imperialism rather than sit down and become people of a conquered nation,' one of the leaflets ran. Ho Ying-ch'in felt that the situation was now beyond his control and conceded that only the creation of a new governing body acceptable to both sides would restore it. On December 11th Nanking announced the establishment of a Hopei-Chahar Political Council to administer the territory, including Peking and Tientsin, which was not already under the East Hopei Council's authority in the Demilitarised Zone.

DEBASING THE CURRENCY

The protesters were at least consoled by the knowledge that they had denied Doihara his ambition to extend Japanese control to Shantung, Shansi and Suiyuan, although their satisfaction would have been somewhat short-lived if they had known the contents of a document issued by the Japanese War Ministry on January 13th 1936 under the title of 'An Outline of Policy to Deal with North China' which was specifically devoted to the incorporation of these three additional provinces under Japan's control.

When Britain and America had expressed some concern at the establishment of the 'Autonomous' Councils, Tokyo replied blandly that 'the Autonomy Movement in North China is essentially a Chinese matter, and Japan is watching it with interest'. There the matter had been allowed to rest and, encouraged by this lack of international response, the Okada Cabinet had no qualms in adopting the document as official Government policy. The U.S. Ambassador, Joseph Grew, reported that there was now a 'swashbuckling temper' in the country at large, accompanied by much talk of Japan's destiny to subjugate and rule the world.

A key rôle in the Japanese plan to undermine the new currency reforms and to consolidate their economic hold over northern China was assigned to the so-called 'special trade' with Japan. This had already grown considerably, not merely in opium and, in the other direction, silver, but also in a wide range of other commodities and manufactured goods since the Nationalist Government had introduced a sharp increase in tariffs in 1933, but it was now boosted to an altogether higher plane with the open encouragement of Japan's minions in the East Hopei Council. Most of this 'trade' had formerly been brought down on the South Manchuria Railway to Shanhaikwan, where it was transferred to waiting lorries and driven across the border under the guise of 'military stores', but the Council made it very much more profitable to bring it in by sea by barring Chinese customs boats from entering East Hopei waters.

Within a month twenty-three vessels ranging up to sixty tons in weight were plying regularly from Dairen, and when the goods were landed the local customs officials were usually bribed to turn a blind eye; on other occasions even this nicety was dispensed with and the smugglers were allowed to go about their business unmolested under the protection of armed Japanese soldiers on the pretext that interference with Japanese ships would constitute piracy. When customs officials in Hopei then began searching Japanese entering from the Demilitarised Zone, the head of the Hopei-Chahar Council was told very sharply to put an end to this 'humiliating practice' or face reprisals.

Presently the Council gave up all pretence of trying to collect customs duty from Japanese importers on Nanking's behalf and instead permitted Japan to impose a 'handling charge'. This preferential treatment naturally led to a drastic decline in trade with other countries, but when they complained to Tokyo the Foreign Ministry assured them that legitimate Japanese traders were also voicing the same complaints.

In this way almost a third of Nanking's usual customs revenue was soon being diverted into the coffers of the puppet Council; this would, so it was promised, lead to the creation of another 'earthly paradise'. The commander of the Japanese fleet in China reported with satisfaction that the loss 'is embarrassing the Nanking Government greatly. If we cleverly utilise this situation, we believe the Nanking Government will reconsider its policy and reduce its unreasonably high tariffs. We should, moreover, be able to open its eyes over its diplomatic policy towards Japan and foster the opportunity to co-operate.' The Foreign Ministry was less happy with the development, for it brought protests from the Powers that Japan was contravening the customs agreement incorporated in the Washington Treaty; Britain and America had particular cause for concern, in that the customs revenue was pledged as security for their loans to China.

Another channel for these funds was found in Master-Spy Tanaka's Inner Mongolian 'independence movement'. This bounty came at a particularly opportune moment, because the flow of slush-money from Tokyo had dried up following Hirohito's fury on learning that the Kwantung Army was preparing a push into Suiyuan just when the negotiations for the establishment of the Chahar-Hopei Autonomous Council were coming to a successful conclusion. On Tanaka's recommendation and with the backing of 'Scrapper' Tojo, then Chief of Secret Police in Manchuria and shortly to become the Kwantung Army Chief of Staff, the campaign was resumed the following month, and when in June 1936 an Inner Mongolian Government was proclaimed under the nominal leadership of Te, Hirohito gave it his personal blessing by elevating him to the title of Prince.

SURPRISE BEDFELLOWS

In the meantime however, the 'Young Warlord' Chang had returned, apparently revitalised by his sojourn in Europe, to reorganise his scattered forces. Chiang Kai-shek had allotted them a major part in his forthcoming sixth, and he hoped final, Extermination Campaign against the Communists, but he now gave them his blessing to concentrate in Suiyuan against the new Japanese puppet. In November, under the direction of one of the German advisers recruited in 1933 to help in the Extermination, they decisively routed Tanaka's Kwantung Army unit and his Mongol allies.

When Tokyo then rejected a request from the Kwantung Army to be allowed to send in further troops to restore the situation, Tojo disavowed any connection with the whole operation and dismissed it as an internal conflict between Mongol tribesmen. In response to international expressions of concern, the Foreign Ministry issued a categorical denial that any Japanese forces had been involved. A month later Te renounced Tokyo's support and proclaimed his allegiance to Nanking.

The frustrated Tojo turned his attention instead to reorganising the economy of 'Manchukuo'. Thanks to the interference of its unqualified military overseers this had so far seen little of the expansion expected of it, and Tojo now called for the assistance of Kishi Nobusuke, a rising star in the Ministry of Commerce and Industry. Kishi drew up an ambitious Five-Year Plan, and in order to implement it he turned to his uncle, Aikawa

Gisuke, the head of the Nissan (abbreviated from Nippon Sangyo or Japan Industry) conglomerate which incorporated the electrical engineering firm of Hitachi. Nissan had risen to prominence in the World War One boom, and as a comparatively recent arrival it did not carry the stigma attached to the older conglomerates in the eyes of the military; under the recent Automobile Manufacturing Law, production licences had been restricted to Nissan and Toyota with the express purpose of giving them sufficient strength to drive their foreign-owned competitors (Ford and General Motors) out of business. Accepting the invitation, Aikawa virtually transplanted Nissan to Manchuria, where with the Kwantung Army's blessing he proceeded to parcel out the colony's economy between himself and the new President of the SMR, 'The Talking Machine' Matsuoka. Five years later Nissan would account for three-quarters of all Japanese overseas investment.

South of the Great Wall, the sudden growth of the 'special trade' had led to a surge in the number of Japanese residents in Hopei. This, coupled with the Communists' successful establishment of a new base in Shensi at the end of their Long March, gave Japan the pretext for more than doubling the size of the Tientsin Garrison for the residents' protection in line, it was claimed, with the 1901 Boxer Agreement. The commander of the enlarged force, which was now retitled the North China Garrison, was to be appointed directly by the Emperor in order, Hirohito explained, 'not to make control inconvenient as was the case when we reorganised the Kwantung Army' (prior to the Manchurian Incident).

Although this move did not draw any official protest from Nanking, it gave rise to a fresh wave of anti-Japanese incidents throughout the country (many of them provoked by the opening of Japanese Consular offices for espionage purposes in areas outside the Japanese sphere of influence), in which a number of Japanese were killed. On August 7th the Inner Cabinet formally adopted the programme for the 'Strike South' envisaging a major war with America within thirty years as a 'Fundamental of National Policy', and when a Japanese shopkeeper was murdered a month later in the southern province of Kwangtung a 'Southern Task Force' of two cruisers and five destroyers was dispatched to the island of Hainan. When three weeks later again a Japanese sailor met a similar fate in Shanghai, the Naval General Staff drew up a plan for a general Sino-Japanese conflict which required that 'the Army should immediately fall into step with the Navy'.

However, the encampment of the Communists so close to its sphere of influence (in February they had actually pushed across the Yellow River from Shensi into Shansi) had revived the Army's preoccupation with Russia. 'If, as is probable, the existing situation continues, Japan is destined sooner or later to clash with the Soviet Union', Itagaki declared in his new capacity as Kwantung Army Chief of Staff. To meet the occasion Mukden drew up an operational plan for a two-pronged attack on

Vladivostok and Lake Baikal; 1941 was set as the deadline for preparations, by which time it was proposed that the bulk of the standing army in Japan should have been transferred to Manchuria. At the same time the other Inseparable, Ishihara, who now held the key post of Chief of Operations Section in the General Staff, drafted a Five-Year Programme for Major Industries. 'In order to prepare for war with the Soviet Union by 1941,' he argued, 'industries essential to the waging of war must be fully developed in Japan, Manchukuo and North China'; this necessarily entailed that the Army should have the lion's share of its budget and that the Navy should wait for a second five-year programme before realising its plans in the South.

The Army therefore declined to support the Navy's call for military operations and opted instead for a policy of using the incidents to back the plan of Hirota, now Prime Minister in the wake of the February Mutiny, to extract a negotiated settlement from Chiang which would commit China to recognise 'Manchukuo', to join Japan in an anti-Communist alliance and to give preferential treatment to Japanese economic expansion in the North. Chiang had given little indication previously that he would ever agree to such terms, and the negotiations broke down completely when he countered with a set of demands of his own, which included the abrogation of the Tangku Truce, the disbandment of the East Hopei Council and an end to the smuggling from Japan and Manchuria.

Japan then promptly concluded the Anti-Comintern Pact with Germany. Publicly the Pact provided for no more than an exchange of information on the Comintern's subversive activities in order to assist in curbing the spread of Communism, but a secret annexe, the existence of which was widely suspected but naturally denied by Japan, pledged assistance for the protection of the two countries' mutual interests in the event of a Russian attack on either. Hitler had made the initial suggestion for such an agreement as far back as 1933, and so anxious was he to divert Russia's attention to the East while he carried out his plans in Europe, that he stretched the principle of Aryan superiority to allow that 'the blood of Dai Nippon contains within itself virtues closely akin to the pure Nordic strain'. Tokyo had begun to respond in earnest after the Government had adopted the Army's plan to split the five northern provinces from Nanking (incorporated in the 'Policy to Deal with North China'). Japan's satisfaction at its successful conclusion was summed up by a Foreign Ministry statement which predicted that it 'ought to prove quite effective in making China decide her attitude'.

TOWARDS A SHOWDOWN

Having successfully overseen the rout of the Japanese in Suiyuan, Chiang returned south to the Shensi provincial capital of Sian to launch the sixth Extermination Campaign against Mao's Red Army. The announcement of the Anti-Comintern Pact, however, had brought an explosive revival of anti-Japanese feeling throughout China, and it was even suggested that Chiang's policy of 'reunification first' indicated that he had concluded a secret deal with Japan. Thus when he arrived to discuss tactics against the Communists, the 'Young Warlord' declined to take part, and when Chiang persisted he was arrested and put under lock and key.

For twelve days, during which he found himself confronted by his old adversary Chou En-lai, his fate hung in the balance. Then suddenly on December 24th he was released and allowed to return to Nanking. No formal statement of what had transpired was ever issued, but it soon became clear that he and the Communists had agreed finally to sink their differences and to join a united front against the Japanese invaders. Chiang submitted his resignation as Head of State and was immediately reappointed, Chang surrendered himself into his protection and on New Year's Day 1937 the Extermination Campaign was publicly called off. 'With the completion of a United Front of all classes and parties and the democratisation of the Chinese Republic, we will commence a defensive war against Japan,' Mao announced. 'War with Japan is inevitable.'

'The Japanese nation seems to be somewhat thunderstruck by the sudden and unexpected determination of China to yield no more to Japanese pressure,' Ambassador Grew reported. The Anti-Comintern Pact was so roundly criticized in the Diet that War Minister Terauchi Hisaichi resigned in protest and thus brought the Hirota Cabinet down with him; he was the son of Terauchi Masatake, who as Prime Minister in 1918 had launched the abortive Siberian Expedition, and his attitude towards the democratic process may be judged by his remark on the opening of the new Diet building two months earlier: 'Wouldn't the money have been better spent on two new divisions?'.

Now in his eighty-eighth year, Last Noble Saionji asked to be excused from his traditional rôle of Premier-maker, but when his request was refused by the Emperor he nominated Ugaki. The Army, however, had still neither forgotten nor forgiven Ugaki for his reduction of defence expenditure as War Minister in the previous decade, and the Big Three declined to nominate a War Minister to serve under him, making it impossible for him to form a Cabinet. The task was then assigned to 'Border-Crosser' Hayashi. Saionji's forthright criticism of the choice recorded by his secretary Harada confirms that it was not his, but that of the Court; clearly, Hayashi's action in having entered Manchuria without Imperial authority was no longer held against him.

The prospect of united resistance from the Nationalist-Communist alliance brought about a profound shift in Tokyo's strategy towards China. 'We should change our policy,' a General Staff memorandum declared. 'Priority should be assigned to economic and cultural policies with the aim of promoting mutual assistance and co-prosperity. At this juncture we should maintain a just and fair attitude towards the movement for national unity in China, and the separation of North China should not be carried out.' As a mark of this 'just and fair attitude', the War Ministry even went so far as to suggest the abolition of the East Hopei Council.

Conversely, the union produced an altogether new robustness in China's attitude towards Japan, so that when a Japanese trade mission arrived in March to discuss possible joint developments (the South Manchuria Railway had already set up a subsidiary in northern China in December), they were confronted with demands of a much wider scope than those which Chiang had put forward in the autumn. In a further gesture of defiance the following month, Chiang sent 5,000 troops into Shantung as a special Tax Supervision Corps to clamp down on the 'special trade'. After their arrival, the Japanese Consul in Tsingtao reported that 'the Chinese have begun to adopt a strikingly offensive attitude, such as we have never before seen.'

The ignominious failure of this new policy of conciliation brought disastrous defeat for Hayashi in the general election at the end of April and his replacement by Imperial Go-Between Konoye; for the first time Saionji was not called upon to nominate a candidate. The new Cabinet included Black Dragon Godson Hirota as Foreign Minister, 'Toilet Door' Sugiyama as War Minister and 'Great Fascist' Suetsugu (as he was dubbed in the Diet for his uncritical admiration of Mussolini) as Home Minister. In a few months Konoye would be promising to 'beat China to her knees', and their collective attitude was graphically described by 'The Talking Machine' Matsuoka thus: 'China and Japan are two brothers who have inherited a great mansion called East Asia. The ne'er-do-well elder brother became a drug addict and a waster, but the younger, lean, rugged and ambitious, ever dreamed of bringing back past glories to the old house ... In a towering rage, he beat up the elder, trying to knock some sense of shame into him and awaken some pride in the noble traditions of the great house. After many scraps the younger finally made up his mind to stage a showdown fight.'

This new fighting talk naturally struck a sympathetic chord among the 'Strike North' element in the Army, particularly when Konoye ordered the release of Mazaki from the prison where he was being held on suspicion of having master-minded the February Mutiny, for they saw a resurgent China as an obstacle which would have to be removed before they could embark on the showdown with Russia. This view was well illustrated in a telegram from Tojo at the Kwantung Army Headquarters to the War Ministry: 'From the point of view of our military preparations against Russia I am convinced that, our current resources permitting, we should deliver a first strike against the Nanking regime in order to remove this menace at our rear.'

For once the Army's 'Strike North'-ers and the Navy's 'Strike South'-ers were in harmony, although their ultimate objectives remained as far apart as ever. Only the Control Group ventured to differ, maintaining that any move against China was fatally premature. Ishihara, who had taken on the mantle of the assassinated Nagata, declared that 'a decisive showdown against China is impossible'. His belief that the anticipators of victory were misled by the ease of the conquest of Manchuria was fortified by intelligence reports of huge Chinese orders for foreign armaments, particularly from Germany. When it was suggested that the North China Garrison should be reinforced as a preliminary move, he replied stoutly that 'not one soldier is going to be sent to China while I am alive'.

Once again, however, the debate was not to be resolved by the decisions of the high command in Tokyo, but by the actions of subordinates in the field.

25

'The China Incident'

THE OPENING SHOTS

On the evening of July 7th 1937 a company of the Japanese battalion stationed in Peking under the terms of the Boxer Protocol moved out towards the Marco Polo Bridge for a 'night exercise'.

The Bridge, dating back to the twelfth century and described by the Venetian adventurer as 'unequalled by any other in the world', marked the traditional crossing point of the Yungting River between the Inner Mongolian provinces and the Gulf of Chilhi. Its strategic importance was underlined by the railway bridge built parallel with it to carry the connection between the main lines from the capital to Hankow and Nanking. The Japanese had designs on building a barracks and airfield in the area, but despite the blandishments offered to them the local landowners had refused to sell. The Japanese response had been to attempt to intimidate them by holding frequent manoeuvres over their land.

The Chinese authorities had been given formal notice of this latest manoeuvre, but when shortly after ten o'clock the Japanese began firing blanks in the darkness it was not difficult to conclude that they had an altogether more serious purpose, and the Chinese troops stationed nearby reacted by loosing off a number of shells in their general direction. The Japanese company commander then held a roll-call. One soldier was found to be missing, and a runner was dispatched to report his absence to battalion headquarters.

The battalion commander, who was a member of the activist Cherry Society, felt it to be a 'grave matter' and ordered the remainder of the battalion into the area; he was also a close friend of the Operations Section Chief on the General Staff, which has led to a suggestion that the affair was not the spontaneous event that it was subsequently portrayed to be. At the same time he sent a demand to the Chinese to be allowed permission to search the nearby town of Wanping, even though the missing soldier had by now reappeared (having, it was generally believed, taken advantage of the darkness to visit a local brothel). This was refused, and as dawn broke the Chinese garrison opened fire on the Japanese, who were now being deployed around the town by a General of the Special Services Agency.

The Japanese promptly counter-attacked, and by noon the Chinese had fallen back inside the town walls.

When news of the incident reached Tokyo, it at once revived the debate between those who, like the Kwantung Army, urged that 'since the northern borders [with Russia] present no problems, we should take this opportunity to render a decisive blow in the Hopei-Chahar area', and those who, like Ishihara, felt that any such offensive in China proper would be fatally premature. Consequently, Chief of Staff Uncle Kanin issued a compromise order that same evening to the North China Garrison 'to avoid further use of force so as to prevent extension of the conflict', while at the same time pledging that if requested 'the Government would dispatch troops sufficient to achieve a quick solution of the incident'. This division surfaced again when the Cabinet met the following morning: the War Minister, 'Toilet Door' Sugiyama, recommended that three divisions should be sent immediately, while the Navy Minister, Yonai Mitsumasa, countered that such a decision could lead to all-out war and should therefore be avoided unless the situation became critical. At that point news arrived that a local settlement had been reached and the meeting was adjourned.

Almost immediately, however, further shooting broke out at Wanping, as did in turn the argument in Tokyo. Two days later a local settlement was again reached on the basis of a joint withdrawal of troops, but by this time events in Tokyo had overtaken it. At a General Staff Conference Ishihara argued that any offensive in China would require a minimum of fifteen divisions to guarantee its success, but the majority took a much more optimistic view of China's fighting capabilities and again called for the dispatch of three divisions from Japan plus another from Korea and two brigades from Manchuria. At a meeting of the Inner Cabinet the same day (July 11th) Yonai again voiced his opposition to the dispatch of troops, but it was approved by the majority with the qualification that it could still be cancelled if there proved to be no need for it.

Seeing the move as a serious threat to their 'Strike South' strategy, the Navy then hastened to reach an agreement with the Army which committed the latter to making three divisions available in Tsingtao and Shanghai 'for the protection of local Japanese residents'. The affair was now officially labelled the 'North China Incident', and Imperial Go-Between Konoye invited representatives of the political parties and the Press to the Prime Minister's Residence in order to secure a 'unified public opinion' in favour of the dispatch of troops. The decision had been made 'not in despair of the situation,' he said, 'but as a call for grave reflection on the part of China'. Thus it was that news of the local settlement was dismissed as a rumour, accompanied by the comment that 'if we, on the basis of a mere oral agreement, should trust the Chinese, we would only be deceived by them again.'

The following day Ishihara again warned the General Staff against creating a repetition of the ill-starred Siberian Expedition, but his argument was not helped by intelligence reports that Chiang Kai-shek's Nationalist Government was moving forces northward to Peking. The outcome was another compromise, which upheld the policy of non-extension of the conflict but at the same time authorised the dispatch of reinforcements 'should the situation warrant it'.

The situation on the ground also took a more ominous turn with the arrival of the Imperially-appointed Kazuki Kiyoshi to take over the command of the North China Garrison. Only the previous day the Garrison's Staff had told Tokyo in some indignation that they had no need for reinforcements, for which their new commander promptly branded them as 'a bunch of cowards'. However, he was persuaded to stay his hand for the moment on being informed that the Emperor had approved the policy of non-extension at the same time as giving his provisional authorisation for the dispatch of reinforcements. During the Imperial audience Hirohito asked Uncle Kanin what would happen if Russia intervened, and the Chief of Staff dismissed the suggestion as improbable. 'But if they do?' Hirohito persisted, to which Kanin replied 'Well, that's the end of it.' This attitude of 'let's see what the Powers will let us get away with' was to be the governing factor in Japanese policy over the next four years.

The Foreign Ministry drew up a set of terms for Nanking's ratification which were broadly in line with those of the local settlement, but these were then withdrawn at the Army's insistence and replaced by a much stiffer set which included the dismissal of the local Chinese commander and the withdrawal of the Chinese troops by July 19th without any corresponding withdrawal by the Japanese.

These were not surprisingly rejected by Chiang, who stipulated that no settlement could be accepted which infringed China's sovereignty and imposed restrictions on the movements of her forces. Echoing the call of Chou En-lai as spokesman of his new Communist allies that the time had now come to open hostilities against Japan, he declared that China was ready 'to throw the last ounce of her energy into a struggle for national survival regardless of the sacrifices'. Ishihara urged that Konoye should fly to Nanking to negotiate with Chiang in person, but his suggestion was rejected, and when on July 20th it was reported that the Chinese had again opened fire the Cabinet approved the dispatch of the three divisions.

ESCALATION

Events now snowballed. On the 22nd the Vice-Chief of the Chinese General Staff arrived in Peking to take command of the forces in the area. Kazuki responded by moving up further forces from Tientsin and another clash occurred on the 25th. He then signalled Tokyo for permission to retaliate and without waiting for a reply ordered an attack, at the same time issuing an ultimatum to the Chinese to withdraw their forces from Peking by the 28th. When his Tientsin units came under fire as they entered the former capital the following day, he informed Tokyo that he was abandoning the policy of non-extension in order to 'chastise the Chinese troops located in the Peking-Tientsin area'.

The high command gave their retrospective approval for these moves and presented the Cabinet with a scheme for the mobilisation of reinforcements. Having been nodded through there, it then received Hirohito's sanction; 'The North China Incident will be over in a month,' Sugiyama assured him. Following the Imperial audience, a Press report spoke of a 'second step' of the greatest importance having been taken in Japan's programme for China, and in the Diet Konoye spoke publicly for the first time of being determined to achieve 'a new order in East Asia', a phrase with an all-too-ominous ring.

The first troops disembarked on the morning of the 28th and immediately advanced to surround Peking. After a fierce aerial bombardment and bitter resistance from the heavily-outnumbered and out-gunned Chinese defenders, the city fell two days later. Tientsin suffered similarly, the famous Nankai University being reduced to rubble even though not a single soldier was there to defend it. The whole of northern Hopei was now under Japanese control, although not before the local Peace Preservation Corps at Tungchow, 20 miles east of Peking, had turned on their Japanese supervisors and killed them together with some 230 Japanese residents.

'The only course now open is to lead the masses of the nation, under a single national plan, into a struggle to the last,' the Generalissimo told his fellow-countrymen. Kazuki's response was similarly unequivocal: 'We shall have to smash the Central Government,' he declared. The Army General Staff drew up a new 'Strategy towards China' which advanced the front line seventy miles south to Paoting, and which also provided for the 'deployment, if necessary, of part of the [additional] forces in the Tsingtao and Shanghai areas'.

The Kwantung Army followed up with an even more comprehensive 'Outline for Solving Current Problems' calling for the dissolution of the Nanking Government and the establishment of puppet 'autonomous' regimes over all the five northern provinces. Ishihara, however, had still not despaired of avoiding an all-out war, and at an Imperial audience on July 31st he advised that 'the Army can reach the Paoting line, but nothing more can be accomplished. The most urgent task awaiting us today is to effect a truce by diplomatic means before we reach that time.' When Hirohito indicated his assent, Ishihara then joined with his opposite number on the Naval General Staff to draft a set of terms to put to the Chinese.

Noticeably generous in spirit in accordance with their desire to bring the conflict to an early close, they offered the abolition of the agreements establishing the Demilitarised Zone and the two Autonomous Councils, an end to the 'special trade', the withdrawal of Japanese reinforcements and the restoration of Chinese sovereignty in Hopei and Chahar, thus largely meeting the demands which Chiang had made the previous autumn. In return China was asked to concede recognition of 'Manchukuo', form an anti-Communist alliance and end the boycott and other anti-Japanese activities. They were eventually approved by the Inner Cabinet after a reluctant Sugiyama agreed to fall in with the majority, and on August 7th an envoy was dispatched with them to Nanking.

Once again, however, the outcome was overtaken by events on the mainland. Negotiations opened two days later, but that very evening two Japanese marines were discovered attempting to inspect a Chinese military airfield on the outskirts of Shanghai by a sentry and shot dead. The commander of the local Japanese forces, Admiral Hasegawa Kiyoshi, did not immediately force the issue; he had only 2,500 men at his disposal, whereas the Chinese had concentrated some 120,000 troops around the city since the shooting had begun at the Marco Polo Bridge.

The following day, however, the Naval General Staff concluded that 'the solution of the current difficulties will ultimately require the use of force', and Navy Minister Yonai asked the Cabinet to prepare for mobilisation in accordance with the recent agreement with the Army to supply troops in Shanghai and Tsingtao. By the 12th Hasegawa was reporting that 'the situation in the area could explode at any moment' and urged that 'the dispatch of army troops be expedited'. The Inner Cabinet met in emergency session that night and agreed to approve the request, and the following morning Chief of Naval Staff Fushimi obtained his cousin Hirohito's sanction.

SECOND FRONT

The dispatch of two divisions to Shanghai was then authorised with the Army's reluctant assent; 'the Navy dragged the Army into it,' Ishihara recorded. Hasegawa was instructed to refrain from using force at least until the reinforcements had landed, but even this caveat came too late, for the Japanese warships anchored in the Yangtse had already exchanged fire with Chinese shore batteries. That night he intercepted a Chinese signal which revealed a plan to bomb the fleet and ordered a pre-emptive strike from air units in Kyushu and Formosa. Bad weather prevented them taking off the next day, but two Chinese aircraft dropped several bombs over the International Settlement which caused more than a thousand casualties, forty of them Westerners. 'With these developments, the policy of non-extension of the conflict has disappeared,' Yonai declared with satisfaction 'The North China Incident has now become the Sino-Japanese Incident.' The following day Japanese naval bombers raided both Shanghai and Nanking, and China ordered a general mobilisation.

Whether the Navy deliberately engineered the initial incident at the airfield in order to widen the conflict is still to this day a matter for debate. Certainly, since its agreement with the Army on July 11th, the General Staff had been drawing up detailed contingency plans, including one for the landing of five divisions in central China in order to seize Nanking, and three days later Hasegawa had declared that the Navy was 'fully prepared to engage in an all-out war with China'. Against that, it has been noted how he did not immediately seize on the incident as a pretext to implement these plans, and it was another event which took place almost simultaneously which was the more likely to have persuaded the General Staff that the situation 'will ultimately require the use of force'.

On July 28th the Kwantung Army had sought permission for a preliminary advance into Chahar in response to a move by Chinese forces into the province, and this had been granted by Hirohito on condition that it did not advance any further westwards. On August 8th, however, it did precisely that, and the following day the high command authorised a general advance into Inner Mongolia; it was spearheaded by the newly-arrived 5th Division under the other Inseparable Itagaki, under the overall command of 'Scrapper' Tojo.

Such a move was bound to have been seen by the Navy as an attempt by the Army to promote the 'Strike North' at the expense of their own long-term strategy, which they therefore felt obliged to counter with a strike into central China even at the risk of its being seriously premature. When Hirohito gave it his sanction on August 13th, he remarked that 'if the Naval General Staff also feel this way, it will be very difficult to settle the matter by diplomatic means.' The 'Strike South' must, he was saying, retain priority.

Another serious risk which must have concerned the Navy was that a move against Shanghai invited a punitive reaction from the Powers with interests in the International Settlement there; the possible invocation of the U.S. Neutrality Act posed a particular danger, for it entailed the cutting off of nine-tenths of Japan's current oil supply. Conversely, such an extension of the conflict held more appeal for China, and the explanation of Madame Chiang Kai-shek, who was responsible for the development of China's fledgling air force, for the 'tragic accident' of the bombing of the Settlement lacked a certain credibility: the planes had been hit by Japanese anti-aircraft fire, she explained, which had loosened the bombs in their racks and eventually caused them to fall.

Other 'accidents', attributable to both sides, inevitably soon followed. On August 20th a stray Japanese shell hit the U.S.S. *Augusta*, flagship of the American Asiatic Fleet, killing one of her crew. Three days later a Chinese bomb fell on a department store in Chapei, causing over three hundred civilian casualties. Three days later again the British Ambassador's official car was strafed by two Japanese fighters, injuring his spine and drawing a protest at last from the Foreign Secretary. On August 30th the American liner S.S. *President Hoover* was bombed by four Chinese aircraft while taking off refugees — mistaken, it was claimed, for a Japanese transport.

On September 2nd the Cabinet in Tokyo, doubtless with the Neutrality Act in mind, declared that the 'North China Incident' was now to be known as the 'China Incident', even though full-scale war was now raging on both the northern and central fronts. On the former the three reinforcing divisions from Japan had all landed by the end of August, to be incorporated with the North China Garrison and Tojo's Kwantung Army force into the 'North China Army' under ex-Prime Minister Terauchi. A month later its First Army under Kazuki had occupied Paoting and was advancing on Tsinan, while Tojo's Second Army had swept through Chahar and into Suiyuan. In Shanghai the two divisions ordered had landed on August 23rd, but they met with such stiff resistance from the city's defenders that it soon became clear that further reinforcements would be needed. All the remaining Reserves were then mobilised.

In Tokyo Ishihara continued to fight an increasingly lonely battle against the dispatch of further troops and the extension of the front lines beyond Paoting and Shanghai, even breaking with his former boon companion and ally Itagaki when the latter asked permission to take the Fifth Division into Shansi. By September 27th his isolation was such that he was dismissed from the General Staff, and he would subsequently put himself so far beyond the pale as to suggest that the Emperor and the Imperial Family should undergo a course in military science in order to give themselves a better grasp of the country's military limitations (for this heresy he would be drummed out of the Army altogether, to pass the rest of his days in the seclusion of a Buddhist monastery).

Two weeks earlier President Roosevelt had banned U.S. Government merchant ships from carrying war material to either China or Japan, and on October 5th he suggested that aggressor nations should be put in some sort of 'quarantine'. The following day the League of Nations passed a resolution accusing Japan of having violated the Washington Treaty and the Kellogg-Briand Pact and calling on the Powers to consider means of lending support to China; at the same time it arranged for a conference in Brussels to formulate the basis for a possible peace settlement. Japan not only refused to participate, but also proceeded to set up an Imperial Headquarters in the grounds of the Imperial Palace in order to facilitate Hirohito's overall direction of the campaign, just as his grandfather Meiji had done at Hiroshima in 1904 at the outset of the war with Russia.

The Navy opposed the participation of Konoye because of his long-standing links with the Army 'Strike North'-ers. When the Prime Minister then threatened to resign, a Liaison Conference was also set up alongside to give him access to the deliberations of the Headquarters, but in order to emphasize that he could not expect thereby to play any part in their decision-making their orders were not required (as they had been in 1904) to be counter-signed by the Prime Minister. Even as War Minister, Tojo related in his post-war testimony, he was only allowed to attend as a 'participant' and not as a member.

In another calculated show of contempt for international opinion, Japan landed a further five divisions north and south of Shanghai in early November while the Brussels Conference was still pondering on what action, if any, the situation demanded. Incorporated with the troops already in the area into a 'Central China Expeditionary Force' under the overall command of Matsui Iwane, they quickly advanced in a pincer movement to cut off the Chinese line of retreat.

Chiang's German advisers urged him to abandon the city and adopt a strategy of tactical withdrawal in order to stretch the Japanese lines of communication, but he refused to accept that the West would be prepared to leave him to his fate and he ordered one battalion to fight to the last while he pulled back the remainder of his forces. Their mission fulfilled, the survivors made their escape under the cover of British guns into the International Settlement, but Japanese bombers continued to terrorise the now defenceless civilian population.

THE WAKING OF THE WEST

On November 19th when the Brussels Conference broke up without even so much as deciding on economic sanctions against the aggressor, Japanese forces were driving at full speed for Nanking, sweeping through the Chinese in their path in a series of 'slaughter battles' — so called because the number of casualties counted afterwards often exceeded the number of arms recovered by a factor of ten or more. 'SUB-LIEUTENANTS IN RACE TO FELL 100 CHINESE RUNNING CLOSE CONTEST' a headline in Tokyo ran. The two contestants 'in a friendly (sic) contest to see which of them will first fell 100 Chinese in individual sword combat before the Japanese forces completely occupy Nanking, are well into the final phase of their race, running almost neck and neck'; the 'score' was reported as being 89 to 78.

It was at this juncture that Hitler stepped forward in the hope of mediating between the two sides; not only was he increasingly embarrassed by the involvement of the German advisers against his co-signatory to the Anti-Comintern Pact, but he was worried that an extension of the war would damage both his increasing trade with China and Japan's ability to threaten Russia's eastern border.

A month earlier the Japanese Inner Cabinet, in a document entitled 'Outline for Dealing with the China Incident', had drawn up a list of minimum requirements for an armistice which included demands for recognition for 'Prince' Te's proposed regime in Inner Mongolia and reparations to cover the cost of the war to date. When these were subsequently put to Chiang by the German Ambassador, he had at first rejected them out of hand, but the Brussels fiasco and the remorseless advance of the Japanese on his capital forced him to reconsider, and on December 2nd he indicated to the Ambassador his willingness to negotiate.

In the meantime, however, Matsui had urged Tokyo that the occupation of Nanking was all that was needed to bring about a total Chinese capitulation. Vice-Chief of Staff Tada Hayao warned that the fall of Nanking would give China 'the strength of a cornered rat in its struggle against Japan', which would then become 'a tremendous drain on the Empire's strength far into the future', but since the disgrace of Ishihara his was an isolated voice of caution in the Army high command. On December 1st the Imperial Headquarters gave Matsui the go-ahead. At the same time they began to draft a greatly-harshened set of conditions, and Foreign Minister Hirota informed the Ambassador that 'public opinion' would no longer permit him to negotiate on the basis of the previous demands.

Nanking was a good deal less easily defended than Shanghai, and Chiang had already moved his administrative arm further up the Yangtse valley to Hankow. The Germans advised him to pull out his forces too in order to deprive the Japanese of a pretext for slaughtering the civilian population, but to surrender the seat of the new Republic and the resting place of its founder Sun Yat-sen without a blow was more than he could bring himself to sanction. However, his remaining army of 200,000 men, disorganised and demoralised after its headlong retreat from Shanghai, was in no condition to offer more than token resistance. By December 9th the Japanese, now under the command of Imperial Uncle Asaka, whom Hirohito had dispatched to take over from the fever-ridden Matsui, were within sight of the ancient walls. A surrender demand was issued, and when no reply was forthcoming another programme of saturation bombing from both ground and air was launched.

The large international community hastened to join the thousands of refugees fleeing in a flotilla of small craft following Chiang up the Yangtse, only to find that Japanese shells were no respecters of diplomatic immunity. An artillery regiment led by Chief Cherry Hashimoto cut across country south of Nanking to reach the river sixty miles upstream, and on December 11th he opened fire on the escorting British gunboat HMS *Ladybird*, killing one of its crew.

The following day, learning that a second convoy of three American oil tankers and the gunboat U.S.S. *Panay* was standing off the city to take on more Western refugees, he ordered a squadron of naval aircraft to attack them with the object of blocking the river. All four ships were disabled in the assault, and as the crews attempted to make good their escape a Japanese launch put out and swept them with machine-guns, continuing to fire even after they had made land. In addition to the numerous Chinese casualties, three Americans were killed and another fourteen seriously injured.

These two attacks excited the attention of the West to events in China as signally as all other manifestations of Japanese ambition had failed to do in the past. Not content with conveying his government's 'shock and concern' to the Foreign Ministry, President Roosevelt sent a personal message to Hirohito to the same effect, while in Tokyo Ambassador Grew, reminded of the sinking of the *Lusitania* which had triggered America's entry into World War One, stood by to pack his bags. As Hirota hurried round with 'profound apologies and regrets', the Foreign Ministry put out an official statement implying that the *Panay* and its convoy had been mixed up with a number of Chinese vessels and that the attack on them was 'purely accidental'.

The Navy voiced a more genuine concern, recalling the pilots responsible and the Admiral commanding the Naval Air Service in Central China. A few days earlier Hirohito had talked of plans to send a division to Canton to further the 'Strike South', which would now obviously have to be postponed in order to allay Western suspicions of their motives. By contrast, the Army seems thoroughly to have approved of Hashimoto's actions, which by blunting the 'Strike South' enhanced their argument for the 'Strike North'. The Chief Cherry was not recalled until over a year later, despite repeated protests from the British Ambassador, Sir Robert Craigie, and then he was commissioned to set up 'The Japan Patriotic Society' as a forerunner to Konoye's one-party Imperial Rule Assistance Association.

'Certainly, war with Japan is inevitable,' Roosevelt's confidant, Secretary of the Interior Harold Ickes, declared, but nobody was more aware than the President how unprepared America was for such a prospect at that juncture, and when Hirota followed his apologies with an offer of generous compensation to the families of the *Panay* casualties, he allowed the book to close on the incident.

NANKING RAPED

For the Army Hashimoto's actions served another purpose, namely, to divert the attention of the world from what was now taking place in Nanking. After four days of bombardment, the city had finally fallen. The defending forces had been warned in the surrender demand to expect 'harsh and relentless' treatment for resisting, and in their frenzy to escape the inevitable retribution thousands were drowned, pushed, trampled and crushed to death. However, these may be considered the lucky ones in the light of the fate which was reserved for those of their comrades who were taken alive.

The most common retribution meted out was to be trussed up and used as live dummies for sword and bayonet practice; others were bound together, doused in petrol and burnt alive or slung on stakes and roasted; still others were buried up to their necks in the ground to be left to rot or to have their skulls squashed by tanks; to be simply taken out and shot was the best that they could hope for. In Tokyo the Press reported that the 'race' between the two blood-letting sub-lieutenants had been extended to 150; the blade of one of them 'had been slightly damaged, its owner explained, as a result of cutting a Chinese in half, helmet and all. The contest was "fun", he declared.'

Non-combatants, by contrast, had been promised 'kind and generous' consideration, and on the strength of this pledge a group of Westerners remained behind to organise a 'safety zone' for the quarter of a million civilians trapped in the city. What then ensued they were powerless to prevent, but at least they were able to record it and eventually pass it on for the outside world to digest.

Inevitably it was the women who suffered most. On the pretext of being wanted 'for questioning', they were removed from the zone and in many cases raped even before they were loaded on to the waiting trucks, in broad daylight; age was no protection, a girl of 10 and a woman of 76 being among the victims. When one of them pleaded that she was too old she was impaled instead with a broomstick; another whose assailant was interrupted by the cries of her baby was obliged to look on while he smothered it before resuming; one poor creature was assaulted ten times every night for six weeks, until she was removed to hospital suffering from virulent symptoms of all three venereal diseases. The diary of one soldier described a typical exercise in an outlying village; 'We tried to capture this most interesting girl. The chase lasted for two hours. We shot one to death because it was her first time and she was ugly.' Even infants were not immune, a favourite 'sport' being to toss them in the air and impale them on bayonets as they came down.

Such, then, was the 'kind and generous' consideration promised. In two months of inhuman butchery the casualty figure, both military and civilian, rose according to one Japanese estimate to 300,000. One of the Western missionaries described how he and his colleagues would 'call every day at the Japanese Embassy and present our protests . . . We are met with suave Japanese courtesy, but actually the officials here are powerless. The victorious army must have its rewards — to plunder, murder, rape at will, to commit acts of unbelievable brutality and savagery on the very people they have come to protect and befriend, as they have so loudly proclaimed to the world. In all modern history surely there is no page that will stand so black as that of the Rape of Nanking.' The poet W. H. Auden, who was also there as a witness, later put it more succinctly: 'Where life is evil now: Nanking, Dachau.'

Like the sinking of the *Panay* and the *Ladybird*, the Rape of Nanking represented no mere 'accident'; it was a coldly-calculated attempt to intimidate the Chinese into surrender. 'You must realise that most of these young soldiers are just wild beasts from the mountains,' was a typical excuse offered to Western observers, but the composition of the Army had not changed from that which had so impressed the world a generation earlier with its discipline and self-restraint in the wake of its victories against the forces of the Tsar. Indeed, the testimony of those Western observers make it clear that far from rampaging out of control, the soldiers were in fact acting on the orders of their superiors. Officers were recorded supervising the looting of shops and homes, reserving the more desirable women for themselves, ordering the mass shooting and burning of captives.

The ultimate authority, in the absence of the bed-ridden Matsui, rested with Hirohito's uncle Asaka. When on December 17th Matsui was sufficiently recovered to lead a formal victory parade in the city, he afterwards delivered a reprimand to the assembled officers which, according to a Japanese correspondent present, was unprecedented in its severity. The following day he was returned to Shanghai, leaving Asaka in sole charge of the still worse atrocities that were to follow. When reports of these reached him there, he remarked pointedly that 'the discipline [of the soldiers] was excellent but the guidance and behaviour [of the officers] were not.'

When it was all over, Asaka returned to report the fulfilment of his mission to his nephew Hirohito. Privy Seal Secretary Kido naturally made no reference to such compromising knowledge in his diary, which permitted him to make the breath-taking claim before the War Crimes Tribunal nine years later that it had only been in 1945 that news of events in Nanking had reached the Court for the first time. The outside world was no longer prepared to play along with such dissimulation and demanded explanations. 'But of course,' Ambassador Grew observed wearily, 'the Japanese have an answer for everything ... As for the cases of rape, they say that hundreds of professional Chinese women had fled from the houses of public prostitution and the soldiers were merely bringing them back to carry on their usual commerce ...'

'A POINTLESS MOVE'

Confident that the sight of Nanking's agony would cow China into submission, Japan presented her on December 21st with a set of peace terms which amounted to little less than a formal submission of surrender, demanding the creation of Demilitarized Zones in northern (to include Peking and Tientsin) and central China, the establishment of a 'special political structure which would not necessarily be under the Government of Chiang Kai-shek' and the payment of reparations to cover not merely losses to Japanese residents but also the entire cost of the war to Japan.

A major hand in drafting them was taken by 'The Great Fascist' Suetsugu, who had joined the Cabinet earlier in the month as Home Minister and thereby gained a voice in the Liaison Conference. 'Unless the peace conditions are very much stiffened, our people are going to be dissatisfied and so are our soldiers at the front,' he told his colleagues. 'Now Nanking has fallen it appears that Chiang's regime is in real trouble, but we still cannot conclude that his authority has disappeared. If we weaken our campaign a little bit, it is evident that his regime will recover again. But if we give just one more little push, it will fall ...'

These terms, moreover, were not subject to negotiation; China had until December 31st to accept them 'in their entirety' otherwise Japan would, Foreign Minister Hirota warned, 'be forced to treat the present situation from an entirely different point of view'. The fall of Nanking had done nothing to lessen the conviction of Vice-Chief of Staff Tada of the disastrous consequences of the protracted war thus threatened, and he succeeded in having the deadline postponed until after the issue had been put before an Imperial Conference, the first to be convened since the war against Russia, on January 11th 1938.

Konoye was not best pleased at the prospect of the Emperor being compromised by openly identifying himself with the proposed terms, and to avoid that danger he informed Hirohito that they had already been unanimously agreed by the Government and that therefore there would be no need for any comment from the Throne. The meeting was opened by Chief of Staff Uncle Kanin, who gave his approval to the terms; when the remainder followed suit Tada felt inhibited in raising his lone voice of opposition in the Imperial presence, and it broke up after less than an hour without a single word from Hirohito.

A new deadline of January 16th was set for China's acceptance of the terms; if Chiang still refused them, he was threatened, his Nationalist Government would face either 'annihilation' or absorption into a new regime 'with which Japan could negotiate the adjustment of mutual relations and co-operate to bring about the regeneration of China.' Before it expired, Tada decided to make one last-ditch attempt to reverse the position at a meeting of the Liaison Conference on the 15th, but he was eventually silenced by Navy Minister Yonai, who told him that if he could not support the terms he should either resign or face the prospect of bringing down the Government. After toying briefly with the idea of a direct appeal to the Throne, Tada finally bowed to the inevitable, although still expressing a hope that 'the Emperor may order the Cabinet to reconsider its position or may call another Imperial Conference'. He was once again to be disappointed.

Contrary to Japanese expectations, however, Chiang gave no sign of acceptance, and when the new deadline passed and still nothing had been heard from him, Konoye issued the historic declaration that 'the Imperial Government will cease henceforth to deal with the Nationalist Government'. The last bridge had been burnt; it was, Hirota declared to the Diet, 'stronger even than a declaration of war'. The German Ambassador reported to Berlin that the protraction of the war was now a *fait accompli*.

Six months and the expenditure of two thousand million yen later, the worst forebodings of Tada and Ishihara would come to pass, moving even Konoye to describe the war as 'a pointless move'.

26

Empty Seat at the Feast

TWIN PUPPETS

While the eyes of the world had been rivetted on Shanghai and Nanking, the North China Army had been pushing steadily further south, and on December 14th a 'Provisional Government' had been declared in Peking to take over from the Peace Preservation Committees and Special Services Agencies which had moved in behind the troops. That Nanking had just fallen was no coincidence, because the North China Army was not prepared to see itself subordinated to any central regime that the Central Army might be planning to establish there.

The new body's writ extended only over Shantung, Honan and the southern sectors of Hopei and Shansi because 'Scrapper' Tojo refused to yield the Kwantung Army's control of the areas to the north, particularly Inner Mongolia, where it had at last succeeded in establishing a Mongolian Federated Autonomous Government under 'Prince' Te, in defiance of instructions from Tokyo. In a move which presaged his entry into the highest political arena, Tojo informed Tokyo that he felt that 'Manchukuo' should formally be made a party to the Anti-Comintern Pact. Vice-Minister of War Umezu, the former commander of the North China Garrison, agreed, but added that the first move should come from the Manchukuan government in order to 'preserve the fiction of Manchukuo's independence'.

The nominal heads of the Provisional Government were dissident warlords, many with a history of collaboration with the Japanese dating back to the First Republic of Yuan Shih-k'ai; they would have few powers because, as the Foreign Ministry official responsible for recruiting them explained, 'the Chinese people have had enough of tiresome regulations'. What powers they did enjoy were largely directed towards the promotion of Japan's economic penetration of the region. A 'Reserve Bank of China' was set up in order to replace the Chinese currency with its own banknotes.

This was followed in March 1938 by the establishment of a Sino-Japanese Economic Council, but effective control of all the more important economic activities had already been subsumed by the North China Development Company, an off-shoot of the South Manchuria

Railway established in 1935. Mitsui, Mitsubishi and the other Japanese conglomerates were invited to subscribe the necessary development capital. In northern Shansi the SMR, with the blessing of the Kwantung Army, took direct control over the Tatung coal mines, whose production was then exported to Japan at a tenth of the price which it had previously commanded on the open market. The Provisional Government financed itself by taking over the collection of customs dues, at the same time cutting the tariff rates to their pre-1931 level to give a further boost to imports from Japan and so eliminate the need for the undercover 'special trade'. Another source of income was provided by the ill-named 'Opium Prohibition Bureau', whose purpose was, far from suppressing the traffic in the drug, to encourage it under a licensing system which channelled the profits into its own coffers.

The Provisional Government was also armed with a propaganda organisation entitled 'The New People's Society' to inculcate the Chinese equivalent of the 'Imperial Road' and to eradicate the influence of Sun Yat-sen's Three Principles — that 'rubbish of Western Thought'. The unit's first objective was to reorganise institutions of higher education (most of whose students had fled into the protection of the Communists in Shensi) and to train civil servants for the Provisional Government. Most of the teachers it employed were drafted in from Japan, and a Textbook Revision Committee ensured that only 'correct interpretations' of previous Japanese activity in China were taught. It soon branched out into a host of other fields, however, organising anti-Chiang marches and demonstrations, speaking contests on themes such as 'How Japan and China Can Be Intimate', radio broadcasts, travelling libraries, medical services, rural co-operatives and the distribution of seeds and implements; according to one observer, 'it even imports pigs for breeding experiments.'

The Central China Army was not slow to set up a rival establishment and on March 28th, without even waiting for formal blessing from Tokyo, it inaugurated the 'Restoration Government of the Republic of China'. This body was first located in the New Asia Hotel in Shanghai, before being moved in June to Nanking; it took over from a somewhat shadowy stop-gap administration whose head, a mayor imported by the Army from Formosa, had rarely shown himself in public and whose leading officers were described by one Western observer as 'a bunch of second-rate racketeers and gangsters, most of whom had previous police records'.

Like its counterpart in the North, it was mainly headed by relics of Yuan's Republic and effectively controlled by Japanese advisers; 'Oh no, the Japanese do everything,' one of its officials told an American diplomat. Financially, however, it was much weaker, because the Western Powers refused to hand over the collection of customs dues in Shanghai, while Britain froze the payment of the remaining Boxer indemnities due to Japan. Learning from the experience in the North, where the Provisional Government's banknotes were so unpopular that even the Japanese

Government-controlled Yokohama Specie Bank refused to accept them, it made no attempt to issue its own currency, and for its income it was forced to rely almost entirely on secret deals with Shanghai's underworld empires. A Central China Development Company was set up, but its modest starting capital reflected the comparative paucity of natural resources in the area, and its main function was to put in hand repairs to public utilities, particularly railways, damaged in the fighting.

CHIANG ENSCONCED

In the field, the two Armies devoted most of the first three months of the year to consolidating their gains before launching a joint operation to link up at the vital junction of Suchow. At the end of January Vice-Chief of Staff Tada presented a 'restrained policy for protracted war' which envisaged three stages of execution: 1938 would be spent strengthening the puppet governments, 1939 and 1940 would see the resumption of large-scale military campaigns and 1941 the extension of the war to Russia with a force of ninety divisions and ten thousand planes. It was immediately opposed by Prime Minister Konoye and War Minister Sugiyama as too dilatory and likely to demoralise the men in the field, but at a stormy Imperial Conference on February 16th Tada won agreement for 'maintenance of the status quo and no further advances'. That he was able to do so was due to the intervention of Hirohito, which forced the War Ministry to admit that any immediate extension of the front in China might jeopardise the longer term plan of the Army against Russia as well as the Navy's 'Strike South'.

When it was handed down to the field commanders, however, the strength of protest was reported to be such that fears were expressed in the General Staff that matters might be taken out of their hands and the war 'converted into another Siberian Expedition'.

The first stage of the 'policy of restraint' was then abandoned forthwith and a General Mobilisation Law, as envisaged by Nagata ten years earlier, introduced to raise the requisite new divisions envisaged by the third stage. At the same time the Government issued a statement explaining that because China's leaders 'were persisting in their blindness' in refusing the terms that Japan had offered to them, they had to be made to 'realise the disastrous consequence of anti-Japanism'.

On April 5th Imperial Headquarters gave the two armies the go-ahead to close in on Suchow. However, the Chinese too had taken advantage of the lull since the fall of Nanking to regroup and raise a considerable number of fresh divisions; their morale had also been boosted by the exploits of Madame Chiang's makeshift Air Force, which not only achieved several spectacular victories but also ventured as far as Formosa and succeeded in knocking out a power station there. On the recommendation of the German advisers, Chiang threw a major proportion of his manpower into the Suchow area in order to draw off possible Japanese attacks on the more vulnerable cities further inland. He concentrated his defence round the small railhead of Taierhchwang; the town was well known to his tacticians, because it had long been used by the Chinese War College for field exercises.

The North China Army's advance, moving down the line of the Peking-Nanking railway, had been spearheaded by Itagaki's 5th Division. In the face of the unexpectedly effective resistance they suffered severe casualties even before they reached Taierhchwang, and the capture of the town itself, which fell after seventeen days of the most intense fighting of the war, was achieved only with the loss of all but Itagaki's entire division.

Even by the Japanese it was seen as a 'signal victory' and the turning point of the whole war for the Chinese, who now, it was reported from the field, 'began to talk boastfully about destroying the Japanese forces'. To the despair of the Germans however, Chiang rejected their pleas to follow up his success and go on to the attack before the Japanese Central China Army could reach Suchow; 'the Chinese cannot get the idea of the offensive into their heads,' U.S. Military Attaché 'Vinegar Joe' Stilwell complained.

In recognition of its importance, Hirohito's uncle, Higashikuni, was drafted in to lead the attack on the city and his brother Chichibu sent on a morale-boosting tour of the front, while troops were hurriedly brought down from the Kwantung Army in order to make good the previous losses. After a further month of bitter conflict, the Chinese pulled out their forces before the Japanese could encircle them.

When they entered the empty city on May 19th, the Japanese commander demonstrated that their behaviour at Nanking had not represented a breakdown in discipline among the common soldiers as was subsequently claimed, but an example of a calculated campaign of terror which was now overseen and co-ordinated for the second time by a senior member of the Imperial Family. Most of the male captives were again made targets for bayonet practice, at which a Western observer noted that an officer 'insists that clumsy thrusts must be repeated'. The women suffered no less horribly: after one had been raped and murdered in quick succession by a soldier, the same writer described how 'an officer runs up and reproves the man for his lack of consideration, arguing that everyone should have his turn and promising to lead the soldiers on to further prey. Another soldier kicks at the breast of the murdered woman and laughs as the blood spurts out.'

The extent of the Japanese casualties gave rise to a sharp division of opinion among the leadership in Tokyo. The hardliners in the Army were all for following up the Chinese retreat with a thrust up the Yangtse to Chiang's new capital of Hankow. Konoye, on the other hand, was reinforced in the doubts that he had already begun to entertain on the

wisdom of the 'annihilation' policy. He had submitted his resignation as
Prime Minister at the end of March in protest at the Army's underhand
formation of the Provisional Government which Sugiyama had presented
as a *fait accompli* to his Cabinet colleagues, but Hirohito, who also
complained of the Army's 'sneaky methods', (but not, of course, of its
bestial behaviour, of which he was still purportedly ignorant) persuaded
him to stay on and reorganise the Cabinet instead. The replacement of
Sugiyama as War Minister presented the major hurdle, and the 'Toilet
Door' resisted all suggestions (even those of the Throne) that he should
step down voluntarily.

In the end a compromise was struck with the appointment of Itagaki
with Tojo as his Vice-Minister. Konoye hoped to use Itagaki, who was the
candidate of Number Two Roadster Mazaki and 'Doctor' Okawa (both
now released from their confinement for their involvement in the 1932 and
1936 mutinies) to curb the influence of the dominant Control Group. In
particular, given the Imperial Roadsters' preoccupation with a war against
Russia, Konoye was confident that he could rely on Itagaki to follow the
formerly-Inseparable Ishihara in supporting the 'policy of restraint' in
China, but he fatally under-estimated the fighting instincts of 'Scrapper'
Tojo. In another *quid pro quo*, Foreign Minister Hirota, the instigator of the
'No more dealings with Chiang Kai-shek' declaration, was replaced by
Demobiliser Ugaki, while the Ministry of Education was given to Head
Roadster Araki.

The compromise, however, did little to heal the divisions. 'One group
says that it wants to end the war, the other says that it will go so far as to
attack Hankow', Hirohito remarked soon after the new Cabinet had been
installed. 'What a pity that there is no liaison between them.' No one was
more acutely aware of the growing atmosphere of crisis, which began to
be reflected in his physical appearance; those in contact with the Palace
spoke of him as appearing 'dispirited', 'haggard' and 'exceedingly
emaciated'. Nor would it have escaped the notice of even the humblest of
His subjects: cotton cloth was withdrawn from the domestic market, iron
became as 'scarce as gold', the shortage of raw materials reduced many
factories to half capacity while in others a 14-hour working day became
the norm, and chemists in the Ministry of Agriculture were reduced to
'tanning rat skins in their search for a leather substitute'. Even the neon
lights in Tokyo's Ginza precinct were ordered to be extinguished, a move
which one acerbic observer approved with unconscious irony as 'an
enlightened act by our unenlightened Military Government'.

As part of the compromise an Imperial Conference on June 15th gave its
approval for an advance on Hankow. The two armies had in fact begun to
strike inland in pursuit of the retreating Chinese after the fall of Suchow,
but they had been brought to a sudden halt by the blowing of the dykes on
the Yellow River which interposed an impassable barrier running all the
way down to the Yangtse. Two million people were rendered homeless by

the flood, but it gave the Chinese armies precious time to regroup and forced the Japanese to divert their line of attack along the much more indirect and less accessible Yangtse valley.

The Japanese lines of supply were now seriously stretched, as a captured diary testified: 'We are having great difficulties in transporting supplies. There seems little hope of us winning the war ...' To surmount the difficulty Uncle Higashikuni called on the Navy to reinforce him with a fleet of transports and aircraft carriers. Resort was also made to the liberal use of mustard-gas and other internationally-outlawed chemical weapons, while 200,000 Chinese dollars was spent on bribing Chiang's secretary to reveal the plans for an attack on the Japanese ships. Despite these less orthodox strategems, it was not until October 25th that Hankow finally fell, by which time the Generalissimo and his administration were safely ensconced a further 500 miles up river in Chungking — a location which was to prove for ever beyond Japanese reach.

WANG SEDUCED

One of Ugaki's preconditions in accepting the post of Foreign Minister had been that the 'no more dealings with Chiang' posture should be abandoned. 'We Japanese are always talking about "China for the Chinese",' he declared. 'If this really is our policy, then we should be satisfied with anyone the Chinese wish to instal and maintain in office ... The strong current behind the political activities in China in recent years has been the concept of a national state, and it was by responding to this current that Chiang became China's leader. We cannot ignore the immense power wielded by this hidden current.' He accordingly set about reopening the lines of communication with Chiang, and in June secret talks were begun in Hong Kong between the secretary of the Nationalist President (Chiang's brother-in-law) and the Japanese Consul-General there.

The first question raised on the Chinese side was whether Japan still demanded Chiang's resignation, and the meeting of the Inner Cabinet on July 8th provided the uncompromising answer that Japan's 'acceptance of the capitulation of the present Central Government of China' was indeed conditional upon it; in other words, the 'no dealings' posture had only been dropped in order that China's surrender could be negotiated.

At the time Ugaki seems to have agreed to go along with the demand as an initial bargaining tactic, for when the Chinese went on to question the demand for the recognition of 'Manchukuo' and for war reparations he indicated that he viewed them as alternatives, asserting that Chiang's resignation would 'really benefit your country more than Japan' on the argument that his rule had brought China nothing but misery. The Chinese replied bluntly that it was simply out of the question, adding for good measure that because of the devastation which the war had already wrought they were in no position to afford any reparations. When the Japanese then came forward with a further demand that the whole of North China could be declared a 'special [Japanese-controlled] zone' the talks tailed off without any conclusion being reached.

When at the end of September Ugaki was heard to exclaim that 'the Chiang regime and his gang must be smashed by increasing our pressure on them', he may have been speaking out of a general sense of exasperation, for he was then on the point of submitting his resignation. The issue which drove him to take such a step was not that of Chiang's resignation, but a proposal by the Inner Cabinet to establish, following the linking up of the North China and Central China Armies, a new central governing body to take over from the Provisional and Restoration Governments. Unknown to Ugaki, a 'Special Commission for China' was set up under 'The Lawrence of Manchuria' Doihara to recruit suitable stooges to front the new body, and it quickly became clear that the Army and Navy intended to monopolize control of it.

Their plans for it envisaged maintaining military control not merely of North China but also of the Yangtse valley, Inner Mongolia and the islands off the South China Coast in order to strengthen 'the strategic position of Japan in preparation for the coming [wider] conflict'. It would also exercise economic control by taking over the functions of the two Development Companies. Ugaki was not against the principle of such a body, but he insisted that it should be under the control of the Inner Cabinet as a whole and, in particular, that the Foreign Minister should continue to be responsible for relationships with the Nationalist Government. When the Army and Navy Ministers refused to concede this at an Inner Cabinet meeting on September 27th, he promptly resigned.

Before his successor could take office, the new body was duly set up by another Imperial Conference under the title of the Asia Development Board to 'administer political, economic and cultural affairs in connection with the China Incident ... until the programme for the reconstruction and development of China and the economic, political and cultural co-operation of Japan, Manchukuo and China have been effected.' The Board was nominally under the Presidency of the Prime Minister, but it was dominated by the Army and Navy and its chief executive member was China-Watcher Suzuki Teiichi; its Secretary-General (another General) was also invited to join the Inner Cabinet whenever its discussions involved China. Four regional offices were set up in Peking, Shanghai, Kalgan (Chahar) and Amoy, all under the direction of Generals and Admirals — in fact, they were merely renamed branches of the Special Service Agency. The Foreign Minister's say in China dwindled to the point where he was informed that his function there consisted of no more than the reception of foreign envoys and the signing of treaties.

Doihara's chosen target as a Chinese front for the Board was Wang Ching-wei, Chiang's former rival who had recovered from the wounds inflicted by his would-be assassin sufficiently to take up the post of Deputy Director-General of the Kuomintang. When he was first sounded out by a Chinese intermediary Wang professed to be shocked and stoutly refused to 'betray Chiang', but after the mass destruction caused by the blowing of the Yellow River dykes and the scorched earth policy borrowed from Mao's Communists which followed it he had gradually become disillusioned with the Generalissimo's strategy.

The breaking point came with the fall on October 21st (almost simultaneously with that of Hankow) of his own former fiefdom of Canton, of which he wrote afterwards that the fire-raising of Chiang's retreating soldiers 'did not halt the advance of the Japanese troops, nor in any way embarrass their positions. It merely destroyed the lives, properties and the livelihood of the Cantonese people themselves.' He accused Chiang of 'merely following the instructions of the Communist Party ... Anybody with a knowledge of history can see that Communist guerrilla warfare is just a euphemism for large-scale robbery.' Events in Europe only strengthened his belief that a change of tack was called for: the surrender of Czechoslovakia to Hitler at Munich meant that nothing could be expected from the West, while the aid being received from Russia was being given merely with the object of seeing China eventually 'brought to ruin by a policy of unending resistance to Japan ... Was it not better to bear the unbearable and conclude peace terms with Japan?'

On November 3rd Prime Minister Konoye publicly called for a 'New Order in East Asia' in which Japan and China would combine against the 'imperialistic ambitions and rivalries of the Western Powers' to bring about 'eternal peace' in East Asia; the Nationalist Government was welcome to participate in the creation of this utopia as long as it 'remoulded its personnel so as to translate its rebirth into fact' — as long as, in other words, Chiang was replaced at its head.

Two weeks later clandestine negotiations got under way in Shanghai between representatives of Wang and members of Doihara's Commission. On November 20th a tentative agreement was reached under which the new Chinese regime would recognise 'Manchukuo', would pay compensation for war damage but not reparation of the cost of the war, would give Japan 'special facilities' for economic development in North China and would allow Japan to station troops in Inner Mongolia and North China as part of a joint defence network against Russia. In return, Japan would withdraw her troops from all other areas within two years and would drop proposals for a Sino-Japanese Joint Economic Committee which would have carried 'special privileges' for Japanese businessmen throughout China. These terms were a good deal less demanding than those formulated at the succeeding Imperial Conference 'For Adjusting to New Japan-China Relations' which set up the Asia Development Board on November 30th, by which time Wang's assent to them had been secured.

In order to avoid the taint of identification with the puppet Provisional and Restoration Governments, it was planned that Wang should establish his regime first in the unoccupied provinces of Yunnan and Szechwan. He was to escape to Hong Kong on December 8th and announce his defection, after which Konoye would make a radio broadcast at Osaka announcing the new 'adjustments'. Wang, however, had still not given up hope of persuading Chiang to enter peace negotiations, but he was obliged to wait until the Generalissimo returned from an inspection tour of the front on the 9th. A 'great and violent debate' ensued between them, at the end of which Chiang was still unmoved. Only then was Wang's mind finally made up, and it was not until the 19th that he was able to organise his flight.

AND UNDECEIVED

Konoye in the meantime had postponed his broadcast and returned to Tokyo pleading illness, and when he eventually made it on the 22nd, it was in language very different from that which Wang had been led to anticipate: not only did it incorporate the 'special privileges' which Wang's negotiators had fought to exclude in Shanghai, but it also, on the insistence of the Army General Staff (where the obstructive Tada had just been replaced as Vice-Chief) made no commitment to any withdrawal of Japanese troops. This reflected not only the 'adjustments' agreed by the Imperial Conference, but also widespread suspicions in Tokyo (enhanced by his failure to keep to the original timetable) that Wang was acting in collusion with Chiang. On the face of the available evidence, it does seem unlikely that Wang could have made his escape without Chiang's knowledge — he had flown from a military airport, while his wife and entourage drove all the way to Hanoi by car — and as late as the 26th Chiang was claiming that his Deputy had only gone 'for medical treatment' and expressed the hope that 'if Mr. Wang had his own views on national policy, he should feel free to return and discuss them with members of the Government and the Party.'

On the motives of the Japanese that lay behind Konoye's statement Chiang was prepared to give no such benefit of the doubt, comparing the reference to the 'non-separability of Japan, Manchukuo and China' to the talk of the non-separability of Japan and Korea which had preceded Korea's annexation in 1910. 'Whenever the word "Japan" is spoken in front of the Chinese people, they immediately think of soldiers of fortune who work in intelligence agencies and criminals. We associate the term "Japanese" with those who engage in opium traffic, selling morphine, making cocaine, distributing heroin, establishing opium dens, monopolizing prostitution, secretly dealing in arms, assisting bandits and protecting undesirable elements.'

'When we attain complete sovereignty (recover our rights, etc.), we may discuss with other countries the possibility of permitting foreigners to reside and engage in commerce in the interior of China,' he went on. 'However, we cannot accept such a proposal from Japan, unless we are willing to overlook their poisonous influence and disturbance, abandon our right to maintain order, permit them to corrupt our good manners, and allow them to exploit our economic arteries.' Even his tolerance of Wang finally snapped when three days later the latter announced that he still considered Konoye's statement to represent a basis for negotiation, and on January 1st 1939 the Deputy Director-General was formally expelled from the Kuomintang.

Wang's position became even more exposed when the warlords of Yunnan and Szechwan failed to declare themselves for him as he had counted on, and he began to apply to Western embassies for a visa in contemplation of exile in Europe. In Tokyo the possibility of any further discourse with Chiang appeared to vanish altogether with the replacement of Konoye as Prime Minister by Big Baron Hiranuma, who informed the Diet that 'as for those Chinese who still refuse to come to their senses and persist in their opposition to Japan, we have no alternative but to exterminate them.' In a final despairing bid to regain credibility for his mission Wang threatened to return to Chungking and carry the argument into the Nationalist headquarters 'should they let the present impasse drag on without coming to a definite conclusion'. The only response was a visit from a party of nocturnal assassins who, however, became confused in the darkness and shot his secretary instead.

Far from being intimidated, Wang announced his determination to continue his peace efforts, 'for the sake of the nation whose existence depends on this policy'. In the meantime the continuing failure of the puppet Provisional and Restoration Governments to gain acceptance had obliged Hiranuma to modify his uncompromising attitude, and he arranged for Wang to be transferred to the safety first of Shanghai, and then of Japan itself, in order to discuss the formation of a centralised 'Anti-Communist National Salvation Party' to take over from them. As far back as the previous July the Inner Cabinet had decided that the two bodies should be 'guided towards incorporation into one regime as early as possible', and two months later a United Council had been inaugurated in Peking. The Kwantung Army had succeeded, however, in seeing that Inner Mongolia was excluded from its jurisdiction, and the continuing rivalry between the North and Central China Armies had effectively emasculated it.

Although the concept of a central government under Wang had the support of Suzuki's Asia Development Board, the high command in Tokyo was by no means unanimously in its favour. The Inner Cabinet on June 6th decided that Wang should be only one of a number of constituent elements in the new body and that he would have to prove his usefulness by 'winning over various powerful forces within the Nationalist Government' — and even then he would have to accept that its influence would not extend to the occupied areas. However, he was to be given 'the impression of a bright future and Japan's complete sincerity by allowing him to carry out his wishes on unimportant matters'.

War Minister Itagaki would not offer him even this pretence, informing him that even if the Provisional and Restoration Governments were nominally abolished, they would have to continue in substance and that it would be necessary to 'preserve by some sort of organisation the relationships that had sprung up between them and Japan'. 'So you're not talking about sovereignty [for the new body] at all?' a shocked Wang replied, and he refused to have any part in its creation unless the two puppet governments were subordinated to it. Instead, he maintained, he would have to 'establish a regime in a new geographical region and await another opportunity to form a new central government.'

On June 15th 1939 Wang had a second interview with Itagaki, at which he presented the War Minister with a 'Request to Japan Concerning Implementation of the Principle of Respect for the Sovereignty of China'. This asked in particular that Japan should not attach political or military advisers to his new government. In return for such a dispensation he was required to make several concessions, including the recognition of 'Manchukuo', the abandonment of the Kuomintang principle of 'one government, one party' and the creation of an 'administrative council' in North China with 'a relatively large degree of autonomy'.

When Itagaki then agreed that Wang would be given unrestricted freedom of action in Central China he was being less than honest, for the attachment of Japanese advisers had been one of the essential preconditions laid down by the Inner Cabinet on June 6th. The interview ended in a heated wrangle over the flag to be adopted by the new regime, Wang arguing for the blue and white emblem of the Nationalists and Itagaki for that used by the puppet Provisional Government. In the end a compromise was struck whereby Wang was allowed the former on condition that he twinned it with a pennant bearing the slogan 'Peace, Anti-Communism and National Reconstruction' (already derided by one of his supporters as 'a pig's tail').

Wang returned to China to seek the co-operation of the leaders of the puppet regimes, but he was sharply rebuffed by both. In desperation he then hatched a plan to set himself up in his former stronghold of Canton with the collaboration of the South China Army (as the invasion force there was now named); once the new regime was established, the Japanese would then hand over to the forces of the warlords of the five southern provinces which he believed were sympathetic to him.

Once again, however, his appeals fell on deaf ears, but the greatest fiasco came with his attempt to convene a 'Sixth Kuomintang Congress' in Shanghai on August 28th. Only 240 'representatives' turned up, and of these the vast majority were 'people who had no connection with Wang and were only yesterday shouting for resistance' (to Japan). Wang worked off his frustration in a magazine article in which he declared that most Chinese feared the Japanese even more than they feared the Communists and Western imperialists; for them Japan was a 'brute among brutes'.

TWINS INTO ONE

Just when it seemed that all Wang's hopes were still-born, they were suddenly revived by two events far beyond his control. The first was the signature of the Nazi-Soviet Non-Aggression Pact on August 23rd, the announcement of which caught Hiranuma so off-balance that the Prime Minister was immediately obliged to resign, to be replaced by the more sympathetic Abe Nobuyuki. The second was the crushing defeat inflicted in September by Marshal Zhukov's tanks when the Kwantung Army created an 'incident' at Lake Nomonhan on the Soviet-Manchurian border, which brought home to the high command the need to settle the 'China Incident' if Japan was ever going to be able to confront Russia on equal terms. The North and Central Armies were accordingly re-formed into a unified China Expeditionary Army under Itagaki's command, and for the first time thoughts in Tokyo turned seriously towards the creation of a central puppet regime to give it the necessary political front.

On September 19th Wang was brought together with the leaders of the two puppet regimes in Nanking to discuss their unification, but little was agreed beyond the formation of a Central Political Congress of 'persons of outstanding virtue and great wisdom' under Wang's Chairmanship. Wang had at first wished to restrict this to members of the Kuomintang, but on Japanese insistence it was thrown open to top officials of the puppet regimes. At the same time their military sponsors were summoned to meet the General Staff's Chief of Intelligence, who informed them that the new Cabinet was committed to backing Wang 'to the end'; until recently there had been some on the General Staff who had still favoured negotiations with the Nationalists, but 'we no longer have those unprincipled elements now. Public opinion will not permit a rapprochement with Chiang Kai-shek,' he told them. 'To abandon Wang now would be to discard *bushido*.'

To frustrate any further Nationalist attempts on his life a heavily fortified residence was prepared for Wang and his entourage adjoining the International Settlement in Shanghai, and it was there on November 1st that negotiations began in earnest. Almost immediately Wang was disabused of any lingering 'impression of a bright future and Japan's complete sincerity' which had been given to him in Tokyo on June 6th.

Japan's terms were, if anything, even stiffer than those which had been originally laid down by the Imperial Conference: not only were the areas to be occupied 'as a defence against Communism' now considerably enlarged to cover Amoy, Hainan and the whole of North China above the Yellow River, but Japan was also to be allowed to station troops elsewhere in China 'wherever necessary until peace and order is restored'; all railways, airports, waterways, harbours and other communication facilities in these areas were to be under Japanese control, although the cost of their upkeep was to fall on China. The attached advisers were to include economists, teachers, customs officials and technicians; the 'special privileges' for economic development in North China were extended to cover the exploitation of all mineral resources for Japanese consumption, although China would be free to use the 'left-over products from the blast furnaces built jointly by Japan and China'; and although the Provisional Government was in theory to be subsumed into the new regime, a new North China Political Council was to be created which would effectively take over its functions and even have the right to raise its own Japanese-advised army.

Even the members of Doihara's Commission were taken aback at the extent of these demands, which constituted 'a dirge that signalled the failure of the peace movement even before the Wang government was established,' one of them warned. 'Japan is asking for everything — from the earth to the sky'. Their leader even returned to Japan in the hope of persuading those responsible to take a softer line, but to no avail.

Here and there Wang was eventually able to gain some minor concession, including the phased withdrawal of troops from the non-occupied areas 'within two years of the establishment of public order', but most of the time he found himself up against a stone wall; when, for instance, he requested the return of confiscated property, he was met with a flat denial that any had been confiscated — 'we have simply taken measures for its protection,' he was told.

At one stage complete deadlock threatened over the inclusion of Hainan in the occupied areas, but so essential was the island for the execution of the Navy's 'Strike South' that an Admiral was sent over to give personal voice to their insistence. After six days of negotiation with him Wang finally caved in. The published version of the agreement would mention only the dispatch of officials there to facilitate Sino-Japanese co-operation, but a secret appendix gave Japan the right to station troops, construct dockyards and exploit the island's underground resources (partly as a cover for secret submarine bays).

After two months of this remorseless humiliation, on December 30th the exhausted and demoralised Wang finally put his signature to the 'Outline for Adjusting to New Relations between Japan and China'. One of his closest aides was moved to mark the occasion with a poem composed, with bitter irony, in the traditional Japanese *tanka* format:

> The north,
> The south,
> The sea,
> And the mountains,

> None of them belongs to China.
> Where shall the Chinese people live?

A few days later the author defected to Hong Kong with a copy of the 'Outline' and exposed to the world Japan's scheme 'to dismember our country and bring about its extinction'.

On January 20th 1940 Wang met again with the leaders of the Provisional and Restoration Governments to co-ordinate the birth of his own regime. Two months later the Central Political Congress of 'persons of outstanding virtue and great wisdom' convened for the first time in Nanking, and on March 30th the new 'National Government' was formally inaugurated. The two original puppet regimes were simultaneously abolished, but while the Restoration was absorbed into the new Government the Provisional was simply renamed the North China Political Council as the 'Outline' demanded.

Only a third of the members of the Congress were drawn from the Kuomintang, and so restricted was Wang in his field of choice of suitable persons for government office that he was reduced to falling back on his own family; the Foreign Ministry, for instance, was allotted to his wife's brother-in-law, a man whose previous claim to fame rested on his invention of a mechanical sparring partner for boxers and a doctoral thesis entitled 'A Study of the Vaginal Vibrations of the Female Rabbit'.

In Japan Abe had handed over the Premiership to Navy Minister Yonai in order to oversee as Ambassador the signature of a 'Basic Treaty' with the new regime, upon which Tokyo would formally concede diplomatic recognition. In his inauguration speech Wang had bravely declared that 'China must maintain the independence of her sovereignty and her national freedom before she will be able to . . . share in the responsibility of building up the New Order in East Asia,' but one of Abe's officials was quick to correct him: the new regime would, he told a Press questioner, be as independent as the Government of 'Manchukuo'.

Abe's instructions, handed down by Suzuki at the Asia Development Board, were that in settling any outstanding differences he should 'proceed gradually, but in no event in such a way as to affect adversely the execution of the war'. Thus it was rapidly made clear to Wang that even those minor concessions which he had wrung with so much effort in his negotiations with the Doihara Commission were now to be withdrawn. 'Japan has extracted from the informal agreements [the 'Outline'] everything that she wants in order to incorporate it into the forthcoming treaty,' he remarked. 'The rest will be turned into wastepaper.'

FEAST INTO ASHES

Formal agreements on the text of the 'Basic Treaty' was reached on August 31st but Tokyo still withheld diplomatic recognition — for the very good reason that it was at one and the same moment conducting secretly-resumed negotiations with Chungking. 'We realise only too well that Chiang Kai-shek is the one outstanding man in China. We should be working through him,' Suzuki explained in an unguarded moment to an American journalist. 'We are aware of Wang Ching-wei's record of deserting those with whom he worked. But he is the best man available to Japan in the circumstances.' In the Diet a veteran member of the Democratic Nationalists spoke even more disparagingly of Wang's regime, describing it as 'shot through with bandits and defeated stragglers'.

The Army in particular had become increasingly concerned at its lack of progress in the field, especially in the face of the guerrilla warfare tactics of Mao's Red Army, and at the increasing diversion of its manpower from the other fields of operations which it had planned. On January 1st it had drawn up a 'Secret Guideline for Solving the Incident'; 'We shall endeavour to settle the Incident by the autumn of 1940,' it declared, and to that end Japan 'should continue its peace overtures to Chungking, seize any opportunity for a truce and lead Chungking into joining Nanking.'

In their keenness to do a deal with Chiang, the high command was prepared to offer him rather more liberal terms than they had forced on Wang. In the words of one of Doihara's Commission, the negotiations with Wang were like a banquet at which the choicest dishes were withheld from the invited guest so that 'a splendid feast' could be set before the uninvited one. For Chiang, however, who conversely felt that the tide of war was now turning in his favour, the terms were by no means liberal enough; not only did he still refuse to recognise 'Manchukuo', but he insisted on the withdrawal of Japanese troops from all areas except Inner Mongolia.

This uncompromising attitude provoked a harder line in Tokyo, particularly after the return in July of Imperial Go-Between Konoye at the head of a Cabinet committed to war against the West (it included 'Scrapper' Tojo as War Minister and 'The Talking Machine' Matsuoka as Foreign Minister), and on July 27th a Liaison Conference decided that where diplomacy failed, Japan would 'use force' to achieve her goals in Asia. At the same time the chances of a military victory over Chiang had suddenly brightened following three new developments: reports of Chiang's troops being involved in clashes with their Communist allies, the successful pressurising of Britain into closing Chungking's vital supply road from Burma and the signature of the Tripartite Pact with Germany and Italy. Chiang held firm, however, and he was rewarded by Britain's reopening of the Burma Road on October 18th.

Still Matsuoka refused to give up, and he reapproached Chungking with terms which were for the second time softened: the recognition of 'Manchukuo' would be relegated to a secret annexe, Japan would withdraw all troops sent to China since the opening of the Incident within six months of a truce taking effect and China would have first claim on her natural resources, any surplus going to Japan at the highest current prices. At the same time he enlisted the aid of his new German ally to confront Chiang with the prospect of a German victory in Europe 'by the spring of 1941 at the latest', which would remove the Nationalists' present sources of support; the Generalissimo should therefore seize this 'last opportunity' of making peace with Japan while it lasted.

This threat, however, had precisely the opposite effect to that intended, for it allowed Chiang to threaten Britain and America in turn with the prospect of a Japan released from its involvement in China and moving on to attack their possessions in the Pacific. When America smartly obliged with a loan of $100 million and a fleet of fifty fighter planes, Matsuoka was finally forced to admit defeat and accept the 'best man available'.

The Basic Treaty was signed on November 30th, and Wang's regime was recognised at last. Its anticipated effect would be to make 'the new Central Government in China collaborate fully in various measures vital to the strengthening of the war efforts of the Japanese Empire. Or, to employ stronger words,' Matsuoka added, never being one to pull punches, 'to make it a regime under semi-military control.'

Even 'The Talking Machine', let it be noted, was at last conceding the truth of Ishihara's prediction that the conquest of all China by force of arms was not a practical proposition; Japan's military presence there was now seen only as a holding operation in support of her conquistadorial ambitions elsewhere. In the words of an officer on the China Army Staff, 'our national policy is now worldwide in scope, having as its objective a Greater East Asia centred around the South Seas. In other words, Tokyo desires to maintain the status quo in China and regards the China Incident as a large-scale protracted war which it hopes may be solved by a political settlement.' That hope was never to be realised, for each fresh overture from Japan was successfully exploited by Chiang to squeeze yet more aid from his British and American allies.

Even the new limited objective was to prove so expensive that it cost Japan whatever prospects of success she might have had in the wider campaign. While Chiang's Nationalists held the line in the centre, Mao's Reds went from strength to strength in the north, so that the occupying forces were hard pressed even to defend the cities and the connecting railways in the area nominally under their control. (Five years later that was still no larger, with the exception of the major part of the southern province of Kwangsi which was overrun in 1944 in an abortive attempt to link up with the forces in Burma). In reprisal the Japanese embarked on their infamous 'Three-All' strategy — Kill All, Burn All, Loot All — which succeeded only in driving still more of the population over to the side of the enemy.

On the day that Japan finally struck at Pearl Harbor, Malaya and the Philippines (December 8th 1941) 29 divisions — exactly half her available manpower — was still tied down in China and Manchuria. It was only after the advance of the 11 divisions committed to the 'Strike South' had finally ground to a halt at Guadalcanal seven months later that a desperate Tokyo began to pull out reinforcements from China — and then no more than three divisions, which was hardly enough to prevent the turn of the tide. When the Surrender finally came in August 1945 the remaining 26 were still on their original station. By a supreme stroke of irony, they then found themselves pressed into battle once more, this time on the side of their former Nationalist enemies in the Chinese Civil War which now ensued.

When in 1972 Hirohito, on the occasion of Japan's final recognition of the Communist victory, spoke of 'certain misfortunes in the past', he perhaps had in mind not so much the death of the twenty million Chinese and Japanese who had lost their lives in the conflict (and which, in 1982, his Minister of Education would attempt to excise from the history books), as that of Japan's hopes of conquest which her involvement in the 'China Incident' had done so much to frustrate.

27

Dalliance of Thieves

'THE COMING GREAT, DECISIVE WAR'

In presenting his 1936 Five Year Programme For Major Industries 'in order to prepare for war with the Soviet Union by 1941', Ishihara had prescribed that 'after the Northern threat has been eliminated, we shall actively accomplish our national policy vis-à-vis China and the South Pacific by force.'

Although the Navy continued to argue against the opening of actual hostilities with Russia, they at least went so far as to concede that it would be necessary to secure the northern flank before they would be in a position to launch their cherished 'Strike South'; as Third Fleet Commander Oikawa Kojiro put it, 'Although we must make our final advance to the South where the pickings are great, the Empire has not yet reached the stage when we can happily bring about a collision with England and the United States.' Until that moment arrived Japan, they advised, 'should for the time being plan a gradual advance in both emigration and the economic field ...' In the face of the restrictions imposed by Australia, Canada and the United States, Central and Southern America had become the particular targets of the emigration programme; in Brazil, for instance, the Japanese population had already reached nearly 200,000, provoking the introduction of a bill to prohibit the arrival of any more.

The Army and the Navy then turned to updating Hirohito's revision of his grandfather Meiji's 1907 National Defence Plan. The new concern with Russia stemmed from the meeting the previous year of the seventh Comintern Congress which had called upon Communists everywhere to unite in opposition to Japan's and Germany's 'imperialistic ambitions of world redivision'. In addition, the second Soviet Five-Year Plan had provided for an enormous increase in Russia's Far Eastern Army to give it a 3-to-1 superiority over Japan's Kwantung and Korean Armies. A portion of these troops were to be stationed in Outer Mongolia which in March had concluded a Pact of Mutual Assistance with Russia, a development which ran directly counter to the Kwantung Army's plans for a Pan-Mongolian Federation.

The Army argued that 'we should first concentrate all our strength on securing Russia's submission, since at present there are many areas in

417

which our preparations for a long-term war are inadequate, and if we do not preserve friendly relations with England and the United States, or at least with the United States, it will be difficult to fight a war against Russia.' Once Russia was eliminated, however, they promised that they would turn their attention south to the British possessions in South East Asia and the Pacific: 'We will attack their bases, liberate the oppressed Asian races and make New Guinea, Australia and New Zealand our territory.' When that had been achieved, Japan would then be in a position to 'prepare for the coming great, decisive war with the United States.'

Armed for the first time with the Army's explicit commitment of support for the 'Strike South', the Navy finally gave their blessing to making the elimination of Russia the first priority. By doing so, they also saw that they would secure for themselves what they regarded as a fair share of the military budget: while the Army would get another five divisions under the draft agreement, the Navy would be allocated funds for a new (Third) Replenishment Plan, which included provision for twelve battleships — including two of the new 60,000-ton leviathans and aircraft carriers.

When it was first submitted to Hirohito, the Emperor refused to give it his approval on the grounds that it would be beyond Japan's resources to prepare for war on both fronts at once; however, Naval Chief of Staff Fushimi was able to convince his cousin that the Navy fully supported the switch. The new strategy, encapsulated in the statement that 'the fundamental diplomatic and defence policy that the Empire must establish is to advance into the South Seas while maintaining the Empire's foothold on the Continent', was formally adopted on August 8th 1936 by Prime Minister Hirota and his Inner Cabinet colleagues, who then voted through the necessary, greatly increased budget. In deference to Hirohito's anxieties, emphasis was laid on the hope that it could be achieved without recourse to arms. The agreement proclaimed that in the North 'thwarting the Soviet Union's aggressive intentions must be achieved by diplomatic means and by completion of a defence build-up'; similarly in the South 'while avoiding the antagonizing of other countries as far as possible, we will undertake our national and economic advance into the South Seas, particularly the outer regions, and we plan to build up and strengthen our national power through advancing our influence by gradual and peaceful means.'

Implicit throughout, however, was the assumption that Japan would not hesitate to resort to force when she was denied by other means, and in 1948 the War Crimes Tribunal concluded that this document, formally entitled 'The Fundamental Principles of Our National Policy', 'proved to be the corner-stone in the whole edifice of Japanese preparations for war'. In condemning Hirota to death as the only civilian Class A War Criminal, the Tribunal reasoned that 'it was a cardinal principle of his policy to have

Japan's preparations for war completed behind the façade of friendly foreign relations'.

Side by side with the new armaments programmes, preparations for war were now stepped up in many other fields. Particular attention was given to the development of submarines designed to carry midget subs and seaplanes, for which the illegal construction of bases in the Mandated Pacific islands (which had first come to the notice of U.S. Ambassador Grew in 1933) was accelerated. The same bases were used by reconnaissance craft disguised as pearling luggers to explore the waters of Australasia, and on at least two occasions they were seen to land parties of Naval Reservists on the Australian coast.

The Special Service Agency had continually expanded the scope of the espionage network established by the Black Dragon at the turn of the century, and it now concentrated its efforts on targets associated with the 'Strike South': Singapore, where the chief steward of the British Officers' Club was eventually unmasked as a full Colonel in the Agency: the Dutch East Indies, where a chain of cheap hotels was set up to attract Dutch servicemen; Panama, where no less than fifty-five of those other fountainheads of information, barbers' shops, were opened; Mexico, where a fishing fleet took up station to monitor U.S. Navy movements from the Californian bases; the United States itself, where agents were put to drawing up a sabotage hit-list of installations along the whole of the West Coast; and, of course, Hawaii, where spies had been in place ever since the arrival of the first Japanese immigrants in the 1870s. At the same time 'Doctor' Okawa was set up as the head of the 'Showa Foreign Language Institute' in order to train administrators for the areas marked for occupation.

ENGAGEMENT TO AXIS

On the domestic front the Government turned its hand to creating what the Minister of Finance described as a 'quasi-wartime economic system'. A Cabinet Research Bureau had already been created the previous year alongside the existing Resources Bureau, while above them was set a Cabinet Deliberative Council whose purpose, it was explained, was to 'remove technical economic matters from political interference'. Its actual effect was to transfer control of economic policy even more openly to the military. In June 1937 a Fuel Bureau was established to formulate fuel policy, promote the development of new sources of energy and administer the Petroleum Industry Law introduced three years earlier giving the Government power to fix prices and requiring importers to stockpile at least six months supply. Although, like the others, this new body was placed under the overall control of MCI, it included for the first time officers on active military service.

A month later, following the outbreak of 'The China Incident', the

Research Bureau and the Resources Bureau were merged to form a single economic overlord, the Cabinet Planning Board. Although still within the orbit of MCI, the military were again strongly represented on this new 'economic general staff', as it soon became known, while many of its bureaucrats were recruited from those who had collaborated with the Kwantung Army in directing the economy of 'Manchukuo' (in 1939 Kishi himself would return to take over the top bureaucratic post, the Vice-Ministry). Under a National Generalisation Law introduced the following year, the Board was given powers which effectively put the economy on to a war-time footing: they included those of controlling all foreign exchange, limiting imports, fixing prices and wages, switching production from consumer goods to munitions, amalgamating smaller companies and transferring their displaced employees to China or Manchuria. Many of these powers would be re-utilised by MCI's post-war successor, MITI, in the drive to establish Japan's economic hegemony.

Similarly, a Cabinet Advisory Council of ten 'men of stature' (including Head Roadster Araki and 'The Talking Machine' Matsuoka) was set up alongside the already-established Bureau of Thought Control in order to promote the 'renovation' of the education system and the encouragement of 'correct' political attitudes. The publication of Kokutai No Hongi or 'The Cardinal Principles of the National Entity of Japan' and its issue to every school and university, both at home and among Japanese settlements overseas, followed some months later. Its purpose, as we saw in the Introduction, was to propagate a theological and historical justification for the newly-agreed programme of world conquest by a spurious interpretation of the 'whole world under one roof' pronouncement which the compilers of the Nihongi had attributed to the mythological Jimmu in an attempt to substantiate the claim that he had been the creator of Japan's nationhood. This was then bolstered by the even more spurious genealogies of the Imperial line concocted by the zealots of the National Learning Movement in the 18th and 19th centuries, which were used to demonstrate that Hirohito, who contributed a personal Introduction, was the direct inheritor of this 'Divine Mission'.

In order to secure its unquestioning absorption by His subjects, the whole was invested with the submissive ideology of Confucianism which Shinto had assimilated over the centuries. 'That the subjects should serve the Emperor is not because of duty as such, nor is it submission to authority, but it is the welling, natural manifestation of the heart and is the spontaneous obedience of deep faith towards His Majesty', it preached. 'Loyalty means to revere the Emperor as our pivot and to follow Him implicitly. By implicit obedience is meant casting aside of the self and serving the Emperor intently ... offering our lives for the sake of the Emperor does not mean so-called self-sacrifice, but the casting aside of our little selves to live under His august grace.'

An 'amazing mixture of mythology, rationalisation and historical fact' it may have been in the words of one leading Oriental scholar, but it would not be long before its effect on the impressionable youth of an already uniquely malleable people would manifest itself in the self-immolation of the airmen of the *kamikaze* squadrons, of the sailors in the 'human torpedoes' and of the soldiers who, faced with falling into the hands of the enemy where they could no longer serve their Emperor, preferred the cut of their own bayonets. And not only the youth — a venerable member of the Diet is recorded as making the remarkable declaration that 'we know it's not true, but we believe it!'

Araki, elevated in due course to the office of Minister of Education, was made directly responsible for its propagation. He lost no time in spelling out just what sort of 'education' pupils could now expect: 'Education of a very intellectual type must be abandoned; stress must be laid upon moral training,' a Ministry directive ordained. 'We must return to the spirit, ideals and moral traditions of old Japan. All ideas from abroad which conflict with the Japanese spirit must be barred ... Our imperiality must be preached and spread over the whole world. All obstacles standing in the path of this must be resolutely removed even if it is necessary to apply real force.'

In addition to the massive defence build-up, it was also planned to intimidate Russia 'by taking steps to give reality to Japanese-German co-operation'. Unbeknown either to the Navy or the Foreign Ministry, the Army had signalled their positive interest in Hitler's suggestion of an agreement; the negotiations were entrusted to the military attaché in Berlin, Oshima Hiroshi, a protégé of Uncle Kanin and one of Hirohito's companions on his tour of Europe in 1921. These had made somewhat dilatory progress until given a new urgency by the bellicose declarations of the Seventh Comintern Conference and the adoption of the Army's plan to hive off North China. As a result, Oshima was soon able to come to terms with Joachim von Ribbentrop, Hitler's ambassador at large (Oshima was later to describe them as having been 'very good friends'). The agreement took the form of a defensive alliance against Russia, but when it was revealed to the Foreign Ministry, the latter argued that any open mention of Russia would be dangerously provocative — particularly as they were then engaged in negotiations with Moscow for a new agreement on fishing in Russian waters to replace the old one due to expire at the end of the year (the significance attached to this was a reflection of the importance that fish occupied in the Japanese diet).

Consequently, the true purpose of the Anti-Comintern Pact eventually signed with Germany on October 23rd 1936 was concealed in the following Articles of a secret protocol: 'I) Should one of the High Contracting Parties become the object of an unprovoked attack or threat of attack by the USSR, the other High Contracting Party obligates itself to take no measures that would tend to ease the situation of the USSR. Should the above situation occur, both Parties will immediately consult on measures to safeguard their common interests. II) For the duration of the present agreement both parties will conclude no political treaties with the USSR contrary to the spirit of this agreement without mutual consent.' The published Articles, by contrast, spoke merely of an agreement to inform one another of and to collaborate against the subversive activities of the Comintern, and of an invitation of co-operation to any third party so threatened.

On the day that the Pact was finally announced, November 25th, the Foreign Ministry issued an accompanying announcement that 'no special hidden agreement exists' and that it was 'not directed against any particular country such as the Soviet Union'. On January 1st 1937 the official *Tokyo Gazette* likewise asserted that 'the agreement provided for a special type of co-operation between the two countries against the Comintern, but that it was not directed towards any particular country'. On January 5th Foreign Minister Arita Hachiro repeated the same lie in a radio broadcast, and again in a speech to the Diet a few days later.

All this prevarication was so much wasted breath, however, for Moscow had all along been kept fully informed of the progress of the negotiations by the German-born spy Richard Sorge, who had obtained the full details of the Pact through his close association with the German military attaché in Tokyo, Eugen Ott. On November 18th *Izvestia* had denounced the Pact as a secret treaty of alliance, and on the very eve of its announcement Moscow abruptly refused to ratify the new fishing treaty which had already been initialled and instead offered no more than a renewal of the old one on a year-to-year basis.

ATTRACTIONS OF MARRIAGE

If the suspicions of the other Powers needed any confirmation, they could hardly have asked for more than the words which Matsuoka used to greet the Pact's announcement. 'The present pact has come to replace the Anglo-Japanese alliance as our guidepost. Since we are struggling against the Comintern, at present the world's gravest problem, we must struggle with firm resolution,' he declared. 'A half-hearted effort will never do. We must go into the battle assisting and embracing one another ... resolved to go forward together, even if it means committing "double suicide".' Prime Minister Hirota remarked with similar satisfaction to Harada that 'most of the Army's wishes have now been met', but when Harada reported back to his master Saionji, the Last Noble was a good deal less enthusiastic. 'It is useful only to Germany and contains nothing of advantage to us,' he pronounced. 'It would be better for Japan, given its geographical position, to have Britain and the United States as its friends.'

One of the Army's wishes, it will be remembered, was to 'preserve friendly relations with England and the United States' until Russia had been eliminated, and in drafting 'The Fundamental Principles of Our

National Policy' in July it had been agreed that 'Japanese-German collaboration must not be a cause of anxiety to any other powers, especially Britain . . . which has substantial influence with other world Powers, and we must at the very least avoid a face-to-face confrontation with her at all costs.' Consequently the British Government found itself being approached by the Japanese Ambassador in London (and first post-war Premier), Yoshida Shigeru, with the sort of invitation envisaged in the Pact's published Articles. Contrary to Tokyo's rather naïve expectations, however, Britain looked on Japan even less favourably as a result of the Pact, which was described by *The Times* as an 'alliance of thieves' and was seen generally as an alignment of fascistic dictatorships against the Western democracies, an impression which was amply confirmed when Mussolini added Italy's signature to it in November.

The outbreak of the 'China Incident' in July served finally to put an end to any such hopes of amity, and Foreign Secretary Anthony Eden assured the House of Commons that there was no basis for any negotiations with Japan. Instead he appealed to America to join with Britain and France in an attempt to bring about a cessation of the fighting. Secretary of State Cordell Hull, however, rejected the proposal on the grounds that it was an axiom of American policy to 'keep entirely away from political commitments' with other countries. After China had formally appealed to the League of Nations in September, Roosevelt modified his attitude somewhat in his 'quarantine' speech, but when ex-Secretary of State Stimson then called for an embargo on the export of scrap iron to Japan (which had amounted to 1.3 million tons in the first half of the year), he promptly denied that it had constituted a repudiation of the Neutrality Act.

Prime Minister Neville Chamberlain then tried another tack, suggesting that the two countries should stage a joint demonstration of their naval strength at Singapore, to which Washington replied that 'though the President and Secretary of State . . . had been doing their best to bring American public opinion to realise the situation, they were not yet in a position to adopt any measures of the kind now contemplated.' 'It is always best and safest to count on nothing from the Americans but words,' the man who would himself go down in history as the Arch Appeaser was driven to expostulate. It has to be admitted, however, that Roosevelt probably possessed a more realistic appreciation of the deterrent effect that such a demonstration would have on the Japanese, for large-scale manoeuvres conducted by the U.S. Navy in the Pacific in 1935 had shown that it would be unable to defend the Philippines against a Japanese naval attack. The British, on the other hand, continued to blinker themselves with delusions that the Japanese suffered from a congenital eye defect which prevented them from flying at night and that, as their naval attaché in Tokyo reported, they 'have peculiarly slow brains' as a result of the strain of having to memorise as children the thousands of characters in the Japanese script.

The Japanese themselves, of course, did everything they could to foster such an illusion of innocuousness. When, for instance, Konoye was asked to confirm rumours of the construction of the two 60,000-ton battleships which had already been laid down behind giant screens, he replied that 'those Press reports are sheer speculation with no foundation whatever'. It was only after the *Panay* and *Ladybird* were sunk in December that both Governments felt confident enough to appropriate sufficient funds for a credible response and to lay down the first tentative plans for collaboration. These would subsequently evolve as 'Rainbow Two' — and even then the Admiralty was forced to admit that in the event of a war with Germany 'we could never take the risk of dispatching to the Far East a sufficient fleet to act as a deterrent to Japanese aggression'.

The decision to expand the 'China Incident' into all-out war as a prelude to the 'Strike South' and the need to cut off Russia's aid to Mao's Communists naturally turned minds in Tokyo to thinking that German-Japanese co-operation should take the form of something more substantial than a merely defensive agreement. Ex-Foreign Minister Arita (who had yielded that position to Hirota when Imperial Go-Between Konoye had taken over the Premiership in June) had already joined Godfather Toyama and other super-patriots in forming an organisation entitled 'Comrades for the Strengthening of the Anti-Comintern Pact'.

In the early days of the war the German Foreign Ministry under von Neurath had not only rejected Tokyo's request for support, but had even gone so far as to declare that Japan's action in China was contrary to the Pact 'because it will prevent the consolidation of China, will therefore further the spread of Communism in China and will drive China into the arms of Russia.' In September, however, Ribbentrop told Hitler that he was convinced that Japan 'will win a decisive victory in the not too distant future'. He had been encouraged in this opinion by Oshima, who, in what was to be the first of many such unauthorised initiatives, had promised that Germany would be given a 'most favoured nation' commercial status in China in the event of a Japanese victory.

The following month, apparently in response to a threat from Japan to withdraw from the Pact if they continued, Hermann Goering ordered the cessation of all supplies of arms to China which had not already been paid for; 'the Fuhrer has decided that an unambiguous attitude towards Japan should be adopted', he reported. On January 2nd 1938, after Hitler had set out his programme of expanding Germany's *Lebensraum* in Europe, Ribbentrop presented a memorandum calling for a full German-Japanese-Italian military alliance which would have the effect of so dispersing Britain's strength as to render her incapable of opposition. Hitler quickly gave it his approval and appointed Ribbentrop in von Neurath's place to carry it out; at the same time Ott was promoted to Ambassador in Tokyo, formal recognition accorded to 'Manchukuo', a total stop put on arms supplies to China and the Wehrmacht advisers there recalled.

PREPARING THE CONTRACT

Oshima lost no time in passing on Ribbentrop's suggestion for a full military alliance to Tokyo, but the response was distinctly unenthusiastic. Ambassador Togo Shigenori in Berlin was instructed by the Foreign Office to withdraw Oshima's unofficial offer of a privileged position in China, and the Army, preoccupied with the increasingly stubborn Chinese resistance, eventually replied in June that any such alliance would have to be directed solely against Russia. Ribbentrop then informed Oshima with equal coolness that Germany had no interest in such a 'one-sided and weak' arrangement, and there the matter seemed destined to rest. Within a few weeks, however, events were to bring about a more receptive Japanese attitude.

Exasperation with the slow progress in China and the elevation of Araki and Itagaki to the Cabinet as Education and War Ministers respectively had revived the argument of the 'Strike North' element in the Army for a trial of strength with Russia. They were then further encouraged by the defection of a Soviet General on June 11th, who reported to the Kwantung Army that the Russian Far Eastern Army had been thoroughly demoralised by Stalin's recent mass purges. Thus when a detachment of Russian soldiers was observed a month later constructing fortifications on a hill over-looking Lake Khassan, situated at the junction of the borders of Korea, Manchuria and Russia's Maritime Province (Ussuri) some 70 miles south west of Vladivostok, the Kwantung Army immediately signalled Imperial Headquarters for permission to expel them by force. The high command's first concern was that nothing should be done to jeopardise the recently-decided advance on Hankow, and Mukden was accordingly instructed that an attempt should first be made to persuade the Russians to withdraw by diplomatic means.

However, both Hirohito and Chief of Staff Kanin then retired to their summer villas, and Vice-Chief Tada, who had recently lost his plea for a 'policy of restraint' in China in order to concentrate for an attack on Russia, was able to take advantage of their absence to win the support of the rest of the Staff for the use of force. Both the Kwantung and the Korea Armies were ordered to mobilise for an assault. Foreign Minister Ugaki, finding himself outvoted, had alerted the Emperor to the decision, and when Itagaki arrived on July 20th to obtain His sanction he was severely reprimanded and informed that 'hereafter, not a single soldier may be so much as moved without my orders'.

The Imperial order to withdraw had to be repeated twice before the local commander of the Japanese forces complied, and when nine days later the Russians began fortifying another hill nearby he gave the order to drive them off, justifying his action with the claim that the Russians had made an 'illicit assault'. When he went to the Imperial villa to report this new development, Tada was highly relieved to receive the Emperor's post-eventum approval, although Hirohito insisted that no further advance should be made.

Two days later the Russians counter-attacked with two full divisions and some 150 aircraft. The heavily-outnumbered Japanese sustained mounting losses as they clung grimly to their hastily thrown up defence works, but Tokyo rejected all Mukden's repeated requests to be allowed to send in reinforcements. In the negotiations which had now started in Moscow the Japanese spokesman attempted to demonstrate by means of faked photographs that the Russians had crossed the border, but when Japanese losses reached over 50% he was instructed to drop the demand for a Russian withdrawal and on August 10th a cease-fire was finally agreed.

Although, in an attempt to save face, the engagement was claimed by the 'Strike North'-ers to have represented a successful 'reconnaissance in force', it was conceded elsewhere to have been a significant defeat and as such only to have reinforced the argument for the 'Strike South'. The invasion of Canton and southern China duly followed in October, and a month later Konoye announced his plans for a New Order in East Asia and a New Structure in Japan under which the people would combine to liberate their neighbours in a holy war against the 'imperialistic ambitions and rivalries of the Western Powers'. The New Structure would eventually evolve into the one-party Imperial Rule Assistance Association, and it was explained that 'the wars of Japan are carried on in the name of the Emperor and are therefore holy wars'; as an alternative to war, the Powers were offered co-operation 'so long as they understand the true intention of Japan and adopt policies suitable for the new conditions'.

In February 1939 the Navy occupied Hainan and the following month annexed the uninhabited Spratley Islands some 650 miles further south. In describing what he claimed to be an authoritative report of the Navy's intentions, a member of the Italian Embassy in Tokyo confided to Ambassador Grew that he 'wouldn't give a nickel for Hong Kong'.

All these moves inevitably brought Japan into further conflict with the West. In September 1938 the League of Nations had finally voted to impose economic sanctions against Japan, and even Roosevelt had declared a 'moral embargo' on the export of aircraft and parts. The following month Grew presented a memorandum listing over 400 causes for protest since the outbreak of the war in China, ranging fron economic discrimination against American business interests to atrocities against American residents and properties (one church in Chungking had been finally destroyed after eight previous bombings).

To this Arita (now Foreign Minister again after Ugaki's resignation on September 30th) replied bluntly that 'an attempt to apply to present and future conditions without any change in the concepts and principles which were applicable to conditions prevailing before the present incident does not in any way contribute to the solution of immediate issues, and furthermore, does not in the least promote the firm establishment of enduring peace in East Asia.' At the same time he announced the closure of the Pearl River to all but Japanese military craft, and he dismissed protests that the Yangtse was being used to force out Western trade with the claim that Japanese non-military goods were being carried only on very exceptional occasions in order to utilise spare space. Almost simultaneously on the other side of the world Hitler was celebrating the surrender of the Czech Sudetenland signalled by Chamberlain's little scrap of paper.

This growing identification of the Western Powers as the common enemy naturally caused Japan to reconsider the possible advantages of a closer relationship with Germany. In July Itagaki had already called for a full military alliance in order to frighten off Western support for Chiang Kai-shek, but both the Navy and the Foreign Ministry had opposed him. On August 26th the Inner Cabinet were eventually able to agree on a compromise proposal whereby the contracting parties were obligated to render 'all political and economic assistance' in the event of an unprovoked attack on one of them, but which pledged them to do no more than 'immediately enter into discussions' on the rendering of military assistance. Four days later Hirohito gave it his conditional approval, making it clear that he would reserve his final judgement until after he had assessed the reactions of Germany and Italy.

COLD FEET IN TOKYO

An important ambiguity arose, however, in the negotiating instructions which the War and Foreign Ministries then telegraphed to Oshima and Togo respectively in Berlin. While they were told that, in line with Japan's previous policy, the preamble of any new agreement should make it clear that it was directed 'primarily against the subversive activities of the Soviet Union and the Comintern', it was also to state that 'countries such as Britain and the United States are not to be direct enemies' — thus inviting the interpretation that the latter could at least be designated as secondary or indirect targets (in line with the Army's wishes). When on September 10th the Foreign Ministry produced its formal draft of the proposed treaty, it stipulated that any discussion of military assistance should be directed only against the Soviet Union. Both the Army and the Navy protested that this represented an emasculation of the understanding agreed by the Inner Cabinet and refused to accede to it.

Prospects of an early resolution of the deadlock took a turn for the better after Ugaki's resignation from the Foreign Ministry in protest at the establishment of the Army-controlled Asia Development Board in China, since his successor Arita was expected, as the signatory of the Anti-Comintern Pact, to be much more accommodating. At the same time Togo was switched to Moscow to allow Oshima (rather than a regular diplomat) to step into his shoes as Ambassador in Berlin, and indeed one of Oshima's first acts was to arrange for the exchange of intelligence between the German and Japanese General Staffs. The Rome Embassy was assigned to Shiratori Toshio, a nephew of ex-Foreign Minister Ishii and intimate of Big Baron Hiranuma, who had a record comparable to Oshima's for taking responsibility into his own hands. In 1934 he had briefly been expelled from the Foreign Ministry following Western outrage at the notorious statement that 'only Japan could judge what was good for China'.

On October 27th Ribbentrop responded with a revised draft that attempted to gloss over the ambiguity in the Japanese instructions by referring to the targets of the agreement as 'one or several non-signatory nations'. In the meantime Arita had consulted with the other members of Inner Cabinet (apart from Itagaki) and he had established with them that the proposed arrangement as submitted to the Throne on August 30th was envisaged as an extension of the Anti-Comintern Pact and therefore was still directed against Russia and the Comintern.

When the Inner Cabinet met on November 11th to consider the Ribbentrop draft, he again confirmed to them that this was so. Itagaki was obliged to add his acquiescence, with the proviso that it would also apply against France if France should become communist; however, when Oshima then protested that this contradicted his original instructions, Itagaki supported him. The Cabinet was thus faced with the problem, as Arita put it, of deciding 'whether we were to change to suit the Army the decision already made by the Government, or convince the Army and have the Ambassador correct his explanation to the Germans.' It was primarily the failure to resolve this that brought about the resignation of Konoye on January 3rd 1939. He was succeeded by Hiranuma, but the rest of the Cabinet remained unchanged. Itagaki made it a condition of the Army's support that the Government should continue to seek a military alliance with Germany and Italy and to work towards the consummation of an 'epochal development' in 1941. 'The situation has entered a new stage,' he explained. 'The time has come when we must put all our efforts into the establishment of a new order which will assure the eternal peace of the Orient ... by creating a new policy under a new cabinet.'

In asking Arita to remain as Foreign Minister, Hiranuma had agreed that the target of any military assistance should continue to be limited to Russia, but on January 19th the Inner Cabinet decided, as a concession to the Army, that political and economic assistance could be directed against other (unidentified) countries; a special mission was then sent to Europe to emphasize to the two recalcitrant Ambassadors that this was as far as they were permitted to go. Oshima remained unabashed, however, insisting that he would resign rather than present such terms, which would lay Japan open to accusations of bad faith. In Rome, Shiratori declared himself likewise, for in the meantime Italy had agreed to join the new treaty on Ribbentrop's terms which, Shiratori had asserted to Foreign Minister Ciano, would force Britain to 'concede the many things she owes to us all'.

'No matter how much and how many years the Army may have studied diplomacy, what right have they to do such a thing without consulting the Foreign Ministry?' the outraged Arita protested. It was, of course, open to him to have them recalled, but such a drastic step was bound to be interpreted by Germany and Italy as a demonstration of Japan's unreadiness to reach an agreement. Italy was now threatening to conclude one with Germany alone, while Hitler had already sent his tanks rolling into the rest of Czechoslovakia beyond the Sudetenland.

On March 22nd the Inner Cabinet met in another attempt to resolve the impasse. This time the instructions governing the application of military assistance were altered to read that it would be directed against Russia 'as a matter of course', but that 'if other nations are involved, although it is a basic principle of this treaty to provide military assistance, circumstances make it in fact impossible for the Empire to do so at present or in the near future'; it was also required that on the publication of the treaty Japan should be allowed to issue an assurance to Britain, France and America that it was not directed against them.

In reporting this to the Emperor, Hiranuma explained that it was seen as committing Japan to provide, at most, a demonstration such as the dispatch of warships against countries other than Russia. He also promised to recall Oshima and Shiratori if they made any further attempt to question their instructions and to break off the negotiations if no agreement could be reached on the Japanese terms as they now stood. In order to ensure compliance with these undertakings, Hirohito took the unusual step of requiring the five Ministers to sign a written memorandum to that effect.

LOST PATIENCE IN BERLIN

Once again, however, when Ribbentrop and Ciano declared that acceptance of the latest Japanese conditions was 'quite out of the question', the two Double Diplomats declined to fall into line and both made statements to the effect that 'Japan is prepared to offer some military assistance, if only to a limited extent', against countries other than Russia. Prompted by Hirohito's observation that their behaviour could be construed as a violation of the Imperial Prerogative, Arita urged at the next Inner Cabinet meeting that they should be made to retract their statements and put an end to the negotiations in accordance with the undertaking of their written memorandum.

Itagaki strongly opposed both these demands, and Arita felt obliged to advise the Emperor that to take the further step of recalling the culprits might lead to undesirable 'complications'. The mounting impatience of the Army at the lack of progress in the negotiations had given rise to rumours of impending mutiny, and as a precautionary measure the Navy had already drawn up contingency plans to land a large body of marines in Tokyo. Hirohito duly agreed not to press the issue, at the same time warning his Military Aide-de-Camp that the Army might precipitate a fall of the Cabinet if they continued to support the stance of the two Ambassadors.

Ribbentrop now issued an ultimatum to Japan that agreement had to be reached by the end of the month; he hinted to Oshima that if no agreement materialised, it might be necessary for him to conclude a non-aggression pact with Russia. Appalled, perhaps, by the very mention of such a possibility, Oshima omitted to pass this information on to Tokyo. The Japanese reply when it came reinsisted that Japan should not be obligated to offer any 'effective [i.e., military] assistance' except against Russia, and that even in that event she should be able to reserve the right to decide when and if to participate. When they received it, the immediate reaction of Oshima and Shiratori was to ask to be recalled.

In a last desperate effort to break the deadlock, Arita suggested to Hiranuma that he should negotiate with Hitler and Mussolini direct. The Prime Minister took up the idea, although in a rather different spirit to that which the Foreign Minister had intended. In a message to Hitler which was prefaced with expressions of admiration for the Fuhrer's 'lofty wisdom and iron will', he went on to give a pledge of unrestricted assistance 'when conditions make it possible'. It was dispatched on May 4th after the Inner Cabinet had met in several stormy sessions to discuss its form; Arita and Navy Minister Yonai had finally given their agreement to it only after they were promised that this compromise represented the end of the road and that negotiations should be broken off if Hitler rejected it. Further hints of 'direct action' no doubt helped to move Hiranuma so much closer to the Army's position; it was also reported to Ambassador Ott that Itagaki had threatened to resign as War Minister and so bring down the Cabinet by the familiar ploy of refusing to nominate a successor.

The two Ambassadors had meanwhile had second thoughts and decided that their goal might still be achieved if they remained at their posts after all; Shiratori informed Ciano that it would first be necessary to force Arita and Yonai to resign. In Berlin Oshima took matters into his own hands once again and set to working out the draft of an agreement in co-operation with the German Foreign Office. Its central feature was a provision that Japan should assume the status of a belligerent in any war concerning Germany and Italy even though initially precluded from rendering military assistance. This essentially met the Army's wish for an unconditional alliance because the Army expected to have the major voice in deciding when circumstances made military assistance possible.

Ribbentrop still found Hiranuma's statement to be too loosely worded for Germany's purposes, and the Oshima draft was therefore referred back to Tokyo in its place for approval. However, its effect was merely to distance the Army still further from the Navy and Foreign Ministry. 'This is outrageous,' Arita expostulated, 'and I won't be responsible [for foreign affairs] if this sort of conspiracy goes on'; likewise, Yonai refused to make the Navy responsible for the conduct of any war that Japan was obliged to enter under such terms. Arita seriously considered resigning, but the Navy's firm attitude was sufficient to dissuade him.

Faced again with their united opposition, the Army, in the person of Chief of Staff Kanin, appealed to the Throne for support, but he received short shrift from Hirohito and was severely reprimanded for his pains. He was followed by Chichibu, who was likewise told by his brother that the Army had no business meddling in the matter. Kido, who had been promoted from Privy Seal Secretary to Home Minister, cautioned the Emperor against taking too hard a line: 'In order to lead the Army but still make it appear as if it were being led by them, we must also make it seem as if we understood them a little more.'

In the absence of any response from Tokyo Ribbentrop warned Oshima that Germany and Italy were now ready to sign a military alliance independently of Japan. This pressure spurred the Inner Cabinet to yet another compromise: it was agreed that it should be formally denied that Japan was committed to any unconditional action except against Russia, but at the same time Oshima's informal commitment to that effect was allowed to stand. Hoping to placate all concerned, they predictably succeeded only in exacerbating the antagonisms. On May 22nd Germany and Italy duly announced their Alliance, and in a speech the following day Hitler spoke of Japan's 'cool and restricted collaboration'. In Tokyo, the police uncovered a plot by some of Toyama's minions to assassinate Naval leaders, including Yonai and Vice-Minister Yamamoto, at the Tsushima Victory Day celebrations on the 27th.

A chastened Inner Cabinet reassembled once more to defuse the situation. From the Palace, Hirohito sent word that Itagaki should come to terms with the views of the Navy and Foreign Ministry. Hitler, for his part, dispatched an Admiral from Berlin to talk the Navy out of its respect for the British and American fleets.

On June 5th the Cabinet finally agreed on a form of words which committed Japan to military assistance in any war involving Germany and Italy but at the same time gave her the right to decide the point of entry. Once again it was clearly all too open to differing interpretations; the Navy in particular, although it seemed to move them nearer to the Army's demands still saw it as offering them a veto on participation.

Once again too it was rejected by Ribbentrop, who insisted that only a 'clear and unconditional alliance' would deter Russia and America. An exasperated Oshima signalled from Berlin that it was 'utterly fruitless' to negotiate on any other basis; an exhausted Cabinet, its bolt shot, was happy to take him at his word.

28

For Better, For Worse

CRUNCH FOR THE 'STRIKE NORTH'

The Army meanwhile had begun to vent its frustration elsewhere. Following the murder of a Japanese-appointed customs inspector in the British Concession at Tientsin, the Japanese Consul-General there on May 31st 1939 had issued an ultimatum to Britain to surrender the four Chinese Nationalists suspected of complicity. When Britain refused on the grounds of lack of evidence and suggested the setting up of an ad hoc tribunal to consider the facts, the North China Army not only rejected this, but also insisted that even if the men were surrendered Britain should withdraw her support from Chiang Kai-shek and collaborate with Japan in the building of the New Order by prohibiting the circulation of the old Chinese currency. In an attempt to enforce this demand, they then (on June 14th) mounted a blockade on the Concession.

In the negotiations which followed, Britain was required to sign a statement committing her to a general policy of non-intervention in the Japanese-occupied areas before the actual points at issue were discussed. In British eyes this represented no more than an acknowledgement of the existing situation, but Hiranuma immediately seized on their agreement to it as a commitment to cease the supply even of economic aid to the Nationalists; such help 'must be regarded in principle as an action aiding our enemy', he asserted.

The object of this manoeuvre had been, in the words of the Director-General of the Asia Development Board, to ensure that Britain 'would make every sacrifice in the Far East to appease Japan in order to solve her problems in Europe', and its apparent success in Japanese eyes encouraged the Army to believe that Russia might be similarly 'appeased' and that perhaps after all an alliance with Germany was not the indispensable requirement which they had hitherto thought it to be.

The border dividing Outer Mongolia from the remote north-western corner of Manchuria had been traditionally regarded as being of academic significance only, having since time immemorial been crossed and re-crossed at will by nomadic tribesmen in search of fresh pastures in this area's barren steppes; however, since the Kwantung Army's occupation of Manchuria and Russia's pact of mutual assistance with Outer Mongolia it

432

had become the source of several minor clashes. Its previously-accepted line had run a few miles to the east of the Halka River, but in 1935 the Japanese had changed their maps of the area to put it on the river itself. In April the Kwantung Army, seeking a pretext to avenge its drubbing at Lake Khassan the previous year, issued a set of new 'Principles for the Settlement of Soviet-Manchukuoan Border Disputes', which stated that 'in areas where the border lines are indistinct, the defence commander shall determine a boundary of his own'. Even more provocatively, it permitted him 'to invade Soviet territory temporarily, or to decoy Soviet soldiers and get them into Manchukuoan territory'.

When a month later a body of Mongolian cavalry crossed the river and skirmished with the Japanese garrison at Nomonhan some ten miles further east, the Kwantung Army seized the opportunity to enlarge the incident. However, the regiment which was dispatched to administer 'resolute and thorough punishment' found itself confronted by a superior force of cavalry and tanks and was all but annihilated. Mukden thereupon moved up an entire division and obtained War Minister Itagaki's permission to launch a full-scale invasion. They omitted to inform him, however, that their plans also included a preparatory bombing raid on the nearest Russian airfield, and when news of that reached Tokyo the Vice-Chief of Staff was summoned to the Palace and severely reprimanded for this infringement of the Emperor's supreme command. Imperial Headquarters then issued an order forbidding any further air raids.

The division's ground units crossed the Halka River in force on July 1st, but they were again met by unexpectedly superior numbers and weight of artillery and obliged to pull back with heavy casualties. Tokyo now began to have second thoughts on the wisdom of continuing the conflict and, after further pressure from Hirohito, issued an order to Mukden to 'endeavour to terminate the incident by the winter at the latest'. After promising to study it, the Kwantung Army command launched a still stronger attack, but this too ended in failure.

Russia now prepared a massive counter-attack to drive the Japanese back to the original border. The leading tank-warfare expert Georgi Zhukov was dispatched from Moscow to direct it, together with seven Tank Brigades equipped with a newly-developed diesel-driven vehicle whose armour was impervious to Japanese anti-tank guns. On August 20th it smashed through the ill-equipped defence, inflicting 50,000 casualties in 'a battle of iron and flesh'.

This awesome demonstration of Russian power finally convinced the Army of the necessity for an alliance with Germany. They were also spurred to this conclusion by persistent rumours surrounding the German-Russian negotiations in progress at the time, and they were not inclined to accept German assurance that any talk of a non-aggression pact was 'pure fraud'. Oshima and Shiratori once more exceeded their brief and issued a joint public statement to the same effect, and the massive demonstrations organised by the activists in its favour caused Yonai to remark to Ambassador Grew that 'the demagogues are getting busy again.'

However, the determination of the Navy and Foreign Ministers to oppose such a call was greatly strengthened by America's decision to abrogate the 1911 U.S.-Japanese Commercial Treaty when it expired at the end of the year, thus clearing the way for the possibility of embargoes on exports to Japan, particularly of oil. At a meeting of the Inner Cabinet on August 8th even Hiranuma supported their joint demand that they should not move from the position agreed on June 5th. Itagaki then addressed an appeal to Ott for German acceptance of that position, and the Ambassador passed it on to Berlin with his approval (the War Minister had told him that otherwise he would be obliged to resign). It was too late, however: the Nazi-Soviet Non-Aggression Pact had already been agreed.

Its public announcement on August 23rd came as a bolt from the blue to Japan. Even Oshima was led to expostulate with Ribbentrop that 'the Japanese government and people will never accept it. The German Government must bear the responsibility for any unfortunate results.' Hiranuma, who had been appointed to the Premiership with the specific objective of bringing an alliance with Germany to fruition, was left with no option but to resign, explaining that 'there has emerged an intricate and baffling new situation in Europe ... Since I cannot justify myself to my Emperor, I shall apologize and resign.' Last Noble Saionji declared that the choice of a successor 'is beyond me. If there is anyone I thought would be better than another I would speak up ... our foreign policy is the biggest failure since the beginning of our history.'

In recognition of its part in this failure the Army put forward the name of Abe Nobuyuki, a figure of such moderation that he was almost unknown to the public at large; alone among the top Generals, he had identified himself with neither the Imperial Roadsters nor the Control Group, instead pursuing a career, in the words of the government organ *Contemporary Japan*, of 'watchful obscurity'. For lack of any other candidate who had not been compromised by the debate, Hirohito eventually approved his nomination with the less-than-enthusiastic observation that 'the Army would co-operate with Abe since he understands matters concerning them, so let's try him out.'

The Emperor instructed the new Prime Minister that he should abandon all thoughts of an Axis alliance and instead 'follow a conciliatory line with regard to Britain and America'. In a further step to ensure that the cause of the 'Strike North' was now finally dead and buried, he went on to insist that his own Aide-de-Camp Hata Shunroku should succeed Itagaki as Minister of War: 'Even if the Big Three decide on someone else and submit his name to me, I have no intention of sanctioning that choice.'

SEEKING TO SHARE THE SPOILS

On September 1st 1939 the unholy pair of proletarian dictators, the national socialist and the international socialist, invaded Poland, Hitler from the west and Stalin from the east. Two days later Chamberlain finally consigned his scrap of paper to the waste basket; Europe was at war.

Abe immediately took the opportunity to publicise his government's new direction: 'The Empire will not intervene in the war in Europe, but will concentrate its efforts upon solving the "China Incident",' he announced. This, of course, was the essential stepping-stone for the 'Strike South', and Abe had already broadcast a warning that Japan would 'inflexibly oppose those who obstructed her mission'. In a further move to consolidate the policy, the vacant Foreign Ministry was allotted to Nomura Kichisaburo, who had retired from the Navy to take up the headmastership of the Peers School, the alma mater of the sons of the Court.

Nomura too quickly followed his appointment with a foreign policy statement that the Government would 'take advantage of the international situation to concentrate its efforts on settling the "China Incident".' The Cabinet accordingly turned down all Mukden's pleas that the Kwantung Army should be allowed the chance of saving its face with another counter-attack at Nomonhan and instead signed an armistice with Russia on September 15th; under its terms a Border Demarcation Committee was set up, which eventually found in favour of the hitherto accepted line.

Even before his resignation as Prime Minister, Hiranuma had transmitted an official protest to Berlin at Germany's palpable violation of the Anti-Comintern Pact — Article II of which pledged the signatories 'not to conclude any political treaties with the Soviet Union without mutual assent'. Oshima, however, was already recovering from the shock, and when he formally presented the protest to Ribbentrop's deputy at the Foreign Office, he allowed himself to be persuaded by the latter, speaking 'between men and soldiers', that he should take it back again since it was bound to receive 'an ill-tempered answer'. Although he replied to Tokyo that he had delivered it as instructed, the Double Diplomat in fact withheld it until September 18th, when he was able to gloss it over with copious congratulations to Hitler on his successful conquest of Poland. These might not have been quite so lavish if he had heard the Fuhrer's current opinion of the Japanese: 'The Emperor is the companion piece of the later Tsars,' he told his Generals the day after the Pact's announcement. 'Weak, cowardly, irresolute ... Let us think of ourselves as masters and consider these people at best as lacquered half-monkeys, who need to feel the knout.'

In negotiating the Non-Aggression Pact Foreign Commissar Molotov had suggested that Germany might like to serve in the role of mediator to improve Russo-Japanese relations. Ribbentrop eagerly took up the idea, seeing it as a means both of tightening the hold around Britain's neck and of composing Japan's ruffled feathers; since the Pact had failed to intimidate the former from going to war in Poland's defence, the Japanese Navy in particular would fulfil an invaluable function, he envisaged, in diverting British naval strength to the Far East.

'I for one believe that the best policy for us would be to conclude a Japanese-German-Soviet non-aggression agreement and then move against Britain,' Ribbentrop told Oshima. 'If this succeeded, Japan would be able freely to extend her strength in East Asia towards the south . . . the direction in which her vital interests lay'. Otherwise, he warned, 'the decisive battle of the world' between Germany and Britain would take place without Japan, in which event she would be left without a share in the spoils of victory. Oshima responded enthusiastically, drawing a picture of Japan gaining self-sufficiency in oil from the Dutch East Indies, rubber from Malaya, cotton from India and wool from Australia.

Ribbentrop instructed Ott in Tokyo to do everything he could to work for a *rapprochement*, and in particular to plead for the retention of Oshima as Ambassador in Berlin (his accomplice in insubordination Shiratori having already been recalled). In this he was unsuccessful, but before Oshima left for home Ribbentrop arranged for him to send back coded telegrams direct via Ott's embassy. Shiratori arrived back in October and promptly embarked on a propaganda tour to urge the resumption of negotiations for an alliance with Germany and Italy; 'In a world on the eve of a great revolution, the co-operation of Japan with the Axis is still a solemn fact,' he informed his audiences.

The following month he joined 'The Great Fascist' Suetsugu and Mukden-Collaborator Koiso (now Minister for Overseas Affairs) in setting up a national movement for an alignment with Russia against Britain. When Oshima returned shortly afterwards, Ott reported that in the opinion of these two accomplices, 'who are working hard for the overthrow of the present Cabinet, two or three transitional cabinets are still necessary to bring about a fundamental change of course'. In the event their prediction was to prove unduly cautious.

America's rejection of Nomura's approaches for a new commercial treaty combined early in the New Year, 1940, with food shortages and soaring inflation caused by the war in China to bring about the downfall of Abe's caretaker Cabinet. He was succeeded by ex-Navy Minister Yonai while Nomura was replaced as Foreign Minister by Arita, the architect of the Anti-Comintern Pact. Arita made it clear, however, that little change in foreign policy was to be expected: 'Japan will continue the previously-adopted policy of seeking a prior settlement of pending problems', he stated, at the same time dismissing the idea of a Japanese-German-Soviet non-aggression treaty as 'a matter for the distant future and not very useful'. The Prime Minister's long-held opposition to an Axis alliance seemed to ensure that the 'conciliatory line in regard to Britain and America' would be maintained. Within a week, however, that prediction too was thrown open to revision.

On January 21st a British warship intercepted the *Asama Maru*, Japan's largest liner, off the Chinese coast and searched her on the suspicion that she was carrying German nationals; twenty-one were found and taken off. When reports of the incident reached Japan, they provided a field day for the pro-Axis elements. 'The news had an electrifying effect on the whole country. Never in my experience have I known such a universal and violent outburst of vituperation', British Ambassador Craigie recorded, and the indignation increased rather than diminished when he pointed out that Japan had already stopped and searched no less than 191 British-owned ships off Hong Kong in the previous four months.

Relations with America turned equally sour soon afterwards over the inauguration of Wang Ching-wei's puppet regime in Nanking; Secretary of State Hull's condemnation of it and his simultaneous announcement of a further loan to Chiang's regime was attacked as 'most regrettable'. As a result the Government thought it prudent to ask Germany to postpone the visit of the Duke of Coburg to take part in the celebrations of the '2600th anniversary of the Accession of Jimmu' for fear that it might be seen as compromising Japan's neutral status. The same considerations, however, did not prevent the arrival of Ribbentrop's special envoy Heinrich Stahmer together with an economic mission, and he reported back to Berlin with satisfaction that 'the influence of the Army, greatly weakened since last summer, is already growing again. A further increase is to be expected.'

COURTSHIP RESUMED

The 'increase' duly came in April after Germany's sweeping victories in Denmark and Norway, which were then followed by the even more spectacular successes in Holland, Belgium and France. The favourable possibilities that these now opened up for a move into the Dutch and French colonies in the 'Southern Areas' also caused sentiment in the Navy to take a markedly more pro-Axis turn, and Germany was told that if she cared to send warships, particularly commerce raiders and submarines, into Japanese waters, they would be given every possible assistance. It was also proposed that German merchant ships at present blockaded in Japan could escape by being chartered to Japan to carry coal from Manchuria. The Duke of Coburg was now given the all-clear to make his postponed visit and was received with ostentatious hospitality, while in Berlin the Japanese-German Cultural Committee held its first session.

Furthermore, it was evident that even the Court was now prepared to drop the 'conciliatory line in regard to Britain and America'. Hirohito's nominee War Minister Hata told the Diet that the Washington Nine-

Power Treaty was now obsolete, and Imperial Go-Between Konoye began to hold regular conferences with Suetsugu and his pro-Axis coterie, who now merged their movement with various other like-minded organisations, including Chief Cherry Hasimoto's Japan Youth Party, to form 'The National Federation for the Reconstruction of East Asia'. In March Konoye had himself recruited over a hundred members of the Diet from all parties as founder members of 'The Federation for the Prosecution of the Holy War' dedicated to the realisation of his New Order. He had also been working simultaneously with Kido on the draft plans for his proposed one-party New Political Structure, and on May 31st Hirohito appointed Kido to the office of Lord Keeper of the Privy Seal, the closest civilian adviser to the Throne. Stahmer returned to Berlin with the prediction of an early change of government to one headed, he hoped, by Konoye.

The fall of Paris and the subsequent armistice with France signed on June 22nd brought this change of sentiment to a head. 'Seize this golden opportunity!', Hata exhorted. 'Don't let anything stand in the way!' Japan had already made tentative inquiries in Berlin about the possibility of being allowed a free hand in French Indo-China, but Ott had advised a cool response in order to precipitate the fall of the Yonai Cabinet in favour of one 'which would be close to us'. Two days later Konoye resigned from the Presidency of the Privy Council in order to make himself available for just such a rôle.

On June 29th Arita had planned to make a public announcement of the Cabinet's intention to adopt a more active policy (although still without resorting to force) in pursuit of the realisation of the New Order, but the Army protested that the original draft was too weak. Then, when he attempted to meet their criticism by strengthening it, they promptly denounced the resultant statement as 'contradictory to the policy that the Cabinet had so far followed and an attempt to forestall the activities of pro-German elements in order to prolong the life of the Cabinet.'

On July 3rd the General Staff issued an 'Outline of the Main Principles for Coping with the Changing World Situation' which called for an improvement in relations with Russia to secure the northern front in order to pave the way for the opening of hostilities against Britain and, 'if the situation requires', America. This was followed up by a petition the next day to Hata declaring that 'it is now deemed imperative to set up a powerful cabinet of the entire nation to execute various policies without vacillation. In this connection we request you, the Army Minister, to take appropriate action.'

By 'appropriate action' they meant, of course, his resignation — the time-honoured method of engineering the fall of a Cabinet. The fanatical activists of 'The Soldiers of God', the perpetrators of the attempted coup of 1933, were preparing to take more direct action still with a wholesale assassination of Prime Minister Yonai, Arita and others whom they regarded as the leading obstacles of an Axis alliance, including senior advisers to the Court — but not, of course, Kido. The plot was uncovered just in time; in reporting it to the Emperor, Kido remarked that 'their actions are blameworthy, but their motives deserve consideration'.

A few days later the Vice-Minister of War informed Kido that 'the character of the Yonai Cabinet is not at all suitable for conducting negotiations with Germany and Italy' and nominated Konoye to form a new one, having first obtained an undertaking of his support for the strategy of the 'Outline'; he then paid a visit to the Secretary of the Cabinet and warned that if the Cabinet did not resign of its own volition, the Army would use Hata's resignation to force it to do so. At a Cabinet meeting on July 16th Hata, as prearranged with Chief of Staff Kanin, called for the Cabinet's resignation. When Yonai refused and instead demanded that Hata himself should resign, the War Minister duly did so. The 'Big Three' refused to nominate a successor and Yonai was left with no option but to follow suit.

Konoye's succession was unanimously confirmed, although Saionji refused to have any part in it and his formal rôle of Premier-maker was taken over by a newly-established Committee of Ex-Premiers. Yoshida Zengo remained at the Navy Ministry, but the War and Foreign Ministries were transferred to the pro-Axis 'Scrapper' Tojo and 'The Talking Machine' Matsuoka, while Double Diplomat Shiratori was assigned to the latter as a permanent adviser. Kido would later claim to the War Crimes Tribunal that Hirohito had advised Konoye 'to be especially prudent' in filling the Foreign Ministry, but the choice of Matsuoka must have led the judges to think this a rather too obvious attempt to suggest the Emperor's non-involvement.

The Foreign Ministry had in the meantime produced a draft 'Proposal for Strengthening Co-operation between Japan, Germany and Italy'. Calling for 'the maximum co-operation possible short of involvement in war', it was approved in principle by the Army and Navy on the same day that the Yonai Cabinet fell. When Matsuoka saw it on assuming office the next day, however, he exclaimed 'This won't do!' and sent it back inscribed with a note saying 'unless you go into the tiger's den, you cannot catch the tiger's cub'. It was a phrase that would become all too familiar to the rest of the world in the next eighteen months.

On July 27th the Liaison Conference, the first since that of February, 1938 which had approved the extension of the China Incident, met to approve the Foreign Ministry draft; from now on it would largely take over the function of the Inner Cabinet in an attempt to improve, through the presence of the two Chiefs of Staff, co-ordination with the forces in the field. Muto 'The Silent', now Chief of Military Affairs on the General Staff, declared that 'if Germany and Italy propose a military alliance, we must accept'. The Navy's representatives, however, not wishing to be pushed into the 'Strike South' before they had completed their preparations, indicated that they were still not ready to take such a decisive step and it was resolved merely that 'Japan will reconsider the possibility of a military alliance if it should be proposed by Germany and Italy'.

This was hardly good enough for Matsuoka, and three days later the Foreign Ministry produced a fresh draft which stipulated that 'in the event that Germany and Italy should express a desire for Japanese military co-operation with them against Britain, Japan will be prepared, in principle, to meet their desire', and, furthermore, that 'in the event of a danger of either contracting party entering upon a state of war with the United States, both parties will confer on measures to be taken'. Its only reservation was that Japan should be allowed to decide for herself when the use of actual force was appropriate. 'The Talking Machine' followed this up with a declaration of his own that Japan was now ready to work for the realisation of her 'heavenly-ordained mission' in league with other friendly powers.

Matsuoka invited Ott to tea in order to sound out the likely German attitude to these new proposals for an alliance; he was also anxious to establish whether Hitler, in the wake of his victories over the motherlands in Europe, was now entertaining any ambitions for seizing their colonies in East Asia, which would conflict with Japan's envisaged New Order. The Fuhrer, however, was on the eve of launching his aerial bombardment as a prelude to Operation 'Sealion', the invasion of Britain. He was confident that this would break the back of her resistance and would therefore eliminate the need for Japanese help in diverting some of her naval strength to the Pacific. The Ambassador's response was accordingly cool, and he even went on to complain forcefully about Japan's interference in German commercial activities in China and her restrictions on exports to Germany of badly-needed tin, tungsten and soya beans. As for acqui-escence in the realisation of the New Order, he made it plain that Germany would expect 'tangible and valuable advantages' in return.

Never one to accept 'no' for an answer, Matsuoka renewed the invitation, and on August 23rd he received the gratifying news that Stahmer was being sent to Japan formally to reopen negotiations.

BETROTHAL

Two events had combined in the interval to bring about this German change of heart: the Luftwaffe's disappointing lack of progress in the Battle of Britain, which had thrown 'Sealion' into jeopardy, and secondly, Roosevelt's Lend-Lease Bill, under which America was to loan Britain fifty destroyers for Atlantic convoy escort duty in return for the lease of military bases on British soil. Furthermore, rumours were reported by Ott to Berlin that Japan was on the point of negotiating some form of non-aggression pact with America. It had been a standing principle of Hitler's foreign policy to do everything possible to forestall America's entry into the war on Britain's side, and such a neutralisation of Japan could only serve to increase the likelihood of such a contingency — as did America's patent unwillingness to cross swords with Japan (in a recent Gallup poll, only 12% had answered that they were prepared to risk war rather than see Japan gain control of China).

The imminence of Stahmer's arrival brought the differences between the Army and the Navy to a head. Navy Minister Yoshida continued to voice his opposition to a military alliance, provoking the following entry in the Army General Staff's Confidential War Diary: 'Negotiations with Germany and Italy stalled. Still being studied by the Navy Minister. Ugh!' Within the Navy, however, Yoshida was finding himself increasingly isolated; the recently-announced American restrictions on certain categories of oil exports had lent considerable encouragement to the 'now or never' attitude already prevalent among middle-ranking officers, while even his senior colleagues were reluctant to see the service cast in the rôle of odd-man-out now that the Foreign Ministry had been brought over by Matsuoka to the Army's side. As the strain mounted, so the Minister's health declined, and on September 3rd it broke down altogether and forced him into hospital and resignation.

His successor, the former Imperial Aide-de-Camp Oikawa, was thus in place when the Inner Cabinet convened three days later to consider a new draft policy presented by Matsuoka (and partially drawn up by Shiratori) laying down the proposed basis for an agreement with the Axis 'in order that they shall mutually co-operate by all possible means in the establishment of a New Order in Europe and Asia'. The 'all possible means' were now to be applied against America also, a proposal which caused Oikawa to voice his reservations but which did not, however, prevent him from adding his approval to the document as a general basis for negotiation. This elevation of America alongside Britain as a target of all-out hostilities had been sparked by the interception of a secret telegram suggesting that she was preparing to impose a total embargo on all exports to Japan, and in Matsuoka's language of diplomacy the only proper answer to a threat was another, bigger threat.

Stahmer arrived in Tokyo on September 7th, to be greeted by Ribbentrop's former accomplice, Oshima. When the Double Diplomat reported back to Matsuoka that Germany was looking to Japan to take the lead in suggesting terms for the proposed alliance, the Foreign Minister remarked that 'neither the Army nor the Navy is taking the initiative on this, though Navy Minister Oikawa is better than Yoshida. But I'll do it even if it costs me my job, and I'll wrap it up in one or two weeks', he declared with his usual confidence.

When he and Stahmer met two days later to inaugurate the formal negotiations, the German made it plain that he was looking for a full and openly-published military alliance rather than a mere declaration of mutual support for their respective New Orders. 'A weak, luke-warm attitude or declaration at this juncture will only invite derision and danger,' he asserted. 'What Germany wishes of Japan . . . [is] to enter into an understanding or agreement with Germany and Italy whereby both of us will be thoroughly prepared to meet an emergency effectively at any moment . . . [and] that will leave neither the United States nor the rest of the world in doubt.' Stahmer therefore proposed that the terms should include a commitment to the effect that 'if one of the three is attacked by a Power not presently involved in the European war or the China Incident, the three countries shall aid one another by every means, political, economic and military.' Matsuoka expressed enthusiastic assent, but he still, of course, had to win the approval of the Inner Cabinet — and of Oikawa in particular.

When the Inner Cabinet conferred on Stahmer's draft, Tojo gave it the Army's blessing, Konoye recorded, but Oikawa 'wanted to think it over'. By the time that they met again the following day, however, the Navy Minister indicated that he was prepared to fall into line, although he still insisted that the contracting parties should be able to reserve the right to decide the time and place of their entry into any conflict. In addition, he sought an undertaking that the former German Pacific islands now mandated to Japan should be recognised as Japanese territory. Matsuoka gave him his personal reassurance on both counts, and the Navy's support for a full military alliance was finally secured. In giving it his Imperial sanction, Hirohito remarked that 'since we have come so far, we cannot turn back.'

The agenda for the subsequent Imperial Conference was as usual agreed with Hirohito in advance, allowing him to remain silent throughout. Matsuoka was able to allay fears expressed by the Navy's representatives at the prospect of war with America with the assertion that since it was Germany's first wish to keep America out of the war, an alliance with her made such a prospect less, rather than more, likely. Turning to the oil problem, he likewise assured them that Germany would make up the shortfall resulting from any subsequent American embargo by pressurising the Russians and Dutch to step up their current supplies to Japan. Finally, the President of the Privy Council, who traditionally served as the Emperor's mouthpiece on these occasions, conferred his blessing, adding that 'even though a Japanese-American clash may be unavoidable in the end, I hope that sufficient care will be exercised to make sure that it will not come in the near future, and that there will be no miscalculations.'

Traditionally such an agreement also required the final approval of the Privy Council, and despite Matsuoka's suggestions to the contrary Hirohito insisted that it should do so on this occasion. At the same time, however, the Emperor also pointed out that in the event of the Council withholding its approval the Cabinet was free to present a counter-petition to the Throne, which all but ruled out the possibility of such an event — thus demonstrating that the process was merely one further device for ostensibly dissociating the Emperor from responsibility.

Meanwhile Matsuoka's negotiations with Stahmer had run into rougher waters following the receipt of a draft of proposed terms from Ribbentrop in the wake of consultations with Mussolini. Il Duce had expressed enthusiastic support for the alliance, declaring that it would have the 'effect of a bomb' on America. The point at issue was Japan's continuing stipulation that she should have the right to decide independently the time and place of her entry into hostilities. Matsuoka had suggested that it should be appended to the published treaty in a secret protocol, but Ribbentrop now dismissed the whole idea of such a proviso as 'rather childish'.

Both Stahmer and Matsuoka, however, were unwilling to see all their efforts brought to nought after being so close to agreement, and after settling the other outstanding differences they reached a compromise whereby Japan was allowed the right to decide not when and where she was to enter hostilities, but whether 'an attack' had taken place on the other two parties of such a nature as to obligate her assistance — which, of course, effectively amounted to the same thing. In addition, the proviso was to be contained not in a secret protocol, but in an 'exchange of notes' between the two countries. In the event, Stahmer decided, in the light of Ribbentrop's attitude, to keep the Japanese note to himself, and by all accounts it was not until long afterwards that Berlin even became aware of its existence.

The formal signing of the Tripartite Pact was set for September 27th 1940, the day after the Privy Council was due to meet to give its approval to the final draft; in this way it was judged that they would be even less likely to demur. Hirohito announced it to His people in an Imperial Rescript, justifying it on the grounds that 'to enhance justice on Earth and make of the World one household is the great injunction, bequeathed by our Imperial Ancestors, which we lay to heart by day and night.'

The thieves were allied at last, and their purpose revealed for all the world to see.

29

'The Whole World Under One Roof'

'THE TIME HAS COME'

'The principle of The Whole World Under One Roof embodies the spirit in which the Empire was founded by Jimmu,' Admiral Yonai declared after his appointment as Prime Minister in January 1940. 'My understanding is that this is the spirit of making the boundless virtues of the Emperor prevail throughout the whole world.'

The Navy, it will be remembered, had finally committed itself to embarking on the voyage of conquest in August 1936 when the Army had pledged its support (embodied in 'The Fundamental Principles of Our National Policy') for the 'Strike South'; the Third Replenishment Plan had been launched in preparation for it, to be followed in due course by the Fourth, resulting in a five-fold increase in warship construction. In 1939 Hainan and the Spratley Islands had been occupied to serve as advance bases and secret submarine pens prepared in the Mandated Pacific islands; detailed reconnaissance had been made in the 'Southern Areas' and plans drawn up, including one for the invasion of Australia, a copy of which was captured in China and forwarded to the Australian Commissioner in Chungking. On November 15th 1939 a new Fourth Fleet had been established to take over these activities and a 'first alert' state of readiness, representing 60% of a full war footing, set for April the next year.

On October 20th 1939 Navy Minister Yoshida had approved a draft 'Outline of Policy Towards America', in which it was stated that 'in view of the unpredictability of American diplomacy, as shown by the sudden notice of termination of the Treaty of Commerce and Navigation, an arms replenishment programme must be promoted to provide against any emergency.' The elaboration of this programme had been entrusted to the head of the General Staff's War Guidance Section, who on the outbreak of the war in Europe in September had proclaimed that 'finally the time has come. This maritime nation, Japan, should today commence its advance to the Bay of Bengal. Moss-covered tundras, vast barren deserts — of what use are they [i.e., the 'Strike North']? . . . We should not hesitate to fight even the United States and Britain . . . Under present circumstances, Japan

444

must advance east of the Dutch East Indies to Malaya (naturally Australia will come under our control) and to the British islands in the South Seas ...'

The 'first alert' preparations were all but completed by the target date of April 1940, and Navy Chief of Staff Fushimi requested Hirohito to sanction a 'second alert' for completion in a further three months. 'At present everything is almost ready, except for air force crews and a few other matters,' he informed his cousin. 'After receipt of the order the Navy will require at least five to six months to prepare for war, needing time to requisition and equip special vessels.'

There was another, equally important, requirement which had to be met, however, before the Navy would be able to pronounce itself ready for war: oil. Nine-tenths of its present supply came from America which, given her 'unpredictable diplomacy' and the embargoes already imposed on aircraft (in June 1938) and certain raw materials (in September 1939), was an obvious target for further reprisal. Although stocks equivalent to eighteen months' supply had been built up, it was essential to secure an alternative source before realisation of the 'Strike South' could be con-templated. It was this consideration which caused Yonai at this time to oppose negotiations for the Tripartite Pact, for fear that a military alliance with the Axis would commit the Navy to a premature opening of hostilities.

Apart from the small field in British Brunei and those in northern Sakhalin which were anyway under lease to Japan, only the Dutch sector of Borneo offered an alternative source within reasonable reach of Japan. The Navy had drawn up a plan in 1936 for the seizure of the island, and in the same year Japan had invited Holland, on the pretext of offering help against the communist-inspired nationalist movement in the East Indies, to join the Anti-Comintern Pact. The Dutch, however, who had already found it necessary to introduce restrictions on Japanese immigration and commercial activities there, politely declined.

The opening of the war in Europe and the threat of a German occupation of Holland offered the disconcerting prospect of British and/or American counter-moves to protect the Dutch East Indies (here-after abbreviated to DEI), and Yonai's Foreign Minister Arita approached Holland with an offer to guarantee their security in return for certain economic concessions, including, of course, an increased supply of oil. This too, however, was rejected, with a pointed reminder that Japan had already given just such a guarantee in the 1922 Washington Treaty. 'If we give the Japanese even a finger's breadth of their demands,' the Dutch Ambassador in Tokyo warned, 'they will quickly ask for the whole of our country'.

This time Japan would not take 'no' for an answer, and when in April Germany invaded Norway and Denmark Arita seized on the occasion to announce that 'the Japanese Government cannot but be deeply concerned over any development accompanying an aggravation of the war in Europe that may affect the status quo of the Dutch East Indies ... [with which] Japan is economically bound by an intimate relationship of mutuality in ministering to one another's needs.' In private the language of the Naval General Staff was somewhat less circuitous: 'the time has come to occupy the Dutch East Indies', they declared, and when Hitler invaded Holland itself on May 10th, the 4th Fleet was ordered the very same day to take up station at Palau in the Caroline Islands.

A few days later the Japanese Consul-General in Batavia presented himself at the colony's Office of Economic Affairs and delivered a catalogue of 'condolences, requests and veiled threats almost in the same breath'. The requests included an annual supply of one million tons of oil — double the current level and approximately one-fifth of Japan's total needs. In the meantime British and French troops had landed, at The Hague's invitation, in the Dutch possessions in the West Indies in order to prevent the oil wells there falling into German hands.

CLEARING THE DECKS

These events caused considerable alarm in Washington, not least because America was relying on significant imports of tin and rubber from the DEI for her own defensive preparations. Roosevelt, supported by the Australian Minister, R. G. Casey (who had good reason for making his voice increasingly heard on developments in the south-west Pacific, for his country's very considerable support for the British armies in the Middle East had left only 7,000 regular soldiers to defend its enormous coastline), had already cautioned against any military intervention in the DEI, and he now lost no time in urging Britain and France to withdraw their troops from the West Indies as soon as they had established trustworthy local regimes in order to avoid giving Japan an excuse for taking similar action in the DEI.

The Japanese Navy simultaneously put this objective to the test in a series of map exercises. Working on the assumption that Roosevelt would impose a total embargo on oil exports even if the attack was confined to the DEI, they concluded that America would sooner or later enter the war, in which event, in spite of having secured possession of the oil wells there, 'Japan would be able to continue the war for a year at most. Should the war continue beyond a year, our chances of winning would be nil.' Such an inference not only had the effect of putting an end to any thoughts (in the Navy, at least) of occupation in the immediate future, but it also awakened fears that Germany might anticipate Japan and help herself to the Dutch and French possessions in the Far East in the wake of her victories in Europe.

In answer to Arita's tentative enquiries, Ambassador Ott replied that Germany 'was not interested in the problem of the DEI'. Thus reassured, the Inner Cabinet felt able when France surrendered the following month to present the Governor-General of Indo-China with demands that all movements of war materials to the Chinese Nationalists should cease (the Hanoi-Chungking railway had already been heavily bombed) and that Japan should be permitted to send military observers to see that this was carried out; if he refused, force was to be used. A week later Britain was presented with similar demands for the evacuation of her troops from the Shanghai International Settlement and for the closure of the Hong Kong frontier and the Burma Road.

Germany was asked at the same time to exert pressure on the new Vichy regime in France to acquiesce, but the response this time (as we saw in the previous chapter) was a good deal cooler. The need now perceived for an arrangement with Germany on the basis of 'the maximum co-operation possible short of involvement in war', which would guarantee German recognition of Japan's envisaged hegemony in Asia in return for that of Germany's right to a similar position in Europe, brought about, as Berlin had intended, the fall of the hesitant Yonai and the return of Imperial-Go-Between Konoye.

In their July 3rd 'Outline of the Main Principles for Coping with the Changing World Situation' the Army General Staff urged that advantage should be taken of American hesitation and the now confidently antici-pated German victory over Britain to drive the British and Dutch out of South-East Asia. 'We should not miss the opportunity to establish a self-sufficient economic sphere. The rapid changes taking place in the world do not permit a moment's hesitation,' it declared. 'Never in our history has there been a time like the present, when it is so urgent to plan for the development of our national power ...' Hong Kong and Malaya were to be the first targets, and the Army even went so far as to mobilise heavy artillery for an attack on the former. When the Naval General Staff considered the plan, they found themselves in something of a quandary, for although it talked of restricting action 'in so far as possible to Britain alone', their own map exercises had shown that any such action would inevitably involve America sooner or later; to veto it, on the other hand, might place the whole 'Strike South' and their share of the military budget in jeopardy. They therefore inserted the following amendment: 'A mili-tary offensive is to be avoided in so far as possible. But if the situation permits, an offensive will be carried out with a firm resolution for war against Britain (or even against the United States).' The extent of the preparations needed for such a war — and in particular, the acquisition of sufficient oil — would, they calculated, effectively give them a veto on its timing.

The final draft was submitted on July 19th to the new Inner Cabinet of Konoye, Tojo (War) Yoshida (Navy) and Matsuoka (Foreign Affairs). It was then formally incorporated at the Liaison Conference a week later into a document entitled 'The Main Principles of Japan's Basic National

Policy' setting out the means by which the New Order, now to be known as 'The Greater East Asia Co-Prosperity Sphere', was to be realised. In addition to establishing a 'political combination' with the Axis and a 'sweeping readjustment' of relationships with Russia, Japan was to maintain a 'stern attitude' towards the United States and to 'take stronger measures against French Indo-China, Hong Kong and foreign concessions in China for the purpose of cutting off aid to the Nationalist regime'. These would then leave her in a position to undertake 'positive steps in order to incorporate into the New Order the English, French, Dutch and Portuguese colonies and their neighbouring islands in East Asia'.

On the domestic front, Konoye's long-cherished one-party New Political Structure was to be introduced under the title of 'The Imperial Rule Assistance Association'. It would serve to guide 'the one-hundred-million-strong nation's march towards the completion of the domestic structure and the construction of a high-tensioned defence state through the co-operation of all strata of society' by the abolition of the existing political parties. All this was to be done with the declared aim 'of establishing world peace in accordance with the lofty ideal of "the Whole World Under One Roof" on which the Empire is founded'. Put more simply, Japan was now clearing the decks for all-out war.

STORM CONES IN WASHINGTON

For all its grandiose scope, its instigators still 'all hold different ideas in regard to the execution of the plan,' so Lord Privy Seal Kido was informed by Hirohito. 'Konoye, believing that The China Incident cannot be settled easily, wants to try to reduce the area of occupation in China and start the southwards advance. Thus he seems to be trying to divert the discontent of the people over the failure in China. The Army wants to leave the situation in China as it is, and to advance south if there is an opportunity. But the Navy seemingly does not wish to advance south until the war in China is settled.' In particular, the Naval General Staff were concerned that an advance into Indo-China would 'increase the probability of a tightening of the embargo against Japan, and the execution of an embargo on scrap iron and oil is a matter of life and death for the Empire, in the event of which the Empire will inevitably have to make a firm decision to invade the DEI in order to acquire its oil fields' — which in turn would provoke 'hostilities with a third country [i.e., America].' They were not to know that they were taking the words out of Roosevelt's mouth.

Ever since the all-out invasion of China in 1937 the President had been wrestling with the converse problem of how to deny Japan the raw materials on which her ambitions depended without provoking her to further adventures to acquire them by force elsewhere and ultimately driving her into a war for which America was still, three years later, both logistically and spiritually very far from prepared. In 1937 he had talked of placing Japan 'in quarantine', but had declined support for economic sanctions; in 1938 the embargo introduced on the export of aircraft had been 'moral' rather than statutory; in 1939 the ban on sale of other armaments had been cloaked under the Neutrality Act; and in January 1940 when Henry Stimson called for a total embargo on the grounds that 'the very last thing which the Japanese Government desires is a war with the United States', he had preferred to accept the contrary advice of his Ambassador in Tokyo.

'If we once start sanctions against Japan we must see them through to the end, and the end may conceivably be war. If we cut off Japanese supplies of oil and Japan then finds that she cannot obtain sufficient oil from other commercial sources to ensure her national security, she will in all probability send her fleet down to take the DEI,' Grew warned. 'It is my opinion that even if worse came to worst there is realisation that Japan has irrevocably committed herself to the continental adventure and is determined to see it through ... Japan is a nation of hardy warriors, still inculcated with the *samurai* do-or-die spirit which has by tradition and inheritance become ingrained in the race.'

Thus when Holland fell in May, Roosevelt ordered the U.S. Fleet, then on manoeuvres off Hawaii, to stand by in Pearl Harbor, but he declined a request from Britain and Australia that it should be dispatched to Singapore. A month later he turned down a similar suggestion from the Dutch Government-in-exile that a detachment should be sent to link up with their naval forces in the DEI. When Britain and Australia again appealed for a show of American support to counter the Japanese demand that all British supplies to the Chinese Nationalists should cease he once more refused. The Burma Road and the Hong Kong border were accordingly closed on July 17th.

However, Stimson had by now rejoined the Administration as Minister of War and was finding increasingly vocal allies for his point of view, and the announcement of Konoye's Cabinet finally tipped the balance in his favour. Grew remarked of the new Cabinet that 'it gives every indication of going hell-bent towards the Axis and the establishment of a New Order in East Asia, and of riding rough-shod over the rights and interests, and the principles and policies, of the United States and Great Britain'. Hardly less disconcerting was a report of the tripling of Japanese orders for motor and aviation fuels, much of it to be delivered in drums to Hainan, the staging post for the 'Strike South'. On July 20th Roosevelt signed the Bill for the creation of separate Atlantic and Pacific Fleets, and on the very day that Konoye was proclaiming his 'Greater East Asia Co-Prosperity Sphere' in Tokyo, he announced an embargo on the export of aviation fuel and No. 1 scrap iron.

INTO INDO-CHINA

Following Germany's profession of uninterest in the DEI, Japan had informed Batavia that she would be dispatching a mission there to negotiate an increase in the exports of raw materials. It was to be headed, on Matsuoka's recommendation, by Mukden-Collaborator and ex-Minister for Overseas Affairs Koiso. However, the Dutch objected to his appointment on the grounds of a statement which he had made in the Press accusing them of having exploited the colony and asserting that 'we cannot tolerate such a condition — it is necessary to emancipate the Oriental races'. Koiso himself expressed reservations about accepting it when the Navy Minister Yoshida refused his request that the mission should be accompanied by a squadron of warships and a force of marines, and eventually Commerce and Industry Minister Kobayashi Ichizo was chosen in his stead.

Anticipating the likely nature of his demands the White House approached the American oil companies operating in Borneo with a request that they should not contract themselves to increase supplies to Japan, but the Dutch expressed concern that such a move would only provoke further, more drastic demands. The other major operator, Royal Dutch Shell, was likewise instructed by London to 'bargain hard both as to time and quantity'.

In Indo-China meanwhile the French Governor-General had acquiesced in the original Japanese demand to close the frontier with China and to permit the presence of Japanese observers, but when this was promptly superseded by further demands for the stationing of troops and the use of military airfields (in support of an invasion of the Chinese province of Yunnan planned by the South China Army) he had referred them to Vichy. The South China Army, which had also drawn up plans for an invasion of Indo-China itself on the grounds that it 'will not only provide a quick solution of the China Incident but will also constitute the basis for a further southward advance', then on its own initiative presented the French with an ultimatum.

In Tokyo too Matsuoka adopted a tone of extreme belligerence, demanding complete freedom of both military and economic action in Indo-China (for the export of raw materials to Japan, in particular) and refusing to give any guarantee to respect the country's territorial integrity. 'Our present requests are based on absolute military necessity,' 'The Talking Machine' informed Vichy's Ambassador. 'Despite the fact that Japan has not declared war against China, if the French authorities do not accept our requests, we may be obliged to violate your neutrality ...' After several further rounds of hard talking, an agreement was signed on August 30th which excluded any guarantee of territorial integrity, but which limited the Japanese presence to 6,000 troops and confined their field of operations to the Chinese border and three airfields. At the request of the French, there was to be no public announcement of the agreement and the details of its provisions were to be settled locally by the commanders in the field.

The South China Army took a predictably dim view of these restrictions and carried on with its plans regardless. Operations Section Chief Tominaga Kyoji, who had taken over in the field, even went so far as to forge a telegram from Chief of Staff Kanin authorising the invasion. The Governor-General was accordingly presented with a new ultimatum to allow the entry of 25,000 Japanese by September 5th; in Tokyo Matsuoka and Tojo gave it their retrospective approval, but the Navy expressed considerable reservations and Tominaga was ordered to await Imperial sanction. At 11 pm on the 4th the Governor-General finally succumbed in principle, although it was agreed that the details should be worked out in the field and that negotiations were to be broken off if the Japanese moved before they were completed. Two days later a battalion 'became lost' and crossed the border into Indo-China, whereupon the negotiations were referred back to Tokyo.

On September 13th the high command issued an ultimatum, approved by Hirohito, that stationing of the 6,000 troops allowed under the August 30th agreement would begin on the 23rd regardless of whether its provisions had been agreed locally. Furthermore, they would now be stationed not on the Chinese border as stipulated but in the Hanoi-Haiphong area; 'if the troops of French Indo-China offer resistance, military force will be used,' the ultimatum warned. Britain suggested to America that military assistance should be offered to Vichy, but Washington, preoccupied now with the run-up to the Presidential election in which both candidates had pledged themselves to non-involvement in foreign wars, preferred to ignore Grew's call for 'a show of force' and declined.

Deprived of any prospect of outside assistance the French, on September 22nd, once more gave way, permitting the use of four airfields and the passage of 25,000 Japanese troops to the Chinese border in addition to the permanent presence of the original 6,000. These last, however, were to be stationed around the airfields rather than in Hanoi-Haiphong.

Still the South China Army was not satisfied and promptly at midnight launched an attack across the border on a French garrison. Tominaga excused it on the grounds that since the agreement had been reached so close to the deadline 'many errors can be anticipated, [and] since we do not know the contents of the agreement, nothing can be done about it.' The fighting went on for a further two days until halted by a personal order from Hirohito; Haiphong was also attacked from the sea, the commander of the landing force having hidden himself under a lifeboat so that the Imperial command could not be delivered to him. A week later both Kanin and his Vice-Chief of Staff resigned, while Tominaga was recalled to Tokyo and dismissed as head of the Operations Division (although he would subsequently rise again to become Vice-Minister of War).

'ANGLO-SAXONISM WILL BE WIPED OUT'

Roosevelt's embargo on aviation fuel had meanwhile caused the Naval high command to reconsider their non-interventionist policy and to contemplate the prospect that the opportunity for the 'Strike South', however limited its chances of success, would be lost for good if they waited until their fuel stocks began to diminish — a prospect which much increased when Kobayashi reported from Batavia that the Dutch Governor-General had refused to negotiate himself with the Japanese mission, but had instead referred them to a subordinate and 'voiced not the slightest interest in sounding out the true intention of the Japanese Government towards the DEI'. Now that the embargo was in place, it was accepted that it would only be a matter of time before it was extended to all categories of oil, which would require an invasion of the DEI and in turn entail war with America — 'for the survival of the Empire, whether we like it or not'.

On August 17th the groundwork for a 'preparatory fleet mobilisation' was accordingly put in hand, although Chief of Staff Fushimi informed his cousin Hirohito that it would take another eight months to complete. By April, according to the Vice-Chief of Staff, 'vessels already built will have been equipped and merchant ships totalling 2.5 million tons will have been converted to warships. Once all these preparations are completed, we have a chance of victory over the United States if we aim for a quick war and a quick victory. But if the United States prolongs the war, then we will face grave difficulties ... In this regard, it is better to fight now.'

It was calculated that the present stock of aviation fuel would only suffice for a year's hostilities, and consequently they were obliged to admit that in the event of a protracted war 'we are not very confident of our capacity for endurance'. Navy Minister Yoshida continued to voice strong reservations, remarking pointedly that in that case 'is this not a very unreliable navy?' By September 4th, however, the strain of his isolation had driven him to resign. As the negotiations for the Tripartite Pact got under way, his replacement Oikawa became increasingly seduced by Matsuoka's argument that Japan would be allowed to reserve the right to choose the time and place of her entry into any war against America (thus preserving the Navy's oft-stated proviso that the war in China should be settled first), and that anyway an alliance with the Axis would make such a war less, rather than more, likely. 'There is a danger that we shall pick Germany's chestnuts out of the fire. But the United States will hesitate to wage a war. I think it's probably safe,' Oikawa declared.

Hirohito too seems to have been swayed by the same argument in giving his approval to the Pact, which he believed, so he told Konoye, 'cannot be helped in the present situation. If there are no other means of dealing with the United States it may be the only solution.' He also showed, however, that he shared the Navy's lack of confidence if the worse did come to the worst: 'What is the Navy going to do in the event of war with the United States? I am very concerned over what would happen if Japan is defeated,' he told the Prime Minister. 'If that should happen, I wonder if you would share the pains and tribulations with me.' Konoye replied stoutly by quoting Ito's pledge to Meiji on the eve of the attack on Russia in 1904: 'I would give up everything and go out to the battlefield as a common soldier to die alone.'

Hirohito appears to have received this with some scepticism, for he remarked to Kido that he would be placed in a most compromising position if Konoye was again to 'run away' (as he had done by resigning in January 1939). Even greater diffidence was expressed by Pearl Harbor Mastermind Yamamoto, now Commander-in-Chief of the Combined Fleet: 'It's out of the question! To fight the United States is like fighting the whole world. But it has been decided, and so I will fight my best. Doubtless I will die on board my flagship and Tokyo will be burnt to the ground,' he added prophetically.

At the Imperial Conference on September 19th which gave the formal go-ahead to the Pact Fushimi reiterated the Navy's proviso that '1) every possible measure will be taken to avoid war with the United States; 2) the southward advance will be attempted as far as possible by peaceful means.' At the meeting of the Privy Council which rubber-stamped it a week later Matsuoka again assured him that its purpose was to 'bring about an international situation favourable to us and thereby to avoid an outbreak of hostilities with America'. (On the other side of the world Ribbentrop was telling Mussolini with equal bombast that America 'would reflect a hundred times before participating in the war').

In answer to questions on the Navy's state of readiness, however, Oikawa implicitly conceded that such a war was in fact inevitable. 'Today our fleets are completely equipped and in no way inferior to those of the United States. But if the war is [to be] protracted, we would have to make more complete preparations,' he declared. 'At present, if we aim at a quick war and a quick victory, we have a good chance of winning.' He attempted to put the best gloss he could on the oil supply position: 'We have enough heavy oil for a fairly long war,' he asserted. 'We are also now testing synthetic substances ... [and] we expect to obtain oil from the DEI by peaceful means.' Konoye informed the Councillors that in giving the Pact his Imperial sanction Hirohito had displayed 'an unusual resolve', and the Imperial Rescript which announced it tacitly conveyed the desirability of a quick victory: 'We earnestly wish that war be ended and peace restored as soon as possible.'

As understood by the terms of the Pact, the 'Greater East Asia Co-Prosperity Sphere' to be recognised by the other partners as Japan's area of hegemony stretched from Burma in the West to New Guinea and New Caledonia in the South and to the Mandated Pacific islands in the East. In order 'to induce the Soviet Union to go along with the policy of the

Tripartite Pact' it was agreed 'to acquiesce in the Soviet Union's future advance in the direction of Afghanistan and Persia (including India if circumstances should demand it).' Matsuoka went on to claim that 'we have made an understanding that this sphere could be automatically broadened in the course of time,' and indeed detailed plans had already been laid for an enormous extension of the 'sphere' — although these were never revealed to the other signatories.

Drawn up by the Ministry of War's Research Section in collaboration with the National Policy Investigation Society, a body funded jointly by the Government and the major conglomerates, they envisaged the incorporation of Australia, New Zealand, southern India, Ceylon and all the other islands in the Indian Ocean except Madagascar; the entire Pacific, including, of course, Hawaii; the western side of North America from Alaska to the State of Washington; the whole of Central America with the exception of Mexico, and the northern half of the Caribbean; and the west coast of South America if the countries there should enter hostilities with Japan. It was appreciated that such a vast domain could hardly be absorbed at a single stroke, and the country would therefore have to prepare to launch a second war some twenty years after the establishment of the original 'sphere'.

The following week Matsuoka sent a statement to the U.S. Ambassador denying that the Pact was aimed at any particular country. His deputy had already given this the lie, however, having informed Grew that 'the Pact is aimed directly against the United States, which ever since the Immigration Act of 1924 and the Manchurian Incident has hampered Japan's necessary expansion; world totalitarianism will take the place of Anglo-Saxonism, which is bankrupt and will be wiped out, and Japan has to ally herself with the other camp which is not intransigently set on preserving the status quo.'

'There are some who say that Matsuoka must be insane,' Secretary Harada remarked to Saionji after reporting the conclusion of the Pact. 'He can only improve if he does become insane,' the Last Noble rejoined. Six weeks later, at the age of ninety-one, this one feeble hand of restraint, who had fought for so long to divert Japan from such 'insanity', lay dead.

OIL SEARCH

The news of the Pact had not taken the rest of the world quite by surprise, because two days earlier, on September 25th, the *New York Times* had carried a story that Germany and Japan were on the point of an alliance and that Hitler was calling for a Japanese attack on Hong Kong and Singapore. On the same day Washington announced a further $25 million loan to Nationalist China and, twenty-four hours later, a total embargo on the export of all categories of iron and steel scrap to all except the British

Empire. Roosevelt rejected the arguments of Stimson and others for tighter limitations on oil exports, however, partly in response to further pleas from the Dutch that such a move would only increase Japanese pressure on them and partly because of similar warnings from Grew. The scrap embargo by itself was a considerable blow to Japan whose own steel production was still only one-tenth that of America's, and in a predictable outburst of bragadaccio and indignation Matsuoka condemned it as 'an unfriendly act'. Any further embargoes 'would not seriously handicap us,' he boasted, but in the next breath he warned that they 'would intensely anger the Japanese people ... [and] future relations between Japan and the United States will be unpredictable.'

A Gallup poll taken five days later showed a remarkable transformation in American public opinion: no less than 88% of those questioned expressed approval for the scrap iron embargo, and 57% now agreed that steps should be taken to prevent Japan from becoming more powerful 'even if this means risking war'. In the next fortnight sixteen million men registered for military duty under the newly-passed Selective Training and Service Act. Britain's response was to reopen the Burma Road, but a repeated offer for the use of Singapore as a base for the U.S. Pacific Fleet was again declined.

Although Roosevelt rejected the further suggestion that the two countries should formally initiate discussions with the Dutch for a joint defence arrangement in the South-West Pacific until the election was out of the way, he did give his approval for some preliminary discussions, and as soon as he had been safely re-elected he authorised 'an exhaustive series of secret staff conversations with the British, for which definite plans and agreements to promote unity of effort against the Axis and Japan could emerge.' He gave his approval for the dispatch of six submarines to the Philippines and, in response to Japan's formal recognition of Wang's puppet 'National Government' in China, for the grant of a further $100 million dollars to Chiang Kai-shek together with fifty fighter planes. He also wanted to supply the Generalissimo with long-range bombers which were capable of hitting Tokyo, but it was found that there were none to spare.

The significance of these moves was not lost on Japan, and in early October the Army finalised its strategic planning under which eleven divisions, to be placed under the direct control of Imperial Headquarters, were earmarked for the 'Strike South'; training was to be completed by February in preparation for joint exercises and mock landings with the Navy the following month. For their part the Navy drafted the order for the 'preparatory fleet mobilisation' initiated by the General Staff in August, the central feature of which was the creation of a new 6th Fleet; it was finally approved by Hirohito on November 15th. The Operations Section calculated that by January 1941 they would be in a position to invade the DEI and by mid-April 'we shall achieve approximately 75%

readiness vis-à-vis the United States. Hence it is the Navy's view that we must commence hostilities against the United States by April or May.' Two weeks later Yamamoto held a table-top exercise for an attack on the DEI, from which he concluded once again that such an operation would inevitably draw America into the war. The high command still refused to be deflected, however, Oikawa remarking only that 'we must handle the situation in anticipation of such developments'. The Foreign Ministry drew up an alternative plan, under which Singapore was to be seized first and the DEI then coerced into declaring their 'independence'; the subsequent administration was naturally to be dominated by Japanese.

In the negotiations in Batavia Kobayashi put forward a demand for an annual supply of 3.75 million tons of oil, over six times the current rate of exports to Japan; the Dutch rejected this on the grounds that it would entail the premature exhaustion of the oil fields and instead offered some 2 million tons on a six-month contract only. Although this was accepted as not unsatisfactory, it was already clear that Japan was after not only a huge increase in actual exports but also the control of the oilfields themselves — and that with a view not only to the exploration and extraction of oil, but to the establishment also of secret military bases. For this purpose they demanded large areas of Borneo, Celebes, Dutch New Guinea and neighbouring islands; a considerable number of Kobayashi's entourage were intelligence officers whose mission was to survey these areas and select landing points for an invasion. The Governor-General continued to refuse to allow the negotiations to cover anything but the subject of exports, and indeed suggested that as contracts had now been agreed they could be formally discontinued. Kobayashi was consequently recalled to Japan and replaced by a senior diplomat, ex-Foreign Minister Yoshizawa Kenkichi.

The negotiations resumed on January 2nd 1941. The Japanese presented a greatly-extended range of demands, including an increased supply of other raw materials, the admission of many more Japanese as residents, assistance in setting up businesses in conjunction with Japanese companies, permission to increase the number of Japanese ships operating in DEI waters and the opening of harbours at present closed to them. Once again, however, the Governor-General refused to discuss them, provoking the exasperated Matsuoka to declare in the Diet that since the DEI were already included in the Greater East Asia Co-Prosperity Sphere a fundamental realignment of their relationship with Japan was called for.

This was merely playing into the hands of the Dutch, who secretly informed the U.S. Consul-General that they would 'endeavour to prolong the negotiations as long as possible in order to give Great Britain more time to bring about a change in the situation in Europe'. Matsuoka's faux pas was then further compounded by a suggestion that Japan would refuse to recognise the Dutch Government-in-Exile in London. They therefore formally protested that the negotiations could not continue under such conditions, and it was mid-February before a suitable apology had been extracted and the negotiations once more resumed.

Yoshizawa cabled Tokyo that he held little hope that he could secure Japan's demands, but it soon became clear that the Navy was not yet in a position to use force, and the Dutch reported to Washington that the new round of negotiations 'were generally characterized by a remarkable lack of strength on the part of the Japanese representatives. Several exaggerated and far-reaching proposals were reduced to much more modest requests.'

'THIEF AT A FIRE'

Any invasion of the DEI entailed the prior establishment of advance bases in Indo-China. To this end on November 21st 1940 the Inner Cabinet had decided to lend their support to demands which Thailand was then making on Vichy for the retrocession of certain territories along the Mekong (see Map 7). 'The Empire will act swiftly to mediate in the dispute between Thailand and French Indo-China and will co-operate with Thailand to recover its lost territories in order to establish a closer relationship with Thailand and, by manipulating France, to advance and expand the influence of the Empire in Indo-China', it was agreed. In return 'Thailand will be induced to co-operate with the establishment of the New Order in East Asia ... [but] if Thailand should not respond positively to our demands, it should be caused to do so by intimations that Japan might otherwise promote closer ties with Indo-China ...' When fighting between the two disputants broke out shortly afterwards, Japan immediately entered the ring with an offer of mediation. The Axis also added its voice in support of the Thai demands, and when Vichy rejected it Tokyo stepped up the supply of planes and armaments to Bangkok.

On December 26th a Liaison Conference moved to increase the pressure on Indo-China still further by the establishment of 'close, inseparable relations between Japan and Thailand' and a 'politico-military pact'. At the same time, they decided, 'negotiations with Indo-China should begin immediately and Japan's economic, military and political demands presented to it. Our economic demands, above all, must be accepted at once ... If France does not accept our demands, we must be prepared to abandon the Matsuoka-Henry Agreement [of August 30th] and take the necessary steps accompanying the destructions of that pact.'

On January 16th an Indo-Chinese attack on Thai troops at the Cambodian border was beaten back with heavy casualties, but in a simultaneous assault at sea the Thai fleet suffered a major defeat. Bangkok appealed to Tokyo for further support, which was not slow in coming: three days later Matsuoka presented the French Ambassador with a second offer of Japanese mediation, informing him that if it was again rejected

Japan would be forced to take 'a very strong attitude'. A Liaison Conference the same day drew up plans to exert the 'necessary pressure' by the dispatch of a force of two aircraft-carriers, eight cruisers and 700 marines.

Its purpose, ostensibly one of intimidation, was intended by the Navy's Operations Section to go a good deal beyond that, as they confided to their counterparts in the Army: 'In fact, our real intention is to use military force in central and southern Indo-China ... The Navy's hope is to secure permanent bases near Saigon and Camranh Bay.' This was necessarily divulged when Imperial approval was sought, and obtained, on February 1st, although, it was explained to Hirohito, 'it cannot be boldly expressed'. Kido also recorded that it was arranged at the same time that, 'in case armed force is resorted to, Imperial sanction will be obtained afresh.'

Thailand, of course, immediately accepted the Japanese offer, and when the French showed signs of hesitation Matsuoka, alleging that they were 'seeking to establish relations with England and the United States' (Britain having also offered to mediate), appealed again to Germany 'to work on the Vichy regime. Japan's southward advance on Singapore is impossible without going through the Malay peninsula, and in order to utilise this land bridge Japan must go through Indo-China and Thailand. For this reason, Great Britain must be prevented from exercising influence upon Thailand.' This was an argument well calculated to appeal to Germany, who at that moment was doing her utmost to commit Japan to an attack on Singapore in order to draw off the Royal Navy from the Atlantic.

Faced with this double pressure the French, as they informed Washington, were 'no longer in a position to refuse'. A truce was duly called and discussions opened on board a Japanese cruiser anchored off Saigon to settle the terms of the mediation. These were soon agreed; an armistice was signed, and the negotiations proper got under way in Tokyo on February 7th.

Thailand immediately presented a demand for the retrocession not merely of the territories along the Mekong, but of all those ceded to Indo-China since 1867. Deadlock at once ensued, and Japan then came forward with a plan of her own. This proved unacceptable to the French and after a second plan had also been rejected Japan set a deadline for its acceptance of March 5th. Another Liaison Conference in the meantime decided that if this too was rejected, 'the Empire will commence military action against French Indo-China ... [and] we will approve freedom of action for Thailand to seize such territory as is awarded in our mediation plan. Military assistance, including weapons, munitions and technical advice, will be supplied to Thailand.' The French held out to the last, capitulating on March 6th. In the subsequent treaty Japan inserted a secret pledge from both sides not to conclude any agreements amounting to a military pact with third parties hostile to Japan.

In giving it his approval, Hirohito cautioned against arousing British and American hostility by implementing it too quickly. He also expressed some distaste at the thought that Japan's actions might be viewed by the outside world as those of 'a thief at a fire', preferring that they should be seen as part and parcel of the realisation of the lofty ideal of 'The Whole World Under One Roof'.

However, the Emperor went on, this was no time for 'mistaken benevolence'.

30

Talking at Cross Purposes

SIGHTS ON SINGAPORE

If the way to the south was now clear, the Army still had to be certain that the northern flank in Manchuria was secure, and the Navy that the supply of Russian oil from North Sakhalin would continue, before they made their next move.

In theory, Germany's participation in the Non-Aggression Treaty with Russia and in the Tripartite Pact with Japan should have effectively guaranteed these, but there were already straws in the wind to indicate that the former might come apart just as quickly as it had been stuck together. One of the declared aims of the Army's July 3rd 1940 'Outline of the Main Principles for Coping with the Changing World Situation' had been that of 'rapidly improving relations with Soviet Russia', which had then been translated by the incoming Konoye Cabinet into a firm decision to 'conclude with that country a non-aggression pact to guarantee the boundaries between Japan, Manchukuo and Mongolia, to remain in effect for a period of five to ten years'. The purpose of such a time limit was made clear by the next sentence: 'During the effective period of the proposed non-aggression pact, Japan will strengthen its military preparedness against the Soviet Union so as to be invincible.'

The inducement offered to Russia was the acquiescence in a Soviet advance into Afghanistan and Persia, and India 'if circumstances should demand it', written into the Tripartite Pact, and it was borne to Moscow by Tatekawa; the former Manchurian Mastermind, now a leading light of 'The Great Fascist' Suetsugu's National Federation for the Reconstruction of East Asia, had been Matsuoka's choice as Ambassador there in place of the career diplomat Togo. However, it was agreed that 'Japanese policy would be best served if the foregoing ideas were presented to Soviet Russia ... as being German suggestions' — understandably, since only two years earlier the two countries had come close to all-out war at Nomonhan. Accordingly, Foreign Commissar Molotov was invited to Berlin for discussions with a view to 'adopting a long-range policy ... by delimitation of their [i.e., of Russian, Japanese, German and Italian] interests on a world-wide scale'.

In reply, Stalin agreed that an arrangement on such a basis was 'entirely possible', and the talks opened in the Reich's capital on November 12th. However, it soon emerged that his price for any arrangement was a good deal higher than either Germany or Japan were prepared to offer: from the former he demanded the right to include the Balkans in the Soviet 'sphere', from the latter the renunciation of Japan's coal and oil concessions in North Sakhalin. Acceptance of such a demand by Germany, which was almost wholly dependent on Rumania for her oil supplies, was out of the question, and it was now that Hitler gave the order to prepare for Operation 'Barbarossa', the invasion of Russia which he had already planned in outline three months earlier. In return for the renunciation of her Sakhalin rights Japan was offered a guaranteed annual supply of 100,000 tons of oil for five years together with a treaty of neutrality, but the Navy, unwilling to forego even such a relatively small contributor to its oil resources, vetoed the proposal.

'The Talking Machine' Matsuoka, as confident as ever of his powers of persuasion, decided to beard Stalin in person on the matter; at the same time he reappointed Double Diplomat Oshima to the Berlin Embassy in the uninformed belief that Berlin was still interested in negotiating a four-power entente with Moscow. Among the terms which he proposed taking with him was an offer to buy the whole of North Sakhalin outright or, if this was not acceptable, to renounce Japan's concessions there in return for 2.5 million tons of oil annually for the next five years. They were approved in principle by the high command except for a proposal that the Army should 'drastically reduce' its front in China, but both services insisted that he should delay his departure for Europe until the negotiations with Indo-China and Thailand had been successfully resolved.

As we saw in the previous chapter, these were not completed until March 6th 1941, and in the interval the straws in the wind pointing to the Nazi-Soviet Pact's collapse grew thick enough to impinge even on Matsuoka's tunnel vision. In the Imperial Palace Hirohito saw their significance a good deal more clearly. 'Should Germany in the near future start a war against the Soviet Union, our alliance obligations make it necessary for us to prepare in the North,' he told Lord Privy Seal Kido. 'With our hands tied in the South, we would be faced with a grave problem. Policies towards the South require very careful consideration.' The degree of confidence placed in Matsuoka's capacity for such 'very careful consideration' may be gauged from the fact that when the Foreign Secretary finally boarded the connecting train for the Trans-Siberian Railway on March 12th, an intelligence officer was planted among his entourage with orders to 'watch that in his talks with the Germans the expansive Minister would not commit the Japanese Army without its knowledge.'

This anxiety related in particular to the attack on Singapore for which Germany had been pressing with increasing urgency since the arrival in Berlin the previous December of a Japanese Naval Commission to promote co-operation between the two fleets. This had already begun with the secret provisioning of German blockade runners and commerce raiders in the Mandated Islands bases, and in November Germany had been able amply to repay the compliment with the gift of a cache of top secret documents captured by the raider *Atlantis* from the British freighter *Automedon*. These had included a highly pessimistic War Cabinet appreciation of British defence capabilities in the Far East and detailed directions for the defence of Singapore. Their significance was such that the Japanese at first refused to believe that they were genuine, and when they were so convinced Hirohito showed his appreciation with the gift of a *samurai* sword to the raider's captain, Bernhard Rogge — one of the only three Germans to receive such a mark of appreciation (the other two being Goering and Rommel) throughout the whole course of the War.

Hitler was at first doubtful of the advantages of such a move, but he was soon persuaded of them by his Naval Commander-in-Chief Erich Raeder. 'The present weakness of the British position in Eastern Asia and Singapore indicates the possibility of a Japanese attack on this main base of Britain in the Far East,' he told the Fuhrer's Conference on December 27th. 'Japan's interest is very great; she has good prospects of success ...' At the next Conference eleven days later Hitler even went against his first principle of maintaining American neutrality in recommending that 'the Japanese should be given a free hand even if this may entail the risk that the United States is thus forced into drastic steps', on the grounds that this would serve 'to keep American forces from the European theatre in addition to weakening and tying down British forces.' Joint studies were accordingly held in January between representatives of the two countries' General Staffs around a sand-table of the island which had been set up in the German Embassy in Tokyo.

In the same month the Japanese Navy began its secret reconnaissance of Pearl Harbor from submarines, and in Mexico City an office was opened to co-ordinate the information being gathered by spies on U.S. Fleet movements. Rumours of a planned attack on Singapore, naturally dismissed by Matsuoka as a 'ridiculous fantasy', had already leaked out (as they had of one on Pearl Harbor, reported by Grew to Washington on January 27th), and at the opening Joint Staff Conference between Britain and America held in Washington at the end of the month the British repeated their request for the dispatch of the U.S. Fleet to Singapore. Once again, however, it was turned down, although Roosevelt did give his agreement to sending a small squadron of cruisers and destroyers as a gesture of reassurance to beleaguered Australia and New Zealand.

The President had every reason for caution at that point. The Lend-Lease Bill was now under consideration in Congress, where it was already being attacked by the isolationists on the grounds that 'it will enable the President to take us into the war'. He did, however, extend the export embargo to cover a number of other raw materials, including copper, zinc and nickel.

TOUCH OF THE BLARNEY

All of these were important contributors to Japan's armaments build-up, and it increased the Navy's fears that it would soon be extended to oil. Nor did the Navy share Hitler's confidence that an attack on Singapore would not draw America into the war. Thus even though the obstacles in Indo-China had now been cleared, it was still refusing to commit itself until alternative sources of oil had been secured.

It was then bolstered in its stand by a pessimistic report of the Army's War Preparation Section, whose head concluded that 'in the end, we are no match for the United States and Britain in the event of war'; the General Staff, which only a month earlier had reaffirmed that 'military operations towards Malaya and the Dutch East Indies would be undertaken', were now, on March 22nd, obliged to agree with the Navy that 'it is better not to undertake military operations in the South. Only if absolutely unavoidable should such operations be allowed.' Both services accepted that there was only one circumstance which could be deemed to make them 'absolutely unavoidable' — a total embargo on oil exports from the United States.

Such a conclusion was extremely unpalatable to Matsuoka, but he was fully aware that his every action was being monitored — indeed, he and his 'tail' had held a discussion as soon as they had left Japanese shores. When he reached Moscow on the 23rd, he therefore made an early call on the U.S. Ambassador to deny that Japan had any intention of attacking Singapore or indeed held any territorial ambitions at all in the area.

The following afternoon he saw Stalin for an hour. According to an informant of Grew, 'The Talking Machine' devoted 58 minutes of it to a lecture in Japanese ideology, winding up with the remarkable assertion that although they did not believe in 'political or economic communism', the Japanese were nevertheless 'moral communists' by tradition. In the two minutes that remained of the interview he was offered not, as he was seeking, a non-aggression pact, but one of neutrality only. He replied that he would give his reply on his return from Berlin where, in his ignorance of German designs (which Hitler had wisely decided that he could not be trusted with), he fondly believed that he would be able to persuade the Fuhrer to talk his rival dictator around.

He arrived in Germany to find instead the conversation immediately diverted to the subject of Singapore. Ribbentrop had already attempted to persuade Oshima that 'Japan would be right to enter the war as soon as possible in her own interest. The decisive blow would be an attack on Singapore ... it must be carried out with lightning speed and if at all possible without a declaration of war'. He had also asked for some maps of the island 'so that the Fuhrer, who must certainly be considered the greatest expert on military matters in modern times, could advise Japan on the best method of attack.' At a Fuhrer's Conference on March 18th Hitler had likewise reiterated that 'Japan must take steps to capture Singapore as quickly as possible, since the opportunity is more favourable than it ever will be again. The entire British fleet is tied down; the U.S.A. is not prepared to wage war on Japan; the U.S. Fleet is inferior to the Japanese Fleet.' In spite of the postponement of 'Sealion' a British surrender was only a matter of time, they both now assured Matsuoka, and in a final effort to secure Japan's commitment Hitler went so far as to give a pledge that 'if Japan got into a conflict with the United States, Germany on her part would take the necessary steps at once [to declare war]'; 'a great Power does not let others declare war on it, it declares war itself', his Foreign Minister added — bombast that 'The Talking Machine' himself might have envied.

Matsuoka, however, was obliged to tell them that he was in no position to give such a commitment; reverting to his favourite analogy, he explained that while he himself was naturally all in favour, there were other more timorous souls among his Cabinet colleagues who 'would like to capture the tiger cub, but were not prepared to go into the den to take it away from its mother'. However, he told them, they should not be deceived by any show of friendship towards the British, which he was assuming in order to mislead not only them, but also 'the pro-British and pro-American elements in Japan, until he (sic) should one day suddenly attack Singapore'. When 'The Talking Machine' then tried to steer the conversation around to his hopes for a non-aggression pact with Russia, Ribbentrop abruptly dismissed them with the opinion that 'in view of the general situation it might not be best to go into things too deeply with the Russians. I don't know how the situation will develop . . .'; furthermore, he advised that 'if possible, you should not bring up the subject in Moscow, since this would probably not altogether fit into the framework of the present situation.'

If these broad hints did not finally remove the scale from Matsuoka's eyes, the news of Hitler's invasion of Yugoslavia in order to pre-empt Russia's control of the Balkans did. He was quick to recover from whatever dismay he might have felt, however, for he realised that such a development gave Stalin a strong incentive to secure his eastern flank with Japan. In addition, the fear of being seen to return to Japan with nothing to show for his travels provided an equally strong motive for displaying some flexibility on his part.

After his request for a non-aggression treaty had again been turned down when the negotiations reopened in Moscow on April 7th, he accordingly indicated that he was prepared to settle for a neutrality pact. Molotov continued to insist, however, that Japan should surrender the mineral concessions in North Sakhalin, but just when it seemed certain that 'The Talking Machine' would return home empty-handed after all Stalin himself intervened on the very eve of his departure and amended the condition to read that Japan should undertake to resolve the question of the return of the concessions 'within a few months'. When the new terms were referred to Tokyo for the Emperor's approval, Hirohito gave it without consulting either the Cabinet or Privy Council in order to allow Matsuoka to catch his train as scheduled. Stalin, in a parade of mutual congratulation no doubt put on for the benefit of the watching German Ambassador, broke all precedent and came in person to the station to see him off.

Matsuoka was not to enjoy his triumph for very long, however, for a most disagreeable discovery was awaiting his return.

AMERICA STANDS PAT

The French capitulation in Indo-China had combined with the successful passage of the Lend-Lease Act through Congress to free Roosevelt's hand for a more positive policy of deterrence. In this he was further fortified by the opinion of Ambassador Grew that 'the principal question before us is not whether we must call a halt to the Japanese southward advance, but when ... The moment when decisive action should be taken, if it is ever to be taken, appears to us to be approaching.' On March 27th the Joint Staff Conferences in Washington concluded with the drafting of an understanding, known subsequently as the ABC - 1 Staff Agreement.

While its main thrust was to confirm the policy of concentrating co-operation in the Atlantic and America's refusal to base her Pacific Fleet at Singapore, she did agree to dispatch some ships to the Philippines and her island bases west of Hawaii; it was also envisaged that the American presence in the Atlantic would enable Britain to release part of her forces to the Far East. The following month the Commands of the American, British, Dutch and Australian defence forces in the region met in the first ABDA Conference at Singapore to work out a joint local defence arrangement.

Suspicions of these developments served to awaken fresh fears in Japan of 'encirclement' and thoughts, particularly in the Navy as the negotiations in the DEI continued to drag on fruitlessly, that war with America was not perhaps so 'inevitable' after all — at least in the immediate future. At an Imperial Conference on April 16th it was therefore decided that for the time being Japan should only resort to arms either if 'the self-existence of the Empire should be threatened by embargoes', or if 'anti-Japanese encirclement by the United States, Britain, Holland and China becomes so tense that it cannot be tolerated in the interests of national defence.'

Ex-Foreign Minister Nomura, who enjoyed a wide range of personal

contacts among high-ranking Americans, had already been chosen as
Japan's Ambassador in Washington by Matsuoka and Konoye as the man
most likely to present a convincing portrait of her 'ultimately peaceful'
intentions. Well aware of its real purpose he had at first refused to undertake so distasteful a mission, but he was eventually persuaded to do so by his
Naval colleagues in the hope that he would be able to negotiate at least a
temporary accommodation. He was assisted in it by two priests from a
Catholic mission in Maryknoll, New York, who had had a conversation
with Matsuoka and had been persuaded that he genuinely wished to
improve relations with America. Secretary of State Hull was by no means
so convinced, considering Matsuoka to be 'as crooked as a basket of fish-
hooks', but he indicated that he was at least prepared to consider any
proposals that they might jointly wish to lay before him.

On April 8th Nomura duly presented the results of their consultations.
Japan, he said, was prepared to pledge that she would only go to war if her
Axis partners were attacked, and that she would employ only 'peaceful
measures' in the South-West Pacific. In return, America was expected to
press Chiang Kai-shek to make peace on the terms already stated by Japan
and to end all assistance to him if he did not; to end all embargoes on
exports to Japan and to help her in obtaining the raw materials that she
needed from other sources in the region; and to guarantee the independence of the Philippines and to help in 'the removal of Hong Kong and
Singapore as doorways to further political encroachment by the British in
the Far East'. Finally he suggested a personal summit between Konoye and
Roosevelt, to be held in Honolulu.

The one-sided nature of the offer would hardly have escaped Hull, and
the news two days later of Matsuoka's Neutrality Pact with Russia must
have led him even perhaps to question its authenticity. In his reply he
therefore confined himself to a list of general principles — namely, those
of respect for territorial integrity, non-interference, maintenance of the
status quo and the 'Open Door' — to be agreed before any negotiations
could usefully commence. When these 'Four Principles' were relayed to
Tokyo, a Liaison Conference decided on a self-contradictory policy of
accepting it as a basis for negotiations while at the same time maintaining
Japan's commitment to the Tripartite Pact and the Greater Co-Prosperity
Sphere; its effect was thus to heighten rather than resolve their dilemma.

When the news of these discussions was broken to Matsuoka on his
return home, his reaction was one of predictable outrage and he retired to
bed for a fortnight on a plea of 'bronchitis'. Konoye, too, found a similar
excuse to opt out and indicated a wish to resign, but Hirohito ignored it
and both of them recovered their equanimity sufficiently to attend a
further Liaison Conference on May 3rd, at which 'The Talking Machine'
managed to win the tacit approval of his colleagues for his suggestion that
before any negotiations took place America should be offered a neutrality
pact (under which she would remain neutral even if Japan attacked

Britain) as a test of her 'sincerity'. In his instructions to Nomura, he added a further message, to be passed on orally, that Japan could do nothing against the interests of the Axis, who were bound to win the war anyway, and that American entry would merely serve to prolong it.

When these were delivered to Hull, however, the Secretary of State 'showed no interest whatsoever' — a reaction made even easier for him by the fact that their contents had already been made known to him via 'Magic', the decoding process which had cracked the top Japanese diplomatic 'Purple' code.

Matsuoka reported this rejection to the Palace in a high state of satisfaction. If Germany came to blows with America, Japan would have to enter the war on Germany's side and attack Singapore or he would resign, he informed Hirohito; similarly, if as a result hostilities should then break out between Germany and Russia, Japan should scrap the Neutrality Pact and launch an invasion into Siberia as far west as Irkutsk. Almost simultaneously he was expressing the opinion to Grew that the 'manly, decent, and reasonable thing for the United States to do would be to declare war openly on Germany since your attitude towards Germany is provocative.' The Emperor was so alarmed by the extravagance of his assertions that he confided to Konoye two days later that he was considering getting rid of him; the Prime Minister assured him, however, that his Cabinet colleagues did not share Matsuoka's views and that they were on the contrary determined to come to some arrangement with America.

As a further obstacle to the negotiations Matsuoka had proposed waiting for the comments of the Axis partners, but when it was rumoured that Roosevelt would declare war on Germany in his Pan-American Day speech on May 14th Konoye ordered Nomura to present the revised Japanese proposals without further delay. On learning this Matsuoka threw another tantrum, while in the German Embassy Ott expressed 'immense regret'. Voicing his fulsome apologies to the Ambassador, 'The Talking Machine' declared his continuing loyalty to the Tripartite Pact and promised to keep Berlin fully informed of the progress of the negotiations, which he was confident would prove fruitless anyway, although he did not go quite so far as to accept Ott's request that Germany should actually be allowed to participate in them.

As it transpired, the new Japanese proposals offered little variation from the original ones. America was still asked to accept that Japan's commitment to the Tripartite Pact was a defensive one and in return to withdraw her assistance to Britain in the Atlantic; as for China, while the peace terms now offered to her showed some modification, Japan was still to have the right to retain troops there; finally, the previous pledge of 'peaceful measures' only in the South-West Pacific was now omitted. 'Very few rays of hope shone from the document,' Hull concluded.

HITLER STRIKES EAST

Berlin's concern to be kept abreast of developments in Washington sprang from the fact that the preparations for 'Barbarossa' were fast approaching completion. As early as April 16th Ribbentrop had confided to Oshima that 'it is possible that Germany may start a war against Russia even during the present year', and six days later the Double Diplomat reported to Tokyo that 'it seems that they have made up their minds to attack Russia'. Matsuoka, dazzled at first by the illusion of his success with Stalin, at first refused to believe in such a possibility, and at a Liaison Conference on May 22nd he even suggested that 'Germany and the Soviet Union will unite against Japan and the United States will join in the war' — provoking Navy Minister Oikawa to ask aloud, 'Is Matsuoka sane?'

In the same week 'The Talking Machine' urged Germany 'to do all in its power to avoid an armed clash with the Soviet Union', but on June 6th Oshima cabled that 'it is reasonable to conclude that the outbreak of war between Germany and the Soviet Union is inevitable ... I think that the Rubicon will be crossed in a short time.' Still Matsuoka, as he told Hirohito the next day, would not put the possibility any higher than 40%. Awaiting his trial before the War Crimes Tribunal in 1946, he was by then sufficiently sobered to concede that his scepticism 'was probably due to my wish not to see it happen'.

When, on June 22nd 1941, it did finally happen, he lost no time in covering his tracks, rushing to the Palace to advise the Emperor that 'Japan should co-operate with Germany and attack the Soviet Union. To carry out the attack, it is better that we refrain temporarily from action in the South. We shall have to fight sooner or later. Ultimately, Japan will have to fight simultaneously the Soviet Union, the United States and Britain.' His suggestion was coolly received, however; Hirohito remarked afterwards to Kido that 'the Foreign Minister's policy would mean Japan's positive advance in both the northern and southern regions', for which he doubted that Japan had the capacity.

For all his flights of oratory — 'he who would search for pearls must dive deep. Let us act resolutely,' he told his colleagues on the Liaison Conference — Matsuoka could find no one else to support him, with the predictable exception of Oshima who spoke from Berlin of 'the perfect opportunity to remove, once and for all, the menace in the North and to settle the China Incident'. When berated later in the evening by the Prime Minister for having gone over his (Konoye's) head, Matsuoka backtracked somewhat, explaining that he was not advocating 'immediate action'.

JAPAN ACCELERATES SOUTH

The high command had in fact already decided to set its face to the south as a result of the continuing failure of the negotiations with the Dutch in Batavia. The point of deadlock had finally been reached when the Dutch sought a guarantee that any supplies of rubber and tin were not to be re-exported to Germany, calculating that the figures that the Japanese were demanding were well above their actual needs — correctly, since during his time in Berlin Matsuoka had given a specific promise to pass on the surplus to Germany. 'For Japan, a major Power to accept the demand of the Dutch, a minor Power, that we promise not to re-export material to Germany would be a humiliation,' he raged. 'Hence we shall never give such a guarantee. Such a demand reveals how arrogant the Dutch have become. We cannot be sure what will happen with respect to Japan's foreign and domestic policies if the negotiations break down ...' The Dutch refused to be brow-beaten, however, and on June 14th Yoshizawa and his mission were ordered back to Tokyo.

Two days after the news of Barbarossa broke the Army and Navy jointly pronounced that 'Japan should not intervene for the time being, but should continue its military preparations against the Soviet Union in secrecy'; only if the new war 'developed extremely favourably for Japan should the northern problem be solved through the exercise of military power.' (The extent of these secret 'military preparations' indicates that the 'Strike North' lobby was still very much alive in the Army's lower echelons — they had drawn up a plan which called for the mobilisation of no less than twenty-two divisions in Manchuria.) The Naval General Staff had decided a fortnight earlier that 'should a new situation arise in German-Soviet relations, Japan should not intervene', and at a Liaison Conference on the 16th agreement was reached with the Army that a demand should be presented to the French for permission to station troops in southern Indo-China. If it was refused, military measures should be taken; 'If and when it is necessary to strike, we will strike,' Chief of Naval Staff Nagano Osami declared, while his Army counterpart Sugiyama stated that 'I'd like to see blitzkrieg diplomacy as soon as the troops are assembled on Hainan.' It was recognised, however, that the Emperor's approval would have to be obtained first, and Matsuoka had expressed concern at Hirohito's possible reaction to the breach of the previous August's agreement with Vichy France that such moves would entail.

A memorandum entitled 'Measures for Accelerating the Southern Policy' and incorporating the demands to the French was approved by the Liaison Conference the next day, June 25th, and by Hirohito that same evening. The Government, it stated, 'keeping in mind existing circumstances, will advance the policy already approved with respect to Indo-China and Thailand. In particular, a military relationship with Indo-China, aiming at the security and defence of East Asia, must be established,' its objectives being 'the creation and use of air bases and ports at specified places in Indo-China and the stationing of necessary troops in southern Indo-China ... Military means will be used if the French

Government or the Indo-China authorities do not accept our demands.'

Only Matsuoka voiced any opposition, and at a further Liaison Conference two days later he called once again for an invasion of Russia and the
abandonment of the Neutrality Pact. 'If we advance in the North and get,
say, to Irkutsk, or even only half that distance, it would have an effect upon
Chiang Kai-shek, and I think an overall peace might ensue,' he argued.
'When Germany wins and disposes of the Soviet Union, we can't take the
fruits of victory without having done something. We have to either shed
blood or engage in diplomacy. It's best to shed blood.' When he was asked,
'Are you saying that we should strike the Soviet Union immediately?', he
replied without hesitation, 'Yes, I am' — thus directly contradicting the
apologia which he had offered to Konoye only three days earlier.

When 'The Talking Machine' went on to declare that 'I insist upon
diplomacy based on moral principles', there must have been others besides
Oikawa among his hearers who doubted whether he was still right in the
head. In a cable to Ott urging support for such an action — now that he had
despaired of persuading Japan to attack Singapore — Ribbentrop invoked
the same 'morality': 'A Japanese action against a Soviet Russia already
beaten to the ground would be quite prejudicial to the moral and political
standing of Japan.'

No reference had been made in 'Measures for Accelerating the Southern
Policy' to the possibility of Britain or America being provoked into
hostilities by a move into southern Indo-China, but in the wake of an
announcement from Washington that the oil embargo was being extended
to cover all exports from the East Coast (where there was actually a
shortage for local consumers) it was realised that such a contingency now
had to be squarely faced, although some held that America's recent
decision to establish military bases in Iceland served to deprive her of the
justification for such an intervention.

Accordingly, an Imperial Conference on July 2nd formally endorsed the
following further memorandum, 'The Outline of National Policies in
View of the Changing Situation'. 'The Imperial Government is determined to follow a policy which will result in the establishment of the
Greater East Asia Co-Prosperity Sphere and world peace, no matter what
international developments take place,' it stated. 'It will continue its effort
to effect a settlement of the "China Incident" and seek to establish a solid
basis for the security and preservation of the nation. This will involve an
advance into the Southern Areas and, depending upon future developments, a settlement of the Soviet Question as well ...'

The Government 'will continue the diplomatic negotiations with respect to the Southern Areas necessary for our self-preservation and self-
defence,' it went on. 'We will first carry out various policies with respect
to Indo-China and Thailand on the basis of "Measures for Accelerating the
Southern Policy" and thereby strengthen arrangements for the advance
towards the south. To obtain these objectives *the Empire will not hesitate to*

engage in war with the United States and Britain' (author's italics). It had, of course, already been approved by the Cabinet and Hirohito the previous day, and at the close of the Conference it was observed that 'the Emperor seemed to be extremely satisfied'.

THE TIGER BARES A TOOTH

Matsuoka, buoyed up by reports of initial sweeping German advances and predictions from Ribbentrop that 'the Japanese Army advancing westward should be able to shake hands at the half-way mark with the German troops advancing to the east', continued to call for an attack on Russia. It was now three months since the negotiations with America had opened, and Ambassador Nomura had very little to show for his efforts. On June 21st Secretary of State Hull had even expressed doubt about the value of continuing them in the light of pro-Axis statements put out by 'certain leaders of the Japanese Government', and three weeks later he remarked of the most recent Japanese proposals that 'Nomura had nothing new to offer'.

At the Liaison Conference on July 12th Matsuoka demanded not only the retraction of the former which he (rightly) took to refer to himself, but also an end to the negotiations altogether. 'The American President is bent on leading his country into war,' he asserted. 'Roosevelt is a real demagogue.' The Army and the Navy, however, committed now to move into southern Indo-China and so worse placed than ever to face the prospect of a total American oil embargo, were unanimous in their opposition, and it was clear that if the negotiations were to proceed, they would have to do so under a new Foreign Minister. Matsuoka himself presented them with a ready-made pretext only two days later when, in defiance of the Cabinet decision, he ordered Nomura to ask Hull for a retraction, provoking the sorely-tried Ambassador to request permission to resign himself.

It was feared, however, that if Matsuoka alone was singled out for replacement, he would use the claim that he was the victim of American pressure to whip up public opposition; it was therefore decided, in consultation with Hirohito, that the whole Cabinet should resign and then be reappointed without him. This manoeuvre was completed in the space of another two days; 'The Talking Machine' was silenced at last. The choice of successor fell on Admiral Toyoda Soemu, another of the select band who had accompanied Hirohito to Europe in 1921; as a Naval colleague of Nomura, he was thought most likely to revive American trust in Japan's intentions. They were not to know that this had already been demolished by the evidence of their own mouths.

The list of new requirements in Indo-China were presented to the Vichy regime. They included the use of eight airfields and the Saigon and Camranh Bay naval bases with all their equipment, total freedom of action and even financial support for the incoming Japanese troops and the withdrawal of Indo-Chinese troops from the areas selected. They were aimed, it was explained, at the 'joint defence of Indo-China', whose sovereignty and territorial integrity 'was previously guaranteed by the Imperial Government . . . we are fully determined to carry it out.' A reply was demanded by the 19th, and Oshima was told to ask Berlin once again to use its influence. On a plea of consulting with Germany and Italy as required under the terms of the Armistice the French asked for an extension of the deadline, but when Japan threatened immediate military action unless all the demands were met by the 22nd they conceded that they 'had no choice but to yield' to them. A message of thanks was cabled from Tokyo to Berlin.

Unbeknown to the Japanese, every stage of this dialogue had been monitored by 'Magic' in Washington, as had the decision of the July 2nd Imperial Conference 'to engage in war with the United States and Britain'. In addition, another intercept on July 14th revealed that after Indo-China had been successfully occupied it was planned 'to launch therefrom a rapid attack . . . next on our schedule is the sending of an ultimatum to the Dutch East Indies. In the seizing of Singapore the Navy will play a principal part.' When, in Nomura's absence, his deputy was asked for his comments, he declared that 'the Japanese had no knowledge whatever of any intention on the part of the Japanese Government of occupying Indo-China', while in Tokyo Toyoda was earnestly assuring Grew that 'Japan has no intention at all of making the southern part of Indo-China a base of armed advancement against adjoining areas'; even in 1947, it may be remarked in passing, the leading defendants were still claiming to the War Crimes Tribunal that their prime motive in doing so had been to secure their supplies of rice, rubber and tin.

Possessed of the evidence of such monumental duplicity, Hull's deputy observed that he could no longer see any basis for continuing the negotiations, while the Secretary of the Treasury, Henry Morgenthau, pressed for a total embargo on all trade with Japan. The Navy, however, was more cautious, arguing that such an embargo 'would probably result in a fairly early attack by Japan on Malaya and the Dutch East Indies, and possibly would involve the United States in early war in the Pacific.' America was indeed still very far from prepared for such an eventuality; for instance, only the first batch of the Flying Fortresses which were designed to constitute the principal defence of the Philippines was yet in place. Hull himself agreed that 'nothing will stop them except force,' but he argued that 'the point is how long we can manoeuvre the situation until the military matter in Europe is brought to a conclusion . . . I just don't want us to take for granted a single word they say, but [I want us to] appear to do so, to whatever extent it may satisfy our purpose to delay further action by them.'

Roosevelt consequently decided to compromise by freezing all Japanese funds held in America, although this came close to being an effective embargo because any purchases by Japan could now only be met from the proceeds of exports to America which were now effectively confined to silk. Britain and the Dominions all followed suit within a week, as also did the Dutch with a further threat of a total suspension of trade if Japan made any further moves.

When Nomura was summoned to the White House to receive the decision, he was also warned that if Japan 'attempted to seize the oil supplies by force in the Dutch East Indies, the Dutch would, without a shadow of doubt, resist; the British would immediately come to their assistance, war would result between Japan, the British and the Dutch, and in view of our own policy of assisting Great Britain, an exceedingly serious situation would immediately result.' To reinforce his words, the President announced that the Philippine Army was being placed under the American command of its military adviser, retired General Douglas MacArthur, who was now returned to the Active Duty list.

CONCENTRIC CIRCLES

The Japanese reaction was much as the U.S. Navy had feared — as they learnt by courtesy of 'Magic' again. On July 31st Toyoda signalled to Nomura and Oshima that 'commercial and economic relations between Japan and other countries, led by England and the United States, are gradually becoming so horribly strained that we cannot endure it much longer. Consequently, the Japanese Empire, to save its very life, must take measures to secure the raw materials of the South Seas. It must take immediate steps to break asunder this ever-strengthening chain of encirclement . . .' Everything was now to be staked on the 'Strike South', and Oshima was told to explain to Berlin that solution of the Soviet problem would have to be suspended for the time being.

Three days later Kwantung Army Commander Umezu reported that a wireless black-out had been imposed on Soviet military units stationed on the Manchurian border and, fearing that this presaged an imminent air attack, asked Tokyo's permission to make a pre-emptive raid. On the same day Soviet sabotage teams blew up a number of the Army's fuel and ammunition dumps. Chief of Staff Sugiyama immediately cabled back: 'In principle, stop counter-attacks at the boundary line. The high command expects the Kwantung Army to act with caution.' Three days later again it was agreed with the Navy that 'while instituting precautionary measures for defence against the Soviet Union, we must strictly avoid provocative actions. If incidents arise, they should be localised so that they will not escalate into hostilities between Japan and the Soviet Union.'

The General Staff now finally decided that no attempt to resolve the 'problem' by force should be made that year. The two factors which dissuaded them were first, an Army Intelligence report that a German victory by the end of 1941 was now out of the question; and secondly, a signal from Nomura in Washington reporting that America 'has suddenly established very close relationships with the Soviet Union. In view of this fact, it is highly doubtful that she would merely watch from the sidelines if we should make any moves to the North.'

For once the Kwantung Army was content to yield to Tokyo's diktat, for it had been agreed that any invasion of Russia was dependent on the transfer of at least 50% of Soviet Far Eastern forces to the European front. In the event, it was reported that only five divisions, representing rather less than 20%, had been moved — doubtless due in no small measure to the spy Sorge's information that the July 2nd Imperial Conference had deferred such an invasion.

Since it was the Navy which would play the main rôle in the 'Strike South' Hirohito turned to Nagano for an assessment of its prospects in the light of the American embargo. The Navy Chief of Staff was not optimistic, calculating that the present stock of oil would be exhausted in two years, or, if America was drawn into the hostilities, a mere eighteen months. If they failed to persuade America to lift the embargo, they would therefore have no choice but to go to war (the other alternative, that Japan should abandon her conquistadorial designs for the Greater Asia Co-Prosperity Sphere, was something that he could not bring himself to consider). Hirohito then asked what the chances of success would be in that event. Nagano doubted whether there was any prospect for victory at all, let alone for a quick knock-out such as they had won against Russia in 1905.

When the Emperor expressed his concern at the implications of this conversation to Kido, the Lord Privy Seal refused, as he recorded in his diary, 'to share Admiral Nagano's simple views'. Instead, he put forward another proposal: Japan should back off from such a conflict and 'go through unspeakable hardships and privations' for the next ten years until she would then be in a position to win it, just as she had done after the Triple Intervention in 1895. To Konoye he also suggested that if the Prime Minister failed to persuade the high command of the need to defer war with the United States, he should pass the responsibility on to them and resign.

Having reshuffled (in theory at any rate) his Cabinet only three weeks earlier Konoye was reluctant to take such a step; in addition, he feared that it would betray to the world the disarray that the embargo had caused. Furthermore, he had a proposal of his own to offer, namely that he should meet Roosevelt in person 'and express straightforwardly and boldly the true intentions of the Empire', while offering the following terms for an agreement: Japan would undertake to guarantee the neutrality of the Philippines, not to advance beyond Indo-China and to withdraw from there when the China Incident had been settled, in return for which America was to drop the embargo, coerce Chiang Kai-shek into coming to terms and to discontinue her defence build-up in the South-West Pacific.

He would, as these terms indicated, 'insist on the firm establishment of the Greater East Asia Co-Prosperity Sphere'; his one single concession was to omit the former demands for recognition of the Tripartite Pact. In making it he was motivated chiefly by the revised calculation of Germany's progress against Russia, which was now showing unmistakable signs of faltering. For this reason also 'the conference must be held soon,' for if the Germans did indeed get bogged down 'the American attitude will stiffen and she will no longer entertain the thought of talking with Japan.'

The proposal was thus merely a ploy to persuade Roosevelt to drop the guard which he had only recently begun to put up in the South West Pacific and thus allow Japan to secure vital sources of oil in the DEI by force. Indeed, while the Army General Staff were finally postponing any military action against Russia, they were simultaneously deciding to pull six divisions back from Manchuria and to bring forward the deadline for the 'Strike South' to the end of November. In making it Konoye even went so far as to canvass the support of the 86-year-old Godfather Toyama, and Hirohito agreed that 'the meeting with the President should take place as soon as possible'. Only War Minister Tojo expressed some reservations, on the grounds that it would cause offence to Germany, and in giving it his reluctant approval he told the Prime Minister not to resign if it ended in failure — 'rather, you should be prepared to assume the leadership in the war against America.'

An advance draft of these terms was cabled to Nomura to present to the White House. They elicited little interest from Hull, who a few hours earlier had received the 'Magic' intercept of the 'immediate steps to break asunder this ever-strengthening chain of encirclement' signal; he was caused to observe that 'there is no occasion for any nation in the world that is law-abiding and peaceful to become "encircled" by anybody except itself.' The President anyway was on the point of departure for a rather more congenial meeting off Newfoundland with the British Prime Minister, which was to result in the declaration of the Atlantic Charter.

Churchill pressed for a warning to be issued in the starkest possible terms to Japan jointly by Britain, America, Holland and Russia, but Roosevelt felt that if it was too strongly worded it might actually provoke Japan into taking the very action which it was designed to deter, and which his nation was not yet sufficiently geared to face — that same day the Bill to extend the term of the Selective Service Act secured the approval of the House of Representatives by a single vote.

Their joint communiqué was therefore amended, then toned down still further by Hull when it was brought back to Washington, to read merely that America 'will be compelled to take immediately any and all steps which it may deem necessary' in response to further military action by Japan. Roosevelt did, however, agree to retain in the Pacific three battleships which he had earmarked for the Atlantic, while for his part Churchill promised to dispatch two battleships and an aircraft-carrier (the ill-fated Force Z) to Singapore. On his return to the White House he also authorised an increase in the number of Flying Fortresses allotted to the Philippines, whose defence forces were now forecast to reach self-sufficiency by February 1942.

In such a context there was clearly no place for Konoye's proposal, and Nomura was referred again to the 'Four Principles' which he had been told in April would have to be agreed before such a meeting could serve any meaningful purpose. The Ambassador had already complained to Tokyo of the 'scorching criticism' in the Japanese Press which had greeted the public announcement of the Atlantic Charter, and he had gone on to say that the 'deteriorating atmosphere' now made any agreement with America improbable. This reply from Hull effectively put an end to the negotiations, although proposals and counter proposals would continue to be exchanged for another four months.

From now on the American tigress (to borrow Matsuoka's analogy) would eye the circling hyena with a full knowledge of its purpose and with a sleepless resolve to ward off its depredations until the Pacific cubs were strong enough to fend for themselves. What she could not guess was that the predator had marked down the one cub that she imagined to be in that happy condition.

31

'Into the Tiger's Den'

IMPERIAL BENEDICTION

The Navy had already been practising the Pearl Harbor attack since early July in Kagoshima Bay, whose matching topographical features required the dive bombers to fly in low over the surrounding mountains in order to drop torpedoes especially designed to run in shallow waters.

The result of these exercises were judged to be so promising that at a joint General Staff conference on August 16th 1941 the Navy recommended that the deadline for the completion of military preparations should be brought forward a month to the end of October. The Army were more than happy to agree to this because their own studies had shown that the optimum period for amphibious landings in the monsoon belt of the 'Southern Areas' was the first half of November; beyond that such landings would get progressively more difficult, until by January they would be out of the question.

Indeed, so impressed were Tojo and his fellow Generals by the prospects for success that they wanted to call an immediately halt to the negotiations with America and to launch the attack as soon as their forces were in place, arguing that preparations could not be fully carried out unless a firm decision to go to war had been taken. However, the Admirals, with the exception of the hawkish Chief of Staff Nagano, still had not abandoned the hope that the DEI oilfields could be secured without entailing American intervention, and they insisted that the negotiations should continue at one and the same time. Eventually the difference was resolved by an agreement that a deadline of early October should be set on the negotiations and that the preparations should be made 'on the basis of a determination not to run away from a war'. The Navy then embarked on an intensive programme of mock exercises for the anticipated battles to come against the U.S. Pacific Fleet.

On September 3rd the two services presented their new schedule of war preparations to the Liaison Conference. The only point of disagreement to arise was the wording of the deadline to be set on the negotiations, which was finally amended to read 'If, by the early part of October, there is still no prospect of being able to attain our demands through diplomatic negotiations, we will immediately decide to open hostilities against the

United States, Great Britain and the Netherlands'; the demands themselves were to remain exactly as before. It was then arranged for an Imperial Conference to give its formal approval on the 6th, and as usual Konoye called at the Palace a day in advance to present the agenda and secure the Emperor's sanction.

'This would seem to give precedence to war,' Hirohito remarked when he saw the discussion papers, but the Prime Minister hastened to assure him that such an impression was merely due to the order in which the proposals had been set down and that the Cabinet intended to work 'till the very end' in its efforts to obtain a diplomatic settlement. The Emperor then indicated that he wished to question the two Chiefs of Staff on the point. Sugiyama and Nagano were accordingly summoned, and both gave similar assurances. Sugiyama was next asked to give a timetable for the Army's advance into the 'Southern Areas', and when he answered 'five months,' Hirohito reminded him that he had given a similar forecast at the beginning of the 'China Incident', which was still being fought four years later. To his explanation that it was only the physical size of China which had caused the schedule to fall behind, the Emperor remarked acidly that 'If you call China vast, what do you call the Pacific?'

This reduced the 'Toilet Door' to silence, but his Naval colleague came to his rescue with an analogy comparing the problem facing the high command to that of a surgeon confronted by the decision of whether or not to operate on a critically-ill patient as the only means left of saving his life. Hirohito then asked if this could be taken to mean that they favoured action only as a last resort, and they both answered in the affirmative. After they had bowed themselves out of the Imperial presence, however, the Emperor indicated that he wished to put further questions in person to them at the Imperial Conference. Lord Privy Seal Kido, fearing that such an unprecedented action might compromise the Throne, persuaded him to follow the usual device of having them put for him by the President of the Privy Council.

The Conference opened the following morning with detailed expositions of the operational plans of the Navy (revealing for the first time to the Cabinet those for Pearl Harbor) and the Army from the two Chiefs of Staff, who repeated the demand for a deadline of October 10th to be set on the diplomatic negotiations in Washington. Rehearsing the arguments for this, Sugiyama confirmed that the Army's plans for attacking Russia had been postponed rather than cancelled, declaring that 'if we finish our operations in the South quickly, I believe that we'll be in a position to deal with any changes in the Northern situation that might take place next spring and thereafter ...'

The President of the Cabinet Planning Board, former China-Watcher Suzuki Teiichi, followed with the latest estimate of the logistical position, giving particular attention to that of oil stocks. Despite a draconian cutback in civilian consumption (that of private motorists had been reduced from an annual rate of 7 million barrels to 1.6 million), he reported that the combination of increased consumption needed for practice manoeuvres, which had reduced the Navy's reserves alone from 29 to 22 million, and the new American restrictions had caused a fall in total reserves from 55 to under 50 million barrels; Japan's own production of crude and synthetic oil still amounted to no more than 3 million. It was therefore more necessary than ever that America 'should restore trade relations with Japan and make available ... materials indispensable to her existence', Suzuki asserted, at the same time recounting the terms which Japan was prepared to offer in return — which had already been so roundly rejected.

The Privy Council President then rose as planned and repeated the Emperor's question as to whether the two services still hoped to settle the issue by diplomacy first. Navy Minister Oikawa confirmed that this was so. At that point Hirohito himself intervened to express regret that it had not been answered by the two Chiefs of Staff. Before his startled audience could recover from their surprise, he then drew a slip of paper from his pocket and recited the following *haiku* *:

> 'Since all the seas of the world are linked with
> one another, why, I wonder, must the wind and
> waves continually disturb them?'

It had been written by Meiji and it was a favourite of his own, expressing as it did, Hirohito explained, his grandfather's 'great love of peace'.

It has been suggested that his purpose in quoting it was to credit himself with a publicly-stated commitment to peace in case the worst came to the worst and the leaders of a defeated Japan were called to account. However, such an interpretation would both ignore the context and its author, not to mention the 'tacit understanding' conveyed between all Japanese by the 'language of the belly'. The only peace in prospect depended on America's acceptance of the negotiating terms endorsed by the Conference, and previously by Hirohito, and it was by now obvious to all those present that there was not the smallest possibility of such an outcome. As for Meiji, the instigator of the annexation of Korea and of the attack on Russia and the author himself of the original blueprint for territorial expansion, the 1907 National Defence Plan, he was the very man who had set Japan on the ineluctable path of conquest, and the word 'peace' in his mouth was synonymous with the 'paradise' that the world would become after it had been united under 'one roof' on the completion of Japan's 'divine mission'.

In this light, the following, rather different, interpretation emerges:

> 'Since all the world is destined to lie under the
> divine protection of Japan, why, I wonder, must
> some other nations so obstinately refuse to
> be brought within it?'

After a further silence in which the doubly-Imperial words were digested,

* A traditional Japanese poetic form of 17 syllables.

Nagano rose to stammer his apologies, explaining that he had thought that Oikawa had been expressing his opinion for him, which remained, of course, the same. The Conference then adjourned.

JUMPING OFF THE CLIFF

Having thus received the Imperial sanction for their timetable, the Army and Navy embarked on a final series of war games for the operations ahead. For his part, Konoye, conscious of his pledge to the Emperor to work 'to the very end' for a negotiated settlement (and perhaps also of the freedom from interruption that the two services required while they perfected their plans), telephoned Ambassador Grew that very afternoon to revive his proposal for a summit with Roosevelt and invited him to discuss it with him alone over dinner at the house of Prince Ito, the adopted son of the Constitution-Maker.

The rendezvous was conducted in great secrecy: unmarked cars were used to take both men to it and all the servants in the building were given the evening off. The Ambassador was surprised to hear the Prime Minister now declare that he, 'and consequently the government of Japan, conclusively and whole-heartedly agree with the Four Principles enunciated by the Secretary of State as a basis for the rehabilitation of relations between the United States and Japan'. Although they were 'splendid as a matter of principle', he realised, however, that 'certain points may need clarification and more precise formulation', and it was as a means of settling the latter that he felt that a meeting with the President would be most effective. The proposal had, he claimed, 'the full support of the responsible chiefs of the Army and Navy', who had agreed to appoint a full Admiral and General to accompany him.

On the face of it, his words seemed to offer a gleam of light after all the talking in the dark of the previous months, but in the subsequent discussions of the 'certain points [that] may need clarification and more precise information' it emerged that the Japanese position had not in fact shifted at all, and that they were still expecting America to put into effect all the concessions demanded before Japan carried out those that she was offering in return. Furthermore, the offer to withdraw from China on the conclusion of any peace treaty with Chiang Kai-shek was heavily qualified by the insistence of the Army and Navy that troops should continue to be stationed in Amoy, Hainan, Inner Mongolia and North China. Ambassador Nomura, knowing that such a demand would finally remove what slim chance remained of reaching a settlement, asked permission to delete it. As a result, it was amended to state that troops should remain 'in certain areas for a necessary period'.

This was hardly sufficient to reassure the White House, however, and by September 28th Roosevelt and Hull both recognised that they were back to square one, concluding together that the only proper response was

15. One of the 9.5 inch howitzers smuggled into Mukden by the Kwantung army before the invasion of Manchuria

16. Hirohito parading with the puppet 'Emperor of Manchukuo' Pu-Yi

17. The remains of the germ warfare factory in 1945, established at Pingtan, near Harbin

18. The cruiser *Idzumo*, the Japanese headquarters during the 'Shanghai Incident' January 1932

19. The trial of the young officers and cadets who assassinated Prime Minister Inukai Ki 15th May 1932

20. The Chapei district of Shanghai burning after mass aerial bombardment August 1937

21. Refugees seeking safety in the French sector

22. Japanese troops parading through the International Settlement 3rd December 1937

23. The scene shortly after a Chinese student threw a grenade into the parade

24. The aftermath of the bombing of Nanking station

25. The sinking of the U.S.S. *Panay* 12th December 1937

26. The incinerated bodies of Chinese civilians burnt alive in Nanking

27. Hirohito's uncle, Prince Asaka (centre), conferring on the city's capture at his headquarters with Generals Matsui and Yamagawa

28. Imperial go-between Prince Konoye in the guise of his ally Hitler at a fancy-dress party

29. 'The Talking Machine' Matsuoko with Stalin at the signing of the Russo-Japanese Neutrality Pact 13th April 1941

once more 'to recite the more liberal original attitude of the Japanese when they first sought the meeting, point out their much narrowed position now, earnestly ask if they cannot go back to their original attitude, start discussions again on agreement in principle, and re-emphasise my hope for a meeting.' While accepting the force of their argument, Grew warned at the same time that its 'logical outcome . . . will be the downfall of the Konoye Cabinet and the formation of a military dictatorship.'

Meanwhile the war games had been completed and their outcome judged eminently satisfactory. From the sidelines of the German Embassy, Ott reported that although there was still an element which sincerely wished for a negotiated settlement, the real purpose of Konoye s sugges-tion was to demonstrate to the people at large that none was possible and so to convince them that war was the only answer.

There were, of course, a great many who needed no such convincing. Some of these a month earlier had attempted to assassinate, of all people, the super-patriotic Big Baron Hiranuma on the grounds of his failure to resign from the Cabinet in protest at Matsuoka's dismissal (the pistol used was afterwards found to have been the property of one of the Blood Brotherhood involved in the attempted 1933 coup). On September 18th, the tenth anniversary of the Mukden Incident, a similar attack was made on Konoye's car, but the assailants were arrested as they attempted to mount the running board. On the same day the high command called for the presentation of Japan's final terms to America and the establishment of a deadline for the decision to go to war if they were not accepted. At another Liaison Conference a week later, they demanded that it should be set at October 15th at the latest.

Konoye complained to Kido the following day that he could not allow his hands to be tied in this fashion, and he talked of resigning. On being reminded by the Lord Privy Seal of his pledge to share the Emperor's 'pains and tribulations', he promised to think it over and retired to his seaside villa. On October 2nd his 'rest' was cut short by the receipt of Roosevelt's response conveying his repetition that no useful purpose could be served by their meeting without a specific commitment to observe the Four Principles.

Its effect was to bring renewed calls from Tojo and the Army General Staff for an October 15th deadline, the War Minister informing Konoye that at some point in a man's lifetime he might find it necessary to jump off a cliff with his eyes shut. The latter retorted that that might be all very well for a private individual, but as Prime Minister responsible for the fate of 100 million people he had to behave rather more responsibly. Navy Minister Oikawa indicated that he would still like to see the negotiations continue, but it was explained on his behalf that he could not say so openly for fear of creating public division and he would therefore leave the decision to the Prime Minister. However, his hesitation more probably stemmed from the fact that he was in disagreement with the majority of his General Staff, who shared the opinion of their Army counterparts. In doing so, they were no doubt influenced by the fact, reported by Grew, that Japan's foreign currency reserves, which could be used to purchase oil from neutral countries, were now exhausted.

TOJO'S 'ONE-MAN SHOW'

The Inner Cabinet met on October 12th at Konoye's private residence to resolve the issue. Foreign Minister Toyoda suggested that a settlement with America might still be possible if Japan were to agree to withdraw from China 'in principle' and to set a limit to the time that troops were to remain in the 'certain areas'. Tojo, however, refused to countenance such a concession, arguing that unless Japan was permitted to retain troops there on a permanent basis she stood to lose all the gains that she had made in the course of the past fifty years, while Oikawa contented himself with repeating that the time had come to take a decision one way or the other but that the Navy would leave it to the Prime Minister. Konoye, feeling the ground slipping away beneath his feet, declared that he would not be able to take the responsibility if the Army was insisting on war, where-upon Tojo accused him of abdication on the grounds that he (Konoye) had been party to the Imperial Conference's endorsement of an 'early part of October' deadline.

The meeting broke up without a decision having been taken, but Hirohito evidently considered that the debate was as good as over, for the following day he ordered Kido to draft an Imperial Declaration of War. He also pointed out that it was vital to secure a German commitment to fight alongside Japan; 'We must use every diplomatic strategy we can to stop Germany from concluding peace separately,' he told the Lord Privy Seal. 'We must have her assistance in our war with the United States.' Later that same day Kido prompted Konoye to put a new proposal to Tojo via Suzuki, namely, that the time limit set at the Imperial Conference should be reconsidered and 'the slate wiped clean'. The War Minister, however, objected that the decision of the Conference was traditionally final — that is to say, it could only be amended by a new Cabinet.

The next morning Konoye called Tojo in for a private discussion prior to the scheduled Cabinet meeting. 'I wonder if we should not make up our minds to readjust relations with America which at the moment are so fraught with risk,' he told him. 'With the China Incident still not settled, I am questioning whether we should extend our hands further towards the South ... The consensus of realistic opinion is that if the arrow should leave the bow it may take five or ten years ...' What he had in mind, he went on, was a 'token' withdrawal from China whereby Japan would agree with America to pull out but then, perhaps by arrangement with the Chinese Government, in fact retain troops in the 'certain areas'.

However, even this deception did not commend itself to Tojo. 'I cannot yield on this,' he replied. 'America's real intention is to control the Far East, therefore one concession would lead to another, and so on.' He went on to accuse the Prime Minister of taking 'too pessimistic' a view of the likely outcome of a war; 'America must have weaknesses of her own', the 'Scrapper' asserted. The meeting ended with his remarking that 'I suppose this all boils down to the difference in our personalities'.

There was certainly some truth in this, Tojo being a man as quick of decision as he was of temper, whereas Konoye habitually preferred to take refuge in his bed whenever the occasion demanded one. The contrast became even starker in the ensuing Cabinet meeting, which Tojo, as Konoye later recorded, turned into 'a one-man show'. He first accused the Navy of shirking its responsibility by passing the decision on to the Prime Minister and of being happy to approve a withdrawal from China because, unlike the Army, it had so few of its forces committed there.

Failing, however, to entice Oikawa from his corner, he then turned his anger on Foreign Minister Toyoda. He asserted that diplomacy could not be allowed to stand in the way of military considerations, and the suggestion that troops could be retained in China under the pretence of a withdrawal was a 'practical impossibility'; to give in to America on the other hand would be equivalent to surrendering. The meeting then broke up with the prospect of agreement seemingly as far removed as ever. In the afternoon a last desperate appeal was made to the Navy to come off the fence on one side or another, but the reply was still the same: because of the Army's attitude the Navy could not say publicly that it was against war; it was for the Prime Minister to decide, and the Navy could only pledge itself to support whatever decision was made.

Tojo then informed Konoye that the only way out of the deadlock now was for the Cabinet to resign. 'Then, if the new men should decide that we are not to fight, that may appear to be the end of it. But,' he warned, 'the Army is straining at the leash ...' He himself favoured the Emperor's uncle, Higashikuni, as the Prime Minister's successor, he added.

Konoye too approved of the choice, and the following morning, October 15th, he took the suggestion to the Palace. 'The Navy does not want war, but cannot say so in view of the decision of the Imperial Conference ... I, as Prime Minister, am thus all the more in disagreement with the idea of war,' he explained. Hirohito, however, expressed reservations about the succession of Higashikuni: 'Since the appointment of an Imperial Prince would make him appear to be my personal representative, it would be bad for an Imperial Prince to take over and decide on war.' On the other hand he queried, 'if peace should be decided upon, will the Army submit to orders?'

When the question was put to Tojo, he replied that he was not in a position to give such a guarantee, but that an Imperial Prince 'would be able to suppress the Army'; in giving his opinion, he was no doubt bearing

in mind Higashikuni's long-standing connections with the Imperial Roadsters. Lord Privy Seal Kido, however, came out strongly against the
choice: not only was he not optimistic about the outcome of a war, but
'should the worst eventually happen, I thought therefore that the Imperial
Family might become the target of hatred by the people, with the result
that Japan's national entity [*kokutai*] itself would be called into question.
The only case in which a Cabinet formed by a Prince of the Blood was
permissible would be that of one organised as a result of the Army being
convinced of its error and deciding to accept a *volte-face*.'
    Seeing no possibility of such an event occurring, Konoye finally threw
in his hand and the next day submitted his Cabinet's resignation.
    Earnest discussions then ensued on the question of a successor. Kido
considered that only the War or Navy Minister was now sufficiently
abreast of all the considerations involved to fill the position, and his own
personal preference was for Tojo on the grounds (so he told the War
Crimes Tribunal) that since leaving the Army to become War Minister
'his character had changed' and he now 'much respected Imperial wishes'.
Such respect, he went on, 'was common to all soldiers, but it was stronger
in Tojo.' It was out of this respect, he explained, that Tojo wanted to
uphold the decision of the Imperial Conference, and if the Emperor was to
order him 'to review the situation on a fresh basis, I had sincere confidence
that Tojo would change his policy in pursuance of Imperial wishes.'
Konoye too agreed because, he felt, the appointment should go to 'the
strongest side' of the two (hinting that the Army might refuse to accept the
choice of Oikawa), and the ex-Premiers too added their approval, as they
did also to the proposal that Tojo should also continue to serve as Home
and War Minister concurrently. His new Cabinet did not contain a single
elected member of the Diet; for the Minister of Commerce and Industry
he turned again to Kishi, whom he had invited five years earlier to
'Manchukuo' as the colony's economic supremo.
    Tojo was accordingly summoned the following afternoon to the Palace
to receive the Imperial Mandate; in addition to the Premiership he was to
retain his post as War Minister — and even for good measure to take on the
Home Ministry as well. 'Bear in mind, at this time, that co-operation
between the Army and Navy should be closer than ever before,' Hirohito
commanded him, as he did also Oikawa a few minutes later. Both men
were also instructed to make a very careful review of all aspects of the
present situation and to feel free, if necessary, to change the decision of the
Imperial Conference. The nation at large, however, had already concluded that no such change was to be expected, if the following patriotic
song which appeared in the English-language *Japan Times & Advertiser* may
be taken as an indicator;
        Siren, siren, air raid, air raid!
        What is that to us?
        Preparations are well done,

Neighbourhood associations are solid,
Determination for defence is firm.
Enemy planes are only mosquitoes or dragonflies.
We will win, we must win.
What of air raids?
We know no defeat.
Come to this land to be shot down.

Hirohito himself also seems to have been touched by the same sense of euphoria: after thanking Kido for the part that he played in securing Tojo's appointment, he went on to borrow Matsuoka's favourite aphorism that 'you cannot obtain a tiger's cub unless you brave the tiger's den ...'

THE DECISION FOR WAR

One man who was certainly not so touched, but who could see the future equally clearly, was the unfortunate Nomura in Washington. Asking for the second time to be recalled, he declared that 'now that I am a dead horse, I don't want to continue this hypocritical existence, deceiving myself and other people.' Tojo's response was to order him to stay put and make greater efforts to reach a settlement — only in the next breath to put such a possibility out of court by telling him that only a change of heart on America's part could bring it about. On a less official level, the Maryknoll missionaries were button-holed to carry another private message from Konoye to the White House warning that an agreement would have to be reached 'very soon or not at all'.

At a Liaison Conference on October 23rd Army Chief of Staff Sugiyama insisted that a final decision must be made in the very near future as the military preparations were now almost complete. The command of the Southern Army which was to carry out the 'Strike South' had been established at Saigon and its eleven divisions were now entering their final training, including the technicians who were to operate the DEI oilfields. He was supported by his Naval counterpart Nagano; 'the Navy is burning 400 tons of oil an hour,' he informed the Conference. 'The situation is urgent.' At a further Conference two days later they estimated that the Army would be able to complete its operations in the South in 4-5 months, the Navy in 6-8 months (additional time being required to seal off Australasia from the U.S. Pacific Fleet) respectively.

The Cabinet and high command convened again for a final review of the situation on November 1st. Three plans were considered. First, Kido's suggestion that Japan should postpone hostilities and endure 'unspeakable hardships' for the five to ten years in the hope that she would then be able to strike. This was rejected when it was concluded that even with the expenditure of millions of yen there was no hope of significantly increasing the output of synthetic oil, and that Japan's stocks, even at a peacetime rate of consumption, would last no more than another two years; it was thus imperative to seize the DEI oil fields, and it was seen now as wholly out of the question that this could be done without provoking American intervention. The second alternative was therefore to attack at once on the grounds that postponement could only work to America's advantage. It was favoured by the two Chiefs of Staff, who expressed themselves now as much more confident than previously of the prospects for success. Not only could they look forward to victories in the initial strikes, they both declared, but there was also a good chance of sustaining a long war through to a final and decisive victory.

They were opposed by Tojo, however, on the grounds that such a move obviously ran counter to the Emperor's injunction to revise the decision of the September 6th Imperial Conference. His objection was accepted, and discussion turned to the question of how much longer the deadline for negotiations could be extended. The Navy suggested a date of November 20th, but the Army were only prepared to see it run to as far as the 13th. The new Foreign Minister, Togo, refused to accept either as practicable, but after a heated debate it was eventually set at November 30th.

There remained only the question of what amendments, if any, should be made in the terms offered to America. It was decided to present two alternatives. The first, Plan A, would be merely a restatement of the old formula, except that in regard to 'the necessary period of time' for which troops were to be retained in the specific areas in China Nomura was instructed, 'in case the United States asks', to reply 'about twenty-five years'. The withdrawal elsewhere would be completed 'within two years of the firm establishment of peace and order' in China, while that from Indo-China would follow the establishment of 'a just peace in East Asia'.

If this was once again rejected Nomura was to offer Plan B for a temporary *modus vivendi*, under which America was to supply Japan with a 'required quantity' of oil annually and to restore trade generally to pre-embargo levels, 'to co-operate with a view to securing the acquisition of those goods and commodities which the two countries need in the DEI', to lift the freeze on Japanese assets and to refrain from any action 'prejudicial to the endeavours for the restoration of general peace between Japan and China'; both countries were to forswear any military activity in 'the South East-Asia and Southern Pacific area except the part of Indo-China where Japanese troops are stationed at present'. In return for all this, Japan merely 'declares that it is prepared to remove its troops now stationed in the southern part of Indo-China to the northern part'. This almost nonsensical proposition was the brainchild of Foreign Minister Togo, who hinted that he might resign if it was not approved. It was indeed at first strenuously opposed by the Chiefs of Staff on the grounds that it would only delay a settlement in China, and it was in order to win them round that the undertaking by America not to obstruct such a settlement was inserted. The Conference finally broke up at 1.30 am in the morning.

When Tojo, accompanied by the two Chiefs of Staff, reported their conclusions to the Palace to obtain the Emperor's approval that afternoon, Hirohito told him, according to Tojo's testimony to the War Crimes Tribunal, that 'if the state of affairs is just as you have stated now, there will be no alternative but to proceed with the [military] preparations, but I still hope that you will also adopt every possible means to tide over the difficulties in the negotiations with America.' He then went on to pose certain questions as to how Japan would justify an invasion of Thailand if it proved necessary and whether the export of oil from the DEI could be guaranteed in the face of enemy counter-attacks, before finally giving his Imperial sanction. Tojo knew now that he could look forward to the scrap to end all scraps.

At Hirohito's request, a meeting of the Supreme War Council was called two days later under the chairmanship of Uncle Kanin to review the final operational plans. They were again assured by Nagano that 'if we start in early December with the strength that we now possess, we have a very great chance of victory in phase one of the war,' while Sugiyama promised that the eleven divisions of the Strike South force were 'all ready to move the moment the Imperial Order is issued'. Tojo, while conceding that a long war was '80% probable', spoke of the possibility of a short war in the event of the destruction of the U.S. Pacific Fleet, consequent loss of American morale accelerated by a German declaration of war, closure of her supplies of raw materials from the Far East and the reduction of Britain to starvation by a successful German blockade in the Atlantic.

Comforted by these optimistic projections, the Council gave its unanimous assent to the decision for war. At the Imperial Conference called the next day, November 5th, to affix its traditional rubber-stamp, Tojo finally ruled out any question of further concessions on China. 'As I understand it, withdrawal of our troops is retreat. We sent a large force of one million men and it has cost us well over 100,000 dead and wounded, the grief of their bereaved families, hardship for four years and a national expenditure of tens of billions of yen,' he declared. 'We have some uneasiness about a protracted war, but how can we let the United States continue to do as she pleases? Two years from now we will have no petroleum for military purposes, ships will stop moving ... We would become a third-class nation after two or three years if we just sat tight.'

Speaking through his usual mouthpiece, the President of the Privy Council, the Emperor agreed that 'we cannot let the present situation continue. If we miss the present opportunity to go to war, we will have to submit to American dictation. Therefore, I recognise that it is inevitable that we must decide to start a war against the United States ...'

The deadline of December 1st for the completion of negotiations was duly confirmed, with the added proviso that the decision for war should then be taken regardless of the current state of negotiations (author's italics).

THE FLEET SAILS

To put him on his mettle, the deadline as signalled to Nomura was put forward to the 25th. 'This time we are showing all our friendship; this time we are making our last possible bargain. In fact, we have gambled the fate of our land on this throw of the dice,' he was informed. 'We have endured what is difficult to endure for more than half a year. Our endurance up to now stems from our desire for peace. But there is a limit to our patience. We should like you to inform the United States that she should seriously reflect on [whether it is wise] to continue to ignore Japan's demands, and that the present situation cannot be overlooked even for a single day.' Togo simultaneously stressed the urgency of the situation to Grew. 'The United States has delayed and delayed. Japan has made concession after concession ... The feelings of the Japanese people won't allow this situation to continue,' he asserted to the Ambassador. 'For the United States to disregard the sacrifices that Japan is making in China is tantamount to telling us to commit suicide.'

Nomura reported back that despite these warnings Hull was continuing to insist that the current negotiations should only be regarded as 'preliminary discussions' and that Japan would have to accept his 'Four Principles' before any settlement could be seriously negotiated. 'That won't do,' he was told sharply, and in case he should again show signs of faltering, it was also decided to dispatch professional diplomat Kurusu Saburo to support him in his hapless task — made all the more so, of course, by 'Magic's' betrayal of the facts which he was required to conceal. Elsewhere on the diplomatic front, Germany was to be told that no action could be expected from Japan against Russia for the time being, while a request was to be made to Thailand for the free passage of Japanese troops; if this was refused, the country would simply be invaded. As a further cover, it was also decided to approach the Dutch for new negotiations on the supply of raw materials from the DEI.

As soon as the Imperial Conference adjourned the two Chiefs of Staff hurried away to issue their respective Secret Operations Order No. 1. The work of drafting that for the Navy had been put in hand by Yamamoto in late September, and for the first time it revealed the precise details of the strategy for the attack on Pearl Harbor. 'Despite the fact that the Empire has always maintained a friendly attitude towards the United States, the latter has interfered in all the measures which we have taken out of self-preservation and self-defence for the protection of our interests in East Asia,' it declared. 'Recently she has blocked our speedy settlement of the "China Incident" by aiding the government of Chiang Kai-shek and has even resorted to the final outrage of breaking off economic relations with us ... The Japanese Empire is expecting war to break out with the United States, Great Britain and Holland. War will be declared on X day; this order will become effective on Y day.'

Five days later the mobilisation order was issued to the Pearl Harbor Task Force directing that battle preparations were to be completed by November 20th, when it would rendezvous at Hitokappu Bay in the Kuriles; 'X day' was also designated as December 8th — the 7th in U.S. Time. On the same day the first group of the fifteen I-Class submarines (the largest category, having a cruising range of 12,000 miles and being equipped with seaplanes for reconnaissance) not required in the attack set out to take up observation posts outside important naval bases, from Madagascar in the West to California in the East. The I-10, for instance, left Yokosuka on the 16th and arrived off Suva in the Fiji Islands on the 29th, while another which was already on station in Australian waters — she had been sighted launching her seaplane off the Great Barrier Reef the previous month — may be presumed to have been assigned to Fremantle, for three sightings of an unidentified seaplane were reported a little further up the west Australian coast during the first week of November. On the 15th an order issued by Sugiyama confirmed that 'on suitable occasions the Navy will carry out air strikes and submarine operations in the Australian and Indian Oceans.'

On November 15th the Liaison Conference met again to approve 'The Draft Proposal for Hastening the End of the War Against the United States, Great Britain, the Netherlands and Chiang', which gave a detailed description of Japan's global strategy. '1. Our Empire will engage in a quick war, and will destroy American and British bases in Eastern Asia and in the South-West Pacific region ... At the appropriate time, we will endeavour by various means to lure the main fleet of the United States [near Japan] and destroy it. 2. We will work for the surrender of Great Britain by a) breaking the connection between Australia, India and the British motherland by means of political pressure and the destruction of commerce; b) promoting the independence of Burma and so stimulating the independence of India ... 3. We will work to destroy the will of the United States to fight by a) dealing with the Philippines, b) disrupting commerce to the United States, c) cutting off supplies from China and the South Seas, d) stepping up strategic propaganda to the United States pointing out the uselessness of a Japanese-American war ...'

TWO-FACED IN WASHINGTON

In Washington meanwhile Nomura presented Plan A, accompanied by a 'vague and uncertain' assertion of the sincerity of Japan's intentions. It was, as he expected, rejected, Roosevelt observing that Japan had only to withdraw her troops from China and Indo-China to prove that she was sincere. The Ambassador signalled back to Tokyo that 'even though I know I will be harshly criticised for it, I feel that should the situation in Japan permit, I would like to caution patience for one or two months in order to get a clear view of the world situation.' The answer was uncompromising: 'I am awfully sorry to say that the situation renders this out of the question. The deadline for the solution of these negotiations is set,' Foreign Minister Togo signalled back. 'There will be no change. Please try to understand that. You see how short the time is, therefore do not allow the United States to sidetrack us and delay the negotiations any further.'

Kurusu then arrived, and he and Nomura together presented a proposal on their own initiative that both sides should return to the position prevailing in July before Japan moved into southern Indo-China and America imposed her freeze. Hull indicated that just possibly here was a basis for negotiation, but it was quickly scotched by an instruction from Tokyo that 'no further concessions can be made' and that Plan B should now be presented. 'When we say "Do not obstruct efforts to achieve peace between Japan and China", we mean that America should suspend aid to Chiang,' Togo added for good measure. At the same time a signal was received from Grew warning of the possibility that Japan would use a surprise attack to seize the initiative.

On November 20th the two envoys duly returned to delivery Plan B. Hull needed only to check it against the version that he had received from 'Magic' before confirming his opinion that it was 'clearly unacceptable'. 'The commitments we should have to make were virtually a surrender,' he later wrote in his Memoirs. In return for all the concessions required of America Japan 'would still be free to continue her military operations in China, to attack the Soviet Union, and to keep her troops in northern Indo-China until peace was effected with China ... The President and I could only conclude that agreeing to these proposals would need condonement by the United States of Japan's past aggressions, assent to future courses of conquest by Japan, abandonment of the most essential principles of our foreign policy, betrayal of China and Russia, and acceptance of the role of silent partner aiding and abetting Japan in her effort to create a Japanese hegemony over the western Pacific and eastern Asia.' If American Intelligence had been able to read the Japanese Naval as well as Diplomatic Code, they would have known that on the other side of the Pacific mobilisation orders were at that moment being issued to the 'Strike South' force.

The White House, however, only too conscious that America's guard, particularly in the Philippines, was still far from fully up, decided against giving a flat rejection of Plan B and instead to put forward a counter-proposal, under which America would offer her services as mediator between Japan and China while supplying Japan with some oil and the promise of more later; in return, Japan was to promise not to move any more troops, to agree not to invoke the Tripartite Pact even in the event of an American-German war and to subscribe to a joint statement of principles. Before presenting it, however, Hull submitted it to the representatives of Australia, Britain, China and Holland and requested them to obtain their Governments' approval, merely informing the Japanese that a counter-proposal was in the offing.

When Nomura relayed this development to Tokyo, he was again told that it would be very hard to extend the deadline 'for reasons beyond your ability to guess', but that 'if you can bring about the signing of the pertinent notes, we will wait until November 29th. After that, things are automatically going to happen.' This reply was once again intercepted by 'Magic', but another signal sent out that same day, the 22nd, to the Pearl Harbor Task Force was not (being, of course, in Naval code): 'The Task Force will move out from Hitokappu Bay on November 26th and proceed without being detected to Rendezvous set for December 3rd. X day will [still] be December 8th.' On the same day also a Liaison Conference decided that if any negotiations did ensue from Plan B, Japan would make a 'concrete demand' for no less than six million tons of oil annually. If on the other hand Plan B was rejected, the decision for war would be taken.

On November 24th, when still no response had been received from any of the ABCD governments (the 22nd being a Saturday), Roosevelt cabled a personal message to Churchill outlining the counter-proposal in more detail. 'I am not very hopeful,' he added, 'and we must prepare for real trouble, possibly soon.' At noon the following day he called a War Council, in which, according to Stimson, he 'brought up the event that we were likely to be attacked perhaps [as soon as] next Monday, for the Japanese are notorious for making an attack without warning, and the question was what we should do. The question was how we should manoeuvre them into the position of firing the first shot without allowing too much danger to ourselves.' The terms of the counter-proposal were approved, on the understanding, however, that they should not be construed as offering to compromise on the oft-stated Four Principles.

TELLTALE EVIDENCE FROM LONDON

During the afternoon the awaited ABCD replies began to come in. From London, Anthony Eden expressed support and confidence in Hull's ability to handle the negotiations for the best, adding that 'our demands should be pitched high and prices low.' The Dutch Minister also reported his Government to be in favour, but warned against supplying enough oil to allow Japan to increase her military potential. Only the Chinese had serious reservations, Chiang Kai-shek saying that any relaxation of the economic restrictions against Japan would be received as a heavy blow to the morale of his forces and might even lead to a total collapse in the will to resist. However, his fears were not taken over-seriously by the White House, for several times in the past the Generalissimo had used such expressions of alarm to extract further commitments of assistance from his allies.

By the following morning (the 26th), however, some new factor had arisen which caused Roosevelt and Hull to rule their idea out of court. Treasury Secretary Morgenthau noted that when he was shown into the President's bedroom at breakfast time 'he hadn't touched his coffee. He had some kippered herring which he had just begun to eat when Cordell Hull called up. He was talking to Hull and trying to eat his food at the same time, but by the time he finished his conversation his food was cold and he didn't touch it.' One hour later, just before 10 am, Hull rang Stimson to say that he 'had just about made up his mind' not to go ahead with the counter-proposal, but 'to kick the whole thing over'. What could this new factor have been, to have brought about such a sudden and dramatic change of heart — in effect to remove the last slender hope that America would not be plunged into a war that she was still so ill placed to fight?

Until the publication of John Costello's book *The Pacific War* in 1981 the cause was generally attributed to the combination of an intelligence sighting of a convoy of between 30 and 50 Japanese troop transports south of Formosa reported to Stimson late in the afternoon of the 25th (as recorded later in his diary) and a discouraging telegram from Churchill received in Washington during the early hours of the 26th. Costello demonstrates, however, from evidence uncovered in a recently-declassified file of Stimson's correspondence that the report in question referred to a convoy of not 30-50 but only 10-30 vessels, and that it was sighted not at sea, but merely in the process of assembling in the mouth of the Yangtse, an event which the Military Intelligence Division further-more dismissed as 'more or less a normal movement'.

As for the telegram from Churchill, which is marked in the main (London) Churchill-Roosevelt correspondence file as having been dis-patched at 3.20 am on the 26th, it read as follows: 'Your message about Japan received tonight. Also full accounts from Lord Halifax of discussions and your counterproject to Japan on which Foreign Secretary has some comments. Of course it is for you to handle this business and we certainly do not want an additional war. There is only one point which disquiets us. What about Chiang Kai-shek? Is he not having a very thin diet? Our anxiety is about China. If they collapse, our joint dangers would enor-mously increase. We are sure that the regard of the United States for the Chinese will govern your action. We feel that the Japanese are most unsure of themselves.'

It is hard to see anything in this most non-committal of Churchillian missives that should have caused the Presidential kippers to go cold, and the reference to having received Roosevelt's telegram of the 24th 'tonight' indicates that it reached London (which was five hours GMT ahead) in the early hours of the 25th and that Churchill's reply was dispatched some time later that same day; furthermore, two of Hull's staff subsequently recalled discussing it with him that afternoon.

There is, however, other evidence to suggest that a *second* message was indeed received from Churchill during the early hours of the 26th and that it was subsequently expunged from the files both in London and Washington. Tucked away in another file in the London Public Records Office and bearing the much less conspicuous title of 'Far East — General: U.S. Policy vis-à-vis Japan' can be found the following cover note from Churchill's Secretary to the Third Secretary at the U.S. Embassy: 'Dear Mr Beam, I enclose a telegram from the Former Naval Person [Churchill] to the President for dispatch as soon as possible. I am so sorry to trouble you at this hour.' Notwithstanding the irregularity of Churchill's working hours, even he would have felt bound to apologise for disturbing the Embassy's slumbers at 3.20 am in the morning. What could it have contained to have justified such a disturbance — and to have caused such a momentous reaction when it reached Washington?

Six days earlier, as the sun was setting off the West Australian coast some 500 miles north of Fremantle, the light cruiser HMAS *Sydney* had encountered the German raider *Kormoran* lying hove to in the water. By an illegal *ruse de guerre* (described in detail in the author's book *Who Sank The Sydney?*) the raider's captain was able to convince his Australian counterpart that his ship, which was flying the Norwegian flag, had been crippled by a raider which had then fled over the horizon, and having thus lured the cruiser into very close range he then launched a surprise attack before she could bring her greatly superior armament to bear. The *Sydney* was, however, able to recover sufficiently to return fire and to set the raider alight, causing her to be rapidly abandoned. The Germans then rowed towards the *Sydney*, herself seriously disabled but still afloat, in the hope of being picked up, but before she could do so she was rent by a massive explosion and disappeared before their eyes.

In sharp contrast to the fate of the *Sydney*'s 645 men, none of whom were ever seen alive again, 318 of the *Kormoran*'s complement of 398 were eventually rescued and brought ashore. After they had been formally interrogated, they were transferred to prisoner-of-war camps in Victoria, where they saw out the remainder of the War. During their time there a sketch was discovered on the person of the *Kormoran*'s Intelligence Officer which was found to conceal a series of shorthand characters. They were deciphered to read as follows: 'Reinforcements arrived . . . in the evening conquered the victim. A Japanese gunfire attack from Japan itself.' It was also recalled that a number of Japanese milk-bottle tops had been recovered from one of the German lifeboats, but the official account of the action maintained that no word was ever received from the *Sydney* and that her loss had been due to the damage inflicted on her by the raider.

However, as early as November 24th — that is, before any of the German survivors had been recovered and interrogated — the Admiral Commanding the Australian Squadron had recorded in his diary that 'the Naval Board are very worried about *Sydney* . . . they think there is a possibility that a Vichy submarine escorting a Vichy ship has torpedoed her.' It would have taken the Naval Board only a few hours to establish with the Admiralty in London that there was no Vichy (or German) submarine nearer to Australia than the Mediterranean at that time, and that if indeed a submarine had been responsible for her loss it could only have been from Japan. Australia then being 11 hours GMT ahead of London, there would thus have been ample time to convey to Churchill, and for him to pass it on to Roosevelt by 3.20 am London time on the 26th, the stunning conclusion that Japan had already in effect entered the war.

At first glance, it may seem improbable that Japan would have risked blowing the whole element of surprise which was so vital to the success of her plans by engaging in an action so far beyond her previous field of activity. However, the I-Class submarines were notorious for their shortage of storage capacity of fresh water, and a rendezvous with a German ship well out of range of any enemy airfield would have seemed a preferable solution than a search of the very barren West Australian coastline. Furthermore, the No. 1 Order issued to the Fleet on November 5th had included the instruction that 'in the case of discovery within 600 miles of the objective against which war is to be declared, make immediate preparations to attack and destroy the unit responsible.'

Such an action would also seem to provide the only satisfactory explanation for the very curious absence of survivors from the *Sydney*, which made her by far the largest warship to be lost with all hands — and that in tropical temperatures — in the whole course of the war. That the news had come to the White House via London would also explain the great lengths gone to subsequently to conceal the fact on both sides of the Atlantic, for both Prime Minister and President knew only too well that their alliance in the coming hostilities hung on the latter's ability to refute the charge of the isolationists that he was allowing Churchill to talk America into the war.

ALL SET

Later that morning, the 26th, the counter-proposal was accordingly 'kicked over' and replaced by a 'Proposed Basis for Agreement' whose terms were altogether less accommodating. Japan was called upon not to advance in any area at all where it had forces stationed and to withdraw all but completely from the whole of Indo-China; on the American side there was no commitment to stop either the flow of aid to China or the defence build-up in the Philippines, and as for oil the supply was to be limited to a monthly allowance to meet civilian needs only.

Hull handed it over, marked 'Strictly Confidential, Tentative and Without Commitment' to Nomura and Kurusu at five o'clock that afternoon. He had no illusions as to the reaction to be expected from them, remarking to the Secretary of War that 'I have washed my hands of it, and it is now in the hands of you and Knox, the Army and the Navy.' The following day final alerts were sent to commanders in the field instructing them to 'be on the *qui vive* for any attack'; that to Admiral Kimmel at Pearl Harbor was additionally labelled 'This Dispatch is to be considered a War Warning'.

For his part Nomura put the best face he could on the American reply, advising his Government to continue negotiation and recalling a remark of Roosevelt that there would be 'no last words'. The professional diplomat Kurusu, however, was altogether less prepared to delude himself, concluding that 'it could be interpreted as tantamount to meaning the end', and that when it was received in Tokyo the Government 'would be likely to throw up its hands'. The Naval and Military Attachés in Washington, acting on their own initiative, cabled Tokyo even more emphatically: further negotiations would be, they considered, 'completely hopeless'. The Liaison Conference that met to consider it duly condemned it as a humiliating ultimatum; as Tojo later argued in his testimony to the War Crimes Tribunal, 'Japan was now asked not only to abandon all the gains of her years of sacrifice, but to surrender her international position as a power in the Far East. That surrender, as he saw it, would have amounted to national suicide. The only way to face this challenge and defend ourselves was war.'

The decision for war required the formal sanction of the Imperial Conference, and Hirohito suggested that the ex-Premiers should be invited to take part in order to convey an impression of national unity. Tojo, doubtless fearing opposition from them, objected to the proposal on the grounds that men who no longer held political responsibility should have no part in decision-making; the precedent of 1904 when Meiji consulted the Elder Statesmen before attacking Russia did not apply here, he argued, because 'the only qualification that the ex-Premiers possess is that they once held the post of Prime Minister, and they are not necessarily able men.' By way of a compromise, it was arranged that the Prime Minister should see them beforehand. Nomura was accordingly sent the following instruction: 'With the report of the views of the Imperial Government that will be sent to you in two or three days, talks will be *de facto* ruptured. This is inevitable. However, I do not wish you to give the impression that the negotiations are broken off ... From now on do the best you can.'

On November 29th Tokyo received a repeated assurance from Hitler that Germany would at once enter any war which arose between Japan and America and Britain; he promised that in the spring the Russians would be chased over the Urals and into Siberia. In return Double Diplomat Oshima was told to inform Berlin that the negotiations with America were now at an end, and that 'there is an extreme danger that war may suddenly break out between the Anglo-Saxon nations and Japan through some clash of arms and that the time of the start of the war may be quicker than anyone dreams.' The ex-Premiers met the same day at the Imperial Palace to discuss the decision for war with Tojo. Most of them, including amongst

them as they did the last relics of parliamentary democracy, expressed a
marked lack of enthusiasm for the war and even Konoye wondered
whether 'it would be possible, while carrying on things as they are, later to
find a way out of the deadlock by persevering to the utmost against all
odds'. The Prime Minister, however, had an answer to all their anxieties;
war 'could not be avoided', he told them, or 'we'll lose our chance to
fight', and while he refrained from disclosing any details of the Pearl
Harbor attack on the grounds that they were 'state secrets', he assured
them that the high command was 'rather confident of victory'.

When the Liaison Conference met that afternoon to settle the agenda
for the Imperial Conference, Foreign Minister Togo learnt for the first
time that the deadline had been set at December 8th. However, his request
that this should be revealed to Nomura was refused. 'Our diplomats will
have to be sacrificed,' he was told. 'What we want is to carry on
diplomacy in such a way that until the very last minute the United States
will continue to think about the problem and we will continue to ask
questions, and our [real] plans will be kept secret . . . At this juncture the
entire population will have to behave like the Forty-Seven Ronin' (who
disguised their true purpose until able to strike down their target).

After the meeting adjourned, Tojo went on to a dinner held to mark the
anniversary of the Anti-Comintern Pact. He used the occasion to make a
speech in which he accused the West of setting the peoples of the Far East
against each other in order to exploit them and declared that 'for the
honour and pride of mankind, we must purge this sort of practice from
East Asia with a vengeance . . . so that a chorus of victory may go up in the
camp of justice as speedily as possible.' Although he claimed subsequently
to have been misreported by the American Press, the effect of his words
was to bring Roosevelt hurrying back to Washington from a Thanksgiving
dinner in Georgia and to evoke an anguished appeal from Kurusu to Tokyo
for 'the Premier and the Foreign Minister to change the tune of their
speeches. Do you understand? Please all use more discretion.' Tojo's
optimistic assertions were contradicted twenty-four hours later by
Hirohito's second brother Takamatsu, then a serving officer in the Navy,
who reported to the Throne that the Naval General Staff 'were not at all
confident of victory'. Hirohito immediately summoned Nagano and
Oikawa to the Palace for confirmation; they were evidently able to
reassure him, however, for when the audience was over he ordered
Privy Seal Kido to 'instruct Prime Minister Tojo to proceed according to
plan. The Chief of Staff and Navy Minister have both given affirmative
answers to my question regarding our war chances.' He also told Kido that
the Imperial Conference arranged for the next afternoon formally to
ratify the decision for war after the expiry of the deadline at midnight that
night should go ahead as planned.

Tojo once again explained how nothing more could be hoped for by
continuing the negotiations, declaring that on the contrary further delay

could only disadvantage Japan and that, regrettable as it was for the deep anxiety that it was causing to His Majesty, the only course now left was war. Nagano added his support with an assessment of the Navy's morale: both officers and men were 'burning with a desire to give their lives for the state' he declared, and they were ready 'to go forth in high spirits to accomplish their great mission.' The Privy Council President was again deputed to speak on the Emperor's behalf, and he rose to put some awkward questions on what precautions were being taken to protect the main cities against incendiary air-raids, but even though he met with no very satisfactory answers he did not persist, and turned instead to abuse the United States, whose attitude, he said, was 'utterly conceited, obstinate and disrespectful. We simply cannot tolerate it. If we were to give in, we would give up in one stroke not only our gains in the Sino-Japanese and Korean-Japanese wars, but also the benefits of the Manchurian Incident ... The great achievements of the Emperor Meiji would all come to nought, and there is nothing else that we can do.' The Conference broke up after only two hours, the momentous decision that Japan was effectively in a state of undeclared war being endorsed almost by default. Sugiyama recorded in his diary that Hirohito 'nodded in agreement with the statements being made and displayed no signs of uneasiness. He seems to be in excellent spirits, and we are all filled with awe.'

DAY OF INFAMY

The next day Nagano and Sugiyama returned to the Palace to confer with Hirohito on the date set for the attack. December 8th was doubly suitable, it was decided, because being a quarter-moon there would be good night time cover for the two task forces, while the fact that it was a Sunday in Hawaii (on the other side of the date-line) should catch American vigilance at its lowest. As soon as the date was confirmed, a signal was flashed to the Fleet ordering the Pearl Harbor force to proceed to its final rendezvous point and the Strike South force to weigh anchor and set out across the Gulf of Thailand for the Kra Peninsula. At the same time all current Fleet Codes were changed; 'Do you mean to say that they could be coming round Diamond Head and you wouldn't know?' Admiral Kimmel in Pearl Harbor exclaimed with uncanny prescience when this was reported to him. Tojo was called to the Palace several times in the next week to discuss the progress of operations; at his trial before the War Crimes Tribunal he naturally denied that Pearl Harbor had been discussed, and at an interview with the Chief Prosecutor in 1948 Hirohito himself denied all prior knowledge of it. Sugiyama's diary, however, records that it was Hirohito himself who had authorised the initial evaluation of the feasibility of the attack eleven months earlier.

In Washington Nomura was instructed to keep up the impression that

Japan still wished to continue the negotiations, but at the same time he was told to burn all but one of the Embassy's code books. The signal was duly intercepted by 'Magic', and watching American agents were presently rewarded with the sight of a plume of smoke rising from the Embassy's back yard.

On December 4th Tojo submitted to the Liaison Conference the draft of his proposed reply to Hull's 'Proposed Basis for Agreement' of November 26th. 'It is the immutable policy of the Japanese Government to insure the stability of the Far East and to promote world peace and thereby to enable all Nations to find each its proper place in the world,' it began, and continued to ramble on in the same vein of posturing righteousness over thirteen lengthy paragraphs. 'The China Incident' was held to have broken out 'owing to China's failure to comprehend Japan's true intention' . . . despite Japan's 'best efforts to prevent its extension, America and Britain had resorted to every possible measure to assist the Chungking regime so as to obstruct the establishment of a general peace' . . . the negotiations in Washington had broken down because the American Government had 'failed to display in the slightest degree a spirit of conciliation' and was 'scheming for the extension of the war in Europe and preparing to attack, in the name of self-defence, Germany and Italy'.

The Japanese Government by contrast, he asserted, had 'always maintained an attitude of fairness and moderation and had made all possible concessions' . . . 'Finally on November 26th, in an attitude to impose upon the Japanese Government those principles it has persistently maintained the American Government made a proposal totally ignoring Japanese claims, [which] Japan viewed as a source of profound regret.' The fourteenth paragraph wound up with an assertion that 'the earnest hope of the Japanese Government to adjust Japanese-American relations and to preserve and promote the peace of the Pacific through co-operation with the American Government has finally been lost. The Japanese Government regrets to have to notify hereby the American Government that in view of the attitude of the American Government it cannot but consider that it is impossible to reach an agreement through further negotiations.'

Foreign Minister Togo argued that no Declaration of War was called for under International Law because Japan had a right to resort to a 'war of self-defence' in response to an 'ultimatum'. In the next breath, however, he declared that the final paragraph in effect amounted to a declaration of war because 'the expression of hope having been lost for an adjustment of relations clearly signified a cessation of peace; that is to say, a resort to war.' None of his colleagues could find fault with this tortured logic, and the argument devolved instead on the timing of the presentation of the Note in Washington. While it should not be allowed to jeopardise the success of the surprise attack, Hirohito had insisted that it should precede the actual outbreak of hostilities. The following day it was set at 12.30 pm Washington time, but the Naval high command then insisted on postponing it for a further half-hour, although they refused to give the reason, claiming that it was an operational secret. It was, in fact, that the first strike in Pearl Harbor had been put back to 1 pm (7.30 am in Hawaii); if the Foreign Minister in Tokyo was not permitted to know that, how much less so was his errand-boy Nomura in Washington.

On the 6th a RAF reconnaissance plane from Singapore sighted the 'Strike South' force half way across the Gulf of Thailand, causing Z Force commander Admiral Phillips to hurry back from Manila to his base 'in order to be there when the war starts'. At much the same time in Washington 'Magic' intercepted a signal to Nomura instructing him to stand by to receive the first thirteen paragraphs of the Note.

While the decoders and the code-breakers waited on their respective sides of Massachusetts Avenue, Roosevelt sat down to compose his last throw, a personal appeal to Hirohito to draw back and respect their joint 'sacred duty to restore traditional amity and prevent further death and destruction in the world'. He had opened with a reminder that 'almost a century ago the President of the United States addressed to the Emperor of Japan a message extending an offer of friendship,' but at the best of times it would not have been calculated to appeal to the great-grandson of that Emperor Komei who had set it as the sacred duty of his Imperial line to avenge the incursion of the 'barbarians' on to the shores of the Divine Land; how much less so therefore was it now when the moment of that revenge was at hand. Nor was it even to reach its destination in time, due to a blanket 24-hour delay imposed by Military Intelligence in Tokyo on all incoming telegrams from abroad.

By 9.30 pm that evening all the first thirteen paragraphs were in the President's hands. Progress in the Japanese Embassy, however, had been much less expeditious, for because of its sensitivity Nomura had been ordered not to entrust its processing to the usual secretarial staff and by the time that the unprofessional two fingers of a diplomat had typed it out, the sun had already arisen to herald the momentous day of December 7th 1941. The fourteenth paragraph then arrived, together with a instruction that Nomura should arrange an appointment with the Secretary of State at 1 pm 'as a matter of extreme urgency' in order to hand over the complete note. Not satisfied with the appearance of his first attempt, he set out to type it all over again ...

By 10 am the fourteenth part had already been unravelled by 'Magic', but by 1 pm still the substitute typist had not completed his second draft. A flustered Nomura rang the State Department and asked to postpone his scheduled meeting with Hull until 1.45. When they finally arrived, he and Kurusu were made to wait a further ten minutes until they were ushered into the Secretary's office. By then the Pearl Harbor task force had been strafing, bombing and torpedoing the U.S. Pacific Fleet with devastating effect for a full hour, but even if the Note had been presented at 1 pm as scheduled, it would still have followed the opening bombardment of the

British defences on the Kra Peninsula by 75 minutes; London was favoured not even by a bogus 'declaration of war'.

Hull pretended to read what he had first seen some four hours earlier before delivering his response of calculated fury: 'In all my fifty years of public service, I have never seen a document that was more crowded with infamous falsehoods and distortions — infamous falsehoods and distortions on a scale so huge that I never imagined until today that any Government on this planet was capable of uttering them.'

In the course of the next seven hours the 'divine soldiery that is sent to bring life to all things' followed up with further surprise attacks on the Philippines, Guam, Wake and Midway Islands, Hong Kong and the International Settlement in Shanghai. When their successes had been reported to Tokyo, Hirohito's Imperial Rescript announcing the opening of hostilities was then broadcast to His people.

'The hallowed spirits of Our Imperial Ancestors guarding Us from above, We rely upon the loyalty and courage of Our subjects in Our confident expectation that the task bequeathed by Our Imperial Ancestors will be carried forward, and that the source of evil will be speedily eradicated and an enduring peace immutably established in East Asia, preserving thereby the glory of Our Empire.'

Six months later that 'confident expectation' would begin to fade after the decisive reverse at Midway, for the 'final war' which had been planned in 1936 to follow in thirty years' time had been launched twenty-five years prematurely.

Three years and three months later again, the One Roof which was to have brought the Whole World under Hirohito's Divine Hegemony fell in on Japan in a cloud of atomic dust.

Epilogue

New Conquests, Old Goals

On August 15th 1945 Hirohito broadcast his decision to accept the Allies' terms of surrender, explaining to His subjects that the war, which had been declared 'out of Our sincere desire to ensure Japan's self-preservation and the stabilisation of East Asia, it being far from Our thought either to infringe upon the sovereignty of other nations or to embark upon territorial aggrandisement ... has not developed necessarily to Japan's advantage.'

Ten days later, and two days before the scheduled arrival of the first forces of the Occupation, the Vice-Minister of the Ministry of Munitions (as the Ministry of Commerce and Industry had become after its merger with the Cabinet Planning Board in 1943) summoned his four senior bureaucrats to a hurried conference. Their mission was to recreate the Ministry under its old guise as the MCI, because it was feared that anyone thought to have been connected with munitions would be liable to arrest or dismissal. The following day was mostly taken up with the destruction of incriminating personal files (as it was in other Government buildings all over the country).

Their efforts were largely successful: not only was the Ministry itself allowed to survive, but only 42 of its total staff (which in 1949 numbered 21,199) were subsequently purged, while the four themselves would all go on in the 1950s to serve as Vice-Minister. The one man that they could not save was their Minister, Kishi, who was imprisoned for four years on charges as a Class A War Criminal. In the mistaken belief that it was they who had held ultimate control over the economy the Supreme Command of the Allied Powers (SCAP) turned its fire instead on the conglomerates and ordered their immediate disbandment. This was backed by the introduction of an Anti-Monopoly Law incorporating the establishment of a Fair Trade Commission, but due to another misconception imported from America (where banks are forbidden industrial or trading affiliates) it was not applied to the conglomerates' banking arms, with the result that much of the intricate network of interlocking subsidiaries and their managements survived intact. They were also assisted by the chicanery of post-war Premier (and pre-war Ambassador in London) Yoshida, who had the SCAP directive ordering the purge of all standing directors translated to apply only to their managing directors; 'By so doing we were able to save many ordinary directors who might otherwise have been purged,' he boasted in his *Memoirs*. 'Which shows that sometimes mistranslations serve their turn'.

The MCI thus emerged from the war with its position as economic overlord considerably strengthened; if the conglomerates wished to continue their clandestine existence, they dared not challenge the diktat of the Ministry as they had done not infrequently before 1939. Its bureaucrats were also quick to exploit American fears of an economic collapse and its natural corollary, a communist revolution (in 1947, for the first and only time, a socialist government briefly held office in post-war Japan), persuading SCAP to extend its powers still further via the Economic Stabilisation Board which was introduced to organise the allocation of the few resources available; the shortage of coal was particularly acute due to the repatriation of 150,000 Chinese and Korean forced labourers who had been drafted into the mines by Kishi, and to relieve it the old MCI Fuel Bureau was reconstituted as the Coal Agency. A further difficulty was the inflation caused by the enormous sums dispensed by the Ministry to factory owners as war compensation. By March 1946 it was running at over 1100 per cent, but when SCAP ordered a stop on them funds were diverted to a Reconstruction Finance Bank which simply continued the payments.

When Yoshida was returned to power in 1948 (after the Prime Minister himself had been arrested for misuse of RFB funds), inflation was still rampant and compounded by a balance of payments deficit of some $400 million made good by the U.S. Treasury. Washington now decided that enough was enough, and that it was time for Japan to begin to pay her way. The Government was ordered to wind up RFB payments and to balance the budget; with inflation thus drastically brought under control, a fixed exchange rate of 360 yen to the dollar was set to encourage exports. These measures were a blow to the influence of MCI, whose share of the national budget had risen to 33% thanks to its manipulation of the RFB. Furthermore, Yoshida was deeply suspicious of MCI's centralised direction of the economy, which in his eyes smacked altogether too much of socialism – he was reported as saying that he 'could not distinguish an MCI official from an insect'. He was determined to bring it under the control of his own alma mater, The Foreign Ministry, and for this purpose he merged the MCI with the Board of Trade which was responsible for the administration of foreign exchange and was staffed by the Foreign Ministry. In order to emphasize its rôle in the promotion of exports, the new body was named the Ministry of International Trade and Industry (MITI).

It was recognised, however, that much had still to be done to rationalise industry and increase productivity before Japan would be in a position to compete successfully in world markets. In addition, the economy was severely depressed by the measures introduced to control inflation, and the relief which the outbreak of war in nearby Korea in June 1950 promised was threatened by industry's desperate shortage of capital. These conditions opened the way for MITI to reassert the control over the economy enjoyed by its predecessor.

Two instruments in particular were employed to achieve this. The Foreign Exchange and Foreign Trade Control Law had been introduced by SCAP to restrict imports of consumer goods and to promote exports by compulsorily channelling all foreign exchange earnings into the import of approved foreign technology; intended as a temporary measure to correct the current balance of payments deficit, it remained on the statute book for the next thirty years constituting, in the words of one commentator, 'the most restrictive foreign trade and exchange control system ever devised by a major free nation'. Similarly the Japan Development Bank (JDB) was set up in 1951 as a short-term cure for industry's lack of capital; it was specifically forbidden by SCAP either to borrow itself or to lend for any purpose other than investment in new machinery. However, when the Occupation ended the following year not only were these restrictions immediately lifted, but the JDB was granted the power enjoyed by the pre-war MCI to draw on Post Office Savings accounts which by 1980, thanks to exemption from tax and generous interest rates, had grown to a sum four times greater than the assets of the Bank of America, the world's largest commercial bank. The combination of these prerogatives gave MITI, according to another commentator, 'weapons of industrial management and control that rivalled anything its predecessors had ever known during the pre-war and wartime periods'.

This power over the direction of investment allowed MITI to switch the support which SCAP had given to export-orientated consumer manufactures such as textiles to its own designated targets in heavy industry. In the three succeeding years no less than 83% of all JDB loans went to the producers of coal, steel, ships, and electricity. Moreover, the seal of JDB approval opened the door to further loans from the commercial banks, so that favoured companies were allowed to borrow even in excess of their net assets; the over borrowing was guaranteed by the Bank of Japan — which, since the Bank fell within MITI's orbit, served to tighten MITI's control still further. The virtue to the companies of this system was that it reduced their reliance on shareholders for capital (by 1963 the proportion raised by equity totalled a mere 10%), and so allowed them to plan for the longer term at the expense, if need be, of short term profits; this would give them an important advantage when they came to compete with publicly-quoted companies in the free world.

The dependence on the banks also had the effect of openly reviving their former associations with the conglomerates and their other affiliates; the last of the Occupation forces had hardly departed in 1952 when the Mitsubishi network was reformed, although it was another three years before Mitsui did so. Now that its control over them was beyond challenge, MITI welcomed this concentration as further facilitating its

direction of the economy. As if this was not enough, it also sponsored the
introduction of an Enterprises Rationalisation Promotion Law. Although
it did not give MITI the power actually to compel one company to merge
with another, its provisions allowed for the withholding of tax concessions
and other favours if the company refused to fall in with this 'administrative
guidance'. The threat proved so effective that MITI was able to reduce
2,800 companies ranking below the conglomerates to no more than 20
cartels, and on November 27th 1952 its Minister, Ikeda Hayato, proclaimed in the Diet that 'it makes no difference to me if five or ten small
businessmen are forced to commit suicide'. When the Fair Trading
Commission objected that such practice contravened the Anti-Monopoly
Law, MITI replied that the Law did not extend to 'informal advice'; it was
then amended by an obliging Diet to permit 'co-operative behaviour' such
as the fixing of production quotas, the arrangement of joint investment
planning and the sharing of new technology to lower export costs among
the new cartels.

   With the fall of Yoshida in December 1954 and the subsequent merger
of the old Seiyukai and Democratic Nationalist parties into the Liberal
Democrats, the party which has governed Japan uninterruptedly ever
since, MITI's political backing grew ever stronger. Yoshida was followed
as Prime Minister by, successively, Hatoyama Ichiro (who had characterized his pre-war tenure of the Ministry of Education with the threat to
close all universities unless academics toed the Government line), Ishibashi
Tanzo (a former MITI Minister), Kishi (having served his time as a War
Criminal), Ikeda (again an ex-MITI head) and Sato Eisaku (the brother of
Kishi who had been born a Sato and then adopted). As early as 1952 30% of
the seats in the Diet were held by former politicians who had been banned
by SCAP from holding public office, and they were bolstered by an
increasing number of ex-bureaucrats; between them they would soon
represent a parliamentary majority, and MITI, together with the Finance
and Foreign Affairs Ministries, was now seen as one of the three
indispensable rungs to the top of the political ladder. MITI's share of the
national budget remained a modest one, but it was kept deliberately so in
order to avoid a dependence on the Ministry of Finance; besides, it bore no
relationship to the size of the funds which it controlled — in 1956, for
instance, MITI itself spent only 8.2 billion yen, but it was responsible for
the distribution of no less than 160.9 million.

   Having thus successfully filled the shoes of the wartime 'economic
general staff', the Ministry has since consolidated its inheritance by
nurturing within its own ranks and those of the conglomerates new
generations of the leading families of that era; in 1983, for instance, the
Chairman of Mitsubishi Motors would be the son of none other than
'Scrapper' Tojo himself. It employs relatively few economists, preferring
instead to draw on the élite of Tokyo University's Law School; it
represents, an *Asahi* journalist has stated, 'without doubt the greatest

concentration of brain power in Japan'. Its influence within the Government is reflected in the fact that since 1955 no budget (with one exception) has been amended in the Diet, while its hold on industry is maintained through the system of *amukudari* or 'descent from heaven' whereby the top flight of MITI bureaucrats move on retirement into executive positions in the conglomerates. If any outsider should be tempted to believe that MITI does no more than any other government agency in the free world commissioned with encouraging economic growth, let him hear the words of one of its former Vice-Ministers: 'It is an utterly self-centred point of view to think that the Government should be concerned only with providing a favourable environment for industries without telling them what to do.'

The end of the Korean War boom landed Japan once again with a serious balance of payments deficit. MITI argued that the key to improving the competitiveness of Japanese goods in order to achieve the necessary increase in exports was first to reduce costs by expanding the home market; it is this philosophy which — coupled, of course, with MITI's panoply of powers to restrict imports — has allowed Japan to maintain a high-growth economy ever since. In order to explore potential overseas markets MITI set up the Japan External Trade Organisation, which eventually established offices in 54 different countries in order to furnish manufacturers with the necessary intelligence and to assist them in marketing their products. The network was funded by the novel expedient of imposing a special tax on the importation of bananas, for which the hungry Japanese were prepared to pay exorbitant prices; in the single year 1955 this tax raised over 100 million yen. Exporters were also helped by an exemption from tax on up to 80% of profits earned from exports; this was preferred to a direct subsidy as being not only more efficient (in being a payment by results, whereas a subsidy was necessarily payable in advance), but also less visible to foreign competitors. When complaints were eventually raised in GATT, MITI switched to an even more invisible system whereby depreciation allowances were increased in direct relationship to the company's export performance.

In the next five years Japan's economy expanded at an average annual rate of 7.6%, and the IMF and GATT Conferences in the autumn of 1959 were dominated by demands that she should remove her restrictions on foreign goods and capital. Promises to accede to them, however, served only to demonstrate that it was the 'language of the Japanese belly' that still had the final word. When Singers, for instance, attempted to regain its pre-war leadership in the Japanese sewing-machine market by setting up a joint production unit with a local company, MITI immediately stepped in with a production quota in order to protect domestic producers. The treatment accorded to IBM, whose possession of all the basic computer patents precluded the development of Japanese local production, was even more uncompromising: 'We will take every measure to obstruct your business unless you licence IBM patents to Japanese firms and charge them no more than a 5% royalty,' MITI's Vice-Minister informed them. Reluctantly, IBM fell in with these terms. Thus was born the Japanese computer industry which, as we shall see, today threatens to dominate the world.

By 1961 the IMF protests had grown to a pitch where they could no longer be ignored even in the 'belly', and in Washington President Eisenhower responded to a flood of cut-price Japanese textiles by giving US Foreign Aid purchases precedence to American products. Prime Minister Ikeda replied with a promise to open 80% of the Japanese economy (the figure was raised to 90% after further pressure) to foreign goods and capital within three years, but in response to Press warnings of 'a second coming of the black ships' and 'a bloodstained battle between national and foreign capital' he simultaneously raised import tariffs to protect the liberalised industries. At the same time MITI set up an Industrial Structure Investigation Council to look into the possibility of further rationalisation in order to beat off foreign competition; it was eventually merged with the body created by the Enterprises Rationalisation Law to form the Industrial Structure Council, which continues today as the chief outlet of MITI's 'administrative guidance'. In theory its recommendations were not legally enforceable, but the array of sticks at its command made them in fact irresistible. When, for instance, Sumimoto Steel refused to comply with a 'recommendation' to cut production by 10%, MITI threatened to reduce its supply of imported coking coal accordingly; again, when a bank protested that it was unable to absorb the full quota of Government bonds earmarked to it, it was warned 'so you think your bank can survive even after Japan collapses?' Similarly with the carrots: Nissan received a generous loan on easy terms from the Japan Development Bank to merge with the Prince car manufacturer.

Yet another body established under MITI's sponsorship was the Supreme Export Council, which set annual export goals for individual industries. As the richest market in the free world America made an obvious starting point. Sony was an early beneficiary, being assisted by a two-year tax holiday while it built up its lead there in transistor radios (the patent for which it had paid Western Electric Inc. a mere $25,000 in 1955), although as a relative newcomer it was obliged to look to a conglomerate (Mitsui) rather than to the Japan Development Bank for development funds.

Another early target was the television market, for which MITI set up a Television Export Council comprising the six leading producers. They first fixed domestic prices at levels which produced sufficient profits to enable them to place their sets on the American market at below cost prices. Asked eventually by U.S. Treasury Department investigators to explain the difference, Sanyo replied that the export models were made by younger workers who earned lower salaries; when some scepticism was expressed at this, the prices on entry were raised but then reduced again on the shop counter by means of rebates paid to the retailers in the form of 'loyalty discounts'. When U.S. manufacturers attempted to hit back by exporting to Japan (where they had every hope of competing successfully against the exorbitantly-priced home products), MITI refused to provide importers with the necessary foreign exchange. The result of this conspiracy was the closure of ten U.S. manufacturers at a cost of 70,000 jobs and the loss to the Treasury of some $800 million (at a conservative estimate) in evaded customs duty. The U.S. Commerce Department eventually (in 1980) claimed back $67 million in lost duty, adding a fine of $11 million for dumping, but by then it was too late to salvage this important industry from the hands of the invaders.

Other areas of the American market were similarly targetted as the companies concerned moved on into fresh fields in order to forestall accusations of dumping. Nevertheless, by 1982 no less than 28 such charges had been substantiated in the courts, and the Commerce Department had imposed anti-dumping tariffs on Japanese manufacturers ranging up to as high as 48.7% (on electrical typewriters, but not before another 21,000 U.S. jobs had been lost in that industry alone). By the same year Japanese imports of computer-controlled machine tools, which had begun after a Japanese producer copied an American patent licensed to it in the Far East, had captured 60% of the U.S. market by means of cut prices subsidised by the $1 billion annual levy culled by MITI from licensed gambling on bicycle racing.

Even more systematic was the strategy employed against the American steel industry. In order first to achieve the necessary economies of scale (and to emphasise to Sumimoto the price of insubordination) MITI brought Yamata and Fuji Steel together to form New Japan Steel, the world's largest producer; its president and senior executives were all former MITI bureaucrats. Almost immediately, its products began to flood across the Pacific. When domestic producers complained, the U.S. authorities introduced a list of minimum prices, but the flood continued unabated, disguised now as having been produced in Canada, Mexico and even Taiwan (which at that date boasted no steel mills) and helped on its way with further 'loyalty discounts'. Although not itself a producer, Mitsui acted as agent for 40% of all Japanese steel imports; when eventually brought to book on 21 charges of fabrication and conspiracy the company was fined a total of $11 million, the heaviest ever imposed by a U.S. court. Within a decade 300,000 American steelworkers would find themselves unemployed.

The impact of cheap Japanese exports on the American car market was similarly dramatic; selling at a price $2500 below the notional cost price of a U.S.-produced small car, they reached an annual figure of over two million units in the same decade. The profit margin at such a level would have been minimal had not MITI protected it by allocating market shares to the six leading manufacturers, thus eliminating the cost of competition. When Congress finally threatened to introduce a fixed percentage of American-made components in all imported cars, MITI stepped in again to impose allocations restricting the total to a 'voluntary' 1.68 (subsequently raised to 2.3) million units per annum, at the same time instructing the manufacturers to boost exports of their small trucks, which were not included in the figure, and to establish production facilities inside America. Estimates of U.S. job losses resulting from these tactics run as high as 500,000.

The extent of MITI's influence was by now winning it considerable enemies, even in Japan itself. Japan's membership of the Organisation for Economic Co-operation and Development committed her to the removal of all existing restrictions on foreign goods and capital, but the Industrial Structure Council immediately set to work drawing up a labryinth of rules and regulations which had the effect of protecting the domestic market except in areas (such as saki and wooden clogs) where no foreign competition could be expected or where no demand for foreign products existed (e.g., cornflakes); the television market, for instance, was declared open to foreign manufacturers — except those of colour sets. Similar steps were taken to fend off the invasion of foreign capital which, it was feared, would only too easily snap up ownership of low-equity, bank-dependent Japanese companies; foreign equity ownership was limited to 20%, at least half the directors of any joint venture had to be Japanese and all such ventures were still subject to MITI approval.

Fearful of being caught in a backlash from the antagonism which this obstructionism created abroad, industry began to loosen MITI's embrace. When the Ministry attempted to rationalise the motor industry further into two groups under Nissan and Toyota, Mitsubishi broke ranks and entered a 63-35 partnership with Chrysler; Isuzu then followed with a similar arrangement with General Motors. The shock created by these novel displays of independence brought about the resignations of two successive MITI Ministers and their replacement by Tanaka Kakuei, a self-made building millionaire and a man far removed from the traditional mould of institutionalised bureaucrat.

The period also saw increasing concern among the public at large at the pollution, highlighted by the permanent smog in the main cities and the deaths caused by the consumption of mercury-poisoned fish, inherited from two decades of indiscriminate industrial growth; in 1967 the Diet had introduced Pollution Counter-measures, but MITI had effectively emasculated them by insisting that they had to be 'in harmony with the healthy (*sic*) development of the economy'. Tanaka saw an opportunity to promote his cause in the forthcoming LDP leadership contest by setting his staff to draw up a scheme to relocate industry in less crowded areas; not only would this answer current criticisms of the Ministry, but it would also serve to channel funds into his own constituency of Niigata.

Published under his own name as 'A Plan to Remodel the Japanese Archipelago', it proved a runaway best-seller and duly secured his election as Prime Minister. In return for his support the MITI post was handed on to a fellow LDP faction leader, Nakasone Yasuhiro (it was alleged in the Press that a considerable sum had changed hands between them). In order to implement the scheme the 1973 budget increased government spending by no less than 24.6%, causing one commentator to describe it as 'the largest pork-barrel in the history of Japanese finance'. The spiralling inflation that inevitably followed brought a barrage of accusations that the conglomerates and MITI were conspiring to corner the market.

Just when it seemed that the day of MITI's over-lordship were numbered, it was rescued by the first OPEC 'oil shock'. Japan, being totally dependent on oil from the Middle East for her energy, was an immediate casualty. Almost overnight such basic commodities as kerosene, detergent and even toilet paper vanished from the market, with the result that MITI was called in to restore order by fixing prices and regulating supply; at the same time Nakasone hurried off to the Persian Gulf with his MITI cheque book to buy credence for Japan's sudden protestations of support for the Arab cause (the largest of his investments was a $3 billion petrochemical complex in Iran; still not complete after being overtaken first by the Khomeini Revolution and then by the Iran-Iraq War, it threatens to rival the 1918 Nishihara Loans as a white elephant). So enthusiastically did MITI seize the opportunity to reassert its authority that the oil companies presently found themselves accused by the Fair Trade Commission of rigging the market. They replied that they had only been acting in accordance with MITI's 'administrative guidance', and by the time that the High Court finally ruled in 1980 that such conduct had been *ultra vires* MITI had succeeded in frustrating attempts to give the Commission more teeth.

Another event in 1974 which helped restore MITI to its pedestal was the resignation of Tanaka as Prime Minister after he had been accused of corruption and tax evasion (two years later he would also be charged with receiving a bribe of $2.2 million from Lockheed over the procurement of a contract to purchase the company's airliners). His replacement was an ex-MITI Minister, Miki Takeo, one of whose first actions was to direct the Ministry to compile each year a 'Long-Term Vision' in order to 'set up guidelines which the people, business sector and government can follow in their concerted efforts ... to open the way for a new age'. Their conclusion, drawing on the themes of pollution-reduction and energy-conservation, was that Japan should switch from heavy to lighter industries, particularly the knowledge-intensive fields such as robotics, computers and, in particular, semi-conductors around which the others were built and which were predicted to become 'the crude oil of the 1980s'.

In 1975 MITI accordingly 'guided' six leading electronics manufac-

turers to set up a research project for the development of a high
performance semi-conductor superior to anything produced in America;
no less than $332 million was made available in low-interest loans. At that
time Japan was producing Random Access Memory (RAM) chips with a
capability of only 4K (that is, able to store 4,000 items of data), and these
were of indifferent quality, while America was about to launch a 16K
RAM chip. Three years later, however, Japan was producing 16K RAMs
of a comparative quality with the American — and bearing a remarkable
resemblance to those whose technology had been bought from America
under licence. Although the Japanese market was in theory 'liberated',
imports of American chips were strictly controlled during this period in
order to give the Japanese manufacturers the advantage of a protected
home base generating the profits which would then enable them to
undercut the prices prevailing in overseas markets.

When Japanese 16K RAMs were launched in America in 1979, they
immediately captured 42% of the market, forcing local manufacturers to
cut back on their research for the next generation of 64K RAMs and to
revise their prospective prices upwards in order to recoup their losses.
Thus when they reached the market the following year at prices between
$25 and $30 each, the Japanese simultaneously launched their 64K RAMs at
a price of $15. As the Americans dropped their prices in an attempt to
compete, so too did the Japanese until by the end of 1982 they were quoting
a price of $4.25 — far below the Americans' cost of production (in filing a
complaint to the Commerce Department, one U.S. manufacturer alleged
that they were selling at *94 per cent* below fair value; the Department
eventually imposed an anti-dumping tariff of 35%). In 1983 they captured
70% of the total world market, forcing all but the largest American
producers out of business and leaving the field in 256K RAMs clear for
themselves.

The development of Japan's computer industry has followed a similar
path. In spite of being forced by MITI to part with its patents, in 1970 IBM
still held three-quarters of the Japanese market. MITI then decided to
rationalise the domestic producers by merging them into three groups, led
by Fujitsu-Hitachi, and 'guided' them into developing machines that
could be used with IBM software; it also instructed the companies
enjoying its patronage to buy only the Japanese products. As a result, by
1979 IBM's market share had shrunk to 27%. When it was learnt that IBM
were planning to counter with a new 'third generation' Hitachi mounted
an operation to steal its trade secrets, only to be caught red-handed by the
FBI; in Japan, however, it was IBM who was accused of 'industrial
espionage' by the Press, and its sales declined still further.

MITI then made a further $130 million available to the same six
companies to develop a super-computer capable of running at least a
hundred times as fast as any then in existence and ready for lauching in
1989, but it was already looking ahead to a fifth generation for the 1990s.

These machines, the research for which was put in hand by MITI as far back as 1978 and is scheduled to cost $500 million in direct subsidies spread over a ten-year programme, will for the first time boast 'artificial intelligence'; they will be able to digest data in both spoken and written form (in different languages) and even in photographs, process them and arrive at an inference. The claim that their successful production would 'provide our country with bargaining power' might be thought a masterpiece of understatement even in Japanese terms.

In response to the growing impatience of her competitors (signalled by America's imposition in 1971 of a 10% surcharge on imports following Japan's failure to fulfil a promise to cut those of cheap textiles), Japan had declared herself in 1973 to be '100% liberalised' — with the exception of 22 specified industries, 17 of which were under MITI's 'administrative guidance'. Three years later the latter too were theoretically opened, but, as with semi-conductors and computers, they continued to enjoy the protection of so-called 'non-tariff barriers'.

The extent and ingenuity of these devices are such that they have passed into folklore among would-be exporters to Japan. To give but a few examples: every imported car has to be individually tested on landing for compliance with local exhaust-emission requirements; all foreign drugs have to be tested either in Japanese laboratories or on Japanese living in their country of origin; a leading British drink was rejected on the grounds that the glue on the bottle label did not conform to Japanese standards, as was a consignment of biscuits which was held to contain an 'unknown additive' because their exporter had mis-spelt one letter in sodium metabisulphite; a new, non-international set of standards has recently been imposed on skis, one of the few markets in which foreign imports predominate, on the grounds that Japanese snow is 'wetter' than that in Europe or North America. Elsewhere, most noticably in the field of wines and spirits, tariffs continue to exist in a disguised form; thus whisky has been divided into seven quality grades, the top grade (which includes all the leading Scotch brands) carrying a duty of 2,100 yen as against one of 362 yen carried by locally-produced whiskies; hardly surprisingly, sales of Scotch have fallen 36% since the system's introduction.

In industries outside MITI's remit, other tactics have been evolved to fend off the intrusion of foreign competitors. For example, after two American manufacturers had accepted the invitation of the Defence Agency to submit plans for the next-generation support-fighter in competition with Mitsubishi, they were suddenly handed a list of 64 additional requirements, one of which stipulated that the plane should be capable of taking off fully loaded at 104° Fahrenheit — a temperature not recorded in Japan for the past thirty years. In 1985 the Ministry of Posts and Telecommunications approved legislation permitting foreign participation of up to one third in the provision of a second international telecom service; however, when Britain's Cable & Wireless and America's Pacific Telesis took shares of 20 and 13 per cent respectively in a bid with four domestic companies, the Ministry first hastily organised an all-Japanese rival and then ordered the two groups to merge into a single consortium, reducing the Cable & Wireless stake to one of a mere 3 per cent and removing their right to a seat on the executive board. In the construction industry contracts are allocated by the time-honoured process of 'designated bidding' whereby potential bidders are first nominated by the Ministry concerned and the contracts then placed after consultations with senior executives of the larger companies, who in turn distribute the awards among favoured subcontractors. The present construction of a new Osaka airport on an artificial island in the Inland Sea is being regarded as a test case for the credibility of Japanese protestations that such a system is not calculated automatically to exclude foreign bidders; they have already been shut out of the first stage, the construction of the island itself, and it will be no surprise if they fail to pick up more than a few minor orders for the second stage.

Of all industries, however, it is agriculture which is the most heavily protected, enjoying the benefits both of rigid quotas on foreign produce and of colossal government subsidies. The Japanese consumer pays a heavy price for the perpetuation of its inherent inefficiency (the average Japanese farm runs to less than three acres); the price paid to farmers for their staple product, rice, is some *ten* times higher than the current market price in America, while for beef they receive five times as much. As a result, the country's total food bill accounts for fully one quarter of all consumer spending (compared with a U.S. figure of 13%). Foreign cigarettes, besides bearing a tariff of 20%, are allowed on sale at less than a tenth of the country's 250,000 tobacconists, and their importers are forbidden to advertise except in English-language publications; when asked for an explanation, the Government cited considerations of health — forbearing to account for the absence of any such restriction on Japanese tobacco.

The real reason behind these barriers is the LDP's dependence on the rural vote, which enjoys a representation in the Diet quite out of step with the massive post-war shift in the population to the cities. When in August 1986 a government committee proposed a modest 3.8% cut in the price of rice (the first for thirty years), Prime Minister Nakasone not only intervened to block it, but at the same time he removed the long-standing right of Japanese seamen to bring home up to 45lbs of foreign rice duty-free. When the United States then attempted to open discussion on the issue, the Minister of Agriculture refused point-blank to negotiate, claiming that any change in the present system would 'lead to wide-scale fluctuations of demand, supply and prices, and make it impossible to ease the financial burden of the Government.' Even more cynical was the pretext offered by MITI for restrictions on the import of leather: their removal, it was pleaded, would 'hurt the Eta, who are the only people in the tanning business' — this oppressed caste, now euphemized by the title of *burakumin* or 'village dwellers', owe their monopoly to the fact that they are still debarred from any more wholesome occupation.

In the financial markets too the story has been much the same. When the 'temporary' 1949 Foreign Exchange and Foreign Trade Control Law was finally repealed in 1980 and the entry of foreign capital into Japan was declared to be 'free in principle', other barriers were swiftly erected in its place. MITI, for instance, was given powers (and a supporting fund of ten billion yen) to organise 'investment-limiting cartels' in six major industries described as 'structurally depressed', while even investment in private property has been made all but impossible for the foreigner. Although 77 foreign banks have been granted licences in Japan, they are still excluded from the management of the country's enormous pension funds and their share of the domestic credit market remains a meagre three per cent (yielding a return on assets of a derisory 0.19%). Of the 14 British firms licensed to deal in securities in Tokyo (compared with 58 Japanese firms licensed to deal in London) only one has so far been granted a seat on the Stock Exchange, other applicants having been turned away on the grounds that 'there is no room available'.

By contrast, the export of Japanese capital flows unchecked in the opposite direction, boosted by the same tactics employed in promoting that of manufactures. In May 1986 the Chairman of Barclays Bank spoke of 'the universal fear of Japanese dumping of financial services'; 'You can dump financial services just like you can dump everything else,' he observed. The high debt-capital ratio permitted to Japanese banks, coupled with the assurance of MITI's support in meeting any short-term losses incurred in establishing themselves in overseas markets, has enabled them to undercut the terms offered by local competitors. As a result, they now account for almost a quarter of all loans booked in the United Kingdom and command nearly forty per cent of all international business done out of the City of London. World-wide, they have easily overtaken America in international banking, having captured fully one third of the world banking market; the five largest commercial banks are now Japanese, while the government-owned Post Office Savings Bank matches the assets of the ten largest American money centre banks put together.

The effect of this centrally-directed programme of protection against foreign imports and penetration of export markets in both manufactures and financial services has been to produce an inexorable rise in Japan's trade surplus since the second 'oil shock' of 1979 created a temporary deficit, until in 1986 it reached a total of 101,400,000,000 dollars in visibles and invisibles combined. Faced with a threat of such magnitude, her competitors have turned an increasingly sympathetic ear to the appeals of their own industries for retaliation, despite the danger that a return to protectionism carries for the world economy. Thus in April 1987 the U.S. Government introduced a tariff of 100 per cent on Japanese personal computers, colour television sets and certain electric tools, while the

European Commission has similarly penalised imports of Japanese out-
board motors, ball bearings, excavators, photocopiers and electronic
typewriters; Britain has concentrated her fire on the financial sector,
threatening to revoke the licences of Japanese banks and other institutions
already established in London.

In an apparent attempt to deflect her critics, Japan has set aside a good
part of the surplus towards the creation of production capacity inside their
own markets. MITI's 'vision' projected that this investment would total
$93 billion by the end of 1986, but such has been the size of the trade surplus
since that by 1985 it had already reached a figure of $129.8 billion.
However welcome it may be in the short term in helping to alleviate
unemployment (partly created by the penetration of Japanese imports in
the first place) in the countries concerned, they should be aware that it is
also being made with longer term considerations in mind. Much of it, for
instance, has been directed towards oil-producing countries, both in oil
exploration and in manufacturing operations, in order to secure her future
energy supplies; of these Indonesia has been particularly favoured, Japanese investment there exceeding that of all other sources combined. Similar
motives underlaid an offer in 1986 to recycle $9 billion in the form of loans
to the Third World, for it was tied to a condition that the money should be
used only for the purchase of Japanese goods; it was aimed in particular at
South America, an area which, as we have seen, has long been a target for
penetration.

In the developing countries generally, particular attention is given to
establishing the local manufacture of products which will enhance the
prospects of success for Japanese bids for major development projects —
for instance, switchgear, turbines, and generators. Advantage is also taken
to extend the market life of products either which are becoming obsoles-
cent in Japan itself or whose penetration in export markets can be
sustained on the back of cheaper labour costs; most of the textiles, for
example, now sold in Japan are the products of Japanese plant located in
China, while a large proportion of Japanese television sets and video tapes
are produced for Western markets by overseas subsidiaries. Many of these
subsidiaries have first opened as joint ventures with local manufacturers,
but then once established in the market through the partner's ready-made
distribution network they have broken away and launched their own
products; a recent leading article in *The Financial Times*, headed 'Beware
Japanese Bearing "Gifts"', quoted examples of Western victims of this
tactic, notably the Sweda Cash Register Company.

Much has been said and written in the West of the need to imitate the
Japanese work ethic in order to be able to compete in the world's markets.
Certainly, this has been a potent factor in her success, but as a product of
that unique blend of Shinto and Confucianism which has moulded the
Japnese character over the centuries its scope for imitation is necessarily
restricted. Western employees of Japanese subsidiaries may be prepared to

don the company uniform and even, with tongue in cheek, sing the company song, but how many would go so far as to behave like the director of Nissho-Iwai who, in order to expiate its involvement in the Lockheed scandal, jumped from the top floor of the company skyscraper with the parting words 'Banzai Nissho-Iwai'? 'The Way of the Warrior' has evolved into 'The Way of the Salaryman'.

Any envy of the security of lifetime employment offered by the major Japanese companies should likewise be tempered by consideration of the conditions attached to it. Although salaries are roughly in line with their Western equivalents, a large proportion is paid in the form of performance-linked 'bonuses' which can be withdrawn at any time; most workers are still tied to a five-and-a-half day week, and although they are entitled to three weeks' holiday the pressures of the workplace are such that few take up their full quota; absence through sickness is penalised by a loss of 'bonus', while those of the supervisors concerned are similarly docked in the event of an accident; finally, pension rights are virtually non-existent, so that a man retired at the mandatory age of 55 must, unless he is lucky enough to be allocated another (lesser paid) job in a company subsidiary, seek a new job elsewhere and start again on the very bottom rung of the pay-scale — according to a recent survey, 45% of men over the age of 65 were still in active employment. The position of women is even less enviable, even those with a university degree being usually confined to decorative or menial rôles commanding on average only half the salary of a man. 'Don't take on divorcees, wives of teachers or writers, women who live alone or wear glasses,' runs the personnel department directive of a leading chain of bookshops. 'Above all, don't employ ugly women'.

Furthermore, 'lifetime' employment even on these conditions is not available to the majority of the workforce who are employed either by the major companies as 'temporaries' or in the vast jungle of smaller units sub-contracted to them (over 70% of the average Nissan car, for instance, is the product of sub-contractors); any downturn in demand is met by transferring work to the main factory, leaving the sub-contractor's work force out on the street. Since very few of them are unionised they have very little chance of redress, and even the workers in the major companies are represented only by company 'enterprise' unions which act as nothing more than as an arm of management — indeed, service in the union is a recognised path of promotion to the company board. Thus while Japanese employers speak fondly of the system's 'three sacred treasures' — lifetime employment, non-pensionable retirement and company unions — it is hardly surprising that in a recent survey only 53% of the workforce were found to be satisfied with their jobs, or that a record 25,524 committed suicide in 1986. If such a system cannot find more favour with the innate complaisance of the Japanese, there would seem to be little to be said for attempting to imitate it elsewhere.

Such widespread dissatisfaction might be expected to be reflected in the polls and the dismissal from office of the ruling LDP which for so many years has presided over the system's post-war revival — and indeed, in the 1983 election the party's share of the vote did in fact fall below 50% for the first time. Another potential threat to its dominance is posed by the belated moves to redraw the parliamentary constituency boundaries as required by the Constitution to reflect the population shift away from the party's rural heartlands. Its calculated response to these has been to fall back on an open appeal to the voters' chauvinistic instincts, which in Japan lie, as ever, so conveniently close to the surface. To judge by the results of the most recent election (on July 6th 1986), in which the LDP won 304 of the 512 seats in the Lower House, such a tactic has proved only too successful; they have also served to fulfil Nakasone's hopes of persuading the Party to amend its rules in order to allow him to serve an unprecedented third term as its leader.

It is in this context that the doctoring of school history textbooks in 1982 and the other more recent revivals of prewar nationalism (described in the Introduction) should be seen. Few are better qualified than Prime Minister Nakasone to launch such an appeal: it was Nakasone who, as Director of the Self-Defence Forces in 1970, introduced Mishima Yukio to the military hierarchy and even permitted his private army of ultra-nationalists to join in official training exercises before the novelist committed his spectacular *hara-kiri* after the failure of his attempted coup for the restoration of direct Imperial Rule; it was Nakasone who first visited the Yasukuni Shrine in his official capacity as Prime Minister after 'Scrapper' Tojo and the thirteen other Class A War Criminals had been secretly enrolled there as 'martyrs'; and it was Nakasone who immediately welcomed the decision of the High Court that the Education Ministry did not behave unconstitutionally over the textbooks, as a result of which the earlier promises to make 'the necessary amendments' have not been fulfilled.

As we saw in the Introduction, the indifference to the reaction of Japan's neighbours to the latter makes it clear that the misrepresentations are not aimed at any outside audience. Rather, their purpose is to exorcise the past in the Japanese themselves in order to give them the confidence to assert a dominant presence in the international field commensurate with their current economic strength. The ground has been additionally fertilised by an uneasy awareness that the benefits of this strength have yet to be translated into any improvement in their everyday lives; as the monthly *Chuo Koron* has put it, 'Japan's apparent wealth is, in large part, nothing but an unsubstantiated juggling of figures which merely testify that the Japanese people are forced to live and do business on land that they must acquire at exorbitant prices.' This sentiment has been given point by a survey which shows that it would now take the average employee seven years to earn the price of a two-bedroom house an hour's commuting distance from Tokyo.

The institution of the Imperial Throne is also being used to lend further authority to this new assertiveness, just as it was a hundred years earlier by the leaders of the Restoration in order to consolidate support for their quest to negotiate the unequal treaties with the West. Almost one fifth of the world's annual gold production was purchased in 1986 for the issue of a commemorative coin to celebrate the sixtieth anniversary of Hirohito's accession (although it was considered that any depiction of him on them would constitute sacrilege), which was also marked by a massive parade through the capital. 'It is an expression of adoration for the Emperor, a living god,' explained the organiser (and special adviser to Nakasone). 'It is like going up to Mount Sinai.' This revival of Emperor worship is inevitably giving rise to renewed expressions of its corollary, the innate superiority of the Japanese race, most notably again from Nakasone himself: the average level of intelligence in America was 'very low, because its population includes blacks, Mexicans, Puerto Ricans and others,' he has remarked, whereas that in Japan was superior 'because we are a homogeneous society.'

The perceived need to maintain Japan's racial purity is as strongly held as ever. The restrictions on immigration are little more relaxed than those maintained under the Tokugawa Shogunate, while the opportunities available to the foreigner for employment in Japanese firms are both temporary and limited to a few specialised categories such as teaching and entertainment. Even for those fellow Asians in distress, the Vietnamese 'boat people', exception was made only with the greatest reluctance, the 3,000 eventually admitted comparing with the 387,000 accepted by America, the 73,000 by Australia and the 18,000 each by Britain, France and West Germany in more distant Europe. Of Japan's 120.8 million inhabitants counted in the latest census, only 841,831 were registered as non-Japanese, and over eighty per cent of these were Korean, the descendants of the forced labourers press-ganged into the mines and other heavy industries after the annexation of their country in 1910. Although most of them are now residents of at least two generations' standing, they are not only still refused Japanese citizenship but are even required to submit themselves to be finger-printed every five years in order to re-register; in the face of their increasingly bitter protests at this humiliating ritual, the Government's only concession to date has been to change the colour of the ink used from black to transparent.

Even for those possessing Japanese nationality there are still obstacles to acceptance as racial equals. The Ainu may have been Japan's original inhabitants, but they remain virtually confined to their northern fastness of Hokkaido as they have been for the past thousand years since being driven from their southern homelands by the 'barbarian-suppressing' Shoguns; their right even to own property there is still subject to the authorisation of the island's Governor, while reference to their cultural origins and subsequent suppression has been excised from today's school history textbooks as completely as the wartime atrocities mentioned in the

Introduction. The barriers faced by the three million Eta are scarcely less formidable: the same 'village rolls' or records of ancestry used by Japanese employers to exclude Eta from their payrolls are scoured just as diligently by the parents of prospective marriage partners for any possible taint of Eta blood, and it has been estimated that some 50,000 engagements are broken off every year as a result. Even to mention the word Eta or the euphemism *Burakumin* in public is considered taboo; when James Clavell's novel *Shogun* was published in Japan, the first print was recalled in order to delete a single reference to the Eta. In spite of this all-pervasive and continuing discrimination, the Japanese Government recently denied to the United Nations that any racial minorities existed in Japan; if only their skin was a little darker, its victims might ruefully reflect, they could receive a portion of the attention devoted by the rest of the world to those of apartheid in South Africa.

The 'alarming trend towards extolling nationalism', as the *Asahi Shimbun* has described it, has carried with it uncomfortable echoes of a new militarism, of which once again Nakasone has been a leading spokesman. 'Military armament,' he announced during his term of office as Director of the Self-Defence Forces, 'was the final guarantee that poor, tiny Japan would confront the white man'; twenty years later as Prime Minister he cited 'the voice of God' to justify the abandonment of the ceiling on defence expenditure (set at one per cent of the Gross Domestic Product; if this does not seem at first a figure of much consequence, it should be borne in mind that the rise in the value of the yen has already put it on a par with the defence budgets of the major European countries). In another move to circumvent the post-war constitutional embargo on the deployment of troops abroad, Nakasone has agreed to contribute military personnel to United Nations peace-keeping operations. MITI too has come forward with a parallel plan for the establishment of a chain of retirement settlements in selected foreign countries. These are seen as serving a dual purpose: besides reducing the claims of the country's rapidly-growing old age population on the limited provisions available to it in Japan, they will serve as bridgeheads for future expansion in the same way that the labour colonies dispatched to Hawaii and elsewhere did in the previous century. The first such site has already been acquired in Spain, while others are being actively sought in Greece, Portugal, Australia and New Zealand.

For the moment, however, it is the problem of finding the means to redress Japan's enormous and destabilising trade balance that is of more immediate concern. In a move to forestall demands for further liberalisation of her domestic markets from his guests at the April 1986 Economic Summit in Tokyo, Nakasone appointed a commission headed by an ex-Governor of the Bank of Japan to recommend ways of reducing the surplus. The commission's conclusion that tariffs should be reduced and the population encouraged to purchase more foreign goods was duly hailed at a meeting with President Ronald Reagan as representing 'an historic change of course', but hardly had the mouth spoken than the 'belly' too began to make itself heard. Dismissing it as 'not Government policy', a Foreign Ministry spokesman added that although he understood that it was 'the Prime Minister's intention to implement large parts of it, when and how has not bet been decided.'

Subsequent events have done nothing either to encourage hopes of progress. On July 31st an agreement was signed with America not to export semi-conductors at less than fair value, but less than three months later Japanese producers were accused of dumping chips in third markets for re-export at prices which even MITI conceded to be 'rather low', and by January 1987 their exports to Asia were no less than 114% up on the previous year. It was this behaviour which finally persuaded the U.S. Government to impose the 100% tariffs already mentioned, although the last straw was also reported to have been a remark by MITI's Vice-Minister to the effect that 'it was a waste of time for the United States to try to sell super-computers to Japanese government agencies or universities, no matter how superior they were in price or quality.' The President of the all-powerful Employers Federation expressed the same attitude even more bluntly: 'There is nothing that Japan really wants to buy from foreign countries, except possibly neckties with unusual designs.'

One hundred and eighty-three years earlier the Shogun had similarly dismissed the offerings of Tsar Alexander with the remark that 'Japan already produced all that he could conceivably want.' Everything that has taken place in the interval should be sufficient to convince the rest of the world that when passed through the Japanese belly 'an historic change of course' is nothing less than a contradiction in terms, and that Japan will remain, in the words of the prescient Li Hung-chang, a 'great and permanent anxiety'.

* * *

How courteous is the Japanese;
He always says, "Excuse it, please."
He climbs into his neighbor's garden,
And smiles, and says, "I beg your pardon;"
He bows and grins a friendly grin,
And calls his hungry family in;
He grins, and bows a friendly bow;
"So sorry, this my garden now."

Ogden Nash

Notes

INTRODUCTION

page
vii Textbook 'corrections': *Daily Telegraph* 29 July 1982; *Japan Times* 6 August 1982.
'The cause of the incident ...': *China Daily* 26 July 1982.
viii 'The necessary amendments ...': *Japan Times* 27 August 1982.
A Seoul newspaper ...: *Japan Times* 4 August 1982.
'Japan, simply to assure ...': *Japan Echo* Vol. XL (1984) Special Issue, 7, 49.
Okinawa: *Japan Times* 3 August 1982.
ix Biological Warfare Research: *Daily Telegraph* 8 April 1982, 16 August 1984; *Guardian* 17 September 1982; *The Observer* 10 April 1983, 24 June 1984, 11 August 1985. Hirohito spared: Bergamini, *Japan's Imperial Conspiracy*, 181.
'There is probably no nation ...': Holtom, *Modern Japan and Shinto Nationalism*, 15.
x Their compilers ...: James, *The Rise and Fall of the Japanese Empire*, 62.
The first function of education: Holtom, op. cit., 6.
xi 'Filled with lies ...': Price, *The Son of Heaven*, 156.
Kojiki and Nihongi not fact: Brownlees, *History in the Service of the Japanese Nation*, 166.
'Subjects have no mind ...': Holtom, op. cit., 10–12.
'The shining example ...': Brownlees, op. cit., 149.
Neolithic finds misinterpreted: Conroy, *Pacific Historical Review* Vol. XX–1 (1951), 37.
xii 'We, the Japanese nation ...': Ogata, *Defiance in Manchuria*, 199.
Kokutai No Hongi English translation: Gauntlett, 3.
'Entails the use of military power ...': Holtom, op. cit., 23.

1. THE MYTH MAKERS

1 'It is six years ...': Gauntlett, *Kokutai No Hongi*, 70.
'The whole speech ...': Aston, *Chronicles of Japan from the Earliest Times,* Vol. I, 131.
2 Shotoku mission to Peking: Tsunoda, *Sources of Japanese Tradition*, 11.
3 Fujiwara dominance of the Court: Bergamini, *Japan's Imperial Conspiracy*, 197.
4 'Japan was the roots and trunk ...': Tsunoda, op. cit., 271.
5 'Only in our country ...': ibid., 279.
6 Hideyoshi's continental ambitions: ibid., 326; Kuno, *Japanese Expansion on the Asiatic Continent,* Vol. I, 144.
7 Iemitsu's isolationist measures: Sansom, *A History of Japan,* Vol. III, 36–7.
8 Hayashi Razan's influence: Tsunoda, op. cit., 351.
'It was the Sun ...': ibid., 373.
9 The development of Bushido: ibid., 394f.
Critics of chauvinism: ibid., 474, 487.
10 The National Learning movement: ibid., 511f., 548.
11 'They are the natural expression ...'; ibid., 519f.
12 *Confidential Plan of World Reunification*: ibid., 575f.

2. 'UGLY AND IMPUDENT BARBARIANS'

13 The Dutch at Deshima: Keene, *The Japanese Discovery of Europe*, 7f.
14 Dutch Learning School: ibid., 32; Tsunoda, *Sources of Japanese Tradition*, 601.
15 'Japan already produced all ...': Lensen, *Russia's Eastward Expansion*, 155.
16 Raffles: Beasley, *Great Britain and the Opening of Japan*, 5f.
   'Today the ugly and impudent barbarians ...': Tsunoda, op. cit., 596f.
17 'If the Shogun issues orders ...': ibid., 548.
19 'How can we know ...': Beasley, op. cit., 37.
20 'Eastern Ethics, Western Science': Tsunoda, op. cit., 603f.
21 'When the safety of Japan ...': Akamatsu, *Meiji 1868*, 91.
   Satsuma's trade with Loochoo: Beasley, *The Modern History of Japan*, 33; Craig, *Choshu in the Meiji Restoration*, 71.
22 'Mediocre leaders ...': Tsunoda, op. cit., 595.
23 Perry's missionary zeal: Bergamini, *Japan's Imperial Conspiracy*, 227.
24 Britain stays on the sidelines: Beasley, *Great Britain and the Opening of Japan*, 93.
25 'The letter of the President ...': Murdoch, *A History of Japan*, Vol. III, 584.

3. 'EXALT THE EMPEROR, EXPEL THE BARBARIAN'

27 The *daimyo* canvassed: Beasley, *Select Documents*, 98.
28 The Americans 'were arrogant ...': ibid., 103–4.
   'There is a saying ...': ibid., 117–18.
29 Shimazu suggests time limit: ibid., 113.
   Keiei rejects opening ports: ibid., 115.
30 The Bakufu's secret instructions: ibid., 123.
31 The Shogun's reply: Murdoch, *A History of Japan*, Vol. III, 600.
   'Commerce brings profit ...': Beasley, *The Meiji Restoration*, 96.
32 Dutch treaty: Murdoch, op. cit., 617–18; Akamatsu, *Meiji 1868*, 101.
33 Mistranslation of the Treaty of Kanagawa: Murdoch, op. cit., 623.
   Townsend Harris finally allowed ashore: Barr, *The Coming of the Barbarians*, 47f.
34 'I am determined to take firm ground ...': Griffis, *Townsend Harris*, 105.
   'It is quite preposterous ...': Murdoch, op. cit., 632.
   The Roju and Hotta memoranda: Beasley, *Select Documents*, 130–1.
35 'Pleased with the letter ...': Akamatsu, op. cit., 106.
   'Even if we were to open hostilities ...': ibid., 165f.
36 'Instantly the whole Castle ...': Murdoch, op. cit. 644–7.
37 'Above all to allow a barbarian ...': ibid., 644.
   'The Imperial mind is deeply concerned ...': Borton, *Japan's Modern Century*, 47.
38 'The American affair ...': Beasley, *Select Documents*, 181.
39 Harris argues against delay: Murdoch, op. cit., 656.
   'If we reject the treaty ...': Beasley, *Select Documents*, 183.
40 'A cruel satire ...': Barr, op. cit., 72.
   The appointment of a 'full-grown and enlightened heir': Murdoch, op. cit., 680.
41 'The treaties providing for friendship ...': Beasley, *Select Documents*, 193f.
   Yoshida Shoin's argument: Beasley, *The Meiji Restoration*, 148–9; Tsunoda, op. cit., 622.
43 Komei's secret appeal: Murdoch, op. cit., 688.
   Yoshida's legacy: Tsunoda, op. cit., 622; Stevenson, *Familiar Studies of Men and Books*, 172.

4. MURDER ON THE HIGHWAY

44 The assassins' manifesto: Murdoch, *A History of Japan*, Vol. III, 702.
The debate on the Shogun's marriage: Beasley, *Select Documents*, 198f.

47 'Of many nationalities ...': Alcock, *The Capital of the Tycoon*, 140; Public Records Office, FO 881/1054.
Advocates of *sonno-joi*: Beasley, *Select Documents*, 152f.
The official Choshu policy: Craig, *Choshu in the Meiji Restoration*, 170.

48 Sakuma's hopes: Harootunian, *Towards Restoration*, 180.
Nagai's dismissal: Craig, op. cit., 181.
Saigo's new plan: Murdoch, op. cit., 720–1.

49 'Our basic policy remains ...': Craig, op. cit., 183.
Kusaka's memorial: ibid., 188–9.

50 Hisamitsu's proposals and their effect: Murdoch, op. cit., 722f.
'In the twinkling of an eye ...': Gubbins, *The Progress of Japan 1853–71*, 142.

51 The Court's demand: Beasley, *The Meiji Restoration*, 191, *Select Documents*, 233.

52 'Expulsion' substituted for 'withdrawal': ibid, 194; Akamatsu, *Meiji 1868*, 164.
The memorial of the eleven *daimyo*: Paske-Smith, *Western Barbarians in Japan and Formosa in Tokugawa Days*, 148–9.
British threats of reprisal: Beasley, *Select Documents*, 238.

53 Yoshinobu's letter: ibid., 247.
Col. Neale's reaction: Satow, *A Diplomat in Japan*, 81–2.

54 Hisamitsu's undertaking: ibid., 93.

55 Extremists' plans: Craig, op. cit., 201; Paske-Smith, op. cit., 168.
'The expulsion of foreigners ...': Akamatsu, op. cit., 172.

56 Iemochi-Komei exchange: Murdoch, op. cit., 738; Beasley, *Select Documents*, 264f.

57 Takasugi replaced by Yamagata: Craig, op. cit., 215.
'We will defeat ...': Hackett, *Yamagata Aritomo in the Rise of Modern Japan*, 19f.

58 Treaty Powers' note: Beasley, *The Meiji Restoration*, 204.
'They did not believe ...': Satow, op. cit., 99.
'Our military preparations ...': Beasley, *Select Documents*, 277.

59 Lord Russell's dispatch: Public Records Office, FO 881/1299.
The terror of future Emperor Meiji: Akamatsu, op. cit., 180.
Takasugi's explanation to the Western envoys and their reply: Beasley, *Select Documents*, 284f.

5. IMPERIAL RULE RESTORED

61 'We have no hatred ...': Akamatsu, *Meiji 1868*, 178–9.
'Somehow to use Choshu men ...': Beasley, *The Meiji Restoration*, 232.

62 The Bakufu's orders: Craig, *Choshu in the Meiji Restoration*, 304–5.
'Of late the Bakufu ...': ibid., 312.

63 Takasugi and Okubo compromise: Beasley, *The Meiji Restoration*, 238–9; *Select Documents*, 83.
The Satsuma-Choshu accommodation: Craig, op. cit., 313f.

64 'The entire country felt relieved ...': ibid., 308.
'If the Shogun returns ...': Beasley, *The Meiji Restoration*, 251.
Japanese assessment of Parkes: Murdoch, *A History of Japan*, Vol. III, 757.

65 The Bakufu's warning: Beasley, *Select Documents*, 302f.
Okubo's letter: Beasley, *The Meiji Restoration*, 253.
'I see, as in a mirror ...': Craig, op. cit., 319.
Satsuma's undertakings: Beasley, *The Meiji Restoration*, 256.

66 'The Tycoon's ministers ...': Satow, *A Diplomat in Japan*, 157.

'Having beaten the Choshu people ...': ibid., 129.
French suspicions: Beasley, *Select Documents*, 84.
Satow's pamphlet: Satow, op. cit., 159.
Naval officer's observation: Black, *Young Japan*, Vol. II, 5.

67 Keiei's warning: Beasley, *The Meiji Restoration*, 258.
The Shogun's 'illness': Black, op. cit., 28.

68 Satsuma's determination stiffened: Beasley, *Select Documents*, 268.
Rumours of foul play: Satow, op. cit., 186.
Iwakura's change of heart: Beasley, *The Meiji Restoration*, 261f.
Yoshinobu's reforms: ibid., 265; Akamatsu, *Meiji 1868*, 206.

69 Opponents impressed: Craig, op. cit., 335; Satow, op. cit., 198.
Yoshinobu's letter to Komei: Beasley, *Select Documents*, 309.
'I hinted to Saigo ...': Satow, op. cit., 200.
Satsuma's offer of land: ibid., 189.

70 Komei's reply: Beasley, *Select Documents*, 309.
'If Sir Harry on his arrival ...': Satow, op. cit., 190.
'It is in every way necessary ...': Beasley, *Select Documents*, 311.
Satow noted that ...: Satow, op. cit., 202.
Parkes' attitude: Beasley, *The Meiji Restoration*, 268; Satow, op. cit., 244.

71 'Orders should be issued ...': Beasley, *Select Documents*, 313.
Ito's letter: Craig, op. cit., 338.

72 'Since the Bakufu is incapable ...': Hackett, *Yamagata Aritomo in the Rise of Modern Japan*, 45.
Okubo's letter: Craig, op. cit., 339.
Goto's proposals: Beasley, *The Meiji Restoration*, 277.
Saigo's and Okubo's letters: Craig, op. cit., 341; Beasley, *The Meiji Restoration*, 284.
'in two or three years' time ...': Satow, op. cit., 254.

73 'If we are robbed ...': Beasley, *The Meiji Restoration*, 285.
Japan 'will fall into the toils ...': ibid., 266.
Yoshinobu's announcement: Murdoch, op. cit., 769.
Parkes' conclusions: Beasley, *The Meiji Restoration*, 281; ibid., 293.

74 '... the territories and cities ...': ibid., 283.
Draft order for Yoshinobu's expulsion: Akamatsu, op. cit., 216; Beasley, *The Meiji Restoration*, 288.
Hisamitsu's assurance: Craig, op. cit., 344.
'All was going on well ...': Satow, op. cit., 284f.

75 Yoshinobu's optimism: Beasley, *The Meiji Restoration*, 293; Akamatsu, op. cit., 218.

76 'He gave but a lame account ...': Satow, op. cit., 301; ibid., 299.
The British Legation's qualified support: ibid., 304f.

77 'No faith can be placed ...': Murdoch, op. cit., 777.
'A private war': Craig, op. cit., 348.
Satsuma's Note to the foreign envoys: Satow, op. cit., 325f.

78 'Walk about accompanied by ...': Beasley, *The Meiji Restoration*, 326.

6. THE SAMURAI'S LAST STAND

83 'It is my intention ...': Harootunian, *Towards Restoration*, 306.
'The Tokugawas were exchanged ...': Pooley, *Japan at the Crossroads*, 38.

84 Council of State created: MacLaren, *A Political History of Japan During the Meiji Era*, 62.
Domestic trivia: Ike, *The Beginnings of Political Democracy in Japan*, 38–9.
'I had in mind ...': Akita, *Foundations of Constitutional Government in Modern Japan*, 8.

85 Satow's complaint: Satow, *A Diplomat in Japan*, 381.

Imperial Rescripts sanctifying Shinto: Holtom, *Modern Japan and Shinto Nationalism*, 5–6; ibid., 60.
86 'Mikado worship was established ...': Pooley, op. cit., 38.
The British Chargé d'Affaires remarked: Beasley, *The Meiji Restoration*, 302.
Ito's and Sanjo's warnings: ibid., 330, 333.
Kido's definitions: ibid., 329.
Iwakura's similar conclusions: ibid., 304.
87 'Two things are essential ...': ibid., 331; MacLaren, op. cit., 75.
Parkes' interpretation: ibid., 332.
88 'The expenditure or budget ...': Borton, *Japan's Modern Century*, 73.
Government Mint established: Roberts, *Mitsui: Three Centuries of Japanese Business*, 95f.
89 'Higo may no longer ...': Beasley, op. cit., 346.
Announcement of the abolition of the *han*: ibid., 347.
Hisamitsu's rage: Mounsey, *The Satsuma Rebellion*, 70.
90 'The frog looking at the world ...': Beasley, op. cit., 315.
'He intended to make ...': Harootunian, op. cit., 378.
'Arbitrarily introduced barbarian customs ...': Black, *Young Japan*, Vol. II, 273.
'We must abandon ...': Mounsey, op. cit., 45; Ike, op. cit., 48.
Iwakura mission's brief: Beasley, op. cit., 367.
91 '... even when foreigners ...': Nish, *Japanese Foreign Policy 1869–1942*, 12.
'If the country ...': Beasley, op. cit., 371.
'A far-reaching scheme ...': ibid., 373.
92 'If a reform is not effected ...': Pittau, *Political Thought in Early Meiji Japan*, 50–1.
Okubo's reply to Kido: ibid., 48-9; Akita, op. cit., 17.
93 The Central Board's veto on discussion: Hackett, op. cit., 97.
'For effrontery and sheer contempt ...': MacLaren, op. cit., 119.
Founding of the Rissisha: Ike, op. cit., 60f.
94 Hisamitsu's resignation: Mounsey, op. cit., 72–3.
The more extreme element dissatisfied; ibid., 81.
'It is a people's duty to overthrow ...': Pittau, op. cit., 68.
95 'Our country differs from all other lands ...': Mounsey, 91–2.
'If in the past ...': Titus, *Palace and Politics in Pre-War Japan*, 20.

7. THE EMPEROR BECOMES 'SACRED AND INVIOLABLE'

96 Influence on Meiji of Motoda Eifu: Shiveley, *Motoda Eifu*, 310f.
97 Arisugawa's constitutional commission: Akita, *Foundations of Constitutional Government in Modern Japan*, 10–11.
Motoda's submissions: Shiveley, op. cit., 322f.
98 'When we seek the reason ...': Ike, *The Beginnings of Political Democracy in Japan*, 70.
Admonition to military personnel: Hackett, *Yamagata Aritomo in the Rise of Modern Japan*, 84.
Order establishing the General Staff: Maxon, *Control of Japanese Foreign Policy*, 22.
Tokyo Azuma's editor: Ike, op. cit., 90.
Yamagata's warning: ibid., 93.
'Constitutional government was not created ...': Akita, op. cit., 12.
'Mobs will rise ...': ibid., 29.
99 Iwakura's and Ito's disapproval: ibid., 11.
'The method to be adopted ...': ibid., 29.
'Of course, initially ...': Hackett, op. cit., 94; Borton, *Japan's Modern Century*, 108.
Ito's and Inoue's suggestions: Pittau, *Political Thought in Early Meiji Japan*, 83, 90.
100 Okuma's proposals: Akita, op. cit., 34.
Ito's reaction: ibid., 36, 51.

The Hokkaido Commission scandal: MacLaren, *A Political History of Japan During the Meiji Era*, 158.

101   'We must settle these problems ...': Akita, op. cit., 43.
       The Councillors' memorial to the Emperor: ibid., 45.
       'Ito and Inoue allowed themselves ...': ibid., 53.

102   'We perceive the tendency ...': Borton, op. cit., 128.
       The people's lack of respect: Akita, op. cit., 61.

103   Roesler's philosophy: Pittau, op. cit., 141.
       'The government plans to reject ...': Akita, op. cit., 56.
       The Emperor 'shall have supreme command ...': Pittau, op. cit., 90.
       'If one gives parliament ...': ibid., 143.
       Motoda's proposals: Shiveley, op. cit., 326.

104   Press criticism: Ike, op. cit., 90, 106.
       'I not only disdain ...': Akita, op. cit., 55.
       Yamagata defined its function ...: Hackett, op. cit., 99.
       Matsukata's economic policies: Johnson, *MITI and the Japanese Miracle*, 84–5; Borton, op. cit., 115.

105   Yamagata's Press restrictions and police reorganisation: McLaren, op. cit., 164; Hackett, op. cit., 104.
       The Peace Preservation Ordinance: MacLaren, *Japanese Government Documents*, 503.
       'If you are not strong enough ...': Ike, op. cit., 185.
       'To put into effect a Prussian-style constitution ...': Pittau, op. cit., 166.

106   'Thanks to the famous German scholars ...': Akita, op. cit., 61; Ike, op. cit., 175–6.
       'I believe this is an absolutely indispensable instrument ...': ibid., 172.
       Court given financial independence: Titus, *Palace and Politics in Pre-War Japan*, 65f.

107   'Is not only against the principle ...': Pittau, op. cit., 163; Akita, op. cit., 65f.
       'Whenever Iwakura and Sanjo ...': Shiveley, op. cit., 319f.

108   Mori's reward: MacLaren, op. cit., 187.
       Ito's guidelines: Pittau, op. cit., 171.
       'Inoue sounded out Roesler's views ...': Akita, op. cit., 235.

109   Heated and protracted discussions: ibid., 237.
       Roesler's final draft: Pittau, op. cit., 151.

110   'From the nature of *kokutai* ...': Ito, *Commentaries on the Constitution*, 10.
       'The first principle of our Constitution ...': Pittau, op. cit., 178.

111   'The Emperor stands above the people ...': Akita, op. cit., 70.
       'Your reform plan, which went beyond ...': ibid., 68.
       In a speech delivered ...: ibid., 73.
       'Ito sought rule by both the monarch and the people ...': ibid., 62–3.

112   'In formulating the restrictions ...': Okuma, *Fifty Years of New Japan*, Vol. I, 128.
       'The executive power is of the Imperial prerogative ...': Hackett, op. cit., 127.
       'In Japan a system ...': Asaji and Pringle, *Lectures Delivered In The Presence of His Imperial Majesty*, 100.
       Imperial Rescript on Education: Hackett, op. cit., 133.

113   'The Monarch is not the ruler ...': Akita, op. cit., 276.

8. FALSE DAWN FOR THE RISING SUN

114   'If we wish the reforms ...': Borton, *Japan's Modern Century*, 71.
       Yamagata's observations of Europe: Hackett, *Yamagata Aritomo in the Rise of Modern Japan*, 51f.

115   'If Yamagata were to receive ...': ibid., 60.
       'The only way for a country like Japan ...': Bergamini, *Japan's Imperial Conspiracy*, 256.

116 Kido's call for a 'recourse to arms': Conroy, *The Japanese Seizure of Korea*, 24; Beasley, *The Meiji Restoration*, 373.
'Our army is presently ...': Hackett, op. cit., 70.
Saigo's plans of conquest: ibid., 31; Borton, op. cit., 88.
Soejima's conversation with Parkes: Jansen, *The Japanese and Sun Yat-Sen*, 23–4.
Meiji's 'warm encouragement': Norman, *The Genyosha*, 265.

117 'No matter what His Majesty says ...': Ike, *The Beginnings of Political Democracy in Japan*, 53.
Yamagata's Army reorganisation: Hackett, op. cit., 72.

118 Private companies invited: Borton, op. cit., 115f.; Ike, op. cit., 74–5.
LeGendre's arguments for territorial expansion: Conroy, op. cit., 38, 389.

119 Soejima's petition to the Throne: ibid., 41.
Li's disillusionment on Japan's motives: Tsiang, *Sino-Japanese Diplomatic Relations*, 5; Ike, op. cit., 49.
The expedition to Formosa: ibid., 24; Conroy, op. cit., 55f.

120 'Unless for the next several years ...': Hackett, op. cit., 74.
'If Japan had not taken steps ...': Sansom, *The Western World and Japan*, 393.

121 Inoue's secret instructions: Conroy, op. cit., 64.
Korea defined as 'self-governing': Hishida, *The International Position of Japan as a Great Power*, 164.
'At last the military foundation ...': Borton, op. cit., 157.

122 'Although Loochoo in itself is insignificant ...': Tsiang, op. cit., 38.
'The Mikado and Ministers were anxious ...': ibid., 44.
'Japan covets Korea and Formosa ...': Stead, *Japan by the Japanese*, 181.

123 The Chief Council's demand to Korea: Conroy, op. cit., 104.
'I can do nothing before finding out ...': Jansen, op. cit., 38.

124 'I find that the Europeans ...': Akita, op. cit., 13; Conroy, op. cit., 112.
'Some Japanese politicians like Goto ...': Stead, op. cit., 189–90; Tsiang, op. cit., 79.

125 'From the very beginning our principle has been *sonno-joi*': Jansen, op. cit., 40.
Takezoe instructed to cultivate Kim: Conroy, op. cit., 143f.; over-zealous: Stead, op. cit., 191.

126 The occasion selected was a dinner ...: Conroy, op. cit., 148f.

127 The Koreans' 'three-hundred-year hatred': Bishop, *Korea and Her Neighbours*, 42.
Okuma put what gloss he could ...: Okuma, *Fifty Years of New Japan*, Vol. I, 108.
The inner cabinet's caution: Conroy, op. cit., 159f.

128 'The Japanese were inside and the Chinese outside ...': ibid., 173.
'It was indeed a victory for Japan': Tsiang, op. cit., 87.

9. DEMOCRACY DEFERRED

130 Yuan 'the biggest man in town': Conroy, *The Japanese Seizure of Korea*, 184.
Criticism of the proposal for mixed courts: Pyle, *The New Generation in Meiji Japan*, 58f., 103–4; Okuma, *Fifty Years of New Japan*, Vol. I, 104.

131 Okuma tricked in the race to greet Yamagata: Hackett, *Yamagata Aritomo in the Rise of Modern Japan*, 121.

132 The Imperial Rescript endorsing Ministers' accountability to the Emperor: ibid., 127–8.
Motoda's acknowledgement of his debt to Yamagata: ibid., 134.
Yamagata's first speech before the House: ibid., 138.

133 Ito's angry reaction: ibid., 141; Akita, *Foundations of Constitutional Government in Modern Japan*, 77f., 242.

134 'European people ridiculed the idea ...': Akita, op. cit., 84.

135 'No matter what is decided ...': ibid., 81.

136 'You may consider this an order . . .': Hackett, op. cit., 148.
Matsukata anecdote: Rikitaro, *The Recent Aims and Political Development of Japan*, 59.
Cabinet division over the military budget: Akita, op. cit., 92f.
137 Yamagata's and Ito's reactions to the dissolution of the Diet: Hackett, op. cit., 149;
Akita, op. cit., 96.
The campaign to rig the election: Norman, *The Genyosha*, 276; Yanaga, *Japan Since Perry*, 218.
138 Shinagawa's transfer to the Privy Council: Hackett, op. cit., 152; Akita, op. cit.,
102; Borton, *Japan's Modern Century*, 201.
New budget impasse: Hackett, op. cit., 154; MacLaren, *A Political History of Japan During the Meiji Era*, 218f.
139 'The appointment or removal of Ministers . . .': MacLaren, op. cit., 224.
140 'The actions taken against the Diet . . .': Akita, op. cit., 116.
'It is useless for the government . . .': Hackett, op. cit., 159.
The Emperor's intervention: Takeuchi, *War and Diplomacy in the Japanese Empire*, 103–4.

10. FIRST RAYS OVER ASIA

141 'On all important military matters . . .': Hackett, *Yamagata Aritomo in the Rise of Modern Japan*, 156–7.
Press enthusiasm for further expansion: Spinks, *Origin of Japanese Interests in Manchuria*, 263.
142 Genyosha 'fire-setters': Conroy, *The Japanese Seizure of Korea*, 227f.; Norman, *The Genyosha*, 281f.
Yamagata's intelligence spadework: Hackett, op. cit., 87, 160; Norman, op. cit., 278.
143 Ito deceived: Conroy, op. cit., 239f.; Hackett, op. cit., 160–1.
Tokyo's instructions to Otori: Conroy, op. cit., 243f; Hackett, op. cit., 161; Akita,
Foundations of Constitutional Government in Modern Japan, 256.
144 The sinking of the *Kowshing*: 'Vladimir', *The China-Japan War*, 350.
145 'They should realise that we are fighting . . .': Pyle, *The New Generation in Meiji Japan*, 173.
'We propose that at the very beginning . . .': Akita, op. cit., 256.
146 'The happiest moment in my life': Hackett, op. cit., 161.
Yamagata's advice to the Emperor: ibid., 163–4.
The Shimonoseki negotiations: 'Vladimir', op. cit., 325; Borton, *Japan's Modern Century*, 207.
147 The propagandists' different account: Okuma, *Fifty Years of New Japan*, Vol. I, 54;
Hishida, *The International Position of Japan as a Great Power*, 186; Okuma, op. cit., 107.
'Their purpose was well concealed . . .': Bishop, *Korea and Her Neighbours*, 28, 210.
Yamagata's petition to the Throne: Hackett, op. cit., 168–9.
148 'In the earliest beginnings of the Empire . . .': Stead, *Japan by the Japanese*, 9.

11. DARK CLOUD

149 Western attempts to mediate: Langer, *The Diplomacy of Imperialism*, 174; *Blackwood's Magazine*, September 1895, 316f.; Yanaga, *Japan since Perry*, 245; Conroy, *The Japanese Seizure of Korea*, 289.
150 Pressure on Japan to retrocede: Kajima, *The Emergence of Japan as a World Power*. 15f.;
Conroy, op. cit., 292f.; Langer, op. cit., 186.
Imperial Rescript to quell protest: Hackett, *Yamagata Aritomo in the Rise of Modern Japan*, 166. (Meiji himself was voted 20 million yen by the Diet 'in gratitude for his wise direction' of the war – Price, *The Son of Heaven*, 182.)

151 'It became to Japan as clear as daylight ...': Asakawa, *The Russo-Japanese Conflict*, 79. Coalition's increase in military expenditure: Borton, *Japan's Modern Century*, 210; Hackett, op. cit., 169; Beasley, *The Modern History of Japan*, 164–5; Asakawa, op. cit., 80.
    Inoue forces 'reforms' on Korea: Conroy, op. cit., 271; Bishop, *Korea and Her Neighbours*, Vol. II, 35–6, 59; Borton, op. cit., 207.
152 Application for a loan: Conroy, op. cit., 281f.
    Mutsu's caution: ibid., 298–9.
153 Pak's over-confidence: ibid., 300f. Inoue replaced: ibid., 284, 303f.
    'The Japanese government would not fail to protect ...': Bishop, op. cit., 61.
154 Acquittal in spite of the evidence: Conroy, op. cit., 318; Bishop, op. cit., 71; Borton, op. cit., 216.
    Apologists' field day: Okuma, *Fifty Years of New Japan*, Vol. I, 119; Hishida, *The International Position of Japan as a Great Power*, 188; Asakawa, op. cit., 260.
    Korea into Russian protection: Conroy, op. cit., 322f.; Sands, *Undiplomatic Memories*, 67–8; Bishop, op. cit., 182; Hackett, op. cit., 174.
155 Russian loan to establish Chinese Eastern Railway: Borton, op. cit., 217–18; Langer, op. cit., 188, 401f.
156 Other railway concessions to the West: Langer, op. cit., 454; Asakawa, op. cit., 130; Yanaga, op. cit., 257.
    'I ardently hope that such a union ...': Conroy, *The Japanese Frontier in Hawaii*, 52.
    'postpone assuming office ...': Hackett, op. cit., 178.
157. 'If you organise a political party ...': ibid., 182f.
158 'I long ago perceived that he was not merely a soldier ...': ibid., 185.
159 Ozaki misrepresented: Yanaga, op. cit., 262.
    Horse-trading with Itagaki: Hackett, op. cit., 191f.; Yanaga, op. cit., 263; Akita, *Foundations of Constitutional Government in Modern Japan*, 124.
160 Other ploys to secure a majority: Yanaga, op. cit., 264; Titus, *Palace and Politics in Pre-War Japan*, 128; MacLaren, *A Political History of Japan During the Meiji Era*, 258.
161 Hoshi calls the price: MacLaren, op. cit., 264f.; Akita, op. cit., 142.
    Yamagata's secret message to Meiji: Hackett, op. cit., 199.
    Imperial Ordinances: Yanaga, op. cit., 266; Borton, op. cit., 146.

12. BLACK DRAGON

162 Russia the target: Langer, *The Diplomacy of Imperialism*, 456; Brown, *Nationalism in Japan*, 135.
    Japanese take-over of Korea's economy: Conroy, *The Japanese Seizure of Korea*, 450f.; Sands, *Undiplomatic Memories*, 206; Asakawa, *The Russo-Japanese Conflict*, 274f.; Langer, *The Diplomacy of Imperialism*, 690–1.
163 Lea, *The Valor of Ignorance*, 249, 290; MacLaren, *A Political History*, 280.
164 Chinese rebels welcomed: Miyazaki, *My Thirty-Three Years' Dream*, 47; Jansen, *The Japanese and Sun Yat-sen*, 52f.
    The Philippines adventure: Jansen, op. cit., 70f.
165 Amoy: Jansen, ibid., 85f.; *Opportunists in South China during the Boxer Rebellion*, 243; Nish, *Japan's Indecision during the Boxer Disturbances*, 450.
    The Boxer Rebellion: Yanaga, *Japan since Perry*, 281f.; Langer, op. cit., 692f.; Hackett, *Yamagata Aritomo in the Rise of Modern Japan*, 205.
167 Amoy again: Jansen, *The Japanese and Sun Yat-sen*, 102–3; *Opportunists in South China during the Boxer Rebellion*, 246; Nish, op. cit., 450.
168 Yamagata's resignation: Hackett, op. cit., 207–8; Jansen, *Opportunists in South China*, 248; Nish, op. cit., 460.
169 Russian consolidation in Manchuria: Langer, op. cit., 696f.; Asakawa, op. cit., 143f.;

Gapanovich, *Sino-Russian Relations in Manchuria*, 459; Yanaga, op. cit., 284.
171 Japanese alarm: Jansen, *The Japanese and Sun Yat-sen*, 94; Okamoto, *The Japanese Oligarchy and the Russo-Japanese War*, 58f.
'A peaceful agreement with Russia will mean a defeat . . .': Langer, op. cit., 716.
Founding of The Black Dragon: Jansen, *The Japanese and Sun Yat-sen*, 110; Okamoto, op. cit., 61.
172. Budget forced through: Hackett, op. cit., 209; MacLaren, *A Political History of Japan During the Meiji Era*, 275; Yanaga, op. cit., 269.
Rising tension with Russia: Langer, op. cit., 720f.; Okamoto, op. cit., 62.
Secret conclave with the Emperor: Kajima, *The Emergence of Japan as a World Power*, 107.
173 'The Curtain Cabinet': Hackett, op. cit., 211; Okamoto, op. cit., 25.

13. ALLIANCE WITH BRITAIN, VICTORY OVER RUSSIA

177 'Sooner or later there will be a collision . . .': Hackett, *Yamagata Aritomo in the Rise of Modern Japan*, 215–16.
'In order to oppose Russia . . .'; Takeuchi, *War and Diplomacy in the Japanese Empire*, 124.
178 British offer of a loan: Nish, *Japanese Foreign Policy*, 275.
Ito hoodwinked: Hackett, op. cit., 218–19; Pooley, *The Secret Memoirs of Count Hayashi Tadasu*, 140f.; Langer, *The Diplomacy of Imperialism*, 763f.; Nish, *Anglo-Japanese Alliance*, 194.
179 'I certainly wish . . .': Hackett, op. cit., 218–19.
180 Alliance signed: Borton, *Japan's Modern Century*, 232; Asakawa, *The Russo-Japanese Conflict*, 127–8; Nish, *Anglo-Japanese Alliance*, 224f.; Hishida, *The International Position of Japan as a Great Power*, 225.
Detached observers: Contemporary Review March 1902, *China Station*, 433; Chung Fu-chang, *Anglo-Japanese Alliance*, 96–7.
181 Russian reaction: Asakawa, op. cit., 210f.; Langer, op. cit., 751; Gapanovich, *Sino-Russian Relations in Manchuria*, 462.
Budget compromise: Hackett, op. cit., 220–1; MacLaren, *A Political History of Japan During the Meiji Era*, 282f.
182 Ito's resignation: Okamoto, *The Japanese Oligarchy and the Russo-Japanese War*, 78; Hackett, op. cit., 224.
183 New Russian assertiveness: Asakawa, op. cit., 235f.; Yanaga, *Japan since Perry*, 304; Gapanovich, op. cit., 466f.
184 'There is no longer room for discussion . . .': Okamoto, op. cit., 251.
Komura's memorandum: ibid., 77f.; Asakawa, op. cit., 298f.; Okamoto, op. cit., 253.
185 Russia's response: Asakawa, op. cit., 301–2; Gapanovich, op. cit., 471.
186 'What positive action has our government taken . . .': Okamoto, op. cit., 86.
Kodama's new post: Hackett, op. cit., 225; Jansen, *The Japanese and Sun Yat-sen*, 110; Okamoto, op. cit., 62.
187 Toyama's visit to Ito: Norman, *The Genyosha*, 272; Okamoto, op. cit., 254, 84.
Press accusations of weakness: ibid., 86f.
188 Kono's sleight of hand: MacLaren, op. cit., 287; Okamoto, op. cit., 90.
'Where in the world is Japan . . .': Asakawa, op. cit., 322.
189 Undeclared war: Okamoto, op. cit., 98f.; Asakawa, op. cit., 343f., 354; Okuma, *Fifty Years of New Japan*, Vol. I, 119; Titus, *Palace and Politics in Pre-War Japan*, 317; Asakawa, op. cit., 354.
190 Port Arthur captured: Hackett, op. cit., 227; Bergamini, *Japan's Imperial Conspiracy*, 281–2; Hargreaves, *Red Sun Rising*, 163.
Peace feelers: Okamoto, op. cit., 261.
192 Treaty of Portsmouth: ibid., 123f., 143f., 264; Brown, *Nationalism in Japan*, 144;

Pooley, *Japan at the Crossroads*, 202.
194 'Japan required peace ...': Kajima, *The Emergence of Japan as a World Power*, 174.
Negotiations with Britain and America: ibid., 153f., 333.

14. KOREA AND BEYOND

195 Collective apoplexy: Okamoto, *The Japanese Oligarchy and the Russo-Japanese War*, 169f., 203f.; Tetsuo, *Conflict in Modern Japanese History*, 258.
197 Saionji-Katsura deal: Okamoto, op. cit., 135, 187f., Pooley, *Japan at the Crossroads*, 148.
198 Martial Law: Okamoto, op. cit., 215f.; Hackett, *Yamagata Aritomo in the Rise of Modern Japan*, 231.
Missions to China and Korea: Kajima, *The Emergence of Japan as a World Power*, 335; Borton, *Japan's Modern Century*, 241f.; Takeuchi, *War and Diplomacy in the Japanese Empire*, 161; MacLaren, *A Political History of Japan During the Meiji Era*, 312.
199 'The Plan of National Defence': Hackett, op. cit., 235–6; Borton, op. cit., 259.
200 Dubious practice: MacLaren, op. cit., 308–9.
Rapprochement with Russia: Pooley, *Japan's Foreign Policies*, 47; Edwards, *Great Britain and the Manchurian Railway Question*, 742; Pooley, *The Secret Memoirs of Count Hayashi Tadasu*, 260–1; Yanaga, *Japan since Perry*, 337.
201 Collaboration in Manchuria: Pooley, *The Secret Memoirs of Count Hayashi Tadasu*, 260–1, 321f.; Kajima, op. cit., 177f.
South Manchuria Railway established: Asakawa, *Japan in Manchuria*, 212, 269f.; Yanaga, op. cit., 334; McMurray, *Treaties and Agreements With and Concerning China*, Vol. I, 551.
202 Fakumen-Hsinmintun rival line: Kajima, op. cit., 193; Asakawa, op. cit., 285–6; Nish, *Alliance in Decline*, 17; Yanaga, op. cit., 341; Asakawa, op. cit., 271.
203 Attempt on Meiji's life: Ike, *Kotoku: Advocate of Direct Action*, 222f.
Yamagata's 'trickery': Hackett, op. cit., 239; MacLaren, op. cit., 327.
204 'Misunderstanding' with America: Asakawa, op. cit., 277; Yanaga, op. cit., 434f., 339.
205 The Root-Takahira Agreement: Reid, *The Manchu Abdication and the Powers*, 13; McMurray, op. cit., 532, 769; Nish, *Alliance in Decline*, 25; Reid, op. cit., 17f.; Edwards, op. cit., 744–5.
206 1904 decision to annex Korea: Kajima, op. cit., 156.
Ito as Resident-General: Conroy, *The Japanese Seizure of Korea*, 337, 419f.; Takeuchi, op. cit., 162.
The King's abdication: Conroy, op. cit., 347f.; Takeuchi, op. cit., 163; Young, *Japan under Taisho Tenno*, 66; Jansen, *The Japanese and Sun Yat-sen*, 128.
208 Ito replaced: Conroy, op. cit., 424f., 36f.; MacLaren, op. cit., 319; Bergamini, *Japan's Imperial Conspiracy*, 284.
209 '... fortunately he was invited ...': Conroy, op. cit., 428–9.
210 'Agreement' finalised: Conroy, op. cit., 430f.; Takeuchi, op. cit., 165.
Conclusions in London: Reid, op. cit., 70; Gooch, *British Official Documents on the Origins of the War*, Vol. VIII, 489–90; Pooley, *Japan's Foreign Policies*, 40.
211 Terauchi in Seoul: Conroy, op. cit., 381; Takeuchi, op. cit., 165.
Excuses advanced: Ishii, *Diplomatic Commentaries*, 80; Reid, op. cit., 376; Pooley, *Japan's Foreign Policies*, 13; Conroy, op. cit., 389.
212 South Korean President's visit to Tokyo: *Observer*, 9 September 1984, *The Times*, 3 September 1984.

15. SPEEDING REVOLUTION IN CHINA

213 Toyama's expansion plans: Jansen, *The Japanese and Sun Yat-Sen*, 111f.; Weale, *The Truth about China and Japan*, 50.
The Sworn Brotherhood: Sharman, *Sun Yat-sen*, 79f., 99; Jansen, op. cit., 117f.; Yanaga, *Japan Since Perry*, 348; Conroy, *Government v Patriot*, 33.

214 Early disappointments: Jansen, op. cit., 125f.; Sharman, op. cit., 107; Wilson, *Radical Nationalist in Japan*, 50; Reid, *The Manchu Abdication and the Powers*, 335; Pooley, *The Secret Memoirs of Count Hayashi Tadasu*, 289; Okamoto, *The Japanese Oligarchy and the Russo-Japanese War*, 73; Jansen, op. cit., 253.

215 Railway concessions for the West: Reid, op. cit., 25f.; Edwards, *Great Britain and the Manchurian Railway Question*, 749; Kajima, *The Emergence of Japan as a World Power*, 195; Nish, *Alliance in Decline*, 30; Yanaga, op. cit., 341.

217 Japan and Russia intervene: Pooley, *Japan's Foreign Policies*, 97; Edwards, op. cit., 763f.; Reid, op. cit., 79–80.
Anglo-Japanese Alliance renewed: Nish, op. cit., 40f.; Kajima, op. cit., 206f.; Nish, op. cit., 83, 51; Reid, op. cit., 235.

218 Four-Power Consortium: Reid, op. cit., 194, 232.
End of the Manchus: Sharman, op. cit., 109f.; Reid, op. cit., 395–6.

220 Tokyo electric light franchise: MacLaren, *A Political History of Japan During the Meiji Era*, 337.
Toyama's support for Sun: Jansen, op. cit., 135f.; McAleavy, *A Dream of Tartary*, 160.

221 Yamagata for Yuan: Hackett, *Yamagata Aritomo in the Rise of Modern Japan*, 272f.
Cabinet compromise: Masaru, *Japan's Response to the Chinese Revolution*, 214f.; Pooley, *Japan's Foreign Policies*, 65.

222 Sun-Yuan rapprochement: Sharman, op. cit., 126f.; Yim, *Yuan Shih-k'ai and the Japanese*, 68; Jansen, op. cit., 145f., 255; Masaru, op. cit., 218f.; Reid, op. cit., 274; Pooley, op. cit., 66–7.

224 Death of Meiji: Pooley, *Japan at the Crossroads*, 64; Bergamini, *Japan's Imperial Conspiracy*, 274f.; Yutaka, *The National Ideals of the Japanese People*, xxviii.

225 Katsura's return engineered: MacLaren, op. cit., 343–4; Pooley, *Japan's Foreign Policies*, 77; Hackett, op. cit., 252f.; Bergamini, op. cit., 294.

226 His downfall: Hackett, op. cit., 258f.; Pooley, *Japan at the Crossroads*, 153; Young, *Japan under Taisho Tenno*, 29.

227 Naval building programme: ibid., 39f.; Nish, op. cit., 87.

228 'Japan is determined on having permanent, exclusive possession...': Dull, *Count Kato and the Twenty-one Demands*, 152f.

229 Sun turns again to Japan: Jansen, op. cit., 158f.; Sharman, op. cit., 146, 156f.; Young, op. cit., 41.

230 *Casus belli*: Jansen, op. cit., 168.
'Positive measures': Kajima, op. cit., 366; Jansen, op. cit., 169f.; Sharman, op. cit., 191f.; Wilson, op. cit., 55.

231 'Japan is going to take advantage ...': Reinsch, *An American Diplomat in China*, 129; Sharman, op. cit., 194; Borton, *Japan's Modern Century*, 279; Pooley, *Japan's Foreign Policies*, 52–3, 130; Hackett, op. cit., 283.

16. WORLD WAR ONE: PERFECT CAMOUFLAGE

233 Sir Edward Grey: Nish, *Alliance in Decline*, 116f.; La Fargue, *China and the World War*, 9f.
Japan's reply and ultimatum: Nish, op. cit., 119f.; Hackett, *Yamagata Aritomo in the Rise of Modern Japan*, 276; La Fargue, op. cit., 14.

235 Curzon's suppression: Dignan, *Australian and British Relations with Japan*, 144f.
'It would shame me more ...': Nish, op. cit., 135.
Japan's motives: Fujisawa, *The Recent Aims and Political Development of Japan*, 183, 78;
Takeuchi, *War and Diplomacy in the Japanese Empire*, 178; Ishii, *Diplomatic Commentaries*, 84.

236 Intervention of the Elder Statesmen: Hackett, op. cit., 277f.; Takeuchi, op. cit., 179.

237 Tsingtao campaign: Nish, op. cit., 126f.; Takeuchi, op. cit., 198; Atkinson, *The History of the South Wales Borderers*, 73.

238 Grey's acquiescence: Nish, op. cit., 145.
Seizure of the Tsingtao-Tsinan railway: La Fargue, op. cit., 23; McMurray, *Treaties and Agreements With and Concerning China*, Vol. II, 1153.
Twenty-One Demands: Hackett, op. cit., 281f.; Borton, *Japan's Modern Century*, 256;
Jansen, *The Japanese and Sun Yat-sen*, 181; La Fargue, op. cit., 44f.

239 Reaction of Reinsch and the *North China Herald*: La Fargue, op. cit., 47.
'Outwardly and inwardly filthy': Pooley, *Japan's Foreign Policies*, 96.

240 'Why does Japan treat China ...': Dull, *Count Kato and the Twenty-one Demands*, 157.
Japanese denials: Pooley, op. cit., 151; La Fargue, op. cit., 47; Reinsch, *An American Diplomat in China*, 135.
The negotiations: Kajima, *The Emergence of Japan as a World Power*, 370; Borton, op. cit., 256; La Fargue, op. cit., 65f.; Jansen, op. cit., 184; Young, *Japan under Taisho Tenno*, 78.

241 Western reaction: La Fargue, op. cit., 74–5; Ishii, op. cit., 85f.

242 Domestic criticism: Jansen, op. cit., 186; Hackett, op. cit., 286f.

243 Yuan as Emperor: Lowe, *Great Britain, Japan and the Fall of Yuan Shih-k'ai*, 708, 715;
Yim, *Yuan Shih-K'ai and the Japanese*, 67; Ishii, op. cit., 94–5.

244 Japanese help for rebels: Lowe, op. cit., 714; Yim, op. cit., 68; Jansen, op. cit., 195–6; Yim, op. cit., 70–1; Reinsch, op. cit., 190–1; Young, op. cit., 88; Storry, *Double Patriots*, 19.

245 Yuan's fall and death: Yim, op. cit., 73; Young, op. cit., 87.
Fourth Russo-Japanese Agreement: Hackett, op. cit., 292f.; Yanaga, *Japan since Perry*, 362; Kajima, op. cit., 240f.; Ishii, op. cit., 106.

246 Okuma ousted: Hackett, op. cit., 298f.; Jansen, op. cit., 197.
Japan's double game: Iklé, *German-Japanese Peace Negotiations during World War One*, 65; Tuchman, *The Zimmerman Telegram*, 96–7; Nish, op. cit., 150, 171, 206.

247 'If we have made an unpleasant virtue ...': Nish, op. cit., 209.

17. VERSAILLES: EASY PICKINGS

248 Nishihara Loans: Reinsch, *An American Diplomat in China*, 225; Young, *Japan under Taisho Tenno*, 99.

250 Lansing-Ishii Note: Reinsch, op. cit., 269, 307f.; La Fargue, *China and the World War*, 132f.; Ishii, *Diplomatic Commentaries*, 112f.; Kajima, *The Emergence of Japan as a World Power*, 253.

251 More loans: Reinsch, op. cit., 301; La Fargue, op. cit., 112; Young, op. cit., 101, 120; Reinsch, op. cit., 318; Yanaga, *Japan since Perry*, 364; Johnson, *MITI and the Japanese Miracle*, 208.

252 'Japan's political and economic supremacy in China': Morley, *The Japanese Thrust into Siberia*, 29–30.

253 Soviet threat: ibid., 50–150; La Fargue, 168.

254 'In order to create a military spirit ...': Morley, op. cit., 156.

255 'Aggressive defence': ibid., 214, 188f.; La Fargue, op. cit., 169.
International expedition: Morley, op. cit., 263; Borton, *Japan's Modern Century*, 286;
Takeuchi, *War and Diplomacy in the Japanese Empire*, 207–8.

256   Second Japanese force: Morley, op. cit., 265f.; Borton, op. cit., 286f.
      'The Empire anticipates . . .': Morley, op. cit., 307.
257   Versailles: Yanaga, op. cit., 367; Reinsch, op. cit., 333; Nish, *Alliance in Decline*, 271.

18.   ENTER HIROHITO

263   Domestic unrest: Jansen, *Japan and China*, 317; Yanaga, *Japan since
      Perry*, 387f; Young, *Japan under Taisho Tenno*, 151, 239, 171.
264   'Maintaining law and order': Young, op. cit., 173, 233; Storry, *Double Patriots*,
      28; Yanaga, op. cit., 491; Young, op. cit., 252; Hackett, *Yamagata Aritomo in the
      Rise of Modern Japan*, 326.
265   'A most misunderstood man . . .': Fujisawa, *The Recent Aims and Political Development
      of Japan*, 32.
      'get rid of foreign products . . .': Pooley, *Japan's Foreign Policies*, 19.
      Taisho's disorder: Bergamini, *Japan's Imperial Conspiracy*, 306; Mosley, *Hirohito,
      Emperor of Japan*, 35.
      'A good physical specimen': Price, *The Son of Heaven*, 10; Mosley, op. cit., 29.
      'China is degenerate . . .': Bergamini, op. cit., 298.
266   Betrothal: Mosley, op. cit., 41f.; Young, op. cit., 156; Hackett, op. cit., 338.
      Tour: Bergamini, op. cit., 317f.; Jansen, op. cit., 344.
268   New ultranationalists: Borton, *Japan's Modern Century*, 326; Wilson, *Radical Nationalist
      in Japan*, 86.
      Kita's *Plan*. Tsunoda, *Sources of Japanese Tradition*, 775f.; Wilson, op. cit., 70f.
269   Eyes on Australia, Siberia, S. America: Storry, op. cit., 38; Tanin, *Militarism and
      Fascism in Japan*, 98.
      'Of all Japan's *Rightists* . . .': Jansen, op. cit., 340.
270   'We do not consider it sufficient . . .': Wilson, op. cit., 98.
      Seiyukai's desperate methods: Young, op. cit., 280.
271   Washington Conference: Yanaga, op. cit., 423f.; Nish, *Alliance in Decline*, 334;
      Young, op. cit., 256; Borton, op. cit., 303.
272   Japanese dissatisfaction: Nish, op. cit., 385; Yanaga, op. cit., 427.
      New defence programme: Takeuchi, *War and Diplomacy in the Japanese Empire*, 237;
      Bergamini, op. cit., 383.
273   Earthquake scapegoats: Taylor, *Shadows of the Rising Sun*, 60; Young, op. cit., 300.
      Assassination attempt: Bergamini, op. cit., 337.
274   Toyama a wedding guest: Bush, *Land of the Dragonfly*, 133.
      New patriotic societies: Yanaga, op. cit., 493; Storry, op. cit., 35.
      Colonists to the Americas: Yanaga, op. cit., 445; Seth, *Secret Servants*, 188.
      'If Japan is only concerned with . . .': Public Records Office, London, ADM 1 18331.
275   'Dangerous Thoughts': Yanaga, op. cit., 476; Young, op. cit., 328.
      'Mitsubishi Government': Yanaga, op. cit., 316; Young, op. cit., 318: Johnson, *MITI
      and the Japanese Miracle*, 94f.
      Treaty with Russia: Yanaga, op. cit., 461; Nicolaevsky, *Russia, Japan and the
      Pan-Asiatic Movement*, 284.
276   Army reforms: Ogata, *Defiance in Manchuria*, 26; Yanaga, op. cit., 405; Mosley,
      op. cit., 96.
      Chemical and bacteriological research: Bergamini, op. cit., 341; *Observer*, 10 April
      1983, 24 June 1984, 11 August 1985; *Guardian*, 17 September 1982; *Daily Telegraph*,
      8 April 1982, 16 August 1984; Television South, *Did the Emperor Know?*, 13 August 1985.
277   Secret funds for the Seiyukai: Tanin, op. cit., 176.
278   Chiang in control: Yanaga, op. cit., 449–50; Sharman, *Sun Yat-sen*, 302f.; Yoshihashi,
      Conspiracy at Mukden, 131; Jansen, op. cit., 297; Boyle, *China and Japan at War*, 21;
      Young, *Imperial Japan*, 15.

279 Fall of Wakatsuki Cabinet: Yanaga, op. cit., 451, 410f; Young, *Imperial Japan*, 22; Johnson, op. cit., 101–2, 118.
280 'My war is Japan's war ...': Bergamini, op. cit., 357.
    Mori's Shantung triumph: Yoshihashi, op. cit., 14f.; Bergamini, op. cit., 357.

19 EXIT DEMOCRACY

281 Eastern Regions Conference: Yoshihashi, *Conspiracy at Mukden*, 21f.; Stephan, *The Tanaka Memorial: Authentic or Spurious?*, 733f.
283 Bargain with Chiang: Yoshihashi, op. cit., 34; Bergamini, *Japan's Imperial Conspiracy*, 361.
    Crackdown on opposition: Young, *Imperial Japan*, 36–7.
    Shantung campaign: Yanaga, *Japan since Perry*, 455; Morley, *Japan Erupts*, 129; Yoshihashi, op. cit., 34.
284 'Said to me in an overbearing tone ...': Yoshihashi, op. cit., 36.
    Target Manchuria: Yoshihashi, op. cit., 39–40; Morley, op. cit., 140.
285 Tanaka's veto: Yoshihashi, op. cit., 42–3; Ogata, *Defiance in Manchuria*, 16.
    Chang assassinated: Yoshihashi, op. cit., 41f.; Dull, *The Assassination of Chang Tso-lin*, 455.
286 Son takes over: Young, op. cit., 45; Iriye, *Chang Hsüeh-liang and the Japanese*, 35f.; Yoshihashi, op. cit., 54; Snow, *Far Eastern Front*, 66.
287 'In the case of monarchies ...': Quigley, *Japanese Government and Politics*, 71.
    'Infringing the Imperial Prerogative ...': Takeuchi, *War and Diplomacy in the Japanese Empire*, 265f.; Quigley, op. cit., 71.
288 'What fools! ...': Yoshihashi, op. cit., 50.
    'Our plans': Dull, op. cit., 457; Crowley, *Japanese Army Factionalism in the Early 1930s*, 313.
    Komoto's protectors: Dull, op. cit., 458; Yoshihashi, op. cit., 58–9.
289 Chang-Chiang accord: Yoshihashi, op. cit., 56; Bergamini, op. cit., 370; Young, op. cit., 45.
290 Tanaka's embarrassment: Young, op. cit., 46–7; Yoshihashi, op. cit., 60.
    'War with China and the United States ...': Ogata, op. cit., 198; Bergamini, op. cit., 373.
291 Pyrrhic victory: Borton, *Japan's Modern Century*, 314; Young, op. cit., 49.
    Ambassador's murder: Yoshihashi, op. cit., 120–1.
292 Naval Treaty debate: Yoshihashi, op. cit., 63–4; SMayer-Oakes, *Fragile Victory*, 95; Yanaga, op. cit., 465.
    Dependence on economic strength: Mayer-Oakes, op. cit., 85; Morley, op. cit., 35; Johnson, *MITI and the Japanese Miracle*, 110.
293 'for the sake of world peace ...': Morley, op. cit., 36.
    Kato's opposition: Morley, op. cit., 41f.; Yoshihashi, op. cit., 67f.; Mayer-Oakes, 111, 121; Morley, op. cit., 59, 70–1.
295 Takarabe's return: Morley, op. cit., 86; Mayer-Oakes, 132, 255, 158.
    Supreme War Council won round: Morley, o. cit., 97, 105–6.
296 Short-lived triumph: ibid., 240; Takeuchi, op. cit., 324; Mayer-Oakes, op. cit., 115, 253f.
297 Young officer radicals: Storry, op. cit., 54; Yoshihashi, op. cit., 96f.
298 Konoye and Kido: Mayer-Oakes, op. cit., 276; Titus, *Palace and Politics in Pre-War Japan*, 196; Maxon, *Control of Japanese Foreign Policy*, 9, 224.
299 'We feel suffocated ...': Ogata, op. cit., 35.
    Mori's planned coup: Yanaga, op. cit., 498; Yoshihashi, op. cit., 87f.

20. KWANTUNG ARMY STEALS A MARCH

302 Occupation plans: Ramsdell, *The Nakamura Incident and the Japanese Foreign Office,* 52–3; Yoshihashi, *Conspiracy at Mukden,* 139; Ogata, *Defiance in Manchuria,* 42f.; Morley, *Japan Erupts,* 154f. 149f., 166f.

303 Situations Estimate: Morley, op. cit., 174–5, 252.

304 General Outline: ibid., 176; Ogata, op. cit., 54.
Conspirators impatient: Ogata, op. cit., 50f.; Yoshihashi, op. cit., 133–4; Colegrove, *Militarism in Japan,* 29; Storry, *Double Patriots,* 73.
Nakamura Incident: Ramsdell, op. cit., 53f; Causton, *Militarism and Foreign Policy in Japan,* 141; Yoshihashi, op. cit., 147.

305 Commanders' Conference: Ogata, op. cit., 56; Yoshihashi, op. cit., 105; Morley, op. cit., 185; Ogata, op. cit., 206; Ramsdell, op. cit., 57; Young, *Imperial Japan,* 73.

306 All set: Ramsdell, op. cit., 62; Morley, op. cit., 183f.; Takeuchi, *War and Diplomacy in the Japanese Empire,* 347; Morley, op. cit., 196–7.

307 'A plot is afoot': Morley, op. cit., 201f.; Maxon, *Control of Japanese Foreign Policy,* 79; Storry, op. cit., 76; Snow, *Far Eastern Front,* 24; Takeuchi, op. cit., 348; Yoshihashi, op. cit., 149, 207; Morley, op. cit., 193, 204.

308 Tatekawa's cover: Yoshihashi, op. cit., 155f.; Morley, op. cit., 205, 224f.

309 Mukden seized: Morley, op. cit., 227f.: Yoshihashi, op. cit., 160f.; Causton, op. cit., 149; League of Nations, *Report of the Lytton Commission,* 71; Snow, op. cit., 73.

311 First reactions in Tokyo: Morley, op. cit., 242f.; Maxon, op. cit., 236; Yoshihashi, 171.

312 Honjo constrained: Ogata, op. cit., 60; Morley, op. cit., 252f.; Yoshihashi, op. cit., 178; Morley, op. cit., 245–6.

313 Promises of containment: Morley, op. cit., 253; Willoughby, *The Sino-Japanese Controversy and the League of Nations,* 30.
Korean Army given the wink: Yoshihashi, op. cit., 172f.; Maxon, op. cit., 83–4; Ogata, op. cit., 61f.; Takeuchi, op. cit., 352; Morley, op. cit., 247.

315 Cabinet hamstrung: Morley, op. cit., 248f.; Takeuchi, op. cit., 356; Willoughby, op. cit., 50; Ogata, op. cit., 69–70; Morley, op. cit., 261f., 251; Ogata, op. cit., 66.

316 Hirohito's connivance: Yoshihashi, op. cit., 181f.; Ogata, op. cit., 66; Price, *The Son of Heaven,* 173; Maxon, op. cit., 85.

21. 'MANCHUKUO'

317 League of Nations: Willoughby, *The Sino-Japanese Controversy and the League of Nations,* 57f.
'The army in Manchuria was proceeding without authorisation . . .': Ogata, *Defiance in Manchuria,* 72.

318 Plan Two: Ogata, op. cit., 76f.; Yoshihashi, *Conspiracy at Mukden,* 180; Willoughby, op. cit., 69f.
'Why on earth don't we withdraw . . .': Yoshihashi, op. cit., 190, 211.

319 Conspirators unrestrained: Ogata, op. cit., 80–1; Yoshihasi, op. cit., 179.

320 Chinchow bombed: Yoshihasi, op. cit., 191; Willoughby, op. cit., 79f.; Morley, *Japan Erupts,* 289; Ogata, op. cit., 87f.; Willoughby, op. cit., 110, 132.
'Bombing those who obstruct reconnaissance . . .': Ogata, op. cit., 82.

321 'We are in real trouble . . .': Yoshihashi, op. cit., 192–3.
October plot: Ogata, op. cit., 92f.; Titus, *Palace and Politics in Pre-War Japan,* 93; Storry, *Double Patriots,* 90; Yoshihashi, op. cit., 195f.; Morley, op. cit., 328.

323 Operation 'Henry': Morley, op. cit., 329f.; Ogata, op. cit., 122; Bergamini, *Japan's Imperial Conspiracy,* 451; McAleavy, *A Dream of Tartary,* 202.
Northern front: Morley, op. cit., 267f.; Ogata, op. cit., 108f.; Yoshihashi, op. cit., 212–13.

326 Doihara's diversion: Morley, op. cit., 292f.; Young, *Imperial Japan*, 111; Yoshihashi, op. cit., 217; Snow, *Far Eastern Front*, 122.
327 Commission of Inquiry: Ogata, op. cit., 115f.; Willoughby, op. cit., 162f
328 Saionji bitterly observed ...; Ogata, op. cit., 106.
     Cabinet undermined: Yoshihasi, op. cit., 223; Bergamini, op. cit., 455; Morley, op. cit., 299; Ogata, op. cit., 138–9.
329 Southern thrust: Willoughby, op. cit., 205f.; Morley, op. cit., 304.
330 'Independence' for Manchuria: Willoughby, op. cit., 365; Morley, op. cit., 333–4; Ogata, op. cit., 140–1; McAleavy, op. cit., 203; Storry, op. cit., 116–17; Seth, *Secret Servants*, 118f.; Snow, op. cit., 225; Ogata, op. cit., 130, 123; McAleavy, op. cit., 217; Snow, op. cit., 264; Boyle, *China and Japan at War*, 11.
331 Lytton Commission: Ogata, op. cit., 144; Willoughby, 370, 415–16; Young, op. cit., 147; Yanaga, *Japan since Perry*, 561; Takeuchi, *War and Diplomacy in the Japanese Empire*, 381f.
332 Left in no doubt; Ogata, op. cit., 159f.
333 No cause for worry: Takeuchi, op. cit., 389f.; Ogata, op. cit., 161f.
     Findings: Willoughby, op. cit., 25, 395, 367, 400; Yanaga, op. cit., 562; Ogata, op. cit., 171–2.
334 Reaction in Tokyo: Takeuchi, op. cit., 399f.; Willoughby, op. cit., 408f.
     'The day is fast approaching ..': Matsuoka, *Dissolve the Political Parties*, 661f.
335 Jehol campaign: Bergamini, op. cit., 537; Snow, op. cit., 240f.; Morley, *The China Quagmire*, 11f.
336 Withdrawal from the League: Ogata, op. cit., 174; Takeuchi, op. cit., 418; Willoughby, op. cit., 597.

22. DISSENSION IN THE RANKS

337 'The Manchurian Incident has developed as expected ..': Bergamini, *Japan's Imperial Conspiracy*, 463.
338 The Shanghai 'Incident': Young, *Imperial Japan*, 132f.; Snow, *Far Eastern Front*, 170f.; Morley, *Japan Erupts*, 307f.; Bergamini, op. cit., 464f.
340 World concern: Willoughby, *The Sino-Japanese Controversy and the League of Nations*, 321f.; Mosley, *Hirohito, Emperor of Japan*, 123; Morley, op. cit., 310f.; Young, op. cit., 143; Maxon, *Control of Japanese Foreign Policy*, 89.
342 Restless radicals: Tanin, *Militarism and Fascism in Japan*, 185; Crowley, *Japanese Army Factionalism in the 1930s*, 314; Byas, *Government by Assassination*, 208; Storry, *Double Patriots*, 114; Ogata, *Defiance in Manchuria*, 147.
343 May 15th Plot; Storry, op. cit., 106f.; Ogata, op. cit., 150–1, 230; Byas, op. cit., 28–9; Bergamini, op. cit., 512.
345 'Chichibu for Hirohito': Young, op. cit., 190f.; Storry, op. cit., 89, 112; Ogata, op. cit., 152; Shillony, *Revolt in Japan*, 97–8; Titus, *Palace and Politics in Pre-War Japan*, 305; Storry, op. cit., 129f.; Shillony, op. cit., 107–8; Byas, op. cit., 43; Maxon, op. cit., 91.
346 'Japan is the greatest country in the world ..': Byas, op. cit., 61.
347 Military Cabinet: Ogata, op. cit., 155; Storry, op. cit., 127; Takeuchi, *War and Diplomacy in the Japanese Empire*, 384; Colegrove, *Militarism in Japan*, 49; Tanin, op. cit., 187; Crowley, op. cit., 315.
348 Military budget doubled: Young, op. cit., 185; Colegrove, op. cit., 43; Johnson, *MITI and the Japanese Miracle*, 119–20.
     Kokutai revived: Storry, op. cit., 136, 147; Tanin, op. cit., 301–2, 186–91; Mosley, op. cit., 122.

23. HIROHITO TAKES COMMAND

350   Araki's brief term: Crowley, *Japanese Army Factionalism in the Early 1930s*, 316f.;
      Storry, *Double Patriots*, 137, 150–1, 142–3.
351   CER purchase: Young, *Imperial Japan*, 208f.
      'War is the Father of Creation . .': Colegrove, *Militarism in Japan*, 51f.; Crowley, op.
      cit., 318.
352   Naval build-up: Pelz, *Race to Pearl Harbor*, 30f.; Maxon, *Control of Japanese
      Foreign Policy*, 78; Pelz, op. cit., 77.
353   'Abrogate the treaties': Pelz, op. cit., 39f.
      Okada's appointment: Storry, op. cit., 155f.; Pelz, op. cit., 50f.
354   Abrogators victorious: Pelz, op. cit., 53f.; Bergamini, *Japan's Imperial Conspiracy*, 581;
      Pelz, op. cit., 150.
355   Military Academy Incident: Shillony, *Revolt in Japan*, 45f.; Storry, op. cit., 159f.
      Organ Controversy: Yanaga, *Japan since Perry*, 507; Storry, op. cit., 163f.; Byas,
      Government by Assassination, 272; Shillony, op. cit., 50–1; Smethurst, *The Military
      Reservists Association and the Minobe Crisis*, 9; Bergamini, op. cit., 592f.
356   Mazaki removed: Storry, op. cit., 169f.; Shillony, op. cit., 48.
357   Radicals' revenge: Storry, op. cit., 175; Byas, op. cit., 97–8.
      Hirohito's intervention: Shillony, op. cit., 53; Mosley, *Hirohito, Emperor of Japan*, 134;
      Maxon, op. cit., 99; Shillony, op. cit., 102.
      Pressure on Okada; Smethurst, op. cit., 12f.; Storry, op. cit., 180.
358   Aizawa's trial: Shillony, op. cit., 54, 113; Byas, op. cit., 111f., 101.
359   New plot: Storry, op. cit., 181; Shillony, op. cit., 71, 111f; Bergamini, op.
      cit., 623.
360   February 26th: Shillony, op. cit., 123f.; Bergamini, op. cit., 634.
361   'This is mutiny . .': Storry, op. cit., 187–8.
363   Martial Law declared: Shillony, op. cit., 149f.; Storry, op. cit., 189; Bergamini,
      op. cit., 640f.
365   Surrender: Shillony, op. cit., 158–206.

24. ACROSS THE GREAT WALL

368   Peking threatened: Snow, *Far Eastern Front*, 254–6; Morley, *The China Quagmire*,
      31f.; Maxon, *Control of Japanese Foreign Policy*, 49.
372   The order to withdraw: Morley, op. cit., 34.
      Tangku Truce: Morley, op. cit., 53f.; Boyle, *China and Japan at War*, 31.
374   Japanese take-over of trade: Morley, op. cit., 62; Young, *Imperial Japan*, 202f.
      'Japan alone must act and decide . .': Morley, op. cit., 79f.; Young, op. cit., 205.
375   Exploiting internal strife: Morley, op. cit., 90f.; Boyle, op. cit., 35.
376   Ho-Umezu Agreement: Morley, op. cit., 99–114; Li, *The Japanese Army in North China*,
      28.
377   Ch'in-Doihara Agreement: Boyle, op. cit., 124; Morley, op. cit., 118f.
      Economic warfare: Morley, op. cit., 148f.
378   Autonomy movement: Morley, op. cit., 141f.
379   'The plain fact is that if Japan would recall General Doihara . .': Boyle, op.
      cit., 41; Morley, op. cit., 153; Li. op. cit., 98.
380   'Dealing with North China': Morley, op. cit., 159f.; Ekins, *China Fights for Her
      Life*, 206.
381   Setback in Mongolia: Morley, op. cit., 168, 217f.; Ekins, op. cit., 157; Yanaga, *Japan
      since Perry*, 571.
      Manchukuo's economy reorganised: Johnson, *MITI and the Japanese Miracle*, 131–2;
      Roberts, *Mitsui*, 311.

382 Army's caution: Morley, op. cit., 174f.; Bergamini, *Japan's Imperial Conspiracy*, 637; Li, op. cit., 30; Morley, op. cit., 196f.
383 Anti-Comintern Pact: Iklé, *German-Japanese Relations*, 28, 37.
384 Nationalist-Communist truce: Boyle, op. cit., 42; Morley, op. cit., 224–5; Ekins, op. cit., 184.
   Shift in Tokyo: Grew, *Ten Years in Japan*, 173; Storry, op. cit., 204–5; Morley, op. cit., 226f.
385 Conciliation overruled: Young, op. cit., 297; Wilson, *When Tigers Fight*, 3; Storry, op. cit., 200; Boyle, op. cit., 49–50.

25.   THE CHINA INCIDENT

387 Marco Polo Bridge Incident: Jones, *Japan's New Order in East Asia*, 31; Morley, *The China Quagmire*, 247; Storry, *Double Patriots*, 221; Boyle, *China and Japan at War*, 136; Wilson, *When Tigers Fight*, 14.
388 Debate in Tokyo: Morley, op. cit., 450, 248f.; Wilson, op. cit., 15; Li, *The Japanese Army in North China*, 59; Jones, op. cit., 40–1; Boyle, op. cit., 51.
389 Events now snowballed ..: Morley, op. cit., 260; Boyle, op. cit., 53; Grew, *Ten Years in Japan*, 189; Butow, *Tojo and the Coming of War*, 99; Wilson, op. cit., 25; Ekins, *China Fights for Her Life*, 224; Morley, op. cit., 452.
390 Ishihara's peace terms: Morley, op. cit., 263.
391 Shanghai: Storry, op. cit., 222; Young, *Imperial Japan*, 296; Ekins, op. cit., 228f.; Morley, op. cit., 266f., 456.
392 'If the Naval General Staff also feel this way ..': Morley, op. cit., 266.
393 Ishihara ostracised: ibid., 275; Boyle, op. cit., 57.
   Western disapproval ignored: Yanaga, *Japan since Perry*, 573; Morley, op. cit., 271f.; Maxon, *Control of Japanese Foreign Policy*, 61; Ekins, op. cit., 254; Wilson, op. cit., 40.
394 Drive on Nanking: Byas, *Government by Assassination*, 145; Bergamini, *Japan's Imperial Conspiracy*, 21; Morley, op. cit., 457, 278f.; Boyle, op. cit., 70f.
395 *Panay* and *Ladybird* attacked: Grew, op. cit., 205f.; Bergamini, op. cit., 25; Storry, op. cit., 227–8; Mosley, *Hirohito, Emperor of Japan*, 173.
396 Rape: Timperley, *Japanese Terror in China*, 19f.; Wilson, op. cit., 76f.; Bergamini, op. cit., 34f.; Mosley, op. cit., 180.
397 'Where life is evil now ..': Auden, *Collected Poems*, 154.
398 'The Japanese have an answer for everything ..': Grew, op. cit., 214.
399 Chiang uncowed: Boyle, op. cit., 71f.; Morley, op. cit., 281f., 344; Ekins, op. cit., 267.

26.   EMPTY SEAT AT THE FEAST

400 'Provisional Government': Boyle, *China and Japan at War*, 85f., 131; Morley, *The China Quagmire*, 321f.; Butow, *Tojo and the Coming of War*, 104; Li, *The Japanese Army in North China*, 54–5, 105.
401 'Restoration Government': Boyle, op. cit., 145, 112f.
402 Pincer movement on Suchow: ibid., 135f.; Byas, *Government by Assassination*, 265; Wilson, *When Tigers Fight*, 89f.
403 Western observer: Wilson, op. cit., 112.
404 Compromise Cabinet: Boyle, op. cit., 145f., 375–6; Storry, *Double Patriots*, 231–2. Hirohito's unease: Boyle, op. cit., 135.
405 Chiang out of reach: Wilson, op. cit., 121f.; Seth, *Secret Servants*, 121.
406 Central overlord: Boyle, op. cit., 148f.; Morley, op. cit., 328; Li, op. cit., 71.
407 Wang won over: Boyle, op. cit., 187f.; Morley, op. cit., 383, 327.
408 Rebuffed by Chiang: Boyle, op. cit., 209f.; Morley, op. cit., 385–6; Boyle, op. cit., 226f.; Wilson, op. cit., 147.
410 Undeceived by Japan: Morley, op. cit., 386f.; Boyle, op. cit., 119, 242f.

413 'National Government': Morley, op. cit., 402f.; Boyle, op. cit., 279f.
416 'Certain misfortunes in the past': Wilson, op. cit., 253.

27. DALLIANCE OF THIEVES

417 Securing the northern flank: Pelz, *Race to Pearl Harbor*, 169f.; *Contemporary Japan*, June 1934, 137; Morley, *Deterrent Diplomacy*, 18; Morley, *The Fateful Choice*, 15; Jones, Japan's New Order in East Asia, 24.
'We should first concentrate all our strength ..': Pelz, op. cit., 174–5.
418 Fundamental Principles: ibid., 173f.; Morley, *Deterrent Diplomacy*, 31; Butow, *Tojo and the Coming of War*, 83, 85.
419 Other fields: Grew, *Ten Years in Japan*, 82; Montgomery, *Who Sank the* Sydney?, 164; Seth, *Secret Servants*, 224, 148, 165, 154, 206; Storry, *Double Patriots*, 278.
Quasi-wartime economic system: Storry, op. cit., 196; Johnson, *MITI and the Japanese Miracle*, 120f., 137, 148, 161.
420 Thought Control: Butow, op. cit., 110–11; Storry, op. cit., 196; Gauntlett, *Kokutai No Hongi*, 67, 80; Holtom, *Modern Japan and Shinto Nationalism*, 24; Price, *The Son of Heaven*, 158.
421 Araki's 'education': Price, op. cit., 126, 147.
Anti-Comintern Pact: Pelz, op. cit., 176; Bergamini, *Japan's Imperial Conspiracy*, 675; Morley, *Deterrent Diplomacy*, 3, 261f.
422 'No hidden agreement': Morley, *Deterrent Diplomacy*, 37–8; Iklé, *German–Japanese Relations*, 40; Morley, *The Fateful Choice*, 16.
Matsuoka's words: Morley, *Deterrent Diplomacy*, 214–15.
Relations with Britain and America: ibid., 35f.; Iklé, op cit., 43; Jones, op. cit., 40; Feis, *The Road to Pearl Harbor*, 10f.; Pelz, op. cit., 182f.
424 Strengthening the Anti-Comintern Pact: Morley, *The Fateful Choice*, 31; Jones, op. cit., 41; Iklé, op. cit., 36; Jones, op. cit., 58–9; Morley, *Deterrent Diplomacy*, 48–9; Iklé, op. cit., 69f.
425 Lake Khassan Incident: Bergamini, op. cit., 691; Morley, *Deterrent Diplomacy*, 142f.
426 New Order: Grew, op. cit., 226, 230; Morley, *The China Quagmire*, 348f.; Feis, op. cit., 14; Butow, op. cit., 123.
427 Towards an alliance: Morley, *Deterrent Diplomacy*, 55f.
428 Oshima and Shiratori over the traces: Iklé, op. cit., 83; Grew, op: cit., 42, 125; Morley, *Deterrent Diplomacy*, 71f.; Butow, op. cit., 135–6; Iklé, op. cit., 89.
429 'No matter how much and how many years ..': Iklé, op. cit., 93.
Impasse: Morley, *Deterrent Diplomacy*, 84f.; Iklé, op. cit., 96f.; Storry, op. cit., 246.
431 Hirohito's hard line: Storry, op. cit., 250; Iklé, op. cit., 111; Feis, op. cit. 31.
Berlin's lost patience; Iklé, op. cit., 112f.; Morley, *Deterrent Diplomacy*, 101f.; Storry, op. cit., 253.

28. FOR BETTER, FOR WORSE

432 Nomonhan Incident: Morley, *The China Quagmire*, 356f., 158f.; Morley, *Deterrent Diplomacy*, 170; Morley, *The Fateful Choice*, 18.
434 Nazi-Soviet Pact: Iklé, *German–Japanese Relations*, 125f.; Morley, *Deterrent Diplomacy*, 191f.; Storry, *Double Patriots*, 256.
New Cabinet: Feis, *The Road to Pearl Harbor*, 36; Morley, *Deterrent Diplomacy*, 194–5; Storry, op. cit., 257; Jones, *Japan's New Order in East Asia*, 128; Morley, op. cit., 175.
435 Oshima and Shiratori recalled: Iklé, 133f.; Morley, *Deterrent Diplomacy*, 192f.; Iklé, op. cit., 143f.; Morley, *The Fateful Choice*, 25.
'The Emperor is the companion piece ..': Iklé, op. cit., 133.
437 Berlin back in favour: Morley, *The Fateful Choice*, 30; Storry, op. cit., 260; Grew, *Ten Years in Japan*, 272; Morley, *Deterrent Diplomacy*, 203; Iklé, op. cit., 149f.

438 Konoye's return: Yanaga, *Japan since Perry*, 543–4; Butow, *Tojo and the Coming of War*, 141; Storry, op. cit., 262f.; Morley, *Deterrent Diplomacy*, 206f.; Jones, op. cit., 191; Feis, op. cit., 80.
439 Matsuoka sets the pace: Morley, *Deterrent Diplomacy*, 213f.; Iklé, op. cit., 165f.; Feis, op. cit., 122.
441 Naval turnabout: Morley, *Deterrent Diplomacy*, 229f.
442 'Since we have come so far ..': ibid., 243.
Imperial Conference: Ike, *Japan's Decision for War*, 13; Butow, op. cit., 178.
443 Tripartite Pact: Iklé, op. cit., 176; Morley, *Deterrent Diplomacy*, 253–4; Holtom, *Modern Japan and Shinto Nationalism*, 22.

29. 'THE WHOLE WORLD UNDER ONE ROOF'

444 'The principle of The Whole World ..': Holtom, *Modern Japan and Shinto Nationalism*, 22.
Naval preparations: Pelz, *Race to Pearl Harbor*, 197; Montgomery, *Who Sank the Sydney?*, 154; Morley, *The Fateful Choice*, 242f.
445 Securing oil: Morley, *The Fateful Choice*, 241; Morley, *Deterrent Diplomacy*, 41–2; Morley, *The Fateful Choice*, 126–7; Feis, *The Road to Pearl Harbor*, 51f.
446 Nod from Germany: Jones, *Japan's New Order in East Asia*, 240; Morley, *The Fateful choice*, 133, 246; Feis, op. cit., 59f.
447 Main Principles: Morley, *The Fateful Choice*, 248f.; Storry, *Double Patriots*, 266; Feis, op. cit., 85; Butow, *Tojo and the Coming of War*, 151; Pelz, op. cit., 215; Butow, op. cit., 159.
448 Naval fears of an American embargo: Feis, op. cit., 87; Pelz, op. cit., 215.
Roosevelt cautious: Feis, op. cit., 41f.; Grew, *Ten Years in Japan*, 262; Morley, *The Fateful Choice*, 134; Feis, op. cit., 70f.
450 Kobayashi Mission: Feis, op. cit., 96; Morley, *The Fateful Choice*, 142.
Into Indo-China: Morley, *The Fateful Choice*, 169f.; Jones, op. cit., 228; Feis, op. cit., 102; Morley, *The Fateful Choice*, 192.
452 Navy's diffidence: Feis, op. cit., 104; Morley, *The Fateful Choice*, 257–8, 276; Feis, op. cit., 116; Jones, op. cit., 199; Butow, op. cit., 168; Morley, *The Fateful Choice*, 269f.; Iklé, *German–Japanese Relations*, 176f.
453 Hirohito's 'unusual resolve': Feis, op. cit., 118.
454 Japan's 'Sphere': Iklé, op. cit., 184; Morley, *The Fateful Choice*, 53; Feis, op. cit., 120 114; Storry, op. cit., 276–7, 317f.
Matsuoka's imposture: Grew, op. cit., 295; Feis, op. cit., 120.
Sterner American stand: Iklé, op. cit., 179; Feis, op. cit., 122f.
455 'Strike South' mobilised: Morley, *The Fateful Choice*, 277f.; Jones, op. cit., 239.
456 Batavia plays for time: Morley, *The Fateful Choice*, 244f.; Feis, op. cit., 130–1; Jones, op. cit., 244; Feis, op. cit., 150–1.
457 Siamese cat's paw: Morley, *The Fateful Choice*, 227, 283–4; Feis, op. cit., 181; Morley, *The Fateful Choice*, 229f.; Butow, op. cit., 198.

30. TALKING AT CROSS PURPOSES

460 Seeking a detente with Russia: Morley, *Deterrent Diplomacy* 208, 218–19; Morley, *The Fateful Choice*, 54f.
461 'Should Germany in the near future ..': Morley, *The Fateful Choice*, 70.
Matsuoka tailed: ibid., 10.
462 'Attack Singapore': Trefousse, *Germany and Pearl Harbor*, 39; *Brassey's Naval Annual 1948*, 161, 172; Feis, *The Road to Pearl Harbor*, 180; Storry, *Double Patriots*, 283.

Pearl Harbor plans: Butow, *Tojo and the Coming of War*, 201; Grew, *Ten Years in Japan*, 318.
Roosevelt still cautious: Feis, op. cit., 153f.

463 Military retreat in Tokyo: Morley, *The Fateful Choice*, 290f.
Matsuoka in Moscow: Grew, op. cit., 327; Morley, *The Fateful Choice*, 72; Feis, op. cit., 183.

464 Crossed lines in Berlin: Jones, *Japan's New Order in East Asia*, 253–4; Feis, op. cit., 182f.; Trefousse, op. cit., 49; Morley, *The Fateful Choice*, 74.

465 Brief triumph: Morley, *The Fateful Choice*, 75f.; Feis, op. cit., 187.
ABDA established: Feis, op. cit., 155, 167; Jones, op. cit., 248.

466 Nomura's sceptical reception: Feis, op. cit., 191, 172f.; Jones, op. cit., 267, 270.
Matsuoka's tantrums: Jones, op. cit., 271f.; Feis, op. cit., 194f.; Grew, op. cit., 336; Morley, *The Fateful Choice*, 89f.

468 Hitler's Rubicon: Morley, op. cit., 90; Butow, op. cit., 208.
Matsuoka before the War Crimes Tribunal: Morley, *The Fateful Choice*, 82.
'Strike North' vetoed: Morley, *The Fateful Choice*, 94f.; Storry, op. cit., 286; Akira, *Power and Culture*, 26; Jones, op. cit., 217.

469 'Strike South' first: Feis, op. cit., 189; Morley, *The Fateful Choice*, 151f., 93, 235; Butow, op. cit., 210; Ike, *Japan's Decision for War*, 56; Morley, *The Fateful Choice*, 96.
Manchurian mobilisation plan: Morley, *The Fateful Choice*, 104.
'Measures for Accelerating the Southern Policy': ibid., 235.

470 'Moral Principles': ibid., 97; Ike, op. cit., 60; Butow, op. cit., 216–17; Morley, *The Fateful Choice*, 100.
Imperial Conference: Feis, op. cit., 206f.; Morley, *The Fateful Choice*, 236; Butow, op. cit., 218.

471 'The Emperor seemed to be extremely satisfied': Ike, op. cit., 90.
Matsuoka silenced: Feis, op. cit., 214, 205, 222f.; Storry, op. cit., 287.

472 American freeze: Morley, *The Fateful Choice*, 236f.; Grew, op. cit., 352; Feis, op. cit., 229f.; Ike, op. cit., 106.

473 'Commercial and economic relations ..': Feis, op. cit., 249.
Kwantung Army cautioned: Morley, *The Fateful Choice*, 12, 104f.; Ike, op. cit., 113f.

474 Nagano's 'simple views': Butow, op. cit., 234f.; Feis, op. cit., 252; Morley, *The Fateful Choice*, 207.
Konoye's summit ploy: Jones, op. cit., 281; Feis, op. cit., 249f.; Butow, op. cit., 245–6.

476 Nomura's complaint: Ike, op. cit., 123.

31. 'INTO THE TIGER'S DEN'

477 October deadline: Feis, *The Road to Pearl Harbor*, 217; Butow, *Tojo and the Coming of War*, 246f.; Feis, op. cit., 264–5; Ike, *Japan's Decision for War*, 135.

478 Hirohito's questions: Feis, op. cit., 266f.; Butow, op. cit., 253f.; Ike, op. cit., 142; Mosley, *Hirohito, Emperor of Japan*, 218.

479 Meiji's poem: Butow, op. cit., 258–9; Feis, op. cit., 267; Mosley, op. cit., 220.

480 Konoye's false prospectus: Feis, op. cit., 270f.; Butow, op. cit., 260–1; Grew, *Ten Years in Japan*, 368f.; Ike, op. cit., 170.

481 'October 15th': Feis, op. cit., 276f.; Butow, op. cit., 251–2, 262f.; Grew, op. cit., 391.

482 Hirohito evidently considered ..: Butow, op. cit., 277–8; Mosley, op. cit., 224–5.
Konoye v Tojo: Storry, *Double Patriots*, 292–3; Butow, op. cit., 282f.; Feis, op. cit., 284.

483 'Then, if the new men should decide ..': Storry, op. cit., 294.

484 Tojo in command: Storry, op. cit., 294–5; Butow, op. cit., 289f.; Mosley, op. cit., 225–6; Johnson, *MITI and the Japanese Miracle*, 38.

485 'You cannot obtain a tiger's cub ..': ibid., 309.
Signals to Washington: Feis, op. cit., 291–2; Butow, op. cit., 311.

486 Final deadline: Feis, op. cit., 292f.; Bergamini, *Japan's Imperial Conspiracy*, 801; Butow, op. cit., 319f.
Plans A and B: Butow, op. cit., 322–3; Feis, op. cit., 309.

487 Imperial sanction: Jones, *Japan's New Order in East Asia*, 297–8; Butow, op. cit., 324.
Supreme War Council: Bergamini, op. cit., 809f.; Butow, op. cit., 325; Feis, op. cit., 294.
Imperial Conference: Ike, op. cit., 229f.; Butow, op. cit., 325–6.

488 'This time we are showing all our friendship. ..': Feis, op. cit., 297; Ike, op. cit., 245–6.
Elsewhere on the diplomatic front ..: Butow, op. cit., 327.
Operations Order No. 1: Feis, op. cit., 296; Butow, op. cit., 326; Bergamini, op. cit., 805–6.

489 Fleet mobilised: Butow, op. cit., 333; Feis, op. cit., 303; Bergamini, op. cit., 819; Montgomery, *Who Sank the* Sydney?, 164f.
'Draft Proposal ..': Ike, op. cit., 247–8.
Plans A and B presented: Feis, op. cit., 304f; Ike, op. cit., 250; Butow, op. cit., 322, 334.

490 American counter-proposal: Feis, op. cit., 312f.; Butow, op. cit., 334f.

491 Some new factor: Costello, *The Pacific War*, 625f.; Public Records Office, Prem 3 469/3, 156/5; Montgomery, op. cit., passim.

493 'The Naval Board are very worried about *Sydney* ..': Imperial War Museum, 69/18/1.

495 'Proposed Basis' rejected: Feis, op. cit., 321f.; Butow, op. cit., 337f.
The decision for war: Ike, op. cit., 257; Feis, op. cit., 328–9; Costello, op. cit., 129; Butow, op. cit., 347.

496 'Our diplomats will have to be sacrificed ...': Ike, op. cit., 262.
Decision ratified: Grew, op. cit., 418; Butow, op. cit., 349f.; Feis, op. cit., 329; Bergamini, op. cit., 830; Titus, *Palace and Politics in Pre-War Japan*, 263.

497 Hirohito 'displayed no signs of uneasiness ...': Ike, op. cit., 283.

498 Declaration of war redundant: Butow, op. cit., 372f.

499 Roosevelt letter delayed: ibid., 388f.

500 'In all my years ...': ibid., 402.
Imperial Rescript: Bergamini, op. cit., 849

EPILOGUE

501 Hirohito's broadcast: Bergamini, *Japan's Imperial Conspiracy*, 112.
MCI in a new guise: Johnson, *MITI and the Japanese Miracle*, 172f.; Wolf, *The Japanese Conspiracy*, 230; Yoshida, *Memoirs*, 155–6.

502 New weapons: Johnson, op. cit., 194f.; Wolf, op. cit., 235.

504. Political entrenchment: Johnson, op. cit., 46, 79.

505 Export offensive: ibid., 229f.
'We will take every measure ...': ibid., 247.
'Administrative guidance': ibid., 250f.

506 America targetted: Wolf, op. cit., 80; Johnson, op. cit., 236; Roberts, *Mitsui*, 409; Wolf, op. cit., 12f.; Johnson, op. cit., 283.

507 Impact on the U.S. car market: *Financial Times*, 5 September 1985; Johnson, op. cit., 286; Wolf, op. cit., 242.
Domestic protection: Johnson, op. cit., 278–9.

508   Resentment of MITI silenced: Johnson, 284f.; Bownas, *Japan's Strategy for the 1980s in Industrial Electrical and Electronic Equipment*, 5.
509   Semi-conductors subsidised: Wolf, op. cit., 85f.
510   Computer manufacturers 'guided': ibid., 42f., 195f.; Feigenbaum and McCorduck, *The Fifth Generation*, 13.
511   Promises to liberalise home market unfulfilled: Johnson 302f.; Taylor, *Shadows of the Rising Sun*, 29–30, 262f.
      Devices to exclude exports: *Financial Times*, 28 July, 23 September 1986, 9, 22 January 1987; *Sunday Telegraph*, 12 October 1986; *Financial Times*, 6 April 1987. Cable & Wireless elbowed out: *Daily Telegraph*, 28 March 1987; *Financial Times*, 21 January, 2 May 1987.
512   Agriculture protected: Wolf, op. cit., 307f.; Taylor, op. cit., 262.
513   Capital markets closed: Johnson, op. cit., 303; Wolf, op. cit., 125; *The Times*, 26 March 1987; *Financial Times*, 28 July, 10 May, 28 July 1986; *Daily Telegraph*, 15 May 1987; *Sunday Telegraph*, 22 February 1987; *The Spectator*, 9 May 1987.
      Measures against Japanese trading tactics: *Financial Times*, 27 August 1986, 18 April 1987; *Daily Telegraph*, 26 March 1987; *The Times*, 2 April 1987.
514   Production established overseas: Bownas, op. cit., 58–60; Taylor, op. cit., 53–4; *Financial Times*, 16 January 1984.
515   Exploitation of labour: Taylor, op. cit., 154, 166, 175f.; Wolf, op. cit., 249, 274–5.
516   Nakasone stirs nationalism: Taylor, op. cit., 283; Bergamini, op. cit., 1075; *Japan Times*, 16 August 1985; *The Times*, 20 March 1986; *Daily Telegraph*, 9 September 1986. 'Japan's apparent wealth ...': *Daily Telegraph*, 23 January 1987.
517   Emperor worship revived: *Financial Times*, 23 April 1986; *Japan Times*, 27 September 1986; *Daily Telegraph*, 6 May 1987.
      Racial purity maintained: *Japan Times*, 28 August 1986; *Daily Telegraph*, 20 September 1986.
      Discrimination against minorities: Wolf, op. cit., 305; *Daily Telegraph*, 17 October, 9 December 1986.
518   A new militarism: Taylor, op. cit., 280; *Daily Telegraph*, 15 December 1986, 17 February 1987; *The Spectator*, 9 May 1987.
      Trade imbalance unlikely to be redressed: *Financial Times*, 25 April 1986; 12 February, 27 March 1987.
519   'a waste of time ...': *New York Herald Tribune*, 27 March 1987.
      'There is nothing ...': *Guardian*, 21 July 1985.

Bibliography

Akamatsu, P., translated by Kochan, Miriam. *Meiji 1868, Revolution and Counter Revolution in Japan*. G. Allen & Unwin, London 1972

Akira Iriye. 'Chang Hsueh-Liang and the Japanese'. *Journal of Asian Studies* Vol. XX-1 (November 1960)

—— *Power and Culture: The Japanese–American War 1941–1945*. Harvard University Press, Cambridge, Mass. 1981

Akita, G. *Foundations of Constitutional Government in Modern Japan 1868–1900*. Harvard University Press, Cambridge, Mass. 1967

Alcock, Sir Rutherford. *The Capital of the Tycoon: a Narrative of Three Years' Residence in Japan*. Longman, Green & Co., London 1863

Asaji, N., and Pringle, Rev. J.C. 'Lectures Delivered in the Presence of His Imperial Majesty'. *Transactions of the Asiatic Society of Japan* Vol. XL (1912)

Asakawa Kanichi. *The Russo-Japanese Conflict: Its Causes and Issues*. Kennikat Press, IUP Reprint, Shannon 1974

—— 'Japan in Manchuria'. *Yale Review* Vol. XVII-2/3 (August/Nov. 1908)

Aston, W.G. *Chronicles of Japan from the Earliest Times to AD 697 (Nihongi)*, Vols I & II. Kegan Paul, Trench & Trubner, London 1896

Atkinson, C.T. *The History of the South Wales Borderers 1914–1918*. The Medici Society, London 1931

Auden, W.H. *Collected Poems*. Faber & Faber, London 1976

Barr, Pat. *The Coming of the Barbarians: the Opening of Japan to the West 1853–1870*. Macmillan & Co., London 1966

Beasley, W.G. *Great Britain and the Opening of Japan 1834–1858*. Luzac & Co., London 1957

—— *Select Documents on Japanese Foreign Policy 1853–1868*. Oxford University Press, Oxford 1955

—— *The Meiji Restoration*. Oxford University Press, Oxford 1973

—— *The Modern History of Japan*. Weidenfeld & Nicolson, London 1963

Bergamini, David. *Japan's Imperial Conspiracy*. Wm. Heinemann, London 1971

Bishop, Mrs. I.L. *Korea and Her Neighbours*. J. Murray, London 1898

Black, John R. *Young Japan 1858–1979*, Vols I & II. Trubner & Co., London 1880

Borg, Dorothy. *The United States and the Far Eastern Crisis of 1933–1938*. Harvard University Press, Cambridge, Mass. 1964

Borton, Hugh. *Japan's Modern Century*. The Ronald Press, New York 1955

Bownas, Prof. G. *Japan's Strategy for the 1980s in Industrial Electrical & Electronic Equipment*. BEAMA, London 1980

Boyle, John Hunter. *China and Japan at War 1937-1945: the Politics of Collaboration*. Stanford University Press, Stanford, Cal. 1972

Braddon, Russell. *The Other One Hundred Years' War: Japan's Bid for Supremacy 1941-2041*. Wm. Collins, London 1983

Brown, Delmer M. *Nationalism in Japan*. University of California Press, Berkeley, Cal. 1955

Brownlees, John S. ed. *History in the Service of the Nation*. University of Toronto Press, Toronto 1983.

Bush, Lewis. *Land of the Dragonfly*. Robert Hale, London 1959

Butow, Robert J.C. *Tojo and the Coming of War*. Princeton University Press, Princeton, N.J. 1961

'By Our Own Correspondent'. 'The Japan Imbroglio'. *Blackwood's* Magazine (September 1895).

Byas, Hugh. *Government by Assassination.* G. Allen & Unwin, London 1943

Causton, E. E. N. *Militarism and Foreign Policy in Japan.* G. Allen & Unwin, London 1936

Chung Fu-Chang. *Anglo-Japanese Alliance.* Johns Hopkins University Press, Baltimore, Maryland 1931

Colegrove, K.W. *Militarism in Japan.* World Peace Foundation, New York 1936

Conroy, Francis Hilary. 'Government v "Patriot": The Background of Japan's Asiatic Expansion'. *Pacific Historical Review* Vol. XX-1 (February 1951)

—— *The Japanese Frontier in Hawaii 1868–1898.* University of California Press, Berkeley, Cal. 1953

—— *The Japanese Seizure of Korea 1868–1910.* University of Pennsylvania Press, Philadelphia, Penn. 1960

Costello, John. *The Pacific War.* Wm. Collins, London 1981

Craig, A.M. *Choshu in the Meiji Restoration.* Harvard University Press, Cambridge, Mass. 1961

Crow, Carl, ed. *Japan's Dream of World Empire: the Tanaka Memorial.* Harper & Bros., New York 1942

Crowley, James B. 'Japanese Army Factionalism in the Early 1930s'. *Journal of Asian Studies* Vol. XXI-3 (May 1962)

Dignan, D.K. 'Australian and British Relations with Japan 1914–1921'. *Australian Outlook* Vol. XXI-2 (August 1967)

Dull, Paul S. 'Count Kato and the Twenty-one Demands'. *Pacific Historical Review* Vol. XIX-2 (May 1950)

—— 'The Assassination of Chang Tso-lin'. *The Far Eastern Quarterly* Vol. XI-4 (August 1952)

Edwards, E. W. 'Great Britain and the Manchurian Railway Question'. *English Historical Review* XXXI-4 (October 1966)

Ekins, H.R., and Wright, Theon. *China Fights for Her Life.* McGraw-Hill, New York 1938

Feigenbaum, A., and McCorduck, Pamela. *The Fifth Generation: Artificial Intelligence and Japan's Computer Challenge to the World.* M. Joseph, London 1984

Feis, Herbert. *The Road to Pearl Harbor: the Coming of War between the United States and Japan.* Princeton University Press, Princeton, N.J. 1950

Gapanovich, J. J. 'Sino-Russian Relations in Manchuria 1892–1906'. *The Chinese Social and Political Science Review* Vol. XVII (1933)

Gauntlett, J. O., translator. *Kokutai No Hongi* (Cardinal Principles of the National Entity of Japan). Harvard University Press, Cambridge, Mass. 1949

Ginsburg, Norton S. 'Manchurian Railway Development'. *The Far Eastern Quarterly* Vol. VIII-4 (August 1949)

Gooch, G. P., and Timperley, H. *British Official Documents on the Origins of the War 1898–1914,* Vol. VIII. His Majesty's Stationery Office, London 1932

Grew, Joseph C. *Ten Years in Japan.* Hammond, Hammond & Co., London 1944

Griffis, William E. *The Mikado: Institution and Person.* Princeton University Press, Princeton, N.J. 1915

Gubbins, J.H. *The Progress of Japan 1853–1871.* Oxford University Press, Oxford 1911

Hackett, Roger F. *Yamagata Aritomo in the Rise of Modern Japan 1838–1922.* Harvard University Press, Cambridge, Mass. 1971

Hargreaves, R. *Red Sun Rising: The Siege of Port Arthur.* Weidenfeld & Nicolson, London 1962

Harootunian, H.D. *Towards Restoration: The Growth of Political Consciousness in Tokugawa Japan.* University of California Press, Berkeley, Cal. 1970

Hishida, Seiji G. *The International Position of Japan as a Great Power.* Columbia University Press, New York 1905

Holtom, D.C. *Modern Japan and Shinto Nationalism: A Study of Present Day Trends in Japanese Religions.* Revised Edition, University of Chicago Press, Chicago, Ill. 1947

House, Edward H. *The Japanese Expedition to Formosa.* Tokyo 1875

Hsü Shu-hsi. *The Manchurian Question*. China Council, Institute of Pacific Relations, Peking 1931

Hull, Cordell. *The Memoirs of Cordell Hull*, Vols I and II. Hodder & Stoughton, London 1948

Ike Nobutake, ed. and transl. *Japan's Decision for War: Records of the 1941 Policy Conferences*. Stanford University Press, Stanford, Cal. 1967

—— 'Kotoku: Advocate of Direct Action'. *The Far Eastern Quarterly* Vol. III-3 (May 1944)

—— *The Beginnings of Political Democracy in Japan*. Johns Hopkins University Press, Baltimore, Maryland 1950

Iklé, Frank N. 'German-Japanese Peace Negotiations during World War One'. *American Historical Review* Vol. LXXX-1 (October 1969)

—— *German-Japanese Relations 1936–1940*. Bookman Associates, New York 1956

Ishii Kikujiro. *Diplomatic Commentaries*, translated and edited by W.R. Langdon. Johns Hopkins University Press, Baltimore, Maryland 1936

Ito Hirobumi. *Commentaries on the Constitution of Japan*, translated by Ito Myoji. Tokyo 1889

James, David H. *The Rise and Fall of the Japanese Empire*. G. Allen & Unwin, London 1951

Jansen, Marius B. *Japan and China: from War to Peace 1894–1972*. Rand McNally College Publishing Co., Chicago, Ill. 1975

—— 'Opportunists in South China During the Boxer Rebellion'. *Pacific Historical Review* Vol. XX-3 (August 1951)

—— *The Japanese and Sun Yat-sen*. Harvard University Press, Cambridge, Mass. 1954

Johnson, Chalmers. *MITI and the Japanese Miracle: The Growth of Industrial Policy 1925–1975*. Stanford University Press, Stanford, Cal. 1982

Jones, F.C. *Japan's New Order in East Asia: Its Rise and Fall*. Oxford University Press, Oxford 1954

Kajima Morinosuke. *The Emergence of Japan as a World Power 1895–1925*. Charles E. Tuttle & Co., New York 1968

Keene, Donald. *The Japanese Discovery of Europe*. Routledge & Kegan Paul, London 1952

Kuno, Yoshi S. *Japanese Expansion in the Asiatic Continent*, Vol. I. University of California Press, Berkeley, Cal. 1937

Kwanha Yim. 'Yuan Shih-k'ai and the Japanese'. *Journal of Asian Studies* Vol. XXIV-1 (November 1964)

La Fargue, Thomas Edward. *China and the World War*. Stanford University Press, Stanford, Cal. 1937

Langdon, Frank C. 'Japan's Failure to Establish Friendly Relations with China in 1917–1918'. *Pacific Historical Review* Vol. XXVI-3 (August 1957)

Langer, William L. *The Diplomacy of Imperialism*. Alfred A. Knopf, New York 1951

Lea, Homer. *The Valor of Ignorance*. Harper & Co., New York 1909

League of Nations. *Report of the Lytton Commission*. Geneva, 1933

Lensen, G.A., ed. *Russia's Eastward Expansion*. Prentice-Hall, New York 1964

Li, Lincoln. *The Japanese Army in North China 1937-1941: Problems of Political and Economic Control*. Oxford University Press, Oxford 1975

Lory, Hillis. 'Recognition of Manchukuo'. *Contemporary Japan* Vol. III-4 (March 1935)

Lowe, Peter. 'Great Britain, Japan and the Fall of Yuan Shih-k'ai'. *The Historical Journal* Vol. XIII-4 (December 1970)

—— 'The British Empire and the Anglo-Japanese Alliance 1911–1915'. *History* Vol. LIV (June 1969)

McAleavy, Henry. *A Dream of Tartary: the Origins and Misfortunes of Henry P'u Yi*. G. Allen & Unwin, London 1963

MacLaren, W.W. *A Political History of Japan during the Meiji Era 1867–1912*. G. Allen & Unwin, London 1916

—— 'Japanese Government Documents 1867–1890'. *Transactions of the Asiatic Society of Japan* Vol. XLII-1 (May 1914)

McMurray, J.V.A. *Treaties and Agreements With and Concerning China 1894–1919*. Oxford University Press, Oxford 1921

Maki, John M. *Conflict and Tension in the Far East: Key Documents 1894–1960.* University of Washington Press, Seattle 1961

Masaharu Anesaki. *History of Japanese Religion,* 2nd edition. Routledge & Kegan Paul, London 1963

Masamichi Ruyama. 'The Meaning of the Manchukuo Empire'. *Contemporary Japan* III-1 (June 1934)

Masaru Ikei. 'Japan's Response to the Chinese Revolution of 1911'. *Journal of Asian Studies* Vol. XXV-2 (February 1966)

Matsuoka Yosuke. 'Dissolve the Political Parties'. *Contemporary Japan* Vol. II-4 (March 1934)

Maxon, Y.C. *Control of Japanese Foreign Policy: a Study of Civil-Military Rivalry 1930–1945.* University of California Press, Berkeley, Cal. 1957

Mayer-Oakes, T.F., transl. 'Fragile Victory: Prince Saionji and the 1930 London Treaty Issue'. In *The Memoirs of Baron Harada Kumao.* Wayne State University Press, Detroit, Mich. 1968

Miyazaki Toten. *My Thirty-Three Years' Dream,* translated by Eto Shinkichi and Jansen, Marius B. Princeton University Press, Princeton, N. J. 1982

Montgomery, Michael. *Who Sank the Sydney?* Leo Cooper, London 1983

Morley, James W. *The Japanese Thrust into Siberia.* Columbia University Press, New York 1957

—— *Japan Erupts: the London Naval Conference and the Manchurian Incident 1928–1932,* Vol I of *Japan's Road to the Pacific War.* Columbia University Press, New York 1984

—— *The China Quagmire: Japan's Expansion on the Asian Continent 1933–1941,* Vol. II of *Japan's Road to the Pacific War* 1983

—— *Deterrent Diplomacy: Japan, Germany and the USSR 1935–1941,* Vol. III of *Japan's Road to the Pacific War* 1976

—— *The Fateful Choice: Japan's Advance into Southeast Asia 1939–1941,* Vol. IV of *Japan's Road to the Pacific War* 1980

Mosley, Leonard. *Hirohito, Emperor of Japan.* Weidenfeld & Nicolson, London 1966

Mounsey, Dr. A.H. *The Satsuma Rebellion.* J. Murray, London 1879

Murdoch, James. *A History of Japan,* Vols I–III. Kegan Paul Trench Trubner & Co., London 1926

Nicolaevsky, B. 'Russia, Japan and the Pan-Asiatic Movement to 1925'. *The Far Eastern Quarterly* Vol. VII-4 (May 1949)

Nish, Ian H. *Alliance in Decline: A Study of Anglo-Japanese Relations 1908–1923.* Athlone Press, London 1972

—— *Anglo-Japanese Alliance.* Athlone Press, London 1966

—— *Japanese Foreign Policy 1869–1942.* Routledge & Kegan Paul, London 1977

—— 'Japan's Indecision during the Boxer Disturbances'. *Journal of Asian Studies* XX-3 (May 1961)

Norman, E.H. 'The Genyosha: a Study in the Origins of Japanese Imperialism'. *Pacific Affairs* Vol. XVII (September 1944)

Ogata, Sadako N. *Defiance in Manchuria: the Making of Japanese Foreign Policy 1931–1932.* University of California Press, Berkeley, Cal. 1964

Okuma Shigenobu, compiler, Huish, M. B., editor. *Fifty Years of New Japan.* Smith Elder & Co., London 1909

Oliphant, Laurence. *Narrative of the Earl of Elgin's Mission to China and Japan 1857–1859,* Vols I & II. Wm. Blackwood & Sons, Edinburgh 1859

Paske-Smith, M. *Western Barbarians in Japan and Formosa in Tokugawa Days 1603–1868.* J.L. Thompson & Co., London 1930

Pelz, Stephen E. *Race to Pearl Harbor: The Failure of the Second London Naval Conference and the Onset of World War Two.* Harvard University Press, Cambridge, Mass. 1974

Pittau, Joseph. *Political Thought in Early Meiji Japan 1868–1889.* Harvard University Press,

Cambridge, Mass. 1967

Pollard, Robert T. 'The Dynamics of Japanese Imperialism'. *Pacific Historical Review* Vol. VIII-1 (March 1939)

Pooley, A.M. *Japan at the Crossroads.* G. Allen & Unwin, London 1915

—— *Japan's Foreign Policies.* G. Allen & Unwin, London 1920

—— ed. *The Secret Memoirs of Count Tadasu Hayashi.* Eveleigh Nash, London 1915

Price, Willard. *The Son of Heaven: The Problem of the Mikado.* Wm. Heinemann, London 1945

Public Records Office, London. FO 881/1054, 881/1299: PREM 3 469/3, 156/5

Pyle, Kenneth B. *The New Generation in Meiji Japan: Problems of Cultural Identity 1885–1895.* Stanford University Press, Stanford, Cal. 1969

Quigley, Harold S. *Japanese Government and Politics: an Introductory Study.* The Century Co., New York 1932

Ramsdell, Daniel B. 'The Nakamura Incident and the Japanese Foreign Office'. *Journal of Asian Studies* Vol. XXV-1 (November 1969)

Reid, John G. *The Manchu Abdication and the Powers.* University of California Press, Berkeley, Cal. 1935

Reinsch, Paul S. *An American Diplomat in China.* Wm. Heinemann, London 1922

Rikitaro Fujisawa. *The Recent Aims and Political Development of Japan.* Yale University Press, New Haven, Conn. 1923

Roberts, John G. *Mitsui: Three Centuries of Japanese Business.* J. Weatherhill, New York 1973

Sadler, A.L. *The Maker of Modern Japan: The Life of Tokugawa Ieyasu.* G. Allen & Unwin, London 1937

Sands, William Franklin. *Undiplomatic Memories: The Far East 1896–1904.* J. Hamilton, London 1930

Sansom, Sir George. *A History of Japan,* Vol. III. Wm. Dawson, Folkestone, 1958

—— *The Western World and Japan.* Cresset Press, London 1950

Satow, Rt. Hon. Sir Ernest. *A Diplomat in Japan.* Seeley & Service, London 1921

Scalapino, Robert A. *Democracy and the Party Movement in Prewar Japan.* University of California Press, Berkeley, Cal. 1952

Scherer, J.A.B. *Japan's Advance.* Hokuseido Press, Tokyo 1934

Seth, Ronald. *Secret Servants: the Story of Japanese Espionage.* V. Gollancz & Co., London 1957

Sharman, Lyon. *Sun Yat-sen: His Life and Its Meaning.* J. Day Co., New York 1934

Shillony, Ben-Ami. *Revolt in Japan: the Young Officers and the February 1936 Incident.* Princeton University Press, Princeton, N.J. 1973

Shiveley, Donald H. 'Motoda Eifu: Confucian Lecturer to the Meiji Emperor'. In *Confucianism in Action,* ed. by Nivisen, David. S., and Wright, Arthur F. Stanford University Press, Stanford, Cal. 1959

Shumpei Okamoto. *The Japanese Oligarchy and the Russo-Japanese War.* Columbia University Press, New York 1970

Smethurst, R.J. 'The Military Reservists Association and the Minobe Crisis'. In *Crisis Politics in Pre-War Japan,* ed. by Wilson, George M. Sophia University Press, Tokyo 1970

Snow, Edgar. *Far Eastern Front.* Jarrolds, London 1934

Spinks, C.N. 'Indoctrination and Re-education of Japan's Youth'. *The Far Eastern Quarterly* Vol. III-2 (March 1944)

—— 'Origin of Japanese Interests in Manchuria'. *The Far Eastern Quarterly* Vol. II-3 (May 1943)

Stead, Alfred, ed. *Japan by the Japanese.* Wm. Heinemann, London 1904

Stephan, John J. 'The Tanaka Memorial (1927): Authentic or Spurious?' *Modern Asian Studies* Vol. VII-4 (September 1973)

Stevenson, R.L. *Familiar Studies of Men and Books.* Chatto & Windus, London 1882

Storry, Richard. *The Double Patriots: a Study of Japanese Nationalism.* Chatto & Windus 1957

Takeuchi Tatsuji. *War and Diplomacy in the Japanese Empire.* G. Allen & Unwin, London 1935

Tanin, O., and Yonan, E. *Militarism and Fascism in Japan.* M. Lawrence, London 1934

Taylor, Jared. *Shadows of the Rising Sun: a Critical View of the Japanese Miracle.* Wm. Morrow,

New York 1983

Tetsuo Najita and Koschmann, J. Victor, editors. *Conflict in Modern Japanese History: the Neglected Tradition*. Princeton University Press, Princeton, N.J. 1982

Timperley, H.J. *What War Means: the Japanese Terror in China, a Documentary Record*. Gollancz, London 1938

Titus, D.A. *Palace and Politics in Pre-War Japan*. Columbia University Press, New York 1974

Trefousse, Hans Louis. 'Germany and Pearl Harbor'. *The Far Eastern Quarterly* Vol. XI-1 (November 1951)

Tsiang, T. F. 'Sino-Japanese Diplomatic Relations 1870–1894'. *The Chinese Social and Political Science Review* Vol. XVII (1933)

Tsunoda Ryusaku, de Bary, William T., and Keene, Donald, compilers. *Sources of Japanese Tradition*. Columbia University Press, New York 1958

Tuchman, B. *The Zimmerman Telegram*. New English Library, London 1967

Uyetsuka, T. 'Immigration to Brazil'. *Contemporary Japan* Vol. III-1 (June 1934)

Vinson, J. Charles. 'The Annulment of the Lansing-Ishii Agreement'. *Pacific Historical Review* Vol. XXVII-1 (March 1958)

'Vladimir'. *The China-Japan War: Compiled from Japanese, Chinese and Foreign Sources*. Sampson, Low, Marston & Co., London 1896

Vogel, Ezra F. *Japan as Number One: Lessons for America*. Harvard University Press, Cambridge, Mass. 1979

Weale, Putnam (pseudonym of A.B. Lenox Simpson). *The Truth about China and Japan* G. Allen & Unwin, London 1921

Willoughby, Westel W. *The Sino-Japanese Controversy and the League of Nations*. Johns Hopkins University Press, Baltimore, Maryland 1935

Wilson, Dick. *When Tigers Fight: The Story of the Sino-Japanese War 1937–1945*. Hutchinson, London 1982

Wilson, George M. *Radical Nationalist in Japan: Kita Ikki 1883–1937*. Harvard University Press, Cambridge, Mass. 1969

Wolf, Marvin J. *The Japanese Conspiracy: Their Plot to Dominate Industry World-Wide and How to Deal with It*. Empire Books, New York 1983

Yanaga Chitoshi. *Japan since Perry*. McGraw-Hill, New York 1949

Yasui Chinhei. *'Bemmo': Exposition of Error*, translated by J.H. Gubbins. Japan Mail, Yokohama 1875

Yoshida Shigeru. *The Yoshida Memoirs: the Story of Japan in Crisis*. Houghton Mifflin Co., Boston, Mass. 1962

Yoshihashi Takehiko. *Conspiracy at Mukden: the Rise of the Japanese Military*. Yale University Press, New Haven, Conn. 1963

Young, A. Morgan. *Japan under Taisho Tenno 1912–1926*. G. Allen & Unwin, London 1928

—— *Imperial Japan*. G. Allen & Unwin, London 1938

Yutaka Hibino. *The National Ideals of the Japanese People*, translated by A. P. McKenzie. Cambridge University Press, Cambridge 1928

Index